Clan Politics and Regime Transition in Central Asia

This book is a study of the role of clan networks in Central Asia from the early twentieth century through 2004. Exploring the social, economic, and historical roots of clans, and their political role and political transformation during the Soviet and post-Soviet periods, this study argues that clans are informal political actors that are critical to understanding politics in this region. The book demonstrates that the Soviet system was far less successful in transforming and controlling Central Asian society, and in its policy of eradicating clan identities, than has often been assumed. Clans increasingly influenced and constrained the regime's political trajectory during the later Soviet and post-Soviet periods, making liberalizing political and economic reforms very difficult. In order to understand Central Asian politics and the region's economies today, scholars and policy makers must take into account the powerful role of these informal groups, how they adapt and change over time, and how they may constrain or undermine democratization in this strategic region.

Kathleen Collins is Assistant Professor of Political Science at the University of Notre Dame. She has been a Postdoctoral Fellow at the Kellogg Institute for International Studies and the Harvard Davis Center for Russian Research. She holds the Notre Dame Junior Chair in Comparative Politics. She has published articles in *World Politics, Comparative Politics*, the *Journal of Democracy*, and several edited volumes. She has received grants from the MacArthur Foundation, the United States Institute of Peace, the International Research and Exchange (IREX), and the National Council for Eurasian and East European Research, among others. Dr. Collins was named a Carnegie Scholar in 2003 for her research. She has been conducting research throughout Central Asia since 1994. Her dissertation won the S. M. Lipset Prize awarded by the Society for Comparative Research, for the best dissertation in comparative politics or sociology in 2000.

Clan Politics and Regime Transition in Central Asia

KATHLEEN COLLINS
University of Notre Dame

CAMBRIDGE
UNIVERSITY PRESS

CAMBRIDGE UNIVERSITY PRESS
Cambridge, New York, Melbourne, Madrid, Cape Town, Singapore, São Paulo, Delhi

Cambridge University Press
32 Avenue of the Americas, New York, NY 10013-2473, USA

www.cambridge.org
Information on this title: www.cambridge.org/9780521114660

First published 2006
This digitally printed version 2009

A catalog record for this publication is available from the British Library

Library of Congress Cataloging in Publication data

Collins, Kathleen.
Clan politics and regime transition in Central Asia / Kathleen Collins.
   p.   cm.
Includes bibliographical references and index.
ISBN 0-521-83950-5 (hardback)
1. Clans – Asia, Central.   2. Asia, Central – Social conditions – 1917–1991.
3. Asia, Central – Social conditions – 1991–   4. Asia, Central – Politics and
government – 1991–   5. Soviet Union – Relations – Asia, Central.
6. Asia, Central – Relations – Soviet Union.   7. Asia, Central – History.   I. Title.
GN487.7.C55C65   2006
929.6'0958–dc22   2004030862

ISBN 978-0-521-83950-1 hardback
ISBN 978-0-521-11466-0 paperback

To my mother, an advocate of justice, truth, and human dignity.

Contents

Tables and Figures

Tables

Figures

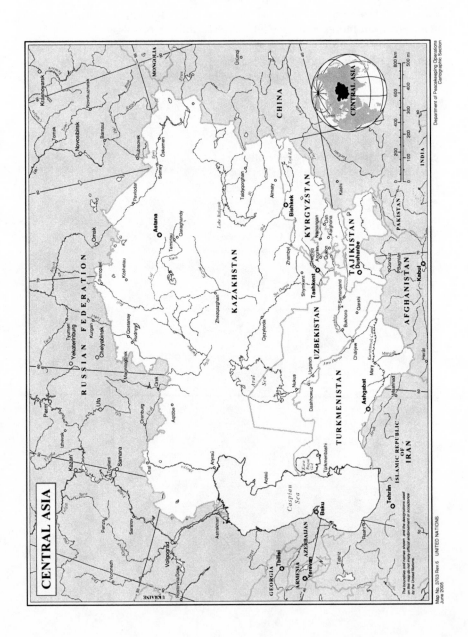

x

Preface

> Trains in these parts went from East to West and from West to East....On
> either side of the railway lines lay the great wide spaces of the desert – Sary-
> Ozeki, the Middle lands of the yellow steppes. In these parts any distance was
> measured in relation to the railway, as if from the Greenwich meridian....And
> the trains went from East to West and from West to East.
>
> Chingiz Aitmatov, *The Day Lasts More than a Hundred Years* (1980)

This is Central Asia, remote, exotic, and harsh. These are the words of
Chingiz Aitmatov, a native Kyrgyz and father of the "Turkestani" movement
in Soviet literature. Aitmatov seeks to capture the barrenness and isolation
of Soviet Central Asia, its physical and metaphorical distance from Moscow,
even at the close of the 1970s, after six decades of Soviet rule. In his sur-
real fantasy *The Day Lasts More than a Hundred Years*, Aitmatov vividly
portrays a land and a people whose history, tradition, and identity were
the victims of relentless Soviet purges but, paradoxically, the beneficiaries
of Soviet development. From collectivization of the nomads' lands to the
elimination of the tribal *bai* (wealthy), to Stalin's war on Islam and his 1937
slaughter of the Ferghana intelligentsia, to Khrushchev's disastrous Virgin
Lands program and cotton campaign, Central Asia incessantly felt the heavy
and destructive hand of Soviet rule.

And yet by 1980, as the Soviet grip began to relax, Central Asia remained at best only haphazardly penetrated by the Soviet system. Everywhere, modernity clashed with tradition. On the Kazakh steppe, camels still
roamed freely on the outskirts of nuclear weapons sites. In the Kyrgyz Republic, Communist Party officials still wore *kalpaks* (traditional felt hats)
and drank *kumuz* (fermented mare's milk). Throughout Central Asia, stalwart Soviet "atheists" still laid their dead to rest under the crescent moons
of Islam, passed on knowledge of the *Qur'an*, and even observed the Muslim
feast of *Ro'za*. And yet all the while, the ever-present steel railroad connected

this vast and persistent expanse of Asiatic steppe, desert, and mountain to modernization, to Soviet politics, industry, education, and culture.

If we leap forward two decades to the late 1990s, the so-called post-Soviet era, we find that presidents have replaced the Soviet first secretaries of each Central Asian republic. The Communist Party has been subsumed by various shades and stripes of "democratic" parties. New ideologies, from consumerism to Islamism, have replaced Marxism-Leninism. Capitalist economic theory is taught by those who once propounded only socialism. The Leninist Houses of Friendship now welcome not brother Soviets, but American, German, and Japanese investors. Changes along the scale of Stalinist industrialization are again under way. And yet Aitmatov's portrayal of Soviet Central Asia is still remarkably fitting. Why is this so? How is this possible? How can so much change so quickly, and yet so much remain the same?

As a political scientist, in this book I look at the transformation of Central Asia in light of such changes and historical processes occurring around the globe. The breakdown of authoritarian regimes, and the democratization that sometimes follows, have been dynamic and ongoing movements for several centuries. In the twentieth century, these issues have often been at the heart of major United States foreign policy efforts. Not surprisingly, these processes are also the focus of much scholarship in the field of political science. Why? Because of the rise of international norms regarding basic human rights, which generally consider freedom from authoritarian rule and a liberal democratic form of government to be integral to human dignity. Although liberal democracy may not, indeed never does, meet the criteria of the classic Aristotelian "best" regime – a regime of participatory rule by the virtuous – liberal democracy has thus far proven to be the closest approximation to the post-Enlightenment Western ideal of a just government. In recent decades, these norms of legitimate government have diffused beyond the West. Thus we have witnessed the courageous deeds that have defined certain cataclysms in world history – East Germans tearing down the Berlin Wall, Hungarians flooding their barbed wire border and heading West, Poles marching behind Solidarity and rallying to the encouragement of their Pope, and Muscovites mounting tanks to defy the 1991 coup against Gorbachev – all this in the name of freedom and democracy.

Deep in the Soviet Union, however, the wave of democratization was slower in coming. Leninism and Stalinism had gripped the Soviet peoples much longer and much more harshly than most authoritarian dictators or ideologies throughout history had been able to do. Yet there was never a lack of dissidents demanding truth and justice. Pasternak's poetry sought space for the personal life. Mandelstam and Akhmatova died in a quest for freedom of self-expression. Solzhenitsyn mocked Stalinism's cowardly attempts to control the human mind and soul. Sakharov survived exile in Gorky and multiple hunger strikes in order to expose communism's brutal disregard for human rights. Writing from Central Asia, Aitmatov and Suleimanov published fantastic tales to call their ethnic peoples to remember who they are, to value their cultural identity, and to keep sacred those very memories Soviet ideology had sought to destroy. By the late 1980s, atomized dissidence in the Soviet Union had surged into mass movements. What had begun with scientists and intellectuals in Leningrad and Moscow soon rippled outward to inspire the popular fronts and civil protests of the Balts and Ukrainians and, eventually, even of the Central Asians. The grip of repressive and corrupt regimes has been strong, but now, after a decade and a half of failed post-Soviet democratization, Kyrgyz and other Central Asians are again renewing the call for democracy.

The post-Soviet political transition of Central Asia is the main concern of this book. Not only theoretically, but normatively, the Central Asian transition is imbued with importance and meaning – for those analytically studying that transition, for those shouldering the responsibility of shaping and directing that transition, and most of all, for the many people who are living that transition. In this book, I hope to contribute to our understanding and remembering of that process.

Acknowledgments

Perhaps the most enjoyable part of finishing a book is finally to have the opportunity to thank all those who were involved in the process. It is with sincere and heartfelt gratitude that I acknowledge the support of so many teachers, colleagues, and friends who have been a part of this work and a part of my life.

My work in Central Asia would never have been possible without the dedication and assistance of many Central Asian scholars, students, and dear friends who gave of themselves so generously. Many hundreds of people, in many regions of Kyrgyzstan, Uzbekistan, and Tajikistan, patiently sat through interview sessions with me, and always offered such warm and overflowing hospitality that it was most difficult to leave. Unfortunately, because of political risks, I cannot recognize by name the countless individuals who made my travels to Central Asia so rich in friendships, conversations, and experiences, as well as a remarkable education. I shall forever be indebted to them, and I trust that if they read this, they will know that I remember them.

Many other friends, also interlopers in Central Asia, graciously gave of their time to assist in my research in multiple ways. I am indebted in particular to Sabri Ergan, Howard Ockman, Michael Wallace, Dick Rechtiene, Sethurman Dinakar, Dmitry Trofimov, John Fox, Aftab Khoker, and Ambassador Ram Mukhija and Mrs. Mukhija, who were hospitable and kind and who never failed to spark interesting discussions during my long stays in Central Asia. Ambassador Stanley Escuadero and Ambassador Joseph Pressel graciously shared their time and extensive knowledge of the region on multiple occasions. Ambassador M. K. Bhadrakumar's keen insight constantly provoked new ways of analyzing my findings and greatly expanded my appreciation of the history and culture of Asia. Ercan Murat thoughtfully provided much-needed technical assistance and his faithful drivers, and shared the practical advice that kept me from many a bad situation during my travels. Shrinivas, Basit, Waseem, and Mohammed kindly offered much-needed help. My loyal drivers/bodyguards – Sasha, Sergei,

Alexei, Aziz, Sasha, Gulam, Kubanbek, and Alisher – ensured that I never had to worry when I was in their hands. Over the course of our friendship, from Stanford to Moscow, Valery Tishkov has offered a wealth of scholarly advice and wisdom. The Institute for Ethnography and Anthropology, which he directs, has been generous with its treasures of experience, knowledge, and resources.

My book is the result of many influences on my education. My mother was perhaps the first to spark my fascination with Russia, through the history and literature she teaches so well. Father Fred Kelly, formerly a professor at the Jesuit University in Baghdad, long ago kindled in me an abiding curiosity about the Middle East and a profound respect for the Islamic faith and peoples. Although my academic studies originally directed me toward Russia, eventually I found myself in the heart of a fascinating mélange of Russian and Islamic culture and history. I cannot forget the inspiration of many wonderful faculty members at the University of Notre Dame, where I spent my undergraduate years of study. With warm gratitude I remember my Russian classes with Thomas Marullo and David Gasperetti. I owe a debt to T. R. Schwarz, Edward Goerner, Walter Pratt, and Marcia Weigle, who encouraged me to go to graduate school, and especially to George Brinkley, who left me a library of Soviet history books that I use to this day. Jim McAdams, my senior thesis advisor, was a constant source of support, not only at Notre Dame, but during the many ups and downs of graduate school as well. He gave me the best advice possible when I left for Kyrgyzstan in June 1994 – to begin field research. He told me to ask people what was important, and just to listen. I thank him for always having faith in me and my work, right through to this book's completion.

I returned to Notre Dame as a Kellogg Fellow, and later as a faculty member. Since then, I have benefited from being a member of a truly great cohort of colleagues and friends. Scott Mainwaring and the Kellogg Institute have provided a research home and exceptional support. Fran Hagopian and Tony Messina each read parts of the manuscript and gave generous advice and support in recent years. I truly thank them. Rodney Hero has been a wonderfully encouraging chairman. Michael Coppedge and Michael Zuckert offered sound advice. I have learned much from Eileen Botting, Al Tillery, and Lou Ayala. They have been great critics and even better friends. Cheri Gray solved many crises during my overseas travel. Many, many more people in the Notre Dame community have together created a wonderful environment for my teaching and research, and I can never thank them enough.

I owe debts of gratitude to many other people, especially at Stanford University, where this book began as a dissertation. The Department of Political Science at Stanford, the Berkeley–Stanford Program in Post-Soviet Studies, the Center for International Security and Cooperation (CISAC), the United States Institute of Peace, the Center for Russian and East European Studies, the Institute for International Studies, and the MacArthur Foundation all generously funded my research. And Jeanette Marino, like a good mother, invariably made sure that I actually received my stipend in crisp American dollars as I traveled through a region where travelers' checks, much less ATMs, are still almost unknown. Jane Edsell was always cheerful, helpful, and kind. CISAC directors and administrators – Scott Sagan, Andy Kuchins, Analia Bond, Lisa Saad, and Helen Sutton – provided a stimulating working environment. CISAC Fellows Chip Blacker, Norman Naimark, Michael Oksenberg, Donald Rothchild, Elizabeth Sherwood Randall, Stephen Stedman, and especially Lynn Eden were always encouraging. I especially thank Gail Lapidus and Roza Otunbayeva, who are largely responsible for my plunge into Kyrgyzstan.

Lisa MacIntosh-Sundstrom, Steven Krasner, Scott Mainwaring, Gerry Munck, Ronald Suny, Alisher Khamidov, Azizulla Ghazi, Richard Pomfret, and David Kang each commented on parts of the dissertation or book manuscript. Valerie Bunce generously critiqued the whole dissertation. Timothy Colton, Yoshiko Herrera, and Rose McDermott were especially supportive during my postdoctoral fellowship at Harvard. I am particularly grateful for the opportunity to have learned much about Central Asia from my conversations with Adrienne Edgar, Roxanna Bonnell, Laura Adams, John Schoeberlein, Scott Levi, Doug Northrop, David Lewis, Alisher, Aziz, and many other Central Asian colleagues and friends. They all offered both great insights and great companionship, along the Silk Road or in Moscow, as I completed this work. Tim Fiorta and Amy Chambers were excellent research assistants.

Jason Cowert and Ted Lee solved many a computer crisis, and Scott Boehnen, Andrey Kounov, and Alexei Sitnikov chivalrously offered much-needed moving assistance as I packed and unpacked for my many trips overseas. My cohort at Stanford – especially Pam Ballinger, Kelly Chang, Erin Jenne, Inna Sayfer, Marie-Joelle Zahar, and Rebecca Bill Chavez – shared laughs along the way. Arthur Khachikian, Lisa MacIntosh-Sundstrom, Flavia Herrod, Bisi Agboola, and Lou Ayala have patiently listened to my travails and exultations and reminded me of the many other joys in life.

It is hard to imagine being blessed with a more wonderful dissertation committee than mine. They genuinely care about scholarship, about their students, and about the real political problems of regime transitions and democratization. Philippe Schmitter was instrumental in framing my ideas about the study of democratization, and has continually given thought-provoking advice. Jean Oi always challenged me to sharpen and clarify my arguments, and to develop both the careful empirical detail and the broader comparative implications of my work. For years, when not saving democracy in Russia, Mike McFaul has always managed to offer insightful academic advice and an abundance of moral support. Most especially, I thank Larry Diamond and David Holloway. Larry probably lost many hours of sleep in so carefully reading and critiquing my lengthy chapters, and in provoking me to develop my arguments and analysis. Perhaps just as importantly, his perpetual encouragement has given me whatever confidence I have in myself, my ideas, and my work. Larry's dedication continually fills me with awe. The world is a far better place because of his commitment to democratization. I can never adequately thank my graduate advisor, David Holloway, who unfailingly exemplifies the true nature of scholarship and the strength of personal integrity. I persevered through graduate school because of his support. He has been a constant inspiration. The Uzbek poet Alisher Navoi once wrote that "an *ustoz* is a more than a teacher; he is a mentor and a friend." David Holloway is a true *ustoz*. Because I had such a wonderful committee of advisors, I completed my dissertation, and now this book, with some sadness. I can only hope to bring such passion and dedication to my own teaching and research.

I presented the dissertation and book manuscript at APSA (the American Political Science Association), ASN (the Association for the Study of Nationalities), AAASS (the American Association for the Advancement of Slavic Studies), the University of Wisconsin, Stanford, Cornell, Princeton, Duke, the University of Chicago, Dartmouth, the University of Illinois, Ohio State, King's College Cambridge, Berkeley, the Kellogg Institute, the Harriman Institute at Columbia University, the University of Minnesota, the Harvard Davis Center for Russian Research, and the Weatherhead Center for International Affairs, among other places. I greatly appreciate the helpful comments I received. An overview of the book was published as "The Logic of Clan Politics: Evidence from the Central Asian Trajectories," *World Politics*, vol. 56, no. 2 (January 2004). Parts of Chapter 2 of my dissertation and Chapter 1 of this book were published as "Clans, Pacts, and Politics in Central Asia," *Journal of Democracy*, vol. 13, no. 3 (July 2002). I am also indebted to two anonymous reviewers from Cambridge University Press, and especially to my Cambridge editor, Lew Bateman, for seeing the book to completion. I was fortunate to have superb editorial assistance from Stephanie Lewis Levy and Phil Costopoulos. There are many aspects of this study that are still incomplete, unknown, or in flux. Some things have necessarily been left unsaid. The many imperfections are solely my own. Yet I hope that in spite of them, those who inspired and guided this work will be proud to have done so.

Finally, I owe an irreparable debt to my family. My parents inspired in me a love of learning and sacrificed much to give me an education. Ryan, Megan, and Anne have patiently endured me and encouraged my endeavors for many years. No words will express what that means to me. Nor would I have survived "my great white whale," as he puts it, without my future husband, Tom, who always makes me laugh. Tom probably never planned to become an expert on Central Asia, but he has listened night after night with loving kindness and patience to the saga of this book, and he has been waiting too long for me to finish it. Most of all, I thank Jayne Collins, a great teacher, scholar, and mom. I dedicate this book to her – for her innumerable hours of worrying, and for her constant support and love.

Notre Dame, Indiana

Note on Transliteration

In this book, I use a modified Library of Congress system of transliteration from the Cyrillic, especially for Russian words and names. There is no standard system for the transliteration of the Central Asian languages. There is even further confusion in transliteration, given that some languages (especially Uzbek and Turkmen) have started to use a modified Latin alphabet in recent years. There is also disagreement among Central Asians themselves over the proper new Latin spelling of some words. Throughout the text, I adopt the Central Asian form based on the Cyrillic script, since the most comprehensive Central Asian dictionaries are still in Cyrillic. A few exceptions are included in the glossary.

I have adopted some changes for the ease of the reader who is not fluent in Russian or the Central Asian languages. I have typically not used accent marks above the letters, though I have retained the Russian soft sign (e.g., *oblast'*). For words commonly used, such as glasnost, I drop the sign.

For the ease of the reader as well as for the sake of consistency throughout the text, I use one form (the Uzbek form) of any Central Asian word that has very similar variants and the same meaning across the languages (for example, *qishloq, oqsoqol, mahalla*). See the Appendix for other forms of these words in Kyrgyz, Tajik, Turkmen, and Kazakh. When using a plural form of a Central Asian or Russian word (such as *qishloq, kolkhoz*), I simply add the English plural form, "s" (*qishloqs, kolkhozes*), rather than use the Central Asian plural, which might be confusing to the reader.

I attempt to use the most common and most readable spellings of Central Asian persons' names (such as Niyazov, not Niiazov). If they retain the Russian spelling, I adopt that. If they have changed to a more traditional Uzbek or Tajik spelling, I use that form. Some names are written in multiple ways in the local press, so it can be difficult to know which is the preferred form for each person. It is important to note that in some cases, individuals and/or families since independence and in some cases since perestroika have opted to drop the Russian endings from their names (e.g., the Pulatov/Pulat brothers).

When using Central Asian place names, I generally adopt the transliteration from the Russian/Cyrillic spelling, except when a particular spelling is common in the Western literature, or when the Russian form is less readable than other forms. For example, I use the Uzbek spelling Jizzak (rather than the Russian Dzhizak) for the Uzbek province. I use Samarkand, the common English spelling, for the city and province of Samarkand. I use the common transliteration of the Russian form of Uzbekistan (not the Uzbek form, Ozbekistan). In discussing the post-1991 period, I use the common form, Kyrgyzstan, rather than the official form, the Kyrgyz Republic, throughout text for the sake of simplicity and to conserve space. Transliteration does not reflect any bias toward one of the many languages used in the region, but only my concern for some consistency and the ease of the general reader.

I

An Introduction to Political Development and Transition in Central Asia

In 1994, I had the opportunity to monitor the local elections in the Kyrgyz Republic. I was then given a first glimpse of clan politics. I talked with local elders who had come in to vote for their twenty or thirty closest relatives. The election monitors didn't mind. "This is our practice here," they said. They did not stop the elders, nor report incidents of fraud. Election observers in other districts recounted the same story. This seemed odd in a country recently deemed a "democracy." The election results were even more odd, as political parties gained less than 20 percent of the seats in parliament and did not even field a candidate in the presidential elections. Just as bizarre were the 1994 and 1999 Uzbek and Tajik parliamentary elections, where new authoritarian regimes had attempted since the Soviet collapse to create mass, pro-regime parties, based on their renamed Communist Party institutions, but had widely failed. As in the Kyrgyz Republic, the majority of seats went to so-called independents. None of these regimes was able to combat the widespread practice of voting for personalistic leaders along clan lines. Moreover, in spite of massive campaigns by all three governments since 1991 to create national, civic identities, at the mass level, in all regions of each country, most people strongly identified with their local clan networks, not with parties, not with ethnic groups, and certainly not with either the democratic opposition or the state. In other ways, the Central Asian presidents actively drew on clan ties and practices during elections. In the subsequent presidential elections, the Kyrgyz government informally pressured local elders to organize a traditional "democratic" *kurultai* to endorse the incumbent president and to use their kin and patronage networks in the villages to vote for him.

The Central Asian elections offer just one example of "clan politics." This study explores the causes, dynamics, and implications of this general type of political behavior – politics organized by and around informal identity networks commonly known as clans. After the Soviet collapse in 1991, neither scholars nor policy makers had anticipated the rise of a primarily informal, clan-based politics throughout Central Asia. While the optimists predicted that democracy could and would spread to the far reaches of the former Soviet Union, the naysayers expected either the rise of Islamic fundamentalism or the persistence of communism even after the Central Asian republics were forced to exit the defunct Soviet Union. Indeed, the basis of such uncertainty and pessimism was strong; Central Asia, the Soviet Union's southern, Islamic, and Asian rim, had never before experienced statehood and nationhood, much less democracy. For 130 years these republics had been colonized, first by the Russian empire and later by the Soviet empire; they thus shared a similar authoritarian political legacy.

While Russia has long viewed this region as its Muslim periphery, Central Asia was at the heart of multiple civilizations long before Russia's entry into the region. The pre-Russian Islamicization, under the influence of Persian and Arab neighbors, and a pre-Islamic history characterized by tribal political alliances and a clan-based social organization are just as important to Central Asia's cultural, social, and political history and identity. Indeed, the complexity of identity and history in Central Asia makes it a region of rich interest for studies of comparative politics.

This book is a study of regime transition, transformation, and state building in Central Asia, from Soviet colonization to decolonization; in particular, the book explores the informal politics that shapes these processes, the political systems that emerge, and the durability of these systems. Creating a democratic regime and creating a durable one are two issues that should be linked, yet most scholars and practitioners of the "third wave" of democracy have focused on building democratic regimes while neglecting the fundamental issue of regime stability.[1] This study integrates these issues.

Building on very similar cultural and social foundations, and coming from nearly parallel experiences with Soviet political and economic institutions and development strategies, the five new states of Central Asia surprisingly embarked on distinct political trajectories. While the Kyrgyz Republic rapidly adopted democratic and market reforms, its neighbors – Kazakhstan, Uzbekistan, Tajikistan, and Turkmenistan – settled into a post-communist authoritarianism. Moreover, while four of the five Central Asian regimes survived the transition and have subsequently maintained internal stability, Tajikistan's regime did not. In 1992, the Tajik regime collapsed in the midst of a bloody civil conflict that would last until 1997, with violent repercussions and flare-ups into early 2004. This is one central puzzle addressed in this book: What explains this initial divergence of trajectories – in both the type and the durability of these emergent regimes? Is democratization possible in Central Asia? And why do some regimes survive decolonization

---

[1] On the democratization wave that began in Portugal in 1971, see Samuel Huntington, *The Third Wave: Democratization in the Late Twentieth Century* (Norman: University of Oklahoma Press, 1991).

and transition? That is, why are some regimes durable while others abruptly collapse in conflict?

Going beyond the transition, this study asks: What kinds of regimes emerge in the longer term? Can they be understood by examining only the formal institutions of the regime, when in fact in-country research suggests that clans play such a critical role? Why and how have clans and clan politics been shaping these political trajectories? We must explain the informalization of power in regimes that had once seemed so solidly institutionalized, consolidated, and even modern under the Soviet system. This book shows how clans have played a major role in this process. The book offers a historical and broader theoretical explanation of the persistence of clans and the rise of clan politics. Clan politics creates an informal regime, an arrangement of power and rules in which clans are the dominant social actors and political players; they transform the political system. Clan networks, not formal institutions and elected officials, hold and exercise real power. Clan politics has a corrosive effect on the formal regime, especially on democratic institutions; it further erodes the durability of both democratic and authoritarian institutions over time, as fragile, personalistic regimes cling to power.

In these respects, understanding clans in certain societies is critical to responding to one of the key theoretical and policy questions of our time: why and how does democratization sometimes fail, and why is political order often a victim as well? Instability, collapse, and conflict are the brutal consequences. Since the late 1990s, the U.S. government, the World Bank, the International Monetary Fund (IMF), and the Organization for Security and Co-operation in Europe (OSCE) have been both intrigued and confounded by democratization and its failures in Central Asia. Scholars and policy makers alike have viewed Central Asia through theoretical models that fail to grasp the complex sociological basis of either its pre-transition politics or its transitional and post-transition regimes. Most observers have viewed the post-communist countries uniformly as cases of democratization, implying that significant forces within society or the state were pushing for democracy. But while Central Europe succeeded, Central Asia failed. Thomas Carothers recently inserted a reality check into the "transitions debate."[2] Carothers countered that Central Asia, the Caucasus, and even Russia have not in fact been struggling toward democracy. They are not temporarily trapped between communist dictatorship and liberal democracy. Rather, like many failed (or half-heartedly attempted) African transitions of the 1950s and 1960s, and again in the 1990s, these regimes have comfortably settled into new forms of authoritarianism that might continue for decades.[3] Not just in post-Soviet

---

[2] Thomas Carothers, "The End of the Transitions Paradigm," *Journal of Democracy*, vol. 13, no. 1 (January 2002), pp. 5–21.

[3] Philip Roeder, "The Revolution of 1989: Postcommunism and the Social Sciences," *Slavic Review*, vol. 58, no. 4 (Winter 1999), pp. 743–755. For similar views on African transitions,

Central Asia, but in Afghanistan, Somalia, the Sudan, and Iraq, tribal and other identity networks have similarly attained greater salience as socialist dictatorships were swept away.[4] The Central Asian cases therefore present a remarkable opportunity for scholars of regime change and democratization. In comparatively tracing three distinct post-communist transitions – democratization in the Kyrgyz Republic, authoritarianism in Uzbekistan, and regime collapse and disintegration in Tajikistan – this study ties together and examines both regime transition and democratization and political order and collapse.

I. AN OVERVIEW OF THE CENTRAL ASIAN TRAJECTORIES

In the heady days of the early 1990s, the Kyrgyz Republic seemed the exemplar of democratization theory; democratization had made significant strides, even in the most unlikely and unfavorable of circumstances. Neither socioeconomic deprivation and decline, nor the "Leninist legacy" of seventy years, nor Islamic or Asian values – all factors that earlier scholarship had highlighted as detrimental to democratization – seemed to have thwarted the spread of democracy. Following the adoption of its new constitution in May 1993, the Kyrgyz Republic was internationally touted by the Western media as "an island of democracy" surrounded by a sea of authoritarianism. The president of the Kyrgyz Republic (more commonly referred to as Kyrgyzstan) was Askar Akaev, a former academic who became renowned in Western circles for his supple references to Alexis de Tocqueville and Thomas Jefferson. Kyrgyz legislators and judges flew to Washington, D.C. for training in democratic principles, the rule of law, and market economics. Where civil society had been nearly nonexistent, nongovernmental organizations suddenly proliferated, defending human rights, supporting women in business, developing a free press, and even creating a Silk Road Internet. Kyrgyz youth watched *Dynasty*, listened to Bruce Springsteen, wore American flag tee shirts, and even studied at Georgetown, Indiana University, and Notre Dame. These changes were foreign not only to communism but also to the region's Asian and Islamic culture. The globalization of capitalism and democracy seemed at its apex.

A neat discussion of the Central Asian transitions would end with 1995; by then, the second set of presidential and/or parliamentary elections had taken place, a point that many democratization theorists use as the marker to end the transition. Kyrgyzstan had liberalized and established an electoral democracy by late 1991, according to Joseph Schumpeter's minimalist

---

see Jeffery Herbst, "Political Liberalization in Africa after Ten Years," *Comparative Politics*, vol. 33, no. 3 (April 2001), pp. 357–375.

[4] Susan Sachs, "In Iraq's Next Act, Tribes May Play the Lead Role," *New York Times*, June 6, 2004.

criterion of free and fair elections. Civil and political liberties were rapidly expanding.[5] While hardly a full-fledged liberal democracy, much less a consolidated one, Kyrgyzstan surprised the world during this early period. In Kyrgyzstan's neighbors, however, elections were manipulated, and some doubted that any transition had taken place. In Uzbekistan, President Islam Karimov won a referendum and appeared to have consolidated his dictatorship, described in the American press as Stalinist. In Tajikistan, the former communist leadership was run from power during the civil war, and the newly elected president, Emomali Rakhmonov, emerged from the chaos of the civil war and recreated an authoritarian regime with Russia's backing.

Yet the story of transition does not end here. As political uncertainty subsided and the new institutions and rules of the game were established, Central Asia's regime trajectories increasingly converged. By 2000, these regimes looked quite similar – similar in their inability to consolidate their formal institutions, similar in their informal division of political and economic resources, and similar in their increasingly precarious grasp on domestic stability. By 2002, not merely democracy, but the durability of these regimes appeared to be in question. Why were these democratic and authoritarian institutions unable to consolidate their power? These cases suggest important implications for our understanding of institutions, the role of social actors in transitions, and the importance of informal politics.

Indeed, we find that, despite the postcommunist regime, institutions turn out to be less significant than the informal clan relationships that organize society and politics. In adopting a more historical and sociological view of political development in Central Asia, this work situates the short-term regime transition within the longer-term political development of this region – from its pre-Soviet and pre-modern society, through Soviet "modernization," to a post-Soviet transition, transformation, and state building. In this light, the post-Soviet transition is indeed a sharp and uncertain break with the past. The divergence of Central Asia's immediate post-Soviet trajectories is puzzling. The post-transition period, from about 1995 to the present, exhibits an ongoing dynamic between the formal and informal elements of politics, and a surprising reemergence of informal organizations embedded in both the Soviet and the pre-Soviet political order of this region.

Clans have not played a political role only in Central Asia. Yet they have greater resilience and political power in some societies than in others. For example, clans declined or disappeared in many states in Western Europe, and have sometimes been controlled by states in East Asia. Yet in post-Soviet Central Asia, we find that clans adapted to the Soviet system, were

---

[5] See Joseph Schumpeter's classic, *Capitalism, Socialism, and Democracy* (New York: Harper and Row, 1975 [1947]).

TABLE 1.1. *Political trajectories in the post-Soviet Central Asian cases*

Short Term: 1991–94		
Case	**Formal Regime Type**[a]	**Regime Durability**[b]
Kyrgyzstan	Electoral democracy	Durable
Uzbekistan	Autocracy	Durable
Tajikistan	Collapsed regime	Not durable
Kazakhstan	Autocracy	Durable
Turkmenistan	Autocracy	Durable

Medium–Longer Term: 1995–2004			
Case	**Formal Regime Type**	**Informal Regime**	**Regime Durability**
Kyrgyzstan	Autocracy	Clan politics	Weakly durable
Uzbekistan	Autocracy	Clan politics	Moderately durable but declining
Tajikistan	Autocracy	Clan politics	Weakly durable
Kazakhstan	Autocracy	Clan politics[c]	Durable
Turkmenistan	Autocracy	Clan politics	Weakly durable

[a] Regime type is measured according to Freedom House scores.
[b] Regime durability scores reflect indicators of collapse in Robert Rotberg, "Failed States, Collapsed States, Weak States: Causes and Indicators," in Robert Rotberg, ed., *State Failure and State Weakness in a Time of Terror* (Washington, DC: Brookings Press, 2003), pp. 2–9. Specifically, I use a broken pact, coup attempts, protest, and violent insurgency as indicators of declining durability.
[c] Clan politics is much more limited and controlled in this case, as a result of economic prosperity.

both repressed and fostered by it, and now play a transformative role in the post-colonial conditions of these new states. (See Table 1.1 for an overview of the cases and trajectories.)

One of the objectives of this book is to explore the relevance of two major theoretical arguments about democratization for understanding regime transition in Central Asia and, by implication, in other clan-based societies. Comparative historical analysis of the Central Asian transitions finds that neither the "preconditions" school nor the "transitions" school adequately explains the type of transition that takes place in these cases.[6] However, this inquiry goes beyond the rather narrow focus of these approaches to post-communist studies, situating these transitions within a broader set of political

[6] For a more precise discussion of each theory's predictions for Central Asia, see Kathleen Collins, "Clans, Pacts, and Politics: Understanding Regime Transition in Central Asia" (Ph.D. dissertation, Stanford University, 1999), chapter 2; and Kathleen Collins, "Clans, Pacts, and Politics in Central Asia," *Journal of Democracy*, vol. 13, no. 3 (July 2002), pp. 137–140.

processes under way.[7] In developing an alternative approach that puts clans at the center of a theory of political development, I draw upon the classic political sociology of Weber and Durkheim, as well as upon insights taken from the more recent literature on political development, informal institutions, norms, and networks, to explain these political processes. Clans are the critical informal organizations that we must conceptualize and theorize in order to understand politics in Central Asia and similar developing states. This work finds that the dynamic interplay among clans and between clans and the state helps to explain the central elements of the political trajectory: (1) regime durability, that is, whether or not the regime will be viable or collapse during and after the transition; and (2) regime type, not just the formal governing arrangements and distribution of power (e.g., democracy, autocracy, state socialism), but more importantly, the informal governing arrangement and distribution of power beneath the formal façade.

II. LINKING POLITICAL TRANSITION AND POLITICAL ORDER

In this book, I bring together two major literatures often treated disparately: studies of transition and democratization, and scholarship on political development and the social foundations of political order. This analysis both builds from and critiques earlier approaches, and contributes to them by offering a theory that connects clans and political trajectories. The post-communist cases are indeed a "laboratory" for theories of democratization.[8] Yet they are also a laboratory for understanding the dynamics of political development and state building in post-colonial and post-imperial societies. Indeed, the two issues are deeply intertwined. Before delving into a discussion of a theory of clan politics and transition, in chapter 2 of this book, it is important to understand what the prevailing paradigms for studying transition tell us, or in fact fail to explain, in these cases.

The Inadequacy of Theories of Regime Transition

Two schools of thought have dominated the literature on regime transition and democratization, as well as the literature on post-communism, for

---

[7] Some scholars have argued that we should view the post-communist cases as transformations, suggesting a deeper change than a mere formal regime transition. See Lazslo Bruzst and David Stark, *Post-Socialist Pathways: Transforming Politics and Property in East Central Europe* (Cambridge: Cambridge University Press, 1998); Katherine Verdery and Michael Buroway, *Uncertain Transition* (New York: Rowman and Littlefield, 1999); and Valerie Bunce and Maria Csanadi, "Uncertainty in the Transition: Post-Communism in Hungary," *East European Politics and Societies*, vol. 7, no. 2 (Spring 1993), p. 262.
[8] George Breslauer, "Introduction," in Richard Anderson, M. Steven Fish, Stephen Hanson, and Philip Roeder, *Postcommunism and the Theory of Democracy* (Princeton, NJ: Princeton University Press, 2001), p. 3.

decades. Since 1989, these schools have shaped the debate about the causes
and failures of democratization in the post-communist transitions.[9] In the
1960s and 1970s, one school of thought, generally known as "preconditions" or alternatively "modernization" theory, emphasized the causal role
of macro-social, macroeconomic, and macro-cultural variables in explaining regime change and democratization.[10] This school looks at rising GDP,
literacy, and economic development, at the rise of a middle class, and at the
presence of a secular, individualist culture as preconditions for democracy.
Focusing on one social structure – class – Barrington Moore formulated
the hypothesis: no middle class, no democracy.[11] He would not have anticipated democratization in Kyrgyzstan, or anywhere else in the former Soviet
republics for that matter. In fact, in 1991, except for their literacy rates (estimated at 97 to 99 percent) and their partial industrialization and urbanization, the Central Asian republics would hardly typify societies on the brink
of democratization. (See Appendix, Tables A.3 and A.4.) Almond and Verba,
representing another strand of the "preconditions" school, would have been
skeptical because of the lack of individualistic and civic values, much less a
civil society, across the region. On the one hand, large segments of society
did remain independent of the state, especially after the Stalinist period. Yet,
much like what has been termed "traditional society" in Africa, Asia, and the
Middle East, Central Asian society is organized around an array of clan, kin,
and Islamic institutions. Social organization is largely ascriptive and involuntary, promoting communal norms and values, unlike the individualist and
voluntary associations that de Tocqueville and others have argued are the basis of Western and democratic civil society.[12] Others have fined-tuned the negative prediction of the modernization school, pointing out that democratization might commence in these low-income, semimodern countries but would

[9] These two theoretical paradigms, their specific hypotheses, and their application to Central Asia are discussed at greater length in Kathleen Collins, "Clans, Pacts, and Politics:
Understanding Regime Transition," pp. 21–99. For a statistical critique of the preconditions literature's variables as applied to the post-communist states, see M. Steven Fish, "Democratization's Requisites: The Postcommunist Experience," *Post-Soviet Affairs*, vol. 14,
no. 3 (1998), pp. 212–247. For a critique of transitology, see Valerie Bunce, "Comparative
Democratization: Big and Bounded Generalizations," *Comparative Political Studies*, vol. 33,
no. 6/7 (August/September 2000), pp. 703–734.
[10] Exemplars include Samuel Huntington, *Political Order in Changing Societies* (New Haven,
CT: Yale University Press, 1968); Seymour Martin Lipset, *Political Man: The Social Bases of
Politics* (New York: Doubleday, 1960); Larry Diamond, Juan Linz, and Seymour Martin
Lipset, eds., *Politics in Developing Countries: Comparing Experiences with Democracy*
(Boulder, CO: Lynne Rienner, 1995); and Kenneth Jowitt, *The New World Disorder*
(Berkeley: University of California Press, 1992).
[11] Barrington Moore, *Social Origins of Dictatorship and Democracy: Lord and Peasant in the
Making of the Modern World* (Boston: Beacon Press, 1966).
[12] Gabriel Almond and Sidney Verba, *The Civic Culture: Political Attitudes and Democracy in
Five Nations* (Boston: Little, Brown, 1965); and Robert Putnam, *Making Democracy Work:
Civic Traditions in Modern Italy* (Princeton, NJ: Princeton University Press, 1993).

probably not be sustainable.[13] An unanswered question, however, is what mechanism or mechanisms undermine democracy in less modern countries.

For the past two decades, the "transitions" school has become the predominant approach for explaining transitions from authoritarianism and democratization. Dankwart Rustow, and later Guillermo O'Donnell and Philippe Schmitter, in a sharp break with their pessimistic predecessors, set out the central argument of democratization theory: elite actors can willfully reject authoritarianism and both initiate democratization and consolidate democracy irrespective of social, cultural, and economic conditions or historical legacies.[14] While giving hope for democracy around the globe, this view often explains the short-term, elite-led initiation of democracy at the expense of anticipating and understanding the medium-term retrenchment toward authoritarianism, especially given the absence of social support for democracy. Indeed, the central hypothesis of this theory is that elite choices, in the form of often-exclusivist elite pacts are, paradoxically, the most likely path to successful democratization. Conversely, paths that involve society, the theory predicts, are more likely to end in failure. A large corpus of subsequent literature has focused overwhelmingly on the formal and elite level, on getting the *formal* institutions right to consolidate democracy,[15] rather than on the often more powerful informal level.[16] Less scholarship has been devoted to explaining the factors working against democratization, much less against consolidation. O'Donnell himself did warn that informal, particularistic relationships lead to low-quality, "delegative democracies" in much of the developing world, but he expects them to be durable regimes.[17]

The Central Asian cases call us to rethink the central hypothesis of O'Donnell and Schmitter, since pacts in Central Asia have generally been followed by autocracy; they were followed by a brief period of democratization only in Kyrgyzstan, where Askar Akaev and a handful of civil society activists, not a pact between regime elites, were mainly responsible for

---

[13] Adam Przeworski and Fernando Limongi, "Modernization: Theories and Facts," *World Politics*, vol. 49, no. 2 (January 1997), pp. 155–183.

[14] Dankwart Rustow, "Transitions to Democracy: Toward a Dynamic Model," *Comparative Politics*, vol. 2, no. 3 (April 1970), pp. 337–363; and Guillermo O'Donnell, Laurence Whitehead, and Philippe C. Schmitter, *Transitions from Authoritarian Rule: Tentative Conclusions about Uncertain Democracies* (Baltimore, MD: The Johns Hopkins University Press, 1986).

[15] On consolidation, see Scott Mainwaring and Timothy Scully, eds., *Building Democratic Institutions: Party Systems in Latin America* (Stanford, CA: Stanford University Press, 1995); and Juan J. Linz and Alfred Stepan, *Problems of Democratic Transition and Consolidation: Southern Europe, South America, and Post-Communist Europe* (Baltimore, MD: The Johns Hopkins University Press, 1996).

[16] Exceptions include Guillermo O'Donnell, "Illusions About Consolidation," *Journal of Democracy*, vol. 7, No. 2 (April 1996), pp. 34–51; and Katherine Verdery and Michael Buroway, *Uncertain Transition*.

[17] Guillermo O'Donnell, "Delegative Democracy," *Journal of Democracy*, vol. 5, no. 1 (January 1994), pp. 55–69.

the democratization that briefly occurred. The Central Asian cases offer a different hypothesis: pacts, when made between clan elites, are not a mode of transition to democracy, but an informal agreement that fosters the durability of the state, irrespective of the regime type.[18]

Recent contributions to the transitions school have often focused on the "post-communist" cases and the peculiarities of the "Soviet legacy," without distinguishing the vast variation in that legacy from Hungary to Tajikistan. Again, they highlight the role of elite actors, ideology, and leadership choice in designing democratic institutions.[19] However, they fail to explain why democratic ideology resonates in some societies and not in others, why some leaders matter and others do not, or how society may constrain transitions.[20] A related problem is that few scholars have systematically incorporated the role of society and social organization, either in driving, facilitating, or inhibiting democratization and democratic consolidation. This is somewhat surprising, given the powerful role of social movements in the political transitions in Eastern Europe and the Baltics, in contrast with the silent role of society in most of Central Asia, where autocracies emerged. Those who have examined society's role in democratization typically focus on class, labor, and parties – *formal* social organizations that are largely irrelevant in Central Asia since the Soviet collapse.[21] Examining the role of *informal* social actors is just as critical.

Studying Central Asia further forces us to examine *nondemocratic trajectories* – either the rise of new autocracies or, conversely, regime collapse. These phenomena have received surprisingly little attention in the transitions literature until recently, as scholars of post-communism struggle to explain

[18] Kathleen Collins, "Understanding Regime Transition," chapter 3; and Collins, "Clans, Pacts, and Politics," pp. 137–145.

[19] Adam Przeworski, *Democracy and the Market: Political and Economic Reforms in Eastern Europe and Latin America* (Cambridge: Cambridge University Press, 1991).

[20] See Michael McFaul, "The Fourth Wave of Democracy and Dictatorship: Noncooperative Transitions in the Postcommunist World," *World Politics*, vol. 54, no. 2 (January 2002), pp. 212–244; M. Steven Fish, "Postcommunist Subversion: Social Science and Democratization in East Europe and Eurasia," *Slavic Review*, vol. 58 (Winter 1999), pp. 794–823; Gerardo Munck and Carol Leff, "Modes of Transition and Democratization: South America and Eastern Europe in Comparative Perspective," *Comparative Politics*, vol. 29, no. 3 (April 1997), pp. 343–362; Gerald Easter, "Preference for Presidentialism: Postcommunist Regime Change in Russia and the NIS," *World Politics*, vol. 49, no. 2. (January 1997), pp. 184–211; and John Higley and Richard Gunther, eds., *Elites and Democratic Consolidation in Latin America and Southern Europe* (Baltimore, MD: The Johns Hopkins University Press, 1992).

[21] For example: Ruth Berins Collier, *Paths towards Democracy: The Working Class and Elites in Western Europe and South America* (Cambridge: Cambridge University Press, 1999); David Collier and Ruth Berins Collier, *Shaping the Political Arena* (Princeton, NJ: Princeton University Press, 1991); and Eva Rana Bellin, "Contingent Democrats: Industrialists, Labor, and Democratization in Late-Developing Countries," *World Politics*, vol. 52, no. 2 (January 2000), pp. 175–205.

democratic backsliding.[22] Explanations have generally treated the return to autocracy as little more than a lack of elite commitment to democracy; elites desire to hold onto power, and do so by creating super-presidential institutions.[23] And yet an array of new autocracies has emerged in this region.[24] In many of them, the president does not act autonomously, despite the hyperconcentration of executive power, but is instead constrained by informal networks, such as clans. Neither democratic nor autocratic power is consolidated. As Samuel Huntington astutely observed in the 1960s, the problem in many new states is consolidating power: "there is a failure to recognize that most countries are suffering from an absence of power in their political systems."[25] The problem of political order becomes fundamental – where is power located, how is it used to govern, and what are the implications for stability? We need to understand the nature and content of these autocracies, and the implications for their stability. In order to do so, we must go beyond the literature's narrow focus and study the informal mechanisms beneath the failed liberalization and declining durability of regimes in Central Asia.

Political Development and Order when "Informal" Politics Prevails

The Central Asian cases challenge us to rethink the democratization literature and to search for better explanations of these political trajectories. Democratization may occur at the initiative of a few elites, and democratic institutions imposed from above may indeed introduce significant reforms, as we have seen in Kyrgyzstan and Russia in the early 1990s. An elite component to democracy is critical. At the same time, a social component is just as critical, if not more critical, to the sustaining of democracy. The social component is to a large extent rooted in social organization and in socioeconomic and cultural conditions. When social actors at the mass level are networked into a clan-based structure of patronage and dependency, they are less likely to check the actions of elites. When power is organized informally in the hands of opaque clan networks, the ideological choices and actions of the best-intentioned elites will ultimately have a very limited effect.

---

[22] O'Donnell and Schmitter's classic work emphasized and the transition "from" the old regime, not necessarily to democracy. Guillermo O'Donnell and Philippe C. Schmitter, *Transitions from Authoritarian Rule* (Baltimore, MD: The Johns Hopkins University Press, 1986). Recent exceptions to the focus on democratic outcomes include Richard Anderson, M. Steven Fish, Stephen Hanson, and Philip Roeder, *Postcommunism and the Theory of Democracy*; Bunce, "Comparative Democratization"; McFaul, "The Fourth Wave"; and Steven Levitsky and Lucan Way, "The Rise of Competitive Authoritarianism," *Journal of Democracy*, vol. 13, no. 2 (April 2002), pp. 51–66.

[23] An elite focus offers a partial explanation of democratic backsliding. See Fish, "Postcommunist Subversion."

[24] Philip Roeder, *Postcommunism*, pp. 11–53.

[25] Samuel Huntington, *Political Order*, chapter 1.

When there is a long historical, institutional, and cultural basis for foster-ing nontransparent clan-based politics, these mechanisms and patterns of political development are not likely to disappear with ease. The "social" focus of the "preconditions" school, then, does have merit. Yet, rather than concentrate on macro-level factors that involve no agency or mechanism for undermining democracy, this inquiry focuses on meso-level social networks and the logic of individual actors within these networks. Those actors seek to maintain their power, prestige, and social stability through creating informal and exclusivist rules of the game that effactually subvert open and inclusive democratic rules.

Given the inability of either the democratization or the preconditions the-ory adequately to explain the Central Asian trajectories, this study proposes a shift in thinking, a turn toward understanding these cases in terms of the *informal politics* of state-society interaction that underlies the dynamics of regime transformation. As Guillermo O'Donnell later argued, the transitions literature and its overwhelming focus on formal institutions and democratic consolidation has neglected the *informal* level of particularistic ties, where power is often located.[26] Still, this powerful critique of the democratization literature has generated few studies of the relationship between informal organizations and regime type and durability, either theoretically or empir-ically. A number of scholars outside of the transitions paradigm do look at informal politics and the state-society dynamic that critically affects political development.

An earlier political-sociological literature on development in the post-colonial world did take the social organization of post-colonial and tran-sitional societies seriously, especially in connection with their prospects for nation and state building. In fact, this literature's framing of these issues, as well as the lessons it offers, give us some insight into the relationship be-tween clans and political trajectories in contemporary Central Asia. While some proclaimed the informal politics of tribalism a primordial curse, oth-ers naively dismissed it as a thing of the colonial or pre-colonial past. The former strand, in overemphasizing the static, unchanging culture and social structure of these regions, assumed the incompatibility of "traditional so-ciety" with modernity or democracy. For example, one scholar wrote that "tribalism is Africa's natural condition, and is likely to remain so for a long time to come."[27] This deterministically anticipated the failure of political transitions in such societies.[28] While highlighting tribalism or the salience of other subnational identities as a problem, few scholars have investigated

---

[26] Guillermo O'Donnell, "Illusions about Democratic Consolidation."

[27] Colin Legum, "Tribal Survival in the Modern African Political System," *Journal of Asian and African Studies*, vol. 5, no. 1–2 (January–April 1970), p. 102.

[28] M. Fortes and E. E. Evans-Pritchard, eds., *African Political Systems* (London: Oxford University Press, 1940).

both the roots of such strong informal politics and the conditions that foster the emergence or continuance of tribalism.[29]

The latter strand of this literature was fused with optimism after the advent of post–World War II decolonization – not unlike that of the 1990s. Arguing against those who had viewed tribalism as an inexorable problem,[30] the optimists asserted that the modernizationist policies of post-colonial states were already breaking down traditional society. Tribalism would disappear, they argued, thereby fostering nation-stateness and democracy.[31] Even Samuel Huntington, who had stressed the challenges of clan, tribal, and religious loyalties, argued that modernizing state policies would shift "loyalties from family, village, and tribe to nation,"[32] although he was pessimistic about the prospects for simultaneously achieving stable democratic outcomes. Others, observing the Indian case of political development, argued that tradition and modernity were not diametrically opposed; rather, subnational identity groups could be integrated into a durable democratic system.[33] The Indian case today stands as one of the few successful models for integrating informal organizations, such as caste, into a durable democratic system in post-colonial states.

Critiquing those who had predicted successful transitions, the establishment of nation-states, and durable democracies, James Coleman and C. R. D. Halisi argued that the elite-centrism of the early post-colonial period had overestimated elites' power and will to transform society.[34] Elites of the early transition, they claim, were a minority whose support of nationalism

[29] Exceptions include Daniel Posner, "The Colonial Origins of Ethnic Cleavages: The Case of Linguistic Divisions in Zambia," *Comparative Politics*, vol. 35, no. 2 (January 2003), pp. 127–146.

[30] See Colin Legum, "The Dangers of Independence," *Transition*, vol. 6, no. 7 (October 1962), pp. 11–12; David Apter, *Ghana in Transition* (New York: Atheneum Publishers, 1963); Aristide Zolberg, "The Structure of Political Conflict in the New States of Tropical Africa," *American Political Science Review*, vol. 62 (March 1968), pp. 70–87; Abner Cohen, *Custom and Politics in Urban Africa* (Berkeley: University of California Press, 1969).

[31] See Thomas Hodgekin, *Nationalism in Colonial Africa* (London: Frederick Muller, 1956); James Coleman, *Nigeria: Background to Nationalism* (Berkeley: University of California Press, 1958); Aristide Zolberg, *Creating Political Order* (Chicago: Rand McNally, 1966); and James Coleman, *Nationalism and Development in Africa: Selected Essays*, edited by Richard Sklar (Berkeley: University of California Press, 1994). Revisionist modernization theory treated social organization as capable of interaction with the state and transformation. Also see James Coleman, "Nationalism in Tropical Africa," *American Political Science Review*, vol. 48 (June 1954), pp. 404–426; and James Coleman and Carl Rosberg, eds., *Political Parties and National Integration in Tropical Africa* (Berkeley: University of California Press, 1964).

[32] Samuel Huntington, *Political Order*, pp. 140–141.

[33] Lloyd Rudolph and Susanne Rudolph, *The Modernity of Tradition: Political Development in India* (Chicago: University of Chicago Press, 1967).

[34] James S. Coleman and C. R. D. Halisi, "American Political Science and Tropical Africa," *African Studies Review*, vol. 24 (September/December 1983), pp. 220–221.

and democracy did not reflect the deep social divisions, informal groups, and informal politics at the subnational level. Indeed, an abundance of research on the "economy of affection," bureaucratic development, corruption, and the developing economies of these regions demonstrates the persistence of informal institutions and social organizations, but generally without linking those issues to questions of regime.[35] The effects on the political economy of African state development have generally been negative.[36] Nor are such phenomena entirely confined to the Third World. A rich literature on political development in southern Italy – which has lagged behind the rest of Europe – has similarly pointed to the negative political effects of the social structure and cultural norms in which "*clientelismo*" is rooted.[37]

The "state-in-society" literature goes further in examining the dynamic relationship between social organization and the state in historical perspective.[38] Joel Migdal, Atul Kohli, and Vivienne Shue have persuasively demonstrated the need to look beyond democratic or authoritarian regimes and states and to examine the complex and multifaceted relationship between society and state. A central insight of this approach is that society and the state are not separate realms; a dynamic "mutual transformation" intertwines them.[39] At times, society can penetrate and transform the state; in other conditions, the state may transform society. Migdal, Kohli, and Shue argue: "States are parts of societies. States may help mold, but they are also continually molded by, the societies within which they are embedded.... Societies affect states as much as, or possibly more than, states affect societies."[40] This approach questions the common assumption of the statist and institutionalist literature that autonomous states shape society. Similarly, Jeffrey Herbst's study of state building in Africa argues that neither colonial nor post-colonial states have effectively governed Africa's dispersed societies.[41]

---

[35] See Robert Price, *Society and Bureaucracy in Contemporary Ghana* (Berkeley: University of California Press, 1975); Goran Hyden, *Beyond Ujaama in Tanzania: Underdevelopment and an Uncaptured Peasantry* (Berkeley: University of California Press, 1980); and James C. Scott, *The Moral Economy of the Peasant: Rebellion and Subsistence in Southeast Asia* (New Haven, CT: Yale University Press, 1976).

[36] Refer to Michael Bratton and Nicolas Van de Walle, *Democratic Experiments in Africa: Regime Transitions in Comparative Perspective* (Cambridge: Cambridge University Press, 1997).

[37] See Sidney Tarrow, *Peasant Communism in Southern Italy* (New Haven, CT: Yale University Press, 1967).

[38] Joel Migdal, *Strong Societies and Weak States: State-Society Relations and State Capability in the Third World* (Princeton, NJ: Princeton University Press, 1988); and Joel Migdal, Atul Kohli, and Vivienne Shue, eds., *State Power and Social Forces: Domination and Transformation in the Third World* (Cambridge: Cambridge University Press, 1994).

[39] Joel Migdal, Atul Kohli, and Vivienne Shue, *State Power*, Chapter 1.

[40] Ibid., p. 2.

[41] Jeffrey Herbst, *States and Power in Africa* (Princeton, NJ: Princeton University Press, 1999); and Mark Beissinger and Crawford Young, *Beyond State Crisis? Postcolonial Africa and Post-Soviet Eurasia in Comparative Perspective* (Washington, DC: Woodrow Wilson Center Press, 2002).

James Scott's seminal work further demonstrates that society often resists powerful states, causing their modernization schemes to fail.[42] State ineptitude is particularly acute when it attempts to control societies organized *informally*. Lisa Anderson's work on tribes and the state in the Middle East is one of the few works in political science that studies the political development and persistence of tribes.[43] In fact, Joel Migdal has recently argued that clans are one of several types of traditional social organization that "vie for power to set rules" affecting social order, but that too little research on clans has been done.[44]

More than political scientists, "new institutionalist economists" have begun to appreciate the economic and political role of informal organizations. Avner Greif and Douglass North, in their works on the economics of collectivist cultures, concur that "pre-modern" collectivist organizations such as clans – despite their suboptimal efficiency and potential long-term deleterious effects – are nonetheless both rational and surprisingly durable, and that they are therefore important variables to be explained.[45] Similarly, Avinash Dixit uses game theory to show that "alternative" informal institutions and organizations (such as clans and mafias) support economic activity when a government is unable or unwilling to provide adequate protection.[46]

The political development and state-in-society approaches, together with the new institutionalist economics, point toward the important dynamic between clans and regimes. Nonetheless, here too, clan politics has been neglected. As Joel Migdal has noted, too little research exists on *how* informal social organizations transform regimes. The literature on clans and clanlike organizations remains scant and is rarely linked to issues of regime type, durability, and transition.[47] Studies of Central Asia by political scientists

---

[42] James Scott, *Seeing Like a State* (New Haven, CT: Yale University Press, 1999).

[43] Lisa Anderson, *The State and Social Transformation in Tunisia and Libya, 1830–1980* (Princeton, NJ: Princeton University Press, 1986).

[44] Joel Migdal, *State in Society: Studying How States and Societies Transform and Constitute One Another* (Cambridge: Cambridge University Press, 2001), p. 50. One exception is Hans-Joachim Lauth, who has categorized the effect of various informal institutions, including clans, on democracy. Hans-Joachim Lauth, "Informal Institutions and Democracy," *Democratization*, vol. 7, no. 4 (Winter 2000), pp. 21–50. Lauth categorizes clans as informal "institutions." He ignores their organization and identity. Nor does he delve into empirical analysis.

[45] Douglass North, "Where Have We Been and Where Are We Going?" in Avner Ben-Ner and Louis Putterman, eds., *Economics, Values, and Organization* (Cambridge: Cambridge University Press, 1998), pp. 491–508; and Avner Greif, "Historical and Comparative Institutional Analysis," *The American Economic Review*, vol. 88, no. 2 (1998), pp. 80–84.

[46] Avinash Dixit, *Lawlessness and Economics: Alternative Modes of Economic Governance* (Princeton, NJ: Princeton University Press, 2004), Chapter 1; and Avinash Dixit, "On Modes of Economic Governance," *Econometrica*, vol. 71, no. 2 (March 2003), pp. 449–481. Dixit argues that more empirical work on specific informal organizations and problems is needed. North similarly accuses the literature of being long on schemas and short on substance.

[47] Analysis of clans has generally been left to anthropologists.

mention the pervasive phenomenon of clans but do not explore it,[48] or alternatively assume that clans were destroyed by Soviet institutions.[49]

Historians of Central Asia have delved into clan and kinship ties much more deeply, but without addressing the broader questions of political development and regime change. This book builds on Gregory Massell's and Adrienne Edgar's significant works on tribe, clan, and kinship in the early Soviet period,[50] and on Olivier Roy's insightful study of the difficulties of nation building in the Central Asian societies.[51] Certainly, clans in the post-Soviet context are not organized as traditionally as they may have been in post-colonial Africa or the Middle East, due to Soviet and now post-Soviet development. In an ongoing state-society dynamic, Central Asia's states exhibit "the modernity of tradition."[52] Informal clan networks still pervade society and play a central political and economic role, but their role and form have changed over time, and not always with positive effects on political development. The task of this work is to conceptualize clans, view them as political actors, and examine the relationship between clans and the formal institutions of the regime. The political dynamics of clans will help to explain the social foundations of order/disorder in Central Asia, and will help us to think about the factors driving negative political trajectories in similar societies.[53]

III. CONCEPTUAL CLARIFICATION IN UNFAMILIAR TERRAIN

Defining Clans

Max Weber observed over a century ago that clans were a historically common form of social organization in the nomadic and seminomadic regions of Eurasia, the Middle East, and parts of Africa.[54] However, Weber, like many social scientists, assumed that clan networks would disappear with

[48] See excellent works by Martha Olcott, *The Kazakhs* (Stanford, CA: Hoover Institution Press, 1988); and Gregory Gleason, *The Central Asian States: Discovering Independence* (Boulder, CO: Westview Press, 1997).

[49] For this view, see Pauline Jones Luong, *Institutional Change and Political Continuity in Post-Soviet Central Asia: Power, Perceptions, and Pacts* (Cambridge: Cambridge University Press, 2002).

[50] Gregory Massell, *The Surrogate Proletariat* (Princeton, NJ: Princeton University Press, 1974); and Adrienne Edgar, *Tribal Nation: The Making of Soviet Turkmenistan* (Princeton, NJ: Princeton University Press, 2004).

[51] Olivier Roy, *The New Central Asia* (New York: New York University Press, 2000).

[52] Lloyd Rudolph and Susanne Hoeber Rudolph, *The Modernity of Tradition: Political Development in India* (Chicago: University of Chicago Press, 1967).

[53] Samuel Huntington, *Political Order.*

[54] Max Weber, *Economy and Society*, edited by Guenther Roth and Claus Wittich (Berkeley: University of California Press, 1978); and Max Weber, *Ancient Judaism* (Glencoe, IL: Free Press, 1952).

the emergence of modern states and the rise of institutionalized politics. As the election story recounted at the beginning of this chapter vividly illustrates, however, clans can act as surrogate political organizations and can thereby play critical roles in the political arena, as well as in the social and economic ones.

Simply put, then, a clan is an informal organization comprising a network of individuals linked by kin and fictive kin identities.[55] These affective ties comprise the identity and bonds of its organization.[56] Kinship ties are rooted in the extensive family organization that characterizes society in this region and in historically tribal societies. "Fictive kinship" ties go beyond blood ties and incorporate individuals into the network through marriage, family alliances, school ties, localism (*mestnichestvo*), and neighborhood (*mahalla*) and village (*qishloq*). Clan ties are neither exotic and primordial, nor inherently negative or undemocratic; they are networks based on the rational calculations of individuals made within a collectivist cultural and institutional context.[57] As anthropologists and historians have often noted, clans are common in tribal and recently tribal regions and in collectivist cultures. In both pre-modern and modern times in Central Asia, clans, tribes, and localist networks have generally defined their groups according to kinship identity ties, even though actual blood ties do not always exist; more important than the objective reality of kinship is the subjective sense of identity and the use of the norms of kinship – such as in-group reciprocity and loyalty – to bind the group and protect its members.[58]

The bonds of clans are vertical and horizontal, linking both elites and nonelites. This bond forms "strong ties" based on tight, predominantly ascriptive relationships and norms; the clan's boundaries, while not fixed and unchanging, are difficult to permeate.[59] Individuals cannot easily enter or

---

[55] See Andrew Shryock, *Nationalism and the Genealogical Imagination* (Berkeley: University of California Press, 1997), pp. 40–41 and 318; Richard Tapper, "Anthropologists, Historians, and Tribespeople on Tribe and State Formation in the Middle East," in Philip Khoury and Joseph Kostiner, eds., *Tribes and State Formation in the Middle East* (Berkeley: University of California Press, 1990), pp. 50–51; and Charles Lindholm, "Kinship Structure and Political Authority: The Middle East and Central Asia," *Comparative Studies in Society and History*, vol. 28 (April 1986), pp. 334–355.

[56] Caroline Humphrey and David Sneath, *The End of Nomadism?* (Durham, NC: Duke University Press, 1999), pp. 26–27; and Andrew Shryock, *Nationalism*, p. 313.

[57] On collectivist culture and institutions, see Avner Greif, "Historical and Comparative," pp. 80–84.

[58] Gregory Massell, *Surrogate Proletariat*; Philip Khoury and Joseph Kostiner, *Tribes and State*; Richard Tapper, "Anthropologists, Historians, and Tribespeople"; and Mounira Charrad, *States and Women's Rights: The Making of Postcolonial Tunisia, Algeria, and Morocco* (Berkeley: University of California Press, 2001).

[59] On the "strong ties" of kinship, see James Gibson, "Social Networks, Civil Society, and the Prospects for Consolidating Russia's Democratic Transition," *American Journal of Political Science*, vol. 45 (January 2001), p. 53; Mark Granovetter, "The Strength of Weak Ties," *American Journal of Sociology*, vol. 78 (1973), p. 1361; and John Padgett and Christopher

exit a clan, as one would a voluntary association or interest group. In practice, the size of clans may vary.[60] For example, Central Asian journalists
estimate that Central Asian clans range from 2,000 to 20,000 individuals.
In more traditional or rural areas, informal councils of patriarchs and elders
govern clans. In more urban areas, both wealthy elites and elders control
clans. An extensive network – poorer relatives and kinsmen, close friends,
women, youth, and children – comprise the nonelite members: Clans typically cross class lines.[61]

Why Write about Clans?

Interestingly, while little scholarship on clans and clan politics exists, scholars and policy makers have many different, contradictory, and often negative
understandings of the term "clan." It is therefore important to explain why
and how I use this term and why I focus on clans at all. Some scholars have
disputed the use of the terms "clan" and "tribe" as derogatory, primordialist, or "orientalist." Others, especially social and cultural anthropologists
and area scholars, would argue that the term "clan" is too general to capture the great variation and local ethnographic detail within Central Asia.
They accurately point to differences between urban and rural communities, recently nomadic and longer-settled populations, and mountain, steppe,
and valley populations. Political scientists, by contrast, typically adopt a far
more general approach and might be more comfortable with the encompassing term "informal institution," "social network," or "clientelism." Some
might even dismiss clans as simply corruption. Depending on one's scholarly
discipline, one might bring these various critical lenses to bear when reading
this work.

Despite these issues, there are good reasons to use the term "clan" to
discuss the general phenomenon that I have defined here. To begin with, I
use "clan" as a neutral term to describe a social organization. The terms
"clan" and "tribe" have long been used by Central Asians themselves. As
the historian Adrienne Edgar observes, in Central Asia and the Middle East,
the terms "clan" and "tribe" have not been viewed as negative, as they have
in Africa. The clan as a social phenomenon may have both positive and
negative effects.

Second, while there has undeniably been both cultural and historical variation in kin-based networks and communities across Central Asia, from
Gorno-Badakhshan to the Kyzyl-kum, the term "clan" gives us a general
concept for use in comparing these societies and states. Most Turkmen,

---

Ansell, "Robust Action and the Rise of the Medici, 1400–1434," *American Journal of Soci-
    ology*, vol. 98, no. 6 (May 1993), p. 1267.
[60] Caroline Humphrey and David Sneath, *The End of Nomadism?*
[61] Adrienne Edgar, "Genealogy, Class, and 'Tribal Policy' in Soviet Turkmenistan, 1924–1934,"
    Slavic Review, vol. 60 (Summer 2001), pp. 266–288.

Kazakhs, and Kyrgyz (as those terms refer to territories and peoples today) were nomadic peoples of the steppe or mountains, and they remained largely nomadic, organized in clan and tribal structures, until the 1920s. Many Uzbeks and Tajiks (again, as those terms are used today) settled as urban traders or subsistence farmers before Russian colonization. Still other Tajiks remained nomadic or seminomadic, inhabiting the many mountainous regions of Tajikistan, even though they did not belong to the large tribal descent groups typical of Turkic peoples. Indeed, Dushanbe, the capital of the Tajik republic, was more than 60 percent Russian at the time of the Soviet collapse. The ancestors of contemporary Uzbeks came from nomadic and tribal Turkic groups. In many areas outside of Samarkand, Bukhara, Khiva, and the agricultural basin of the Ferghana Valley, Turkic tribes, both nomadic and seminomadic, persisted into the nineteenth century. Urban emirs and khans had little direct control over the steppe, though there was frequent interaction between the urban and nomadic peoples.

Many have oversimplified the social variation in Central Asia by bluntly separating the "settled" Uzbeks and Tajiks from the "nomadic" Kyrgyz, Kazakhs, and Turkmen. Instead, the greatest variation appears to have been, and to continue to be, between the inhabitants of urban and rural/nomadic regions. Both sets of peoples, however, placed an enormous importance on kin and fictive kin ties, and their living patterns – whether in the urban *mahalla*, the rural *qishloq*, or the nomadic *aul* – were organized around affective networks into the twentieth century. The twentieth century, and the shared Soviet experience across Central Asia, moreover, imposed a far greater homogeneity on informal networks than had existed during the pre-Soviet era.

Chapter 2 goes into greater detail in distinguishing clans from other more conventional concepts in political science that do not capture the intrinsic meaning of a clan. Clans differ from clientelism, a dyadic economic tie; from corruption, an illegal practice; and from mafias, groups perpetrating illegal and violent activity. "Social network," a term in vogue in political science in recent years, captures some elements of the clan, but it could refer to any type of network – university, business, Internet, party, youth group, church group, or kinship, voluntary or involuntary.

Recognizing that there are differences between social networks, and even among types of clan ties, I adopt the general term "clan network" to capture the critical role that informal social networks rooted in kin and fictive kin ties play in Central Asia. Throughout this inquiry, I note the differences between the rural and urban nature of clans, and between the elite level and the social, nonelite level. Differences do remain – for example, in size, practices, historical experiences, visibility, and the role of women. Yet these are variations on a general theme – the informality and identity power of clan networks. Despite the differences, clan networks are an important phenomenon; they need to be conceptualized and empirically explored.

Political Trajectories: Regime Type and Regime Durability

Some other definitions are in order. This study explains "political trajectories," a term I use to capture the dynamic element of both the creation and institutionalization of a new regime type, and the collapse and disintegration of a regime and state. "Trajectory" thus refers to two elements of political order: the *new regime type* and *regime durability*. While "transition" refers to the period of high uncertainty during which there is a change from one regime type to another, "trajectory" refers to a longer-term process, entailing the direction and durability of the polity, and not assuming a fixed end point or outcome.[62] Second, we must distinguish between regime, regime type, and state. A "regime," as Valerie Bunce states, is the "organization of political power"; "regime collapse" is "the disorganization of power."[63] I use "regime type" to refer to the particular nature of the regime and the organization of power – democracy, autocracy, or some variation of these. The "state," following Weber, is the set of institutions that govern and control a territory and monopolize the use of force. In contrast to Weber, however, I do not assume all states to be bureaucratic, rational, or autonomous. State and regime are closely intertwined, especially in transitional and post-colonial countries. If the regime collapses, state collapse – "the total loss of the state's coercive monopoly"[64] – may well follow.

"Political regimes are complex," and definitions of "democracy" are much debated.[65] I adopt a developmentalist approach that marks the threshold of democracy with a minimalist definition: electoral democracy demands only a constitutional system and free and fair elections.[66] A fuller, "liberal democracy," however, demands a political system "that allows the free formulation of political preferences through the use of basic freedoms of association, information, and communication for the purpose of a free competition between leaders to validate at regular intervals, by nonviolent means, the claim to rule without excluding any office of national decision-making from that competition."[67] Larry Diamond argues that this definition falls short of the

---

[62] Guillermo O'Donnell, Lawrence Whitehead, and Philippe Schmitter, *Transitions from Authoritarian Rule*.

[63] Valerie Bunce, *Subversive Institutions* (Cambridge: Cambridge University Press, 1999), p. 11.

[64] Ibid., pp. 11–12.

[65] Adam Przeworski et al., *Democracy and Development: Political Institutions and Well-being in the World, 1950–1990* (Cambridge: Cambridge University Press, 2000), p. 1.

[66] Joseph Schumpeter, *Capitalism, Socialism, and Democracy.* On problems with measuring democracy, see Gerardo Munck and Jay Verkuilen, "Conceptualizing and Measuring Democracy: Evaluating Alternative Indices," *Comparative Political Studies*, vol. 35, no. 1 (February 2002), pp. 5–34.

[67] Juan Linz, cited in Larry Diamond, *Developing Democracy: Toward Consolidation* (Baltimore, MD: The Johns Hopkins University Press, 1999), pp. 13–14. This definition draws on Robert Dahl, *Polyarchy: Participation and Opposition* (New Haven, CT: Yale University Press, 1971).

civil liberties of a more deeply liberal democracy, but it is still useful for categorizing regimes that have adopted fundamental democratic liberties.

Regime "consolidation" refers to the deep institutionalization of a regime, whether democratic or autocratic. The far-too-sanguine literature on "democratic consolidation" tends to focus narrowly on measures of formal institutions.[68] That none of the Central Asian regimes has consolidated points us to the problem of "nonconsolidation" – the absence of regime institutionalization. Likewise, we need to explain regime durability, and conversely, declining durability and collapse. "Durability" is the persistence over time of institutions and norms.[69] As the following chapters will argue, the Kyrgyz and Uzbek regimes, while being undermined internally, were fairly durable at the formal level. Eventually, even formal durability was shaken. Durability can also refer to the persistence of the state itself – its avoidance of collapse. The Kyrgyz state is still durable, although warnings signs of its collapse into civil violence are increasing.

Summary of the Argument

The central argument of this book is that clan networks are meso-level actors, profoundly impacting both the nature and direction of regime transition and the potential for regime viability during and after the transition. The transitions literature and formal institutionalist approaches cannot explain regime transition in Central Asia or, in many cases, in the developing world, because they mistakenly assume a homogenous social context. New regimes are not, however, writings upon a tabula rasa. Informal organizations and institutions critically matter. They can undermine regime consolidation and make the choice of a new regime type and new institutions relatively superficial. Clan structure does not determine outcomes, but it strongly shapes and constrains the preferences and decisions of individual actors. Clan networks infiltrate, penetrate, and transform the formal regime, creating an informal regime based on the informal rules of clans. In this way, even formally diverse regimes, like Kyrgyzstan and Uzbekistan, are likely to converge toward a pattern of informal, clan-based politics shortly after the "regime transition." Clan-based politics does not inevitably preclude long-term change, growth, and democratization, but it does make it unlikely. Until economic or political conditions give clans substantial incentive to invest in the state, they are unlikely to do so. In the meantime, clan-based politics is all too likely to instigate a negative cycle that can move from clan conflict over political and economic assets, to armed violence between clans in pursuit or defense of their clan's interests.

[68] Deborah Yashar, "Democracy, Indigenous Movements and the Postliberal Challenge to Latin America," *World Politics*, vol. 52, no. 1 (1999), p. 98.

[69] On regime endurance and durability, see Deborah Yashar, "Democracy," p. 98–99; and Stephen Krasner, *Sovereignty: Organized Hypocrisy* (Princeton, NJ: Princeton University Press, 1999), p. 56.

Overview of the Book

The book proceeds chronologically and thematically. Chapter 2 sets out
the logic of an alternative model for understanding regime change in these
informally clan-networked societies. I call this model of social and political organization "clan politics," and I hypothesize the nature of political
relationships between formal and informal institutions in societies thus organized. I discuss in depth the nature of a clan-based regime and the implications for political trajectories over the longer term. Chapter 3 provides an
ethnographic discussion of pre-Soviet social organization, and demonstrates
the relationship between informal clans and formal state institutions during
the early Soviet period. Chapter 4 addresses the rise of clans under Brezhnev
and their role in creating informal pacts during the late Soviet period. Chapter 5 discusses the causes and process of decolonization and independence
and lays the backdrop for the political transitions. Chapter 6 compares the
short-term, post-independence trajectories that diverge in both regime type
and regime durability. Chapters 7 and 8 shift to an exploration of the longer-
term trajectory, examining the rise of clan politics at the social, meso, and
elite levels in each case. They examine the process by which clans penetrate
and weaken the regimes. Chapter 9 is a broader comparison of the political
role of clans in other cases and regions. It contrasts the decline of clans in
Western Europe with their persistence in parts of Africa, Central Asia, and
the Caucasus. This chapter highlights certain conditions that may transform
or break down clan politics. Chapter 10 offers some conclusions. Throughout these discussions, this book hopes to contribute to our knowledge and
understanding of the processes that lead to good government and hence to
greater political stability and security in a little-understood region of the
developing world.

2

Clan Politics and Regime Transition in Central Asia

A Framework for Understanding Politics in Clan-Based Societies

The previous chapter introduced the core questions of this book. First, what explains the persistence of clans under modern states? Second, what is the impact of clans upon the political trajectories of new regimes? In Chapter 1, I suggested that the empirical reality on the ground in Central Asia forces us to look at clans, rather than simply at the formal institutions that are the typical target of political scientists' attention. This chapter lays out a theoretical framework for understanding what clans are, and for explaining when and why clans persist and what impact they have upon regime trajectories in modern states. This chapter also makes a theoretical argument for taking clans seriously, even within the context of the modern nation-state. The propositions of this argument are explored empirically in the Central Asian cases and then probed in other contexts in subsequent chapters.

The first question is primarily an historical one that asks why clans are important actors to begin with. That is, why should we even take clans – these supposedly pre-modern groups – seriously? This chapter looks at the conditions under which clans are likely to persist and affect regimes, even under modernizing states. This analysis lays the groundwork for looking at clans of the contemporary period, under transitional regimes and newly independent states. This is the focus of the second question: Why and how do clans affect the political trajectories of independent, transitional states? Put another way, under what conditions does "clan politics" emerge, and what are the consequences for regime type and regime durability? In explaining both the emergence and effects of clan politics, I also demonstrate that in clan-based societies, formal institutions and elite decisions have limited power. Under certain conditions, they do not prevent the rise of clan politics, and unless conditions change, they are unlikely or unwilling to control the negative effects of clan politics. Hence, although we may see an initial divergence of new regimes during the short-term transition, we are likely to see a subsequent and increasing convergence of regime trajectories to a similar pattern of informal politics in which clan interests and deals pervade and even dominate the formal regime. This kind of political order has a logic of its own that has a decidedly negative effect on democratization, as well as a negative effect on regime consolidation and durability in both democratizing and authoritarian systems.

Explaining the persistence of clans, the emergence of clan politics, and the consequences for political order is critical to the study of Central Asia's political development. These questions are also critical to theorizing about the durability of the regimes in other regions that share similar social foundations. I have already shown that existing literatures do not provide an adequate explanation for these cases. This chapter lays the groundwork for the rest of the book by developing the concept of the clan, seeking to clarify its social, economic, and political implications.[1] Then the chapter lays out some propositions for explaining political trajectories in Central Asia, and for exploring these issues in similar clan-based societies.

This chapter is divided into five major parts. Section I develops the concept of the clan theoretically, and argues that clans are affective networks but rational organizations. Section II distinguishes the clan from related concepts. Section III lays out the historical evolution of clans and the modern state and suggests the conditions under which clans survive into the modern era. Section IV elaborates the central propositions of the book and develops the logic of clan politics. Section V addresses the limitations of several alternative lenses for understanding Central Asian politics.

I. CONCEPTUALIZING CLANS: INFORMAL ORGANIZATIONS, IDENTITIES, AND NETWORKS

Only an approach that puts the informal level of politics – especially the informal organization of clans and their informal practices – at the center of the analysis will get at an understanding and explanation of the real nature of political order and disorder in Central Asia and in similar developing regions. Rather than apply lenses and theories that ignore the key players and dynamics in Central Asia, we must develop a theory of clan politics, and in order to do so we must conceptualize the clan. I defined clans in Chapter 1 as informal identity organizations with a kinship basis. Because the literature in political science has failed to develop a conceptual or theoretical understanding of clans, I begin the analysis here by doing so.

The Key Elements of Clans: Kinship, Networks, and Trust

In what sense is the clan both an organization and an identity? Understanding clans requires that individuals be treated sociologically; that is, they must

[1] One of the central problems of the literature both on Central Asia and on clans is the lack of clear and consistent usage of the term, along with the absence of an historical explanation of the term.

be perceived as part of a broader social network and as forming interests and preferences in accordance with that social and normative context.[2] Two principles mark clan relations and identity: *Kinship* is the core foundation of clan relations and identity, and a *network* is the organizing principle of this unit. The clan is thus an informal organization built on an extensive network of kin and fictive, or perceived and imagined, kinship relations. The kinship units typical of Central Asian societies in many ways embody a non-Western, more expansive and fluid notion of kinship.[3] Multiple individuals are connected by kin-based bonds (sometimes distant and sometimes immediate), with concomitant responsibilities for the members of that identity network.[4] The Turkic and Persian languages of Central Asia have an extensive vocabulary for precisely naming one's kin relations and related obligations, thereby reinforcing this broader notion of kinship and the corresponding norms.[5]

From a core of kin elites, the clan then extends itself through both vertical and horizontal ties incorporating more and more extended kin relations,

[2] For a critique of rational choice assumptions about identity, see Peter Katzenstein, *Culture, Norms, and National Security: Police and Military in Postwar Japan* (Ithaca, NY: Cornell University Press, 1996). On the need to examine preferences within a social context, see Kathleen Thelen, Sven Steinmo, and Frank Longstreth, eds., *Structuring Politics: Historical Institutionalism in Comparative Analysis* (New York: Cambridge University Press, 1992); Susan Rose-Ackerman, *Corruption and Government: Causes, Consequences, and Reform* (New York: Cambridge University Press, 1999); Alexander Wendt, *Social Theory of International Politics* (New York: Cambridge University Press, 1999); and Dennis Chong, *Rational Lives: Norms and Values in Politics and Society* (Chicago: University of Chicago Press, 2000). See also Avner Greif, "Historical and Comparative Institutional Analysis," *The American Economic Review*, vol. 88, no. 2 (1998), pp. 80–84; and Avner Greif, "Self-Enforcing Political Systems and Economic Growth: Late Medieval Genoa," in Robert Bates, Avner Greif, Margaret Levi, Jean-Laurent Rosenthal, and Barry Weingast, *Analytic Narratives* (Princeton, NJ: Princeton University Press, 1998), pp. 23–63. Greif uses a rational choice approach, but he acknowledges that a context-specific analysis is necessary and that actors in collectivist societies place interests, such as security and cooperation, above economic maximization.

[3] See Andrew Shryock, *Nationalism and the Genealogical Imagination: Oral History and Textual Authority in Tribal Jordan* (Berkeley: University of California Press, 1997); Richard Tapper, "Anthropological Theories of Tribe and State Formation in the Middle East," in Philip Khoury and Joseph Kostiner, eds., *Tribes and State Formation in the Middle East* (Berkeley: University of California Press, 1990), pp. 148–73; Dale Eickelman, *The Middle East and Central Asia: An Anthropological Approach* (Upper Saddle River, NJ: Prentice Hall, 1998), pp. 123–171; and Mounira Charrad, *States and Women's Rights: The Making of Postcolonial Tunisia, Algeria, and Morocco* (Berkeley: University of California Press, 2001).

[4] Many new institutionalists assume that networks are relations of nonhierarchical contracting between players of equal or relatively equal status. For example, see Oliver Williamson, ed., *The Nature of the Firm: Origins, Evolution, and Development* (New York: Oxford University Press, 1991), p. 291.

[5] Kin and clan were once more meaningful categories in the West than they are today. See Betty G. Farrell, *Elite Families: Class and Power in Nineteenth-Century Boston* (Albany: State University of New York Press, 1993); and Eileen Hunt Botting, *Family Feuds: Wollstonecraft, Burke, and Rousseau on the Transformation of the Family* (in press).

including kin by marriage, close friends, and their relations.[6] One expert on Central Asia and the Middle East described clans in this way: "Imagine multiple concentric circles. The center and smallest circle is the immediate family. Then comes the extended family. Then it extends outwards."[7] Marriage is one mechanism for enhancing the clan's political and economic power; like kinship, marriage bonds are "strong ties," as opposed to the "weak ties" of *blat* and clientelism that bind the network together and enhance trust.[8] In Central Asian societies, the extended family alone typically includes hundreds of people. Marriage and more expansive notions of fictive kinship extend the boundaries further.

Political scientists have often disputed "essentialist" notions of identities. Benedict Anderson, Ronald Suny, Crawford Young, and others have forcefully demonstrated that ethnicity and nation are categories constructed by elites, intelligentsia, and states. Kinship and clan differ in that they entail both relatively fixed and constructed elements. Yet, as Ted Hopf argues, some identities are "congealed reputations" that are not continually fluid and continually changing.[9] The historians Mounira Charrad and Adrienne Edgar have observed that tribal and clan identities are family and blood-based at one level, but clearly constructed at other levels.[10] Kinship is defined primarily by birth, and fictive kinship emerges from long-standing ties based on very concrete ties of historic family alliances; a shared *mahalla* (local community), village, or regional network; and school and business colleagues who have been integrated into such a network. Even in parts

---

[6] On the political and economic importance of marriage and business partnerships in clan network ties, see John Padgett and Christopher Ansell, "Robust Action: The Rise of the Medici: 1400–1434," *American Journal of Sociology*, vol. 98, no. 6 (May 1993), pp. 1259–1319; and Greif, "Self-Enforcing Political Systems," pp. 23–65. For an anthropological view of fictive kinship, see Shryock, *Nationalism and Genealogical Imagination*; and Eickelman, *The Middle East and Central Asia*, especially, pp. 123–146.

[7] Author interview with Stanley Escadero, former ambassador to Uzbekistan, Tajikistan, and Azerbaijan, conducted in Baku, Azerbaijan, August 1998.

[8] On *blat*, see Anna Ledenevna, *Russia's Economy of Favors* (Cambridge: Cambridge University Press, 1998). David Stark, in *Postsocialist Pathways: Transforming Politics and Property in East Central Europe* (New York: Cambridge University Press, 1998), writes about the weaker ties of business networks in Eastern Europe. On strong ties of clan and kinship versus weak ties, see James Gibson, "Social Networks, Civil Society, and the Prospects for Consolidating Russia's Democratic Transition," *American Journal of Political Science*, vol. 45, no. 1 (2001), p. 53; and Mark Granovetter, "The Strength of Weak Ties," *American Journal of Sociology*, vol. 78 (1973), p. 1361. Also see John Padgett and Christopher Ansell, "Robust Action," p. 1267; Greif, "Self-Enforcing Political Systems," pp. 42–43; and Walter Powell and Paul DiMaggio, eds., *The New Institutionalism in Organizational Analysis* (Chicago: University of Chicago Press, 1991).

[9] On constructed identities, see Ted Hopf, "The Promise of Constructivism in International Relations Theory," *International Security*, vol. 23, no. 1 (Summer 1998), pp. 171–200.

[10] Charrad, *States and Women's Rights*, pp. 17, 18, 68–72.

of Uzbekistan and Tajikistan, where more traditional "tribal" notions of kinship had evolved to a greater degree with earlier sedentarization, the phenomenon is very similar. As the Uzbekistani scholar Demian Vaisman writes, "The core clan consists of blood relatives of the family of the clan head, who occupy important positions. The core is extended by marriage connections. Clans usually strengthen their positions through family connections among several regional elite groupings. This cements the clan's power and helps to extend it."[11]

At the periphery of the clan, particularly of powerful clans, the network is composed of more indirect and hierarchical forms of kinship, including subclans or lineages that are dependent upon the patronage of core clans. Kin groups generally cut across class lines.[12] In Central Asia, for example, clans traditionally included both a few wealthy "*bais*" and the more dependent members.[13] Social heterogeneity of wealth and power creates hierarchy both within and between clans. Kin and clans of a lower social or economic status are linked to more significant clans in a patronizing, clan-to-clan relationship. Patronage is a key element of clans and a mechanism that clan elites use to bind members to each other, rationally as well as culturally. Unlike ordinary patron-client relations, kin-based clan relations embody a shared identity. Kinship is an organizing device for stabilizing social ties across time and space.[14] A pattern of repeated, frequent interaction – dense interaction – over time leads to the social embeddedness of kinship and clan relations.[15] From embeddedness emerges trust,[16] which is the basis for mutual reciprocity and interdependence.

---

[11] Demian Vaisman, "Regionalism and Clan Loyalty in the Political Life of Uzbekistan," in Yaacov Ro'i, ed., *Muslim Eurasia: Conflicting Legacies* (London: Frank Cass, 1995), p. 112.

[12] Adrienne Edgar, *Tribal Nation: The Making of Soviet Turkmenistan* (Princeton, NJ: Princeton University Press, 2004).

[13] See Gregory Massell, *The Surrogate Proletariat* (Princeton, NJ: Princeton University Press, 1974); Adrienne Edgar, *Tribal Nation*; and Charrad, *States and Women's Rights*.

[14] See Michael Buroway and Katherine Verdery, eds., *Uncertain Transition: Ethnographies of Change in the Postsocialist World* (Lanthan, MD: Rowman and Littlefield, 1999), p. 6. They argue that kinship norms and other informal networks become more important during transitions. On *asabiyya* (*esprit de clan*) as a "unifying structural cohesion," see Charrad, *States and Women's Rights*, p. 23.

[15] On the importance of trust, see Douglass North, *Institutions, Institutional Change, and Economic Performance* (Cambridge: Cambridge University Press, 1990), pp. 38–39; Avner Greif, "Reputation and Coalitions in Medieval Trade," *The Journal of Economic History*, vol. 49, no. 4 (December 1989), pp. 857–882; and Avner Greif, "Historical and Comparative Institutional Analysis," *The American Economic Review*, vol. 88 (May 1998), pp. 80–84. Durkheim explained dense networking as the overlapping of ties in different spheres. Padgett and Ansell adopt this concept in explaining Italian family and clan networks, in "Robust Action," p. 1280.

[16] On embeddedness, see Mark Granovetter, "Economic Action and Social Structure: The Problem of Embeddedness," *American Journal of Sociology*, vol. 91, no. 3 (November 1985),

Kin-based societies are characterized by the interconnectedness of social, economic, and political relations and a consequent blurring of the public and private spheres.[17] Exchanges among clan members occur in almost every sphere; they are social (familial, marital, and communal) as well as economic and political.[18] Clan ties are therefore more enduring than those of purely political or economic interactions. The latter are often ephemeral; they easily dissolve once the designated material goal has been attained. Those embedded in a broader environment of trust, whether of familial or religious networks, find that communal trust can be carried into other spheres.[19] Moreover, the clan's boundaries, while not fixed and unchanging, are difficult to permeate. Individuals cannot simply choose or change them at will. As one Uzbek sociologist states, "even if you want to change your clan, another clan will not accept you."[20] This cohesive kin-based identity is the basis of a clan culture and collectivist society.

The Socioeconomic Rationale of the Clan

The clan is of particular theoretical interest because of its resiliency in persisting into the modern era in many developing countries. Institutionalist theory often asks why institutions persist.[21] Avner Greif pushes the agenda, asking why collectivist societies persist rather than adopting the more successful institutions of "individualist" (typically "Western") societies.[22] The answer involves both rationality and norms, or "rational norms," to borrow Dennis Chong's term.[23] Rational decisions are made within the clan's normative and

pp. 481–510; and Oliver Williamson, *The Economic Institutions of Capitalism: Firms, Markets, and Relational Contracting* (New York: Free Press, 1985).

[17] Charrad, *States and Women's Rights*; Lisa Anderson, *The State and Social Transformation in Tunisia and Libya, 1830–1980* (Princeton, NJ: Princeton University Press, 1986); Eickelman, *Middle East and Central Asia*.

[18] See Padgett and Ansell, "Robust Action"; Rose-Ackerman, *Corruption and Government*; and David Kang, *Crony Capitalism* (New York: Cambridge University Press, 2002).

[19] Sociologists and political scientists have similarly found that trust emerges with a high density of exchanges in different spheres. See Gibson, "Social Networks"; Paul DiMaggio and Hugh Louch, "Socially Embedded Consumer Transactions," *American Sociological Review*, vol. 63, no. 5 (October 1998), pp. 619–637; and Michael Macy and John Skvoretz, "The Evolution of Trust and Cooperation between Strangers: A Computational Model," *American Sociological Review*, vol. 63, no. 5 (October 1998), pp. 638–660.

[20] Author's interview with the Uzbek sociologist Bakhodir Musaev, Washington, D.C., July 2004.

[21] Powell and DiMaggio, *New Institutionalism*.

[22] Greif, "Historical and Comparative," pp. 80–84.

[23] In line with Chong, I assume that "rationality is based on subjective calculations of self-interest, that individuals are motivated by both material and social goals, and that calculations of interest are contingent on the history of one's choices, including the values, identifications, and knowledge that one has acquired through socialization." According to this definition, adhering to both social norms and habit is not at odds with self-interest. See Dennis Chong, *Rational Lives* (Chicago: University of Chicago Press, 2000), p. 6.

structural context. To explain the clan's role in shaping regime trajectories, we must first examine the properties endowing clans with such broad social, economic, and political roles.

If kin-based trust and identity are ascriptive qualities, why then are clans rational? In fact, however, there are compelling *rational* reasons for kin to trust each other in a society containing many pre-modern or semimodern elements – elements that the Soviet Union and the post-Soviet Central Asian states preserve. The new institutionalist literature can offer some insights into the organizational properties and internal workings of the clan network and the rational basis of clans.[24]

While some emphasize the psychic benefits of following a collectivity's norms,[25] clans also include rational elements – selective incentives and sanctions.[26] Elites need the support of their networks to maintain their social status, protect the group, and make gains within an overarching political or economic system. Nonelites need clan elders and patrons to assist them in finding jobs, dealing at the bazaar, gaining access to education, getting loans, obtaining goods in an economy of shortages, and obtaining social or political advancement.[27] Clan elites also resolve disputes, guarantee economic transactions, and provide security. Clan norms and practices are reinforced through sanctioning.[28] Clan members can monitor other members of the network, given that the organization's size is relatively small. Informal coercion (e.g., social pressure, shame) is used to maintain loyalty. Elites and nonelites do not gain equally from clan politics, but both have incentives to maintain their bonds. Even if nonelites wanted to exit the network, they would have difficulty in surviving outside of a clan or in joining another clan in which they have no basis for membership.

The new institutionalism's focus on organizational behavior, contracting, and transaction costs helps to explain clan rationality. The literature posits that there are two principal organizational mechanisms for contracting or mediating economic transactions: markets and bureaucracies. The former consist of contractual relationships, whether "on-the-spot exchanges"

---

[24] Williamson has argued that the New Institutional Economics' insights should be extended to deal with a richer set of organizational relations, including networks; see Oliver Williamson and Scott Masten, eds., *Transaction Cost Economics* (Brookfield, VT: Elgar Publishing, 1995), pp. 220–221. See also Avinash Dixit, *Lawlessness and Economics: Alternative Modes of Economic Governance* (Princeton, NJ: Princeton University, Press, 2004), Chapter 1; and Avinash Dixit, "On Modes of Economic Governance," *Econometrica*, vol. 71, no. 2 (March 2003), pp. 449–481.

[25] Jon Elster, "Rationality and the Emotions," *The Economic Journal*, vol. 106, no. 438 (September 1996), pp. 1389–1390.

[26] Chong, *Rational Lives*.

[27] Shryock, *Nationalism and Genealogical*; Padgett and Ansell, "Robust Action."

[28] Jack Knight argues that "self-enforcement" is a key attribute of informal institutions in a paper presented at Harvard University, April 5, 2002.

or commitments to reciprocate in the future.[29] Goal incongruence between parties is high, and either actor may cheat, making transactions costs high. In some instances, the bureaucratic organization of the firm or state solves the market's problems – particularly its risk factor and lack of trust – by instituting the long-term employment relation, ensuring "credible commitment" of contracts through monitoring and punishment.[30] Formal institutions and organizations typically resolve these problems in developed states.

What happens when such organizations are absent or too costly to create? The *clan* provides another mode of socioeconomic transaction. The clan's institutions and networks serve transactional purposes. Within the clan organization, individuals share common goals and are imbued with a collective identity. This high goal congruence arises from established trust, high socialization, and the socioeconomic dependence upon the clan. Likewise, the clan's internal social mechanisms can reduce differences between individual and organizational goals. When individual and organizational interests overlap, opportunism and rent seeking are less likely. Group identity ensures greater self-discipline in contributing to the collective. Moreover, the clan's ability to evaluate performance and monitor behavior is critical to its organizational effectiveness.[31] The informal monitoring, norms, and social pressure from peers and elders within the clan guard against opportunism. Formal institutional arrangements are thus not always necessary to discourage malfeasance. State force and violence are not typically mechanisms to which the clan elders and elites resort.[32] Thus the transaction costs of economic and political exchange are lowered.[33]

---

[29] Williamson, *The Economic Institutions of Capitalism*; and William Ouchi, "Markets, Bureaucracies and Clans," *Administrative Science Quarterly*, vol. 25, no. 1 (March 1980), pp. 129–141.

[30] An older organizational literature looks at these issues. See Chester Barnard, *The Functions of the Executive* (Cambridge: Harvard University Press, 1962), and Herbert Simon, *Administrative Behavior* (New York: Free Press, 1945), on "the employment relation." On credible commitment, see Paul Milgrom and Barry R. Weingast, *The Journal of Political Economy*, vol. 102, no. 4 (August 1994), pp. 745–776.

[31] See Mancur Olson, *The Logic of Collective Action* (Cambridge: Harvard University Press, 1965). Olson hypothesizes that weak monitoring and the lack of penalties reduce individual incentives to contribute to the common good, thus engendering the free rider problem. On sanctioning, see Jack Knight, *Institutions and Social Conflict* (Cambridge: Cambridge University Press, 1992).

[32] Granovetter, "Economic Action and Social Structure," p. 498.

[33] These features are typically found in Japanese and Korean corporate firms, organizations often noted for their clannish mentality. See William Ouchi, "Markets, Bureaucracies and Clans," *Administrative Science Quarterly*, vol. 25 (1981), pp. 129–141; Gary Hamilton and Nicole Biggart, "Market, Culture, and Authority: A Comparative Analysis of Management and Organization in the Far East," in Marco Orru, Nicole Biggart, and Gary Hamilton, eds., *The Economic Organization of East Asian Capitalism* (London: Sage, 1997), pp. 111–150; and Kang, *Crony Capitalism*.

Internal Clan Norms – Reinforcing Identity Networks

Any particular formation of a clan network includes both elites and nonelites, or masses. Clans cut vertically through class divisions and include individuals at different places within a social hierarchy.[34] Lenin viewed this, mistakenly, as the basis for class struggle.[35] What then explains the ongoing cohesiveness of the clan, the perpetuation of relationships that comprise the network? What deters nonelites from defecting, that is, from leaving the network, joining another network, or merely living independently? And why is there no intra-clan revolt of nonelites against elites? The new institutionalist explanation – that the clan provides economic and social goods that cannot be attained elsewhere – is powerful but limited. It does not explain why clan members choose to stay within the network, either when economic conditions are so bad that they receive no payoff, or when conditions are optimal and they have no need of patronage. Even if the networked structure of society were to restrain them from defection to other networks – and it often does, because other networks reject them as alien, as nonkin – these individuals still have the option of public protest, an option that has been utilized throughout Russia and Eastern Europe. Even though the collective action problem is minimal within the clan organization, such protest has been rare in clan-based societies. Explanations of peasant compliance have focused on rural poverty and lack of education. Yet in Central Asia's highly literate population (approximately 97 percent literacy in 1991), such explanations are inadequate. Clan elites rarely wield overt force to demand clan loyalty, even in Uzbekistan. In Kyrgyzstan and Tajikistan, they have often lacked the means to do so.

Intra-clan cohesiveness and survival entails more than the economic dependency of clan masses upon each other and upon elites.[36] A fuller explanation is linked to the identity and structure of the clan, which engenders the rise of certain norms; those norms in turn reinforce the clan. Neither mere mental constructs nor cultural epiphenomena, norms are "collective social facts" that make cognitive and behavioral claims on individuals.[37] Norms do not float freely in space, but are crystallized in institutions.[38] The more dense the environment they pervade, the thicker they tend to be. Hence, norms are more operative at a national level than the international

---

[34] See Bruce Cummings, *Korea's Place in the Sun* (New York: Norton, 1997), p. 51; Shryock, *Nationalism and Genealogical*; Edgar, *Tribal Nation*; and Charrad, *States and Women's Rights,* who argue that clans undermine class mobilization.

[35] Adrienne Edgar, "Clans, Nomads, and Class Struggle: Bolshevik Theory Meets Turkmen Reality," Chapter 3 in "The Creation of Soviet Turkmenistan" (Ph.D. dissertation, University of California at Berkeley, 1999), pp. 85–144.

[36] Shryock, *Nationalism and Genealogical*, pp. 318–320, Edgar; "Clans, Nomads, and Class," Chapter 3.

[37] Katzenstein, *Culture, Norms*, pp. 17–19.

[38] Ibid., pp. 15–30.

level.[39] Following this logic, norms are likely to be stronger at local than at national levels. Norms become nested, and the more nested, the more powerful.

Social hierarchy within clans has traditionally been a widely accepted social norm and is often mutually beneficial to elites and nonelites within the identity group.[40] Wealthy clan members protect their less well-off cousins. At the same time, however, such inequality can be exploitative.[41] Nonetheless, in contrast to individualistic and predatory elites with no social constraints and to autonomous, predatory states, clan elites have traditionally been limited in abusing their power vis-à-vis their own group. Within a clan structure, they need social legitimization from their dependents – albeit not of a Western, democratic form. While they do pursue personal interests, they must also pursue the interests of the clan as a whole, lest they jeopardize the very base from which they derive their power and maintain their reputation. Networked into a larger clan structure that constrains their decisions and actions, they continually look both inward and outward in a skillful balancing act. This complex agent-structure relationship entails both mutual dependence and transformation, the mutuality of power and compliance.[42] Clan members constitute the clan. The clan constitutes their identity and social universe.[43]

Peter Katzenstein has argued that constitutive norms, as opposed to mere regulatory ones, are thick or deeply embedded norms. Like regulatory norms, constitutive norms link values and action, but they are far more powerful in shaping preferences and behavior.[44] Such norms establish "focal points" within a certain sociocultural environment.[45] Constitutive norms have the power to express, validate, and legitimate actor identities. Their institutionalization further embeds collective identities.[46] Norms situate the individual

---

[39] Ibid., especially Chapters 1 and 2.

[40] Shryock, *Nationalism and Genealogical*; and Edgar, *Tribal Nation*.

[41] On the cultural norm of hierarchy in clan/lineage groups in Asia, see Cummings, *Korea's Place in the Sun*, pp. 50–51; and Orru, Biggart, and Hamilton, eds., *Economic Organization*.

[42] Williamson, *Transaction Cost Economics*, p. 181, elaborates the concept of resource dependency, based on sociological notions of power.

[43] On the relationship between structure and agency, and constitutive variables, see Alexander Wendt, *A Social Theory of International Politics* (Cambridge: Cambridge University Press, 1999).

[44] On regulatory norms in the international sphere, see Peter Katzenstein, ed., *The Culture of National Security* (Ithaca, NY: Cornell University Press, 1993). On the rise of norms, see James Coleman, *The Foundations of Social Theory* (Cambridge, MA: Harvard University Press, 1990).

[45] Ibid.

[46] On collective identity, see Anthony Giddens, *The Consequences of Modernity* (Stanford, CA: Stanford University Press, 1990); Katzenstein, *Culture, Norms*; and David Laitin, *Hegemony and Culture: Politics and Religion among the Yoruba* (Chicago: University of Chicago Press, 1984).

within a particular social environment, and individual actions and preferences are framed within that context. The constitutive norms that form and
shape clan identity place trust, communal loyalty, and stability at the top of
one's preferences. Repetition of norms over time leads to their embedding
stronger ties within the clan, and harder boundaries between those within
the network and those without. As James Gibson argues, the clan is the basis of a strong, but narrow and exclusivist, and therefore noncivic, social
organization.[47]

The Rationality of Clan Norms

A merging of normative/cultural and rational approaches is in fact possible, especially in certain environments.[48] A networked identity such as the
clan provides an environment conducive to the formation and embedding
of strong constitutive norms. While the socioeconomic conditions of pre-
modern or semimodern societies do not directly give rise to norms, a process
involving agency, they do give rise to the kin-based clan network. The latter
fosters an identity and its related constitutive norms that constrain the individual within the collective network. The self is not an autonomous agent,
but a "social self."[49] Identity is neither fixed nor ascriptive, but socially embedded and constrained. Individuals make rational choices, but their preferences, choices, and actions are shaped by the normative social structure
within which they are situated.[50] Thus, furthering the longer-term interests
of the clan network, rather than maximizing short-term individual utility, is
indeed rational.[51] The clan's tight-network properties, its shared language
and symbols, and the geographical proximity of its members create dense
networks that facilitate the rapid transmission of norms. This information
system perpetuates normative beliefs and actions.

[47] Gibson, "Social Networks," pp. 52–53.
[48] Chong, *Rational Lives*, pp. 221–222; Jon Elster, "Rationality and the Emotions," *The Economic Journal*, vol. 106, no. 438 (September 1996), pp. 1386–1397, especially pp. 1389–1390;
and Jon Elster, "Social Norms and Economic Theory," *Journal of Economic Perspectives*,
vol. 3, no. 4 (Fall 1989), pp. 99–117.
[49] Katzenstein, *Culture, Norms*, p. 14.
[50] See Giddens, *Consequences of Modernity*; Anthony Giddens, *The Constitution of Society:
An Outline of the Theory of Structuration* (Cambridge: Polity Press, 1984); and Wendt, *A
Social Theory*.
[51] Elinor Ostrom argues that trust and reciprocity can enable actors to forego short-run for
longer-run interests that are "better than rational." See Ostrom, "A Behavioral Approach
to the Rational Choice Theory of Collective Action," *American Political Science Review*,
vol. 92, no. 1 (March 1998), pp. 1–22. See also Avner Greif, "Cultural Beliefs and the
Organization of Society," *The Journal of Political Economy*, vol. 102, no. 5 (October 1994),
pp. 912–950; Greif, "Reputation and Coalitions"; and Greif, "Historical and Comparative,"
on actors' preferences within a collectivist society. On limits to rational choice explanations,
see Robert Bates, Avner Greif, Margaret Levi, and Barry Weingast, *Analytic Narratives*
(Princeton, NJ: Princeton University Press, 1998).

Furthermore, intra-clan transactions are not a one-round game, but iterated games in which reputation is critical for the future.[52] Repeated stable interaction and stable expectations over extended periods of time enhance mutual identity and loyalty, making it normative. Normative practices then develop into shared beliefs, understandings, and expectations about human behavior. They become an essential aspect of a collectivist culture. How "reciprocity of exchange" develops as a clan norm exemplifies this process. Reciprocity of exchange is central to maintaining internal clan unity and identity, as well as relations between clans.[53] Clan members who are parties to a transaction feel strong social pressure to fulfill their commitment and make good on their promises. Repeated reciprocity becomes normative, enhancing communal trust, even when there are time lags between interactions. The repetition of such practices, made rationally possible through kin-based trust and the safeguards provided by a clan's monitoring ability, is critical to transforming the mere practice of reciprocity into a communal norm.[54]

Actors adhere to norms in a process that satisfies socioeconomic needs and maintains social identity. The process provides both ontological and physical security. It enables one to make choices without continual rational calculation.[55] Over time, shared cultural symbols and meanings reinforce norms, and their "self-sustaining" persistence reinforces kin-based communal trust, endowing fundamentally rational social behavior with what appears to be nonrational overtones or mere "culture."[56] Norms and reason reinforce each other. The very habitual nature and unconscious use of certain norms reflects their embeddedness and strength. When norms are strong, they are uncontested and hence "invisible."[57] The social-level ethnographic study discussed in Chapter 7 shows that rarely do people consciously think about clan norms. They simply take them for granted and act accordingly. We should view the clan as a variable involving both social structure and agency. Within the informal structure of the clan, clan members (elites and nonelites) make rational decisions that are informed and constrained by their norms and structure. In Alex Wendt's terms, agency and structure are mutually "constitutive."[58] The structure of the clan, and of an overarching clan-based society, limits and frames individuals' choices.

---

[52] On iterated games and reciprocity, see North, *Institutions, Institutional Change*, p. 38.

[53] On the importance of "mutual exchange reciprocity" in maintaining stability, see Donald Rothchild, *Managing Ethnic Conflict in Africa: Pressures and Incentives for Cooperation* (Washington, DC: Brookings Institution Press, 1997).

[54] Some organizational and institutional theorists have theorized the importance of "habit," rather than a cost-benefit analysis for each decision. See Chester Barnard, *The Functions of the Executive* (Cambridge: Harvard University Press, 1938); and Herbert Simon and James March, *Organizations* (Cambridge: Blackwell, 1983).

[55] Chong's model reinforces this view. See Chong, *Rational Lives*, p. 47.

[56] DiMaggio and Powell, *New Institutionalism*; Greif, "Historical and Comparative," pp. 80–84.

[57] Katzenstein, *Culture, Norms*, pp. 5–7. Chong, *Rational Lives*, makes a similar argument.

[58] See Wendt, *Social Theory of Politics*; and Giddens, *Consequences of Modernity*.

Norms of Interclan Dynamics

Externally, clans act vis-à-vis each other and the state. Understanding internal clan dynamics helps to explain clan interests in the political system. Clans do not pursue an ideological agenda; in marked contrast to transitional politics in Russia, much of Eastern Europe, and elsewhere, clan preferences cannot easily be understood in terms of ideology, whether a left-right spectrum or a pro-communist or pro-democracy platform.[59] The contrast with Russian and Eastern European transitional actors is stark.[60] Instead of supporting broad social movements, a nationwide policy agenda, or even ideological platforms and parties, clans narrowly pursue their own economic and political interests. At the aggregate level, clan interests and preferences are self-maximizing; they seek economic gains for the clan. Clan elites must nonetheless attract sufficient resources from the external environment so as to maintain their own status as notables/leaders and to preserve the internal hierarchy of the network. They must provide the goods necessary to sustain at least a minimum level of subsistence. Beyond that, they seek power in order to ensure their access to resources, vis-à-vis other clans.

One of the key norms of stable interclan relations emphasized by Central Asians, as well as by theorists of clans, is "balance" between clan factions.[61] Balance does not equal direct representation of individuals, as in the Western notion of democracy, but it does refer to the need for inclusion and representation of major clans in any national or state political system. This balance is in some ways reminiscent of the loose inclusion of various tribes within traditional tribal confederations. Even under the Soviet system, something of a balance between factions was preserved in the division of top-level Communist Party positions (e.g., the first secretary of the republic-level Communist Party Central Committee, the chairman of the republic Supreme Soviet, and the head of the republic Council of Ministers).[62] The call for such balance has been a key issue for tribal, ethnic, and regional factions in the interim government and constitutional process in Afghanistan as well – the one Central

---

[59] For similar observations, see Olivier Roy, *The New Central Asia* (New York: New York University Press, 2000); Muriel Atkin, "Tajikistan: Thwarted Democratization," in Karen Dawisha and Bruce Parrott, eds., *Conflict Cleavage, and Change in Central Asia and the Caucasus* (New York: Cambridge University Press, 1997), pp. 277–312; Barnett Rubin, "The Fragmentation of Tajikistan," *Survival*, vol. 35 (1994), pp. 71–72; and Charrad, *States and Women's Rights*.

[60] See Valerie Bunce, "Comparative Democratization: Big and Bounded Generalizations," *Comparative Political Studies*, vol. 33 (August 2000), pp. 703–734; Michael McFaul, "The Fourth Wave of Democracy and Dictatorship: Noncooperative Transitions in the Postcommunist World," *World Politics*, vol. 54 (January 2002), pp. 212–244; and Michael McFaul, *Russia's Unfinished Revolution: Political Change from Gorbachev to Putin* (Ithaca, NY: Cornell University Press, 2001).

[61] Based on author interviews in Kyrgyzstan, Uzbekistan, and Tajikistan.

[62] Makhammed-Babur Malikov, "Uzbekistan: A View from the Opposition," *Communist and Post-communist Studies*, vol. 42, no. 2 (March/April 1995), pp. 19–23.

Asian state that was engaged in a democratic transition in 2003. Violating the external norm of balance, as well as the internal norms of patronage and reciprocity between elites and nonelites, is likely to generate social resentment if not immediate instability. The rise of certain powerful clans during the post-Soviet period has increasingly generated resentment among several groups: other elite clans excluded from power and resources, and nonelites excluded from those circles.

II. CLANS, INFORMAL POLITICS, AND RELATED CONCEPTS

The next chapter will discuss some of the variations in the Central Asian context, across and within the cases. First, however, clans should be conceptually distinguished from other concepts often confused with clans. Indeed, some terms (such as "tribe" and "mafia") are loosely related to "clan" in a family of concepts, all connected to informal politics more broadly. While empirically these phenomena are sometimes difficult to pin down, the theoretical distinctions are important for analysis.

Clans and Tribes

Historically and theoretically, clans are closely related to tribes, so a conceptual distinction should be made. Tribal kinship is both real and fictive, reflecting large, loose, military-political organizations. The boundaries of these groups have historically been fluid. Boundaries shifted with military alliances and conquests that incorporated new lineages and led to the rewriting of genealogies.[63] Still, this belief in common descent, whether mythical or actual, has been the source of powerful norms, values, and symbols of kinship and tribal loyalty. Tribes are typically larger conglomerations of interrelated clans (sometimes through actual blood, sometimes through political, military, and marital alliances) who nonetheless claim to be of the same patrilineal descent line. Before the rise of the nation-state in Central Asia and the Middle East, tribal groupings formed confederations, and in some cases broad ethno-linguistic or ethno-national groups (e.g., Arabs, Kurds, and Turkomen).[64]

Tribes and clans vary in size and composition across regions. In Africa, contemporary tribal groups sometimes comprise entire socially defined ethno-linguistic groups, and hence the term "tribe" may be confused with "ethnic group." In other cases, such as the Sudan and Somalia, ethnicity is a larger, state-defined identity, encompassing multiple tribes and clans. The prevalence of smaller, subethnic, kin-based clans (divisions of historic tribes)

---

[63] Khoury and Kostiner, *Tribes and State*, pp. 4–5; and Albert Hourani, "Tribes and States in Islamic History," in Khoury and Kostiner, eds., *Tribes and State*, pp. 303–304. On the importance of rewriting genealogies, see Shryock, *Nationalism and Genealogical*.
[64] Tapper, "Anthropological Theories," pp. 52–53.

that we see in contemporary Central Asia is generally more comparable to the Middle East, North Africa, and the horn of Africa than to most of sub-Saharan Africa, where social organization is more varied and the terms used to describe it less consistent.[65]

I do not adopt the term "tribe" for two reasons. First, the term "tribe" often has negative and "primordial" connotations, suggesting endorsement of the view that this region is atavistic and incapable of modernization. Scholarship in anthropology and political science has nearly disposed of the term, in the belief that it is derogatory, and treats the developing societies of Africa, the Middle East, and South and Central Asia as primitive. The historian Adrienne Edgar points out that "among scholars of the Islamic world, however, 'tribe' is a more neutral term that refers to a society organized on the basis of patrilineal dissent."[66] Certainly, a neutral understanding of the genealogical and fictive kin organization of Central Asian society is crucial to this study.

Second, and more importantly, using the term "tribe" would be historically inaccurate in a study of the Soviet and post-Soviet trajectories of these cases. The Soviet system broke apart nomadic tribes in many areas of Central Asia.[67] Earlier sedentarization patterns broke down tribal groups into smaller kin-based settlements – the urban *mahalla*, and village *aul, awlad,* and *qawm* – in yet other areas.[68] Since most traditional "tribes" and "tribal confederations" had splintered by the 1930s, I focus on smaller subdivisions of tribes. I use the sociological term "clan" to discuss these units.[69] I use

---

[65] Dale Eickelman, *Middle East and Central Asia*, pp. 123–124.

[66] See Edgar, *Tribal Nation*, pp. 5–9. "Tribe" has recently become perceived as a negative term in Central Asia as well, especially with Central Asian elites who dislike comparisons between Central Asia and Africa and the Middle East.

[67] See Massell, *The Surrogate Proletariat*, pp. 12–13, 15–17; Caroline Humphrey and David Sneath, *The End of Nomadism?* (Durham, NC: Duke University Press, 1999); Francine Hirsch, "Empire of Nations: Colonial Technologies and the Meaning of the Soviet Union, 1917–1939" (Ph.D. dissertation, Princeton University, 1998); and Michael Ochs, "Turkmenistan: The Quest for Stability and Control," in Karen Dawisha and Bruce Parrott, eds., *Conflict, Cleavage and Change in Central Asia and the Caucasus* (Cambridge: Cambridge University Press, 1997).

[68] Roy, *New Central Asia*, p. 87. On the similarity of social organization and communities in rural, semiurban, and urban areas – whether of nomadic or sedentary heritage – see Massell, *The Surrogate Proletariat*, p. 6. Massell argues that all groups were organized around "kinship units." Certainly, distinctions between rural and urban groups and between recently nomadic and long-sedentary groups do exist. Yet the similarities in social and political organization are still significant, and they have become even greater as a result of Soviet sedentarization of all groups. For the purposes of this book, I will treat these groups as similar, since my aim here is to explain elite and mass politics rather than to provide an anthropological study of these communities.

[69] In much of Asia and the Middle East, this subdivision of ethnic group into tribe and then clan is common. See Tapper, "Anthropological Theories." However, the terminology of ethnicity, tribe, and clan varies significantly across Africa. Often the terms are used interchangeably,

the term descriptively, not pejoratively, for it reflects a real identity group and building block of sociopolitical organization. Like all identity groups, its boundaries are somewhat fluid, but the ascriptive bonds of a clan give it greater rigidity than more constructed or voluntaristic identity groups. Finally, the term itself is important, since it is used throughout Central Asia, positively to discuss cultural traditions, family values, and social order, and negatively to criticize political behavior that includes kin patronage and corruption.

Clans, Clientelism, and Corruption

At this point, we should distinguish clans from several other concepts often linked to them (mafias, clientelism, and corruption), and then clarify the relationship between them. There are important conceptual and definitional differences that must be explicated. First, clans should not be equated with clientelism and corruption, which are informal *institutions* (i.e., practices), *not identities or organizations*.[70] Like ethnicity, caste, and tribe, clans are identities. Clientelism and corruption have often been confused or loosely equated with theses identities. Instead, "clientelism" (often used interchangeably with "patronage" or "patron-client relations") is defined as the informal exchange of goods and services through an asymmetric, dyadic tie between patron and client, based *not* on ascription or affection but on need.[71] Clientelism is "based on a direct exchange of favors between two actors[,] . . . the direct exchange of short-term material benefits."[72]

---

in part because there are numerous distinct ethno-linguistic groups that are often smaller in size. Those African cases most similar to the Asian ones are the Sudan and Somalia, where clans and tribes within the major ethnic groups are operative sociopolitical units. See David Laitin and Said Samatar, *Nation in Search of a State* (Boulder, CO: Westview Press, 1986).

[70] There is an extensive literature on clientelism and corruption, but it lacks conceptual clarity and consistency. The central assumption of the literature, however, is that clientelism is an *economic* phenomenon, not a group identity. See James Scott, "Patron-Client Politics and Political Change in Southeast Asia," *American Political Science Review*, vol. 66, no. 1 (March 1972), pp. 91–113; Judith Chubb, *Patronage, Power, and Poverty in Southern Italy: A Tale of Two Cities* (Cambridge: Cambridge University Press, 1982); and Simona Piattoni, ed., *Clientelism, Interests, and Democratic Representation* (Cambridge: Cambridge University Press: 2001), especially pp. 2–4. On clientelism and problems with democratic consolidation, see Frances Hagopian, *Traditional Politics and Regime Change in Brazil* (Cambridge: Cambridge University Press, 1994); O'Donnell, "Illusions about Consolidation;" and Hans-Joachim Lauth, "Informal Institutions and Democracy," *Democratization*, vol. 7, no. 4 (Winter 2000), pp. 21–50.

[71] Luis Roniger, *Patrons, Clients, and Friends: Interpersonal Relations and the Structure of Trust in Society* (New York: Cambridge University Press, 1994); and Luis Roniger and Ayshe Gunes-Ayate, eds., *Democracy, Clientelism, and Civil Society* (Boulder, CO: Lynne Reinner, 1994), pp. 3–4, 11.

[72] Simona Piattoni, *Clientelism*, p. 212.

Some scholars have used the term "clientelism" to describe Central Asian society and politics. For example, Muriel Atkin writes that "clan" connotes an essentialist, "primordial" group; she chooses to refer to these groups instead as "patron-client networks linked to extended families."[73] Michael Rywkin, Boris Rumer, and Olivier Roy, for example, regularly interchange their use of the term "clan" with "patronage" and "extended family" or "tribe." The kinship identity and network elements (the core of the definition of a clan) are central even in Atkin's definition. Yet reducing the familial network to clientelism is problematic, since the latter is explicitly tied to a political and economic inequality that trades political support for public goods. That relationship dissolves when its economic cause disappears.[74] Clientelism is a strategic response by individuals to state or market inadequacies.[75]

Second, "corruption" is often a closely related term (especially from a "Western" perspective); corruption is an informal and illegal practice that involves exchanging money in order to obtain a public good or decision for private use.[76] Third, a similar "Soviet" practice is known as "*blat*," a Russian term that refers to the informal institution of obtaining goods through weak, transient ties. *Blat* represents an individual's strategic response to Soviet (and post-Soviet) economic inefficiencies, but unlike clientelism, it is an immediate or short-term exchange of favors or goods.[77]

---

[73] Atkin, "Thwarted Democratization," p. 292, and Barnett Rubin, "Russian Hegemony and State Breakdown," in Barnett Rubin and Jack Snyder, eds., *Post-Soviet Political Order: Conflict and State-Building* (London: Routledge Press, 1998), pp. 128–161, similarly dispute the essentialist connotations of "clan." However, both use the terms "clan," "clientelism," "region," and "extended family" almost interchangeably. Most scholars and observers of Central Asian politics have used the terms descriptively, not analytically, with little conceptual clarity.

[74] See Scott, "Patron-Client Politics"; Chubb, *Patronage, Power*; Simona Piattoni, *Clientelism*; and Roniger, *Patrons, Clients*.

[75] See Chubb, *Patronage, Power*, Chapter 1. Earlier approaches focused less on the strategic side of clientelist behavior and more on the culture of poverty that fostered clientelist behavior. On "amoral familism," see Edward Banfield, *The Moral Basis of a Backwards Society* (Glencoe, IL: Free Press, 1958).

[76] Susan Rose-Ackerman, *Corruption and Government: Causes, Consequences, and Reform* (Cambridge: Cambridge University Press, 1999); Simona Piattoni, ed., *Clientelism, Interests, and Democratic Representation*; Paul Hutchcroft, *Booty Capitalism: The Politics of Banking in the Philippines* (Ithaca, NY: Cornell University Press, 1997).

[77] Anna Ledenevna, *Russia's Economy of Favors* (Cambridge: Cambridge University Press, 1998). Lucan Way makes an excellent distinction between weak ties that use *blat* or corruption, and strong ties of kin/clan, in Lucan Way, "Weak Ties in Moldova," manuscript, Harvard University (April 4, 2002). See also Andrew Walder, *Communist Neo-Traditionalism* (Berkeley: University of California Press, 1986). For earlier arguments about informal, traditional practices in the Soviet system, see Kenneth Jowitt, "An Organizational Approach to the Study of Political Culture in Marxist-Leninist Systems," *American Political Science Review*, vol. 68, no. 3 (September 1974), pp. 1171–1191. This perspective views clientelism as a *reactive* informal institution that emerges in response to the shortages of the socialist economy. Waldner and Jowitt both argue that the Soviet and Chinese socialist

The theoretical and empirical distinctions among these practices are often blurred. For example, in simple corruption, a government minister could steal $10,000 from the customs office and deposit it in a Swiss bank account. In a clientelist practice, he could give jobs in the customs office to 100 people and then "persuade" them to vote for him or his friend. In yet another scenario, he could use the $10,000 he stole to give loans to his employees, with the intention of hitting them for votes at a later date. This instance would involve both corruption and clientelism. These practices establish an unequal and typically exploitative relationship between two individuals. None of these practices necessarily involves an identity or organization, much less kinship. These are informal institutions, *not* organizations.

Clan networks, clientelism, and corruption do overlap to some extent, especially when we talk about the role of clans in elite-level politics, as empirical examples throughout this text will illustrate. However, in any given case, clan ties are evolving over time. Nonetheless, not all "clans" and "clan behavior" can be described, or dismissed, as mere corruption. Nor does all corruption occur on the basis of clans. Clientelism, or patronage, is typically seen as one type of corruption; it is also one type of mechanism that clans use to promote themselves. All three phenomena are treated in this book, and all three are seen as largely corrosive to the state. The focus here, however, is on the *social organization and the actors*, not on instances of corruption; this book examines the *informal organization of clans* and the informal practices by which they conduct political and economic exchanges, either in opposition to or in symbiosis with the state.

The lenses of clientelism and corruption focus on the *practice*, not on the *actors*. Yet *who* engages in these practices, and *why* they do so, are critical issues. Clans are organizations and actors; their repertoire of behavior includes clientelism and corruption. The concepts are theoretically distinct but not mutually exclusive. Clientelism and corruption, entirely distinct from clan networks, do exist in Central Asia, and they often intersect with clan politics. Such simpler forms of clientelism and corruption exist in most political systems to some degree. Yet, beyond this, there are the more pervasive and potentially destructive forms, in which clan elites, both within and outside the state, use clientelism as a regular means of promoting, or patronizing, their network and thereby of enhancing their legitimacy. As Rose-Ackerman

---

systems promoted clientelism and were therefore "neo-traditional." While Soviet practices may have done so, intentionally or inadvertently, in Central Asia, they in fact reinforced clan networks and a culture of informal institutions already present. In Russia, the Soviet system created *blat*; in Central Asia, it created *blat* on top of reinforced clan networks. Arguing that clans came into existence only as a result of Soviet inefficiencies is an ahistorical and inaccurate view. (See the discussion in Chapter 3.) For a more historical view of early Soviet networks, see Gerald Easter, *Reconstructing the State: Personal Networks and Elite Identity in Soviet Russia* (New York: Cambridge University Press, 1996).

puts it, "trusting, personalized relationships facilitate corrupt deals."[78] Kin-based patronage is not just strategic behavior; it is driven by group norms.

The lenses of clientelism and corruption are certainly useful for understanding Central Asian politics, in that they suggest negative implications for the quality of democracy. However, eliding the important distinctions between clans, clientelism, and corruption presents problems in explaining Central Asia's political trajectories. O'Donnell, for example, has argued that clientelism merely promotes "delegative democracy," a low-quality democracy. His focus on dyadic clientelist ties and corruption does not predict – as the focus on clans here does – that informal politics in fact undermines regime type and weakens regime durability. Democracy is not merely low-quality; it no longer exists. Corruption and clientelism that are not practiced by *identity groups* have less significant implications for the regime and state. By empowering group actors, clan patronage has much wider, *systemic* implications – for the centralization of state power, representation, and the legitimacy of the regime itself. Clans have a more factionalist and destabilizing effect upon the regime than the more limited ties of clientelism that most scholars describe. As the Tajik, Chechen, and Somali cases vividly illustrate, interclan tensions may lead to group mobilization and violence, group conflicts with the identity of the nation-state, and even regime and state breakdown.[79]

Finally, clans are not mafias. The latter are organizations (not institutions), like clans. Some, such as the Italian mafia, rely heavily on kinship and clan ties.[80] However, not all mafias need have a kinship element. Most critically, mafias are explicitly criminal organizations that regularly use violence, whereas clans do not. As noted earlier, however, clans are not static organizations. They evolve over time and in different circumstances. We shall see that in Central Asia, some elite clans are increasingly involved in mafialike activity. In what we might call a *mafiosization* of more traditional networks, they even sometimes use violence to pursue or defend their political and economic interests.

Understanding clans, their kin-based identity bonds, and why they use patronage enables us better to explain why clans often persist through fluctuating economic circumstances. Neither a clan elite nor a nonelite simply abandons his family in times of plenty; by most accounts, relatively

---

[78] Rose-Ackerman, *Corruption and Government*, p. 97. Rose-Ackerman further observes that the strength of the Italian mafia lies in its "family" ties, which embed loyalty, kinship norms, and trust in the mafia organization.

[79] Rubin, "The Fragmentation of Tajikistan," *Survival*, vol. 35 (1993–1994), pp. 71–72.

[80] See Judith Chubb, *The Mafia and Politics: The Italian State under Siege* (Ithaca, NY: Cornell University Press, 1989); and Diego Gambetta, *The Sicilian Mafia* (Cambridge, MA: Harvard University Press, 1993). Rose-Ackerman, *Corruption and Government*, pp. 121–122, notes that kinship and trust strengthen mafia organizations.

good economic conditions in Central Asia from the 1960s to the 1980s only strengthened clans. By contrast, the literature on clientelism generally argues that clientelism disappears when economic conditions improve; no durable bond or identity links patron and client. Hence, we would expect the informal organization of the clan to be a more durable informal organization than the informal practice of clientelism. The analysis of clan politics thus builds on the insights of earlier studies on the informal economies and practices of clientelism, but it goes beyond this literature in the direction of identity politics and political trajectories.

Misuses of the Term "Clan"

There are indeed variations in the types of clans found at different levels and in different regions of the state, and in their degrees of fictiveness (e.g., historically tribal versus sedentary). Despite such variation, these networks do have a commonality of form and meaning, rooted in anthropological and historical understandings that must be distinguished from misuses of the term "clan." Because the term "clan" has recently come into vogue, especially in the media and among foreign policy analysts, to describe corrupt power groups, oligarchs, and even mafia groups in Russia, the Ukraine, and elsewhere, we should briefly contrast this very loose use of the term with the more sociological meaning that I use. Some examples from the Russian case highlight the differences between the shifting oligarchs and mafias comprising the Russian government and the clan-based system in Central Asia.[81] "Yeltsin's clan" refers to the power clique that surrounded Boris Yeltsin. In the early years, it was believed to include the "reformers," such as Yegor Gaidar, his key economic advisor, and leaders of the democracy movement. By late 1992, Gaidar was out of power and expelled from the Kremlin clique as Yeltsin appointed the centrist Victor Chernomyrdin to the post of prime minister. Gaidar eventually came to represent Yeltsin's liberal opposition. The "liberal clan" was superseded by Yeltsin's notorious bodyguard, Alexander Korzhakov, and his shady entourage.[82]

Yeltsin's so-called clan was shifting almost by the month during his later years in power.[83] At one moment, Yevgeny Primakov, an old-guard Soviet apparatchik, was brought into the heart of the Yeltsin clique as prime minister

---

[81] Boris Rumer points out that there is an overlap between clans, mafias, and black marketers in Central Asia, going back to the Soviet period; however, he stresses the cultural basis and stability of these groups. See Rumer, *Soviet Central Asia: A Tragic Experiment* (Boston: Unwin Hyman, 1989), p. 146. This is in marked contrast to the Russian mafia's purely criminal basis (without an identity group behind it). See David Hoffman, *The Oligarchs on Russia: Wealth and Power in the New Russia* (New York: Public Affairs, 2001). The Central Asian mafias have a greater basis in the extended family and social structure, as does the southern Italian mafia. See Chubb, *The Mafia*.

[82] Lilia Shevtsova, *Putin's Russia* (Washington, DC: Carnegie Endowment, 2003), p. 26.

[83] On Yeltsin's shifting "clan," see Lilia Shevtsova, *Putin's Russia*, Chapter 1.

and given unprecedented control over the government. In the next breath, he was out. The oligarch Berezovsky was included and then infamously expelled.[84] Yeltsin's designated successor, Vladimir Putin, was then surprisingly drawn from the ranks of the KGB, not because of his connection to or influence upon Yeltsin. Based in part on ideology and in part on money and corrupt politics, Yeltsin's "clan," if it may loosely be called this, was highly fluid. In sharp contrast with the Central Asian clans, it had no core, no identity, and no stability. It shifted continually on the basis of transitory business deals, corruption, and sometimes ideology. Central Asian clans foster an even greater overlap of political and economic ties. In contrast to the fluidity of the weaker ties evident in Russia, a more stable identity underlies the clan network.

In sum, clans are a different type of social actor, with powerful rational and normative elements that reinforce each other. Although as organizations they predated the modern state, their normative content, informal structure, and rational elements enable them to adapt in many circumstances to the advance of the state. They have persisted despite the breakdown of their larger tribal organizations, and they have used clientelism and patronage as strategies for advancement and survival.

III. CLANS FROM THE PRE-MODERN TO THE MODERN ERA

Why do clans still exist as relevant actors today? The clan is generally perceived to be a "traditional" social organization with roots in the pre-modern era. Weber discusses the central social, economic, and political role of clans in structuring the social order in pre-modern Asia and the Middle East.[85] He did not, however, expect clans to survive the onslaught of modernization and the rise of state bureaucracies.[86] Similarly, modernization and institutionalist theories have often neglected or even denied the relevance of clans in the modern era.[87] Nonetheless, historians and anthropologists have often observed tensions between clans and both colonial and post-colonial states.[88] This book looks at the politics of clans within the context of the modern state. I argue that clans are not confined to the traditional, pre-modern era; in fact, in many ways, clans are very modern organizations. In Lloyd and Susanne

---

[84] Ibid. See also Hoffman, the *Oligarchs*.

[85] Max Weber, *The Theory of Social and Economic Organization* (New York: Oxford University Press, 1947).

[86] Ibid.

[87] Alec Nove and J. A. Newth, in *The Soviet Middle East: A Communist Model for Development* (New York: Praeger, 1967), typify the view that the Soviets successfully modernized Central Asia, both economically and culturally. One recent study has similarly argued that Soviet institutions destroyed old identities and replaced them with new Soviet ones. See Pauline Jones Luong, *Institutional Change and Political Continuity: Power, Perceptions and Pacts* (New York: Cambridge University Press, 2002), Chapters 1 and 2.

[88] Khoury and Kostiner, *Tribes and State*, pp. 16–19.

Rudolph's terms, clans exhibit the "modernity of tradition" in their ability to adapt and persist from earlier to later political systems.

Several factors related to the intrinsic attributes of clans explain this persistence. As discussed earlier, clans are a powerful identity and organization, and both identities and organizations are often slow to change. This is especially so when they provide meaning, are necessary for survival, and/or are kept in place by the actions of elites within those organizations. First, clan identities are rooted in kinship, and kinship bonds have significant staying power because they carry meaning and cultural content for the members of the kin organization. In addition to their affective content, however, the earlier discussion stressed the rational importance of clans in addressing the problems of an economy of shortages. Finally, a rich anthropological and historical literature has stressed the role of patriarchal elites in preserving kinship groups and hierarchies.

Beyond the internal properties of clans, we must look at the external conditions under which clans have survived and persisted into the modern era. Certainly, not all clans in all regions and countries have successfully adapted to the modern state. Clans should not be seen as an exotic social form found only in Kyrgyzstan or Afghanistan. In the pre-modern era – usually defined by historians as the period prior to the 1500s – clans were a form of social organization well beyond Central Asia, in large parts of Europe.[89] Yet clans have not persisted in these regions. They have been transformed both by the state and by economic forces over centuries. In Scotland, Ireland, and parts of continental Europe, powerful clans and extended kinship networks gradually declined or disappeared. Even Italy, once a bastion of clan politics, has seen significant social transformation, albeit later and less completely than the other European cases.[90]

Why have clans persisted in Central Asia? What are the conditions that make them likely to persist? I propose that three critical conditions present in the Central Asian cases enable and foster clan persistence: (1) late state formation, due in large part to colonialism; (2) late formation of a national (i.e., nation-state) identity; and (3) the absence of a market economy (and in its place, the existence of an economy of shortages). These conditions characterize the Central Asian cases and the conditions of their political development. These conditions are similar in many respects to the conditions of many African, Middle Eastern, and South Asian countries. In these respects, the cases that are the focus of this work differ significantly from the European

[89] For example, on clans in fourteenth-century Italy, see Greif, "Self-Enforcing Political"; and Padgett and Ansell, "Robust Action." Likewise, in parts of East Asia – especially Japan, Korea, and China – clans and lineages were important politically, economically, and socially. See Bruce Cummings, *Korea's Place in the Sun* (New York: Norton, 1997).

[90] On how Italy's social and political change in the twentieth century is burdened by path dependency, see Chubb, *Patronage, Power*; and Putnam, *Making Democracy Work: Civic Traditions in Modern Italy* (Princeton, NJ: Princeton University Press, 1993).

cases where clan identities were meaningful in the pre-modern era, but declined and disappeared well before the twentieth century. Chapter 9 will explore the conditions of clan persistence and breakdown cross-regionally in greater depth.

As Samuel Huntington has powerfully argued, the Western European model of political development was atypical.[91] By contrast, early state formation, national identity and nation-stateness, and capitalist economic growth did not characterize the Central Asian path of political development. Nor did most of the African, Middle Eastern, and South Asian cases, where kinship, clan, tribe, and related identities have also been historically important, follow the path of Europe. Generally, these regions can be characterized by a history of very late state formation. Although various pre-modern state structures had encompassed the Ferghana Valley region of Central Asia, the first modern states appeared in Central Asia only in 1991, after seven decades of Soviet colonialism and half a century of Russian colonial rule. Likewise, modern, independent states emerged across most of Africa, the Middle East, and South Asia only after the decolonization of the European empires during the 1950s and 1960s. Meanwhile, the colonial experience, despite some institutional variation, has had significant similarities from case to case, especially in its relative disinterest in social transformation. Charrad writes of the Maghrib:

[A]t the time the world historical setting was such that colonizers primarily were interested in the economic advantages provided by colonies. They were concerned with matters of social organization such as kinship or the family only insofar as these matters facilitated or hindered colonial rule and economic domination. Often, the objective of the colonizer was to make tribal kin groupings serve as conservative, stabilizing elements of the social order, as political power at the center was monopolized by colonial authority. Among the colonized, the extended kinship unit acquired further value as a refuge from those dimensions of society being transformed by the colonizer. Kin-based solidarities were therefore reinforced in response to the experience of colonial domination.[92]

---

[91] See Samuel Huntington, *Political Order in Changing Societies* (New Haven, CT: Yale University Press, 1968). Even in Latin America – as opposed to Africa, Asia, and Eurasia – decolonization began much earlier, with consequences for state formation and democratization. See Deborah Yashar, *Demanding Democracy: Reform and Reaction in Costa Rica and Guatemala, 1870s–1950s* (Stanford: Stanford University Press, 1997).

[92] Charrad, *States and Women's Rights*, pp. 23–24. Also on the Middle East, see John Waterbury, *The Commander of the Faithful: The Moroccan Political Elite – A Study in Segmented Politics* (New York: Columbia University Press, 1970); William Zartman and William Habeeb, eds., *Polity and Society in Contemporary North Africa* (Boulder, CO: Westview, 1993); William Zartman, "A Review Article: The Elites of the Maghreb," *International Journal of Middle East Studies*, vol. 6, no. 4 (October 1975), pp. 495–504; Roger Owen, *State, Power, and Politics in the Making of the Modern Middle East* (London: Routledge, 1992); and Martha Mundy, *Domestic Government: Kinship, Community, and Polity in North Yemen* (London: Tauris, 1995).

Charrad's analysis resonates with historical and political analysis of colonial Africa and Asia. Herbst also observes that although colonialism seemed
to change everything in Africa, significant continuities with the pre-colonial
past remain.[93] Even Adeeb Khalid, who has ably demonstrated that the
Russian conquest of Central Asia brought this region into contact with
modernity, emphasizes the Russian colonial administration's focus on economic exploitation and its policy of ignoring Islam and other traditional
identities and local, native control.[94] So long as nothing interfered with
Russia's economic and geopolitical control, Russia was not interested in
social transformation until the Soviet era. As Chapter 3 will demonstrate,
even under the Soviet regime, the Communist Party's colonial-like rule of
Central Asia more often reinforced than undermined traditional kin and clan
identities.

The path of Western European national formation sharply contrasts with
that of Central Asia, where national identity formation began only in the
twentieth century. The nation-state identities that exist in Central Asia today were both constructed and imposed by a hostile regime. The Soviet
government both created and destroyed national consciousness. Although
the Soviet regime promoted affirmative action for certain nations,[95] it also
destroyed pre-Soviet scripts.[96] Despite seventy years of Soviet rule, a period
during which national identities did take on some meaning, in 1991 the new
states of Central Asia found themselves scrambling to create anew these
national identities. They had to give depth and legitimacy to the somewhat
superficial "ethno-national" titular identities they had inherited from the Soviet system, identities that often conflicted with other layers of identity and
loyalty – supra-national Soviet and Islamic identities, and subnational clan
identities and localism. In contrast to the Baltics, Eastern Europe, or Georgia
and Armenia, the Central Asian nations had no pre-Soviet history of nationness. Hence, the new regimes launched campaigns to forge a nation-state
and nationalism through the creation of myths, language, history, culture,
and festivals.[97]

Moreover, as in many African, Middle Eastern, and South Asian cases,
the Soviet state's relatively recent imposition of ethno-national boundaries and ethno-national identities did not eliminate or replace pre-national
identities.[98] These cases of late decolonization and independence were

---

[93] Jeffrey Herbst, *States and Power in Africa* (Princeton, NJ: Princeton University Press, 1999),
pp. 28–30.
[94] Khalid, *Muslim Reform*, pp. 58–60.
[95] Terry Martin, *The Affirmative Action Empire: Nations and Nationalism in the Soviet Union,
1923–1939* (Ithaca, NY: Cornell University Press, 2001).
[96] Benedict Anderson, *Imagined Communities* (London: Verso, 1991), p. 46.
[97] Gleason, *Central Asian States*.
[98] On the limits of imposing late boundaries, see James S. Coleman, *Nationalism and Development in Africa: Selected Essays*, edited by Richard Sklar (Berkeley: University of California
Press, 1994); and Herbst, *States and Power*, p. 25.

plagued by artificial boundaries and populations that lacked a cohesive state identity.[99] Nation-states and nationalism had not taken shape over centuries. Unlike the European nation-states that had begun to define their own boundaries and national identities during the early modern period, newly independent elites (in the late 1940s on the Indian subcontinent, in the 1950s and 1960s in Africa and the Middle East, and in the 1990s in Central Asia) were typically scrambling to build nations. In doing so, they often faced the challenge of integrating preexisting ethnic, tribal, and clan groups. As Ken Jowitt has argued, Western notions of individualism, capitalism, and nation-stateness were not the norm and could not easily be implanted.[100]

The third distinguishing factor is the pre-modern, nonmarket economy that characterized life in these regions. These conditions continued throughout the colonial/imperial period despite some industrialization and agricultural modernization. In spite of its immense military-industrial development and a general rise in living standards, the Soviet state, as Janos Kornai has powerfully argued, was characterized by an "economy of shortages."[101] In fact, in some ways economic circumstances in the Central Asian periphery worsened for the indigenous population, since colonizers typically sought to extract economic resources (e.g. gold, cotton, diamonds, and oil) rather than to develop the economy and infrastructure or to govern the population. The parallels with colonial Africa are significant in this respect. In most of these cases – whether as a legacy of colonialism, as a consequence of geography and poor access to markets, or often as a result of socialist economic planning – this economy of shortages persisted into the post-Soviet period. Economic conditions thus continued to provide an economic rationale for the persistence of clan organizations in most Central Asian cases.[102] One exception is Kazakhstan, which is characterized by greater market reforms leading to significant economic growth – reforms in large part driven by the need for foreign investment in the energy sector. Kazakhstan is the only Central Asian case where a more cohesive state and regime consolidation are developing, and where clan identities may have a less corrosive effect on political stability, and may be in the process of transformation to weaker ties.

The similar legacies of colonialism are important in distinguishing cases in which clans are more likely to have survived into the twentieth century and to be poised to play a role in post-colonial politics, from those

[99] On decolonization and state building in Africa, see Coleman, *Nationalism and Development*; Herbst, *States and Power*; and Crawford Young, *The African State*. On the Middle East, see Anderson, *Tribe and State*; and Charrad, *States and Women's Rights*. On South Asia, see Rudolph and Rudolph, *Modernity of Tradition*. On Central Asia, see Roy, *New Central Asia*, pp. 161–165.

[100] Jowitt, *New World Disorder*.

[101] Janos Kornai, *The Socialist System* (Princeton, NJ: Princeton University Press, 1992), pp. 229–233.

[102] See Buroway and Verdery, *Uncertain Transition*, pp. 7–9.

in which clans have historically declined in influence over centuries. In the late colonial, transitional, and post-colonial periods, the state is typically weak. Fragile new regimes are in the precarious position of holding disparate clan networks together as well as defining their role in an independent state. In post-colonial regions such as Africa, Central Asia, and the Caucasus, where independence forces a political and economic transition, the state may hold vast endowments but still have low institutional capacity. The state is especially challenged when faced with a strongly networked and semimodern society. Western-style regimes are often a poor fit for such a society. Indeed, scholars have attributed various labels to this phenomenon – from "shadow states," to "prebendalism," to "virtual democracy" and even "failed states."[103] Such descriptive labels, however, fail to capture the dynamic processes at work both within the state and between the state and society during the short-term transition and longer political trajectory.

IV. PROPOSITIONS ABOUT THE POLITICS OF CLANS

Building on this discussion of clans, we can construct some general propositions for exploring the relationship between clans and the regime under both colonial and post-colonial states, and for explaining the effect of clan politics upon the political trajectories of newly independent states. This section elaborates the logic of the propositions introduced in Chapter 1 and develops an alternative framework for explaining the political dynamics of clans and their effect on political trajectories, including both *regime durability* and *regime type*. This framework addresses the effect of clans over time, from colonial rule to late colonialism/independence, the transition, and the post-transition period.

Clan Persistence and Pacts

Proposition 1: Clans may persist under strong colonial states under certain conditions, and may gain power under weak, declining ones. The first piece of the puzzle is this: why and under what conditions are clans likely to persist under strong colonial and modernizing states – even when those states seek to destroy them? Kin-based bonds are often viewed by political scientists as pre-modern or primordial, or at best cultural and normative organizations that disappear with modernity. Yet there are compelling reasons for the salience of clans in the modern era, even within the context of formal

---

[103] See Richard Joseph, "Democratization in Africa after 1989: Comparative and Theoretical Perspectives," *Comparative Politics*, vol. 29, no. 3 (April 1997), pp. 363–382; Michael Bratton and Nicholas Van de Walle, *Democratic Experiments in Africa: Regime Transition in Comparative Perspective* (New York: Cambridge University Press, 1997); and Mark Beissinger and Crawford Young, *Beyond State Crisis? Postcolonial Africa and Post-Soviet Eurasia in Comparative Perspective* (Washington, DC: Woodrow Wilson Center Press, 2002).

political institutions, and under both repressive and modernizing states. As noted earlier, late state formation in large parts of Asia, the Middle East, and Africa allowed clans to survive into the twentieth century.[104] When states did emerge in these regions, they came in the form of external powers – colonial or imperial states that initially focused on resource extraction, not on state building or social transformation.[105] When either colonial states or their successors, twentieth-century nation-states, did finally attempt to "modernize" society, they often faced challenges from deeply embedded informal organizations.[106]

The informality of clans enables them to adapt to and resist repressive modern states. Because clan members are not formally registered or catalogued by the state, most state officials have difficulty in identifying or locating the membership and boundaries of clans.[107] Since their institutions and practices are also primarily informal, the state cannot easily target and punish or control them. Indeed, punishment of kin may simply make the identity groups less trusting of the state and more dependent upon the clan. Clans are likely to persist under strong and repressive states under certain conditions: when the state, although outlawing and denying clan existence, does not actually dismember them; when clan identity provides a base of resistance to the regime; and when the state's own institutions inadvertently allow clans access to resources that enable survival. By contrast, state recognition or co-optation is more likely to diminish or transform them.[108]

Clans become increasingly important politically within weakening states (such as late colonial, transitional, and post-colonial ones), when the regime is losing power. Where formal institutions are illegitimate and the regime

---

[104] Contrast the timing, mode, and pattern of state formation in these regions with that of Western Europe. See Charles Tilly, *Coercion, Capital, and European States, 990–1990* (Cambridge: Blackwell, 1990); Herbst, *States and Power*; Crawford Young, *The African State in Comparative Perspective* (New Haven, CT: Yale University Press, 1994); Huntington, *Political Order*; and Beissinger and Young, *Beyond State Crisis*. The simultaneous growth of capitalism and the state in Western Europe is also unparalleled in Central Asia. See Chapter 9 for more cross-regional discussion.

[105] Edward Allworth, ed., *Central Asia: 130 Years of Russian Domination* (Durham, NC: Duke University Press, 1994); Daniel Brower and Edward Lazzerini, *Russia's Orient: Imperial Borderlands and Peoples, 1700–1917* (Bloomington: Indiana University Press, 1997); and Herbst, *States and Power*, pp. 73–80.

[106] James Scott, *Seeing Like a State* (New Haven, CT: Yale University Press, 1999); and Goran Hyden, *Beyond Ujaama in Tanzania: Underdevelopment and an Uncaptured Peasantry* (Berkeley: University of California Press, 1980). On the limits of colonial states, see Herbst, *States and Power*, pp. 76–96.

[107] Humphrey and Sneath note that in rare cases, such as inner Mongolia, the state succeeded in formalizing lists of clans and their members and thereby disempowering them. Caroline Humphrey and David Sneath, *The End of Nomadism?* (Durham, NC: Duke University Press, 1999), pp. 26–27.

[108] Caste-state relations in India in the 1960s also suggest this logic. See Rudolph and Rudolph, *Modernity of Tradition*.

is fluctuating, unpredictable, or lacking in social trust, the role of clans as identities becomes more important. Where bureaucracies cannot adequately provide basic social services, an "economy of shortages" prevails and efficient markets are lacking.[109] Clans fill the gap as networks for social, economic, and political exchange. Credible commitments critical to political and economic deal making are easier to obtain within or through the clan than outside of it. While clans may survive strong, repressive states, they are likely to flourish in weaker transitional and post-colonial states, which often suffer from declining economies and weak or incipient institutions.[110]

Proposition 2: Clan pacts respond to threats and foster regime durability.
Second, clans foster the durability of the regime when they make informal pacts and thereby stabilize relations between groups; they informally – outside the formal institutions of government – arrange a pattern of governance over resources. These pacts are especially important when a strong state weakens or collapses, as in the process of sudden decolonization, and leaves no system to manage the interests of competing clans. Clans will be likely to make pacts when three conditions are present: (1) a shared external threat induces cooperation among clans who otherwise would have insular interests; (2) a balance of power exists among the major clan factions, such that none can dominate; and (3) a legitimate broker, a leader trusted by all factions, assumes the role of maintaining the pact and the distribution of resources that it sets in place. Clan pacts are a response to instability, not a mode of political transition. Pacts do not make democratization more likely, as the transitions literature has argued.[111] If a transition takes place – instigated by an exogenous shock, such as sudden independence – the informal pact will foster a durable but not necessarily democratic transition.

Once in place, clan pacts foster a durability that preserves the interests of the clans who participated. *Clan balancing,* as we will see in Chapters 4 and 8, is an informal mechanism used – typically in a nontransparent way – to include various powerful clans in the regime, and thereby to preclude serious clan opposition to the regime. These pacts give clans informal access to power and resources and make them key players in post-colonial politics. As long as the broker can and does balance their demands and feed their

---

[109] Kornai, *Socialist System.* See also Ouchi, "Markets, Bureaucracies and Clans," pp. 129–141; and Oliver Williamson, *The Economic Institutions of Capitalism* (New York: Free Press, 1985).

[110] Beissinger and Young, *Beyond State Crisis.*

[111] See O'Donnell and Schmitter, *Transition from Authoritarian Rule;* Terry Karl and Philippe Schmitter, "Modes of Transition in Latin America, Southern, and Eastern Europe," *International Social Science Journal,* vol. 128 (1991), pp. 269–300; John Higley and Richard Gunther, eds., *Elites and Democratic Consolidation in Latin America and Southern Europe* (Baltimore: Johns Hopkins University Press, 1992).

networks, the pacts are likely to be stable. The absence of these conditions inhibits a pact. Without a clan pact, a precarious imbalance of clan power and disputes over resources will remain. A sudden shock, such as independence and transition, will likely undermine stability, leading to regime collapse and civil violence.

The Impact of Clans

As clans rise in prominence under a weakened post-colonial state, what is their impact on regimes? How do clans affect institutional choices in the short term and regime trajectories over the longer term?

Proposition 3: Elites, ideology, and formal institution have only a short-term effect. Clan pacts (or their absence) explain one element of political trajectories – the *durability* or *nondurability/collapse* of the regime during the transition – but not *the new regime type*. The cases do not offer a definitive argument about what does cause democratization, although the evidence suggests that elite, actor-oriented views explain the short-term transition.[112] Instead, the argument here is that elites and ideology face significant constraints in clan-based societies. Independence often brings a forced transition. Some pacts are followed by democratization and others by a transition to a new form of autocracy. Pacts, modes of transition, leaders' ideological orientations, and formal new political institutions – the variables highlighted by the transitions school – have only a short-term effect on regime type and political trajectory.[113] They are unlikely to lead to democratic deepening and consolidation in societies pervaded by clan networks. The initial divergence is unlikely to last over the long term, or to break down the informal regime of clan politics that has increased in power under the transitional state.

Proposition 4: Under transitional uncertainty clan politics emerges, pervading formal regimes and weakening regime durability in the longer term. Why and how do clans negatively impact the longer-term political trajectory? The conditions of transitional and post-transitional states, defined by a weakened state and political and economic uncertainty, make it more likely that clan politics will emerge and gain strength at this time. The

[112] M. Steven Fish, "Democratization's Requisites: The Postcommunist Experience," *Post-Soviet Affairs*, vol. 14, no. 3 (July–September 1998), pp. 212–247; and Michael McFaul, "The Fourth Wave."

[113] Gerardo Munck and Carol Skalnik Leff, "Modes of Transition and Democratization: South America and Eastern Europe in Comparative Perspective," *Comparative Politics*, vol. 29 (April 1997), pp. 344–345. They argue that the "identity of the actors in the transition and their strategies" explain how democracies emerge and consolidate. In clan-based societies, the identity of the transitional actors is critically different.

pact itself puts clans informally behind the levers of power of the formal regime. While the new regime is *formally* institutionalized in the constitution, the presidency, and the visible rules of the game, clans, especially those involved in the pact, are *informally* institutionalized, establishing informal rules of the game. There are several mechanisms by which clans pervade, transform, and undermine the type and durability of the regime, even while new presidents seek autonomy and regime consolidation: kin-based patronage, asset stripping, and "crowding out" of formal institutions through clan-based mobilization.[114]

First, since clan norms demand strong loyalty to and patronizing of the clan, these norms can conflict with the identity of a modern bureaucratic state. Clans turn to the state as a source of patronage and resources, with negative effects on the regime. Clan members with access to state institutions patronize their kin by doling out jobs on the basis of clan ties, not merit. Clan elites steal state assets and direct them to their network.[115] Building a circle of clan supporters provides a clan leader with security. Under good economic conditions or a strong state, this practice may just weaken the state institutions (e.g., depleting the tax agency) and create resentment among excluded clans against those with access. Under negative economic circumstances and transitional or weak states, the pressure for clan elites to feed their network increases. Clans begin to strip assets at a faster rate, with more serious consequences for state capacity. In both democratizing and autocratic regimes, if clan networks pervade the state bureaucracy informally, the regime will lose legitimacy as clans steal state resources, and will lose power as clans informally decentralize control. Clans use the assets to fortify their group, effectively bankrupting state coffers, decentralizing state power, and creating competing wealth and power centers where they govern through an informal regime. Although the effect on the state is clearly suboptimal and depletes the future resource base for clans, the actions of individual clan elites are rational. They are investing in their network and base of power, rather than in a sinking state ship.

Clans also engage in "crowding out," a process by which they participate politically through their networks; clans effectively crowd out nonclan forms of association or participation. Clans use this mechanism (inclusion of members/exclusion of nonmembers) as a means of low-cost mobilization and political participation and competition. Clan elites use the clan to mo-

---

[114] On "crowding out" as a causal mechanism, see James Mahoney, "Causal Mechanisms, Correlations, and a Power Theory of Society" (paper presented at the annual meeting of the American Political Science Association, August 31, 2002), p. 9.

[115] On asset stripping by individuals, not groups, see Steven Solnick, *Stealing the State: Control and Collapse in Soviet Institutions* (Cambridge, MA: Harvard University Press, 1998).

bilize social support for their agendas, thereby avoiding the costs of creating new organizations, such as political parties, unions, and class organizations, which would have broader but less reliable constituencies.[116] In democratizing regimes especially, clan-based representation detracts from open competition that would cut across insular groups.[117]

The politics of clans is insular, exclusionary, and nontransparent. While the extensive networks involved in clan politics suggest that this informal governance may be more participatory than some forms of authoritarianism – for example, military juntas, despotism, and totalitarianism – clan politics is not democratic. Even if civil and political liberties exist, clan politics creates informal political and economic rules that are not pluralist, equally and fully participatory and representative, or transparently contested. Clan politics therefore undermines formal civil and political liberties. By pervading formal regime institutions, clan politics inhibits the agendas of both democratic and authoritarian regimes and prevents their consolidation. Finally, clan politics is likely to become self-reinforcing; it is a vicious cycle, difficult to end without some intervening variable (such as dramatic economic growth or the intervention of an external patron). As regime durability becomes uncertain, clans strip assets more quickly, and the regime and state become weaker still.[118] Declining state coffers will likely lead the president to break the pact by excluding clans he cannot now afford to patronize. A broken pact weakens regime durability (see Fig. 2.1). In sum, clan politics emerges as an informal regime under the uncertain political and economic conditions of transitional and post-transitional regimes; its effect is to transform regimes and to weaken or even undermine durability.

The role of clan networks in Central Asia will exemplify the formal and informal dynamics between clans and the formal regime institutions – dynamics leading to the emergence of an informal pattern of politics, the hegemony of *clan politics*. The following chapters will examine the power of these propositions by illuminating the role of clans during several historical periods: the colonial/state socialist period (the early 1900s through the Soviet era), the decolonization period (the end of the Soviet system, 1989–91), the transition period (the immediate post-Soviet period, 1991–95), and the post-transition, post-colonial period (the longer-term trajectory, from 1995 through early 2004).

---

[116] Charrad, *States and Women's Rights*, and Edgar, *Tribal Nation*, pp. 167–175, both argue that kinship groups undermine class organizations and mobilization.

[117] Lauth, "Informal Institutions," p. 30; and Gibson, "Social Networks," p. 59.

[118] Similar conditions lead to state failure. See Robert Rotberg, ed., *State Failure and State Weakness in a Time of Terror* (Washington, DC: Brookings Press, 2003), pp. 20–22.

◆ Given a clan-based society, under conditions of weak state and declining resources:

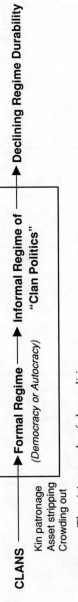

CLANS ——→ **Formal Regime** ——→ **Informal Regime of** ——→ **Declining Regime Durability**
  (Democracy or Autocracy)   **"Clan Politics"**

Kin patronage
Asset stripping
Crowding out

FIGURE 2.1. The vicious cycle of clan politics.

V. ASSESSING ALTERNATIVE APPROACHES TO STUDYING CENTRAL ASIA

Because the clan is an unfamiliar concept to most political scientists, I must briefly address what the clan is not, but is sometimes confused with – ethnic groups and nations, and regions. Alternative approaches to understanding Central Asia based on these concepts have ignored the role of clans. Although they explain elements of Soviet and post-Soviet politics, they ultimately offer unsatisfying explanations for the post-Soviet political trajectories in Central Asia.

The literature on ethnicity, nationalism, and ethnic conflict has provided a major theoretical lens though which many scholars have analyzed and explained the post-Soviet transitions, especially transitions in the non-Russian successor states.[119] This approach has built on an extensive literature on the Soviet legacy of defining ethno-national groups, creating republic boundaries endowed with institutional structures, and Soviet nativization and affirmative action policies.[120] Ironically, ethno-nationality became the frame within which nationality movements arose in opposition to the Soviet system.[121] Ethnicity characterized several communal clashes in Central Asian republics during the later Soviet period.[122] And ethno-national republic boundaries became the lines along which the Soviet Union eventually fell apart into independent states.[123] For these reasons, it is important to take ethnicity/nationality seriously, and an abundance of scholarship on the former Soviet Union has done so.

Why, then, distinguish clan from ethnicity, focusing instead on the former identity as a causal variable? First, we should distinguish the concepts and their political implications. Like ethnicity, the clan is an ascriptive, collective identity; however, the clan is typically a *subethnic* unit, and its essential element is real or fictive "kinship."[124] The discourse of ethnicity

---

[119] See Gail Lapidus, *The New Russia: Troubled Transformation* (Boulder, CO: Westview Press, 1995); David Laitin, *Identity in Formation* (Ithaca, NY: Cornell University Press, 1998); Valery Tishkov, *The Mind Aflame* (Oslo: PRIO, 1997); Gregory Gleason, *The Central Asian States: Discovering Independence* (Boulder, CO: Westview Press, 1997), Olivier Roy, *The New Central Asia* (New York: New York University Press, 2000); and Mark Beissinger, *Nationalist Mobilization and the Collapse of the Soviet State* (Cambridge: Cambridge University Press, 2002).

[120] See Suny, *Revenge of the Past*; Yuri Slezkine, "The USSR as a Communal Apartment, or How a Socialist State Promoted Ethnic Particularism," *Slavic Review*, vol. 53, no. 2 (Summer 1994), pp. 414–452; Martin, *Affirmative Action Empire*; and Edgar, *Tribal Nation*.

[121] Beissinger, *Nationalist Mobilization*.

[122] Tishkov, *The Mind Aflame*; and Nancy Lubin, "Islam and Ethnic Identity in Central Asia: A View from Below," in Ro'i, *Muslim Eurasia*, p. 70.

[123] Valerie Bunce, *Subversive Institutions* (Cambridge: Cambridge University Press, 1999); and Beissinger, *Nationalist Mobilization*.

[124] Tribe, clan, and ethnicity are not equivalent in Central Asia or the Middle East, although these concepts are frequently treated interchangeably in the context of sub-Saharan Africa.

and nation is about language, culture, cultural rights, and sometimes religion. The discourse of nationalism is about territory and sovereignty for a cultural group.[125] Further, ethnic groups, unlike clans, do not necessarily involve a network, although in some contexts ethnic entrepreneurs may attempt to create networks in seeking to attain their political goals. Benedict Anderson argues that most ethnic and national groups make political demands on the basis of a community that members "imagine but never see." He writes: "the member of even the smallest nation will never know most of their fellow members, meet them, or even hear of them, yet in the minds of each lives the image of their communion."[126] In this sense, ethnonationalist groups are distinctly different from clans; the former are overtly political. The political implications of ethno-nationalism are powerful, as Gellner and others have argued. Nationalists pursue the contiguity of a "nation" and a political unit, or territory.[127] The nationalist movements of the Baltics, Eastern Europe, Armenia, Moldova, and Georgia, for example, pursued this goal, triggering the waves of mobilization that shockingly undermined Soviet control.[128] Clans, by contrast, seek political and economic resources for the particularistic ends of a group, within an overarching state. Clans do not inherently oppose the boundaries of a state, or seek their own state.

Although a wealth of scholarship has studied the remarkable twentieth-century creation of nations in Soviet Central Asia, it is not clear that ethnicity or nationalism has become a hegemonic or centrally defining force in the politics of this region. First, contrary to many expectations in the late 1980s, ethno-nationalism did not drive secessionism in the Central Asian republics, as it did elsewhere in the Soviet empire. Rather, these were cases of the "failure" of nationalist and secessionist mobilizational efforts; secession was a de facto outcome of successful nationalism in other Soviet republics and of the collapse of the Soviet center.[129] Indeed, the post-Soviet nation-building projects that Central Asian leaders suddenly took up reflect the relative newness and weakness of their Soviet-defined ethno-national identities (in comparison to the much older ethno-national identities of the Armenians

---

Edgar points out that ethnic groups in Central Asia and the Middle East – "whether they be Arabs, Pashtuns, Kurds, Druze, or Turkmen – may be divided into many constituent tribes." As noted earlier, tribes are subdivided into clans. See Edgar, *Tribal Nation*, p. 36, fn. 17; and Eickelman, *Middle East and Central Asia*, pp. 124–127.

[125] Ronald Suny, "The Empire Strikes Out: Imperial Russia, 'National' Identity, and Theories of Empire," in Ronald Suny and Terry Martin, eds., *A State of Nations: Empire and Nation-Making in the Age of Lenin and Stalin* (Oxford: Oxford University Press, 2001), pp. 59–60.

[126] Anderson, *Imagined Communities*, pp. 5–7, cited in Shryock, *Nationalism*, p. 311.

[127] Ernest Gellner, *Nations and Nationalism* (Ithaca, NY: Cornell University Press, 1983); and Ernest Gellner, *Nationalism* (New York: New York University Press, 1997).

[128] Beissinger, *Nationalist Mobilization*.

[129] Ibid., pp. 210–211, 238–239.

or Georgians, for example) and the need for the new states to build nations
to reflect their new borders.[130]

A second reason for looking beyond ethnicity is that ethnic and ethno-
national conflicts have not erupted during the post-Soviet period,[131] despite a
peak of nationalist discourse in the late 1980s and early 1990s that led many
experts and policy makers to anticipate ethnic and ethno-national conflict.[132]
Criticizing this perspective, Valery Tishkov has stated: "Western scholars are
going to create ethnic conflict by talking about it so much."[133] The war in
Tajikistan was intra-ethnic, unlike the conflict in Nagorno-Karabagh. With
the exception of Kazakhstan, where the Russian population was close to
50 percent in 1991, ethnic lines have not been a critical political cleavage
in the Central Asian cases, especially not in the contest for political and
economic power. Ethnicity has clearly played a role in Central Asian politics
in the debate over language and citizenship laws, and in the Ferghana Valley
riots of 1989 and 1990. Yet, perhaps surprisingly in light of the literature's
expectations, ethnicity does not explain two major issues of the Central
Asian transitions: the durability or collapse of these regimes, and the failure
of democratization and the rise of authoritarianism. Ethnicity has not been
the cause of most group conflict/competition over resources; even the Russian
minorities have not seriously challenged the dominance of the titular ethnic
groups. Conflict has primarily occurred along *intra*-ethnic lines. Although
some tensions remain (e.g., between Kyrgyz and Uzbeks in Osh), Central
Asia's new governments have *not* been characterized by legal oppression of
or discrimination against certain ethnic groups. Although ethnic identity and
nationalism are important elements of Central Asian politics, and do explain
some issues, ethnicity is not a hegemonic identity. Multiple layers of identity
exist and shift in Central Asia, as elsewhere. Since an approach centered on
ethnicity is not helpful in explaining the rise of informal politics in Central
Asia, we should go beyond ethnicity and explore the informal politics of clan
identities.

A focus on regions and "center-regional relations" represents a second
lens recently used to analyze post-Soviet politics.[134] In this view, regions

[130] Helene d'Encausse, *The Great Challenge: Nationalities and the Bolshevik State, 1917–1930*
(New York: Holmes and Meier, 1992); Ronald Suny, "Provisional Stabilities: The Politics of
Identity in Post-Soviet Eurasia," *International Security*, vol. 24 (Winter 2000), pp. 139–178.

[131] I refer to conflict as violent conflict, whether civil war, pogroms, or riots. Certainly political
tension and debate have occurred.

[132] Those who disagree with the overemphasis on ethnic conflict include Martha Brill Olcott,
Central Asia's New States (Washington, DC: United States Institute for Peace, 1996); and
Kathleen Collins, "The Political Role of Clans," *Comparative Politics*, vol. 35, no. 2 (January
2003), pp. 171–173.

[133] Author interview with Valery Tishkov, director of the Institute for Ethnology and Anthropology, Russian Academy of Sciences, Moscow, August 1998.

[134] For example, see Katherine Stoner-Weiss, *Local Heroes: The Political Economy of Russian
Regional Governance* (Princeton, NJ: Princeton University Press, 1995); Luong, *Institutional Change*.

are formal institutions defined by the state. Regional elites often compete with central elites over resources and policy agendas, especially in federal systems. Katherine Stoner-Weiss and Steven Solnick, among others, have written about center-regional relations in Russia. In doing so, particularly in the context of studying federalism, they have focused on the formal institutional bases of power: Soviet and post-Soviet central and regional institutions. This approach encounters several problems, however, when applied to Central Asia. Some blur the distinction between region and clan, while emphasizing informal identities and the importance of kin-based ties. Others, such as Luong, focus only on the formal institutional level, leading to several faulty assumptions: that regions are equivalent to identities; that regions are the only salient political identities in post-Soviet Central Asia; and that the administrative-territorial institutions of the Soviet regime created regional identities. Luong further asserts that by setting up administrative districts within republics, the Soviets thereby eliminated or made irrelevant pre-Soviet identities and cleavages – clan, tribal, and Islamic.[135] However, she neither demonstrates a mechanism by which pre-Soviet identities broke down, nor provides evidence that such identities no longer exist.

A second problem with this approach is that a "region" is a geographically bound territory, not an identity. In the Soviet schema, a region (*oblast'*) is defined by formal institutions of the state, and is very often redefined by the state. Luong assumes that regions have an identity, but ignores the mass level – the attitudes, identities, and opinions of nonelites within the regions. Unlike ethnicity or nations – also defined by the Soviet state – regions are not given any cultural meaning or content. They lack the intrinsic meaning, bonds, network, and staying power of an identity group. "Regional" elites can become "central" elites, and their power base shifts, as Boris Yeltsin's career exemplifies. Clans, by contrast, have a less fluid, ad hoc basis. They have an intrinsic meaning, identity, and legitimacy and cannot merely change their social constituency.

Regions, per se, do not link elites and nonelites in any network or organizational structure. Multiple clans coexist within a region, and may create divisions within a region. For example, in Tajikistan, the civil war was largely fought between clan-based identity groups coexisting within Soviet-defined regions, not between unified regional blocs.[136] Within the Soviet-created "center" of Dushanbe, Garmi and Pamiri clans fought with Kulabi clans, as they also did within the southern "regions" of Kurgan-Tyube and Kulyab. At the same time, as Olivier Roy has pointed out, Soviet policies settled and territorialized clans, thereby giving them a village, local, and

---

135 Luong, *Institutional Change*, pp. 17, 52–53.
136 See Rubin, "The Fragmentation of Tajikistan"; Roy, *New Central Asia*; and Shahram Akbarzadeh, "Why Did Nationalism Fail in Tajikistan?," *Europe-Asia Studies*, vol. 48, no. 7 (November 1996), pp. 1105–1129.

(loosely) "regional" basis.[137] "Localism," Roy argues, refers to the village and region one comes from; it is a close approximation of one's genealogical roots. Villages were often named after tribal ancestors. If a person is a "Samarkandlik" (someone from Samarkand), his clan is not the several million inhabitants of Samarkand *oblast'* but a particular network of kin and fictive kin relations originating in that territory. Native Central Asians often loosely use their region or village of birth when identifying themselves. Locality can be an approximation for clan, especially when distinguishing one's group from other groups, at the national level. As one Tajik political leader observed, "Regionalism is a collective name for the organization of local clans and its elite in charge of some territory, its life and problems, protection of its interests through promotion and placement of its representatives in governmental structures."[138] As with "tribe" and "clan," scholars have often blurred the distinction between clan and region. Yet, conceptually and operationally, the distinction is important. It is not the formal institution – the Soviet-created region – that matters; rather, it is the informal organization of the multiple personalistic networks and identity groups *within* that region that is the operative variable.

Finally, those who focus on the state or colonial creation of identities often ignore the identities that already exist; they treat society as incapable of reacting to and shaping the colonial project.[139] To the extent that a region may be characterized as an identity, the region's identity is a reflection or amalgamation of other preexisting characteristics.[140] The Soviet state did create ethno-national republic boundaries, but those boundaries largely reflected preexisting ethnic and religious identities, such as Armenian, Georgian, and Chechen.[141] Although the Soviet Union's boundaries changed, these social identities persisted. As Kanchan Chandra has argued, colonial governments create institutions that reflect existing cleavages and identities.[142] The British

---

[137] Ibid.

[138] Tajik political leader, quoted in Saodat Olimova, "Regionalism and Its Perception by Major Political and Social Powers of Tajikistan," in Luigi De Martino, ed., *Tajikistan at a Crossroad* (Geneva: CIMERA, 2004), p. 89.

[139] For example, see Nelson Kasfir, "Explaining Ethnic Political Participation," *World Politics*, vol. 31, no. 3 (April 1979), pp. 365–388.

[140] This view neglects the more pervasive social identities underlying regions, even as regional boundaries change. Moreover, the study describes only regional elites, not regional identities.

[141] On differences in formation and depth of national identities, see Ronald Grigor Suny, *Looking toward Ararat: Armenia in Modern History* (Bloomington: Indiana University Press, 1993); Ronald Suny, *The Making of the Georgian Nation* (Bloomington: Indiana University Press, 1994), Suny, "Provisional Stabilities"; and Norman M. Naimark, *Fires of Hatred: Ethnic Cleansing in Twentieth-Century Europe* (Cambridge, MA: Harvard University Press, 2000).

[142] Kanchan Chandra, *Why Ethnic Parties Succeed: Patronage and Ethnic Head Counts in India* (New York: Cambridge University Press, 2004).

did not create Hindus and Muslims in India, although their policies reflected and reified a split already there. Despite being dispersed within regions of the Indian subcontinent, distinct ethnic, linguistic, and religious identities – not state-defined regions – were most salient. Similarly, Roy writes that:

> one of the paradoxes of the Soviet system was that the project of destroying traditional society and the implementation of 'social engineering' with a view to creating a new society translated, at least in the Muslim republics, into a recomposition of solidarity groups within the framework imposed by this system, and also into the creation of a two-level political culture. . . . if the new [Soviet] elites tended to function in ways that were traditional, this was because kinship and clan networks were recomposed on the basis of the territorial and administrative structures put in place by the Soviet system.[143]

Region matters insofar as it is a reflection of, and a venue for, the deeper, traditional ties of kinship and clan. In sum, although the center-regional framework may help to explain narrow questions about formal institutions, most political power in Central Asia does not actually lie in formal institutions.[144]

In short, these other frameworks offer insights into the study of Central Asia, but they do not provide an adequate explanation for either the theoretical questions or the empirical phenomena that this book seeks to explain. The focus on ethno-nationalism crucially explicates the nature of the Soviet collapse, and the variation in nation state identities across the former Soviet space; this lens points us toward the critical problem of post-colonial, post-independence nation building. Yet, neither lens explains the big questions of post-Soviet regime type and regime durability, and both ignore the role of informal actors and informal politics.

SUMMARY

Clan politics, while not sufficient to explain the whole of the transitional process, is critical to explaining post-transition regime convergence – why and how elites and their reform programs are constrained, and why and how new regime institutions, of whatever type, are penetrated and transformed so that they fail to serve the ideological or bureaucratic purposes of the state. Exploring the power of these informal institutions and the nature of their interaction with each other and with the formal regime, suggests that the prospects for achieving long-term regime viability, much less consolidation, are increasingly bleak. Behind their formal facades, all three Central Asian regimes are moving toward government by roughly the same kind of informal politics – a regime type that might best be termed the hegemony of "clan politics."

[143] Roy, *New Central Asia*, p. 85.
[144] Luong, *Institutional Change*, uses a central–regional bargaining model to explain the creation of the post-Soviet electoral laws.

In clan-based societies, then, we should anticipate that formal political institutions are very constrained; informal organizations, the same clan networks that shape the transition, will reemerge, penetrate formal political ones, and subtly disable them. The following chapters will empirically show that clan power in the post-Soviet Central Asian cases increases under the conditions of new, transitional, and post-colonial states, and that clan-based politics transforms and in some ways undermines the political development of both democratizing and authoritarian regimes. At both elite and mass levels, clan networks impede both post-transition regime and state consolidation and longer-term viability. In Central Asia, the initially distinct regimes of the early 1990s converge over the medium- to longer-term transition; informal clan-based regimes arise in each case. These longer-term political trajectories shaped by clan interests are likely to be characterized by authoritarianism, nonconsolidation, and declining regime durability.

3

Colonialism to Stalinism

The Dynamic between Clans and the State

> "They took our identity, our names. What is a man if he can not remember his name?"
>
> *One Hundred Days There Are No More* (1981), Chingiz Aitmatov

Understanding the post-Soviet trajectories in Central Asia, and why they differ so markedly from the post-communist and post-authoritarian transitions elsewhere, demands that we first understand the bases of social and political order in Central Asia – social organization and identities. For the twentieth century, this demands that we explain this social order in terms of the distinctiveness of the Soviet legacy *in Central Asia*.[1] Rather than assume that the Soviet regime successfully made "mankurts" of its Central Asian peoples – to borrow Aitmatov's term – we should examine how pre-Soviet identities and social organization interacted with and adapted to the new Soviet order.

An abundant literature on the nature of the Soviet system and its legacy exists; however, that literature generally assumes a uniform Soviet system and culture, and a uniform legacy. Yet neither the Soviet system nor its legacy is so straightforward. The legacy is far more complex and varied than formal Soviet institutions, ideology, and political culture imposed from above. The twelve time zones of the Union of Soviet Socialist Republics included a vast array of languages and cultures, more than 100 ethnic groups, many more sub-ethnic groups, and significant religious differences. In Central Asia, the Soviet legacy is one of the interaction between the strong and often brutal state policies of the Communist Party and the pervasive informal

---

[1] On communist legacies, see Karen Dawisha and Bruce Parrott, *Russia and the New States of Eurasia* (Cambridge: Cambridge University Press, 1994); and Karen Dawisha and Bruce Parrott, eds., *Conflict, Cleavage and Change in Central Asia and the Caucasus* (Cambridge: Cambridge University Press, 1998). See also Kenneth Jowitt, *The New World Disorder* (Berkeley: University of California Press, 1992).

organizations of society and their institutions and norms. That interaction is dynamic and often surprising. In fact, it forces us to rethink our understanding of the nature and power of the Soviet system, which was at once devastatingly strong and surprisingly weak.

Soviet rule of Central Asia, from 1917 through its demise, does not bolster an image of the Soviet state as uniformly totalitarian, uniformly effective in its reach, and uniformly modernizing.[2] We must, therefore, understand not just "the Soviet legacy," but the Soviet legacy in Central Asia and why it is distinct from Soviet rule, institutional change, and the Soviet legacy elsewhere. The roots of this difference suggest why Central Asia's trajectory does not follow the transitional paths of Eastern Europe, the Baltics, or even Russia, but instead looks increasingly like the post-colonial paths of many African states. This chapter calls for a rethinking of the Soviet period in Central Asia and its legacy for post-Soviet Central Asia. In Chapter 2, I proposed that clans can adapt and persist into the modern era, even under repressive and modernizing states, if certain conditions exist. Late state formation and the late formation of national identities allow the persistence of kinship identities and clan networks, rationally rooted in an economy of shortages typical of the pre-modern period, into the twentieth century. This chapter argues that clans did persist under the Soviet socialist system, despite its severe repression and forced modernization. Clans were able to adapt and persist because (1) state repression of the region fell short of physical destruction of the social system and the extended family structure;[3] (2) the clan organization provided a cultural identity that could become a basis of resistance; and (3) from the 1920s onward, clans had access to state resources that fostered their survival. More generally, the "indirect" nature of first Russian and then Soviet rule in Central Asia fostered the preservation and adaptation of clans as a form of social organization with political and economic consequences.

Following the previous chapters' discussion of clans as social organizations historically rooted in Central Asia, this chapter starts with a discussion

---

[2] On the Soviet system, see T. H. Rigby and J. Miller, *The Disintegrating Monolith* (New York: Augustus, 1968); and J. P. Nettl, *The Soviet Achievement* (New York: Harcourt, Brace, 1967). On Soviet modernization in Central Asia, see Alec Nove and J. A. Newth, *The Soviet Middle East: A Communist Model for Development* (New York: Praeger, 1966); and Charles Wilber, *The Soviet Model and Underdeveloped Countries* (Chapel Hill: University of North Carolina, 1969). For an opposing view, see Gregory Massell, *The Surrogate Proletariat: Moslem Women and Revolutionary Strategies in Soviet Central Asia, 1919–1929* (Princeton, NJ: Princeton University Press, 1974); and William Fierman, ed., *Soviet Central Asia: The Failed Transformation* (Boulder, CO: Westview Press, 1991).

[3] Contrast Soviet policy with communist rule in Cambodia, where the regime intentionally broke apart families and clans. See Kevin McIntyre, "Geography as Destiny: Cities, Villages, and Khmer Rouge Orientalism," *Comparative Studies in Society and History*, vol. 38, no. 4 (October 1996), pp. 730–758.

of clans under the Russian empire, leading up to the early Soviet period.[4] Clans were not the only form of social organization during this period, and some variation in the types of kinship and communal networks existed, but clan networks (in both their more traditional and less traditional forms, as defined in Chapter 2) were strong and pervasive elements of the social structure. Nation-states did not exist, and ethno-national identities were nascent at best. Economic conditions were characterized by scarcity, a factor that made kinship networks critical to economic survival and social well-being. Although Russian rule introduced significant changes in nineteenth-century Central Asia, Russian colonial governance in Central Asia was indirect, limited, and often weak. Consequently, and unsurprisingly, clans persisted during this period.

Second, this chapter grapples with how and why clans persisted under the strong Soviet regime.[5] How did these organizations survive the Soviet era – alternately waxing and waning in power – and then reestablish influence toward the end of the Soviet era, making them potentially powerful players during the post-Soviet period? Clans challenged the Soviet regime in many unexpected ways. Clan identity did not fit neatly into Marxist theory and the communist model of development, and the imposition of Soviet institutions often had unintended consequences. The chapter looks at several major Soviet institutional changes in Central Asia from 1917 through the 1950s. It examines how these institutions sought to eradicate what the Bolsheviks believed to be a "pre-modern" social system, antithetical to the socialist system. Several critical institutions – sedentarization and collectivization (which involved a "tribal policy"), nationalities policy, and the related cadre policy – were central to Soviet modernization of Central Asia. Yet all had the ironic and unintended consequences of reinforcing clan identities and empowering clan networks. These formal institutional reforms, and the ways in which they were implemented, under a state plagued by a constant economy of

[4] For historical and anthropological treatments of kinship affiliations in pre-Soviet Central Asia, see S. M. Abramzon, *Kirgizy i ikh etnogeneticheskie i istoriko-kul'turnye sviazi* (Frunze: Kyrgyzstan, 1990 [1971]); V. V. Bartol'd, *Four Studies on the History of Central Asia* (Leiden: E. J. Brill, 1962 [1956]); Paul Georg Geiss, *Pre-Tsarist and Tsarist Central Asia: Communal Commitment and Political Order in Change* (London: Routledge Curzon, 2003); Adeeb Khalid, *The Politics of Muslim Cultural Reform* (Oxford: Oxford University Press, 1998); Daniel Brower and Edward Lazzerini, eds., *Russia's Orient: Imperial Borderlands and Peoples, 1700–1917* (Bloomington: Indiana University Press, 1997); Yuri Bregel, *Khorezmskie turkmeny v XIX veke* (Moscow: Izd-vo Vostochnoi Literatury, 1961); A. M. Khazanov, *Nomads and the Outside World* (Cambridge: Cambridge University Press, 1984); William Irons, *The Yomut Turkmen: A Study of Social Organization among a Central Asian Turkic-Speaking Population* (Ann Arbor: University of Michigan, 1975); and Dale Eickelman, *The Middle East and Central Asia: An Anthropological Approach* (Upper Saddle River, NJ: Prentice Hall, 1998).
[5] See S. M. Eisenstadt, "Multiple Modernities," *Daedalus*, vol. 129, no. 1 (Winter 2000), pp. 1–29.

shortages, prompted clans to deal with their new conditions by relying on traditional networks of support. Although forced underground by Soviet policies, clans managed to survive and in many cases to thrive off the Soviet system, by manipulating Soviet policies and institutions in order to reinforce their informal networks. Central Asia was indeed transformed by the Soviet system, but Soviet institutions were also transformed in the process of their own implementation. What we find, then, is a story of clan adaptation and persistence.

Third, the Soviet center's unraveling in 1991, discussed in the following chapters, would eventually trigger independence and regime transition; however, the subtle, informal transformation of Central Asia, from communism to something else, grew out of earlier Soviet policies and the trajectories that they set in motion. The rise of informal politics and economics, based largely on clan ties and antithetical to the ideals of the socialist system, is rooted in the 1920s. Informal networks become especially salient after Stalin's death, from the 1960s to the early 1980s, as clans became informally entrenched in the Central Asian power structures under Brezhnev. The Brezhnev era's "stability of cadre" reinforced and even spurred clan politics. This chapter focuses on the dynamic between pre-Soviet informal organizations and formal Soviet institutions across the Central Asian cases from the 1920s to the 1950s. The following chapter will then discuss the Brezhnev era and differences that emerge across the cases in the 1980s as a result of varying state policies toward clan patronage.

Scholars of Central Asia have debated whether Soviet rule in Asia was colonialist rather than communist. The Soviet regime was no doubt communist in ideology and structure, and it incorporated its citizens under a legal and ideological framework that theoretically treated all Soviets as equals. However, the Soviet center also incorporated significant elements of colonialism in its relationship to its peripheral Muslim territories. Colonialism is not a perfect metaphor for Soviet rule; Soviet colonialism in Central Asia was in many ways less discriminatory, less economically exploitative, and more developmental than European colonialism in Africa and Asia.[6] Modernizing policies adopted by the Bolsheviks were not uniformly harsher toward Central Asians than toward Russians. Electrification and improved infrastructure meant that standards of living increased significantly, especially after the 1930s. Literacy approached 100 percent, even in rural areas, during the 1980s. The study of the Soviet-imposed titular languages and cultures and the creation of titular histories and museums were encouraged. Moreover,

---

[6] Nove and Newth, *Soviet Middle East*, pp. 14, 110–111. They argue that Soviet developmentalism in Central Asia dramatically increased literacy rates, industrialization, and access to electricity, telephones, and other infrastructure, and that in the 1950s and 1960s, the Central Asian republics compared favorably to the Muslim states to the south of the Soviet border (e.g., Iran and Afghanistan).

the republics' governing structures were increasingly staffed by their own ethnic cadre, not Europeans.

At the same time, Soviet policy was imbued with a hierarchical view of its Muslim subjects.[7] A central theme of this chapter is that – in contrast both to the central and western Soviet republics and to Italy, Scotland, and other European states where clans had declined or disappeared by the twentieth century – Central Asian social and political development was thwarted by various forms of colonial rule until the end of the twentieth century. Because Central Asians moved from one colonial empire to another during the twentieth century, they did not experience modern, independent statehood until 1991. Although the Soviet Union was not a typical colonial empire, the Central Asian republics experienced socialism, from the 1920s through the 1980s, as colonies.[8] As Douglas Northrop writes, there was great irony in the Bolshevik Party's "vocally anticolonialist" rhetoric and ideology, in light of its colonialist policies in Central Asia.[9] Like other European colonizers, the Bolsheviks viewed their mission in the "backward and primitive" regions of Central Asia as a "civilizing mission."[10] Promoting "friendship of the peoples" within the Soviet "multiethnic" state often meant Russification and the elimination or Sovietization of Asian and Muslim values and traditions, despite other policies that gave new opportunities to the Central Asian peoples. In particular, Islam, clan, and kinship – all at the heart of Central Asian culture and way of life (*byt*) – were viewed as antithetical to

[7] Contrast the Soviet understanding of Central Asians with their view of Russians and of European nations. See Ronald Grigor Suny, *The Revenge of the Past* (Stanford, CA: Stanford University Press, 1993).

[8] Soviet scholars emphasizing the developmental successes and advantages of Soviet nationalities policy in Central Asia argue that these republics were equals in the communist system. See Nove and Newth, *Soviet Middle East*. Specialists on the region, however, often stress the Soviets' "colonial" treatment of the Central Asians, even though it was not as hierarchical as that of the European colonial empires of the eighteenth and nineteenth centuries. See Teresa Rakowska-Harmstone, *Russia and Nationalism in Central Asia: The Case of Tadzhikistan* (Baltimore, MD: The Johns Hopkins University Press, 1970); Boris Rumer, *Soviet Central Asia: A Tragic Experiment* (Boston: Unwin Hyman, 1989); Michael Rywkin, *Moscow's Muslim Challenge: Soviet Central Asia* (New York: M. E. Sharpe, 1982, revised ed. 1990); and Edward Allworth, *Central Asia: 130 Years of Russian Dominance, A Historical Overview* (Durham, NC: Duke University Press, 1994). Recent historiography and political science emphasize this point. See the discussion of Soviet colonialism in the *Russian Review* (2000); and David Laitin, *Identity in Formation* (Ithaca, NY: Cornell University Press, 1998), who observes the distinction between the core Soviet republics and the colonized ones. Bunce notes this critical difference in Eastern Europe. The decolonization process complicated the transitions in numerous ways. See Valerie Bunce, *Subversive Institutions* (Cambridge: Cambridge University Press, 1999).

[9] Douglas Northrop, *Veiled Empire: Gender and Power in Stalinist Central Asia* (Ithaca, NY: Cornell University Press, 2004), p. 17.

[10] Ibid., p. 13. Northrop argues that the attack on the veil in Uzbekistan exemplifies the colonial nature of Bolshevik rule.

the ideals of the new Soviet socialist society. Not unsurprisingly, Bolshevik policy generated strong resistance, both open and subversive, to the new occupiers during the first few decades of Soviet rule.

The "colonial" metaphor further describes the political and administrative relationship between the Soviet center and its Muslim periphery. Despite massive repression and forced modernization, distance and demographics made the relationship between Moscow and the republics of Central Asia one of indirect rule in which the Soviet center had weak control. Despite the imposition of identical Communist Party and state institutions across all republics, enforcement was neither equally strong nor equally successful. Even as late as the 1980s, "of all the republics of the Soviet Union, the Central Asian republics most closely resembled a traditionally colonial model," observed Mark Beissinger.[11] Soviet leaders were often more interested in collecting revenues from Central Asia than in fully implementing Soviet reforms and modernizing policies. Ironically, the colonial-like dynamic between Soviet central policies and local politics preserved and even fostered Central Asia's clan-based social structure.

In sum, the Soviet system failed fully to modernize Central Asia, at least according to its own terms and model of modernization, which expected kinship and other traditional identities to disappear with the imposition of modern ethnic, national, and Soviet identities. A critical legacy of this period, then, is the persistence and reemergence of clan politics. The informality of clan networks made them difficult for the Soviet state to control, and therefore inherently durable as organizational forms. Their identity roots, not only in the traditional, pre-Soviet tribal past but also in ongoing and evolving kin and fictive kin groups, made them a natural source of resistance to the Soviet regime's colonial-like repression. And critically, the political and economic institutions of the Soviet state itself gave clans at various levels the means to sustain themselves. Soviet modernity, it turns out, sometimes inadvertently and sometimes knowingly incorporated kin and clan in significant ways.

I. COMMUNAL IDENTITY AND KINSHIP IN CENTRAL ASIA

Central Asian identity is multilayered and multifaceted. According to Adrienne Edgar:

The demographic structure of Central Asia took shape over a period of many centuries, as successive waves of nomadic Turkic migrants from the East conquered and mingled with settled agricultural populations speaking the Indo-European languages. The result was a rich patchwork of peoples, tribes, languages, and cultures, all living intermingled within a diverse landscape of deserts, mountains, and oases.

---

[11] Mark Beissinger, *Nationalist Mobilization and the Collapse of the Soviet State* (Cambridge: Cambridge University Press, 2002), p. 257.

The diversity existed within a framework of broad cultural unity, an Islamic Central Asian civilization that was a synthesis of Turkic and Persian elements.[12]

The "ethnic" identities of the Soviet "national" republics were largely products of the communist era. Prior to 1917, as Edgar argues, "it is difficult to identify distinct, let alone cohesive, ethnic groups in Central Asia." Rather, "subethnic and supraethnic loyalties were generally more important to people."[13] Islam and kin or village were more central to identity, and *intra*ethnic rather than *inter*ethnic group boundaries were typically the lines of conflict.

Before the twentieth century, intraethnic tribes, clans, kin-based villages, and a small sedentary population comprised the predominant elements of social and political organization in Central Asia.[14]

Historically, clans are socially generated organizations. They interact with the state, but their form pre-dated the state throughout Central Asia and the Middle East.[15] Although today clans are largely dependent upon state resources, they did not simply emerge in response to the state.[16] Nor were clans constructed by the state. Rather, clans are rooted in the informal kin-based communities, tribal and non-tribal, of traditional society organized around extended family units that engage in social, economic, and political activities. For example, leaders in clan villages were responsible for implementing *adat* (customary law) prior to the emergence of modern states. In many regions, this local role of clans persisted with the sanction of the state, as in tsarist Central Asia. Yet this form of social organization has also adapted and changed over time to become more politicized, especially at elite levels during the later Soviet and post-Soviet periods. Today, as Central Asian scholar Rafis Abazov notes, while some clans are increasingly characterized more by the shared political and economic goals of an identity network and less by genealogy, other clans embody the more traditional ties of kinship.[17] The fact that the discourse of clan is used throughout the region, even as the

---

[12] Edgar, *The Tribal Nation*, p. 18.

[13] Ibid.

[14] See Khalid, *Muslim Reform*, p. 189–190; T. Koichuev, V. Mokrynin, and V. Ploskikh, eds., *Kirgizy i ikh predki: Netraditsionnyi vzgliad na istoriiu i sovremennost'* (Bishkek: Glavnaia redaktsiia kirgizskoi entsiklopedii, 1994). Also see V. V. Bartol'd, *Istoriia kul'turnoi zhizni Turkestana* (1927), in V. V. Bartol'd, *Sochineniia* (Moscow: Izd-vo Vostochnoi Literatury, 1977), vol. II, no. i.

[15] Khazanov, *Nomads and the Outside*.

[16] Most contemporary scholarship has assumed that informal institutions and organizations are reactive, emerging in response to the state. Helmke and Levitsky, however, also discuss "spontaneous" informal institutions as those that originate in society, not as a response to the state. See Gretchen Helmke and Steven Levitsky, "Informal Institutions and Comparative Politics: A Research Agenda" (Working Paper no. 307) (Notre Dame, IN: Kellogg Institute, September 2003).

[17] Rafis Abazov, *Historical Dictionary of Kyrgyzstan* (Lantham, MD: Scarecrow Press, 2004), p. 106.

concept itself evolves, suggests that clans continue to be relevant social and political networks and identities.

Although I use the term "clan" throughout this book to refer to the general social organization, we should nonetheless observe variations in the types of informal, kin-based networks that we find across the Central Asian region. Such variation was evident during the pre-Soviet era, just as it is in the post-Soviet period.[18] "Pure clans" do not exist today at the national or local level, in rural or urban areas. In fact, anthropological and historical studies of kinship in Central Asia and elsewhere argue that neither tribes nor clans were "pure" kinship units even during the pre-modern era. Kinship in Central Asian and Middle Eastern societies has always been fluid and semi-fictive.[19] In many ways, it is more dynamic than in Western Europe and North America, where a stable "nuclear" family became the core unit of society, at least since the early nineteenth century. Some historians even argue that the nuclear family structure emerged in the West as early as the seventeenth century, as a consequence of Enlightenment ideas.[20] By contrast, Paul Geiss and Adrienne Edgar both note that the extended family and clan network remained both fluid and critically important in Central Asia. Precise genealogies were not possible even during the pre-tsarist and tsarist periods, given the merging and splitting of tribes; the incorporation of slaves, orphans, and other outsiders; and shifting political alliances.[21] Changes in clan form have also taken place over time, as clans have "modernized" or adapted to new social and political circumstances. The "purity" or "fictiveness" of clan groups is not a dichotomous characteristic, but a continuum, suggesting multiple variations of the clan. Moreover, this notion of kinship is understood as normal in Central Asian society.

A common but simplistic characterization of the variation in Central Asia communal identities emphasizes historically sedentary Uzbeks and Tajiks in opposition to nomadic and tribal Kyrgyz, Kazakhs, and Turkmen. In this view, clans are seen as "real," and therefore more significant, in the latter cases than in the former, where society is portrayed as more modern and clan identities as only fictive. A fundamental problem with this view is that

---

[18] A. M. Khazanov, "Underdevelopment and Ethnic Relations in Central Asia," in Beatrice Manz, ed., *Central Asia in Historical Perspective* (Boulder, CO: Westview Press, 1994), pp. 147–149.

[19] See Charles Lindholm, "Kinship Structure and Political Authority: The Middle East and Central Asia," *Comparative Studies in Society and History*, vol. 28 (April 1986), pp. 334–355; Edgar, *Tribal Nation*, Chapter 1; Geiss, *Pre-Tsarist and Tsarist Central Asia*, pp. 45–85; Lawrence Krader, "Principles of the Asiatic Steppe-Pastoralists," in S. M. Eisenstadt, ed., *Political Sociology* (New York: Basic Books, 1971), pp. 150–156; and Philip Khoury and Joseph Kostiner, eds., *Tribes and State Formation in the Middle East* (Berkeley: University of California Press, 1990), pp. 5–8.

[20] Eileen Hunt Botting, "Family Feuds: Wollstonecraft, Burke, and Rousseau on the Transformation of the Family," in press, pp. 55, 46.

[21] See Geiss, *Pre-Tsarist and Tsarist Central Asia*; and Edgar, *Tribal Nation*, pp. 9, 25.

it assumes a false and stark distinction between these two groups. Tribal names and traditions, and the practice of learning one's genealogy seven to ten generations back, do remain stronger among the more recently nomadic tribes (the Kyrgyz, Kazakhs, and Turkmen). Yet even among the Turkmen there was some variation between nomadic and settled tribesmen (*charva* and *chomry*), and historians have also documented that many Uzbeks were tribal as well.[22]

There were ninety-two nomadic Uzbek tribes during the tsarist period, according to a nineteenth-century genealogy of the "Ozbeks," a term that referred to a supra-tribal "Tatar" group of Turko-Mongolian descent.[23] Other records have enumerated up to 111 Uzbek tribes.[24] Tajiks living outside of the valley oases had nomadic, if not always tribal, roots.[25] Only a small population was urban-dwelling. Typically referred to as "Sarts,"[26] these peoples inhabited the ancient cities of the Silk Road – Samarkand, Bukhara, and Osh. Adeeb Khalid notes the complexity of the Sart population and the difficulty of categorizing this group, since the meaning of the term "varied over time and place." "Sart" was synonymous neither with "Tajik" nor with the modern "Uzbek" population; "Sart" had no clear ethnic, national, or linguistic identity.[27]

The critical distinction historically is in fact between the sedentary urban populations and the nonurban populations (including rural agriculturalists, pastoralists, and raiding nomads). The Sarts either had no historic tribal identity or had begun to lose it by the nineteenth century.[28] The *mahalla* was the traditional form of urban communal organization; its form has persisted into the post-Soviet era. The *mahalla* is a neighborhood unit that typically includes an informal network of families, relatives and extended kin, and neighbors who consider themselves members of a local community. This urban residence group is a clan neither in the traditional anthropological sense nor in the more political sense. However, it should be noted that the

---

[22] Geiss, *Pre-Tsarist and Tsarist Central Asia*; and Kh. G. Gulamov and A. S. Tatibayev, *Central Asia and World History* (Tashkent: Tashkent State University, 1997).

[23] Edward Allworth, *The Modern Uzbeks* (Stanford, CA: Hoover Institution Press, 1990), pp. 31–35. The nineteenth-century historical record of Central Asia, especially for the pre-tsarist period, is relatively thin.

[24] Khalid, *Muslim Reform*, pp. 205–206; and Allworth, *Modern Uzbeks*, pp. 14–15, 28–29.

[25] Rakowska-Harmstone, *Russia and Nationalism*. Tajik tribes, as opposed to Turkic ones, were typically of Persian/Iranian descent. On the contested meaning of "Tajik," see Khalid, *Muslim Reform*, pp. 199–201.

[26] They were referred to as "Chaghatay" in Bukhara. See Khalid, *Muslim Reform*, p. 189.

[27] For thorough historical and anthropological discussions of the complexity of defining "Sarts" and "Tajiks," see Khalid, *Muslim Reform*, p. 188–190, 199–202; and John Schoeberlein-Engel, "Identity in Central Asia: Construction and Contention in the Conception of 'Özbek,' 'Tâjik,' 'Muslim,' 'Samarqandi,' and Other Groups" (Ph.D. dissertation, Harvard University, 1994), p. 141.

[28] Roy, *New Central Asia*, p. 16.

mahalla does embody kin-based ties and an identity network in many areas today, especially where there has been less interethnic mixing with Slavic populations.[29] Although it is outside the focus of this study, one should note that the strong localism of the *mahalla* does resemble the kinship ties typical of the clan-based villages.[30]

Tribal Uzbeks became sedentarized in stages, mainly prior to Soviet rule; their tribal connections are more remote. Rural Uzbeks, therefore, speak less about "clan" ties than about "localism," although their villages similarly are rooted in the traditional kin-based "*avlod*" and "*urugh*" (extended family/lineage or clan).[31] Similarly, many rural Tajiks were sedentarized in such a way that their village includes their traditional *avlod*. Like rural Uzbeks, their group also reflects kin ties and an identity network, although in Tajikistan people generally refer to localistic *avlod* identities rather than to the term "clan." The Tajik sociologist Saodot Olimova writes that "an *avlod* is a patriarchal community of blood relatives who have a common ancestor and common interests, and in many cases shared property and means of production and consolidated or coordinated household budgets."[32] The *avlod* is widespread in rural areas and has some influence in cities. In a nationwide poll carried out in Tajikistan in 1996, 68.3 percent of the 1,500 respondents said that they belonged to an *avlod*; this is approximately the same percentage of the population that is rural. In a survey of 4,000 respondents in 2003, 67.5 percent claimed to be part of an *avlod*. Outside of the urban centers of Dushanbe and Sughd, the percentage was even higher.[33]

Those inhabiting the steppe, desert, and mountains of most of contemporary Kyrgyzstan, Uzbekistan, Kazakhstan, and Turkmenistan, lived within more traditional clan and tribal units and were often part of a larger tribal confederation.[34] For some – especially Kyrgyz, Kazakhs, and Turkmen – nomadism persisted into the early years of Soviet rule. "Native loyalties had never been linked to formal political boundaries drawn by Tsarist officials or by their Communist successors. These feelings . . . were manifest in the *mahalla* and the *qishloq*. . . ."[35] In 1869, the Russian historian V. V. Radlov drafted the most comprehensive history of the tribes that had

---

[29] David Mikosz, "Manual for *Mahalla* and Community-Based Organization Leaders in Uzbekistan" (World Bank, 2003), pp. 5–10.

[30] *Mahalla*s were also governed by committees of *oqsoqols*.

[31] Roy, *New Central Asia*, pp. 87–89. On the *avlod*'s importance even after the civil war, see Saodat Olimova and Igor Bosc, *Labor Migration in Tajikistan* (Dushanbe: IOM, July 2003), pp. 49–50.

[32] Olimova and Bosc, *Labor Migration*, p. 49.

[33] Ibid.

[34] Allworth, *Modern Uzbeks*, pp. 34–36.

[35] Donald Carlisle, "Soviet Uzbekistan: State and Nation in Historical Perspective," in Beatrice Manz, ed., *Central Asia in Historical Perspective* (Boulder, CO: Westview Press, 1994), p. 114.

settled north and east of the Syr Darya River, in present-day Kazakhstan and Kyrgyzstan.[36] Radlov writes about the integrated social, economic, and political organization of the Asiatic steppe peoples and argues that the core was the family. The family included various levels of extended members. The smallest social group was found in the *aul*, which incorporated the nuclear family with all siblings and their marital relations and progeny, in a patriarchal line. The *aul* was also known as the kin-village. The Kazakh, Kyrgyz, and Turkmen *aul*s were nomadic. Several *aul*s comprised a clan. Oral genealogies were extraordinarily important in determining both clan membership and an individual's position within the clan. The leaders of each clan were senior members, respected elders who served as political leaders, representatives to tribal meetings, and mediators in disputes. Leaders also governed a system of patronage by which they distributed sheep and herds of cattle.[37] Strong kinship norms, patrimonialism, and mutually beneficial networks of exchange were central to these traditional clans.

Radlov provides the best concrete ethnographic evidence of the divisions and location of the Kyrgyz tribes and clans. The Kara-Kyrgyz (now known as the Kyrgyz) were divided into two major groups or tribal wings, the Ong and the Sol; each consisted of several tribes that were further divided into clans and *aul*s. By the 1800s, the Kara-Kyrgyz had been driven from neighboring Uzbekistan and Kazakhstan by competing groups. These Kyrgyz tribes extended from Kashgar through the Chu Valley, to the Talas River in the west, and into the Ferghana Valley in the south. According to Radlov and more contemporary ethnographers, the Ong consisted of six smaller tribes: the Bugu, the Sary Bagysh, the Solto, the Adygine, the Chon Baysh, and the Cherik. The Sol branch was less numerous; most of its tribes roamed the western Talas Valley.[38] These larger tribal groupings were further divided into multiple smaller tribes and clans. The Adygine, for example, had several smaller branches, most prominently including the Ichkilik. A third major tribal grouping that crossed Kyrgyzstan, Uzbekistan, and Tajikistan was the Qipchaq. Each tribe occupied particular areas of what is contemporary Kyrgyzstan, giving a regional territorial aspect to tribal identity well before the Soviet period. Abramzon, a Soviet ethnographer writing in the 1950s, observed the persistence of the same phenomenon of clan identities, albeit

---

[36] See V. V. Radlov, cited in Lawrence Krader, "Principles of the Asiatic Steppe Pastoralists," in S. M. Eisenstadt, ed., *Political Sociology* (New York: Basic Books, 1971), pp. 150–156.

[37] See Nazif Shahrani, "The Kirghiz Khans: Styles and Substance of Traditional Local Leadership in Central Asia," *Central Asian Survey*, vol. 5, no. 3/5 (1986), p. 258.

[38] V. V. Radlov, "*Obraztsi narodnoi literatury tiukskikh plemen, chast' 1,*" in S. Aliev, R. Sarypbekov, and K. Matiev, eds., *Entsiklopedicheskii fenomen eposa "Manas": sbornik statei* (Bishkek: Kirgizpoligrafkombinat, 1995), pp. 25–26. See also T. Koichuev and V. Mokrinin, *Kirgizy i ikh predki*, pp. 53–55.

in a sedentarized population.[39] Many of these groups retained knowledge of their tribal heritage, although their living patterns had broken into smaller clan and kin-based units, coming to resemble those of the longer-settled peoples of Uzbekistan and Tajikistan.[40]

In the contemporary period, a third dimension affects the character of clans and their kin or fictive kin nature. Although most clans do include both wealthy and poor members, clans do exist at both the elite and nonelite levels, especially in the post-Soviet era. The rural *avlod* typifies the nonelite level of clans. In some cases, however, an *avlod* becomes wealthy through control of a *kolkhoz*'s resources. Most traditional urban *mahallas* are also rarely included in elite circles. Elite clans are kin-based networks that have access to political and economic power under the modern state. They may have roots in a particular *mahalla* or *kolkhoz*, but typically they do not exist in a concentrated geographical district. Elite-level clans began to emerge during the Brezhnev era, as Central Asians regained control over many elements of the Soviet system. Today, elite clans are those that control urban or rural resources. Central Asians across the region, whether in tribal Kyrgyzstan or in nontribal Tajikistan, refer to these power networks as "clans." The more urban elite clans appear to incorporate more fictive kin ties through marriage, school, and friendship. Rural elite clans have a stronger kinship basis. Kyrgyz, Kazakh, and Turkmen elite clans typically reflect more traditional descent groups, whereas Uzbek and Tajik elite clans have a less traditional notion of kinship.[41]

These distinctions are variations on a theme. All groups use their networks to serve narrow group interests, both political and economic.[42] Anatoly Khazanov writes of post-Soviet identity that "in internal ethnic relations his [an individual's] parochial and/or kin-based tribal and clan affiliations still play an important role. Parochial divisions are particularly conspicuous in Tajikistan and Uzbekistan, while in other Central Asian republics one meets with rather pure forms of tribalism."[43] Further, as we will see,

---

[39] S. M. Abramzon, *Kirgizy i ikh etnograficheskie i istoriko-kul'turnye sviazi* (Bihkek: AN Kirgizskoi SSR, izdatel'stvo "Kirgizstan," 1971). See also Abazov, *Historical Dictionary of Kyrgyzstan*, pp. 8–9, 29–30.

[40] Ibid.

[41] Uzbek society, even today, is further complicated by the existence, historically, of caste distinctions as well. Certain surnames are still associated with elite castes and those families are frequently seen to be in positions of power. For example, the "*Sayyid*" caste is said to be the lineage of the descendents of the prophet Muhammad. The "*Khoja*" caste is said to be of Arab descent. The "*Mir*" caste is believed to represent warriors. See Mukhammed-Babur M. Malikov, "Uzbekistan: A View from the Opposition," *Communist and Post-communist Studies*, vol. 42, no. 2 (March/April 1995), p. 20.

[42] Given the political and economic conditions in contemporary Central Asia, they often do this illegally. For this reason, clans operating at the elite level are often referred to as "mafias" in public discourse.

[43] Khazanov, "Underdevelopment," pp. 147–148.

the Soviet *kolkhoz* structure imposed a certain homogenization on networks across the region and enhanced the kinship and "tribal" nature of rural Central Asia, even in cases where traditional tribal groups had not existed.[44]

Identity and kinship have always been complex in Central Asia (as in the Middle East and South Asia).[45] Writing of the nineteenth century, Adeeb Khalid argues that:

Individuals felt themselves to be Ozbek or Turk or Tajik not through some abstract sense of belonging to a national group but through the concrete fact of being born in a family that was located socially in a ramified structure of relationships conceived in kinship terms. Tribal designations were far more significant to individual identity than broader categories such as 'Turk' or 'Tajik'. . . . Among the sedentary population without tribal divisions, geographical designations played a similar role. . . . Group identities in pre-Russian Central Asia presented a complex mosaic of fragmented identities intimately intertwined with the social and economic fabric of the land.[46]

This multiplicity of identities and complexity of language and tribal origin continues to exist today. In the 1970s, Alexandre Bennigsen classified these identities as subnational (clan and tribe), national (the Soviet-created ethno-nationality of the titular republics), and supra-national (a broader Islamic community), and argued that the subnational level continued to be important during the Soviet period.[47] Adrienne Edgar also observes the political importance of subnational kinship ties in the twentieth century, despite their often varying and semifictive basis. Edgar writes that "tribal genealogies often reflect current political and social relationships as much as they do biological kinship. When groups establish close and enduring political relationships, they may eventually 'discover' common ancestors and rewrite their genealogies accordingly."[48] Furthermore, "even in the absence of biological kinship[,] . . . genealogy was the most important idiom on the basis of which solidarities and conflict were understood and justified."[49]

The situation in post-Soviet Central Asia is often viewed as more "modern," given the imposition of national and nation-state identities during the Soviet and now post-Soviet periods. Tribes have broken down; clans of the pre-Soviet period are not necessarily the same clans of 2003. Some fled to China or Afghanistan in 1917. Others were annihilated in collectivization and the purges. Marriage, Russification, and new party and friendship ties have changed the boundaries of others. Most importantly, the Soviet system,

---

[44] Roy, *New Central Asia*, p. 89.
[45] On the complexity of identity in the Middle East, see Bernard Lewis, *The Multiple Identities of the Middle East* (New York: Schocken Books, 1998); and Khoury and Kostiner, *Tribes and State*.
[46] Adeeb Khalid, *The Politics of Muslim Cultural Reform: Jadidism in Central Asia* (Berkeley: University of California Press, 1998), p. 190.
[47] See Rywkin, *Moscow's Muslim Challenge*, p. 116; and Alexandre Bennigsen, "Several Nations or One People," *Survey* (London: 1979), no. 108.
[48] Edgar, *Tribal Nation*, p. 50.
[49] Ibid., p. 51.

for reasons not entirely known, selectively promoted some and demoted others.

At the same time, however, Khalid's observations about the centrality of relationships conceived in tribal, kinship, and geographical ties (or, as I call their more modern form, "clan networks"), rooted in the "social and economic fabric," are equally applicable to Soviet and post-Soviet Central Asia.[50] "Despite the pain and disruption inflicted... the Soviet regime did not transform the social structure in Central Asia as it did in European parts of the former USSR. In Central Asia Soviet totalitarianism adapted itself.... [N]otwithstanding some variation among the Central Asian countries, in all of them ties of family, tribe, clan, and locality are far stronger elements than in more developed societies."[51] These networks are important sources of identity and social organization across the region. Although religion, ethno-nationality, and civic nationality also provide identities, these broader groups include larger numbers of members, and often lack the network ties that advance political and economic interests.

The complexity of subnational identities and kinship relations should not be underestimated. Figure 3.1 illustrates the main variation in the form of clan networks in the twentieth century. Yet the variation occurs less by ethnicity or republic than by the degree to which communal groups are (1) rural/urban, (2) sedentary/nomadic (or recently so), and (3) elite/nonelite. These factors, in turn, are the result of socioeconomic and historical developments, especially from the seventeenth to the twentieth century. Traditional notions of kinship (designated here as a "high kin basis") are clearly stronger in some groups than in others ("low kin basis").

Differences between groups and their respective notions of kinship – nomadic and sedentary – were very likely more pronounced during the pre-Soviet period. As a result of Soviet policies and modernization, the communal ties and networks remain but are more similar in content, form, and function across the region and cases. Despite continuing variation, these networks share several common features: (1) the notion of an identity and some basis in kinship; (2) shared norms rooted in traditional communal ties; (3) informality of both identity and practices; and (4) insularity and narrowness in pursuing their political and economic interests. In the modern era especially, clan elites actively "construct" kinship and fictive kinship bonds as a source of protection and a means of attaining and keeping political and economic power.[52]

---

[50] Khazanov, "Underdevelopment," pp. 147–148.
[51] Dawisha and Parrott, *Russia and New Eurasia*, p. 148.
[52] The element and method of construction is far more informal and far narrower than is construction of national identities, as discussed by Benedict Anderson, *Imagined Communities* (London: Verso, 1991). National identities and their corresponding communities are typically much broader. Yet the goal of using and manipulating identities to attain some form of power is similar in the two cases.

High Kin Basis ←——————————————————→ Low Kin Basis

Blood   "Fictive"   Patron-Client
Kinship Ties   Kinship   Networks

Kyrgyz, Turkmen, Kazakh elite networks
Kyrgyz, Turkmen, Kazakh non-elite networks (*aul, qishloq*)

Uzbek elite networks
Uzbek non-elite networks (*qishloq, avlod, mahalla*)

Tajik elite networks
Tajik non-elite networks (*qishloq, avlod, qawm, mahalla*)

FIGURE 3.1. Variation in types of clan networks.
Note: The chart does not represent the actual degree of kinship in these networks. Spatial location signifies those networks that more explicitly emphasize their genealogical basis, and those that more explicitly incorporate fictive kin and patronage ties.

These similarities, as well as the frequent use of the term "clan" (as well as "*rod,*" "*avlod,*" and "*urugh*") by Central Asians themselves, suggest that we consider these networks variations on the theme of informal clan organization.[53] In all of these groups, the metaphor of kinship provides an important bond and establishes norms of behavior.[54] Furthermore, one should not overemphasize the differences in kinship form, because the Soviet period destroyed much of the heterogeneity of communal ties that existed during the nineteenth century.[55] All groups were sedentarized, educated, and to some extent modernized, although some cultural differences remain. Finally, as mentioned in Chapter 1, the goal of a political science approach is to understand broadly, across the region, what the implications of this general phenomenon are for political trajectories, rather than to examine particular variations within each case.

II. SOCIOPOLITICAL ORGANIZATION IN NINETEENTH-CENTURY CENTRAL ASIA

Modern state structures did not emerge in Central Asia until the twentieth century. Traditional social organizations such as clan and tribal groups

[53] Olivier Roy, although presenting a very nuanced picture of informal networks in both the rural and urban sectors, alternately refers to these groups as "solidarity groups," "tribes," "clans," and "regional networks," thus leaving the reader unclear about the conceptual similarities and differences. Because of the similarities across the cases, and the need for conceptual clarity, I adopt the common term "clan." See Chapter 2.

[54] Geiss, *Pre-Tsarist and Tsarist Central Asia*, distinguishes between residence groups and descent groups.

[55] On greater clan heterogeneity during the pre-Soviet period, see ibid., p. 240.

(groups typically associated with the pre-modern, pre-state era), therefore, had the social and political space to survive much later than they had in other regions. The city-based principalities existing at the time of the Russian conquest (including the khanates of Khiva and Kokand and the emirate of Bukhara) were pre-modern systems of government that had not disrupted kinship ties and clan organization.[56] They did not attempt to modernize the population, declare fixed state boundaries, or impose a national or civic identity. These "states" were feudal organizations at best; they exerted little control over the territory or the population, especially over the rural and no-madic population of the steppe and mountains. Gregory Massell writes that:

as a rule, the region's largest historical units made for a segmental rather than unitary political universe, while the smallest and primary communal structures were essen-tially segmentary rather than hierarchical in nature. In such a milieu, the vertical link-ages between ruling elites (princely-theocratic, religious, military, and merchantile) at the supra-communal level and the communal leadership of tribes, clans, and villages (including the mass of peasants and nomads) at the grassroots were decidedly weak.[57]

The emirs often struck feudal-like bargains with clans on which they relied for tax collection or military might.[58] Theresa Rakowska-Harmstone simi-larly observes that "the various mountain principalities of Eastern Bukhara such as Darvuz, Karategin, and Gissar were, until the 1870s, ruled by hered-itary *beks* who recognized the sovereignty of Bukhara only nominally."[59] Tajik mountain tribes and clans experienced little direct rule. Russian assis-tance in the 1880s, in fact, gave the Bukharan emir greater ability to subdue the Tajik kin groups.[60]

During the nineteenth century, especially from the 1860s to the 1880s, the Russian empire moved progressively south and east into the Asian steppe.[61] In 1865, Russia conquered the khanate of Kokand and created the governor-generalship of Turkestan. The Russian empire then incorporated the emirate of Bukhara and the khanate of Khiva as tsarist protectorates. Russian rulers conquered vast territory and made deals with the indigenous elites, but they did not significantly transform society.[62] Nor did they seek to. Initial attempts

---

[56] See Massell, *Surrogate Proletariat*; and Roy, *The New Central Asia*, p. 10.

[57] Massell, *Surrogate Proletariat*, p. 11.

[58] See Daniel Brower and Edward Lazzarini, eds., *Russia's Orient*; and Massell, *The Surrogate Proletariat*, p. 12.

[59] Rakowska-Harmstone, *Russia and Nationalism*, p. 15.

[60] Ibid., p. 16.

[61] Seymour Becker, *Russia's Protectorates in Central Asia: Bukhara and Khiva, 1865–1924* (Cambridge, MA: Harvard University Press, 1968).

[62] See Poliakov, *Everyday Islam*, p. 13–15; Brower, *Russia's Orient*, p. 131; and Rakowska-Harmstone, *Russia and Nationalism*, pp. 13–14. Geiss, *Pre-tsarist and Tsarist*, gives greater weight to the social effects of Russian rule.

to integrate and convert the frontier population were replaced by Moscow's policy of ruling minimally and indirectly. It governed through its envoys in the Turkestan district and their contacts with local, traditional authorities (tribal and clan elders). The empire had little hands-on control outside of a few urban centers. Like most colonial empires, it was mainly interested in geostrategic expansion, new tax revenues, and economic exploitation of the region's resources, especially cotton.

Russian officials, inspired by Enlightenment scientific queries as well as by colonialism's use of ethnicity for control of its subjugated peoples, did attempt to create ethnic categories and classification systems for Central Asians. Yet "tribal confusion and Moscow's lack of knowledge of the native kinship-based societies continued to defy Russian attempts at naming and classifying the natives."[63] The main distinction that Russians were able to draw was between the Sarts and the rural and nomadic populations, which retained strong tribal affiliations.[64] To their frustration, Russian ethnographers found that language did not necessarily mark clear distinctions between "ethnic" groups, and that most of the indigenous population did not identify itself according to ethnic categories. According to Daniel Brower, by Western and Russian standards of the time, the Sarts were the most "advanced" in that they had ceased to use their tribal affiliations. Meanwhile, ethnographers found that "the Uzbeks seemed to be at a transitional stage of semi-nomadic life with strong tribal loyalties, and the Turkmen and Kyrgyz nomads (occasionally refined to distinguish between Kyrgyz-Kazakh and Kara-Kyrgyz) clearly occupied a lower rung on the ladder of human evolution. Beyond that there was always the residual category of 'Turk'...."[65]

This intense interest in ethnography was driven by the state largely in order to prevent the spread and deepening of Islam among the population. Still, despite their categorizations, the Russian rulers did not seek to alter the social structures of the region, either by eliminating traditional clan elites or by eradicating Islam.[66] Governor-General von Kaufman (1867–81) did view the colonial administration as an agent of modernity and social transformation, but he nonetheless resisted pressure to exert more direct control and to force assimilation.[67] For example, he adopted a policy of "disregard" of Islam, rather than implement forced conversion or control of religion, because he believed that tolerance was the key to control. "If progressive colonial policies encouraged social development, animosity based on religious beliefs

---

[63] Michael Khodarkovsky, "Ignoble Savages and Unfaithful Subjects," in Brower and Lazzarini, *Russia's Orient*, pp. 9–26.

[64] Brower, *Russia's Orient*, p. 129.

[65] Ibid., pp. 129–130.

[66] See Khalid, *Muslim Reform*, Chapter 2; Edgar, *Tribal Nation*, Chapter 3; and Virginia Martin, *Law and Custom in the Steppe* (Richmond, Surrey: Curzon, 2001).

[67] Brower, *Russia's Orient*, p. 119–123; and Khalid, *Muslim Reform*, pp. 57–59.

would lessen."[68] The Russians were less interested in directly controlling the population than in keeping Islam tame.

Russian administrative structures and institutions in Turkestan further emphasize the primarily indirect nature of colonial rule. Khalid points out that the Russian presence in the frontier region was minimal; it existed at the level of the *uezd* (district) and higher, not in the villages or *mahallas* (neighborhood communities).[69] Russian imperial law, meanwhile, applied only to European inhabitants.[70] Russian administrators in the steppe even attempted to codify *adat* (indigenous customary law) for the native population.[71] In settled and urban areas, local *oqsoqols* (elders) were "elected" to act as local governing committees, a practice that pre-dated the Russians. *Volost'* chiefs were also elected. A "parallel system of administration was created among the nomadic population with electors choosing leaders at the *aul* and *volost'* levels."[72] Khalid argues that this system created a "native tier" and a "Russian tier" of administration. Sometimes the election system reinforced local control and minimized Russian influence. Russia even used local elites to collect taxes and administer justice at both the village and *volost'* levels.[73] Edgar notes that "instead of imposing the Russian legal system on the region, colonial authorities dispensed justice to natives based on local codes of Islamic and tribal customary law."[74] A colonial experiment known as the Temporary Statute of 1868 sought to introduce elections of *volost'* officeholders in the Kyrgyz steppe and to decrease the influence of kinship elders. According to Dov Yaroshevski, however, the system in fact produced networks of clan elders who created early "political machines" to support their groups' candidates.[75] The effect seems to have been slow progress in implementing reforms and even, as Yaroshevski argues, the subversion of reforms altogether. Tribal leadership remained influential at the local and district levels, even though larger tribal configurations broke down.

In sum, the tsarist colonial government was indirect; local identities persisted, and many native institutions continued to function; the system operated much in the way that the British empire operated in British India. Even when the Russians sought to introduce new local institutions, society did not submissively accept them. Local elites sometimes resisted with force, and often transformed those structures and integrated them into their own

---

[68] Brower, *Russia's Orient*, p. 122.
[69] Khalid, *Muslim Reform*, p. 58.
[70] Geiss, *Pre-Tsarist and Tsarist Central Asia*, p. 200.
[71] Martin, *Law and Custom*, pp. 4–5.
[72] Khalid, *Muslim Reform*, p. 58.
[73] Edgar, *Tribal Nation*, p. 56.
[74] Ibid., p. 57.
[75] Dov Yaroshevski, "Empire and Citizenship," in Brower and Lazzerini, *Russia's Orient*, pp. 58–79.

kin- and clan-based institutions. Yet the Russian administration was content to live with this system into the 1900s as long as it kept social stability. Not until after 1917, when the Bolsheviks placed Turkestan and the rest of Central Asia under the directorate of the Central Asian Bureau of the Central Committee of the Communist Party, would a modern state attempt to eradicate the clan system.[76]

III. THE SOVIET WAR ON CLANS AND PRE-MODERN IDENTITIES (1917–1953)

Establishing the Soviet System in Central Asia

The formal configuration of political, economic, and social institutions was nearly identical throughout the Soviet republics. However, the regime's authority over Central Asia's vast economic, social, and political system waxed and waned throughout the Soviet period, albeit for different reasons at different times. In fact, close examination reveals what Joel Migdal has called, in other cases, a "mutual transformation" between formal Soviet institutions and informal, indigenous Central Asian institutions.[77] The continued colonial nature of Central Asia's relationship with Moscow and the central Soviet regime allowed for and fostered an interaction and transformation of institutions over time. The legacy of that interaction would have distinct consequences for the regime transition.

Soviet rule in Central Asia introduced dramatic change, and far exceeded the attempts of tsarist policies to control the empire's Muslim subjects. The first major institutional change included the creation of national republics. The new borders were designed to facilitate administrative control and, just as importantly, to reflect and promote "modern" ethno-national identities that would become the basis of modern socialist identities.[78] Between 1917 and 1920, the Bolshevik army had gradually taken control of Turkestan and the Muslim dynasties of Bukhara and Khiva. In 1918, Turkestan became

---

[76] Francine Hirsch, "Empire of Nations: Colonial Technologies and the Making of the Soviet Union, 1917–1939" (Ph.D. dissertation, Princeton University, 1998), Chapter 1.

[77] Joel Migdal, *State in Society* (New York: Cambridge University Press, 2001); and Joel Migdal, Atul Kohli, and Vivienne Shue, *State Power and Social Forces* (New York: Cambridge University Press, 1994). They focus on "society" more narrowly, rather than on informal organizations, but the phenomena are similar. The top-down view of the Soviet Union is exemplified by Luong. She assumes that the formal Soviet institutions destroyed or made irrelevant indigenous Central Asian identities, and that only Soviet-imposed administrative identities subsequently mattered. See Luong, *Institutional Change*, p. 63.

[78] Suny, *The Revenge of the Past*, Chapter 1; and Yuri Slezkine, "The USSR as a Communal Apartment, or How a Socialist State Promoted Ethnic Particularism," *Slavic Review*, vol. 53, no. 2 (Summer 1994), pp. 414–452. Earlier scholars viewed the delimitation as part of a "divide-and-conquer strategy" designed in response to pan-Turkic and pan-Islamic threats.

a Soviet republic, and in 1920 the nominally independent Bukharan and Khivan republics were incorporated into the Soviet state. In 1924, however, as part of the Soviet nationalities policy, the "national delimitation" dissolved these three republics. In their place, the Soviet government created five entities based on the idea of "national homelands."[79] The Uzbek and Turkmen territories were created as republics in 1924. In 1929, the Tajik Republic was separated from the Uzbek SSR and given full republic status. Finally, in 1936, the Kyrgyz and Kazakh republics were endowed with full republic status (according to Soviet terminology, they "seceded" from the Russian republic), bringing the number of Central Asian Soviet socialist republics to five. Lenin established the Central Asian Bureau (*Sredazbiuro*) to direct Party activities in Central Asia during the early Soviet period.

The centralization of the Soviet system had enabled it broadly to replicate its power structures in each of the Soviet republics. The new Uzbek, Kyrgyz, and Tajik Soviet Socialist Republics, like the other national republics (the Kazakh and Turkmen in Central Asia, and Ukraine, Belarus, and others in the western regions), were each endowed with a parallel governing party and state apparatus, although, as in Moscow, real power was concentrated in the former. Each republic had its own Party structure, extending from the Central Committee of the Communist Party of the Uzbek Soviet Socialist Republic, headed by a first secretary, to the *ob'kom'partiia* (the oblast/regional committee of the Communist Party), to the lowest-level party cells.[80] The republican state structures paralleled the central Soviet system. Each republic was largely under the control of the Party first secretary and the Central Committee. In institutional changes instigated by Gorbachev's decrees, these structures would be transformed in the late 1980s in tandem with the restructuring of party and governmental organs at the Soviet center. That central transformation set in motion a similar institutional process in each union republic during its subsequent transition. Yet how that process unfolded in Central Asia proved to be dependent on the informal legacy of Soviet power – the mutual transformation of Soviet political and economic institutions and indigenous Asian ones at the republic and local levels.

The institutionalization of communism was a revolutionary and dynamic process that took place over decades. Consolidating control during the 1917 revolution was fraught with challenges. The Leninist regime had hoped to "liberate" the suppressed masses of Central Asia with ease, but the Bolsheviks found themselves consumed with subduing the part tribal, part Islamic Basmachi opposition movement, thwarting nascent pan-Turkism, controlling the borders, and establishing formal control in the urban centers.[81]

[79] Ronald Grigor Suny, *The Revenge of the Past*, ch. 1.
[80] Nove and Newth, *Soviet Middle East*.
[81] See Rywkin, *Moscow's Muslim Challenge*; and Massell, *The Surrogate Proletariat*.

Central Asia's ability to subvert Moscow's control certainly varied over time, often as a result of the Soviet regime's capacity and willingness to use force to demand compliance. Several historians have pointed to the co-optation of some local elites, and even the support of socialism among others, especially urban intellectuals and Muslim reformers such as the Jadids.[82] Repression was a more common mode of Soviet annihilation of un-Soviet elements to promote social transformation. The first two decades of Soviet rule – including the Red Army's conquest, war communism, collectivization in the 1920s and 1930s, and the purges of 1937 – were the most brutal and destructive period of communist power in Central Asia, as they were elsewhere in the USSR. The death toll as a result of collectivization and purges did massive damage to the Central Asian way of life.[83] At the same time, repression of Islam and kinship ties engendered substantial, if informal, resistance against the Soviet regime.[84]

Even after the civil war and the Basmachi resistance ended, "the new revolutionary regime confronted in Central Asia a highly diverse and multilayered universe. In this universe the largest (supra-communal) – and hence the most heterogeneous – historical subdivisions were on the verge of disintegration, while the smallest – and hence the most homogenous, including clans, extended families, and village communities – were relatively intact."[85] By the early 1920s, the Soviet regime had created both new political structures in Turkestan and a new social and economic order. Modernization and Sovietization began in force. Yet, as Massell argues, Central Asian societies, because they were fragmented, insular, and informally organized, were "particularly elusive to attempts not merely to establish a mechanism of power, but to legitimize it and use it for rapid revolutionary transformation and efficient integration."[86]

As he embarked upon the social engineering of the Soviet Union, Lenin emphasized the *institutional*, rather than merely the *elite* transformation of the empire.[87] Radical agrarian policies sought a novel and effective mode of social change for a predominantly peasant country. Hence the Central Asian republics were internally organized in a hierarchy of controlling administrative territorial units: the *avtonomnaia oblast'* (autonomous region), the *oblast'*

---

[82] See Khalid, *Muslim Reform*, pp. 285–288.
[83] Kazakhstan was the hardest hit. See Martha Olcott, *The Kazakhs* (Stanford, CA: Hoover Institution Press, 1988); and Robert Conquest, *The Harvest of Sorrow: Soviet Collectivization and the Terror-Famine* (New York: Oxford University Press, 1986). Conquest writes that approximately one million (of a total of over four million) Kazakhs were killed, p. 190. Other estimates are even higher.
[84] Shoshanna Keller, *To Moscow, Not Mecca: The Soviet Campaign against Islam in Central Asia, 1917–1941* (Westport, CT: Praeger, 2001); and Edgar, *Tribal Nation*, pp. 193–195.
[85] Massell, *The Surrogate Proletariat*, p. 37.
[86] Ibid.
[87] Jowitt, *New World*, pp. 27–28.

(province), and the *raion* (district). Just as important were the institutions of collectivization: the *kolkhoz* (collective farm) and *sovkhoz* (state farm), the *sel'sovet* (rural council), and the *selo* (village).[88] And at the most local level of governance within each village were the *kombedy*, committees of poor peasants responsible for the distribution of social welfare. These new administrative institutional structures were the basis of Soviet control. They were also the basis of Soviet modernization that would eventually bring not just Communist Party cells, but electricity, water, irrigation, industrialization, and literacy to the underdeveloped republics of Central Asia. Scholars such as Alec Nove and J. A. Newth have argued that, in fact, most indicators suggest that the Soviet regime had successfully modernized this region by the 1960s, and that levels of development in the Soviet Muslim world far exceeded levels in the Muslim world across the Soviet Union's southern border.[89]

On one level, the administrative, political, and economic changes of early Soviet rule were revolutionary. On another level, however, these institutions were predominantly constructed on the basis of natural territorial divisions and preexisting boundaries between local peoples.[90] *In theory*, these political and economic institutional changes Central Asia had been radically transformed.[91] Numerical indicators of development, however, only partially support this view.[92] Demographic rates continued to be high, and despite some urbanization, a majority of the population of each republic was still rural (Kyrgyzstan, 63.2 percent; Tajikistan, 66 percent; Uzbekistan, 75 percent).[93] The urban population was still predominantly European. Kyrgyzstan's higher urbanization in large part reflects its larger Russian population (21.4 percent). After 1959, Russian immigration slowed and indigenous birth rates increased.[94] In many areas the indigenous population

---

[88] In the Central Asian languages, which were often used by the republican-level Communist Party apparatchiks, and which have been used since 1991, these institutional divisions were called *mustakil viloyat* (autonomous province), *viloyat* (province), *shakhar* (city), *qishloq* and *aul* (village). In addition to the Soviet rural councils, there were committees within each village known as the *aul* or *qishloq komiteti*.

[89] Nove and Newth, *Soviet Middle East*, pp. 110–111 and Appendix.

[90] Luong, *Institutional Change*, Chapter 2, notes in detail the strength of tribal and clan units during the pre-Soviet period and describes the Soviet regime's attempt to keep them together during collectivization. However, she asserts that despite this, the Soviet institutions and policies eradicated clan power and identity. Recent archival work by historians, however, supports the view argued here, that Soviet politics were not successful in this attempt. See Edgar, *Tribal Nation*, pp. 167–196; Hirsch, "Empire of Nations, ch.3 "; and Abramzon, *Kirgizy i ikh etnogeneticheskie*.

[91] M. Vakhabov, *Formirovanie Uzbekskoi sotsialisticheskoi natsii* (Tashkent: Gosizdat, 1961).

[92] See UNDP annual country human development reports.

[93] *World Development Report 2004* (New York: UNDP, 2004).

[94] Edward Allworth, "The New Central Asians," in Edward Allworth, ed., *Central Asia: 130 Years of Russian Dominance* (Durham, NC: Duke University Press, 1994), pp. 527–72;

had experienced relatively little Russification or Sovietization. For example, religious belief remained widespread, even under Soviet repression.[95]

In contrast to common Western assumptions about the totalitarian nature of Soviet rule and the success of Soviet modernization, a post-Soviet perspective on the history of Soviet Central Asia reveals that this region retained a significant level of unofficial or informal self-governance that enabled it to resist substantive transformation by Moscow.[96] In spite of Moscow's intense efforts to create socialism from scratch, the very social and economic institutions created by the communist regime instead fostered social, economic, and consequently political subversion. Citing Soviet analysts, Massell writes that "after nearly ten years of Soviet rule Central Asian traditional elites (religious, tribal, and communal) still commanded 'respect,' 'influence,' and 'authority' among the natives; the Soviet regime did not."[97]

Several key Soviet institutions unwittingly allowed clans to adapt to the Soviet system. Furthermore, the nature of Moscow's relations with its Muslim borderlands – whether viewed as the indirect rule of colonialism or as imperfect totalitarianism – helps to explain the persistence of clans throughout the Soviet era. By the 1940s and later, especially after Stalin's death, Soviet decentralization in general would give more power to the periphery.[98] The level of repression in Central Asia subsequently declined. Patterns established in the 1920s and 1930s through the institutions of collectivization, nationalities policy, and cadre policy would continue from the 1960s through the 1980s with less surveillance from the center. We turn now to an examination of these institutions and the dynamic between them and society's clan-based organization. We must also examine how these formal institutions promoted, intentionally or inadvertently, a colonial-like indirect rule of Central Asia, and their impact on clan networks.

Institutions of Economic Modernization: Sedentarization and Collectivization

Economic modernization went at a stop-and-go pace in the 1920s. Recognizing that war communism had attempted to create a new socialist economy

---

Nancy Lubin, *Labor and Nationality in Soviet Central Asia: An Uneasy Compromise* (Princeton, NJ: Princeton University Press, 1985) pp. 28–38.

[95] See Keller, *To Moscow, Not Mecca*; and Rakowska-Harmstone, *Russia and Nationalism*.

[96] Older scholarship generally makes little distinction between the nature of Soviet rule in Russia and in other regions of the Soviet Union. More recent scholars of Soviet history often view the Soviet Union as an empire, with a central regime that sometimes had difficulty in demanding compliance, much less loyalty, from its peripheral republics.

[97] Massell, *Surrogate Proletariat*.

[98] T. H. Rigby, "The Deconcentration of Power in the U.S.S.R. – 1953–1964," in J. D. B. Miller and T. H. Rigby, *The Disintegrating Monolith* (New York: August M. Kelley Publishers, 1968), pp. 17–46.

too quickly, Lenin halted his attempt at immediate collectivization of land and property and introduced the New Economic Policy (NEP), a program meant to introduce a socialist economy more gradually. The result, unsurprisingly, was very slow economic change during the 1920s in Central Asia, a region where private ownership of land by the *bai* (wealthy individuals and leaders within the clan structure) and a thriving bazaar economy had existed for centuries.[99] In areas where much of the population was still nomadic, as in the mountainous regions of Tajikistan, Kyrgyzstan, and southern Uzbekistan and the steppe and desert areas of Kazakhstan, implementing Soviet policies was especially difficult.[100] In Turkmenistan, for example, the Party adopted a "tribal policy" in order to integrate tribes into the collectivization and modernization process.[101] By 1929, however, Stalin's Five-Year Plan insisted on rapid sedentarization and the mass and rapid collectivization of Central Asia; from 1929 through 1933, collectivization ensued with a vengeance.[102] The forced settlement of the steppe resulted in a phenomenal number of deaths, estimated at half the population of the Kazakh SSR, as well as a large exodus of nomads to China and Afghanistan.

In spite of these cataclysmic events, in many areas traditional social structures – clan-based villages and economic units – were able to survive the onslaught of collectivization and the repression that followed in the 1930s.[103] Two critical aspects of collectivization made this possible. First, most local villages and settlements remained largely in place. The *kolkhoz* (collective farm) and *sovkhoz* (state farm) established the central Soviet economic, social, and political (i.e., governing) institution of the rural regions (approximately 75 percent of Central Asia).[104] In long-settled regions, such as the Ferghana Valley, the *kolkhoz* was often little more than a name given to one or several local villages – the *auls* (villages in Turkic, non-Sart areas) or the *qishloq* or *mahalla* (villages and neighborhoods in long-settled, agricultural areas). Some villages or groups of villages had settled centuries earlier and others much more recently, during the late tsarist period. In the valley of Osh *oblast'* of the Kyrgyz Republic, for instance, one village leader claimed

[99] Massell, *Surrogate Proletariat*, p. 75.

[100] Keller, *To Moscow, Not Mecca*. On the local clan and tribal divisions, see Abramzon, *Kirgizy i ikh etnogeneticheskie*; and Aleksandr Sobianin, "*Aktualnye voprosy natsional'noi bezopasnosti Kirgizii*," *Profi*, no. 11 (1999), pp. 15–16.

[101] Edgar, *Tribal Nation*, p.167.

[102] On collectivization in Kazakhstan, see Martha Brill Olcott, *The Kazakhs* (Stanford, CA: Hoover Institution Press, 1988).

[103] Poliakov, *Everyday Islam*; Gleb Pavlovich Snesarev, *Sem'ia i semeinye obriady u narodov Srednei Azii i Kazakhstana* (Moscow: Nauka, 1978); and V. I. Bushkov, *Naselenie Severnogo Tadzhikistana: formirovanie i rasselenie* (Moscow: Institute etnologii i antropologii RAN, 1995).

[104] Some estimates are higher. According to one scholar from the Academy of Sciences in Uzbekistan, many areas considered "urban" by the official statistics are in fact based on rural economies.

that his *mahalla* was composed of the kin descendents of the Adygine, a Kyrgyz tribe that had settled in the region 100 years before the Russian revolution.[105] In the foothills just across the border of Uzbekistan, a village elder of a Kipchak clan recalled that his clan had been nomads in the region until the 1920s, and then had settled in their current *qishloq*.[106] In either case, rural villages were composed of descendents of Turkic and Persian tribal peoples.[107] Some identified themselves by their traditional clan name, and others by their *"lik"* (local place name), that is, by their *aul, qishloq*, or *mahalla*. In the steppe and semimountainous regions, the *kolkhoz* was generally created from nomadic groups. Small subgroups of tribes, or more traditional "clans," were settled in villages that became the base for a *kolkhoz*. Although variation in the size and composition of villages and *kolkhozes* certainly existed across the Central Asian republics, villages and *kolkhozes* were primarily kin-based units with a clan and more extended tribal history. Inhabitants identified themselves by that descent-based lineage, rather than by class, nationality, or citizenship.[108]

These settlements officially recognized Soviet authority, but initially only minimally reorganized their agricultural production and social structure. They did so without significantly altering their village structure, living patterns, or kin-based network. In fact, archival records indicate that throughout Central Asia, the party attempted to create tribal and clan *kolkhozes* and *sovkhozes*.[109] Clans and tribal lineages were often integrated into the *kolkhoz* as individual brigades.[110] Ironically, for reasons connected with its nationalities policy (to be discussed), the Soviet state had thus fostered this preservation of clan and kin units within the *kolkhoz* and *sovkhoz* structures.

At the most local level, within the collective farms – where a "Soviet" transformation of the worker was expected to take place – life remained

---

[105] Author's interview and oral history with an *oqsoqol* who was a member of the *mahalla* committee of the village, Kara su *raion*, Osh *oblast'*, Kyrgyzstan, May 1998.

[106] Author's interview and oral history with an *oqsoqol* who was a member of the *qishlaq* committee of the village, Andijan, Uzbekistan, May 1997.

[107] On Tajik clans, villages, and social structure, see L. V. Oshanin, *Antropologicheskii sostav naseleniia Srednei Azii i etnogenez eë narodov* (Erevan: izd-vo Erevanskogo universitet, 1957–59); V. I. Bushkov, *Naselenie severnogo Tadzhikistana: formirovanie i rasselenie* (Moscow: Institut etnologii i antropologii RAN, 1995); and N. N. Ershov, *Kul'tura i byt Tadzhiksogo kolkhoznogo krest'ianstva* (Moskva: izd-vo AN SSSR, 1954).

[108] See Roy, *New Central Asia*; and Collins, "The Political Role of Clans." Dragazade, in *Kinship in Georgia*, notes a very similar situation in the Caucasus region at this time. Fitzpatrick observes that even in the Russian republic, prior to collectivization "Russian" peasants identified themselves by locale rather than by "nation." See Sheila Fitzpatrick, *Stalin's Peasants* (Oxford: Oxford University Press, 1994).

[109] Soviet resolutions creating and organizing clan and tribal farms (*kolkhozes* and *sovkhozes*) were common in the 1920s and early 1930s. See Hirsch, "Empire of Nations."

[110] Roy, *New Central Asia*, p. 87.

much the same. The Soviets had created the *kombedy* (committees of the poor) in order to exert local control, as well as to perform social functions such as distributing social welfare and mediating disputes. Yet these "Soviet" institutions were typically merely the renamed *qishloq, aul, or mahalla komiteti* (village or neighborhood committee), that is, the committees of local village elders that had informally governed the community during the pre-Soviet era. These informal institutions of local governance had been ubiquitous in both rural and urban settlements even during the tsarist period. They continued to survive as such throughout the Soviet period, and in that way maintained their moral and rational legitimacy within the village communities.

The party loyalty of this level of society is questionable at best. Low levels of literacy among members of the rural party cells meant that few actually understood the ideology and program of the Communist Party.[111] Furthermore, as Edgar writes, party members to staff the "new" state and party institutions "were frequently drawn from the wrong social classes."[112] Rather than the poor and landless peasants – the proletariat from whom the Soviet regime hoped to gain support – wealthy and influential members of dominant lineages, some of whom were literate, joined the Party as a means to power. These "nominal communists," argues Edgar, "continued to dominate their villages in their traditional roles as ogsogols, or elders, [while] the party cell often existed only on paper. 'Despite the great personal influence of its individual members,' one investigator wrote, 'the cell as such has no connection with the population and does not take part in the public life of the village.'"[113] Throughout Central Asia, representatives of powerful clan lineages who had neither fled nor been killed in the civil war now typically joined the Party to obtain its material and political benefits.[114]

Despite these challenges, by 1934 the Soviet regime had already declared the success of collectivization, and the regime's assault on the rural regions of Central Asia began to subside. During the 1940s, with the onset of World War II, Stalin's attention was diverted from Central Asia and monitoring the progress of collectivization. Although little archival work has been done on this period, surviving informants claim that few changes occurred in the structure of the rural political and economic system. Only in the late 1950s and 1960s, after the death of Stalin, did Khrushchev place renewed focus on energizing Soviet agriculture, and implement new changes.[115] New and

---

[111] Edgar, *Tribal Nation*, pp. 107, 210.

[112] Ibid., p. 107.

[113] Ibid., pp. 188–189.

[114] Edgar's findings were reflected in the view expressed in author's conversations with former communist elites and rural Party members in each republic (1994–2000). See Edgar, *Tribal Nation*.

[115] Valerie Bunce, "The Political Economy of the Brezhnev Era: The Rise and Fall of Corporatism," *British Journal of Political Science*, vol. 13 (April 1983), pp. 129–158.

larger *kolkhoz*es were formed from the amalgamation of several smaller ones. Hence, a new *kolkhoz* was essentially the merger of several villages.[116] For example, in the Andijan *oblast'* of the Uzbek Republic, the Lenin *kolkhoz* (after 1991 renamed the Atakhanov *kolkhoz*, after a renowned elder and *kolkhoz* director) was created in 1951 from five smaller collectives. Each of these collectives, formed between 1929 and 1931 from neighboring qishloqs, consisted of approximately sixty households; the villagers were descendents of a Turkic tribe that had settled in that area 150 years before the Russian Revolution.[117]

To some extent, Soviet policies transformed traditional life and kinship groups. By the 1930s, tribes – the large, somewhat fluid groups including multiple clans claiming common ancestry – had generally been broken down through forced sedentarization.[118] For example, the Kipchak tribe, which had included Kyrgyz, Uzbeks, and Tajiks during the pre-Soviet era, and which inhabited parts of the Ferghana Valley, was divided by Stalin's delimitation of borders into smaller groupings within each of the three republics of the Ferghana Valley. Throughout the rural areas (which included at least 70 percent of the population until the 1960s), the *kolkhoz* and *sovkhoz* were a recomposition of the pre-Soviet tribal and subtribal clan organization to suit the new institutional conditions in which Central Asians were forced to exist. Olivier Roy has argued that the *kolkhoz* became the "new tribe."[119] Certain key changes were evident. The boundaries of the pre-Soviet tribe had changed; the tribe become significantly smaller. Now both traditional blood ties (rooted in the *avlod* and *urugh*) and fictive kinship ties existed within the *kolkhoz*, or across several *kolkhoz*es.[120] The *kolkhoz* also enhanced the pre-Soviet practice of extending fictive kinship to those within the local area, creating a communal identity referred to as "localism" (*mestnichestvo*). Finally, those clan elites who were in positions of favor with the Party in the 1920s and 1930s (as opposed to those who resisted) benefited and were given power within the new territorialized economic and political structures.[121]

Yet in spite of significant agricultural modernization and the changing form and size of the *kolkhoz* during the later Soviet period, the local

---

[116] See Boris Rumer, *Soviet Central Asia: "A Tragic Experiment"* (Boston: Unwin Hyman, 1989); and Snesarov, *Sem'ia i semeinye*.

[117] Author's interview and oral history with an *oqsoqol* and pensioner who was a member of the *mahalla* committee of the village and a former director of the *kolkhoz*, Andijan, Uzbekistan, July 2000.

[118] Refer to Chapter 2 of this volume. Also see Edgar on tribal sedentarization in Edgar, *Tribal Nation*, Chapter 2.

[119] Roy, *New Central Asia*, pp. 86–90.

[120] Author interview with Sergei Abashin, ethnographer, Russian Academy of Sciences, Moscow, July 2000.

[121] Roy, *New Central Asia*, p. 91–92.

population, its social structures, and its living patterns were neither annihilated nor significantly uprooted. In fact, in several areas of forced migration within the Uzbek and Tajik republics in the 1950s and 1960s, villages and the kin networks that inhabited them were moved in entirety, thereby preserving the identity group and in many cases reinforcing the clan ties and sense of solidarity.[122] Sedentarization and collectivization had not accomplished the social transformation of identities and loyalties that the Communist Party had sought.

Institutions of Identity Modernization: *Korenizatsiia* and Creating a Native Cadre

Korenizatsiia, the nativization and indigenization of local elites, was a third Soviet institution that interacted with clan identities in an unanticipated way. As early as 1917, "nationalities policy," as this sociopolitical institution was commonly known, began to evolve as a key element of the Bolshevik program. Initially, *korenizatsiia* was clearly linked to the internationalist socialist goal of freeing subdued nations from colonial rule. Under Stalin, the Peoples' Commissariat of Nationalities (*Narkomnats*) issued declarations "to all Muslim toilers of Russia and the East" in the hope of gaining their support for the socialist revolution.[123] Yet the policy also genuinely embodied a Leninist and Stalinist vision of making all "nations" equal members in the common Soviet socialist experiment.[124] As Terry Martin has convincingly argued, the Soviet Union introduced "affirmative action" programs for its national minority populations.[125] Creating nations was a step toward the party's goal of "the rapproachment (*sblizhenie*) and eventual merging (*sliianie*) of nations" into one Soviet nation.[126]

Ronald Suny's work has shown, however, that the Soviets did not merely promote nations; Soviet nationality policy created nations where none had

---

[122] Ibid., p. 95.

[123] E. H. Carr, cited in Suny, *The Revenge of the Past*, p. 84.

[124] In Soviet scientific terminology, a "nation" is the equivalent of an ethnic group. Most Soviet ethnographers from the early twentieth century (until today) have subscribed to a "primordialist" or biological understanding of ethnic groups as having fixed, natural boundaries defined by culture, language, religion, and way of life. See Yuri Slezkine, "N. Ia. Marr and the National Origins of Soviet Ethnogenetics," *Slavic Review*, vol. 4, no. 4 (Winter 1996), p. 862, for an extensive discussion of Marr's views. Slezkine notes that Marr was the key Soviet ethnographer of Central Asia and that his work shaped Soviet study and policy of the region. See also N. Ia. Marr, *Plemennoi sostav naseleniia Kavkaza: trudy Komissii po izucheniiu plemennogo sostava nasleneiia Rossii* Vol. 3 (Petrograd: Rossiiskaia Akademiia Nauk, 1920). For another discussion, see M. A. Bikzhanova, *Sem'ia v kolkhozakh Uzbekistana* (Tashkent: AN UzSSR, 1959).

[125] Terry Martin, *The Affirmative Action Empire: Nations and Nationalism in the Soviet Union, 1923–1939* (Ithaca, NY: Cornell University Press, 2001).

[126] Suny, *The Revenge of the Past*.

previously existed.[127] It also gave existing ethnic groups territorial units and administrative boundaries (at the republic or subrepublic level). In making a Georgian SSR for the Georgians or an Armenian SSR for the Armenians, the Soviet regime gave de jure (but not de facto) legitimacy to preexisting ideas of nationhood or nationalism, the belief or principle that an ethnic group is a nation and thus deserves a congruent political-territorial unit.[128] In other cases, such as in Kyrgyzstan, the Soviets created ethnic groups that had not previously existed as distinct entities. As noted earlier, during the 1920s and early 1930s the Soviet regime created five national republics: Kyrgyzstan for the Kyrgyz, Uzbekistan for the Uzbeks, Tajikistan for the Tajiks, Turkmenistan for the Turkmen, and Kazakhstan for the Kazakhs. Prior to 1917, these five Central Asian ethnic groups, much less these "nations," had not existed. In creating nations, the Soviets denied the existence of subnational groups, such as tribes and clans. Under Soviet rule, each titular republic was endowed not only with its own political institutions, but also with its own theater, language, schools, and an array of other cultural institutions designed to promote the titular nation. The long-term effect of nationality policy was the "making of nations," a legacy of the Soviet regime that would have profound consequences; with the onset of perestroika, many of these "national republics" would demand greater sovereignty and eventually even independence on the basis of their right to national self-determination.[129] For reasons I will discuss in the following chapter, the Central Asian states did not demand independence on that basis.

In practice, *korenizatsiia* resulted in several unanticipated consequences. First, nativization involved a struggle to find Central Asian cadres to fill Party and state posts. Communist Party records from the Central Asian Bureau reveal that Moscow had little hands-on control.[130] Because of the lack of party cadres, a "crash-training of natives to man important posts" took place.[131] Communiqués regarding the appointment and removal of cadres went back and forth between the Bureau in Moscow and the republic-level Party officials. They reveal the Bureau's reliance on a largely indigenous

[127] Ibid., p. 88.
[128] Gellner, *Nations and Nationalism*.
[129] Suny, *The Revenge*, Chapter 1.
[130] Based on observations of memos and communications between Moscow and Central Asia in Fond 17, Central Asian Bureau of the Communist Party Archives, RTsKhIDNI, Moscow. Frequent memos between Party leaders in Moscow and in the Central Asia republics revealed that there were few trained communists or Russians in the Central Asian governments and party structures in the 1920s and 1930s. Moscow's leaders also lacked the ability to judge the backgrounds and the commitment of the native cadre they had quickly to create. They therefore relied enormously on the recommendations of local elites. Michael Rywkin comes to a similar conclusion about the later, post-Stalin period in *Moscow's Muslim Challenge*, pp. 116–118, 151, despite significant use of Russians as "second secretaries" at most levels.
[131] Critchlow, *Nationalism*, p. 12.

cadre at the republic level. In part, this was due to a simple lack of resources. The Party typically considered Russians to be greater Party loyalists than the indigenous population, but the Russian, much less "Bolshevik," presence was minimal.[132] After 1917, several waves of Russians migrated to Central Asia on Soviet orders, but this typically technical cadre was highly concentrated in industrial centers and "closed" defense cities.[133] Just as it was during the tsarist period, when Russians had acted primarily as a colonial presence in Turkestan, the Soviet presence was dominated by Russians at first, was based in urban areas, and ruled indirectly by relying on a local staff.

Second, *korenizatsiia* had meant the Russification of the titular *nomenklatura*, but correspondingly less Russian control in the party and state apparatis.[134] By the 1980s, the Russian language had become so widespread in Kyrgyzstan that few elites knew their native language. Although this was less typical in Uzbekistan and Tajikistan, Russian was a first language for many elites. According to Soviet standards of modernization, the Russification, de-Islamicization, and secularization of the Central Asian population indicated some success. By the 1980s, this titular elite had become increasingly dependent on Moscow for its access to political, economic, and cultural resources. However, by the 1960s, Soviet *korenizatsiia* of local Party structures had become real, because of the gradual out-migration of Russians (those not born in Central Asia). The Party elite was increasingly dominated by the titular nationality. One study notes the increase in the percentage of Uzbek and other Muslims in the Uzbek Party's Central Committee between 1965 and 1985 (from 69 percent to 80 percent).[135]

Third, for all of the above reasons, nationality policy increasingly gave the native cadre dominance in the elite and local-level (*oblast'*, *raion*, and *kolkhoz*) politics of the Central Asian republics. Although constant turnover from the 1920s through the 1950s within central republic Party organizations did enhance Moscow's control, at the local level the directors of the rural soviets and collective farms were almost exclusively Central Asians. In fact, they were almost exclusively "locals," that is, appointees of their own district. In contrast to the general view that "elections" of *kolkhoz* directors, like most Soviet elections, were entirely controlled by Party officials,

---

[132] Adeeb Khalid, "Tashkent 1917: Muslim Politics in Revolutionary Turkestan," *Slavic Review*, vol. 55, no. 2 (1996), p. 272.

[133] These included several closed cities that produced uranium for nuclear use and that housed other defense-related industries.

[134] The policy was adopted at the CPSU's Tenth Party Congress in 1921. On the creation of a new Tajik *nomenklatura* and educated elite, see Saodat Olimova and Muzaffar Olimov, "*Intelligentsiia drevniaia i novaia: obrazovannyi klass Tadzhikistana v peripetiiakh XXv.*," *Tsentral'naia Aziia i Kavkaz*, <http://www.cac.org/datarus/st_15_olimova.shtml>.

[135] See James Critchlow, *Nationalism in Uzbekistan: A Soviet Republic's Road to Sovereignty* (Boulder, CO: Westview Press, 1991), p. 26–28; and Rywkin, *Moscow's Muslim Challenge*.

informants claimed that people had some measure of choice. If the committee of the *sel'sovet* (on the order of the *raion* Party cell) nominated a candidate (and there was only one candidate) whom the local population opposed, the *kolkhoz* could vote down his candidacy. Occasionally, this did occur; it was most common when a candidate was not local.[136] A more common way of contesting the Party's candidate, however, was through subtle, subversive resistance – by creating problems on the collective until the Party committee put forth a new candidate whom the *kolkhoz* would accept.[137] Hence control of the rural population was almost entirely carried out by the local Central Asian cadre. Russian (and sometimes Central Asian) Party apparatchiks based in the capital cities served as links to Moscow but were heavily dependent on the rural cadre, among whom Party membership was low and superficial. One *oqsoqol* estimated that on his *kolkhoz,*

no more than 5 percent were Party members. None of the kolkhozniks (ordinary rural workers) were Party members, but even Party members on our kolkhoz were all local. None of them ever did anything bad. They just had official authority. People were interested in being Party members because it gave them and their relatives access to better jobs, like the kolkhoz secretary, accountants, brigade leaders, machinists, and engineers.[138]

It was primarily through this cadre that the Party received information about the development of vast rural areas. And it was through this cadre that Soviet decrees were carried out.

In the 1930s, *korenizatsiia* in Central Asia became very intertwined with sedentarization and collectivization. Francine Hirsch's analysis of the collaboration between Soviet ethnographers and the Soviet regime during this period sheds light on the complexity and unintended consequences of nation making and collectivization in this region.[139] Since nations were critical units in Lenin's theory of socialist development, nations had to be defined throughout the new Soviet empire. At least some elements of the Soviet regime were keenly aware of the difficulty of creating nations in Central Asia, Siberia, and much of the Caucasus. Hirsch finds that Academy of Science ethnographers dispatched on a series of nation-defining expeditions in 1925 reported to the Soviet government that creating nation-based republics would be extremely difficult in the Muslim sphere, since nations did not exist. Rather, *subnational* and *subethnic* (or even mixed ethnic) groups were the critical political, economic, and social categories inhabiting the area from the Caspian Sea to the border with China. The relevant groups were tribes and clans. According

---

[136] Author interview with an *oqsoqol*, Syrdarya *oblast'*, May 1997.
[137] On peasant resistance in the Russian collectives, see Fitzpatrick, *Stalin's Peasants*, pp. 65–67.
[138] Author's interview/oral history with an *oqsoqol* who was the son of a *kolkhoz* director in Uzbekistan, Andijan *oblast'*, July 2000.
[139] See Hirsch, "Empire of Nations," especially Chapters 5 and 6.

to Nikolai Marr, a prominent Soviet ethnographer, this vast array of tribes and clans together "composed a *narodnost'* (a people)."[140] However, they could not be defined and separated according to the ethnographic criteria for demarcating ethnic groups or nations. Language was not a clear marker. While "in some instances religion and cultural-historical differences bound people of some tribes together, in other instances they divided peoples of the same ethnic group."[141]

The Soviet regime, however, considered clans and tribes to be pre-modern identities and therefore a threat to the Bolsheviks' modernizing project that had to be eradicated.[142] It was the adept work of the ethnographers that convinced the regime that these pre-modern identities were a legitimate and necessary stage of social evolution. Clan and tribal identities, they argued, would develop into nations, and Soviet policies must foster and accommodate that development. To deal with this "problem," in the mid-1920s the Soviet government created a Commission on Tribal Studies.[143] Under Marr and his team of ethnographers, the commission was given the task of defining and territorially demarcating the complex array of ethnic, tribal, and clan groups inhabiting these regions. These ethnographers further became involved in the creation of governing structures at the local levels. They argued for creating local soviets on the basis of traditional councils. These *aul* soviets (*aul'nye sovety*), also called clan soviets (*rodovye sovety*), fell under the larger Sovietized traditional structures – the "clan *kolkhozes*" and the indigenous executive committees (*tuzriki*) of the native soviets (*tuzemnye sovety*).[144] The policy of promoting clans was in some ways a natural extension of *korenizatsiia*.[145] Clans, like nations, should wither away through Soviet modernization. Yet ironically, the work of the commission in fact contradicted a nationalities policy that had sought to identify in all regions a primeval ethnicity, and to preserve and empower those ethnonational units (and not other units) in Soviet territorial and administrative structures.

From 1931 to 1934, the work of the ethnographers expanded as they were assigned the task of studying the relationship between the development of nations and collectivization. They worked under the Kolkhoz Center, an organ of the Ministry of Agriculture. In short, the ethnographers were told to "rationalize collectivization," which had seen disastrous results in the non-Russian and formerly nomadic regions, where, according to

---

[140] Ibid., p. 173.

[141] Ibid.

[142] Ibid.

[143] Slezkine, "USSR as a Communal Apartment," pp. 414–452.

[144] Ibid, pp. 430–431.

[145] Adrienne Edgar, in *Tribal Nation*, notes that in the Turkmen SSR (and this seems more broadly true of Central Asia), clan and tribal policies were in fact a natural extension of *korenizatsiia*, pp. 167–168.

ministry officials, "it proceeds in especially difficult circumstances" because of "specific economic, everyday life, cultural, and socio-political conditions."[146] The director of the Kolkhoz Center, Ali Bogdanov, opposed Stalin's "dizzy with success" approach to collectivization and argued that "collectivization in national regions had fared best when 'the comrades in charge' understood and acknowledged local custom and concerns.'"[147] Intense discussions about "the clan *kolkhozes*" took place between ministry officials and ethnographers. The former were concerned about the survival of clan structures and the potential for clan ties to undermine Soviet goals. Clan and tribal leaders (known as *bi, bai,* or *manap*), they claimed, were "*kulaks*" (wealthy peasants) and consequently class enemies. By contrast, many ethnographers argued that "'the clan system,' might be 'used for *kolkhoz* construction' if it could be preserved in its pure form without class divisions."[148] Wealthy clan leaders could presumably be eliminated through class conflict and "de-*kulak*ization." However, Francine Hirsch finds that despite clear distinctions between the *bai* (wealthy) and the *bedniaks* (poor) within descent groups (whether small clans or larger tribes),[149] the Soviet regime had very limited success in "creating class," much less class conflict.[150] Members of clan *kolkhozes* "'asserted that it is better to be subordinate to our own *bai* than to another clan's *bai*.'"[151] In contrast to the situation in rural Russia, poor members of a clan were bound by norms of loyalty and dependency to the *bai*; they rarely aided Soviet attempts to identify and eliminate *kulaks*.

According to Hirsch, in order to resolve these disputes, in 1931 the Ministry of Agriculture called for studies on social and economic relations and productivity within the clan collectives. The Kolkhoz Center subsequently carried out detailed surveys to document the transition from clan to nation, and to evaluate how clans inhibit socialist construction. The center's report, published in October 1932, reveals several important processes under way. First, the study found that many *kolkhozes* had in fact been created on the basis of clan structures, although in some cases "national" *kolkhozes* incorporated several clans. Second, collectivized agriculture had not eliminated clan loyalties and identities. "The report noted that 'all *kolkhoz* members know their clan origins . . . even young children, when stating their

[146] Hirsch, "Empire of Nations," pp. 213–214. Based on materials from RGAE f. 7446, op. 13, d. 7, 11, 6, 32.
[147] Hirsch, "Empire of Nations," p. 214. Also see Moshe Lewin, *Russian Peasants and Soviet Power: A Study of Collectivization* (New York: Allen and Unwin, 1968).
[148] Hirsch, "Empire of Nations," p. 249.
[149] See Edgar, *Tribal Nation*, Chapter 3.
[150] Fitzpatrick, *Stalin's Peasants*, p. 41, notes that "now kulaks . . . found themselves in the position of lepers."
[151] See details of the "Records of the Scientific Research Kolkhoz Institute in 1931," in Hirsch, "Empire of Nations," p. 247.

name, add the name of their clan.'"[152] Third, the report observed that
clan organization of labor prevailed despite Party attempts to "rationalize"
work; *kolkhoz* brigades were generally organized along clan lines. *Kolkhoz*
leadership was frequently changed, and young, educated men – trained
"communists" – were increasingly appointed as directors. The study found,
however, that these chairmen continued to defer to their elders, "a bunch
of old men and idlers."[153] Moreover, clan rivalries persisted and were intensified by competition on the *kolkhoz*. Since multiclan and international
(e.g., Russian-Kazakh) *kolkhozes* were seen as causing "dangerous conflict"
between stronger and weaker clans or ethnic groups, single-clan *kolkhozes*
were preferred.[154]

The further development of the clan *kolkhozes* and of the transition from
clan to nation is not well documented. In the 1930s, the Soviet regime declared the success of the collectivization campaign, and presumably of the
tribal/clan modernization campaigns in Central Asia as well. The 1930s and
1940s saw a shift of focus to a concerted attack on the Islamic problem.[155]
Massell views this attack as yet another strategy for undermining traditional
social ties and kinship loyalties. In the 1950s, the regime began to declare the
success of nation building, just as it had declared the success of collectivization in the late 1930s. Over the next few decades, the Soviet regime simply
denied the existence of subnational clans and tribes. Whereas the 1926 census identified 194 subnational groups (including tribes and clans), the 1989
census included only 128 such categories.[156] Furthermore, ethnographers
were no longer permitted to study these phenomena.[157] Despite the break
in scholarship, we do know that even after the devastating famines of the
late 1920s and 1930s, the destructiveness of sedentarization and early collectivization, and the terror of 1937–38, clan identities remained important,
albeit altered and reconfigured by the Soviet assault. And the ironic interaction of Soviet nationality policy and collectivization, sometimes inadvertently

[152] See the IPIN Kolkhoz report, cited in Hirsch, "Empire of Nations," p. 249.
[153] L. P. Potapov, *Poezdki v kolkhozy Chemal'skogo aimaka Oirotskoi avtonomnoi oblasti,
Trudy instituta po izucheniiu narodov SSSR* (Leningrad: Nauka, 1932), cited in Hirsch,
p. 249.
[154] Hirsch, "Empire of Nations," pp. 249–253.
[155] Keller, *To Moscow, Not Mecca*; and Northrop, *Veiled Empire*, pp. 13–14.
[156] Smaller identities were aggregated into larger ones. Most "subnational" groups were from
the Caucasus and Central Asia. See Tishkov, *The Mind Aflame*, pp. 15–19, for an extensive
list of clans and tribes compiled by Soviet ethnographers.
[157] Author interviews with Kyrgyz sociologists Bakyt Seitbayev, August 19, 1995, and Raya
Osmonova, Kyrgyz National University, September 5, 1995. One Soviet scholar's work was
banned from bookshelves for dealing with the "clan question." See S. M. Abramzon, K.
I., Antipina, G. P. Vasil'eva, E. I. Makhova, and D. Sulaimanov, eds., *Byt kolkhoznikov
kirgizskikh selenii Darkhan i Chichkan: kolkhoz imeni K.E. Voroshilova ("Ala-too")
Pokrovskogo raiona Issyk-Kul'skoi oblasti Kirgizskoi SSR* (Moscow: Akademiia nauk SSSR,
1958); and also Abramzon, *Kirgizy i ikh etnogeneticheskie*.

and sometimes openly, fostered the preservation and adaptation of clans to the Soviet system.

The Party's economic plan, together with its desire for social control, re-inforced divisions between Central Asia and the European regions. Several Soviet institutions in some sense froze traditional patterns and networks, especially among the nonelite, mass population. Severe Soviet restrictions on internal movement and the elaborate difficulties of obtaining an official permit to relocate or exit the rural economy enforced the territorialization of these pre-Soviet identity groups. Clans were thus forced to maintain their internal ties from the pre-Soviet period into the post-Soviet period.[158] These restrictions were even tightened during the latter years of perestroika, so as to prevent rural migration and social instability. Yet the policy also rein-forced localism and kinship networks and the political "tribalism" of the *kolkhoz*. This in turn reinforced pre-Soviet traditionalism, including conser-vative living patterns and hierarchical family and community relationships, kinship bonds, exogamy and arranged marriages (generally to facilitate clan ties), high birth rates, and community-bonding cultural rituals (such as eat-ing *osh*).[159] The restrictions on movement further precluded a high level of interethnic mixing (especially with the Slavic, non-Muslim populations, who lived primarily in cities), posed challenges for Russification, and dis-couraged the mobility and individualism that often accompanies modern-ization and increased literacy. Even after service in the Soviet army, most rural Central Asians returned to their home villages. Only a select elite, primarily Communist Party members, could circumvent the restrictions on movement.

IV. MOSCOW'S INDIRECT RULE – INSTITUTIONALIZING A POWER BASE FOR CLANS

As we have seen, at the lowest echelon within each republic, in the rural areas and collective farms, Central Asians had almost exclusive control over the implementation of policies and economic resources. Only a very small percentage of the rural population was European, and so, de facto, the ru-ral cadre was ethnically Central Asian.[160] Moreover, few Central Asians, especially in the rural regions, were Party members or candidates. One local clan elder said of his village, "everyone here is related; we are family. We cooperated in deceiving the party officials whenever they came. It was quite easy, since they did not come often."[161] In fact, the *kolkhoz* provided a

---

[158] See Chapter 2 for a more extended discussion of local-level social structures.

[159] Poliakov, *Everyday Islam*, pp. 39, 53, 76–80.

[160] Life in the rural sector remained very "traditional." See T. Kh. Tashbaeva and M. D. Savurov, *Novoe i traditsionnoe v byte sel'skoi sem'i uzbekov* (Tashkent: FAN, 1989).

[161] Author interview with a local clan elder, Andijan province, Uzbekistan, August 2000.

significant source of resources and therefore of power in the regions.[162] Whether by using their positions to steal funds from the collective to support kinsmen, or by penetrating the hugely profitable cotton sector, clan elites redirected massive amounts of Soviet assets to their networks. By having clan relations in positions of power, many Central Asians were able to survive economic hardship, although their asset stripping was checked by fear of the Party. An elder whose clan entered the Party system after the 1930s said, "we lived very well under the Soviet system, even though few believed in it."[163]

Even at the level of the *raion*, the Party had difficulty filling positions with committed Bolsheviks. Given that few Central Asians had supported the party during the revolution – and many (especially in the Ferghana Valley) had actively opposed it in the Basmachi revolts – Moscow's inclination, at least in the 1920s and 1930s, seemed to be to trust Russians rather than locals in positions of power. A truism about Party politics in the republics was that the first secretary was always a titular national, while the second secretary was a Russian who was a Moscow appointee and held the real power. This ethnic division was generally the case, though the balance of power between the two was not clearly in favor of the Russian secretary, especially after the 1950s. In fact, well into the 1980s, despite the implementation of affirmative action for locals, Moscow continued to position Russians or Slavs in "deputy" positions so that they could monitor the behavior of the titular head.[164] Edgar observes that this policy created a rift between the Central Asian and European communists. The rift was exacerbated by the fact that the European communists sent to the Asian republics knew little about the local culture and rarely learned the language. While their job was to increase central control by reporting to the Central Asian Bureau or even directly to Moscow, they moved with frequency between the republics and Moscow.[165] This created a problem of low continuity in monitoring the republics. Meanwhile, local officials and those in lower-level positions, usually staffed by members of the titular ethnic group, would spend most of their careers within the borders of their own republic. Although their opportunities for advancement within the union were low, they could develop a base of power within their own republic and region, more so than Russians.

Whether because of the center's inability to fill positions with a Russian cadre, or because Moscow supported a nativization policy, communist officials serving in the Central Asian republics felt understaffed and frequently

---

[162] Roy, *New Central Asia*, pp. 84–90.

[163] Author interview with the son of a former Communist Party apparatchik and powerful clan leader, Tashkent, Uzbekistan, May 1997.

[164] Rakowska-Harmstone, *Russia and Nationalism*; and Rywkin, *Moscow's Muslim Challenge*, pp. 123–125.

[165] Edgar, *Tribal Nation*, p. 203.

urged the Central Asian Bureau in Moscow that the Party train and incorporate locals at a greater rate. This was true even in the creation of key institutions of state control, such as the Ministry of Justice and the courts. A memo written in August 1926 by Secretary of the Executive Bureau Sheger, for the Orgbiuro of the KP/bUz (the Organizational Bureau of the Communist Party), highlights this problem. Sheger suggests:

to the People's Committee of Justice (of the OrkSud) to organize an instructional apparatus for training qualified workers by locality. . . . [and suggests] . . . that only in the most remote situations they undertake to shift the places of juridical workers, especially if these workers are local, aboriginal inhabitants and [that NarKomYu] aspire to begin to fill all those places in the periphery with workers from the local aboriginal population.[166]

Sheger adds that the Party must adhere to strict nomination and appointment procedures – even though these inevitably relied largely on the recommendation of locals. The small number of Central Asian Party members, even as late as the 1960s and 1970s, together with the declining number of Europeans in the republics during the Brezhnev years, made filling such posts difficult. Furthermore, the Party's dual system of rule and "second-class" treatment of its Central Asian communist comrades very likely made the Party loyalty of Central Asians questionable; many still viewed Moscow and the party as outsiders and colonizers, even though they no longer openly resisted.[167]

The highest echelons within each Central Asian republic reflected several other elements of colonial rule. Party cadre policy, part consciously and part unconsciously, incorporated and reified preexisting identity divisions, as did the British in ruling India. Although Soviet control was certainly harsher and more heavy-handed from the mid-1930s to the 1950s, when turnover of elites was high, later patterns of recruitment and personnel suggest an attempt to appease the indigenous population. "Central" party and state positions were generally internally divided among particular clan groups. Clans had become territorialized during the 1920s (earlier in some regions) as the Soviets sought to create administrative boundaries that reflected the territorial identification and living patterns of major clan and tribal identity groups.[168] Hence, at the

---

[166] Supplement to protocol no. 26 of the meeting of the Orgbiuro KP/bUz, August 5, 1926, Fond 17, op. 28, delo 3.

[167] Edgar, *Tribal Nation*, pp. 221–222.

[168] See Hirsch, "Empire of Nations"; Edgar, *Tribal Nation*; Rywkin, *Moscow's Muslim Challenge*; and Luong, *Institutional Change*. Edgar notes that among the Turkmen this was especially difficult, since they did not identify with the land. In most other regions, however, clans had varying levels of identification with territory during the nineteenth century. Even nomadic Kyrgyz tribes had a rough identification with a particular territory in the north or south of contemporary Kyrgyzstan. On the contemporary period, see Alisher Khamidov, "Hizb ut-Tahrir" (M.A. thesis, University of Notre Dame, 2002), Chapter 2. On the Soviet and pre-Soviet eras, see Abramzon, *Kirgizy i ikh etnogeneticheskie*.

elite level of politics – both the *oblast'* centers and the republic's central institutions – central elites were an amalgamation of regional elites, and the latter of local elites.[169] Since these "elites" were extensively networked into their respective clans, the republic institutions became a power center within which "favored" clans could interact with and manipulate the Soviet state. This process often forced multiple clans into one territory, but the harsh Soviet presence prevented overt clan competition by repression of such "antistate" behavior.

The policy of favoring and promoting particular clans, within each *oblast'* and within each republic's center, allowed certain clans significant access to state political and therefore economic resources. Why the regime favored some over others is not entirely clear. In some cases, it may have been accidental. In other cases, it was intended to create a balance. In still others, it was meant to promote those who appeared to be more Russian or Soviet. In yet other cases, especially under Brezhnev, Soviet favoritism may simply have been linked to corruption. Although *korenizatsiia* had meant that elites had been heavily indoctrinated with socialist training and education, and although the *nomenklatura* and intelligentsia had been significantly Russified,[170] the Soviet regime had to some extent recognized its inability to eradicate clans within the *kolkhoz*es and representative structures of the republics. The system itself thus reinforced the traditional clan-based organization of society and politics.

SUMMARY

This chapter began by exploring the dynamic relationship between informal institutions of the pre-Soviet era and the Soviet institutions of the 1920s onward, seeking to explain how and why clans persisted under a modernizing and repressive state such as the Soviet Union. Nationality policy and economic modernization had made the Soviet regime distinctly different from many colonial regimes in Africa and Asia, where a distinct hierarchy separated the indigenous population from the colonizers, who dominated all key state institutions. The Soviet system sought to modernize and, at least in theory, to make all its citizens equally socialist. So why did the Soviet state and policies have such colonial-like effects?

From the 1920s onward, clans were a source of resistance to the Soviet state. They used state institutions to adapt and persist, albeit in a more

---

[169] The elite-mass division often used to categorize political actors was less relevant, since networks and loyalties crossed the class and rural-urban distinctions that normally separate elites and masses.

[170] The percentage of Russians in the party structure of Central Asian republics (with the possible exception of Kazakhstan) declined substantially from the 1940s to the 1980s. Rywkin, *Moscow's Muslim Challenge.*

underground manner. Although the Soviet state affected the balance of power among clans, and between clans and the state, it did not succeed in destroying clans or rendering them meaningless. In the process of fixing administrative units and Party cells, traditional relations were no doubt strained. The disruption of the local socioeconomic system and, in particular, the elimination of the *kulaks*, led to the redistribution of power among clans, the destruction of tribes and some traditional clans, and the empowerment of new ones.[171] Yet, given the weak reach of the Soviet government into Central Asia in the 1920s and the inherent challenges of fitting together a modern institutional structure and a peasant social organization, traditional local power structures and social cleavages were very often reinforced.[172] The weakness of local Party institutions, especially in the peripheral republics and their rural areas, furthermore, gave local cadre ample possibilities to manipulate the Party to serve their demands.[173] The upshot was the creation of institutional structures that were always Soviet in form – both communist and nationalist – but largely Central Asian in content. As Kenneth Jowitt has argued of the entire Soviet space, this was Lenin's "ingenious error"; Lenin focused on institutional form but failed to transform the underlying social structure, leading to the Party's "traditionalization,"[174] as much as society's modernization.[175]

The mutual transformation of clans and Soviet economic, social, and political structures sets the historical context for the transitions that would begin under perestroika. How clans survived the Soviet period is a question not likely to be fully answered, given the dearth of ethnographic scholarship on clans during the Soviet period, limited access to archives, and the increasingly underground nature and activities of these groups after the 1930s. Nonetheless, I have argued that the processes of sedentarization and collectivization, as well as the actual implementation of nationality policy and cadre policy, paradoxically fostered clan survival despite the Soviet goal of destroying these pre-modern identities. As we shall see in the next chapter, Brezhnev-style socialism – synonymous with both stagnation and stability – turned a blind eye to clan-based corruption. Thus, the Soviet system inadvertently

---

[171] Author's conversations with a local *bai*, a *sovkhoz* director and deputy, Talas *oblast'*, Talas, Kyrgyzstan, June 1998. In some cases, especially in the Kazakh SSR, entire clans may have been decimated in the process of collectivization and the famine that resulted.

[172] Sobyanin, "*Aktualnye voprosy.*"

[173] On the traditionalization of the *kolkhoz* in Tajikistan, see Bushkov, *Naselenie Severnogo Tadzhikistana*. His conclusions, based on extensive ethnographic field research over many years in the Tajik SSR, coincide closely with my own in Uzbekistan and Kyrgyzstan. For their detailed discussion of Tajikistan, see V. I. Bushkov and D.V. Mikul'skii, *Anatomiia grazhdanskoi voini v Tajikistane: etno-sotsialnye protsessy i politicheskaia borba, 1992–1996* (Moskva: Institut etnologii i antropologii RAN, 1997), pp. 39–41 and 50–51.

[174] Jowitt, *New World*, p. 61.

[175] Soviet ethnographers discuss this phenomenon at length in reference to Tajikistan.

made clan ties important mechanisms of advancement at the local, regional, and central levels of the republics, and also gave them institutions within which to flourish.[176]

The persistence of clans well into the Soviet era suggests that Soviet socialism in Central Asia was markedly different from Soviet socialism, in theory or in practice, in other regions of the USSR. It was less totalitarian, or more imperfectly totalitarian, than in Russia and the western republics. Other scholars have noted this of the post-Stalinist era, but a look at Central Asia from the 1920s onward suggests that Soviet rule, despite its brutality, was limited in many respects even before Stalin's death. Indirect rule characterized many key spheres of the Party and state apparatus, supporting the metaphor of "colonialism." Despite dramatic Soviet changes, at the informal level, Central Asian society managed in many creative ways to resist Soviet attempts to transform its social system, values, and identity.

[176] Khazanov, "Underdevelopment," p. 149, also concludes that the Soviet system unexpectedly reinforced clan and tribe.

4

The Informal Politics of Central Asia

From Brezhnev through Gorbachev

> "Which leaders were the best for your country?"
> "Brezhnev and Rashidov."
> > Conversation with a former *kolkhoz* chairman, Andijan, 2000

In the mid-1990s, I was surprised to learn from Central Asian colleagues that Leonid Brezhnev, the stolid-faced Soviet leader known for sending political prisoners to psychiatric wards even long after the death of Stalin, was actually quite popular in these republics. This was not because he had converted most Kyrgyz or Tajiks to Leninism and scientific atheism, but because he more or less left them alone. And leaving them alone allowed many in these republics to prosper.

So what happened to clans under the later decades of Soviet rule, when mature socialism allegedly finished the task of modernizing Central Asia and therefore should have eradicated clan identities and networks? Not only Brezhnev, but also many Western scholars and policy makers and Central Asians themselves, argued that the Soviet Union had successfully modernized the USSR. First, this chapter, building on Chapter 3, argues instead that despite, or perhaps *because of*, the contradictions of Soviet modernization, clans adapted and survived. Brezhnev's policies reinforced and further entrenched the clan networks that had persisted during the very early decades of Soviet rule. Thus, Soviet policies "modernized" clans, by driving them underground and linking them with corruption, mafioso activities, and the second economy, but did not seriously attempt to eradicate them. Soviet policies furthermore gave some clans greater access to state and party resources. Consequently, these social networks persisted in a symbiotic relationship with the state until the arrival of Gorbachev.

Second, I show that the dynamic between Soviet central reforms and the republics – from 1983–91, the end of the Brezhnev era to the entrée of Gorbachev and the escalation of perestroika – set the stage for the drama of 1991 and later in the Central Asian union republics. The unraveling of the Party-state Soviet system in Moscow under the direction of General Secretary Mikhail Sergeevich Gorbachev rippled down to the level of the republican governing structures very quickly, and with powerful consequences. How Gorbachev's reforms played out in Central Asia is extremely ironic. As Gorbachev liberalized, he also cracked down on clan politics and its related corruption in Central Asia, but his purges spurred resistance and the rise of clan pacts in opposition to the Soviet center. Understanding the informal politics of clans enables us to clarify the obtuse nature of the Central Asian clan pacts.

Third, the interaction of formal and informal politics – between the Party-state and clans – during the Soviet period, and especially in the 1980s, allows us to grapple with a central puzzle of this period and the later transitional trajectories: why did clans negotiate pacts in two Central Asian cases, Uzbekistan and Kyrgyzstan, but not in a third, Tajikistan? This chapter illustrates the conditions under which clan pacts occur, and argues that arriving at such a pact is essential to maintaining transitional regime durability. As we shall see, however, there is nothing inherently democratic about pacts between clans; they are therefore unlikely to lay the foundations for a democratic transition. As subsequent chapters will demonstrate, pacts do not lead to democratization. Indeed, in Central Asia they were negotiated prior to any idea of regime transition. Pacts are a mechanism for uniting clan factions against external threats, and for ensuring stability and balance of governance. Critical pacts among key clan factions occurred during this period and set the stage for the post-Soviet trajectories.

Finally, in anticipation of the next two chapters, I show that the pacts of the late Soviet period are not linked to independence or transition. Rather, the immediate causes of regime change did not emerge within the Central Asian republics. That change would come from Moscow. While perestroika did not directly cause the specific transitional paths embarked upon by Central Asian leaders from 1990 to 1995, Soviet liberalization provided the immediate political context and catalyst for the first stages of regime change in Central Asia.

The ironic perseverance and growth of clans despite Soviet repression and modernization is one critical element of the distinctive Soviet legacy for this region. A second element is the Soviet regime's effect on the relative balance or imbalance of clan power within each republic. Both are key to understanding the Soviet legacy for post-Soviet Central Asian politics. Gorbachev's attempts to break *"zemliachestvo"* in Central Asia came decades too late. Eastern Europe and the Central Asian republics had already gone in opposite directions in terms of social development and its effect on the political and economic system.[1] Gorbachev did, however, reshape the balance of power within most Central Asian republics, eliminating most of the exclusivist,

---

[1] Valerie Bunce, *Subversive Institutions* (New York: Cambridge University Press, 1999).

Mobutu-like clan and patronage networks that had emerged under Brezhnev. And perestroika critically affected the Central Asian republics' relationship with Moscow. Together, these issues compose a prelude to the transition that would begin with the Soviet collapse and Central Asian decolonization in late 1991.

I. THE RISE OF "SOVIET CLAN POLITICS" – CADRE POLITICS AND THE BREZHNEV ERA

The *"kadrovyi vopros"*[2] (cadre question) or *kadrovaia politika* (cadre politics) was one of the most sensitive issues one could raise to the Central Asian Bureau or later to the Party's *OrgOtdel* (Organizational Department), the bodies that dealt with appointing Party cadres.[3] And yet, *zemliachestvo* or *mestnichestvo* – the patronage of one's family, kin, and close friends from one's birthplace (i.e., one's clan), or "localism" – was the dominant principle of appointments in Central Asia.[4] Clan politics diminished and even subverted the primacy of Party loyalty and Leninist doctrine in cadre appointments and promotions.

While clans had infiltrated the rural economic system during the 1920s and 1930s, they were kept in check at the upper echelons of power during the Stalinist era. As elsewhere in the Soviet Union, Party secretaries were quickly replaced to prevent any opposition from nesting within the system (see Table 4.1). Such turmoil prevented clan elites from fostering their networks over long periods of time. They nonetheless attempted to promote kin, and were often removed or reshuffled to other posts on charges of promoting "family groups."[5] The frequent turnover among cadres in the 1930s and 1940s began to have a very negative impact on the economy and stability of the Central Asian republics. Agricultural output was dropping. Social resentment was growing. The new post-Stalinist leadership grew concerned.

Once the turmoil of Stalinism had quieted, the nature of the Soviet system changed. What began as an anomaly became the norm. Khrushchev's agricultural innovations sought to increase productivity by easing the burden on the countryside.[6] In the process, his grip on cadre politics also loosened,

---

[2] The "cadre question" referred to the system of appointments of officials by the Party.
[3] The Central Asia Bureau was the body established in 1922. It was dissolved in the 1930s and appointments were made through the general CPSU *OrgOtdel*.
[4] See Olivier Roy, *The New Central Asia* (New York: New York University Press, 2000); Michael Rywkin, *Moscow's Muslim Challenge*, revised ed. (London: M. E. Sharpe, 1990); and Boris Rumer, *Soviet Central Asia: A Tragic Experiment* (Boston: Unwin Hyman, 1989).
[5] On these practices during the 1940s and 1950s, see Teresa Rakowska-Harmstone, *Russia and Nationalism in Central Asia: The Case of Tadzhikistan* (Baltimore: Johns Hopkins University Press, 1970), pp. 174–175.
[6] Valerie Bunce, *Do New Leaders Make a Difference?* (Princeton, NJ: Princeton University Press, 1980), pp. 188–189.

especially under I. R. Razzakov's secretaryship in Kyrgyzia, during which the Ichkilik clan came to power. In the Uzbek SSR, a Jizzak/Samarkand network began to arise under Sharof Rashidov, the Uzbek first secretary appointed by Khrushchev as part of the new generation of Soviet leaders. Khodjenti clans, meanwhile, maintained control in the Tajik Republic.

Khrushchev's success in reviving the rural sector had cost him debts that would constrain his power, and by 1964 Khrushchev was being widely criticized for "disrupting politics as usual."[7] Yet many of his policies in Central Asia continued under Brezhnev. The Central Committee exerted even less direct control over the borderlands, under the stagnation and endemic corruption of the Brezhnev period, which resulted from what Valerie Bunce has called Brezhnev's "corporatist model" of interest mediation and modernization. An essential aspect of socialist corporatism was Brezhnev's tacit contract with society and the Party, involving a "stability of cadre."[8] "Co-optation [of Party members, economic interests, workers, and peasants] was to replace conflict, and a premium was placed on stability and growth."[9] In practice, this policy meant that the central state's power vis-à-vis the republics (and Eastern Europe) declined. The *OrgOtdel* increasingly ceded control of appointments to republic and local-level figures in the Party. James Critchlow stresses the cultural practices that resurfaced as a result: "the patrimonial character of the regime" and the authority of "white beards."[10] The stagnation engendered by nearly a quarter-century of Brezhnev's stability fostered a soft state and conditions ripe for corruption, rent seeking, and the persistence of *blat*, the Russian mode of informal exchange of goods and services through one's personal relations.[11] Within these macro-institutional conditions, *zemliachestvo* and clan-based patronage intensified. A re-traditionalization of Central Asia was the unintended consequence of Brezhnev's social contract.

During the 1930s and 1940s, there had been significant and often rapid turnover of Party elites in Central Asia, at least at the higher levels of power. By the 1950s, turnover had slowed. Certain clans rose to power and began to consolidate a network. In Uzbekistan, a clan from the more Russified area of Ferghana (as opposed to the old trading elites of Kokand and Margilan), represented by Usman Usupov and later by Amin Niyazov, gained preeminence from 1937 through 1955. It was purged in the mid-1950s, and a

---

[7] Ibid., p. 199.

[8] Djumagyl Saadanbekov, *Sumerki avtoritarizma: zakat ili rassvet?* (Kiev: Nika-Tsentr, 2000), pp. 222–223.

[9] Valerie Bunce, "The Political Economy of the Brezhnev Era: The Rise and Fall of Corporatism," *British Journal of Political Science*, vol. 13 (April 1983), p. 135.

[10] James Critchlow, "Prelude to Independence," in William Fierman, ed., *Soviet Central Asia: The Failed Transformation* (Boulder, CO: Westview Press, 1991), p. 19.

[11] On *blat*, see Anna Ledeneva, *Russia's Economy of Favors* (Cambridge: Cambridge University Press, 1998), pp. 35–37.

Tashkent-based network ascended for several years. As mentioned, in Kyrgyzia, the Ichkilik clan based in Osh, a southern *oblast'* of the republic,
gained significant control over republican politics when its leader, Razzakov, consolidated a power base from 1950 to 1961. Although there was
some balancing during this period, especially with the Adygine clan, Razzakov and his network were removed. In the Tajik Republic, not long after
it was carved out of the Uzbek SSR, the Khodjenti factions quickly gained
dominance. Khodjentis, especially the elite urban families of Khodjent, had
historically been connected to the more Russified Ferghana Valley. Under the
Kokand khanate, and then under tsarist Turkestan, Khodjent had been part
of the privileged, settled population. Moscow's desire to keep control in the
hands of the small, settled, educated, and more Russified (and Uzbekified)
population was clear from early on.

The Brezhnev era ushered in a new period of cadre stability. In some cases,
Brezhnev appointed new republic first secretaries; in others, he kept those
recently appointed by Khrushchev. Brezhnev, reacting against the instability
of Stalin and even Khrushchev, allowed one clan faction to remain virtually
hegemonic in each republic of Central Asia for nearly a quarter of a century
(see Table 4.1).[12] In Uzbekistan, the Rashidov clan, which came from the
Jizzak villages near the Samarkand region, predominated. Rashidov initially
balanced promotion of his own clan with the fostering of economic development in other regions of the country, most of which were more agriculturally
productive than the steppe/semidesert from which he came. Nonetheless, the
vast majority of positions in the Party and state apparatus went to Rashidov's
network. In 1973, he even granted his clan its own fiefdom by creating the
Jizzak *oblast'* (it was dissolved after his death).

In Kyrgyzia, the Usubaliev/Kochkor clan and its vast patronage network
from the Naryn region controlled the republic. Turdakun Usubaliev had
become a favorite of Brezhnev because of his willingness to enforce Russification, at least at the formal level, in terms of language use in educational and
government institutions. At the same time, Usubaliev shifted power and resources from the Slavic cadre to the native Kyrgyz, and bolstered a powerful
and largely exclusivist patronage network around his clan.[13] In the words of
one parliamentary deputy, Usubaliev was "the father and mother of tribalism
and localism."[14] Even during Brezhnev's era, he was frequently criticized by
Kyrgyz for promoting too many of his own Kochkor clan. Although he threw
some bones to the Sarybagysh clan (based partly in Talas and partly in Chu

---

[12] Brezhnev's cadre stability also affected other republics, especially in the Caucasus. See Ronald
Grigor Suny, *The Revenge of the Past.*

[13] On Usubaliev's informal politics, see Eugene Huskey, "The Rise of Contested Politics in
Central Asia: Elections in Kyrgyzstan, 1989–1990," *Europe-Asia Studies,* vol. 47, no. 5
(July 1995), pp. 814–818.

[14] Author interview with a Kyrgyz deputy, Bishkek, June 1998.

oblast's),[15] Usubaliev mostly brought his direct kin and extended clan into Bishkek to occupy profitable government and economic posts. However, given that real economic development had to come from the less remote areas of the country, Usubaliev also directed investment in the development of two other northern regions, especially Chu and Issyk-Kul. Usubaliev's politics was about patronizing his kin and friends and building a servile and loyal cadre.

Even Soviet-era politics revealed a certain clan consciousness on the part of republican elites. It is not clear to what extent Moscow understood interclan norms, but the Party may have been conscious of the necessity to preserve an intra-clan and regional balance of power as well, since top Party posts in each Central Asian republic – the first secretary, the chairman of the republic's Supreme Soviet (the legislature), and the chairman of the central committee (head of state) – were often filled with representatives of different clans.

In the Tajik case, the clan and regional division of power and resources was far more heavily skewed in favor of the northernmost Leninabad region from early on.[16] As part of the Ferghana Valley, but bordered by the Pamiri Mountains on the south, the Leninabad *oblast'* was barely accessible to the rest of the Tajik Republic, and its culture and economy were more closely linked to that of the Uzbek Republic than to those of other Tajiks. Moscow initially favored the Leninabad region because of its greater accessibility and earlier sedentarization. Ironically, although the inhabitants of the region were more traditionally Islamic, the Soviet regime became accustomed to using "communist" Leninabad as a counter to the "fundamentalist" Garmis and Badakhshanis, who were more difficult to control.[17]

In the 1930s, purges and intense Soviet suspicion of the Tajik people led to a high turnover of elite and increased Russian control of the Tajik Party and state apparatus. Still, by the 1940s, a powerful Tajik first secretary, Bobojon Gafur Gafurov, had garnered favor with Moscow and used his position to increasingly take control of the Tajik Party apparatus. Like Rashidov in Uzbekistan, Gafurov was a product of the Soviet system; he had gained status in the Party through his work at the Institute of Oriental Studies in Tajikistan. He became secretary of ideology, and eventually ascended to the post of first secretary. Gafurov then used that status to rise in the local party apparatus and build a patronage network based on his clan.

Although officially a communist stalwart, Gafurov is known to have informally been one of the initial proponents of a "clan ideology" in the cadre

[15] Author interviews with democracy activist Tolekan Ismailova, Notre Dame, Indiana, 2003; with Deputy Cholponbaev, Bishkek, 1998; and with journalists, 1995–98.
[16] Shahrbanouh Tadjkbakhsh, "Causes and Consequences of the Tajik Civil War," *Central Asia Monitor*, vol. 2, no. 1 (1993), pp. 10–14. Also see Barnett Rubin, "The Fragmentation of Tajikistan," *Survival*, vol. 35 (1993–1994), pp. 71–72.
[17] Based on author's meeting with Tajik NGO activists and scholars, Moscow, July 1998; and with S. Panarin, journalist from Tajikistan, Moscow, 1998.

system.[18] In this way, he actively "constructed" a Khodjenti clan identity based in part on kin ties and aristocratic lineages and in part on localism.[19] His goal was both to reassert the Khodjenti network, which had suffered from the purges of the late 1930s, and to exclude from power anyone from Garm or Badakhshan. He even replaced the Russian in charge of cadre policy with his own local appointee. Gafurov's successor, Tursunbai Ul'dzhabaev, similarly maintained control of cadre policy. In his early years, he was accused of forming "family groups," a common Tajik practice. Eventually, he was removed for association with Tajik leaders who were "guilty of 'hoodwinking and direct deception,' 'gross distortion of Leninist principles of leadership,' 'incorrect practices in selection and assignment of personnel,' and 'padding of report figures of cotton procurement.'"[20] Even so, the Soviet regime continued to trust the Leninabadis over the other factions, in part because Gafurov had successfully painted other factions as Islamists. Brezhnev perpetuated the special patronage relationship and increasingly turned a blind eye to the "personnel practices" in which the Tajik leadership engaged.

Among the Leninabadis, several urban Khodjenti clans had dominated since the mid-1940s (see Table 4.1). According to Communist Party officials of the 1980s, almost all the Communist Party first secretaries of the Tajik republic were from the Khodjenti clans of the Leninabad region. Keith Martin points out that although the term "Khodjenti" is typically used to refer to this network, not all areas, ethnic groups, or kin groups within the Leninabad region were part of the Khodjenti clan. In fact, "there are significant differences between various parts of the region itself."[21] According to one journalist, the most powerful (and historically aristocratic) families of the Khodjenti elite came from the city of Khodjent and even from a particular *mahalla*.[22] Several such families frequently intermarried in order to strengthen their clan ties.[23]

The Khodjenti network increasingly consolidated power in the Party and state under its own hands, neglecting to balance clan, regional, and ethnic representation, as the first party secretaries had sought to do until the mid-1940s.[24] First Secretary Jabbor Rasulov was appointed in 1961 and stayed in power until his death in 1982. During that period, as had Usubaliev

[18] Davlat Khudonazar, "The Conflict in Tajikistan: Questions of Regionalism," in Roald Sagdeev and Susan Eisenhower, eds., *Central Asia: Conflict, Resolution, and Change* (Chevy Chase, MD: CPSS Press, 1995), pp. 249–264.

[19] On the constructed elements of clans, refer to Chapter 3 of this volume.

[20] Rakowska-Harmstone, *Russia and Nationalism*, p. 161.

[21] Keith Martin, "Welcome to the Republic of Leninabad?" *Central Asia and the Caucasus*, vol. 4, no. 10 (1997) <www.ca-c.org/dataeng/st_ob_martin.shtml>.

[22] Author interview with a Tajik journalist from the Leninabad region, Moscow, July 1998.

[23] Roy, *New Central Asia*, pp. 18–22.

[24] Khudonazar, "Conflict in Tajikistan," p. 252.

TABLE 4.1. *First secretaries/presidents of the Central Asian republics*

a. The Kyrgyz Republic's Leaders

First Secretary/ President	Years in Office	Nationality	Clan Origin
M. D. Kamensky	1924–25	Russian	–
N. A. Uziukov	1925–27	Russian	–
V. P. Shubrikov	1927–29	Russian	–
M. M. Kulkov	1929–30	Russian	–
A. O. Shakhrai	1930–34	Russian	–
M. L. Belotsky	1934–37	Jewish	–
M. K. Ammosov	1937–38	Russian	–
A. V. Vagov	1938–45	Russian	Osh
N. S. Bogolyubov	1945–50	Kyrgyz	Frunze (Chu)
I. R. Razzakov	1950–61	Kyrgyz	Batken (Ichkilik)
Turdakun Usubaliev	1961–85	Kyrgyz	Naryn (Sarybagysh, Kochkor)
Absamat Masaliev	1985–90	Kyrgyz	Osh (Ichkilik)
Askar Akaev (president)[a]	1990–present	Kyrgyz	Chu (Kemin, Sarybagysh)

[a] Akaev was first elected president, under the new law on the presidency, in indirect elections by the republic Supreme Soviet. At the same time, D. Amanbaev was first secretary of the Kyrgyz Republic Communist Party Central Committee until August 1991.

b. The Uzbek Republic's Leaders

First Secretary/ President	Years in Office	Nationality	Clan Origin
Akmal Ikramov	1929–37	Uzbek	Tashkent
Usman Yusupov	1937–50	Uzbek	Ferghana
Amin Niyazov	1950–55	Uzbek	Ferghana
Nuritdin Mukhidinov	1955–57	Uzbek	Tashkent
Sabir Kamalov	1957–59	Uzbek	Tashkent
Sharof Rashidov	1959–83	Uzbek	Jizzak
Inomzhon Usmonkhodzhaev	1983–88	Uzbek	Ferghana
Rafiq Nishanov	1988–89	Uzbek	Tashkent, no strong clan
Islam Karimov: (first secretary, president)[a]	June 1989–December 1991; December 1991–present	Uzbek (Tajik)	Samarkand

[a] As of 1990, Karimov simultaneously held the posts of first secretary of the Uzbek Republic Communist Party Central Committee and president. The 1990 presidential election was indirect.

TABLE 4.1 *(cont.)*

c. The Tajik Republic's Leaders			
First Secretary (President)	Years in Office	Nationality	Clan Origin
Abdukadir Mukhiddinov	1924–25	Bukharan	Bukhara[a]
Boris Tolypigo	1925–27	Russian	–
Mumin Khodjaev and Ali Shirvani (secretaries in charge)	1927–29	Azerbaijani	–
Mirza Daud Guseinov	1929–34	Azerbaijani	–
Grigoryi Broido	1934	Russian	–
Suren Shadunts	1935–36	Armenian	–
Urumbai Ashurov	1936–37	Tajik	Ferghana (Pamiri)
Dmitryi Protopopov	1937–46	Russian	
Bobojon Ghafur Gafurov	1946–56	Tajik	Leninabad (Khodjent)
Tursunboi Ul'jabaev	1956–61	Tajik	Leninabad (Khodjent)
Jabbor Rasulov	1961–82	Tajik	Leninabad (Khodjent)
Rakhmon Nabiev	1982–86	Tajik	Leninabad (Khodjent)
Kakhar Makhkamov (first secretary; first secretary and president)[b]	1986–90; December 1990–August 1991	Tajik	Leninabad (Khodjent)
Kadriddin Aslonov (acting president)[c]	September–November 1991	Tajik	Garm
Rakhmon Nabiev (president)	November 1991– September 1992	Tajik	Leninabad (Khodjent)
Akbarsho Iskanderov (chairman of the coalition government, acting president)	September 1992– November 1992	Tajik	Gorno Badakhshan (Pamiri)
Imomali Rakhmonov (chairman of the Supreme Soviet; president)	November 1992– November 1994; November 1994– present	Tajik	Kulyab (Dangharin)

[a] Prior to 1929, Tajikistan was an autonomous republic within the Uzbek Union Republic. In 1929, Tajikistan became a Union republic. The region of Leninabad, including the city of Khodjent, was transferred from the Uzbek Republic to the Tajik Republic at this time.

TABLE 4.1 *(notes continued)*

---

[b] Makhkamov was first secretary from 1985 to 1990. Gaibnazzar Pallaev was temporarily appointed president under the new law on presidency. When Makhamov decided to occupy both posts, he was elected president in December 1990, after Pallaev stepped down. Presidential elections were indirect elections in the republic Supreme Soviet. After becoming president, Makhkamov also retained the post of first secretary of the Tajik Republic Communist Party Central Committee.

[c] Aslonov was also chairman of the Tajik Republic Supreme Soviet, 1990–91. The chair of the Supreme Soviet filled in as "acting" president after Makhkamov stepped down, and while presidential election campaigns were under way. Rakhmon Nabiev then assumed the position of chairman of the Supreme Soviet.

Note: The birthplaces and Party histories of individuals were regularly published during the Soviet period, although specific clan names were not. Informants claim that one could guess clan identity from province (*oblast'*), since they usually overlapped. During the post-Soviet period, both clan and provincial origin are considered "secret" information and are no longer published.

Sources: Compiled from *Bol'shaia Sovetskaia Entsiklopediia; Malaia Sovetskaia Entsiklopediia; Kirgiskaia SSR Entsiklopediia; Uzbekskaia SSR Entsiklopediia; Tajikskaia SSR Entsiklopediia*, FBIS reports, Abazov (2004), Abdullaev and Akbarzadeh (2002), Carlisle (1976), Rakowska-Harmstone (1974), Khamidov (2002), <www.centrasia.ru>, and author interviews.

and Rashidov, Rasulov developed an extensive patronage network around his clan and other elite Khodjenti networks. Moscow's patronage of Leninabad led to a path dependency of Leninabadi control; as Moscow endowed the Khodjenti elite with greater resources, the Khodjentis disproportionately developed the infrastructure and economy of their own region, enriching their clan and making it even more valuable to Moscow. The rest of Tajikistan remained significantly underdeveloped by comparison, and increasingly resentful.[25] As the Tajik journalist Khabib Nasrulloev has argued, "there was apparent equality, but it did not however, preclude the dominant clan from working both for itself and against all other parts of the Tajik republic."[26] Moscow thus continued, even during the perestroika years, to patronize and rely on this network of Khodjent clans.[27] Over time, the result was the creation of a Mobutu-like regime that was totally dependent on Moscow for its position.[28]

[25] Author's interview with a Tajik opposition journalist, Moscow, August 2000. Most Tajik scholars as well as Russian (Soviet and post-Soviet) scholars agree on this point. See Grigorii Kosach, "Tajikistan: Political Parties in an Inchoate Space," in Yaacov Ro'i, ed., *Muslim Eurasia: Conflicting Legacies* (London: Frank Cass, 1995); and V. I. Bushkov and D. V. Mikul'skii, *Anatomiia grazhdanskoi voini v Tajikistane* (Moscow: Institut Etnologii i Antropologii, PAH, 1997).

[26] Khabib Nazrullaev, "Strakhi o Tajikistane," *Nezavissimaia gazeta*, March 10, 1993, p. 4.

[27] Author's conversation with an official in the Ministry of Trade and Economics under Nabiev and later a refugee in Kyrgyzstan, Bishkek, 1995. Like most Leninabadis, she shared the view that only they had the expertise to run the Tajik Republic.

[28] I owe this comparison to a conversation with Dennis Galvan.

This pattern of cadre politics reflected the indirect rule of Moscow and the Party over the political and economic system in Central Asia. The pattern had begun in large part because of the Soviets' inability during the 1920s and 1930s to use the small Russian population living there to control the periphery directly. It had intensified because of *korenizatsiia* and the commitment to bringing titular groups into the Party. Brezhnev's patronage politics was a phenomenon that had come to pervade the Soviet system as a whole.[29] His disinterest in direct governance allowed clan networks to develop vast patronage networks that relied on the state and to become deeply entrenched. The growth of patronage and the strengthening of informal networks in Central Asia was not an errant thread. Yet the syncretism between Brezhnev's policy and the Central Asian clan system – which was still officially anathema to Soviet ideology – meant that the system had departed from the Soviet ideal to a far greater extent than elsewhere.

II. GORBACHEV'S ENTRÉE: BREAKING *ZEMLIACHESTVO* AND SHIFTING THE BALANCE OF POWER

Uzbek First Secretary Sharof Rashidov's extensive clan and patronage network illustrates the depth of the clan-cadre phenomenon in Central Asia and the informal acquiescence of the highest level of the Soviet system itself.[30] After Khrushchev's ouster in 1964, Rashidov had become a favored client of Brezhnev, perhaps because Brezhnev himself was tied to an endemic system of corruption in Central Asia.[31] Brezhnev's son-in-law was actively involved in cotton corruption, especially in Uzbekistan.[32] As one Uzbek scholar has observed, Rashidov played the role of a "nineteenth-century khan," delivering resources to the tsar while ruling independently within his territory.[33] Assuaged with Uzbek cotton and gold, Brezhnev ignored internal Uzbek

---

[29] On the rise of patron-client ties within the Soviet system, see T. H. Rigby and Bodhan Harasymiw, eds., *Leadership Selection and Patron-Client Relations in the USSR and Yugoslavia* (Boston: Allen and Unwin, 1980); and Valerie Bunce, "The Political Economy of the Brezhnev Era: The Rise and Fall of Corporatism," *British Journal of Political Science*, vol. 13 (April 1983), pp. 129–158. Walder has noted a similar phenomenon in China, which he views as "neo-traditionalism." See Andrew Walder, *Communist Neo-Traditionalism: Work and Authority in Chinese Industry* (Berkeley: University of California Press, 1986).

[30] Personal conversation with Oleg Grinevsky, former Khrushchev and Brezhnev aide, Stanford, California, May 1999.

[31] The Soviet prosecutors, T. Gdlian and N. Ivanov, avidly pursued Rashidov during this period. For a critical view of the prosecutions, see V. Iliukhin, *Oborotni: Kak bylo nadumano "Uzbekskoe" delo* (Tashkent: Uzbekiston, 1993). Also see James Critchlow, *Nationalism in Uzbekistan: A Soviet Republic's Road to Independence* (Boulder, CO: Westview Press, 1991); and Donald Carlisle, "Power and Politics in Soviet Uzbekistan: From Stalin to Gorbachev," in Fierman, ed., *Soviet Central Asia*, pp. 18–33.

[32] Author's interview with an Uzbek specialist, Tashkent, November 2003.

[33] Ibid.

politics. However, "the linkage in Central Asia between corruption and localism prompted the center to intervene in local politics and law enforcement in the wake of Brezhnev's death."[34] Yuri Andropov, longtime chief
of the KGB, became the new Party secretary and introduced a sea change
in Moscow's relations with Central Asia. When Yegor Ligachev, director
of the Party *OrgOtdel*, brought forth extensive reports of Central Asian
corruption – foremost among them a massive file of complaints about the
personalization of the Uzbek Party under Rashidov – Andropov initiated a
chistka (purge) of the Uzbek SSR.[35] Ligachev's exposure of massive cotton
corruption came to be known as the "*Khlopnii skandal*" (the Cotton Scandal). It ultimately led to Rashidov's demise.[36] The scandal exemplified the
complex overlapping of kinship networks and patronage in pursuit of corrupt practices and illicit gain even under a strong, repressive, and ideological
Soviet state. Ligachev branded Rashidov a "state criminal."[37] Even Brezhnev's son-in-law was eventually implicated, charged with corruption, and
later imprisoned. Many believed that Rashidov committed suicide in order
to avoid prosecution.

Although the scandal widely implicated Uzbekistan and its nepotistic social structure as the source of the worst corruption in the Soviet system,
it is also important to note that the depth of patronage, nepotism, and
corruption was in part a result of Moscow's persistent colonial-like attitudes and policies toward Central Asians. Most Central Asians still feared
and distrusted Moscow and the Party. Their loyalty was, very rationally,
directed toward benefiting themselves and their kin, and toward creating
circles of loyal friends and cadres around them who would not betray
them to the Party. Michael Rywkin describes this sort of corruption as the
"modus operandi" of the system in Central Asia. He views it as a cultural
response that enabled Central Asians to cope with Moscow's repressive and
inequitable policies, and to develop their own assets and region. "As explained by James Critchlow, 'When one takes a close look at the corruption
in the Central Asian republics, from the standpoint of local public interests,
it resembles not so much an abstract evil as a mixture of positive and negative
components.'"[38]

Andropov had died before the *chistka* was completed. Yet Gorbachev,
who was similarly unsympathetic to the reasons behind the abuses, picked

---

[34] Huskey, "Rise of Contested Politics," p. 816.
[35] Personal communication with an aide to Andropov and Ligachev during the 1970s and
1980s. Both Ligachev and his aide noted the immediacy and favoritism with which Rashidov
was treated by Brezhnev. On complaints to the party, see RTsKhIDNI, Fond 17, o. 154,
d. 2846, p. 50.
[36] See the memoirs of Yegor Ligachev, *Inside Gorbachev's Kremlin* (New York: Pantheon Press,
1993).
[37] Y. G. Kul'chik, *Respublika Uzbekistan v seredine 90-kh godov* (Moskva: RAN, 1995), p. 26.
[38] Critchlow, cited in Rywkin, *Moscow's Muslim Challenge*, p. 150.

up the mantle. He sought to root out corruption and patronage, particularly in Central Asia, where he believed the culture of kinship and family relations had undermined Party loyalty and the communist ideology and had therefore made the problem worse than in other regions. In the wake of Rashidov's death, Gorbachev appointed Inomzhon Usmonkhodzhaev to be first secretary of the Uzbek Communist Party. He was instructed to reverse the problems of *korenizatsiia*, which Ligachev saw as fostering abuses. Usmonkhodzhaev, however, was slow to reform the system. In late 1985, at the Tashkent City Party Conference, Boris Yeltsin – the envoy of Gorbachev – forcefully demanded "criticism and self-criticism" within the Uzbek Party, and "a new cadre of party leaders."[39] He called for admitting to "unprincipled behavior, corruption, and patronage of careless workers, friends, and relatives of mercenary motives." Accusing Uzbek Party members of "making bribe-taking a habit," he demanded internal reform of the Party "in entirety."[40] The *raikom* and *gorkom* organizations were especially guilty of "poor selection of cadre"; they were the least subject to oversight and thus responsible for the "rise of militant and avant-garde organizations."[41] Hence, under strict orders from Gorbachev to carry out a *chistka*,[42] Usmonkhodzhaev presided over a massive KGB investigation. Between 1985 and 1987, the purge swept from the top party posts down to the secretaries of almost every *obkom, raikom*, and *kolkhoz*.[43] Approximately 30,000 people were removed or arrested. Individuals from the Jizzak, Samarkand, and Bukhara – those most closely connected to Rashidov's clan – were the most severely struck.[44] And the victims were not merely Party apparatchiks in official posts; they included many family and kin, members of the accused officials' clans who were the beneficiaries of the resources to which they had

[39] RTsKhIDNI, Fond 17, o. 154, d. 2846, pp. 142–143.

[40] Ibid., pp. 137–138.

[41] Ibid., pp. 149–150.

[42] Ligachev discusses the somewhat cryptic circumstances of Usmonkhodzhaev's appointment. Andropov was apparently ailing, and Chernenko, with Ligachev's advice and the support of Gorbachev, who had become knowledgeable about corruption in Central Asia while responsible for agricultural affairs, put forth Usmankhodzhaev's candidacy to the Politburo. As was regular practice, at this point the Politburo merely approved the appointment (personal communication with Oleg Grinevsky, former assistant to Brezhnev, 1999). Romanov and other dissatisfied members of the Politburo accused Ligachev of leaving them out of the decision-making process for high-level Party positions. See Ligachev, *Inside Gorbachev's Kremlin*, p. 241.

[43] For a detailed discussion of those charged with corruption, see Vladimir Ilyukhin, *Oborotin: Kak bylo nadumano "Uzbekskoe" delo* (Tashkent: Uzbekistan, 1993).

[44] The investigation targeted powerful local bosses, clients, distant kin, and relatives of Rashidov, who often occupied positions of power (such as the directors of the Bukhara *Gorpromtorga* and the Bukhara UBD, a branch of the MVD). Personal communication from a relative of Rashidov whose family had been largely displaced by the purge. See also Ilyukhin, *Oborotin*.

access; this was "the system of the Uzbek KGB."[45] In 1986, it was rumored that 27,000 Russian party workers, referred to by Moscow as "mature cadres," would take the place of the Uzbeks.[46] Usmankhodzhaev was scornfully called a "slave of Moscow."[47]

In the summer of 1988, just prior to the Nineteenth Party Conference, Usmonkhodzhaev himself was accused of offering bribes to Moscow elites and of filling the government with Ferghana cadres. Charged by Ligachev with corruption, he too was removed. On October 18, 1988, Gorbachev replaced Usmonkhodzhaev with Rafiq Nishanov,[48] a member of the Tashkent elite and a longtime Moscow-based Party apparatchik. Most of his career had been spent in the Soviet foreign ministry, far removed from the Uzbek Party cadre. Nishanov proceeded with the purge. Some estimates suggest that 90 percent of Uzbek apparatchiks were removed or arrested.[49] He then initiated, in compliance with Gorbachev and in an attempt to gain local legitimacy, limited recognition of an emerging nationalist intelligentsia in the Uzbek SSR. However, Nishanov was still a spokesman for Moscow, not for the Uzbeks. He permitted Gorbachev, in 1988, to install the infamous "*krasnyi desant*" ("red landing"), a cadre of several thousand Moscow appointees – predominantly Russian – who filled most critical posts of the Communist Party of Uzbekistan (CPU). Such repression by Moscow had not taken place in Central Asia since the Stalin years; it effectively delegitimized both the CPU and Nishanov,[50] who was increasingly excluded from the informal functioning of the Uzbek political system.[51]

In the Kyrgyz Republic, a similar though less extensive purge took place. In comparison to the Uzbek Republic, clan-based corruption was seen as less destructive of the economy, probably because cotton production was greater in Uzbekistan. Nonetheless, in 1985 Gorbachev and Ligachev initiated a "*glubokaia proverka*" (extensive investigation) and called Turdakun

---

[45] Personal conversations with several prominent figures from Tashkent whose family members had been arrested during the scandal of the late 1980s.

[46] Rywkin, *Moscow's Muslim Challenge*, p. 151.

[47] Interview with the family member of an accused but later rehabilitated victim of the Uzbek purge.

[48] See Ligachev, *Inside Gorbachev's Kremlin*, pp. 241–242, for the details of Usmonkhodzhaev's arrest and removal from power. Usmonkhodzhaev seemed shocked that after giving up so much for Moscow – i.e., backing Moscow in its sweep of the CPU – he too would be a victim of the Uzbek purge. See also Kul'chik, "*Respublika*," p. 27.

[49] A. M. Khazanov, "Underdevelopment and Ethnic Relations in Central Asia," in Beatrice Manz, ed., *Central Asia in Historical Perspective* (Boulder, CO: Westview Press, 1994), pp. 151–152.

[50] Author's interview with Ambassador Sodyq Safaev, ambassador from Uzbekistan to the United States, Stanford, May 1999; and with political experts in Tashkent, Uzbekistan, 1998.

[51] Dmitry Trofimov, *Tsentral'naia aziia: problemy etno-konfessional'nogo razvitiia* (Moscow: MGIMO, 1994), p. 30.

Usubaliev to be accountable to the Politburo for failing to fulfill the plan (in reality, embezzlement of state assets) and spoiling the Party cadre. Despite his protestations of forty-five years of high-level service to the party, Usubaliev was forced to resign, and a purge followed. Over 80 percent of higher-level workers in the party and state apparatus lost their positions.[52] On November 2, 1985, Usubaliev was replaced by Absamat Masaliev,[53] whom Ligachev had recommended as a staunch Party loyalist.[54] Charged with the task of cleaning up corruption, Masaliev and "the Moscow brigade" soon disrupted the longtime dominance of the northern clans that Usubaliev had patronized – his own Kochkor and Sarybagysh networks, and to a lesser extent the Buguu clan.[55] Over time, it appeared that Masaliev was shifting resources to Osh and the Adygine and Ichkilik clans – his own base of power. Hence, even northern deputies and intellectuals, including Askar Akaev, began openly to accuse Masaliev of "tribalism."[56]

In the Tajik SSR, the transfer of power was different. In fact, it was entirely contained within the same network of certain Khodjenti clans. The Tajik Party leader Rakhmon Nabiev was a northerner, the successor to Rasulov's Khodjenti network. Nabiev ruled from 1982 until 1985, when he was ousted by Gorbachev during the *chistka* of the Central Asian party first secretaries. Although removed on charges of corruption, Nabiev was not arrested. Many Tajiks speculate that Nabiev made a deal with the KGB to create the appearance of a purge in which Nabiev sacrificed power.[57] Indeed, in contrast to the deep purges of the Rashidov and Usubaliev clans, in the Tajik SSR Nabiev's successor was a Khodjenti from the same clan. Moscow had disproportionately promoted Leninabad since 1929, because the KGB apparently did not trust other clans or regions of the republic. Local scholars and journalists claim that Moscow considered other parts of Tajikistan to be too Islamic, or too ethnically close to the Afghans, and therefore hard to control.[58] Makhkamov, the new first secretary, neither prosecuted Nabiev nor removed most other Khodjentis from power. The superficial battle against corruption and the transfer of power had no serious consequences for reforming the republic.

[52] Huskey, "Rise of Contested Politics," p. 816.
[53] Usubaliev's regime was known to have brought most of the first secretary's Naryn kin to Bishkek, to fill party posts, since there were few spoils to be had in Naryn.
[54] Absamat Masaliev, *Stranitsy, zhizni, i bednoe nashe otechestvo* (Bishkek: "AZ-Mak," 1992), pp. 240–242.
[55] Turdakun U. Usubaliev, *Kak menia presledovali Gorbachevtsy: moralnyi i politicheskii terror*, vol. 3 (Bishkek: "Sham," 1997), pp. 56–57. Usubaliev, unsurprisingly, claims the investigation was not objective.
[56] Author interview with Dastan Sarygulov, editor of the *Kyrgyzstan Chronicle*, Bishkek, November 1994.
[57] See *Etnopoliticheskie protsessy* (Moscow: Panorama, 1992), p. 90.
[58] Author interview with a former ORT journalist covering Tajikistan, Tashkent, August 1997. Author meeting with Tajik sociologists, Academy of Sciences, Moscow, July 1998.

Moscow's role in disrupting the clan and patronage system of Rashidov in the Uzbek SSR and of Usubaliev in the Kyrgyz SSR (and similarly of Kunaev in the neighboring Kazakh SSR) was a critical factor in shaping the interaction of formal and informal institutional structures and in setting the stage for the major transition to come.[59] In both the Uzbek and Kyrgyz Republics, Moscow's intervention led to a greater balancing of power and resources among the clan factions. In the Tajik Republic, however, the power and hegemony of one clan network remained, barely shaken by Moscow. Moscow's intervention only reinforced the power imbalance, already long in place, in favor of Leninabad and a network of Khodjenti families. Furthermore, the intensity of perestroika's *chistka* in the Uzbek Republic, as opposed to the milder transfer of power in the Kyrgyz Republic, led to bitter resentment of Moscow's intervention and of Gorbachev in particular.[60] Nonetheless, by 1989 both Uzbekistan and Kyrgyzstan had felt the heavy hand of Moscow's intrusion upon their system of self-rule. Tajikistan had not. This factor would be a precursor to social instability and the second round of elite changes yet to come.

The Central Asian republics thus went into the major political transformations of the late Gorbachev period with a particular formal and informal institutional configuration of politics and balance of power that would dramatically shape the elites governing the transition. The clan-based structure of domestic politics would suggest who the dominant actors of the transition would be, and how these actors would make transitional choices and opportunities. A look at the particular clan elites controlling central Party structures as perestroika began will illuminate this interaction.

III. THE LATER PERESTROIKA YEARS IN CENTRAL ASIA

The Beginnings of Instability: The Ferghana Valley Riots of 1989

From 1988 to 1991, a series of "ethnic" riots and clashes broke out across the southern Soviet republics, from the Caucasus to Central Asia. While the various outbreaks were not necessarily related, nor identical in content and form, all of them did manifest a certain ethnic content and reverberations of ethno-national resentment against the Soviet regime.[61] The extent to which the conflicts did in actuality have "ethnic" causes – as opposed to ethnic consequences – is questionable. The bloody consequences of the violence created significant ethnic tension, and were a clear harbinger of the threat of

---

[59] On critical junctures, see Collier and Collier (1991).

[60] Author's interview with Safaev.

[61] For an in-depth discussion of these conflicts in the Caucasus, and their roots in Soviet nationalities policy, see Suny, *The Revenge of the Past*.

rising instability to Gorbachev and the Moscow leadership, and even more so to the untried republican leadership.

In Central Asia, the first such conflict took place in Uzbekistan, in the Ferghana Valley, in June of 1989, in the Tashlak district of Ferghana City. A conflict between Meskhetian Turks, an ethnic minority, and local Uzbeks broke out in a bazaar over an argument about the price of strawberries.[62] The riot escalated into bloody violence, resulting in the burning of a Turkish *mahalla* and perhaps hundreds of deaths among both Uzbeks and Turks. Rumors that the Meskhetian Turks were killing Uzbek babies quickly spread. Similar pogroms soon took place in several nearby cities – in Kokand, in Namangan, and in Andijan. About the same time, clashes between Uzbek and Kyrgyz villagers in those areas also occurred. The conflict ceased within days, but only after local *oqsoqols* (elders) stepped forth, appealed to traditions of interethnic peace and harmony, and demanded an end to the violence.[63]

Almost a year later, in June of 1990, a remarkably similar event took place between Kyrgyz and Uzbeks. Conflict erupted in Osh and Uzgen, part of the southern Osh *oblast'* of the Kyrgyz Republic.[64] Although many scholars and policy experts have focused on the "ethnic" nature of this clash,[65] there were other factors as well.[66] The conflicts were linked to a transfer of land from ethnic Uzbeks to ethnic Kyrgyz.[67] As in Uzbekistan, the socioeconomic situation was dire and the shortage of land acute. Ethnic tension was already high, since under Masaliev's patronage local Kyrgyz government officials had consistently given lucrative government positions and control over the bazaar to their ethnic Kyrgyz kin.[68] When officials decided to take one further and more drastic step and redistribute collective farm land to the traditionally

---

[62] The Meskhetian Turks were just one of many such unwanted ethnic groups to be deported by Stalin.

[63] Author's conversations with *oqsoqols* and local inhabitants of Kokand, Namangan, and Ferghana, 1997.

[64] Author's interviews with Zh. Rustembekov, *akim* (governor) of the Osh *oblast'*, and with the *akim*'s deputy for nationalities questions, Osh, Kyrgyzstan, July 1995.

[65] For example, see Nancy Lubin and Barnett Rubin, *Calming the Ferghana Valley* (New York: Council on Foreign Relations, 1999).

[66] Tishkov gives an anthropological account that analyzes land issues, ethnic stereotyping, social problems, and rivalries among clans who sought to generate social tension. Tishkov blames the extent of the violence on elite entrepreneurs' manipulation of violent (and sometimes intoxicated) Kyrgyz and Uzbek youth who turned a protest into a pogrom. Valery Tishkov, "Don't Kill Me I Am Kyrgyz," in his *The Mind Aflame* (Oslo: PRIO, 1997).

[67] See Olga Brusina, "*Agrarnoe perenaselenie kak odna iz prichin Oshskogo konflikta,*" *Profi*, no. 11, 1999, pp. 20–23. Brusina notes that the ethnic population of the region had shifted dramatically as Kyrgyz migrants from the mountains settled after the 1960s, increasingly crowding out long-settled Uzbeks; this shift ultimately erupted in the crisis of 1990.

[68] Author's interview with Dmitri Esenbai, Osh *oblast'* journalist for *Slovo Kirgizstana*, Osh, Kyrgyzstan, July 1995. See also Abilalbek Asankanov, "Ethnic Conflict in the Osh Region in the Summer 1990: Reasons and Lessons," <www.iles.umn.edu/faculty/bashiri/Osh/osh.html>.

mountain-dwelling Kyrgyz herdsmen, they ignited a conflict. The authorities turned over a *kolkhoz* inhabited by an Uzbek *avlod* for nearly ten decades and gave it to the landless Kyrgyz herders, who had little employment and had been flocking to the city demanding housing and jobs. The transfer ignited protests from the Uzbek residents as well as their kin across the border in the Uzbek Republic. A vicious conflict characterized by ethnic slurs and hatred soon broke out, with devastating consequences.[69] Most experts estimate that about 300 people were killed in Osh and the Uzbek village of Uzgen.

In the Tajik Republic, some smaller conflicts have been reported between the titular population and other ethnic groups. In the summer of 1988, there were apparently demonstrations by urban Russians against a proposed re-settlement of Armenians, refugees from the devastating earthquake, in the Tajik capital. The resettlement never took place. A minor cross-border con-flict, however, did take place between Kyrgyz and Tajiks at the village of Isfara-Batken in the summer of 1989. The clash was directly linked to a dispute over water use between Tajik villagers and Kyrgyz villagers on dif-ferent sides of the Tajik and Kyrgyz borders.[70] A similar skirmish was to take place on November 2, 1991, in Pandzhikentskii *raion*, between a Turk-ish village and a Tajik-Barlas (Barlas is one Uzbek clan) village. As in the other republics, the clash appeared to be fundamentally economic; it was a dispute over thirty-six hectares of land that the Tajik government sought to take from Turks and give to Tajiks.[71] The incidents attracted less atten-tion and did not significantly delegitimize or undermine the efficacy of the Makhkamov regime.

Explaining and Resolving the Conflicts

When Rafiq Nishanov attempted to dismiss the Ferghana violence as a fight over strawberries, both locals and Moscow elites saw him as incompe-tent in dealing with the horror of the violence.[72] Most serious treatments of this "ethnic violence" understand the events as conflicts over land that took on ethnic dimensions.[73] Certainly, a common thread was the escalat-ing economic crisis. After almost two decades of demographic explosion,

[69] Author's interviews with Bakyt Beshimov, political scientist and rector of Osh State University and a deputy to the national parliament, the Jogorku Kenesh, Osh, Kyrgyzstan, July 26, 1995, and May 26, 1998.

[70] Author's interview with Erik Asanaliev, special officer for Tajik Affairs, Ministry of Foreign Affairs, Kyrgyz Republic, Bishkek, July 1995.

[71] Bushkov and Mikul'skii, *Anatomiia*, p. 52. See also A. Elebaeva and Saltanat Imanova, *Etno-natsionalizm: istoriia i real'nost'* (Bishkek: Ilim, 2001), p. 26.

[72] Kul'chik, *Respublika Uzbekistan*, p. 27.

[73] For a more extensive discussion of the conflict and its ethnic, economic, and clan di-mensions, see Ainura Elebaeva et al., *Oshskii mezhnatsional'nyi konflikt: sotsiologicheskii analiz* (Bishkek: AN, 1991); T. Baicherikov and V. Nishanov, "Problemy mezhetnicheskikh otnoshenii'," in E. Shukurov, *Renessans ili Regress* (Bishkek: Tsentr issledovannii mira

coupled with decades of Soviet abuse of Central Asia's land and water system, the situation was particularly acute in this region. By 1990, the population's traditional reliance on private plots for food had become severely
strained. Unemployment was high. When the local governments could not
provide sufficient housing and land for local inhabitants, unrest over the
redistribution of scarce resources to outsiders was not surprising. Increasing
uncertainty about the direction of nationalist movements against the Soviet
center strained interethic relations.[74] In Central Asia, nationalist movements were relatively weak, but they did heighten the awareness of ethnic
inequalities.

One prominent Kyrgyz journalist argues that the riots were inspired by
the publication in a local Osh newspaper of a report on the severe ethnic
imbalance in political and economic positions of power in Osh *oblast'*.[75]
Ethnic Kyrgyz, who comprised less than 50 percent of the Osh city population, nevertheless controlled the local and *oblast'* government, the police,
and the overwhelming majority of Party posts. Ethnic Uzbeks, by contrast,
who were the majority of the population, controlled the bazaar and many
collective farms, yet had little power.[76] The blatant exposure of such statistics was certainly unwise, and it did contribute to general dissatisfaction
with the economic and ethnic situation. However, the article was circulated
in February of 1989, and the riots took place over a year later. These declining socioeconomic conditions were typical throughout Central Asia and
the Union more generally. Indeed, other areas were suffering more severely
from Soviet abuses; yet such violence did not erupt more widely. Neither
primordialist nor economic explanations of "ethnic violence" explain why
the conflicts erupted when they did, or why the violence has ceased since
1990, despite a worsening economy.[77]

Others argue that the conflicts may have been orchestrated by hard-line
Moscow forces, using local police and the KGB to discredit Gorbachev and
his appointees. Local inhabitants often claim that the instigators of the conflicts were not locals but outsiders who had fabricated stories of murder
and rape in order to spur violence between local groups.[78] Although such

Kyrgyzstana, 1996), pp. 94–95; Tishkov, "Don't Kill Me I Am Kyrgyz"; Kul'chik, *Respublika
Uzbekistan*, p. 9; and Brusina, "*Agrarnoe perenaselenie*," pp. 20–21.

[74] On nationalist movements, see Beissinger, *Nationalist Mobilization*.

[75] Author interview with Dmitri Esenbai, Osh, August 1995.

[76] Zamira Sydykova, *Za kulisami demokratii po-kirghizski* (Bishkek: Res Publika, 1995),
pp. 13–14.

[77] Such theories tend to prevail in the Western, Soviet, and post-Soviet press. Theories of
"Islamic" violence coincide with primordialist ethnic arguments. For an excellent critique,
see Elise Guiliano, "Who Determines the Self in the Politics of Self-Determination? Identity
and Preference Formation in Tatarstan's Nationalist Mobilization," *Comparative Politics*,
vol. 32, no. 3 (April 2000), pp. 295–316.

[78] Author's conversations with locals from the sites of conflict in Kokand, Ferghana, and
Andijan (Uzbekistan) and Uzgen and Osh (Kyrgyzstan), 1997 and 1998.

accounts are difficult to verify, the local police played a passive role at best, suggesting complicity. According to some, they actually fomented the violence.[79] Indeed, Askar Akaev himself publicly stated that the Party Central Committee and the USSR KGB had been fanning ethnic conflicts and tensions.[80]

Valery Tishkov observes that not only the security forces, but also local mafias and various clan elites were displeased with Gorbachev's new Central Asian appointees and had motives to instigate unrest. Investigating the Osh violence, Tishkov writes:

The conflict may have been related to the activities of an economic 'mafia' and the situation in the high-ranking power structures of the republic. As a result of political changes brought about by perestroika, a balance was violated in Kirgizia with respect to the distribution of high-ranking and prestigious positions between the leading regional clans. This was a balance that had been in effect for decades and to some extent reflected former tribal distinctions as well as culturally specific groupings within the Kirgiz. The former first secretary of the Kirgiz Communist Party, Jumgalbek Amanbaev, underscored this in conversation with me: 'In the past we had tried to keep track of how our three major groups divided positions between themselves. The new leaders started to forget about that. It was a signal for them.'[81]

Certain local elites were unhappy with the exclusive control of resources under Masaliev and the *krasnyi desant*, whose loyalty was to Moscow.[82] In Kyrgyzstan, clan opposition to Masaliev seems to have come not only from the northern clan elites, whom he had displaced, but from non-Kyrgyz residents of Osh as well. Hence, Masaliev was doubly weakened by the riots.[83] The situation was similar in the Uzbek Republic. The new Party leadership had little support from either clan elites or the population at large. The Ferghana Valley elites had been increasingly excluded from power. The Rashidov clan had similar grievances against Nishanov, who had undercut the power of the Jizzak *oblast'* and stripped much of their resource base. Nishanov was viewed as undoing Rashidov's well-developed system of regional and clan relations. Given the Party's sensitivity to the "national

---

[79] Brusina, "*Agrarnoe perenaselenie*," p. 22. See also Martha Brill Olcott's insightful discussion, in which she argues that the "ethnic" component has been overblown and that the conflicts were in part manufactured. Martha Brill Olcott, "Ethnic Violence in Central Asia: Perceptions and Misperceptions," in Sagdeev and Eisenhower, eds., *Central Asia: Conflict*, pp. 115–116.

[80] "Minorities' Lawful Interests Will Be 'Reinforced'," Interfax, in FBIS-SOV-91-192, October 2, 1991.

[81] Tishkov, *The Mind Aflame*, p. 137. Tishkov conducted interviews with both Party elites and participants in the violence in Osh and Uzgen shortly after independence.

[82] Also see Khazanov, "Underdevelopment," pp. 156–157.

[83] Based on author's interviews with local elders and local government representatives, Osh and Uzgen, Osh *oblast'*, June 1998. Masaliev's account downplays the conflict: *Absamat Masaliev: Sovettik doorodon uzundulor* (Bishkek: Goskonsern "Uchkun," 1996), pp. 250–251.

question," riots with ethnic overtones were one method of publicly delegit-
imizing any republic's leadership, and when Nishanov and Masaliev handled
the riots so badly, Gorbachev could no longer support them. The new Central
Asian first secretaries were severely weakened.

IV. SHIFTING THE BALANCE OF POWER AND CREATING
CLAN PACTS

Reclaiming Stability

The reaction to the Ferghana and Osh events was rapid, both in Moscow and
among the republics' elite bodies of power. Moscow was finally forced to
realize the enormous volatility of the republics in question, and the severity
of the economic situation. More importantly, Gorbachev and his advisors
in the *Orgbiuro* now understood that if they wanted to maintain stability
in Central Asia, they had to return control to the local cadres.[84] Moreover,
Ligachev had been removed in the internal struggle between hard- and soft-
liners, so the major impetus for attacking clan patronage in Central Asia
was gone. Hence, when republican elites in the Uzbek and Kyrgyz Republics
met in 1989 and 1990, respectively, and decided to propose new candidates
to Gorbachev for the position of first secretary, this time they met little
resistance from Moscow.

The Rise of Karimov: A Preliminary Uzbek Pact

The Uzbek Republic was the first to initiate a change of power, and it did
so immediately in the wake of the June 1989 riots. According to various
members of the Uzbek elite, representatives of the major clan and regional
divisions of the republic met to discuss their united opposition to Nishanov
and to Moscow's interference in Uzbek internal affairs. Certain key regional
elites, from Tashkent and from several other regions, are known to have
strongly influenced the discussions.[85] Most prominent were Ismoil Jurabekov
and Abdulaziz Komilov of the Samarkand network. Others included in informal deals were Shukrullo Mirsaidov, a powerful figure in the Tashkent elite,
and Rustam Akhmedov of Ferghana. Informal negotiations took place behind the scenes, outside of the Party structures and parliament.[86] The group
decided to propose its own local candidate to replace Nishanov as first secretary. They debated several potential candidates, initially including Mirsaidov
and Jurabekov, but both were seen as too entrenched in their own clan and
regional networks to have broader legitimacy. Jurabekov was inextricably

---

[84] Author's interview with Oleg Grinevsky, Stanford, May 1999.
[85] Author's interview with B. Malikov, May 2004.
[86] Author's interviews with Uzbek elites and with diplomatic personnel, Tashkent, Uzbekistan,
   1996–98.

linked to Rashidov, and Mirsaidov to a more narrow "Tashkent clan."[87] Foremost on the agenda were three demands: (1) a strong leader who would serve the Uzbeks and not Moscow; (2) a leader with local legitimacy; and (3) one who would guarantee their interests and uphold informal deals. The leader should therefore not be so embedded in one regional or clan faction that he would neglect to maintain a balance of clan factions at the center of republican politics. Further, the Uzbek elites sought to find a candidate with expertise in economic affairs, since the spiraling downturn in the agricultural sector was seen to be the primary threat to stability and growth in the republic.

The clique settled on Islam Karimov, the first secretary of Kashkadarya *oblast'* and a former minister of finance and economics and head of Gosplan for the Uzbek SSR under Rashidov. Karimov was both a local, networked into the Rashidov clan, and a communist apparatchik, a technocrat whom Moscow would be unlikely to oppose. Although Karimov did not initially support nationalist movements or independence, he did favor greater sovereignty and Uzbek political control. His recent demotion by Nishanov had both won him the respect of Uzbeks and had removed him from the purview of Moscow's purge.[88] Further, like Akaev, Karimov lacked an independent power base giving him autonomy from the clan leaders who supported him and who would expect to be rewarded once he was in power. His candidacy was the work of adroit political maneuvering by certain Uzbek clan elites – especially by Jurabekov, who wanted to restore the Rashidov network's place in power and who saw Karimov as tied by birth to a powerful Samarkand group, but not to the clan of former first secretary Rashidov.[89] Jurabekov thus orchestrated a pact to support Karimov, and even convinced a few "reformers," including the all-union deputy *Mufti* Muhammad Sodyq Muhammad Yusuf, to approach Gorbachev about their decision. In July 1989, Karimov was brought to power with little opposition from Moscow.[90] The Politburo had realized that it could no longer oppose internal Uzbek power networks and expect the situation to remain stable.[91] Jurabekov, meanwhile, became known as the "gray cardinal" behind the throne of Karimov.[92]

---

[87] Based on Trofimov's personal communications with the author, Tashkent, 1997; and author interview with B. Malikov, Washington, D.C., May 2004. Also see Dmitry Trofimov, *Tsentral'naia Aziia: Problemy etno-konfessional'nogo razvitiia* (Moscow: MGIMO, 1994).

[88] Author's interview with a Uzbek journalist, Tashkent, August 1997.

[89] Kul'chik, *Respublika Uzbekistan*, p. 26. Even though no direct kinship link between Karimov and Jurabekov is known, both belong to an elite Tajik Samarkandi clan. Their tie appears to be one of fictive kinship.

[90] Author's conversations with several elites closely connected to Karimov, Tashkent, Uzbekistan, 1997, 1998.

[91] Author's interview with a high-level government official, 1999, 2000.

[92] Khaknazarov, February 2003; personal communication, July 1998.

Shifting Power: The Institutional Context for Change in Central Asia

The year that elapsed between Karimov's appointment and Akaev's rise to power saw significant institutional changes within the Soviet system. When Gorbachev began to use the rhetoric of *demokratizatsiia* and "all power to the soviets" at the Nineteenth Party Congress in June 1988, neither he himself nor most observers, inside or outside the Soviet Union, understood him to be introducing a revolution, or even a gradual regime transition. Gorbachev failed to grasp the implications of his words. On the surface, he appeared to be calling for a return to the ideals and principles of Leninism; in reality, his words were the "spark" that would eventually lead to the unraveling of the first Russian revolution and the beginning of a second Russian revolution.[93] In 1989, Gorbachev began a radical restructuring of the central, parallel political institutions of the Soviet system – the Communist Party and the government/state apparatus. His strategic moves at the center were essentially designed to reform the system by shifting the locus of power from the Party to the state. In doing so, he recreated his personal power base; by 1990, he had become both the general secretary of the Party and the president of the Union, the head of state. A declaration of the 1990 Party Plenum had created the post of president, which Gorbachev increasingly used to expand and legitimize the executive functions and powers of the state under his executive presidency. He then employed his executive powers to decrease the power and relevance of the Party.

In creating a Congress of People's Deputies (CPD) by a decision of the Supreme Soviet session of December 1988, Gorbachev further shifted power to new, non-Party institutions. Although the Congress's first elections, held on March 26, 1989, were not multiparty elections and did preserve a large bloc (100 seats) for the Communist Party and its related social organizations (750 seats), the Congress nonetheless brought together a number of new, non-Party leaders and intellectuals. From Central Asia, these included Askar Akaev, then a prominent Kyrgyz physicist, and the renowned writers Chingiz Aitmatov and Muhammad Salih.[94] All three were to become leading reform figures in Central Asia by 1990. Akaev and Aitmatov became members of Andrei Sakharov's group of deputies in the Congress, and were likewise active supporters of Gorbachev.[95] It was this newly elected

---

93 Scholars debate whether the Soviet transition was a transition or a revolution. Michael McFaul, "Revolutionary," in David Holloway and Norman Naimark, eds., *Reexamining the Soviet Experience* (Boulder, CO: Westview Press, 1995), argues that it was a revolution because of the scale and scope of items on the agenda: social, political, and economic. Most transitions discussed in the democratization literature are narrow political transitions.

94 Chingiz Aitmatov and Muhammad Salih were prestigious members of the Soviet Writers' Union, elected from the bloc of seats reserved for social organizations. Aitmatov was also a member of the Presidential Council of Mikhail S. Gorbachev in Moscow.

95 Author's interview with Askar Aitmatov, presidential advisor, Bishkek, June 1998; also see the account of Akaev's political work in Moscow in A. Erkebaev, *1990 God: Prikhod k vlasti A. Akaeva* (Bishkek: BBK Kirghizstan, 1997), pp. 99–100.

Congress that yielded to Gorbachev's urging and made the fateful decision on March 6, 1990, to amend Article 6 of the 1977 Soviet Constitution, the clause preserving the hegemony of the Communist Party in the Soviet government. The Party monopoly having been eliminated, elections to the Supreme Soviet and to local soviets were convoked in each republic. These elections were multicandidate (although many districts in Central Asia put forth only one candidate), and they initiated a turnover within each of the Central Asian Supreme Soviets from Party apparatchiks to both local notables (such as *kolkhoz* directors) and "reformers."[96] Over 88 percent of the seats of the new Kyrgyz Supreme Soviet were contested in the February 25, 1990 election, and 91.4 percent of the electorate voted. Approximately one-third of the new deputies in 1990 were considered "reformers."[97]

The Rise of Akaev: A Preliminary Kyrgyz Pact

Democratizatsiia had drastically weakened Moscow's control of Central Asia. Yet democratization without regional enforcement had, ironically, allowed Central Asia to take its own course, democratic or not. While Karimov opted to consolidate his authoritarian grasp on power in the Uzbek Republic, Askar Akaev, a noted "reformer," rose to prominence in the remote Kyrgyz Republic. Akaev's entrée is both more understandable and more puzzling when contrasted with that of Karimov. Though of a far higher, and more widely recognized, intellectual and personal caliber, Akaev was nonetheless an outsider. A physicist who had spent nearly twenty years outside of his native republic, at the Leningrad Polytechnic Institute, he had little political experience and indeed had turned down the request put to him by several Kyrgyz deputies to run for president in 1990. In the spring of 1989, Akaev had become a representative of the Academy of Sciences to the newly formed Congress of People's Deputies in Moscow, but he was not a Party member. He thus seemed an unlikely candidate for the most influential position in the Kyrgyz Republic.

In fact, Akaev's moderation seems to have been a prevailing reason for the support of his candidacy. Despite his reputation as a liberal and reformer, Akaev was not in favor of independence. His ideological views were not at stake; his moderation was chiefly desired for the sake of bringing stability to the tense interethnic and interclan situation in the republic.[98] Although appointed for his party credentials, Masaliev had disastrously exacerbated

---

[96] Huskey, "Rise of Contested Politics."

[97] A. Erkebaev, *1990 God*, pp. 19–22. The Supreme Soviet seats were significantly more contested than the soviet seats in the local elections. The percentage of "*bezal'ternativnye okrugi*" (districts with only one candidate) were as follows: 12 percent of the Supreme Soviet seats; 18.3 percent of the *oblast'* soviet seats; 31.3 percent of the city soviet seats; 41.2 percent of the *raion* soviet seats (p. 19).

[98] Author's interviews with Dmitry Esenbai, journalist, *Slovo Kyrgyzstana*, Osh, July 31, 1995; and with M. Sorokin, chairman, Slavic Fund, Bishkek, September 4, 1995.

problems by promoting Kyrgyz clans from Osh at the expense of other ethnic, clan, and regional groups. Finally, as a northerner by birth and marriage, Akaev was an insider. As a scholar, not a Party apparatchik or local power broker, he was also an outsider to Kyrgyz clan rivalries. He was considered a neutral force and was widely seen as legitimate, even among southerners who had become disillusioned by Masaliev's failures.

In the Kyrgyz SSR, as in the Uzbek Republic almost a year earlier, the rise to power of the new leader was the result of a process of local dialogue among varying clan elites, informally representing different areas of the republic. Initially, the discussions took place within the Kyrgyz Supreme Soviet, which discussed several possible candidates, including Amanbaev, a powerful Issyk-Kul clan elite, and Apas Jumagulov, one of the most powerful members of the Chu clan elite, as well as Masaliev, whom the Osh wing of parliament still supported. When the parliament voted on these three candidates, however, no one candidate received a majority of votes. According to one participant in the Supreme Soviet session, "clan tensions ran very high." Since no candidate was seen as legitimate and acceptable to all regional and clan factions, "the republic was close to breakdown."[99] At this point, Chingiz Aitmatov, the "father of Kyrgyz literature" and a renowned patriarch of Kyrgyz society, intervened. He convened an informal "council of elders" to continue the dialogue.[100] Aitmatov was the most prominent participant, but the council also included, among others, Turdakun Usubaliev (the former Party first secretary ousted by Gorbachev and the representative of Naryn); Tursunbek Chinguishev of the Kochkor clan and Issyk-Kul region; Dastan Sarygulov of a prominent Sary clan from Talas; Chingiz Aitmatov's sons (Sanjar and Askar), both powerful members of the Sarybagysh clan elite; and Feliks Kulov and Apas Jumagulov, both of more "modern" Chu clans.[101] According to Askar Aitmatov, who defended this informal and opaque practice of clan negotiating and balancing, "this meeting of the elders was a Kyrgyz tradition" and had "great popular legitimacy."[102] It is not clear whether the advice of any southern representatives was sought, although participants claimed that Masaliev himself was not involved in the discussions.[103] The informal group, at Chingiz Aitmatov's recommen-

---

99 Author's interview with member of the Ministry of Foreign Affairs, Bishkek, August 1994; author's interview with Askar Aitmatov, Bishkek, June 1998.
100 This is a traditional form of Kyrgyz self-governance; it still prevails in the rural areas.
101 Kulov and Jumagulov were known to represent clans created by Soviet rule, especially by their connections with the KGB apparatus, which is sometimes loosely referred to as a clan. Author's conversations with journalists, Bishkek, 1998 and 2000.
102 Author's interview with Askar Aitmatov, Bishkek, June 1998.
103 In fact, Erkebaev, a young reformist deputy, noted the injustice with which Masaliev – whom he claims had faithfully served the Kyrgyz SSR in the footsteps of Razzakov, the Party first secretary from Osh in the 1950s – was excluded from the discussions. See A. Erkebaev, *1990 God*, pp. 96–97.

dation and urging, decided on Askar Akaev, and with some difficulty located him in Moscow to inform him that they were recommending him as a candidate.[104]

Aitmatov went personally to Moscow to propose a change of leadership to Gorbachev, and specifically to recommend Akaev. Presumably, Aitmatov's influence with Gorbachev, as a member of the Soviet Union's Presidential Council, together with Akaev's reputation in the Congress of People's Deputies as a scholar and reformer, were sufficient to win the general secretary's approval.[105] Even so, by the time these discussions had advanced – the summer of 1990 – the parade of sovereignty had begun. In the spring of 1990, the Kyrgyz Supreme Soviet had already followed other republics in declaring "sovereignty" for the Kyrgyz SSR, thus initiating a period of dual governance.[106] Akaev's candidacy was put to the Nineteenth Session of the Communist Party of the Kyrgyz SSR, in June 1990, and subsequently to the Kyrgyz Supreme Soviet. The parliament simultaneously adopted a law establishing a presidency. Akaev's appointment was easier than Karimov's, since by the summer of 1990 non-Party candidates could compete in elections. Had Akaev's candidacy been proposed a year earlier, his lack of Party membership might have undermined his entry into politics.

The Kyrgyz Supreme Soviet voted in August 1990, and Akaev was elected the first president of the Kyrgyz Republic. With strong support from the "movement of 114," the newly elected reformist deputies, and a critical mass of clan elites opposed to Masaliev, Akaev won the election with just over 50 percent of the vote.[107] The split was unsurprising, particularly given that Masaliev was still chairman of the parliament, and 41.5 percent (142) of its 350 deputies came from Osh.[108] Their vote went to Masaliev, the only other candidate, who had a monopoly on the southern clan vote.

[104] This material is based on author's interviews with Askar Aitmatov, a special advisor to the president. The author corroborated his account in interviews with Askar Sarygulov, head of the state property fund; Bakyt Sarygulov, director of *Kyrgyzstan Chronicle* and *Vechernii Bishkek* news agency; Feliks Kulov, *akim* (governor) of Chu *oblast*'; and several members of the Kyrgyz parliament, Bishkek, Kyrgyzstan, 1995–98.

[105] Dj. Asankulov, "*Askar Akeav kak otkritaia kniga*," in Melis Eshimkanov, ed., *Askar Akaev* (Bishkek: "Asaba," 1993), notes this factor, as does Askar Aitmatov. General Asankulov was a former chairman of the Kyrgyz Republic's Committee on State Security. His close knowledge of the discussions suggests that the security forces backed the decision.

[106] For a history of these legal changes, see A. Asankanov, *Kyrgyzstan: nashe otechestvo: istoriia vzaimosviazei i uprocheniia edinstva narodov Kyrgyzstana v usloviiakh stanovleniia nezavisimogo gosudarstva* (Bishkek: "Muras," 1997); and Dzh. M. Malabaev, *Istoriia gosudarstvennosti Kyrgyzstana* (Bishkek: "Ilim," 1997).

[107] Author's interview with Jaspar Jeksheev, leader of the *Demokraticheskoe dvizhenie "Kyrgyzstana"* (Democratic Movement of "Kyrgyzstan"), Bishkek, November 1995 and August 2000. Also see A. Khazanov, "Underdevelopment and Ethnic Relations in Central Asia," in Beatrice Manz, ed., *Central Asia in Historical Perspective* (Boulder, CO: Westview Press, 1994), p. 148.

[108] A. Erkebaev, *1990 God*, pp. 22–23.

Although the Communist Party's candidate, Masaliev did not win the support of the majority of the communist voters, who were concentrated in the North, Akaev's clan base. The party was split along both clan and regional lines.

Establishing Legitimacy and Consolidating Power

Karimov and Akaev both faced the immediate need to consolidate their power and legitimacy at the elite level. They had to demonstrate that they would carry out the informal pacts and the political and economic deals they had incorporated. The new presidents both needed to demonstrate sensitivity to local elite interests, and to maintain a balance of power among the various significant clan actors in the provinces. Thus, even though they did not trust certain clan or regional factions, they included them in the new distribution of power at the center. Both Akaev and Karimov began systematically to replace the Moscow (primarily Russian) appointees of their predecessors, a move that rapidly enhanced their legitimacy with the local power elites. For Karimov, faced with the post-purge situation of the Uzbek Communist Party, this was a bigger task, but one that allowed him quickly to fill with his own appointees the numerous openings left by the exit of the *krasnyi desant*.[109]

Karimov was in the unfortunate position of having to balance the interests of numerous large regions (the most important of which were the Ferghana Valley [including three *oblast*'s], Samarkand and Jizzak, Kashkadarya, and Khorezm) and more regionally based clan elites, some of whom were traditional rivals of his own power base in Samarkand. He did so by incorporating at least token members of each regional elite into the new government. He sought both to appease the most powerful kin networks of each region (for example, the Rashidov and Jurabekov clans of Jizzak and Samarkand), and to promote and patronize clans that were not loyal to his rivals. From the Ferghana Valley region, he included representatives of the more Sovietized Ferghana and Kokand clans (for example, the Akhmedov and Azimov families), rather than those from Andijan or Namangan, who were linked to the religious opposition. He also made gestures to less powerful Khorezm clans (including, initially, the national poet and figurehead Muhammad Salih of the Erk Party). After 1991, however, these networks would receive only token representation in the government.[110] Finally, diverging from more traditional informal politics, Karimov sought to create new clans in Tashkent whose members would be his clients and therefore loyal to him.[111]

---

[109] Author's interview with Sodyq Safaev, Washington, D.C., May 1999.
[110] Author's conversations with journalists, Urgench, October 1997.
[111] Uzbek journalists and scholars debate whether Karimov was ultimately interested in a long-term balance of clans or intended from the start to centralize and personalize power. Usman Khaknazarov argues that Karimov was playing the balancing game of clan politics. See Usman Khaknazarov, "Vozrozhdenie 'Serogo Kardinala' Uzbekskoi politiki,"

In the spring of 1990, ostensibly following the example of Gorbachev, Karimov became the first Communist Party first secretary of a Soviet republic to propose the creation of the office of republican-level president. The Supreme Soviet of the Uzbek Republic quickly adopted Karimov's proposition as law, the "law on creating a presidency" and the "law on electing a president."[112] In an election within the Uzbek Supreme Soviet on March 24, 1990, Karimov was elected president of the Uzbek SSR. No other republic first secretary had been so bold. Gorbachev reportedly telephoned Karimov directly, angrily denounced his action, and demanded the nullification of both the law and the election. Even Boris Yeltsin's dramatic election to the newly created post of president of the Russian Federation, on June 12, 1991, did not occur until several months later.

Karimov initially won the presidency indirectly, in the Supreme Soviet election of March 1990, an election often painted in the Soviet and Western press and scholarship as "communist." Although indeed, in communist style, there was no opposition, there was likewise no real ideological dimension to his candidacy.[113] The election did, however, reveal a struggle between Karimov with his clan backing, and his one opponent, Mirsaidov, a leader of the Tashkent Communist Party elite. After winning the Supreme Soviet election, Karimov named Mirsaidov vice president in an attempt to appease, balance, and also control the Tashkent party elite.[114] Karimov would win a second, partially contested and popular election the following year. On December 31, 1991, just shortly after independence was declared from the defunct Soviet Union, the first post-Soviet Uzbek presidential election took place. Karimov first banned his most threatening opposition, the Birlik Party, from taking part. One opposition candidate, Muhammad Salih, the leader of Erk, was permitted to run, but the vote was widely believed to be rigged.[115] Nonetheless, Salih won considerable support from his own province, where he had entrenched contacts and clan-based support. The election once again suggested that both support for Karimov and opposition to him were not of an ideological nature – communists versus democrats – but instead had clear provincial and clan roots.[116]

<www.muslimuzbekistan.com/rus/rusnews/2003/02/analit21022003_1.html>, February 21, 2003. Malikov argues that Karimov never intended to share power for long; author interview with B. Malikov, Washington D.C., May 2004.

[112] *Vedomosti verkhovnogo soveta Uzbekskoi SSR* (Moscow: Verkhovnogo Soveta Uz SSR, 1990).

[113] See Y. G. Kul'chik, *Respublika Uzbekistan*, p. 20.

[114] Within several months Karimov eliminated the post of vice president and cracked down on Mirsaidov and his kin, arresting some and causing others to flee the country. Author conversation with former party elite, Tashkent, March 1997. See Kul'chik, *Respublika Uzbekistan*, pp. 28–29, for details.

[115] Author's conversations with Erk Party members, Tashkent, Uzbekistan, October 1996 and October 1997; and with Birlik Party members, Washington, D.C., March 1998 and May 2004.

[116] Author's conversation with Erk Party members, Urgench, Uzbekistan, October 22, 1997.

Akaev was in the somewhat less difficult position of incorporating two major clan groupings in the north (often referred to in Kyrgyzstan as supra-clan or "tribal" groups descending from the Sol and Ong wings), each of which had several principal representatives among those who had bargained to engineer Akaev's election. Most of the powerful or lucrative positions were given to those who had helped Akaev to power: Tursunbek Chinguishev, Jumagulov, Chingiz Aitmatov, Askar Aitmatov, and Dastan and Askar Sarygulov. For example, the appointment of Feliks Kulov, a powerful northern clan leader, to the vice presidency was part of the deal that had brought him to power. Akaev initially gave the premiership to Isanov, a member of the Osh southern elite (including the powerful Adygine and Ichkilik clans) in order to create some balance and enhance his legitimacy.[117]

No Pact in Tajikistan: Nabiev's Reappointment and Persistent Regime Illegitimacy

One perspective at this time might have seen the Tajik Republic of 1989–90 as more stable than its neighbors. While its economic situation was somewhat worse, the republic seemed more cohesive in other respects. First, it had suffered no major repression under the early perestroika purges. Second, as a consequence, the Khodjenti elite had maintained its foremost position in the republic, as well as its subsidies from Moscow. Was Tajikistan then poised for a stable transition and viable regime change in 1991? The answer to this question was soon to be demonstrated as negative. In actuality, the lack of warning signs in the Tajik Republic, and the failure to redistribute power and resources in a more balanced fashion among competing clan elites was to become a serious handicap to the Tajik regime.[118] An indication of the Tajik elite's failure to perceive the need for a balancing of forces and a more legitimate regime is its failure to adopt a "law on the presidency" until November 1991, after its de facto independence from the Soviet Union. In the meantime, however, the Tajik Supreme Soviet had conducted an indirect election in a manner similar to that of the Kyrgyz and Uzbek soviets. The election, however, brought little change. The Khodjenti-dominated Supreme Soviet merely elected Makhkamov in 1990 with little internal discussion or contest.[119] Nabiev's successor since 1985, Makhkamov still had the backing of the Khodjenti clan, which refused to recognize signs of instability around it. Like his Kyrgyz and Uzbek neighbors, Makhkamov was seen to have little internal legitimacy, due to his appointment by Moscow and his weakness in

---

[117] Author's interview with Mukhtar Cholponbaev, speaker of the Kyrgyz parliament and deputy, Issyk-Kul *oblast'*, Bishkek, Kyrgyzstan, June 13, 1998.

[118] Author's interview with Stanley Escadero, Ambassador from the United States to Tajikistan, 1992–95, Baku, August 1998.

[119] V. I. Bushkov and D. B. Mikul'skii, *Anatomiia Grazhdanskoi Voini v Tajikistane* (Moskva: IEIA, PAN, 1997), pp. 51–52.

dealing with several small-scale protests. Yet the Khodjent elite did not act to replace him with another Khodjenti, much less with a candidate from a different clan or region.[120] Their failure to use the presidential election to broker a pact and establish a stable balance of internal power only fostered the Tajik regime's delusions of legitimacy and stability. Soon to lose Moscow's backing and subsidization altogether, the Tajik regime was ill-equipped to deal with the consequences of its long exclusion of non-Khodjentis from the Tajik republic's resources and power.[121]

SUMMARY

A central theme of this work is the critical role of Brezhnev's colonial-like, indirect style of rule in Central Asia. His rule fostered, either intentionally or inadvertently, the growth of clan patronage networks and clan politics. At the same time, his policies "modernized clans."[122] The roots of post-Soviet politics were thus largely defined well before the end of the Soviet era. What Valerie Bunce has noted of Eastern Europe is true of Central Asia as well: both regions can be seen as colonies of the Soviet empire and victims of its totalitarian ideology.[123] In neither region was socialism fully implemented. The way in which state socialism evolved, guided by Brezhnev's policies of nearly a quarter-century, allowed a significant decentralization of power to take place. Hence, strongly divergent trajectories were well under way in the Soviet space as early as the 1970s. The Eastern European trajectory was generally toward capitalism, anti-communist nationalism, political liberalization, and eventually democracy. Western ideas already permeated this region. The Central Asian trajectory, by contrast, headed toward the traditionalization and informalization of politics. It reflected decentralization of party and state power without capitalism, strong nationalism, and democratization, and without a pull or influence from the West. In the mid to late twentieth century, Soviet Central Asia already embodied many of the problems of colonial regimes in Africa and the Middle East. This would be a critical legacy for post-Soviet political development.

Second, in the mid-1980s Gorbachev was faced with a challenging society in Central Asia. Thus, his policies there differed from his reforms in other regions. Moreover, Central Asians interpreted his policies in light of their past experiences under Moscow's rule. Rather than openness and democratization, perestroika really meant the reassertion of Moscow's control over Central Asia. Only later did it suddenly mean the rapid undoing of that con-

---

[120] Bushkov and Mikul'skii, *Anatomiia*, pp. 46–47.

[121] Author's communication with Tajik historians and sociologists, Academy of Sciences, Moscow, July 14, 1998. For a good summary of the Tajik case, see Barnett Rubin, "Russian Hegemony and State Breakdown: Causes and Consequences of the Tajik Civil War," in Barnett Rubin and Jack Snyder, eds., *Post-Soviet Political Order* (London: Routledge, 1998).

[122] Author interview with Vladimir Berezovsky, journalist, Tashkent, May 2004.

[123] Bunce, *Subversive Institutions*.

trol. The transformation of power in the late 1980s followed changes at the Soviet center. The simultaneous dwindling of the purges and sudden opening of political space – both of which were due to the severely attenuated reach of the Soviet regime – created the structural context within which Central Asian clan elites were able to reassert themselves, and then to mimic and take advantage of the all-Union reform process. They now had the political leeway to bring about their own transition, which, as in Eastern Europe, first and foremost involved central elements of decolonization – such as removing the colonizer's ruling clique. In Eastern Europe, these were the Soviet-backed ideologues of the communist parties. In Central Asia, they were the primarily Russian cadres controlling the Party and state. By 1990, the delegitimized first secretaries of the late 1980s, along with their Moscow-installed cadres, had exited. Stronger and more legitimate Central Asian presidents – equipped with either a new local cadre or in some cases with a rehabilitated Brezhnev-era cadre – replaced them in a move that significantly enhanced regime durability prior to the next phase of transition.

Third, an analysis of the nature and role of the pact in regime change is central to understanding these transitions. In the cases discussed in this chapter, the pact was not a "mode of transition," as the transitions literature postulates, but rather an outcome of regime change itself. Achieving an informal political pact amongst the various competing clan elites de facto established a regime in which the central element, the division of resources, was agreed upon and managed by clan elites. Both the possibility and the need to form pacts was triggered by outside factors, by changes at the Soviet center that had repercussions for the republics. As in other cases of late colonialism, pacts among local actors were the result of united opposition to the colonial regime. In Central Asia, clans formed pacts in opposition to Moscow's purges.

The critical balance of power among clan elites, or the lack thereof, was likewise shaped by the Soviet regime's interference in the economic and political development of Central Asia. In analyzing the role of pacts as the major outcome of regime change, a fundamental question must be addressed: Under what conditions do pacts occur? Why did the Uzbek and Kyrgyz elites create pacts, while the Tajiks did not? Several elements critically affected the ability of elites to arrive at a stable pact. First, the historical context – and specifically, the role of the colonial regime in shaping a balance or imbalance of clan power within the republics – created the general context for regime change. Increasing repression by the Party destabilized the hegemony of clans in the Uzbek and Kyrgyz Republics that had ruled with minimal power sharing for nearly twenty-five years. Second, the external threat posed by Gorbachev's purges and the "red landing" instigated a united backlash that increased the likelihood of clan elites' successfully negotiating an inclusive pact. Third, successfully concluding a pact demanded the presence of a legitimate leader to facilitate and broker the agreement, and to continue

TABLE 4.2. *Explaining clan pacts and transitional regime durability/collapse in Central Asia*

Cases	Balance of Clans	External Threat	Legitimate Broker	Clan Pact	Durable Regime
Kyrgyzstan	Y	Y	Y	Y	Y
Uzbekistan	Y	Y	Y	Y	Y
Tajikistan	N	N	N	N	N
Kazakhstan	Y	Y	Y	Y	Y
Turkmenistan	Y	Y	Y	Y	Y

Note: Y = yes/present; N = no/absent

in a leadership position as the guardian of that pact. Askar Akaev, whose respected status as both an outsider and an insider vis-à-vis the clan politics of Central Asia, was such a figure. To a somewhat lesser extent, Islam Karimov enjoyed legitimacy as a loyal Uzbek, but outside of clan politics. Although informal, the pacts of 1989 and 1990 stabilized internal politics in these republics. As we will see in Chapter 9, a similar process occurs in neighboring Kazakhstan and Turkmenistan.

In the Tajik Republic, perestroika was less harsh. The Soviet-era regime of the Khodjenti clan did not lose hegemonic control. Consequently, the ruling Tajik clan had no incentive to negotiate a pact introducing a more inclusive and stable division of power and resources among competing clan elites. With an imbalance of power and no legitimate leader, an unstable hegemony persisted; it would quickly break down once Soviet backing evaporated in 1992 (see Table 4.2). These cases illustrate that the process of reaching a pact could take place apart from and independent of either an elite or societal push for regime democratization.

Finally, this chapter highlights the remarkable ease with which Central Asian Party elites made the transition from the Soviet system and a power base in the Communist Party to non-Party presidentialism and executive-concentrated rule, from 1989 to 1991. The informal undermining of decades-old communist policy suggests the lack of loyalty to the Party and its ideology. The contrast between the transfer of power within the Central Asian republics and the Russian republic and Eastern Europe is centrally important to the different types of transitions they were to embark upon. In Russia, for example, the Party's unraveling led to a dramatic undoing of centralized power and the polarized division of elites along ideological lines – hard-liners versus soft-liners – within the Russian parliament.[124] In Central Asia (with the partial exception of Kyrgyzstan, where reformists backed Akaev), the republic Supreme Soviets generally did not experience strong ideological

[124] McFaul, *Russia's Unfinished Revolution.*

splits,[125] and the Party first secretaries retained greater control over both the government and parliament. Indeed, as of the summer of 1989, Karimov had already abandoned any appeal to the legitimacy of the Communist Party and its ideology. Furthermore, he did so without inciting a hard-line faction within the Uzbek Republic's government or Party structures.

By mid-1991, the first stage of Central Asia's transition was complete. Even before official independence, the elite clans of Central Asia had effectively decolonized their regimes by reclaiming political power. Where clan pacts were established during this pre-independence period, the subsequent process of political transition, whether to a democratic or an autocratic regime, would more likely be stable; where no clan pact existed, the threat of instability was already great. In the following two chapters, I will examine the divergent political trajectories upon which these republics embarked.

[125] Huskey, "Rise of Contested Politics"; and author interview with B. Malikov, 2004.

5

Transition from Above or Below? (1990–1991)

> We wanted democracy and freedom. We read Jefferson and Madison. We knew more about democracy than Americans. We knew your history better than you. Yes, all that was forbidden, we read. And then we followed Sakharov, who led the way.
>
> An Uzbek intellectual and former political activist, Tashkent, 1997

The year 1991 meant different things to different people and groups in Central Asia. To some, like this Uzbek activist, it meant a chance for democracy. To others, it meant freedom from Soviet colonization, Russian dominance, or scientific atheism, and to many others it primarily meant an end to subsidies. Indeed, Central Asia experienced a far more complicated transition than states that had undergone this process in earlier waves of regime change in other regions of the world. Chapter 4 demonstrated that the nature and timing of the political pacts in the Central Asian cases were only the first element marking these cases as different from transitions in Latin America, Southern Europe, or even in Poland and Hungary, their former communist neighbors. The multilayered and multiphased nature of the Central Asian transitions, like those of the Eastern European and other post-Soviet cases, involved several almost simultaneous political processes – not only political liberalization, but also independence, decolonization, and nation and state building.[1] At the same time, the Central Asian transitions were far less driven by mass ideological movements for democracy or nationalism than those in the Eastern European states or in the other former Soviet republics.[2]

---

[1] See Claus Offe, "Capitalism by Democratic Design? Democratic Theory Facing the Triple Transition in East Central Europe," *Social Research*, vol. 58 (1991), pp. 865–892.

[2] Social mobilization or imposition from below was often a positive factor in transitions in East Europe, the Baltics, and the Caucasus. See Michael McFaul, "The Fourth Wave of Democracy and Dictatorship: Noncooperative Transitions in the Postcommunist World," *World Politics*, vol. 54, no. 2 (January 2002), pp. 212–244; Valerie Bunce, "Rethinking Recent Democratization: Lessons from the Postcommunist Experience," *World Politics*, vol. 55,

The Central Asian cases must be understood within the overarching sociohistorical context – the Soviet Union's liberalization and ultimate demise. The Central Asian republics' independence and subsequent transitions were not internally driven; they were de facto consequences of the exogenous shock of the Soviet collapse. In marked contrast with the Baltic, East European, Armenian, Azeri, Georgian, Ukrainian, and Russian cases, in Central Asia neither society nor elites played a significant role in breaking with the Soviet regime. Despite feelings of resentment against colonial rule and despite the purges of the 1980s, only weak and limited nationalist-secessionist movements emerged. Nor were there significant democratic ones.

This chapter and the next discuss the agents pushing for and engaging in regime change during the late Soviet period. I address two elements of the "mode"[3] of political transition in Central Asia: (1) "change from below," which ultimately failed; and (2) "change from above," which first involved significant political changes prior to independence, but actual regime change only after independence.[4]

"Change from below" refers to a transition in which society plays a key role. Scholars of democratization and transition in the 1980s, studying earlier waves of democratization, warned that social mobilization was likely to lead to violence and thereby to undermine the likelihood of successful democratization. Yet scholars of "fourth wave" transitions have often highlighted the importance of society's role in pushing for change and tilting the balance of power in favor of the reformers, as well as in laying the foundation for an active political and civil society after the authoritarian regime's collapse.[5] Social mobilization may take various forms. In its most positive form, this mode of change is driven and dominated by a society

---

no. 2 (January 2003), pp. 167–192; and Valerie Bunce, "Comparative Democratization: Big and Bounded Conclusions," *Comparative Political Studies*, vol. 33 (August–September 2000), pp. 703–734. See also Deborah J. Yashar, "Democracy, Indigenous Movements, and the Postliberal Challenge in Latin America," *World Politics*, vol. 52, no. 1 (October 1999), pp. 76–104.

[3] On "modes of transition," see Terry Karl and Philippe Schmitter, "Modes of Transition in Latin America, Southern, and Eastern Europe," *International Social Science Journal*, vol. 128 (1991). Many post-Soviet specialists argue that the Soviet and Russian cases do not neatly fit into any of the modes elaborated.

[4] Steven Fish argues that the post-communist transitions have two main components, society (change from below) and the state (change from above). See M. Steven Fish, *Democracy from Scratch: Opposition and Regime in the New Russian Revolution* (Princeton, NJ: Princeton University Press, 1995), pp. 4–29.

[5] See Karen Dawisha and Bruce Parrott, *Russia and the New States of Eurasia: The Politics of Upheaval* (New York: Cambridge University Press, 1994); Timothy Garton Ash, *The Magic Lantern: The Revolution of 1989 Witnessed in Warsaw, Budapest, Berlin, and Prague* (New York: Random House, 1990); Elisabeth Jean Wood, *Forging Democracy from Below: Insurgent Transitions in South Africa and El Salvador* (New York: Cambridge University Press, 2000); and Michael McFaul, *Unfinished Revolution* (Ithaca, NY: Cornell University Press, 2002).

supporting liberalization, democratization, and sometimes anticolonialism and nationalism. Society may seek a compromise-driven transition from the ancien regime to democracy.[6] Its success is contingent not only upon the willingness of the regime, or of reformers within the regime, to compromise, but also upon the strength and moderation of society as a political actor. In yet another formulation of society-driven transitions, radicals or hard-liners in society direct the push from below, insisting upon revolution and the destruction of the regime. Such a path is similarly contingent upon the strength of society in mobilizing a mass movement in opposition to the regime.

Society and social movements played various roles in the post-communist transitions. The round table negotiations between Solidarity and General Jaruzelski in Poland in 1989 in many ways exemplify society's success in pressuring a regime to reform. Solidarity was sufficiently strong, and soft-liners within the regime sufficiently influential, to sustain a negotiated, peaceful transition to democracy. Likewise, in the Baltics thousands of citizens mobilized against their Soviet colonizer, but social protest did not lead to negotiations; instead, democratic-nationalist movements led to secession in August 1991, and then to regime change. The transition in the Russian republic from 1988 to 1991 has been described as "revolutionary"; it involved hundreds of thousands of pro-democracy demonstrators rallying on the streets.[7] The Romanian revolt in 1989, which ended in a revolutionary uprising and the violent toppling of the Ceaucescu regime and the execution of its sultanlike dictator, is perhaps the best example of a violent revolution in the former communist sphere. In a more virulent form, not uncommon in transitional and post-colonial or post-imperial states, change from below may involve radicals creating "ethnic" (not civic) nationalist social movements and/or pushing for secession in a violent manner, often without regard for democratization.[8] In Armenia, Azerbaijan, Georgia, the Ukraine, and to some extent in Moldova, perestroika and glasnost' triggered substantial nationalist, although not necessarily democratic, social mobilization.[9] Far worse, in the former Yugoslavia, ethno-nationalism became a strategy that unified Milosevic's elite circle and radicals in Serbian society behind a strategy of keeping the ancien regime in power through ethnic cleansing. A decade later, however, in October 2000, Serbian society played a key role in Slobodan

---

[6] Bunce points out that social movements can also be virulent, involving exclusivist nationalism. Nationalism may in fact take many forms, depending on the context and the goals of the elites who use it. See Valerie Bunce, *Subversive Institutions* (Cambridge: Cambridge University Press, 1999), pp. 107–109.

[7] McFaul, "The Fourth Wave."

[8] Bunce, *Subversive Institutions.*

[9] Ronald Grigor Suny, *Looking toward Ararat: Armenia in Modern History* (Bloomington: Indiana University Press, 1993); and Georgi Derlugian, "Georgia's Return of the King," CSIS Working Paper Series #22, PONARS (2004), pp. 9–11, http://www.csis.org/ruseura/ponars/workingpapers/022.PDF.

Milosevic's ouster, and in November 2003 a democratic movement brought about the fall of Eduard Shevardnadze and the Rose Revolution in Georgia.

"Change from above" refers to transitions that are driven by elites, not society. They may involve what Terry Karl and Philippe Schmitter call the "imposition" of a transition and new regime by the elites who dominate the ancien regime, or they may involve "elite pacts," in which hard- and soft-liners agree to implement reforms. In both scenarios, elites strategically choose to *impose* a transition, and thereby to control and shape the transition, rather than allow it to run astray. The balance of power and causal impetus in this model lies with the regime rather than society.[10] Many scholars have argued that elite pacts were the mode of transition that led to successful democratization in Latin America and southern Europe, whereas elite imposition without significant social checks has often led to backsliding (e.g., Turkey, Pakistan, Russia).

Although Gorbachev initiated change from above, society played a critical role in the demise of communism and the subsequent democratization in both Eastern Europe and the Soviet Union (and its successor state, Russia).[11] In fact, in contrast to earlier waves of pacted or elite-driven transitions from authoritarianism, the post-communist transitions involved society to a greater degree. Gorbachev himself had sought to mobilize society in support of perestroika, and in opposition to the hard-liners and apparatchiks who opposed reform. Gorbachev's attempts at economic and then political institutional reform from 1986 through 1989 can be seen as the imposition of liberalizing and later democratizing measures on an obdurate Communist Party and state apparatus. However, in Russia and the Baltics, where a strong intellectual and social base for a democratic movement existed, Gorbachev's reforms opened the political space for a social opposition to mobilize. In allowing social movements and proto-parties to co-opt the democratic agenda, Gorbachev and his strategy of imposition eventually lost control of the reform process.[12]

In Central Asia transition was very much intertwined with the Soviet transition, but the mode was distinct, because it involved both regime change and decolonization. One might have expected the emergence of a strong elite and social movement touting an anti-colonial, anti-communist, and strongly nationalist platform. To some extent, glasnost' and perestroika did mobilize society. The rise of mass opposition movements in Russia and the Baltics was at first replicated by the Kyrgyz, Uzbek, and Tajik intelligentsia, although the nationalist social movements in Central Asia were not clearly democratic

---

[10] McFaul, "The Fourth Wave."
[11] Russell Bova, "Political Dynamics of a Postcommunist Transition: A Comparative Perspective," *World Politics*, vol. 44, no. 1 (October 1991), pp. 113–138; and McFaul, *Unfinished Revolution.*
[12] Bova, "Political Dynamics," pp. 135–136.

and anti-communist. Generally they were not of a virulent nationalist form, either.[13] They were primarily movements of the intelligentsia who shared an anti-colonial agenda and sought greater ethnic, cultural, political, and (in Tajikistan) religious rights, and limited sovereignty.

Leaders of social movements in Central Asia mimicked the organizational structure and the nationalist-democratic agendas of their counterparts in the Baltics, the leaders of the "informals." Yet the proto-parties and social movements of Central Asia failed to mobilize a mass social base. As Mark Beissinger points out, the level of nationalist mobilization was lower in Central Asia than in any other region of the former Soviet Union.[14] In December 1986, the Alma-Ata demonstrations against Moscow's removal of First Secretary Kunaev reflected anger at Moscow's interference in local affairs, but they were not clearly nationalist, much less secessionist or democratic. The events occurred outside the "glasnost' mobilizational cycle"; they were spontaneous protests rather than part of a "movement organization" with a proactive agenda; they principally reflected "outrage" at the replacement of the Kazakh first secretary by an outsider, a Russian.[15] The republic-level regimes generally reacted to incipient social movements by co-optation; unlike the situation in other regions of the Soviet bloc, this strategy was relatively successful. The republic leaders both increased their power vis-à-vis Moscow and prevented the escalation of nationalism and demands for secession from the USSR – which they all opposed.

In the Baltics and in East Central Europe, mass nationalist, democratic, and anti-communist social movements often played critical roles in overthrowing the ancien regime, driving political transition, and fostering democratic consolidation.[16] Where civil society was weaker (e.g., in Russia), despite initial successes, communist cultural and institutional legacies have nonetheless inhibited the development of civil society after the transition.[17]

---

[13] Scholars debate whether nationalism in Tajikistan especially was directed at harming or expelling Russians. Most agree that the ethnic riots in Osh, Uzgen, Ferghana, and Isfara were primarily over land and water, not nationalism. See Olga Brusina, "*Agrarnoe perenaselenie kak odna iz prichin Oshskogo konflikta,*" *Profi,* no. 11 (1999), pp. 20–23; and refer to Chapter 4 in this volume.

[14] See the exhaustive study by Mark Beissinger, *Nationalist Mobilization and the Collapse of the Soviet State* (Cambridge: Cambridge University Press, 2002); and Gregory Gleason, *Central Asia's New States* (Boulder, CO: Westview Press, 1997).

[15] Beissinger, *Nationalist Mobilization,* pp. 73–74.

[16] On the success of econationalist movements in the Baltics and Ukraine, see Jane Dawson, *Econationalism* (Chapel Hill, NC: Duke University Press, 1996). On the role of civil society, see Grzeorg Ekiert and Jan Kubik, *Rebellious Civil Society: Popular Protest and Democratic Consolidation in Poland, 1989–1993* (Ann Arbor: University of Michigan Press, 1999). See Dawisha and Parrott, *Russia and the New States,* on greater civil society development in the western NIS than in the southern NIS.

[17] See Marc Morje Howard, *The Weakness of Civil Society in Postcommunist Europe* (New York: Cambridge University Press, 2003).

In Central Asia, both pre-communist and communist legacies inhibited the development of civil society. There, democratic social movements gained far less momentum at the height of perestroika and transition. Central Asian "informals" do, however, have a limited effect on the transition. This is most evident in Kyrgyzstan and Tajikistan. In the former case, the democratic movement fosters liberalization. In the latter case, given the weakness of the Tajik regime, a coalition of movements ultimately fosters authoritarian regime breakdown and plays into (but does not initiate) the civil violence.

In the first part of this chapter, I discuss the origins, agenda, development, and limits of Central Asian social movements during the perestroika period, and then analyze the responses and choices of regime elites. In the second part, I discuss the Soviet transition in which the Central Asian republics were embedded. I argue that the real trigger for decolonization and transition in Central Asia was not agency but a structural shock, the Soviet collapse. This chapter further highlights the colonial-like character of these transitions and the generally weak role of society in supporting nationalism or democratization, and discusses the pre-independence elements of the transitions and their legacies for the post-1991 transitions (to be discussed in Chapter 6).

I. THE AGENDA, DEVELOPMENT, AND FAILURE OF CHANGE FROM BELOW

I have already noted the remarkably different evolution of perestroika throughout Central Asia. Central Asian "informals" and civil society had minimal, if any, effect on the clan pacts negotiated in 1989 and 1990. Since a certain push from below did develop and increase in strength from 1989 to 1992, it is worth examining why these movements emerged but failed, and what the implications of a weak civil society and a weak sense of national identity would be.[18]

Gorbachev and the Roots of Central Asian "Civil Society"

At a conference of the Institute of Philosophy and Law of the Kyrgyz SSR Academy of Sciences convened in November 1986, Gorbachev told the Kyrgyz intelligentsia that "[i]f we talk about the deficits in today's civilization, there are many. But the very biggest – it is a deficit of the *novoe myshlenie* (new thinking)."[19] Continuing, the new first secretary claimed that "only those of us who are gifted to distinguish the hidden, will be able

---

[18] Dawson, *Econationalism*, Chapter 1.
[19] *Izvestiia akademii nauk*, no. 1 (1987), pp. 27, 31. The Issyk-Kul forum took place on November 10, 1986, on one of Gorbachev's first visits to Central Asia, shortly before the purges of Central Asian party officials got under way.

to accomplish the impossible...and it is the ability to see the hidden, the murky, but existing – that is the most important principle of the new thinking."[20] Gorbachev had set out a challenge for reformers in Central Asia, where politics was even more obtuse than in the rest of the Soviet Union. The rise of civil society was in many ways a predictable response to the relaxed political environment introduced by Gorbachev; after the Party conference of June 1988, liberalization escalated from mere slogans about increased economic productivity to open discussions of political reform, captured in the rhetoric of glasnost', *demokratizatsiia*, and perestroika.

Although civil society was relatively less developed and Gorbachev's political opening considerably more circumscribed in Central Asia, a significant diffusion of ideas from neighboring social movements had occurred. According to a leader of Birlik, they in large part adopted and adapted platforms from their Slavic and Baltic counterparts.[21] The issues were primarily ethnonationalist, and initially linked with ecological demands.[22] The Central Asian organizers of such movements were primarily intellectuals, often with strong ties to Moscow and sometimes with long careers in Moscow.[23] From the outset, they were exposed to the ideas and actions of the popular and national fronts, such as Sajudis in Lithuania, as well as to the wave of civic and democratic movements emerging in Russia. Some were affiliated with the electoral bloc of the opposition, Democratic Russia.[24] The development of a civic opposition thus took similar forms across Kyrgyzstan, Uzbekistan, and Tajikistan and, interestingly, often elicited similar regime responses – generally, co-optation.

The Kyrgyz Movement

In the Kyrgyz SSR, neither democratic nor nationalist movements were quick to emerge with the onset of glasnost'. The first independent social organization with significant social standing to develop was initially socially and

---

[20] Ibid.

[21] Author's interviews with Abdurahim Pulat and Abdummanob Pulat, Washington, D.C., March 1998; and with Abdurahim Pulat, Washington, D.C., May 2004. See also V. Ponomarev, *Samodeiatel'nye obshchestvennye organizatsii Kazakhstana i Kirgizii 1987–1991* (Moscow: Institut issledovaniia ekstremal'nykh protsessov [SSSR], 1991), pp. 87–88.

[22] See "*Programma*," the program of Birlik and Erk in Uzbekistan, *Etnopoliticheskaia panorama* (Moscow, 1995); author's interview with Abdurahim Pulat and Abdummanob Pulat, leaders of the Birlik movement and party, Washington, D.C., March 1998; author's interview with former Erk members, Tashkent, Uzbekistan, and Urgench, Uzbekistan, October 1997; author's interviews with Jaspar Jeksheev, leader of the Democratic Movement of Kyrgyzstan (DMK), Bishkek, Kyrgyzstan, November and December 1994 and July 2000.

[23] This process within the Soviet Union is an interesting twist on Huntington's argument about the causal role of diffusion of ideas and demonstration effects in democratization. See Samuel Huntington, *The Third Wave* (Norman: University of Oklahoma Press, 1991), pp. 102–103.

[24] Author's interview with members of the DMK, Bishkek, Kyrgyzstan, November 1994.

economically oriented. In 1989, calling itself "Ashar," this group included a number of primarily ethnic Kyrgyz students and squatters living in the capital city. They began by protesting housing shortages, which were acute by the late 1980s as a result of severe economic difficulties in rural areas, where most Kyrgyz lived.[25] The problem was exacerbated by the relocation of Armenian and other victims of the 1988 earthquake, who were given priority for apartments. Following Gorbachev's call for reform on the collectives in 1987 and 1988 – plans that introduced "cooperatives" without a change in land ownership or management – attempts had been made to mitigate the huge unemployment problem in the rural areas. These included a mild loosening of the *propiska* system that had traditionally tied laborers to a particular *kolkhoz* and district. Consequently, a small number of Kyrgyz youth migrated to the capital city to find work, established urban connections, and sent money home to their families. The number of shantylike dwellings on the outskirts of Bishkek grew from several hundred to several thousand.[26] Ashar emerged as a social movement, not a party or political organization, but its small group of student leaders organized several protests that further discredited the unpopular First Secretary Absamat Masaliev. Masaliev recognized the group's demands and took measures to address the problem, so as to preempt the consolidation of a poor and disaffected youth population. Yet Masaliev's strategy soon backfired. Ashar represented the type of proto-civil society that was emerging through a process of action, protest, and reaction to the regime's response over time.[27] Although it initially disbanded in response to the government's promises and half-hearted attempts to provide better housing, the group reincarnated itself as a political movement in Bishkek in early 1990, when it put forth several candidates in the March local elections. Its success was minimal. Again the group appeared to recede, but in the summer of 1990, following the ethnic riots in the Ferghana Valley, Ashar emerged in a different form. Because the Ferghana conflagrations had underscored the housing and land crisis, Ashar assumed a more defined nationalist and democratic agenda, staging protests in several cities.[28]

Although still primarily composed of poorly educated peasants and rural students, Ashar's leadership merged with intellectuals and various elites who were also opposed to the ineffective Kyrgyz regime. Russians, critical of Masaliev's poor management of ethno-national relations, feared the

---

[25] Author's interview with member of the DMK who had formerly been involved in Ashar, Bishkek, Kyrgyzstan, September 1994. See also Ponomarev, *Samodeiatel'nye obshchestvennye organizatsii*, pp. 87–89, 93–95.

[26] Author's interview with member of the Ministry of Labor, Bishkek, Kyrgyzstan, July 1995.

[27] Fish, in *Democracy from Scratch*, similarly argues that state institutions shape the type of movement organizations that emerge during liberalization.

[28] Author's interview with a Kyrgyzstani journalist for *Delo gazeta*, Bishkek, Kyrgyzstan, October 1994.

outbreak of further conflict, especially against Slavs. Several thousand emigrated to escape the uncertain situation left by the Osh violence.[29] Ethnic Uzbeks resented Masaliev's catering to ethnic Kyrgyz clans in the southern *oblast*'s of the republic. Some Uzbeks even organized an ethno-national group that demanded the return of several *raion*s of the Osh and Jalalabad *oblast*'s of the Kyrgyz SSR to the Uzbek SSR – a form of separatism rather different from that typical of republican-level politics at the time.[30] However, the "separatists" were few, and their goals were chiefly organized not against Moscow, but in opposition to the Masaliev regime. Hence, the Uzbek population focused on supporting the wider and growing opposition to Masaliev.

The ethnic Kyrgyz component of the opposition was itself a conglomeration of multiple factions, of which Asaba (Banner) – a political movement (later a party) that began by demanding that the government defend the Kyrgyz culture – emerged as a leader. Activists such as Chapyrashty Bazarbaev, the chairman, Turash Dyusheev, and Melis Eshimkanov became founders of Asaba. Soon it made explicitly ethno-nationalist demands favoring the ethnic Kyrgyz population.[31] Primary among these was the adoption of the Kyrgyz language as both the national and state language of the Kyrgyz Republic, and a rapid shift to using Kyrgyz in both educational and government institutions.[32] Their most radical and controversial demand, however, was the adoption of a new land law, one that would "return the land of Kyrgyzstan to the Kyrgyz."[33] This formulation of land reform, which had its primary support among Kyrgyz clan elites and peasants of the southern oblasts, where the riots had taken place, would likely have serious consequences for interethnic relations.[34] Asaba further sought greater sovereignty – but not full independence – for the republic. The group put forth general provisos for economic and political change, but it did not articulate a program for implementing reforms.

Ultimately, certain members of the ethnic Kyrgyz intelligentsia, many of whom had close connections with democratic and nationalist movements in other parts of the Soviet Union in 1980 and 1990, provided leadership to the emerging opposition movement, the Demokraticheskoe Dvizhenie Kyrgyzstana (Democratic Movement of Kyrgyzstan, hereafter DMK). The

---

[29] Valery Tishkov, *The Mind Aflame* (Oslo: PRIO, 1997).

[30] Author's interview with Bakyt Beshimov, parliamentary deputy, Legislative House of Jogorku Kenesh, and rector, Osh State University, Osh, Kyrgyzstan, August 1995.

[31] Rafis Abazov, *Historical Dictionary of Kyrgyzstan* (Lantham, MD: Scarecrow Press, 2004), p. 76; and author's interviews with members of Asaba Party, Bishkek, Kyrgyzstan, November 1994.

[32] A clear distinction was made between "national" (i.e., cultural and ethnic) and "state" (i.e., political and governmental). Debate over the language law was ongoing in 2003 and 2004.

[33] Author's interview with members of Asaba, Bishkek, November 1994.

[34] Zamira Sydykova, *Za kulisami demokratii po-Kyrgyzski* (Bishkek: Res Publika, 1996).

leaders of the DMK, the umbrella organization for this mélange of disaffected groups, and those who engaged in the movement's actions and protests during early 1990 were generally members of the Academy of Sciences and university faculty members who had enjoyed significant exposure to Moscow's intellectual circles.[35] Topchubek Turgunaliev, the leader of the DMK and a proponent of the democratic nationalist agenda of Democratic Russia, was the rector of the Bishkek Humanities University. Ironically, Turgunaliev had been a high-ranking member of the ideology (and propaganda) division of the Central Committee of the Communist Party of Kyrgyzstan under Usubaliev. Turgunaliev was elected a deputy to the Kyrgyz Supreme Soviet in 1990. The DMK's other principal leaders, including Jasper Jeksheev and Erkin Tekebaev, were likewise intellectuals from Bishkek. The former had a career in journalism, publishing, and education and was closely tied to pro-democratic Moscow intellectuals.[36] Tekebaev, who was later to break away from the DMK and form his own party, Erkin Kyrgyzstan, originally emerged as a strong supporter of Akaev and also as a "reform deputy" in the Kyrgyz Supreme Soviet.[37]

The Osh riots in the summer of 1990 generated such resentment toward Masaliev that they spurred the formation of civil society in the Kyrgyz Republic and facilitated cooperation among various opposition factions.[38] Together, the disparate members of the DMK included thirty-four political organizations, clubs, and NGOs (based mainly in the capital). According to the DMK, supporters totaled up to 300,000, but other observers claim that they were no more than a few thousand. Nonetheless, the DMK staged several demonstrations against Masaliev, joined the effort to establish a presidency in place of the first secretaryship in the Kyrgyz SSR, and strongly supported Akaev's candidacy for the post of president of the republic in the October 1990 election. Not long after the election, the DMK began to splinter, primarily along personal lines.[39]

[35] Author's interview with Kamila Kenenbaeva, a former leading member of the DMK and one of the founders of the Ata-Meken Party, Bishkek, Kyrgyzstan, November 1994. She was invited by Akaev to become a state advisor on political parties and social movements in the presidential apparat, as part of his effort to incorporate the democratic opposition.
[36] See Ponomarev, *Samodeiatel'nye obshchestvennye organizatsii*, pp. 96–97, and author interview with J. Jeksheev, a former Leader of the DMK, Bishkek, Kyrgyzstan, July 1995.
[37] Author's interview with Topchubek Turgunaliev, former head of the DMK, Bishkek, Kyrgyzstan, October 1994. Turgunaliev apparently split with Jeksheev due to leadership conflict.
[38] Eugene Huskey, "The Rise of Contested Politics in Central Asia: Elections in Kyrgyzstan, 1989–1990," *Europe-Asia Studies*, vol. 47, no. 5 (July 1995), p. 827.
[39] Masaliev at first opposed any restructuring of the government and party. Then, in April 1990, at the first session of the Kyrgyz Supreme Soviet, Masaliev and his supporters from Osh attempted to create a chairmanship of the Supreme Soviet in addition to the secretaryship of the Party. He would fill both positions, as head of state and head of the Party. The "democratic faction" in parliament, together with Chingiz Aitmatov, was instrumental in

Akaev's Response: Defusing Nationalism and Promoting Democracy

When Askar Akaev assumed the post of president and head of state in September 1990, he quickly recognized both Ashar and the broader Democratic Movement of Kyrgyzstan. He took concrete steps to address the housing crisis and to initiate a program of economic reform intended to go beyond measures advocated by Party liberals. In fact, Akaev's major point of disagreement with the Union Treaty was not over political sovereignty, but over economic sovereignty. In the wake of the Osh riots, Akaev had initiated small-scale land reform at the local level. Yet Akaev rejected the draft law on land proposed by certain ethno-nationalist deputies and supported by Asaba and Erkin Kyrgyzstan. Instead, he reworked the law "in defense of the rights and freedoms of national minorities" and pursued "the creation of a real and effective legal mechanism for the defense of rights and freedoms of all citizens."[40] In an interview with a Russian journalist about interethnic relations in Kyrgyzstan, Akaev remarked that:

The deputies of the Supreme Soviet insisted that the land be allocated only to the Kyrgyz, and that if we turn over the land for private property or lifetime possession, then only to the Kyrgyz. I had to veto this decision, and I managed to pass [my draft law on land] only on the third attempt. I put everything at stake, and if I had not achieved my task then I would have resigned. Thus the Russians, and other nationalities, think that I not only declare equal rights for all nationalities, but actually defend them.[41]

Akaev's revisions to the land law and code substantially increased the number of private plots – which came from collective farm land – and decreased restrictions on farmers' production on their own plots.[42] He did so without upsetting the traditional ethnic balance in the southern *oblast*'s, and without dislocating villagers of any ethnic group or clan.[43] Finally, Akaev began (and would continue after independence) discussions with the Tajik Republic to resolve the dispute over a water reservoir in the Batken region, the source of conflict between Tajik and Kyrgyz villages.[44]

blocking this move. See A. Erkebaev, *1990 God: Prikhod k vlasti Askar Akaeva* (Bishkek: BBK, "Kirgizstan," 1997), pp. 32–34.

[40] D. Z. Malabaev, *Istoriia gosudarstvennosti Kyrgyzstana* (Bishkek: Ilim, 1997), p. 188.

[41] Author's interview with Vladimir Medvedev, in Melis Eshimkanov, Kanybek Imanaliev, Atay Altymshev, Kubatbek Zhusubaliev, Azimzhan Ibraimov, and Bakyt Orunbekor, *Askar Akaev* (Bishkek: Kyrgyzstan, 1993), p. 97.

[42] Author's interview with K. Imailov, specialist on land reform, legal division, presidential *apparat*, Bishkek, conducted in Bishkek, Kyrgyzstan, August 1995.

[43] Author's interview with the *raion akim* (district governor), Uzgen, Osh *oblast'*, Kyrgyzstan, July 1998.

[44] Author's interview with Erik Asanaliev, special officer for Tajik affairs, Ministry of Foreign Affairs, Bishkek, Kyrgyzstan, 1995.

By thus addressing – at least temporarily – the fundamental land and water issues, Akaev deftly separated the economic roots of demands posed by Ashar's supporters from ethno-nationalism. His opposition to the draft law on land for ethnic Kyrgyz only kept the law from a vote in the Supreme Soviet.[45] Second, Akaev did not attempt to revoke the Kyrgyz Language Law adopted by the legislature in 1989; however, he did push for legal recognition of Russian as well. On the broader political agenda, Akaev sought to encourage democratic reformers within the republican Supreme Soviet and to introduce more open political dialogue in the republic at large.

At the same time, Akaev deemed a strong hand and strong central government necessary for leading the republic through the reform period. Hence, he simultaneously began to strengthen the executive branch's control of the *oblast'*- and *raion*-level administrative and legislative institutions. He primarily did so by appointing his reformers from the center to newly created posts, while disempowering if not displacing individuals he considered to be old-school Party apparatchiks. His 1990 reorganization of the Kyrgyz SSR's Soviet of Ministers (the executive organ of the Kyrgyz Communist Party) into a new Cabinet of Ministers strengthened the executive apparatus's ability to carry out work at lower administrative levels of power and the state.[46] In effect, in these very early stages of his presidency, Akaev followed the path of Gorbachev: he relocated power from the Party to the government, and did so in the name of democratization and economic reform.

Shortly after Akaev's election, the DMK was registered first as a political organization and then as a political party (the DMKP) with a platform supporting democratic reform.[47] However, by 1991 the movement had already begun to splinter and decline, and it never regained the prominence it had in the spring and summer of 1990.

The Uzbek Movement

The formation of independent social organizations and a nascent civil and political society began somewhat earlier in the Uzbek Republic. Although, as in the Kyrgyz SSR, no mass social movements or demonstrations occurred on the scale of the events under way in Riga or Leningrad, the Uzbek "informals" were significantly affected by these same external models of protest. The first civic movement began with a similar thrust; it was anti-regime and

---

[45] *Vedomosti verkhovnogo soveta Kyrgyzstana*, 1991. This draft law was discussed in the Supreme Soviet in 1991.

[46] *Narodnyi Deputat*, no. 1 (1992), pp. 18–20. Cited in Malabaev, *Istoriia gosudarstvennosti*, p. 198.

[47] See *Ustav partii demokraticheskogo dvizheniia Kyrgyzstana* (PDDK), <http://www.ca c.org/datarus/pddk.shtml>.

pro-democratic. As the leaders of the informal group Birlik (Unity) would write in their founding document:

In our deciding move, we stood out in support of the collapse of the multigenerational world system of totalitarian socialism. The expression of politics of the new thinking (*novoe myshlenie*) has demanded its collapse, and which by giving to the people new freedoms, opened before them the possibility to define freedom for themselves. The Democratic Fronts of the countries of Eastern Europe and the Baltic republics, with the help of just elections and revolutionary movements, took power in their own hands and are moving to a truly historical, just path of development.[48]

Yet, like their contemporaries in the western republics of the USSR, both Birlik and the wider opposition in Uzbekistan initially assumed the form of a mixed nationalist and ecological movement. They very likely did so for similar reasons: the environment was a relatively safe area for public discussion, and nationalism was an ideology in many ways encouraged by the Soviet system; discussion of both was liberalized by glasnost'. General social dissatisfaction with the Uzbek regime had begun somewhat earlier than in the neighboring Kyrgyz and Tajik republics, in part because of the repression of the cotton scandal. By 1988, "informals" had begun discussing the deteriorating economy and ecological crises – especially the Aral Sea – resulting from Soviet exploitation of Uzbek natural resources. Such issues evolved into demands for a revival of the national culture, language, and identity. Birlik's leaders, the brothers Abdurahim and Abdumannob Pulat(ov),[49] sought to resurrect the "Uzbek nation" from Soviet colonialism and repression. Composed of individuals based in the Uzbek Academy of Sciences and Tashkent State University – that is, primarily the Uzbek intelligentsia – this "opposition" was neither an organization nor a potent social or political force. By early 1989 it was gaining attention, however. In the summer of 1989, the Uzbek authorities even sought Birlik leaders' assistance in calming the violence in the Ferghana Valley. Although primarily based in Tashkent, the Pulats claimed to have supporters there among both intellectuals and rural youth.[50]

Birlik's demonstrations may have weakened Nishanov, but they played no role in influencing the pact that had brought Karimov to power. Unlike Akaev, who had ties to the intelligentsia and the democratic movement, Karimov was a Party apparatchik with no ties to nationalist or democratic

---

[48] *Programma narodnogo dvizheniia Uzbekistana "Birlik,"* May 1989, in *Etnopoliticheskaia programma Uzbekistana* (Moscow: Panorama, 1991), p. 13.

[49] The Pulat(ov)s were academicians in the fields of mathematics and cybernetics from Tashkent State University (TashGU). Much of the mathematics and engineering faculty was involved in the opposition group. Author's conversation with an economist from TashGU who declined to participate in Birlik because they were "unrealistic, especially when they began demanding independence," Tashkent, April 1998.

[50] Author's interview with Abdurahim Pulat(ov), Washington, D.C., March 1998.

activists. As Communist Party first secretary of the Kashkadarya *oblast'* during the mid-1980s, he was little known to Uzbek intellectuals. In fact, Birlik members considered Nishanov closer to their views. In toadying to Gorbachev, Nishanov had introduced a limited glasnost' and had even initiated a dialogue with econationalist "informals" in late 1988.

On May 28, 1989, after its founding congress, Birlik became the first major sociopolitical movement and organization in Uzbekistan. As a people's movement, Birlik's goal was to advocate the moral, spiritual, and environmental defense of Uzbekistan. In the group's program, Birlik's leaders set forth their position on three burning sociopolitical issues: (1) ecological reform, (2) military reform, and (3) the adoption of an Uzbek language law.[51] Birlik's platform became a focal point for other "informals" and thus aided in centralizing and mobilizing the previously scattered opposition.

Several months after Karimov's rise to power in June of 1989, Birlik began to organize for the upcoming 1990 elections to the local and republic-level soviets.[52] Although they did not register as a political party or run opposition candidates, a limited number of nonparty "reformers" did compete and succeed in obtaining seats in the soviets. Initial support was not insubstantial. In March 1990, 5,000 Birlik members protested electoral fraud as well as the resettlement of Meskhetian Turks.[53] Ministry of Internal Affairs (MVD) troops fired on them. Outrage at the government crackdown briefly mobilized the organization, and members continued to meet throughout 1990, but support declined thereafter. Not long after the elections, a split emerged in the movement. One prominent leader, the Uzbek writer and poet Muhammad Salih, left Birlik. Salih had a strong following among students and intellectuals in Tashkent, as well as broader support from his regional base in Khorezm. Salih himself was elected to the Supreme Soviet of Uzbekistan and to the Congress of People's Deputies of the USSR, where he became allied with the liberal bloc. Ostensibly, the schism, as in Kyrgyzstan, was between the "radicals" (the Pulatov brothers), who increasingly demanded not only sovereignty but complete independence from the Soviet Union, and the "moderates" (Salih), who advocated reform of the system. Salih founded Erk Partiasi (the Erk Party), an independent social organization that carried Salih's social base with him. Erk members argue that Salih was no longer able to work with the "radical Pulatovs";[54] Birlik loyalists, however, claim that Salih was co-opted and corrupted by Karimov.[55] For both organizations,

---

[51] *Programma narodnogo dvizheniia Uzbekistana "Birlik,"* in *Etnopoliticheskaia programma,* p. 14–15.
[52] Author's interview with Abdurahim Pulat, Washington, D.C., March 1998. The brothers were exiled from Uzbekistan again in 1997, not long after the OSCE attempted to negotiate their return and recognition.
[53] Beissinger, *Nationalist Mobilization,* p. 354.
[54] Author's conversation with former Erk members, Khorezm, October 1997.
[55] Author's interview with Abdurahim Pulat, Washington, D.C., March 1998 and May 2004.

democratization was inextricably tied to nationalism, decolonization, and self-determination for Uzbeks; few non-Uzbeks were involved in either group.

One final social movement to emerge at this time, one that posed a threat to both the Karimov and Makhkamov regimes, was the Islamic Renaissance Party (IRP). Not unlike the Basmachis of the revolutionary period, the IRP drew on Islam as its legitimizing principle. Founded in June 1989 in Astrakhan, in the Tatar autonomous republic, as a social organization, the IRP soon began to operate branch organizations throughout the Caucasus and Central Asia. In particular, the IRP developed active ties in southern Uzbekistan, generally in the Ferghana Valley region, and in Tajikistan. Under Gorbachev, Islam was enjoying a limited cultural and spiritual revival, particularly within the Russian republic, where Tatarstan housed the Soviet-created formal Islamic structure, the Spiritual Directorate of Muslims for the Caucasus and Tatarstan. In Central Asia, Islam's development was primarily organized and regulated through the official religious channel of SADUM (the Central Asian Spiritual Directorate of Muslims), which was further divided into five republic *qaziyat*s (branches).[56] Two *madrassas* operated in the Uzbek Republic, but they carefully remained unconnected to politics or to social movements such as Birlik. Initially, the IRP was intimidated by officials, but it was not banned from operating in any of the Soviet republics. However, when attempting to register as a "social-political organization and party" (in the Tajik SSR in June 1990 and in the Uzbek SSR in January 1991), the IRP hit a wall of resistance.[57] Nabiev and Karimov both refused to allow the group legal recognition and began to crack down on the IRP's activities. In their view, even the cultural aspects of Islam posed a threat to the state. Karimov's response to the IRP was particularly harsh because its social base was the Ferghana Valley, a region partially excluded from the pact that had brought him to power, and consequently an area where he lacked support.[58] As early as 1990, Karimov began to stereotype the Ferghana Valley as the base of an "Islamic mafia."[59]

---

[56] Author's interview with *imam*, Tashkent Central Mosque, Spiritual Directorate of Muslims of Uzbekistan, Tashkent, Uzbekistan, October 18, 1997. After the dissolution of the Union, Karimov established an independent Uzbek *muftiat*.

[57] On the IRP, see Aleksandr Verkhovskii, *Srednaia Aziia i Kazakhstan: Politicheskii spektr* (Moskva: Panorama, 1992), pp. 67–68, 86–87.

[58] The IRP was suspected of operating from the Namangan and Andijan regions of the valley, the most conservatively Islamic areas of Uzbekistan or Central Asia.

[59] Karimov's response is not unlike the Russian "Orientalist" view of the Islamic world. Whether or not the Karimov regime genuinely feared Islam as a political force, it cleverly used the specter of Islamic fundamentalism to justify repression. The Uzbek government actively continued to support members of the Soviet-installed communist government of Afghanistan. Uzbekistan further played on the threat of Islam to win aid from the West. Author's interviews with former members of the Najibullah and Rabbanni regimes of Afghanistan, Tashkent, Uzbekistan, 1997 and 1998.

Karimov's Response: Co-opting the Nationalist Agenda

As noted earlier, Karimov's response involved increasing repression of the democratic, nationalist, and Islamist movements. However, he also began to co-opt the nationalist agenda as a means of defusing the opposition, enhancing his own legitimacy, and asserting limited autonomy from Moscow. Islam Karimov was actually the first of these leaders to do so, in an astute political maneuver, denying his earlier toeing of the party line. In fact, shortly after he was elected first secretary in 1989, in the wake of the ethnic outbreaks in the Ferghana Valley, Karimov recognized the need to defuse the "national question." Imposing a strong hand and relying on Soviet troops was one method; but Karimov had begun to recognize the popularity of the nationalist agenda put forward by Birlik. He was also forced to deal with a local environment in which his predecessor, Nishanov, had begun a dialogue with such groups, and with an all-Union context in which the Party's recognition of such demands was becoming the norm. Moreover, the central issues at hand were more threatening to Moscow's control of the Uzbek Republic than to his own. To the contrary, he knew that to appear to be a Moscow toady would unravel the network of support that had brought him to power. He had to act as a representative of the *vatan* (motherland). Karimov astutely recognized the greater payoff in becoming the people's champion. Rather than allowing the nationalist opposition to take credit for inevitable reforms, he supported a national language law in 1989, policies to advance cultural revival, and a "declaration of sovereignty" in June 1990. Yet Karimov initially rejected calls for full independence. He also categorically rejected Islamicization of the state. Both issues had already lost Birlik and the IRP much support. In doing so, Karimov astutely portrayed these groups as radical threats to national security.

As Moscow became immersed in its own chaotic political turmoil in 1990 and 1991, its control over the republics dwindled. Karimov manipulated the split in the opposition so as to weaken the movement. Shortly after independence, in October 1991, Birlik the movement transformed itself into Birlik the party, and the Ministry of Justice gave it legal registration in November 1991. Karimov's tactics became harsher as Birlik initiated preparations for the post-coup presidential elections. Many Birlik adherents were harassed or arrested, and others were exiled. The party was declared illegal. Only Erk, which was permitted to register as a political party on September 4, 1991, would compete in the founding presidential elections, the first to be based on a popular vote.

The Tajik Movement

It has become commonplace not only in the Russian and Western media, but even in academic scholarship, to characterize the Tajik opposition and social movements, as well as the ensuing civil war of 1992–97, in ideological terms – the democrats, Islamists, and nationalists versus the communists.[60] The opposition sought to portray itself as democratic, while the Tajik regime and its Moscow supporters painted the movement as fundamentalism, or at best ethnic separatism. In fact, the Tajik opposition emerged in much the same way as the opposition throughout Central Asia, according to the pattern of post-Soviet opposition movements generally.

The year 1989 saw the first real stirrings of informal social and political organizations in the Tajik Republic. The first began as a circle of intellectuals – artists, writers, and scientists, who, inspired by Gorbachev's call for national revival, sought greater cultural autonomy for the Tajik Republic. The "national renaissance," from which the Rastokhez Popular Front movement took its name, initially involved three components: (1) the adoption of Tajik as the official language of the republic; (2) the revival of "Tajik" culture; and (3) the relaxation of government restrictions on the practice of Islam.[61] The first of these demands merely echoed the central goal of other republican national fronts. The pursuit of a Tajik renaissance was likewise a manifestation of Soviet nationality policy's success in creating a titular intellectual class who believed in the naturalness of their ethno-national identity. In reality, the "Tajik" people were the product of Soviet borders.[62] The Tajik Republic was composed of multiple ethnic groups and Iranian and Turkic lineages. Although by 1989 some 64 percent of the population was legally registered as ethnic Tajik, they included various Persian-speaking and other peoples, the majority of whom did not share a strong identity of "Tajikness."[63]

Rastokhez was a classic illustration of an elite that sought to create what Benedict Anderson has called an "imagined community."[64] Like nationalist movements within the other republics, Rastokhez was not a rebirth or renaissance of a previously existing identity, but rather a belief in the titular group's "nationness" and right to ethno-national autonomy. Rastokhez was a misnomer in a second respect: as is common of newly "imagined" nationalist movements, Rastokhez was led by the intelligenstia, not by the *narod* (the people). It had little social backing apart from the intelligentsia of the two major urban centers, Leninabad and Dushanbe. Its leaders were

[60] See, for example, G. Shipit'ko, *Izvestiia*, June 5, 1990; and for a more nuanced but still "Orientalist" Russian view, see Aleksei Malashenko, "Religioznoe ekho etnopoliticheskikh konfliktov," *Svobodnaia Mysl'*, no. 17 (1994).

[61] Author's interview with the ORT journalist who covered Tajikistan and the civil conflict from 1990 through 1993, Tashkent, Uzbekistan, October 1997.

[62] See Muriel Atkin, "Tajiks and the Persian World," in Beatrice Manz, ed., *Central Asia in Historical Perspective* (Boulder, CO: Westview Press, 1994). Author's discussions with Tajik and Russian sociologists, Moscow, July 1998, reinforced this view.

[63] Shahram Akbarzadeh, "Why Did Nationalism Fail in Tajikistan?," *Europe-Asia Studies*, vol. 48, no. 7 (November 1996), pp. 1105–1129; and Barnett Rubin, "The Fragmentation of Tajikistan," *Survival*, vol. 35 (Winter 1993–94), p. 71.

[64] Benedict Anderson, *Imagined Communities* (London: Verso, 1991).

highly educated, avowedly "pro-Western" intellectuals.[65] Foremost among them was the filmmaker Davlat Khudonazar(ov), who was to become the opposition candidate in the first presidential election in November 1991.[66] Rastokhez further called for an end to the "clannish, tribal, and regional loyalties" that pervaded the Communist Party and political leadership.[67] Still, Rastokhez's leader supported the preservation of the Union.[68]

As had Birlik, within a year of its formation the Rastokhez front fractured. In August 1990, the Democratic Party of Tajikistan (DPT), under the leadership of Shodmon Yusuf, split off. Both factions eventually received permission to register as legal political organizations.[69] Both maintained a base among the intelligentsia, although the DPT and Yusuf had stronger ties with the Khodjenti elite. Makhkamov's regime infiltrated and co-opted the DPT. Abdumalik Abdullajonov – a Makhkamov ally and the leader of a clan faction in Khodjent – appropriated the DPT leadership and platform. The flexibility with which the former communist apparatchiks of Khodjent transformed themselves into leaders of the "democratic" front indicated the superficiality of the DPT's ideological platform.[70] Despite the vigor of the Tajik intellectuals who used the openness of this period to "resurrect" their ancient Persian and Sogdian roots, they had little social base.

The Islamic Renaissance Party (IRP) was the third and strongest element of the Tajik opposition to emerge publicly during the late perestroika period. The Islamist movement had greater social resonance in Tajikistan than in any other republic, and broader social appeal than the Tajik nationalist or democratic opposition. The IRP had emerged well before the registration of parties was permitted anywhere in the USSR. In fact, Mullah Sayyid Abdullo Nuri, the leader of the IRP, had been active in organizing an underground Islamist network from the 1970s onward. To a greater extent than elsewhere,

[65] Davlat Khudonazar, "The Conflict in Tajikistan: Questions of Regionalism," in Roald Z. Sagdeev and Susan Eisenhower, eds., *Central Asia: Conflict, Resolution, and Change* (Chevy Chase, MD: CPSS Press, 1995), p. 257.
[66] Khudonazarov changed his name to the Tajik form, Khudonazar, dropping the Russian suffix (ov). Shodmon Yusuf did the same. This practice became common among nationalists.
[67] Mavlon Makhkamov, "Islam and the Political Development of Tajikistan after 1985," in Hafeez Malik, ed., *Central Asia: Its Strategic Importance and Future Prospects* (New York: St. Martin's Press, 1994), p. 199.
[68] Muriel Atkin, "The Politics of Polarization in Tajikistan," in Malik, *Central Asia*, pp. 214–215.
[69] Permission was granted late in 1991 by the Ministry of Justice under Makhkamov's weakened regime. Makhkamov had turned over the ministry, generally considered one of lesser import, to a clan faction from Dushanbe in a half-hearted late attempt to include non-Khodjentis in the regime. The new minister was connected to Yusuf and quickly recognized the organization.
[70] Author's discussion with the sociologists M. Olimov and S. Olimova, "Sharq Center," Moscow, Russia, July 1998.

an unofficial Islamic clergy had survived in the Tajik Republic, especially in central Tajikistan.[71] Many scholars as well as government officials argue that the Tajik Republic – whether because of its Persian heritage, Iranian influence, sympathy with its ethnic kin in Afghanistan, or lower level of development than the other republics – remained more traditionally Islamic than other Central Asian regions.[72] The Soviets had failed to create a strong, secular Tajik national identity[73] – in fact, the Soviet regime had pitted Islam against "Tajikness," thereby allowing Islam – which historically had a strong social base, legitimacy, and network – to become the basis of an alternative social movement.

Although the IRP's agenda was similar in many ways to that of Rastokhez – both advocated a greater role for Islam in society and politics – the Islamist appeal was less elitist. Like Rastokhez and the DPT, the IRP advocated greater autonomy (but not secession) from the Soviet Union; moreover, the IRP advocated Islam in the Tajik Republic, not an all-Union or pan-Islamist agenda. In this respect, its demands were moderate, not radical or fundamentalist. Nonetheless, in early 1990 the Presidium of the Supreme Soviet of the Tajik Republic banned the IRP both from organizing activities and from registering as a political or social organization.

Two characteristics distinguished the IRP. First, it was recognized and supported by the official Muslim clergy of the Tajik SSR.[74] The overlap between the IRP and the official clergy was far more extensive than in the neighboring Uzbek Republic, where the *qaziyat*, as the center of SADUM, had been subject to greater Party supervision than elsewhere. Under the direction of SADUM's pro-establishment *mufti*, Muhammad Sodyq Muhammad Yusuf, the Tajik *qaziyat* nonetheless actively promoted the cultural and spiritual flourishing of Islam during the later perestroika years. By 1991, the *qaziyat* had opened more than ten *madrassas*, primarily in the central regions of the Tajik Republic. Yusuf supported the esteemed Muslim cleric Akbar Turajonzoda, who had been the "unofficial *qazi*" of Tajikistan since 1988, and who became the official *qazi* after 1993. Turajonzoda would become a significant player in supporting the IRP and in leading the "democratic-Islamic" opposition movement.[75]

---

[71] Author's interview with Mullah Sayyid Abdullo Nuri, Dushanbe, Tajikistan, August 2002.
[72] Teresa Rakowska-Harmstone, *Russia and Nationalism in Central Asia: The Case of Tadzhikistan* (Baltimore: Johns Hopkins University Press, 1970); and V. I. Bushkov and D. V. Mikul'skii, *Anatomiia grazhdanskoi voiny v Tajikistane* (Moscow: Institut Etnologii i Antropologii, RAN, 1997).
[73] Shahram Akbarzadeh, "Why Did Nationalism Fail?".
[74] Mark Saroyan, *Minorities, Mullahs and Modernity: Reshaping Community in the Former Soviet Union*, ed. Edward Walker (Berkeley: International and Area Studies, University of California, 1997).
[75] Saodat Olimova, "The Islamic Renaissance Party," *Central Asia and the Caucasus* (Winter 2001), <www.ca-c.org/dataeng/bd_eng.shtml>.

Second, in contrast to the other opposition groups, the Tajik IRP developed a rural network.[76] *Qazi* Turajonzoda's influence played a significant role in garnering the rural base. He himself was from a sacred lineage of influential Islamic leaders. His father and brothers were all associated with the *Rakhat* (Renaissance) mosque in Dushanbe.[77] Mullah Nuri also came from a sacred lineage, which had a more extensive rural network in one region of Garm.[78] He was not Russified. Nor was he well-educated in Islamic theology, but he had significant local legitimacy. Together with such socially active clerics and local leaders such as Davlat Usmon, the Turajonzoda-Nuri clique was the influential core of the IRP and eventually also of the religious wing of the opposition movement.[79] Other religious leaders included Mirbobbo Mirrahim and Jurabek Aminov, each of whom represented a particular local region and clan network. These figures were loosely united with religious leaders from Karategin, Garm, and Kurgan-Tyube. While overarching Islamist interests united them, sub-Islamic clan and village ties persisted among multiple distinct factions within the Islamic opposition.[80]

Despite its factionalized network, the *qaziyat*'s social influence was to become increasingly threatening to the regime. As of 1992, however, the presence of Islamic clerics in the IRP and its emphasis on Islamic mores had not led to the adoption of a fundamentalist agenda. *Qazi* Turajonzoda, who emerged as one of the most prominent leaders of the umbrella "Islamic" movement after independence, was still an advocate of moderate Islam, not of an Islamic state.[81] Even the IRP itself had called for a merging of Islamic values with a secular state, perhaps even under the Soviet state.[82] The IRP itself was not clear on how it envisioned an "Islamic state" and its concrete political goals.

Makhkamov's Response: Recognition or Repression?

Unlike either Akaev or Karimov, First Secretary Makhkamov responded to the various opposition actors in a mixed fashion, sometimes recognizing and acquiescing to their demands and sometimes repressing them. In an

[76] Author's interview with *imam* of mosque, Namangan, Uzbekistan, April 1998.
[77] On the "cultural capital" of sacred lineages in Central Asia, see Adeeb Khalid, *The Politics of Muslim Cultural Reform: Jadidism in Central Asia* (Berkeley: University of California Press, 1998), pp. 5–6.
[78] Author's interview with Muhiddin Kabiri, deputy leader of the IRP, Dushanbe, March 2001.
[79] See Davlat Khudonazar, "The Conflict in Tajikistan: Questions of Regionalism," in Roald Sagdeev and Susan Elsenhower, eds., *Central Asia: Conflict, Resolution and Change* (Chevy Chase, MD: CPSS Press, 1995), p. 257, for an extensive discussion of the clan basis of politics in Tajikistan. Khudonazar himself derived his support from his Pamiri clan, as well as from a small circle of intellectuals.
[80] Khudonazar, "Regionalism."
[81] In fact, Turajonzoda became an actual member of the IRP only in 1997.
[82] Author's interview with Kabiri, Dushanbe, March 2001.

attempt to co-opt the Islamist and nationalist agendas, Makhkamov had originally allowed the revival of many cultural and religious aspects of Islam, as part of the revival of "the Tajik identity" and the "Tajik nation." In 1989, Makhkamov permitted the Tajik *qaziyat* to open the first *madrassa* in Dushanbe,[83] and organized the purchase of Arabic editions of the Koran from Saudi Arabia, ending a nearly seventy-year ban.[84] He supported the "law on language," and on July 22, 1989, the Tajik Supreme Soviet made Tajik the official language of the republic.

At the same time, the Communist Party of Tajikistan publicly blamed the IRP for instigating the February 1990 student riots in Dushanbe – riots over rising bread prices, not over Islamic values or support for the IRP. Makhkamov further accused Rastokhez, the IRP, and the DPT of inciting "religious fundamentalism" and "criminal elements."[85] As in Tashkent, Ferghana, and Osh, Soviet troops were called into Dushanbe to put down the protests and disperse the rioters. Yet, unlike Nishanov and Masaliev, Makhkamov was never removed. On the one hand, he felt secure in Moscow's backing and in Khodjenti hegemony; on the other hand, both he and the communist-dominated Supreme Soviet did feel a need to appease the opposition. They adopted a "law on sovereignty" on August 24, 1990. On December 8, 1990, the Tajik government adopted the draft "law on freedom to gather in religious organizations," and on December 12, 1990, it accepted the "law on social organizations in Tajikistan."[86]

Makhkamov's wavering, however, lost the support of the hard-liners in the Tajik government and the Khodjenti elite. Former first secretary Nabiev and his Khodjenti faction positioned themselves to retake control. The roots of instability thus remained. Furthermore, the regime's policies counterproductively promoted the fusion of democratic, nationalist, and Islamist elements of the opposition.[87] Prior to 1991, these nascent groups had remained fragmented and incapable of driving regime change. The Soviet collapse and the regime crisis that ensued, however, would give them the opportunity to play a greater role.

By the end of 1990, Birlik was demanding full independence for Uzbekistan; Birlik's hard-line position had instigated regime repression, not

---

[83] During the Soviet period, most *madrassas* in Central Asia had been closed, with the exception of the two "official" *madrassas*, one in Bukhara and one in Tashkent – both in the Uzbek SSR.

[84] Bushkov and Mikul'skii, *Anatomiia grazhdanskoi*, p. 105. In a sign of the value it placed on the traditional Qur'an, the *qaziyat* paid the substantial sum of 218,000 rubles (1989 currency) for the books.

[85] Author's interview with K. Mukhkmanov, first secretary, Embassy of Tajikistan in Uzbekistan, Tashkent, Uzbekistan, April 21, 1998.

[86] Bushkov and Mikul'skii, *Anatomiia grazhdanskoi*, p. 53.

[87] A similar pattern of Islamic resistance and government repression has been seen in Algeria and Egypt, and more recently in Indonesia and Turkey.

broader social support. The Kyrgyz and Tajik nationalist groups were not so radical. They primarily directed their demands at the republic-level regime, not at Moscow. Yet once the nationalists had achieved their primary goal – making the titular language the official state language – they lost both their internal cohesion and their popular following. Hence, by late 1991, when the Central Asian republics were abruptly confronted with independence and the need to establish a modicum of legitimacy, the "opposition" would be poised to play only a marginal role in the transitional elections and post-Soviet trajectories.

II. CHANGE FROM ABOVE: FORCED DECOLONIZATION AND INDEPENDENCE

The Union Treaty and the August Coup

In contrast to the failure of the movements from below, change from above – from the very center of Soviet politics – was to have an enormous impact on the Central Asian regimes, and particularly on the perceptions of Central Asian elites about their strategic interests and options. Their possible choices were changing as quickly as the Soviet core.

In early March 1991, Gorbachev presented a draft of the Union Treaty to the fifteen union republics for comment. On March 17, he put the treaty to a vote by popular referendum. The results, published on March 21, unambiguously showed that the Central Asian republics were those most in favor of accepting the treaty and preserving the Union. Although one cannot dismiss the possibility that the vote was falsified, the difference between the Central Asian region (including Azerbaijan) and the other regions of the Union was striking. The Baltics, Georgia, and Armenia – who rejected the referendum – each had far stronger nationalist movements, based on pre-Soviet national identities. Central Asian elites, including a part of the intelligentsia as well as most Communist apparatchiki, supported the treaty. Some understood that membership in the Soviet Union was in their economic interest. Soviet subsidization of budgets was so great that it was not always clear whether Russia exploited them, or they Russia (see Table 5.1).

Others saw their identity as bound to Russia. Soviet-educated and culturally Russified in many respects, this elite class had integrated its traditional norms with a lifestyle more akin to that of the Moscow intelligentsia than to that of rural Central Asia. In mid-1991, Akaev, despite his initial reservations about the Union Treaty, unequivocally stated: "... our forefathers reached a firm decision: that the fate of the Kyrgyz people would only be successful politically, economically, and in all other ways under the wing of Russia, or in union with Russia ... so we have adopted a constructive attitude towards the treaty."[88] Furthermore, independence was not an issue of contention for

[88] Melis Eshimkanov, *Askar Akaev, Chelovek bez serediny* (Bishkek: Kyrgyzstan, 1995), p. 77.

TABLE 5.1. *Budget transfers and inter-republic trade levels of the Central Asian republics*

Soviet Republic	Budget Transfer from the Union as Percent of Total Republic Revenue Estimate (1991)	Inter-republic Trade Deficit (or Surplus) as Percent of Inter-republic Trade at World Prices (1990)
Kazakh SSR	23.1%	26.5%
Kyrgyz SSR	35.6%	19.7%
Tajik SSR	46.6%	30.5%
Turkmen SSR	21.7%	5.4%
Uzbek SSR	42.9%	22.9%

Note: By comparison, the Slavic republics received few subsidies. Moldova and the Baltic republics, at the low end, received no transfers, while the Belorussian Republic, at the high end, received 16.3 percent of its budget in subsidies. The inter-republic trade deficit of the Central Asian states likewise exhibited the highest regional deficit of the Soviet sphere. Elsewhere, the deficit ranged from 3.6 percent in the Belorussian Republic to 29 percent, at the highest level, in Moldova.

Source: Barnett Rubin, "Tajikistan from Soviet Republic to Uzbek Protectorate," in Michael Mandelbaum, *Central Asia and the World* (New York: Council on Foreign Relations, 1994), p. 209. Source is World Bank, *Statistical Handbook, States of the Former USSR, 1992* (Washington, DC: World Bank, 1992).

most ordinary Central Asians, who were proud to be part of the Soviet state. The referendum clearly reflected these material interests, rather than the ethnic or national demands of the various entrepreneurs advocating separatism, much less pan-Turkism or pan-Islamism. The referendum results (Table 5.2) suggest the inordinate shock that the events of the upcoming fall were to present for every level of Central Asian politics and society. The referendum was a harbinger of the difficulty the new Central Asian states would have in instilling their citizens with new civic "national" identities. Nearly a decade later, many Central Asians still regretted that they had lost their Soviet citizenship. They continued to refer to themselves as "*Soiuzniki*" (literally, Unionists, or people of the Union), not as Uzbekistani, Kyrgyzstani, or Tajikistani.[89]

The "9 + 1 Agreement" between Gorbachev and the leaders of nine union republics, which resulted from a meeting on April 23 at the Novo-Ogarevo estate, was an agreement by those participating to keep working toward a revised Union Treaty. However, the event also forced Gorbachev to recognize that the republics that were not participating could "decide their own fates, thereby sanctioning the partial breakup of the USSR."[90] A draft Union Treaty

[89] Author's interview with Uzbek sociologists who conducted a government survey on national identity in Uzbekistan, Tashkent, Uzbekistan, June, 1998. According to the sociologists, the majority of the population preferred the Soviet system and lived better under the Soviet Union. Unsurprisingly, the results of the survey were not published.

[90] Beissinger, *Nationalist Mobilization*, p. 422.

TABLE 5.2. *Results of the referendum on the Union Treaty (March 17, 1991)*

Republics Passing the Referendum	For	Against
Azerbaijan	93.3%	5.8%
Belarus	82.7%	16.1%
Georgia (only Abkhazia)	98.6%	0.9%
Kazakhstan	94.1%	5.0%
Kyrgyzstan	94.6%	4.0%
Russia	71.3%	26.4%
Tajikistan	96.2%	3.1%
Turkmenistan	97.9%	1.7%
Ukraine	70.2%	28.0%
Uzbekistan	93.7%	5.2%
(Karakalpakia)	97.6%	1.8%
Republics Rejecting the Referendum	**For**	**Against**[a]
Armenia	1%	99%
Estonia	10%	90%
Latvia	25%	75%

[a] Percentages appear to have been rounded.

Note: Armenia, Estonia, Latvia, and Lithuania boycotted the elections, but some, particularly Russians, voted anyway.

Source: Doklad komiteta po referendumu, March 25, 1991 (unpublished document of the Ministry of Foreign Affairs, Kyrgyzstan), and *Pravda*, March 21, 1991. For a discussion of the results throughout the Soviet Union, and observers' comments, see "Referendum of the Soviet Union: A Compendium of Reports on the March 17, 1991 Referendum on the Future of the USSR" (Washington, DC: CSCE, April 1991).

was prepared over the summer of 1991, and five republics (the Russian, Kazakh, Uzbek, Tajik, and Belorussian republics) were scheduled to sign it on August 20. The Azeri, Turkmen, Kyrgyz, and (possibly) Ukranian republics were to sign at a later date.[91] Although most Central Asian leaders (except Akaev, who was not a Party member) were seen as hard-line communists, they supported Gorbachev's endeavor and did not boycott the negotiations, as did their more nationalist and liberalizing neighbors. Elsewhere, especially in Moscow, the process produced a widening gulf between soft-line and hard-line ideologues. The latter group saw the treaty as irreparably compromising the Party and the state, while the liberals, led by Yeltsin, expressed the view that the treaty did not go far enough in decentralizing power. Yeltsin might have backed out of the agreement if Ukraine had refused to sign,[92] in effect leaving the Soviet Union with only the Belorussian republic and Central

[91] Ibid.
[92] McFaul, *Unfinished Revolution.*

Asia. Still, Gorbachev's shrinking camp pushed for the treaty as essential to reforming the Party and retaining at least a rump Union.

This polarization culminated in the cataclysmic coup of August 19, 1991, in which a clique of putschists seized control of the state. Led by KGB chief Vladimir Kriuchkov, the hard-line communists formed the GKChP (State Emergency Committee), invoked a national state of emergency, placed President Mikhail Gorbachev under house arrest, and declared the Union Treaty defunct.[93] The Central Asian leaders' reactions to the coup reflect less their support for preserving communism, than their economic pragmatism, the weakness of nationalism, and their lack of preparation for independence.

Kyrgyzstan: Defying the Coup

In the Kyrgyz SSR, the reaction to the coup was strikingly different than in the rest of Central Asia, and was characterized by Akaev's personal relationship with Gorbachev and the reformers in Moscow. According to both Akaev's supporters and various opposition figures, the news of the coup was received in Bishkek with grave concern.[94] Although Akaev and the Kyrgyz elite had never supported the dissolution of the Union, Akaev, alone of the Central Asian leaders, was personally committed to the goals of perestroika, to democratizing and reforming the Soviet system. Rather than maintain silence or support the coup, Akaev almost immediately spoke out on public radio, signaling to the public his loyalty to Gorbachev and the law. Following his lead, the local newspapers carried the story with headlines that would be unacceptable anywhere else in the Soviet Union. "Mikhail Gorbachev has been ousted from the post of President. A State of Emergency has been proclaimed. What does all this mean? A Military coup?" wrote the major republican newspaper, *Vechernii Frunze*, on August 19, 1991.[95] Speaking before the Supreme Soviet of the Kyrgyz Republic, Akaev pledged support for Gorbachev as an elected leader, for the Constitutional law and order of the Soviet Union, and for the Constitution and integrity of the Kyrgyz Republic.[96] He stated:

In view of the above, (the decree of the putschists) I, as President of the Republic of Kyrgyzstan, elected in accord with the Fundamental Law (the Constitution) of the Republic of Kyrgyzstan and acting on the basis of the Declaration of State Sovereignty,

[93] Other key GKChP members were Vice President Gennady Yanaev, MVD chief Boris Pugo, Prime Minister Valentin Pavlov, Minister of Defense Dmitry Yazov, and the chair of the Defense Committee, O. Baklanov. On the putsch, see *Ukaz Vitse-prezidenta SSSR* (August 18, 1991), in Eshimkanov and Imanaliev, eds. (1995), pp. 36–37.

[94] The Russian name of the Kyrgyz Republic's capital, Frunze, was changed to Bishkek by Kyrgyz law in early 1991.

[95] *Vechernii Frunze*, August 19, 1991, p. 1.

[96] *Vedomosti verkhovnogo soveta*, August 19, 1991, cited in Eshimkanov et al., *Askar Akaev*, p. 41.

appeal to the people of Kyrgyzstan with words imbued with anxiety, alarm, and simultaneously with hope for the triumph of wisdom and democracy....

....As the Head of State, I will do everything possible to defend the state sovereignty of the Republic, to preserve social law and order.

I call the people of Kyrgyzstan to maintain during these difficult times tranquility, reason, and wisdom, unity and solidarity, and respect towards the Constitution of and Laws of the USSR and the Republic of Kyrgyzstan.[97]

Akaev emphasized the Fundamental Law of the Kyrgyz Republic, before that of the USSR. Hence, he received a telephone call on August 20 from General Kriuchkov, commander of the central USSR KGB and a key figure of the putsch emergency committee. Kriuchkov demanded assent. He threatened Akaev with an invasion by Soviet troops or special security forces, and notified him that the Turkestan battalion based in Tashkent was on alert. General Fuzhenko, commander of the battalion, called Akaev himself to intimidate him.[98]

Akaev responded over the subsequent two days by enacting several critical measures, as would Karimov, to strengthen his executive power and correspondingly to decrease the power of the Party, the leadership of which he did not trust.[99] The first secretary of the Kyrgyz Communist Party, Jumagalbek Amanbaev, and the apparatchiks who had no power base outside of the party supported the coup and planned to remove Akaev. In a Party document of August 19, 1991, Amanbaev urged "complete and comprehensive support to the State Committee on the State of Emergency and all its activities."[100] Yet, as Amanbaev's deputy Arzymat Sulaimankulov stated, the Party's crisis was not about ideology, but about the loss of resources. In his view, the Party apparatus supported the coup because it was necessary "to get back the power to rule, to appoint, and to distribute."[101]

Akaev countered the Party's attempt to return to power by going before the government and legislature and declaring that an anti-constitutional coup d'état had taken place on August 19. He professed unity with President Boris Yeltsin of the Russian Republic, and later with President Nursultan Nazarbaev of the Kazakh SSR, both of whom had taken a stand against the coup by August 21.[102] Most critically, during this time Akaev rapidly secured control over the security forces in a "Decree on Urgent Measures to Protect the Sovereignty and Security of the Republic of

---

97 *Deklaratsiia prezidenta respubliki Kyrgyzii* (August 19, 1991), in Eshimkanov et al., *Askar Akaev*, p. 38.

98 "President Akaev's Anticoup Actions Reported," *Komsomolskaia Pravda*, August 23, 1991, p. 1, in FBIS-SOV-91-166, August 27, 1991.

99 Author's interview with Askar Aitmatov, Bishkek, June 1998.

100 Document of the Bureau of the Central Committee of the Communist Party of Kyrgyzstan, cited in Eshimkanov et al., *Askar Akaev*, p. 45.

101 *Vedomosti verkhovnogo soveta*, August 1991, cited in ibid., p. 45.

102 *Deklaratsiia prezidenta*, cited in ibid., p. 38.

Kyrgyzstan." He seized the opportunity to remove the commander of the republican division of the KGB, General Jumabek Asankulov, whom he suspected of being a toady of Moscow conservatives and loyal to the coup plotters. Asankulov was replaced with a local Russian of Akaev's cadre.[103] While decreasing the power of the KGB, Akaev elevated the Ministry of Internal Affairs (MVD). The latter organization had been under one of his major clan supporters, Feliks Kulov, since fall 1990. On August 20, Feliks Kulov's specialized militia troops occupied the Government House in order to defend it in case of possible attack.[104] Meanwhile, Akaev had already secured control of the republic's branches of the armed forces, which had traditionally been run from the north of the country. The military commissar of the Republic, Colonel Karabanov, declared that the republic military would be loyal to the Constitution of Kyrgyzstan. The commander of special troops (in Frunze), Lieutenant Colonel Anarbek Shamkeyev, also professed loyalty to the president. On the evening of August 20, following Kriuchkov's threat, Akaev deployed the special forces to guard arms warehouses in Frunze, the most likely targets of an attack by the Soviet OMON (special forces). When Akaev informed Kriuchkov of these measures, the latter, by that time probably realizing his impotence, did not challenge the Kyrgyz leader.

Fortunately for Akaev, as for the other Central Asian leaders, General Fuzhenko did not comply with the putschists' order to occupy the Central Asian capitals. The regiment in Ryazan had received word from the putschists to occupy Bishkek, but it similarly failed to comply.[105] Given that the battalion's commanders were predominantly Russian, it seemed likely that their loyalty would lie with Moscow, not Central Asia.[106] However, they were probably aware of the army's hesitation in Moscow, and that general confusion in the chain of command inhibited the implementation of orders.[107] Instead, Akaev stood unchallenged; within two days the putsch had been reversed, and Akaev's legitimacy within the Kyrgyz Republic – amongst most clan, regional, and civil society groups – had been significantly enhanced.

---

[103] Ibid., p. 46. Party Secretary Aitbaev also resigned.

[104] Eshimkanov gives an insider account of the coup, hour by hour, in *Askar Akaev*, p. 48.

[105] Voice of America, Bishkek, Kyrgyzstan, August 21, 1991.

[106] Interview with U.S. military attaché, U.S. embassy, Bishkek, June 1998. He had received this information from a retired high-ranking Kyrgyz military officer.

[107] See William Odom, *The Collapse of the Soviet Military* (New Haven, CT: Yale University Press, 1998), pp. 317–319, on the military's role during the coup. While the lack of compliance by military commanders seems difficult to explain, it is certainly in line with a similar situation within the Russian Federation and throughout the USSR during the days of the coup. As William Odom notes in an extensive discussion of the coup from the Russian end, according to General Lebed the GKChP had ample resources to carry out a successful coup; yet the lack of coordination and the uncertainty in the chain of command of the MVD, MO, and KGB ultimately led to lack of compliance by lower-level commanders.

By August 27, Akaev had initiated criminal proceedings against Amanbaev and the Central Committee members who had abetted the coup.[108]
Akaev also rapidly began to "de-partyize" the MVD, the KGB, and the
Ministry of Justice.[109] He replaced both ethnic Russian and Kyrgyz coup
backers.[110] In doing so, he quickly centralized control of the armed forces
and decapitated the Party.

Uzbekistan: Supporting the Coup

Although Uzbekistan was later to become the most fiercely independent of
the former Soviet republics of Central Asia, initially the Uzbek leadership
was extremely hostile to independence. Islam Karimov, his apparat, and the
Communist Party of the Uzbek Republic were united in their opposition
to the Union Treaty. Hence, on August 20, 1991, after a day of silence,
Karimov, like Nishanov and Makhkamov, backed the putschists and their
agenda. Little is known about the internal decision-making process in the
Uzbek Republic during the coup, particularly since Karimov's original stance
ultimately turned out to be politically inept and this period of Uzbek history
has since been officially rewritten. The Tashkent-based Turkestan Battalion
had no reason to unseat Karimov, since, unlike Akaev, he had not defied
the orders of Kriuchkov. Instead, Karimov took advantage of the coup's uncertainty to consolidate his regime. He shifted power from the soviets to
the executive, and from the Russian-dominated army and KGB to the special presidential security forces and the local Uzbek Committee for Defense,
which he had created in early 1991.

Only after Karimov realized that the coup was to fail did he retract his
position. He resigned from the Communist Party of the Soviet Union (CPSU)
Central Committee Politburo and suggested that the preservation of the
Soviet Union, at least in its present form, was not in the interest of the Uzbek
Republic.[111] After standing against Gorbachev, Yeltsin, and the now victorious democratic opposition, Karimov had clearly compromised his position
within the Union. Nonetheless, in the wake of the coup, Karimov quickly
asserted control over the Soviet military forces on the territory of the Uzbek
SSR, placing them under General Rustam Akhmedov, the chair of the Defense
Committee and the only high-ranking Uzbek officer.[112] Karimov adeptly used
the coup, both while he was initially supporting it and later when he was condemning it, as a pretext for further crushing of the opposition. The prevailing

[108] "President Akaev's Anticoup Actions Reported," FBIS, August 27, 1991.
[109] Ibid.
[110] "Resolutions, Charges, Dismissals, Following Coup," *INTERFAX*, August 23, 1991, in
FBIS-SOV-91-167, August 28, 1991.
[111] "President Resigns from CPSU Politburo," *Izvestiia*, August 26, 1991, p. 4, in FBIS-SOV-
91-166, August 27, 1991.
[112] By early 1992, this body would become the Uzbek Ministry of Defense.

view of many high-ranking Uzbek officials is that their primary concern during late 1991 and early 1992 was holding the republic together. Elements of the pact of 1989 still seemed uncertain. Hence, Karimov unleashed a campaign to convince the majority of the population that in order to prevent state breakdown, a "strong hand" – far stronger than that of Gorbachev or even the GKChP – was necessary. The putsch thus triggered a crackdown that would become more intense as chaos in neighboring Tajikistan escalated.[113]

Tajikistan: Denying the Coup

The ruling Tajik elite, the Khodjenti clan, likewise supported maintaining the status quo and the clan's privileged place vis-à-vis Moscow. Hence, in concert with Karimov and Turkmen President Saparmurat Niyazov, the president of the Tajik SSR initially remained silent at the news, while indicating his tacit support.[114] When it appeared that the putschists had indeed taken control, Makhkamov vocally backed the GKChP. Although Gorbachev had put Makhkamov in power in 1985, his clan-based regime had for decades been tied to and patronized by the Soviet KGB apparatus. Owing his position to them, Makhkamov acceded to the pressure applied by the GKChP. Furthermore, the 201st Motor Rifle Division of the Soviet Army was stationed in Dushanbe, and it was unclear where its loyalty would lie.[115]

Indeed, the Tajik regime had few options. Unlike Karimov and Akaev, the Tajik leadership could not hope for widespread popular support, since the Khodjenti clans had long excluded those who did not belong to their network, or had kept them in a dependent and clientlike position. They did, however, assume that they could count on the continued support of the Kulyabi clan, which had long been called their "little brothers." The economic and political prizes not absorbed by Leninabad went to the Kulyabi clans, which filled many secondary bureaucratic posts in Dushanbe.[116]

---

[113] Both had left the government in order to avoid conflict with Karimov, but both supported Karimov's strategy for keeping order and stability. Author's conversations with a former government official and former journalist in Uzbek television and radio, Tashkent, Summer 1997.

[114] Author's conversation with ORT journalist who covered the coup period in Dushanbe, Tashkent, Uzbekistan, August 1997.

[115] The 201st Motor Rifle Division would later play an active role in supporting the Rakhmonov regime, probably because the Russian KGB encouraged it to do so. Largely controlled by Russian commanders, but staffed by Tajik troops, the unit was a wild card; it was actively engaged in drug trafficking and arms trafficking, activities that only prolonged the conflict. Author's interviews with a UN representative for drug control, U.S. embassy personnel in Tajikistan, and Uzbek businessmen who frequently traveled to Dushanbe, 1997, 1998.

[116] Author's interview with Tajik expatriates of the Leninabad region and interviews with members of the Tajik Ministry of Foreign Affairs, who were Kulyabis, Tashkent, Uzbekistan, May 1998. They discussed their long resentment against Khodjent's domination.

Makhkamov thus advocated the preservation of the Soviet Union, and he continued to do so even after the coup had failed and his Central Asian counterparts had accepted their fate and declared independence.

As events would soon reveal, however, not only was this stance unrealistic, it was fatal to the regime. Makhkamov's position led to a tense standoff between "the opposition" and the Khodjenti network over the fate of the Tajik Communist Party. In a major show of strength, the DPT and Rastokhez mobilized thousands outside the parliament in Dushanbe and demanded First Secretary/President Makhkamov's resignation and the dissolution of the Tajik Communist Party. The Tajik *Qazi* Turajonzoda likewise called for regime change. Even the hard-line Tajik party members began to demand Makhkamov's resignation, blaming his weakness for the chaos.

On September 7, two weeks after the coup, the opposition forced Makhkamov to step down. In his place, acting President Kadriddin Aslonov (Supreme Soviet chairman), a rival clan and regional leader, belatedly declared independence, resigned from the CPSU, banned the Tajik Communist Party, and announced that the first popular presidential elections would be held in November 1991.[117] Aslonov's moves represented the interests of both the democratic opposition and the Garmi and Pamiri clan networks, who opposed Khodjenti/communist control.

The Khodjentis, however, did not retreat from power. They initiated an almost immediate restructuring at the center. Like Karimov and Akaev, they also sought to demote the Communist Party and the legislature, which were stacked with a handful of ideologues and many client or competing clans. On September 23, the Khodjenti leader and former first secretary Rakhmon Nabiev, who had emerged as head of the Supreme Soviet, took power under a state of emergency. The coup brought the Khodjenti faction back into power, claiming to restore order. Nabiev did support independence and the call for new elections, in order to gain legitimacy. In fact, however, the Khodjentis had no intention of ceding power to the competing clan factions, who were invigorated by the collapse of the Party's power. The November 24 elections, which Nabiev's faction probably rigged, still gave Nabiev only 58 percent of the vote. His main opponent, the Rastokhez leader Khudonazar, garnered only 30 percent, and other candidates of the fragmented opposition won even less.[118]

Thus, in the Tajik Republic, the coup culminated in interclan competition, the mobilization of the democratic-nationalist opposition against the communist apparatchiks, and an invigorated Islamist opposition. Regime destabilization quickly ensued.

---

[117] "Decree Banning Communist Party," Dushanbe radio, September 22, 1991, in FBIS-SOV-91-185, September 24, 1991.

[118] Atkin, "Tajiks," p. 218.

De Facto Decolonization: The Alma-Ata Summit

The failed coup sowed confusion not only in Moscow, but in the republics as well. Those who had supported the putschists suddenly abandoned their positions, declaring the coup invalid and illegal; but since leadership in Moscow was unclear, they seemed unsure of whom to support. Boris Yeltsin, not Mikhail Gorbachev, appeared to be the new figure of strength. Yeltsin, rather than Gorbachev, had seized the initiative during and after the coup, standing with the *narod* (the people) on a tank before the Kremlin, calling for full democracy, and demanding the granting of all power and sovereignty to the republics – words that would haunt him in years to come.[119] Just as Gorbachev's call for "power to the soviets" had resonated throughout the Union, so too did Yeltsin's words. The Baltics declared independence within days of the coup, and most other republics quickly followed their example. Ukraine's key decision to secede came on August 24. The Central Asian republics, long opposed to full independence, were the laggards. Yet they too opted not to be left in the defunct Union, under the rubble of a collapsed empire. On August 30, 1991, Islam Karimov followed suit, almost denying that the Uzbek Republic had ever supported the preservation of the Union. On August 31, at Akaev's urging, the Kyrgyz Supreme Soviet declared Kyrgyzstan independent.[120] Tajikistan waited several weeks, issuing its declaration of independence on September 8, 1991. Turkmenistan followed only on October 28, 1991, after holding its own referendum on independence. Kazakhstan was the last to officially declare itself independent of the Union. Nonetheless, as Beissinger observes, "it was obvious by mid-September that the Soviet government had become little more than a legal fiction."[121]

Despite the revisionist version of this history promoted during the subsequent process of state building, the Central Asian republics did *not* voluntarily choose to leave the Soviet Union. Even after their independence declarations, they were still hanging on to varying degrees. Although Askar Akaev rapidly moved to ban the Communist Party of Kyrgyzstan, and others dissolved or renamed Communist Party structures, they were still not proactive separatists. Noting that the fate of the Central Asian republics depended on "the three Slavic republics, Russia, Ukraine, and Belarussia,"

---

[119] Yeltsin's initial support for such decentralization of power, both within the Union and within the Russian Federation, fostered the breakup of the USSR as well as the seizure of power by certain republics (e.g., Chechnya and Tatarstan). Yeltsin was charged by the Duma with destroying the USSR and causing the war in Chechnya, and was almost impeached in June 1999.

[120] "Declaration of State Independence," *Vedomosti verkhovnogo soveta Kyrgyzskoi respubliki*, August 31, 1991.

[121] Beissinger, *Nationalist Mobilization*, p. 430.

Akaev still pursued a revised Union Treaty,[122] but one with increased guarantees of the rights of ethnic minorities.[123] Nazarbaev, meanwhile, sought to join a new union of the core Slavic states.

The dramatic decision of the Central Asian states to abandon the Soviet Union ultimately came several months after their de facto independence. They were forced into independence because the Union no longer existed, and its center, the Russian Republic, no longer cared to be burdened with subsidizing its southern tier. The Belovezhskoe Forest meeting of December 8, 1991 led to the final dissolution of the USSR and the creation of a new entity, the Commonwealth of Independent States (CIS). The agreement was signed by the leaders of Russia, Ukraine, and Belarus.[124] President Nazarbaev of Kazakhstan was later invited to join them, but refused. Belovezhskoe ultimately forced upon Central Asians the realization that their independence was a fait accompli. A few weeks later, on December 21, 1991, the leaders of the newly independent Central Asian republics, Belarus, Armenia, Azerbaijan, Moldova, and Russia met in Alma-Ata, now the capital of Kazakhstan, to reaffirm the Belovezhskoe decision.[125] Their agreement was the last step in the burial of the Soviet Union. In a somewhat ironic but nonetheless dramatic declaration four days later, on December 25, 1991, Mikhail S. Gorbachev resigned from both the presidency and the general secretaryship of the CPSU of the Union of Soviet Socialist Republics, now a nonexistent state. Central Asia's decolonization, after more than a century of Russian and Soviet rule, was sudden and decisive.

SUMMARY

While the "informals," the democratic proto-parties, and the nationalist and Islamist movements that emerged during this period could be considered a nascent civil society, ultimately they remained within narrow intellectual circles; they would never become mass social movements that would drive transitions from colonialism and authoritarianism to independent nation-states or democracy, much less to political Islam.[126] Mass social movements had swept across Eastern Europe, the Baltics, Russia, and even parts of the

---

[122] *Programnaia rech' prezidenta Kyrgyzstana Askar Akaeva*, Government House, Bishkek, Kyrgyzstan, December 1991, in Eshimbaev et al., *Askar Akaev*, p. 57.

[123] Ibid., pp. 123, 125.

[124] Stanislau Shushkevich, Boris Yeltsin, and Leonid Kravchuk, "Agreement on the Creation of a Commonwealth of Independent States," December 8, 1991, reprinted in Alexander Dallin and Gail Lapidus, eds., *The Soviet System: From Crisis to Collapse*, rev. ed. (Boulder, CO: Westview Press, 1995), pp. 638–641.

[125] For greater detail, see Beissinger, *Nationalist Mobilization*, p. 440.

[126] See Akbarzadeh, "Why Did Nationalism Fail?"; and A. Khazanov, "Underdevelopment and Ethnic Relations in Central Asia," in Beatrice Manz, ed., *Central Asia in Historical Perspective*, (Boulder, CO: Westview Press, 1994), pp. 154–155.

Caucasus. Yet, as Beissinger has aptly observed, "meanwhile Central Asia slept."[127]

Explaining the *absence* of popular support is always difficult, and several factors were clearly important. Regime repression and co-optation, especially in the Uzbek case, is one explanation. Yet in other republics, state elites tried both co-optation and repression with far less success. In fact, repression may have generated a backlash and invigorated social opposition in other republics.[128] Focusing on the state provides only a partial explanation. A fuller explanation must take into account the social characteristics that distinguished the five Central Asian republics (and, in part, Azerbaijan), where nationalist, separatist, and other social movements failed or never even materialized, from those republics where nationalism became a salient and unifying force. Even in the Kyrgyz Republic, where the Akaev regime had sought to accommodate and foster civil society, the democratic movement had little resonance with the bulk of the population, which was rural, poor, and little concerned with the politics of democratization or nationalism. The lack of widespread nationalism (of either a civic or ethnic variety), despite Soviet affirmative action politics, reflected the relatively recent creation of these nations, in contrast to other republics such as Georgia or Armenia, where distinct national languages, literatures, and cultures had existed centuries before the Soviet conquest.[129] The Baltic and Eastern European cases, meanwhile, had a history of independent statehood in the twentieth century. Weak nationalism in Central Asia also reflected the continued strength of subnational clan identities and broader patronage networks, which Soviet nationalities policy, as Chapter 3 demonstrated, had ironically preserved.[130] Finally, limited support for Islamist alternatives in the Tajik case further fragmented the opposition.

While the absence of social support cannot be definitively explained, contrasting the Central Asian cases of weak or failed social movements with the Eastern European and Baltic cases of successful social movements is useful. In the latter group of cases, society played a critical role in driving the transition, demanding national independence, overthrowing communism, and (excepting Yugoslavia) supporting democracy. In the former set, however, the weakness of civic nationalist movements pointed to the difficulty that post-independence elites would face in consolidating nation-states with a unified national identity. Not unlike many late colonial and post-colonial African cases in the 1950s and 1960s, the nationalist project remained the

---

[127] Beissinger, *Nationalist Mobilization*, p. 347.

[128] Ibid., p. 366.

[129] See Ronald Suny, "Provisional Stabilities," *International Security*, vol. 24, no. 3 (Winter 2000), pp. 139–178; and Olivier Roy, *The New Central Asia: The Creation of Nations* (New York: New York University Press, 2000).

[130] On civil society as opposed to the "tyranny of cousins," see Ernest Gellner, *Conditions of Liberty: Civil Society and Its Rivals* (New York: Allen Lane/Penguin Press, 1994).

interest of a handful of intelligentsia and elites, and subnational divisions challenged national unity.[131] Moreover, the lack of social support for democratic movements was a bad omen for the possibility of rapid or successful democratization in the post-independence period. In short, the "revolution from below" never really occurred in these republics, and the mild push that society and reformers gave to the regime had little effect on the truly dramatic events of late 1991. Consequently, the transitions and post-independence politics would be left largely in the hands of regime elites and the clan elites who had embedded themselves in the informal, behind-the-scenes pacts of the pre-transitional period.

---

[131] Thomas Hodgekin, *Nationalism in Colonial Africa* (London: Frederick Muller, 1956); James S. Coleman, *Nigeria: Background to Nationalism* (Berkeley: University of California Press, 1958); and James S. Coleman, *Nationalism and Development in Africa: Selected Essays*, Richard Sklar, ed. (Berkeley: University of California Press, 1994).

6

Central Asia's Transition (1991–1995)

> We have democracy here. Yes, we have stability.
> Brigadier, Great October *kolkhoz*, Syrdarya, Uzbekistan

> No, in Kyrgyzstan they have democracy. Here we have stability. Yes, we have peace... But, all the same, in my opinion, freedom is better.
> Librarian, Great October *kolkhoz*, Syrdarya, Uzbekistan

> What kind of democracy! We don't have democracy! We have chaos!
> Private farmer, Osh, Kyrgyzstan

The third phase of Central Asia's "transition" – often mischaracterized by Western observers as pointing toward either democracy or communism, with other possibilities ignored – was the creation of new regimes in clan-based societies. Not only Westerners but the Central Asians themselves, as these comments from some Kyrgyz and Uzbek villagers illustrate, had difficulty in understanding what types of regimes were emerging and whether they were democratizing.

In this chapter, I address two central questions of the study: why were some transitional regimes durable, and why did some collapse and then disintegrate into civil violence during the transition? And of the durable regimes, why did one democratize while others established a new authoritarianism? What role can elites play within clan-based societies? Despite the brevity of this period and its failures, understanding the causes and limits of these distinct transitions, and especially Kyrgyzstan's brief foray into democratization, is important for the historical record as well as for what it tells us about the theories and practices regarding democratization that are currently popular in Western academic and policy circles.

This chapter demonstrates, in line with the propositions laid out in Chapter 2, that two critical variables determined whether Central Asian countries would be stable and move toward democracy in the early 1990s.

The first was the *presence or absence of a pact* and thus of an informally legit-imized regime (at least temporarily, as the previous chapters have shown) that allowed some elite consolidation of power to take place, and thus allowed a durable transition to occur. The second was *leadership*, or, more specifically, the choices that the region's powerful presidents made concerning liberal-ization versus the reinforcement of authoritarianism. The pacts agreed upon during the pre-transition period become critical preconditions for maintain-ing regime durability and legitimacy during the transition. Where pacts oc-curred before 1991, in Kyrgyzstan and Uzbekistan, the post-Soviet regime transition was stable. Where a pact did not occur, the president was seen as illegitimate and various clans remained excluded from power. These con-ditions would set the backdrop for regime collapse in Tajikistan, as soon as the Soviet center ceased to prop up the hegemonic Khodjenti clan. The subsequent unraveling of the security forces would ultimately tip the Tajik case from instability to full-fledged civil conflict.

Despite the social structural challenges to democratization in Central Asia, during the initial post-Soviet period elites and elite ideology had the greatest ability to influence the transition. The moment of transition in Central Asia was characterized by enormous uncertainty, due to the unexpectedness of the August 1991 Soviet hardliners' coup and the suddenness of independence. With the collapse of the CPSU, the new presidents had a brief window of opportunity. In the midst of such institutional chaos, in which the costs and benefits of various reforms were not entirely clear to clan factions within the republics, they had a chance to seize and shape the transition, at least in the short term. The importance of presidential leadership (or lack of leadership) at sensitive moments underscores the transitions literature's focus on elites and the uncertainty and contingency of transitions.[1] Leaders make three key decisions during the pre-transitional and transitional periods. As noted in the previous chapters, leaders must choose whether or not to create or con-tinue a pact to maintain balance among clan factions. The Kyrgyz and Uzbek leaders did so; the Tajik leader did not. At the time of independence, leaders must then decide to consolidate the security forces, if possible. Third, lead-ers choose the ideological direction of the new regime. Understanding the ideological preferences of a leader is a difficult and risky task, as analysts of

---

[1] Valerie Bunce and Maria Csanadi, "Uncertainty in the Transition: Post-Communism in Hungary," *East European Politics and Societies*, vol. 7, no. 2 (Spring 1993), pp. 240–275; M. Steven Fish, "Democratization's Requisites: The Postcommunist Experience," *Post-Soviet Affairs*, vol. 14 (1998), pp. 212–247; Michael McFaul, "The Fourth Wave of Democracy and Dictatorship: Noncooperative Transitions in the Postcommunist World," *World Politics*, vol. 54 (January 2002), pp. 212–244; George Breslauer, "Introduction," in Richard Anderson, M. Steven Fish, Stephen Hanson, and Philip Roeder, *Postcommunism and the Theory of Democracy* (Princeton, NJ: Princeton University Press, 2001), pp. 1–10; and the classic work, Guillermo O'Donnell and Philippe Schmitter, *Transitions from Authoritarian Rule* (Baltimore: Johns Hopkins University Press, 1986).

Gorbachev and Yeltsin have often observed. Leaders' words do not necessarily mirror their beliefs or reflect their actions. The international climate alone gave Central Asian leaders a strong incentive to talk up democracy, whatever their real intentions. Since leaders' positions and their capacities regarding democratization both often change over time, assessing the sincerity and likely effect of leaders' intentions at any given moment is a daunting task.

In introducing new regime types, Akaev and Karimov defined the new ideology and institutions of their respective regimes. Although their intentions cannot be judged, we can assess several factors: (1) their stated ideological positions vis-à-vis communism, authoritarianism, and democracy; (2) the stated beliefs of each president concerning the relative benefits and costs of democratization; and (3) most importantly, the institutions that each established during the first few years of independence. This chapter first examines elite choices that fostered durability (or fomented collapse), and then turns to elite choices about regime type.

I. MAINTAINING REGIME DURABILITY DURING THE TRANSITION

As Chapter 2 argued, a stable pact managed by a legitimate leader is critical to transitional regime durability in clan-based societies. The presence of a negotiated pact, together with a leader who has the legitimacy and skill to manage its competing factions, is key to consolidating rather than fragmenting security forces and arms during the uncertainty of the transition. How were the brokers of the clan pacts in Kyrgyzstan and Uzbekistan able to avoid such a breakdown in the short term? If clan tensions were nonetheless present in the latter cases, how did these brokers preclude violence from occurring in the longer term?

One element of a viable transition is often overlooked in the post-Soviet cases: the role of the military and security forces.[2] This is somewhat understandable: in the former USSR – unlike the situation in, say, Latin America, Turkey, or Southern Europe – the military has generally played a minor role in transitions. Despite the involvement of the highest-ranking military commanders and civilian chiefs of the security forces in the failed August putsch, neither the Red Army nor the KGB played an active role in initiating or thwarting a transition. By refusing to fire on civilian demonstrators in Moscow on August 19, 1991, their actions at least tacitly supported Gorbachev, and then Yeltsin.[3] Many scholars and analysts have

---

[2] On this factor in Eastern Europe, see Zoltan Barany, "Democratic Consolidation and the Military: The East European Experience," *Comparative Politics*, vol. 30, no. 1 (October, 1997), pp. 21–43.

[3] See William Odom, *The Collapse of the Soviet Military* (New Haven, CT: Yale University Press, 1998).

attributed this to the short leash – backed up under Stalin by vast purges of the officer corps – on which the civilian-run CPSU had always kept the Soviet military.

In Central Asia, as elsewhere across the former territory of the USSR, the regional military and security units remained under the civilian control of the respective Communist Party Central Committees, and thus, throughout the perestroika period, in most cases they contributed to a stable and peaceful transition. Some variation in this respect, however, began to emerge during the late perestroika years, and must be noted, for it was to play a significant role during the period immediately following independence. No independent ministries of defense or internal affairs existed in individual republics prior to the Soviet breakup; however, each republic was equipped with local security forces under its division of the Ministry of Internal Affairs. Most housed battalions of the Soviet army. Further, each had a police force, which was generally locally trained and staffed. By granting greater republican-level control over security forces as part of perestroika, Gorbachev initiated a process of significant local militarization in certain republics, especially in the Caucasus and Tajikistan. By 1990 and 1991, the Baltic republics' "parade of sovereignty" had reached Central Asia, where it fed an increased decentralization of power. In some post-Soviet cases, the problem was not a lack of *civilian* control. Rather, as scholars have observed in the breakdown of Yugoslavia and Moldova, there was a deficit of *centralized* control over the state's multiple armed units.[4] Lack of centralized military control did not feed nationalists or Islamists, who did not have access to arms at this stage, even in Tajikistan; rather, it fed the struggle for power between clan networks, who had become the main political players by late 1991. The disintegration of centralized control over the military in this case again exhibits the shift of power from formal institutions to informal networks, to be used for narrow interests.

The Kyrgyz SSR appeared to be the least affected by the decentralization of military and security forces. Kyrgyzstan had never hosted a large Soviet military presence, and both the local branch of the KGB and the internal ministry troops of the MVD were strictly under the control of Feliks Kulov, a northern clan elite of the Chu region. An Akaev supporter in the 1990 pact, he had been rewarded with the vice presidency in December 1991.[5]

---

[4] On the fracturing of the military and territorial security forces in Yugoslavia, see Valerie Bunce, *Subversive Institutions* (Cambridge: Cambridge University Press, 1999). On Georgia, see Ghia Nodia, "Putting the State Back Together in Post-Soviet Georgia," in *Beyond State Crisis: Postcolonial Africa and Post-Soviet Eurasia in Comparative Perspective*, Mark Beissinger and Crawford Young, eds. (Washington, DC: Woodrow Wilson Center Press, 2002), pp. 413–444. A similar phenomenon took place in Albania in the 1990s.

[5] See a compilation of documents about the August coup and the security and armed forces in Kyrgyzstan in Melis Eshimkanov, *Askar Akaev: Pervyi prezident nezavisimogo Kyrgyzstana* (Bishkek: Asaba, 1995), pp. 37–50.

Also in December, Akaev created a National Guard for the defense of the president, under the supervision of his relative Abdygul Chotbayev. When Akaev eventually created a Ministry of Defense in 1993, the defense minister, Major General Myrzakan Subanov, was a professional Soviet military officer with loyalties to northern clans.[6] According to Kyrgyz journalists, he was half-Russian and half-Kyrgyz, and therefore not an "entrenched" clan elite.[7] Likewise, the State Committee on Emergency Situations, also created in 1993, was put under the control of another loyal Akaev supporter, who was Jewish and who also lacked clan ties. Under such supervision, Kyrgyzstan's military forces were weak but increasingly professional.[8] With security forces relatively small, tightly and centrally controlled, and under the auspices of a mutually acceptable pact, Akaev's regime did not experience a devolution of the means of force to clan elites, the mafia, or local warlords.[9]

Although little specific information is available, we do know that in Uzbekistan, the presence of the Soviet army and intelligence and security forces was both significantly stronger and more centralized than in the rest of Central Asia. Tashkent was the headquarters of the military district that encompassed all of Central Asia. Moreover, in the 1980s, the Uzbek Republic's position as a launching pad into Afghanistan gave it particular strategic relevance. In the spring of 1991, subsequent to the Uzbek declaration of sovereignty but prior to independence, Islam Karimov established an independent defense committee within his government. Rustam Akhmedov, the only high-ranking Uzbek military officer in the Soviet army, was elevated to the post of chairman of defense.[10] Despite his roots in Ferghana, a traditional clan rival of Karimov's regional support base, Akhmedov initially became a client of Karimov, and the military became increasingly centralized even before independence. On January 14, 1992, just after Uzbek independence,

---

[6] Akaev replaced Janybek Umetaliev, the chair of the State Committee for Defense Affairs, with Subanov in 1992. In 1993, the committee became the Ministry of Defense, and Subanov became the minister. Although (1) the military had few resources (about 10,000 troops), and (2) Umetaliev was very pro-Western, in line with Akaev's foreign policy, Umetaliev was from Osh. Akaev gradually purged all Osh elites from critical positions in the regime. Dmitry Trofimov, *Etno-konfessial'nye konflikty v Srednei Azii* (Moscow: IMEMO, 1994), p. 38. Subanov, by contrast, was very anti-Western and a hard-line communist, but he remained in this post for seven years. Author's interviews with Sabri Ergan, NATO attaché to Kyrgyzstan, Bishkek, July and August 1995.

[7] Other reports claim that Subanov was a distant relation of Akaev's wife. One side of his family was from Talas, the northern region that Akaeva's clan dominated.

[8] Author's interview with a member of the Ministry of Foreign Affairs, Kyrgyzstan, Bishkek, July 1994.

[9] Author's meeting with former military personnel and members of the Institute for Strategic Studies, Bishkek, 1997.

[10] Author's interview with Sodyq Safaev, ambassador from Uzbekistan to the United States, May 1999, as well as conversations with U.S. embassy personnel in Tashkent.

Akhmedov assumed control of all Soviet forces, including the former Turkestan Division of the Soviet army, on Uzbek territory.[11] His appointment also solidified Karimov's incorporation of all prominent Uzbek clan and regional factions within the government. In both Uzbekistan and Kyrgyzstan, although for very different reasons, the regime was able to maintain control over the military and security forces despite Gorbachev's initiatives.

In the Tajik SSR, the legacy of Soviet military and security forces was significantly different. Gorbachev's decentralization in this arena had serious consequences for the transition following independence in September 1991. Because Tajikistan had not been used as a major military base for the Soviet Union's southern front – due to the Party's distrust of Tajik Muslims – the military and security forces were less important and, ironically, less strictly and centrally controlled than in Uzbekistan. Corruption was widespread and had allowed draft evasion and other forms of resistance to recruitment to become common. The further decentralization of security forces had particularly ill consequences when coupled with the failure to achieve a stable pact in Tajikistan between 1989 and 1990.

Neither Makhkamov nor Nabiev was able to control rising disputes over power and resources between clan factions that drew support from their regional base. Republican-level security forces thus increasingly broke into factions along regional and clan lines. Nabiev created a new Ministry of Defense in December 1991. Not granting the new ministry much importance, Nabiev appointed a Pamiri as head. The latter proceeded to recruit and staff his ministry and troops almost entirely with Pamiris from Gorno-Badakhshan.[12] Nabiev had mistakenly assumed that the minister would remain a loyal client of Leninabad. Meanwhile, the minister of internal affairs, a traditionally powerful position, had staffed his forces with Kulyabis. At the time, the Kulyabi clans were still the "little brother" clients of the Khodjenti clans – but this would not last very long. Local KGB and MVD leaders likewise formed their own armed units.

Finally, by late 1991 and early 1992, Nabiev had begun creating his own militias. He stacked these with more Kulyabis. The most notorious would become the People's Front (PF) militia, under the Kulyabi ex-convict Sangak Safarov. Even the PF would eventually split along clan lines, however, between Kulyabis and non-Kulyabis.[13] The various militias would increasingly

[11] J. Ergash, *"Uzbekistan: Geopoliticheskie faktori natsional'noi bezopasnosti i stabil'nosti"* (unpublished paper prepared at the Institute of Strategic Studies, Tashkent, 1998).

[12] Based on author's interviews with Stanley Escadero, ambassador from the United States to Tajikistan, 1992–95, Baku, Azerbaijan, July 1998.

[13] Barnett Rubin, "Tajikistan: From Soviet Republic to Russian-Uzbek Protectorate," in Michael Mandelbaum, ed., *Central Asia and the World* (New York: Council on Foreign Relations, 1994), pp. 216–218; and author's conversation with a Western diplomat in Tajikistan, July 2000.

come under the control of so-called local warlords, who were to play a ruthless role in mobilizing villagers during the riots, demonstrations, and fighting that would break out only six months after independence.[14]

Where leaders did not preserve a pact and quickly consolidate control over the use of armed force, the regime not only collapsed but disintegrated into civil violence – with obviously disastrous consequences for any prospective transition from communism to democracy.

II. THE KYRGYZ CASE: DEMOCRATIZATION IN CENTRAL ASIA?

The year 1990 had already brought a different "local regime" to power in Kyrgyzstan.[15] Although appointed by the communist-era Supreme Soviet, Akaev's regime was based not on the Communist Party, but rather on the new institution of the presidency. With independence, the year 1991 saw the Kyrgyz Republic become a nation-state with Akaev at the helm. Just as critical, though less sudden, was the shift away from communism as the basis of the regime. With a relatively stable pact of clan factions supporting Akaev's government, the regime was not likely to collapse into clan-based factions. Bolstered further by support from the democratic social movement, liberalization under Gorbachev became democratization under Akaev.

By December 1991, with the first free and popular presidential elections in history, Kyrgyzstan was no longer a hesitantly liberalizing Soviet republic but a democratizing post-Soviet state. By 1995, when a second presidential election marked the end of the short-term transition, democratization would be far from complete, and a fully "liberal," much less "consolidated," democracy would not yet have emerged. International praise for Akaev's new little Switzerland surrounded by a sea of authoritarianism was probably overdue.[16] Nonetheless, during this window of opportunity of four to five years a far-reaching *process* of democratization did get under way.[17]

Although scholars argue about how best to measure a democracy, much less the stages of democratization, the Kyrgyz government established at the

[14] Author's interview with former U.S. ambassador Stanley Escadero, July 1998. See also Kamoludin Abdullaev, *Historical Dictionary of Tajikistan* (Lanham, MD: Scarecrow Press, 2002).

[15] "Local regime" refers to the republic level institutions of the Kyrgyz SSR, as opposed to the national institutions of the USSR in Moscow. By 1990, after the constitutional dismantling of the CPSU's hegemony, the Central Asian regimes were no longer merely an administrative extension of a single, unified Soviet regime.

[16] "Little Switzerland," *Forbes Magazine*, September 1994.

[17] On democratization as a "process," see Dankwart Rustow, "Transition to Democracy: Toward a Dynamic Model," *Comparative Politics*, vol. 2 (April 1970), pp. 337–64; and Juan Linz and Alfred Stepan, *Problems of Democratic Transition and Consolidation* (Baltimore: Johns Hopkins University Press, 1996).

very least a minimalist "electoral democracy," as defined by Huntington.[18] This process involved the institutionalization of most key dimensions of a democratic regime: (1) free and fair elections (presidential, parliamentary, and local); (2) a democratic constitution with a separation of powers between the executive, legislative, and judicial branches; (3) full and equal citizenship; (4) autonomous political parties; (5) autonomous civil society and media; (6) economic liberalization;[19] and (7) civilian control of the military.[20] Juan Linz and Alfred Stepan further argue that another key dimension of a democracy, especially of a liberal and consolidated democracy, is the "rule of law." Although this element is notoriously difficult to measure, most observers agree that the rule of law was only partially implemented during this period.

Akaev's Ideology: A Jeffersonian Commitment to Democracy?

Kyrgyzstan's first popularly and democratically elected president seized the initiative in driving the post-Soviet transition. As noted in the previous chapters, the political pact that had brought Askar Akaev to power had exhibited a general lack of interest in the ideology of the regime, along with a preoccupation with maintaining stability and dividing resources. Nonetheless, Akaev himself, with a certain amount of support from Chingiz Aitmatov, his primary patron, appeared to be far more interested in bringing an ideological dimension to his politics.

Even before August 1991, Akaev had been an intellectual, not a Party apparatchik. He was among the most active of the republican leaders in promoting glasnost', perestroika, and *demokratizatsiia*.[21] As early as 1989, he pushed for more open ties with the West and for market reforms. One of the strongest indicators of his ideological orientation and commitment is the fact that Akaev was elected to the new all-Union Congress of People's

---

[18] As mentioned in Chapter 1, for the purpose of distinguishing a boundary between the authoritarian and democratic periods, I adopt a minimalist definition of democracy, in line with that of Schumpeter or Huntington. A continuation of the democratization process leads to the adoption of a deeper and fuller conception of democracy, typically referred to by scholars as "liberal democracy."

[19] On the importance of economic liberalization in transitions from communism, see Anders Aslund, *Building Capitalism: The Transformation of the Former Soviet Bloc* (Cambridge: Cambridge University Press, 2002).

[20] These key dimensions of democracy roughly correspond to those outlined by Linz and Stepan, *Problems with Democratic Transition*; Karl and Schmitter, "What a Democracy Is and Is Not," in Larry Diamond and Marc F. Plattner, eds., *The Global Resurgence of Democracy* (Baltimore, MD: The Johns Hopkins University Press, 1995), pp. 49–62; and Larry Diamond, *Developing Democracy: Towards Consolidation* (Baltimore: Johns Hopkins University Press, 1999).

[21] Eugene Huskey, "The Rise of Contested Politics in Central Asia: Elections in Kyrgyzstan, 1989–1990," *Europe-Asia Studies*, vol. 47, no. 5 (July 1995), p. 828.

Deputies in the semicompetitive elections of 1989 as a pro-Gorbachev, "non-[Communist] Party candidate."[22]

As the new president of the Kyrgyz Republic, Akaev had sought to go beyond Gorbachev's commitment to reform, both economically and politically. In fact, the chief of the Kyrgyz KGB, General Asankulov, had reported to Moscow in 1990: "[Akaev's] entrance to power, in my opinion, marked the beginning of a strong turn in the social life [of the country], and he was the first to come into history as a bearer of a democratic consciousness."[23] Akaev had criticized the Union Treaty as "passionless in its political nature," as failing sufficiently to guarantee democratic political rights.[24] He had proposed the incorporation of a passage recognizing that the Soviet Union had been founded on the ruins of an empire and had been a "prison of nations."[25] Unlike Gorbachev, Akaev did not support the halfway house of "democratic socialism." Instead, as early as mid-1991 he was advocating "full democracy" and integration with the West and capitalist economies.[26] His speeches were replete with references to Thomas Jefferson.[27] By 1993, Akaev had created powerful international images of his republic, painting it as an "island of democracy in a Central Asian sea of authoritarianism"[28] and portraying himself as the founding father of Kyrgyz democracy.[29] Kyrgyzstan's intelligentsia was almost unanimously supportive of Akaev's reforms.

Pragmatic Motivations for Democratization

Whatever Akaev's ideological commitment to democracy, he also knew that Kyrgyzstan needed foreign assistance and that the West would be more likely to aid a democratic regime. Unlike Uzbekistan, Turkmenistan, and Kazakhstan, Kyrgyzstan has neither large oil and gas reserves nor a strategic

[22] Regine A. Spector, "The Transformation of Askar Akaev, President of Kyrgyzstan," Berkeley Program in Soviet and Post-Soviet Studies Working Paper Series (Berkeley: University of California Press, 2004), p. 6.

[23] Jumanbek Asankulov, "*On dlia menia raskritaia kniga . . . ,*" in Eshimkanov and Imanaliev, eds., *Chelovek bez seredini* (Bishkek: Kyrgyzstan, 1993), p. 147.

[24] See "*Vystuplenie prezidenta,*" in Eshimkanov and Imanaliev, eds., *A. Akaev: Chelovek bez seredini*, the speech of President Akaev on the Union Treaty, June 1991, p. 122.

[25] Ibid., p. 123.

[26] Ibid., pp. 123–125.

[27] See, for example, Askar Akaev, "Kyrgyzstan: Central Asia's Democratic Alternative," *Demokratizatsiia*, vol. 2, no. 1 (1994), p. 16.

[28] See the *Financial Times*, May 1993. The comparison with Switzerland was prompted by its similarly mountainous terrain, and its similarly multiethnic and multilingual population, within a unified democratic state. It also inspired Akaev's interest in the consociational democratic model.

[29] See T. Koichuev and V. Ploskikh, *Askar Akaev: Uchenyi politik: shtrikhi politicheskomu portretu pervogo prezidenta Kyrgyzskoi Respubliki akademika Akaeva* (Bishkek: "Ilim," 1996), for the intelligentsia's view of Akaev during the transitional period. Koichuev was head of the Academy of Sciences and a strong supporter of Akaev.

location athwart pipeline or shipping routes.[30] Its industrial and agricultural production had plummeted with the end of Soviet subsidies and imports, its traditional Soviet-bloc markets had dried up, and its landlocked geography made trade and transport difficult. Kyrgyzstan had to be able to turn abroad.

By 1992, Akaev had convinced his circle of advisors, and especially those clan elites to whom he was bound by the informal pact of 1990, that massive foreign aid was necessary to save the economy and preserve stability,[31] and that in order to attract such aid, Kyrgyzstan must demonstrate radical economic and political reform. Although the informal clan interests generally cared little about democratization, the clan leaders who had brought Akaev to power continued to support him. The president had gotten Moscow out of local politics and stabilized domestic affairs without undermining their fiefdoms, and his economic and political reforms were giving them access to flows of foreign funds as well as newly privatized state and party assets. His reform strategy was initially successful, both domestically and internationally, and the first wave of foreign assistance would soon enable Akaev to keep the backing of both central and regionally based clan elites.

Presidential Elections: Establishing Popular Legitimacy

It is not clear to what extent Akaev himself believed in the reforms he was initiating, and to what extent Kyrgyz democracy was merely a tool to manipulate the West for money. That Akaev began implementing democratic reforms *before* August 1991, however, should count as evidence of his commitment to reform apart from such pragmatic motivations. Shortly after the Soviet hard-liners' August putsch failed, Akaev astutely determined to hold national, popular presidential elections. His election in 1990 had been indirect, within parliament, and only narrowly victorious. On October 12, 1991, by contrast, Akaev won the presidency unopposed in a popular election that gave him 94.6 percent of the vote amid 99 percent turnout.

Parliament had banned the Communist Party from running a candidate, though such a figure would likely have garnered little support.[32] No other

---

[30] Terry Lynn Karl powerfully argues, in *The Paradox of Plenty: Oil Booms and Petro-States* (Berkeley: University of California Press, 1997), that a lack of energy resources is actually beneficial to a developing country; those states endowed with undeveloped natural resources invariably have misused them to foster corrupt transitional regimes, to the detriment of the economy and polity over time. Nigeria, Iran, and Venezuela, to name just a few "petro-states," have fallen prey to these problems, and Azerbaijan and Kazakhstan are prone to the same trajectory of political corruption and economic mismanagement.

[31] Based on author's interview with Askar Aitmatov, advisor to the president, presidential apparat, Bishkek, Kyrgyzstan, June 9, 1998; and author's conversations with Askar Sarygulov, head of the Kyrgyz Committee on State Investment and State Property Fund and presidential advisor, Bishkek, Kyrgyzstan, July 1995 and June 1998.

[32] See T. Koichuev et al., *Sovremennye politicheskie protsessy* (Bishkek: NAN, 1996), p. 15, for a discussion of the political landscape at this time.

opposition party or candidate was banned, and there was no intimidation by Akaev or any of his allies and backers. The neophyte democratic and nationalist parties had no large followings of their own and so backed Akaev, who had met many of their demands since becoming president the year before. As a leading Kyrgyz democracy and human rights advocate, Tolekan Ismailova, has argued, the democratic activists and the DMK strongly supported Akaev and did not put forth an alternative candidate.[33] Despite the lack of a contest, the elections were widely recognized, both within Kyrgyzstan and abroad, as free and fair.[34] As the first step toward democracy, they gave Akaev a level of legitimacy and proven popular support that he thitherto had lacked.

The core of the opposition to Akaev still lay in the south of the republic with Masaliev's network. Yet even there, Akaev was widely liked for having stabilized the social and political situation following Masaliev's ouster. Leading Kyrgyzstan to full independence had endowed Akaev with the status of a charismatic founding father – above politics, party competition, ethnic divisions, and even regional and clan factionalism. In 1991, not unlike Lech Walesa, Vaclav Havel, or Boris Yeltsin, Akaev virtually embodied in his person the then-twin causes of democracy and statehood. Akaev further symbolized the birth – or rebirth – of the Kyrgyz nation.[35] He was likened to Manas, the epic warrior-hero who, according to legend, had united the Kyrgyz tribes in defense of their land and freedom. In 1991, Akaev was very likely an unbeatable candidate. With this founding presidential election, the Kyrgyz Republic crossed at least the lower, electoral threshold of democracy and seemed poised to make further progress toward becoming a fuller-fledged democracy modeled along liberal-constitutionalist lines. Indeed, 1992 and 1993 would see rapid advances in this direction.

A Constitution for a New Kyrgyzstan

One of the first tasks of the post-Soviet state, eager both to establish its legitimacy and to deal with the pressing issues of the transitional period, was the drafting of a new constitution. Akaev delegated this task to a committee of legislators, representatives of social organizations, and the legal division of the presidential apparat, all working under the chairmanship of a respected judge and chairman of the Arbitrage Court, Daniyar Narumbaev. The Constitutional Committee worked for over a year, relying heavily in

---

[33] Author's interview with Tolekan Ismailova, Notre Dame, Indiana, February 2003.

[34] There were no international monitors during this election, so accounts of fairness are difficult either to verify or to challenge.

[35] Kyrgyz history has been rewritten to discuss the rebirth or resurrection of the Kyrgyz nation, when in fact no nation existed prior to the Soviet era. See Chapter 4 for a discussion of this issue.

the process on the study and comparison of various Western models. The French, German, Swiss, and U.S. models got the most attention. Of particular interest were the relative merits and demerits of presidential as opposed to parliamentary forms of government. By early 1993, a draft had appeared in a main government newspaper, and the committee began to solicit and collect comments and opinions from the media, social organizations, intellectuals, and ordinary individuals.

The discussion of three successive drafts was a public process. From late 1992 to May 1993, most political parties took part, as did social organizations, business associations, religious and ethnic cultural groups, and most major representatives of Kyrgyzstan's growing civic and political society.[36] The vast majority of those who did participate, however, as in Russia and throughout the former Soviet Union, were former members of the Communist Party *nomenklatura* who had simply adopted new formal affiliations and presented themselves as "democrats." Nonetheless, most parties and other nongovernmental actors involved appeared to be satisfied that the drafting was an open and transparent process, and that society had a voice in the process.[37]

The initial debate focused on whether or not the standing parliament – a body elected during the Soviet era – could legitimately participate in the process, much less vote to adopt a new constitution. No new electoral law had yet been adopted, thus creating a doubly complex situation. Leading members of the "democratic fraction" of deputies, many of whom had belonged to the same "Movement of 114" of June 1990, argued that a new electoral law must either be adopted first, or be included in the constitution itself. Abdygany Erkebaev lobbied strongly for an electoral system based upon proportional representation of political parties. Yet such a restriction would have undercut the popular basis of the majority of deputies, who did not belong to political parties (since the expiration of their Communist Party membership in 1991); only the intelligentsia, the members of an array of newly created and highly urban, elite-based parties, supported him.

Most deputies, however, especially those elected as Communist Party candidates, did not want to face reelection. Erkebaev and his supporters, not surprisingly, lost their initiative, and the electoral law was temporarily put aside. The reform contingent continued, however, avidly to participate in the constitutional process. Akaev himself, unlike his counterpart Boris Yeltsin, who sought to monopolize the drafting process within the executive branch, strongly promoted the national Constitutional Committee

---

[36] Author's interview with the legal scholar and historian A. Dordoyev, Academy of Sciences, Kyrgyzstan, Bishkek, Kyrgyzstan, July 1994; author's interview with Judge Karabaev, chairman of the Arbitrage Court and main drafter of the Constitution, Bishkek, Kyrgyzstan, August 1994.

[37] Author's interview with Jaspar Jeksheev, leader of the DDK, Bishkek, October 10, 1994; and with the chairman of the Slavic Fund, Bishkek, September 4, 1995. Discussions with Kyrgyz journalists and NGO members in 1994 and 1995 confirmed this view.

as a consociational mechanism of democratic transition and governance.[38] Ultimately, the constitution itself focused on citizenship and the separation of powers, in ways that showed the influence of the Swiss and American models.

Defining Citizenship and Managing Nationalism

The related issues of citizenship, "nationality," and language were hotly debated, but resolved more civilly than in most post-communist republics. Certain representatives of Erkin Kyrgyzstan (Free Kyrgyzstan) and Asaba (Banner) sought to privilege the ethnic Kyrgyz over other ethnic groups, especially the "colonialist" Russians. The Osh elite also sought to privilege the Kyrgyz over the Uzbek minority, which held fertile land and power in the bazaar.[39] After Kazakhstan, Kyrgyzstan had the largest ethnic minorities in Central Asia; in 1991, Russians comprised approximately 24 percent (and more than 50 percent of Bishkek), while Uzbeks comprised 13 percent (more than 50 percent of the population of the Osh and Jalalabad regions). At Akaev's urging, nationalist clauses were removed from the draft constitution, while the state's name was changed from Kyrgyzstan ("land of the Kyrgyz") to the less controversial Republic of Kyrgyzia. Akaev stressed the civic, not ethnic, basis of citizenship. Although the constitution established Kyrgyz as the official language, Russian "and other languages" were recognized and protected from discrimination.[40] While the Russian share of the population slipped from about 22 percent in 1989 to 18 percent in 1995 – an exodus that Akaev sought to stem – Russian remained the speech of the elite and of interethnic communication.[41]

Akaev's rhetoric about the strength of multiethnic societies gave constitutional standing to his even-handed and non-ethnocentric position on the land and language laws. Interethnic relations rapidly became more stable.[42] In fact, the exodus of the Russian and German populations, which had reached almost 300,000 from 1989 to 1993, largely as a result of the Osh violence, slowed substantially following the adoption of the new constitution.[43]

---

[38] Author's interview with Toiar Koichuev, president, Academy of Sciences, Kyrgyzstan, Bishkek, March 1997.

[39] Author's interview with Bakyt Beshimov, rector of Osh University and parliamentary deputy, Osh, August 1995; and author's discussion with a journalist and scholar from the Osh Academy of Sciences, Osh, August 1995.

[40] *Konstitutsiia Kyrgyzskoi Respubliki*, Article 5.

[41] Russian would later be named a state language as well. In 2004, ten years later, the language issue was again opened in the Kyrgyz parliament.

[42] The government did not recognize Uzbek. As a concession to the Uzbek population (estimated at 13 percent in 1991), the government funded the publication of several major newspapers in Uzbek, permitted the broadcasting of an Uzbek television station, and opened an Uzbek-Kyrgyz University. The Akaev government feared that Uzbekistan was promoting Uzbek separatism in the Ferghana Valley. Author's interview with Uzbek deputy, Bishkek.

[43] Similar statistical and qualitative information about emigration was provided by the Ministry of Labor and Migration, Bishkek, Kyrgyzstan, 1995. Exact figures were difficult for the

Separation of Powers

The separation of powers was another time-consuming constitutional issue. Recognizing the separation principle as a mainstay of democracy, the
commission began the difficult process of distributing power, primarily between the executive and legislative branches.[44] As in most former Soviet
republics experiencing a transition to democracy, the executive–legislative
battle reflected the balance of power of the Gorbachev era, during which
the reformists were concentrated in the newly established presidential and
executive structures, while the Party *nomenklatura* dominated the Soviet-era
legislature. In Kyrgyzstan, however, the initial period of transition presented
Akaev with an enormous window of opportunity. Not only did the pact of
regional and national clan elites back him in his reforms, the reformists in the
executive and in parliament also advocated his agenda – albeit for different
reasons – thus uniting various elements behind him. The conservatives or
anti-reform elements consisted only of discredited Communist Party members who were not networked into any major clan faction. Hence, Akaev was
able, with great legitimacy, to move the overall constitutional process toward
a more balanced but presidential democratic system. He sought to endow
the presidency with enough power to push through economic and political
reforms, but simultaneously sought to ensure that it would be checked.

Some in the presidential apparat, including Feliks Kulov and Apas
Jumagulov, wanted a smaller and weaker legislature.[45] Akaev nonetheless
refused all temptations to seek "super-presidential" powers like those found
in the December 1993 version of the Russian Constitution.[46] In fact, the

government to assess, since after 1993 a large number of Russians returned to Kyrgyzstan,
but they often settled in different homes. The city of Bishkek was once about 80 percent
Russian, and in 1997 was estimated to be 50 percent Russian. In the south of the country,
the emigration was faster and the numbers higher. See also the data presented in V. Bushkov,
"*Tajikistan i Kyrgyziia: Reemigratsiia – real'nost' ili fantaziia,*" in V. Tishkov, ed., *Vynuzh-
denye migranty: integratsiia i vozvrashchenie* (Moskva: RAN, 1995), pp. 257–267.

[44] See U. K. Chinaliev, *Realizatsiia printsipa razdeleniia vlastei v sovremennom Kyrgyzstane*
(Kiev: "Dovira," 1998), pp. 22–31, for an extensive discussion.

[45] Koichuev notes that very few saw the need for a smaller or two-house legislature. He himself
supported the latter. See Koichuev and Ploskikh, *Askar Akaev: uchenyi politik,* p. 34.

[46] Author's interview with Daniyar Narumbaev, the chief of the Arbitrage Court, Bishkek,
Kyrgyzstan, August 1995. According to Narumbaev, neither the president nor the executive branch understood fully in 1993 the necessity for stronger presidential powers during
the transition period. Akaev was guided by Western models of democracy. In fact, he had
originally favored a more consociational model, such as that of Switzerland. On the risks of
super-presidentialism, see Stephen Holmes, "Super presidentialism and Its Problems," *East
European Constitutional Review* (Fall 1993/Winter 1994), pp. 123–126. Legal scholars and
political scientists debate the merits of designing presidential versus parliamentary democracies. Most post-Soviet republics have established presidential systems that have built on the
institutional legacy of the executive presidency established during perestroika. Most Eastern
European democracies, which have adopted parliamentary systems and rejected a strong
executive, have been more successful in sustaining democracy.

only significant change made to the institutional structure of the executive was the elimination of the vice presidency, an office created in December 1991 and filled by presidential appointment. Some power seemed to shift from the central executive to the *oblast' akim*s (regional governors), who were appointed by the president without parliamentary oversight.[47] Feliks Kulov, a key Akaev supporter since 1990, and vice president since 1991, became the *akim* of Chu *oblast'* when the vice presidency was eliminated and a premiership adopted.[48]

Restructuring the organization and powers of the judicial branch was a secondary issue. At Akaev's urging, the constitution created a new judicial body, the national Constitutional Court, which would include nine judges appointed by Akaev and approved by the parliament.[49] Some deputies sought radically to revamp the entire judicial system as well, to model the courts on the American system, and to displace the cadre of judges trained during the communist era; however, given the dearth of qualified judges and the magnitude of such a task, neither Akaev nor the majority within the legislature supported this approach. Other than the Constitutional Court, which was specifically created to deal with disputes between the legislature and the executive, the Soviet court system remained intact. While there may have been concern that a strong judicial branch would detract from the effectiveness of the executive, a more basic explanation is both cultural and institutional: Given the lack of a developed legal culture, there was little recognition at the time, even among the lawyers and judges who participated in the process, that a strong judicial branch was an essential element of a democracy. Neither Narymbaev nor Cholpon Baekova, another prominent judge who would later be appointed chair of the Constitutional Court, fought for a common-law tradition under which federal and local judges would have more power.[50] The executive, not the judiciary, was seen as the holder and guardian of the law. Akaev's revival of a Soviet-style justice ministry to take over many judicial functions underlines the emphasis he put on the governmental, not the judicial, role in developing a legal system and fostering a rule of law. Second, the Soviet court system left the judiciary hampered by a debilitating institutional structure. Most judges and prosecutors were

[47] The *akimiat* (governorship) essentially restructured and renamed the Soviet *oblast'noi ispolkom*, the regional executive political committee, which was headed by the regional Party secretary. The *akim* system, however, was a return to a pre-Soviet traditional form of Central Asian government.

[48] The move was ostensibly a demotion; in reality, the *akimiat* was a more lucrative and powerful position.

[49] *Konstitutsiia Kyrgyzskoi Respubliki*, Article 79.

[50] Based on author conversations with Cholpon Baekova, Bishkek, June 1998; with D. Narumbaev, August 1995; and with CEELI/ABA advisor Howard Ockman, 1994–95. It is unclear exactly why this is the case with Narumbaev. Baekova was connected by kin to the president and may have been influenced by him.

networked into a local clan system from which they derived their positions, power, and prestige; therefore, they were less concerned than the reformist legislators, who often lacked such a social power base, with changing the judicial institutions or system.

In institutional form, the democracy created by the Kyrgyz Constitution of 1993 was a presidential system, in part modeled on the American system of checks and balances, and in part a holdover from the Soviet era. The American model, as opposed to European models, seemed both to reflect the desired distribution of power and to appeal to the United States and Western donors. The primary problem with the constitution was not the de jure distribution of power, but the lack of clarity in the relationship between the branches, and the inefficacy and inexperience of the legislature and judiciary in implementing checks on the president and the executive branch.[51] The constitution also represented a compromise between the president and the legislature, the two primary actors in drafting the document. Neither had been elected under the rules of the new constitution (although the president had at least been elected a second time after independence, rather than prior to August 1991). Yet a law passed by the legislature together with the constitution on May 5, 1993, explicitly preserved the legislature and the presidency intact. The constitution represented an agreement between Akaev and the deputies to retain these bodies and institutions for a transitional period, until the next elections.

The Electoral Law and Political Parties

Although advocating the early adoption of an electoral law for parliament, Akaev neither dissolved nor restructured the legislature. A Soviet-era institution, the Kyrgyz Supreme Soviet was a single chamber of 350 deputies, elected according to the population-based districts and "multicandidate," but not multiparty, electoral law of 1990. As would be expected in any democratizing country, the legislature's power increased under the new constitution. Instead of merely rubber-stamping presidential *ukazes* (decrees) in the Soviet manner, or taking a secondary role in drafting legislation – as had been its practice since early 1991, several months prior to independence – the legislature, now renamed the *Jogorku Kenesh*, assumed real authority to draft, debate, and adopt legislation. Indeed, the president had already clashed with the legislature over differences in views on the Land Code, the Law on Privatization, and the Law on Foreign Investment in 1992 and 1993. The ongoing debate over the Law on Elections complicated matters. Akaev understandably wanted to preserve the standing legislature, since it included

[51] Author's interview with Omurbek Tekebaev, deputy, Legislative House, Jogorku Kenesh, Bishkek, June 1998; and author's interview with Howard Ockman, CEELI/ABA advisor, Bishkek, August 1994.

a majority of his supporters, especially from the intelligentsia; he thus agreed with the majority in the *Jogorku Kenesh* who claimed that a larger legislature was more representative and that a bicameral system was not necessary in a small, nonfederal state. Unlike the situation in Russia, federalism was not an issue, which greatly simplified matters. In a session of the *Jogorku Kenesh* on April 16, 1993, just three weeks before the vote on the draft constitution, Akaev articulated his support for preserving the unicameral body.[52] To get rid of it would have involved "undemocratic" moves – perhaps its forcible dissolution by the president, as Yeltsin had done in December 1993, in clear breach of democratic principles. Akaev chose not to take such measures.

The Constitution of 1993 did not incorporate an electoral law, although it did note in its concluding transitional provisions that one would be adopted to elect a new *Jogorku Kenesh* and local *kenesh*es within two years. Hence, not long after the constitution's adoption, the executive apparatus again brought the issue to the attention of the standing parliament. In January 1994, a law was finally adopted; the date of elections, however, remained a question. To the displeasure of the political party advocates, such as Erkin Tekebaev and Jaspar Jeksheev, the law mandated that elections be held according to a majoritarian, single-member district rule, not a proportional representation system.[53] While the latter rule was recommended by international electoral consultants, and would likely have brought more political parties into parliament, the former seemed more suited to the personalistic political context. As already noted, most deputies in the *Kenesh* did not have a party affiliation and relied instead on their local clan networks. The upshot of the decision, however, was not the discouragement of a multiparty democracy, but the encouragement of fewer, larger parties in which personalities would play a greater role – not unlike the American system. The law on the election of deputies to the *raion* and *oblast' kenesh*es, adopted in October 1994, followed the model of the national *kenesh*.[54]

The law on political parties and elections required that parties register with the Ministry of Justice and produce the signatures of at least 5,000 members. Although the ministry was not particularly encouraging of new party development, fourteen parties had registered by 1997, and more than forty by 2000. The twelve parties registered before the 1995 presidential and parliamentary elections did not complain of difficulty or harassment in the registration process. Several parties – including the Social Democrats

[52] U. K. Chinaliev, *Realizatsiia printsipa razdeleniia vlastei v Sovremennom Kyrgyzstane* (Kiev: Izd-vo, "Dovira," 1998), p. 28.

[53] *Zakon o vyborakh deputatov Jogorku Kenesha Kyrgyzskoi Respubliki*, January 12, 1994 (Bishkek, 1994).

[54] See *Polozhenie o vyborakh v raionnie i oblastnie keneshi Kyrgyzskoi Respubliki* (Bishkek, October 1994), p. 41.

and Ata-Meken – were splinters of the DMK.[55] Some were members of parliament and actively involved in the transitional regime, although Akaev himself eventually declined to affiliate himself with a particular party.[56] Only specifically religious or ethnic parties were refused registration, on the grounds that they violated the separation of church and state or promoted interethnic strife. These restrictions were aimed at the IRP and both pro-Uzbek and anti-Uzbek parties. The Kyrgyz "nationalist" parties – Erkin Kyrgyzstan, Asaba, and Ata-Meken – were thus careful to take a nonconfrontational stance on ethnic issues, and even attempted to include Russians and Uzbeks among their members.[57] By late 1993, the Communist Party was re-registered as a legal political organization, although the government had confiscated much of its property and eliminated its former privileges.

Parties faced the usual problems of scanty funding and lack of experience during the transition of 1991 to 1995, but they enjoyed almost unfettered political openness and acceptance by the regime. They actively participated in the October 1994 local *raion* and city *kenesh* elections, although they were far outnumbered by "independent, self-nominated" candidates.[58] They even more aggressively put forth candidates for the 1995 parliamentary elections, which in fact had been pushed back to February of that year from the fall of 1994 after party leaders brought complaints about lack of time to organize and campaign to the Central Electoral Commission (CEC).[59]

Developing Autonomous Civil Society and Media

No less critical than the legal reforms requisite for institutionalizing democracy were less formal, but more substantive, efforts to create and promote a civil society, the social basis of a strong democracy.[60] On the part of the regime, this primarily involved restraint – a retreat from the Communist Party's attempts to control civic life. A significant liberalization of the press, social organizations, civil society, and universities had occurred in

[55] Author's interviews with Topchubek Turgunaliev, former leader of the DDK, Bishkek, July 14, 1995; with Kamila Kenenbaeva, former head of the Ata-Meken Party, who became an advisor to Akaev on political parties, social organizations, and civil society, Bishkek, August 8, 1994; and with Omurbek Tekebaev, chairman, Ata-Meken Party, Bishkek, November 21, 1994. The DDK appeared to have split along personal and strategy lines. According to Tekebaev and Kenenbaeva, her joining the government had given Ata-Meken greater political influence.

[56] Author's interview with the chair of the Social Democratic Party, of which Akaev had discussed taking the lead in 1992, Bishkek, December 1994.

[57] Author's interview with the chair of Ata-Meken, Omurbek Tekebaev.

[58] Author's interview with Kamila Kenenbaeva, presidential advisor. Author's interviews with various party representatives confirmed this view.

[59] Author's interview with Markel Ibraev, chairman of the Central Electoral Commission, Bishkek, November 22, 1994, and July 12, 1995.

[60] Diamond, *Developing Democracy*.

1990 and 1991, shortly after Akaev came to power. After 1991, this trend continued at a faster pace. Newspapers proliferated and readership was high, although distribution was often limited to urban areas because of financial burdens on publishers.[61] The government continued to print its official newspaper, *Slovo Kyrgyzstana*, but without the ideological bent of the communist regime. Meanwhile, a number of "independent" and even genuinely opposition-oriented periodicals began to appear.

Other forms of free association and open information flourished as well. Multiple civic groups, especially ethnic cultural organizations, began to register, receive modest aid from the government, and act as independent community groups. The Slavic and German funds, both active in Bishkek, unofficially lobbied the government on behalf of the Slavic population.[62] The Uzbek National Group pursued the interests of the Uzbek population in opposition to government policies. Ethnic Uzbek parliamentary deputies demanded that the government address the decline in educational and employment opportunities.[63] The government responded to these demands by founding the Uzbek-Kyrgyz University in Osh and the Slavic-Kyrgyz University in Bishkek in 1995. Religious organizations operated freely, and many mosques received foreign aid. The central Islamic institution, the *muftiat* of Kyrgyzstan, was no longer a state institution, although the *mufti* acted as a consultant to the president on religious affairs and pursued projects of interconfessional cooperation.[64] Foreign-sponsored and grassroots NGOs proliferated. By 1994, more than 200 were registered with the Counterpart Consortium and the USAID office for the support of local NGOs; according to Counterpart, before 1995 none reported interference from the government.[65] The Kyrgyz Open Society Institute worked actively. Several human rights groups operated throughout the country. The Kyrgyz Bureau of Human Rights and the "Uchkuduk" Human Rights Center reported almost no human rights violations from independence until late 1994. Other governmental problems, such as police corruption and instances of abuse, did occur, although without government sanction. The social abuse of women was rampant. Yet until late 1994, when the first restrictions on the press

---

[61] Based on author's interviews with editors of *Res Publica*, an opposition paper, and *Vechernii Bishkek*, the largest newspaper published in Kyrgyzstan (Russian-language).

[62] Author's interview with M. Sorokin, chairman, Slavic Fund, Bishkek, September 4, 1995.

[63] Author's interview with Alisher Sabirov, people's parliamentary deputy from Jalal-Abad, Bishkek, Kyrgyzstan, October 1996.

[64] Author's interview with the *imam-khatib* of the Osh Central Mosque, Osh, Kyrgyzstan, June 1998. This was the largest and most active mosque in Kyrgyzstan. The *imam*, the most authoritative religious figure in the mosque, was actively involved in working with the government to promote good interethnic relations and inter-confessional peace.

[65] Author's interview with the Counterpart Consortium director and review of list and materials of Counterpart-sponsored NGOs, Bishkek, Kyrgyzstan, August 1994 and August 1995.

were introduced, no politically motivated violations of human rights had been documented.[66]

Connecting Economic Reform and Democracy

In 1992, Kyrgyzstan became the only post-Soviet republic to adopt radical economic reforms.[67] Akaev's leadership was critical to the introduction of such a program, which risked losing the support of both elites and his mass following.[68] After Akaev signed on to the IMF stabilization program in May 1993, a team of economists from the Sachs/Balcerowicz project in Warsaw arrived in Bishkek to counsel the government on the implementation of a similar reform program. Defying the temptation to sequence economic and political reform, over the course of the next two years (1992–94) Akaev pushed forward several key ingredients of a radical reform strategy: price liberalization, cessation of subsidies to most state enterprises, severe cuts in social benefits, and, most importantly, the introduction of an independent and convertible Kyrgyz currency and a privatization program for small and medium-sized enterprises.[69] On May 5, 1993, the Kyrgyz government introduced the first Central Asian currency, the Kyrgyz som.[70] Two years of hyperinflation, a drastic decline in industrial production (about 30 percent per year), and a 20 to 30 percent decline in agricultural output and livestock production were the immediate consequences of these measures; however, by 1995 the economy saw a leveling of the current account deficit and a stabilization of the currency and prices.

The next phase of economic reform was designed to bolster democratization and civil society through advancing the growth of an independent

---

[66] Author's interview with a Uchkuduk Center for Human Rights representative, Bishkek, Kyrgyzstan, August 1995. See also U.S. government country reports, Senate Committee on Foreign Relations, and reports by Amnesty International, Freedom House, and Human Rights Watch, 1994–2004.

[67] Gregory Gleason, *The Central Asian States: Discovering Independence* (Boulder, CO: Westview Press, 1997).

[68] Spector, "The Transformation of Askar Akaev," p. 14.

[69] Press conference with Leszek Balcerowicz, Polish economist, Minister of Finance, and architect of economic restructuring in Poland in 1989, Ministry of Foreign Affairs, August 1994. Balcerowicz and Sachs advised the Kyrgyz government in 1993 and 1994. A team of IMF, World Bank, and USAID economists gave Akaev similar counsel. In the author's conversation with Balcerowitz, it was clear that price liberalization and the cutting of government subsidies were the two key aspects of the reform agenda. No thought, at that time, had been given to a social safety net. Only in late 1995 did the World Bank begin to consider the severe social implications of the IMF's program. Author's interview with Balcerowicz, Bishkek, August 1994; author's interview with World Bank consultants, Bishkek, August 1995.

[70] Turkmenistan, Uzbekistan, and Kazakhstan left the ruble zone later in November 1993. Only Tajikistan, whose economy was almost entirely dependent on Russia, stayed with the ruble. However, because the Soviet ruble did not circulate any longer, Tajikistan was effectively cut off from Russia. Tajikistan thus introduced the Tajik ruble in May 1995.

economic society.[71] As early as 1992, Akaev had proclaimed private property a basic human right and building block of democracy, and had initiated a privatization program. Small business was immediately privatized, as was housing.[72] With aid from the United States, a privatization program for medium- to large-scale enterprises was adopted and rapidly implemented in 1993 and 1994, although U.S. consultants would soon find that, as elsewhere in the former communist world, the sale of substantial state assets would be stalled and corrupted by insider involvement. Nonetheless, by 1994 Kyrgyzstan had made substantial progress toward creating a market economy and satisfying the international community's demands.

Satisfying Clan Expectations of Reform

By February 1993, barely a year after independence, Akaev had met with missions of the World Bank, the International Monetary Fund (IMF), the European Bank for Reconstruction and Development (EBRD), and the U.S., Japanese, and German governments and donor agencies. Meanwhile, 107 states and multiple international organizations and institutions had recognized Kyrgyzstan (formally now called the Kyrgyz Republic) as a democratizing sovereign state and member of the international community.[73] With such international recognition and the promise of a capital influx, Akaev gained significant domestic credibility, especially among those clan elites competing for state resources.[74]

Clan leaders, expecting to gain from international aid and investment, agreed at least superficially that massive democratic political and economic reforms would be needed. Those closest to Akaev by kinship, marriage, or region of birth, such as the Sarygulov clan, gave the strongest support for his reforms. Those from Osh, Masaliev's clan, and some more remote regions were more skeptical about what they stood to gain. Yet Akaev's success in

---

[71] Schmitter, "Some Propositions about Civil Society and the Consolidation of Democracy" (unpublished manuscript, Stanford University, 1995), argues that an independent economic society is a critical component of civil society.

[72] One government official reported that he had bought his up-scale Bishkek apartment in 1993 for twelve dollars. Yet, due to cuts in government subsidies and salaries, he could barely afford the sum on his monthly income of twenty dollars. Personal communication, Bishkek, 1994.

[73] Akaev announced this in *Slovo Kyrgyzstana*, September 2, 1992, p. 1. The Department of International Organizations, Ministry of Foreign Affairs, Kyrgyzstan, July 1994, provided me a complete record of Kyrgyzstan's extensive multilateral and bilateral agreements during this period. From 1992 through 1995, this department grew by 300 percent per year. The main goal of Akaev's foreign policy at this time was to make Kyrgyzstan an active member of the international community, to pursue an identity independent of Russia, and to attain recognition as a democratic state. Based on discussions with Roza Otunbaeva, foreign minister, 1994–97.

[74] T. Koichuev and V. Ploskikh, *Askar Akaev: Uchenyi politik* (Bishkek: "Ilim," 1996), p. 37.

maintaining social stability during the transition, his inclusion of all major clans in the government, as well as the prospect of future Western aid and investment, were sufficient to garner their support, at least for the short term.

Akaev thus adroitly used this window of opportunity virtually to impose an agenda of radical political and economic reform on the country. And the world community wanted to make Kyrgyzstan a showcase for the successful achievement of rapid and simultaneous political and economic reform. By 1993 Akaev had convinced the World Bank, the United Nations, and the Western embassies of his commitment to democracy and the market, and the aid packages and programs began to grow.[75] From 1993 to 1996, the U.S. Agency for International Development (USAID) gave more per capita aid to the Kyrgyz Republic than to any other former Soviet republic, and in 1994 the international donors together announced a $580 million aid package. In the second half of the 1990s, however, with foreign debt mounting, international aid would begin to decline and Akaev would lose his ability to appease internal factions with the promise of hard currency. Both he and the clan elites who surrounded him would increasingly undermine the cause of political and economic reform.

Summarizing the Kyrgyz Transition

By minimalist, electoral definitions of democracy, Kyrgyzstan had met the democratic threshold by late 1991. According to the more demanding institutional accounts of Freedom House, the Kyrgyzstan of the initial post-Soviet years also scores relatively well. It had moved from a monopolistic communist regime to a multiparty constitutional regime governed by a separation of powers. From 1992 through 1994, Kyrgyzstan even approximated – though it did not reach – more substantive definitions of democracy ("liberal democracy"). Table 6.1 summarizes the indicators of democratization progress in the Kyrgyz Republic.

Kyrgyz democracy still fell short of a fully free and independent press, and although institutional mechanisms of accountability certainly existed, they were often too weak to meet their goals. Both vertical and horizontal accountability are crucial for movement toward greater consolidation.[76] The former comes from the ballot box, but by itself it can too easily be suborned by "delegative democracy."[77] Horizontal accountability requires that

---

[75] Author's interview with an NGO leader, Bishkek, August 2004.
[76] Andreas Schedler, Larry Diamond, and Marc F. Plattner, eds., *The Self-Restraining State: Power and Accountability in New Democracies* (Boulder, CO: Lynne Reinner Publishers, 1999).
[77] Guillermo O'Donnell, "Delegative Democracy," *Journal of Democracy*, vol. 5, no. 1 (January 1994), pp. 55–69. O'Donnell views delegative democracies as more stable than I do. This form of government, embedded in personalistic ties, has a high propensity to become increasingly illiberal.

TABLE 6.1. *Indicators of Kyrgyzstan's democratization*

Type of Democracy[a]	Indicators of Democracy	1993	1995
Electoral democracy (Huntington 1991)	1. Elections (free, fair, regular)	Yes	Yes
Liberal democracy (Diamond 1995)	2. Civilian regime	Yes	Yes
	3. Constitutional regime	Yes	Yes
	4. Multiparty regime	Yes	Yes
	5. Elections (free, fair, regular)	Yes	Yes
	6. Universal suffrage	Yes	Yes
	7. Organizational and informational pluralism	Yes	Yes
	8. Extensive civil liberties	Yes	Partial[b]
	9. Effective power for elected officials	Yes	Partial[b]
	10. Functional autonomy for legislative, executive, judicial organs	Yes	Partial[b]
Liberal democracy (Schmitter and Karl 1991, 1993)	11. Citizenship (participatory, by elected representatives)	Yes	Yes
	12. Accountability of elected officials	Yes	Partial[b]

[a] Various definitions with higher or lower thresholds have been put forward by different scholars. Huntington's definition is minimalist, and requires only free elections to qualify as an electoral democracy. Diamond, Karl, and Schmitter advocate a fuller definition of "liberal" democracy.

[b] In late 1994, we see the beginnings of curbs on civil liberties (namely, on the press) and on the effective autonomy of parliament. Events in 1995, before and after the elections, reverse this trend for a short while, but in 1996 executive curtailing of civil liberties, especially of the press, begins again.

Note: Assessments are based on Freedom House annual reports (1993–1996).

dynamic processes of checks and balances work within the state itself. Both kinds of accountability will be greatly bolstered if an autonomous and active press and civil society demand them.

On many dimensions, Kyrgyzstan had met international democratic norms and standards. As the second set of presidential elections took place, it was clear that the democratic "rules of the game" had been accepted, at least formally, by all the major political players. No one challenged the system through violence, and minimal fraud was reported. In fact, in 1994 Freedom House ranked Kyrgyzstan a "3," just beneath the most liberal postcommunist regimes and far ahead of its Central Asian neighbors. Yet Kyrgyz democracy was largely "delegative" in nature. It remained at risk both from formal restrictions imposed by the executive, and from informal manipulation by those behind the scenes who sought to maintain their power despite the imposition of democratic institutions. A semiliberal delegative democracy could easily slide toward authoritarianism. By most formal measures, Kyrgyzstan was well above the threshold of democracy. Yet signs of democratic weakening beneath the surface would appear all too soon.

III. UZBEKISTAN'S TRAJECTORY: REMAKING AN AUTOCRATIC REGIME

The story of the Uzbek transition is brief in comparison. Transiting from a dependent republic dominated by the CPSU to an independent autocratic state dominated by renamed communist structures and ex-Party elites seemed a far less complex task. Nonetheless, the Uzbek transition was neither simple nor easy, as the level of state oppression from 1991 through 1995 indicates. The particular mode of constructing a new autocratic regime deserves to be explored.

Calculating Uzbekistan's Post-Soviet Path: Why Not Democracy?

Three predominant factors went into Islam Karimov's assessment of Uzbekistan's post-independence trajectory. First, unlike Askar Akaev, Karimov was not ideologically committed to pluralism, much less to democratization. Unlike Akaev, Karimov was a classic Communist Party apparatchik; he had risen to power and prominence through the rank and file of the CPSU, as well as through his connections with the Ismoil Jurabekov and the Rashidov clan, by virtue of his birthplace, Samarkand.[78] Karimov spent most of the purge years in Kashkadarya, a remote region of the Uzbek Republic; unlike Akaev, he did not interact with the Sakharovs and Havels of the perestroika years.

Second, unlike Akaev, Karimov had great confidence in Uzbekistan's ability to survive on its own – without Russia and without the West. The role of economic resources in the Uzbek transition in many ways illustrates the flip side of the Kyrgyz. Although GDP per capita was slightly lower in Uzbekistan than in Kyrgyzstan, and although the population was generally more agricultural, the Uzbek elite was convinced that it had the natural resources, in the form of oil, gas, gold, and cotton, to finance its own economic and political development and to attract Western aid.[79] Hence, there seemed to be little need to curry international approval in order to attain loans. From 1991 to 1995, Uzbekistan defied IMF recommendations for economic reform, and it likewise remained impervious to international pressure to comply with

---

[78] See Leonid Levitin with Donald Carlisle, *Islam Karimov, President of the New Uzbekistan* (Vienna: Grotec, 1995).

[79] James Critchlow makes a similar observation in *Nationalism in Uzbekistan: A Soviet Republic's Road to Independence* (Boulder, CO: Westview Press, 1991).

world norms regarding human rights.[80] The economic model adopted by Karimov, who had been elected in part for his economic expertise, advocated sequencing of economic and political reform as vital to ensuring domestic stability. In a fairly compelling argument – especially in 1999, a decade after the introduction of simultaneous political and economic reform in Russia – Karimov and his supporters declared that they had opted for something like "the China model," or even the Korean or Singaporean path: gradual privatization and marketization of the economy. Like Singapore's Lee Kwan Yew, Karimov presented himself as the "strong hand" necessary to stave off domestic chaos, interethnic conflict, and religious fundamentalism; unlike his Asian counterparts, however, Karimov professed to be setting Uzbekistan on the road to democracy.[81] While keeping a tight grip, he claimed to be raising national consciousness, preparing Uzbekistan for phased reform. Although some privatization of apartments and small plots of land did take place from 1990 to 1992,[82] for the most part industrial and agricultural privatization was extremely slow.[83] In the first four years of independence, economic reform involved much less government decentralization than the government had suggested, and the "China model plus democracy," seemed increasingly unlikely to come about.[84]

A third important element of Karimov's calculus was the sociopolitical environment within which he was operating. Again unlike his neighbor Akaev, Karimov was at the center of a relatively unstable pact. The forces that had ushered him into power in 1989 were highly tenuous and fluctuating. Karimov was at the epicenter of several powerful clans, most of which had a strong territorial basis (e.g., the Samarkand, Ferghana, and Tashkent clans). Even though he had succeeded by 1991 in consolidating control over the various armed forces, Karimov had to choose a course of political and economic development that would retain all the major players in the pact and suppress those excluded (e.g., the Khorezmlik and Namanganlik clans), and still exert control over a unified state. In order to do this, he sought to centralize economic and political resources, while at the

---

[80] Human Rights Watch was refused entrance and registration until 1996. The National Democratic Institute, an American NGO for promoting democracy and civil society, was expelled from Tashkent in 1992.

[81] The collected works of Karimov address this issue extensively.

[82] *Zakony Respubliki Uzbekistan o zemle, o predprinimatel'stve, o razgosudarstvlenii i privatizatsii* (Tashkent: "Adolat," 1996). The law on land was adopted on July 20, 1990. See especially restrictions on land in Articles 3 and 11. According to Articles 12 and 13, private plots were allowed. According to peasants in the rural areas, these plots of land allowed them to survive.

[83] Author's interviews with World Bank and IMF representatives in Uzbekistan, Tashkent, July 1997.

[84] Author's interview with A. Khodjaev, a clan subordinate of Karimov, appointed to the lucrative post of rector, University of World Economy and Diplomacy, Tashkent, Uzbekistan, March 1997. Khodjaev was also an economic advisor to Karimov.

same time doling out enough goods to every powerful party to deter its defection.

Karimov's task was further complicated by the structural nature of the clan networks he sought to balance. There had been little interaction between and among the major Uzbek networks during the course of the Soviet period. Resentment against Rashidov's clan by networks from Ferghana, Tashkent, and Khorezm was high, due to the long period of hegemonic control exercised by Rashidov. While blood ties and intermarriage often united large family networks within regions, rarely did they cross networks and link members of different regional factions. In Uzbekistan more than elsewhere in Central Asia, even within a given clan the network would be large and hierarchical, so that clan elites shared the wealth with a narrow stratum of kin and quasi-kin, not with the entire district or region.[85] Especially on the collectives, moreover, elite clans kept nonelite clans in a position of clientelistic dependency.

At all levels of society, mistrust was high and the ability of the center to enforce social monitoring and compliance was low, at least in comparison to Kyrgyzstan, where the sociopolitical structure of clan networks both at the center and in the regions was far more tight-knit. Karimov, calculating that democratic reform, or even widespread economic privatization without democratization, would destabilize the country's internal situation, fracture the 1989 pact, and oust him from power, opted instead for even tighter autocratic measures than he had been able to implement during the Gorbachev years.

Constructing an Autocratic Regime: "New" Institutions and the Fusion of Power

Foremost on Karimov's agenda in the wake of the failed August 1991 hardliners' coup, and likewise central to those elites most loyal to him, was the neutralization of the Uzbek Supreme Soviet. The Soviet was dominated by members from Tashkent, many of whom had opposed Karimov's appointment as first secretary and president until a deal was cut to make one of their leaders, Shukrulla Mirsaidov, the new vice president. In September 1991, the same "Tashkent clan" that backed Mirsaidov published a letter condemning Karimov for seizing power and suggested that Mirsaidov should succeed him.[86] Not yet strong enough to attack directly with arrests or a closure of the soviet, Karimov struck back obliquely.[87] He banned the Communist Party of

---

[85] Author's conversations with Uzbek sociologists, Tashkent, 1997.

[86] Dmitry Trofimov shares this interpretation. See Dmitry Trofimov, *Tsentral'naia aziia: problemy etno-konfessional'nogo razvitiia* (Moskva: MGIMO, 1994), pp. 30–31.

[87] Kul'chik, *Respublika*, p. 36; and *Moskovskie novosti*, September 26, 1991, and October 2, 1991. After 1991, the legislature's name was changed to the traditional Uzbek appellation, Oliy Majlis.

Uzbekistan (CPU), thereby stripping many deputies of their assets as Party *nomenklatura*. In the CPU's place, he created by decree on September 14, 1991, and under the supervision of loyal deputies, the People's Democratic Party of Uzbekistan (NDPU). Shortly thereafter, the government, albeit less directly, established several other parties.[88] These were curious moves for a leader who in 1991 had proclaimed himself loyal to the hard-line communists in Moscow, had opposed Uzbek nationalism and secession, and had initially supported the coup.[89] Karimov's version of the new constitution, which would be adopted the following year, further consolidated his control over the legislature by slashing the number of seats from 450 to 250. Those who were to be elected in the fall 1994 parliamentary elections would have to face the scrutiny not of the Communist Party, but of Karimov. His actions from 1989 through 1992 underlined the nonideological nature of his new authoritarianism.

After the Mirsaidov letter, Karimov decreed the abolition of the vice presidency. In October, the executive apparatus began to organize the "founding" popular presidential elections, scheduled for December 31, 1991. As noted earlier, only one "opposition" candidate and party were permitted to register. Muhammad Salih, the leader of Erk and a notable of the Khorezm *oblast'* and clan, garnered a surprising 12.45 percent of the vote, primarily from Khorezm, although some Tashkent intelligentsia supported him as well.[90] While Karimov picked up 84 percent of the vote (with 94 percent turnout) in what international agencies generally judged to be a highly controlled election, Salih's support was deemed worrisome enough to justify a severe crackdown on the Khorezm region. Salih went into exile and has continued his protests from Turkey, Romania, and the United States.

Karimov's tactics additionally shifted power away from the cabinet, which he increasingly put under the control of young "technocrats" with little factional base.[91] Instead, he shifted power both to special advisors within the executive apparatus and to regional *hokims* (governors), a new institution that he had created to replace the party's regional first secretaries. The *hokims* were directly appointed by Karimov, with no oversight from

---

[88] See Aleksandr Verkhovskii, *Srednaia Aziia i Kazakhstan: Politicheskii Spektr* (Moscow: "Panorama," 1992), pp. 68–74. All were constructs of the regime. Only the NDPU, which was the CPUz's immediate successor, had a real organizational structure, which had changed very little by 1994, despite the fact that the party itself had almost no power or resources. Note the similarity to the CPU's structure in the party statement of the December 1993 congress: Kurbanov, ed., *Ideologiia natsional'noi nezavisimosti narodno-demokraticheskoi partii Uzbekistana* (Tashkent: Ozbekiston, 1994).

[89] A key government figure noted that in reality, Karimov had rejected the communist ideology as early as 1989. Personal communication, 2000.

[90] Author interview with Erk activists and supporters of Salih, Urgench, October 1997.

[91] Author conversations with Tashkent elites (businessmen and former government officials), Tashkent, Uzbekistan, August 1997.

any other institution.[92] In this way – by making the leading bosses of
Khorezm, Ferghana, and Samarkand dependent on the executive and his authority – Karimov attempted to ensure the loyalty of the predominant clan
factions.

Karimov's treatment of the judicial structures was unsurprisingly similar;
his intent was not to reform, but to keep the court system immobilized,
to use it when necessary to bestow popular legitimacy on the regime, and
to take advantage of its inherent rent-seeking properties. Unsurprisingly,
since December 8, 1992, when the constitution was quickly adopted, the
courts have played no role independent of the executive. Instead, the main
functions of the judicial branch have been concentrated in the Ministry of
Justice, whose central responsibility has been the issuing and revoking of the
registration licenses of "independent" political organizations; in 1993, the
ministry once again refused to grant legal status to Birlik and Erk.

In early 1992, student protests over rising bread prices spurred Karimov to
launch a campaign aimed at the suppression of any political society. By 1993,
Karimov's rule by decree had obliterated most of the freedoms gained in this
realm under Gorbachev before 1990.[93] The freedoms of political speech and
organization were virtually eliminated. In the social and economic spheres,
restrictions were far looser, with the regime's policy resembling that of a
traditional noncommunist autocracy.[94] The law on religion legalized and
destigmatized Islamic worship – a radical change from the Soviet era – but
nonetheless ensured tight regime control of the *muftiat*, which was subject
to continual censorship by the security services.[95] By 1993, Karimov had further succeeded in replacing the long-standing Namangan-based *mufti* with
a Samarkand-based *mufti*. The Samarkand/Bukhara clerical network was
considered more deferential to the regime. Karimov's crackdown on independent social organizations took its heaviest toll yet again in Namangan
and Andijan, which continued to be problematic regions for the president.
In late 1991, local village leaders and mullahs reportedly had organized village demonstrations against the regime.[96] They were strongly opposed to

[92] This practice by Karimov was later incorporated into the electoral law, Article 20. See *Ozbekistan ovozi*, November 12, 1994.
[93] The typical process of legislation was the following: the president issued a decree; the parliament then adopted it as a resolution and passed it as a law. Hence, almost all legislation was initiated and generated by the presidential executive.
[94] For an extensive discussion of this legislation and decrees, see William Fierman, "Political Development in Uzbekistan: Democratization?," in Karen Dawisha and Bruce Parrott, eds., *Conflict and Change in Central Asia* (Cambridge: Cambridge University Press, 1998), pp. 360–400.
[95] Based on author's observations and interview with *mufti*, Spiritual Directorate for Uzbekistan, Tashkent, Uzbekistan, October 27, 1997. Numerous "independent" mullahs were arrested or disappeared in Namangan in 1992 and 1993. See Human Rights Watch reports for 1993 and 1994.
[96] Author's interview with a correspondent for Radio Free Europe, May 2004.

their exclusion from the circle of power surrounding Karimov.[97] Mobilizing its increasingly powerful security force, the regime arrested and imprisoned or shot hundreds of "mafia criminals" from the Ferghana Valley in 1992 and 1993.[98] According to many Ferghana and Tashkent sources, Karimov still could not eliminate the problem, and hence made a deal with the most powerful elites of the Ferghana Valley clans.[99] As in Kyrgyzstan, in a blow directed at the IRP and the Ferghana Valley, the law on religion banned Islamic and other religious parties. By 1994, the region had quieted down. By this time, the regime's record of human rights abuses was quite abominable.[100]

A New Statist Economy

In the economic realm, Karimov's autocratic state took a somewhat looser form than did the Soviet state. Private property was legalized and a limited economic civil society was permitted to operate, although even small businesses felt the surveillance and intrusive hand of the government. The dual land system persisted, as the great bulk of agricultural land remained underproductive in the hands of state farms. Small-scale trade and private plot production, however, were more independent than during the Soviet era. Karimov's decision in 1991 to give every household a small private plot (six to eight hectares) enabled most to attain a subsistence level of existence. Substantive land reform, however, would be far more difficult, since it would directly cut into the profits and power of certain vested clan interests at both the national and regional levels.[101] The cotton sector was again becoming a major source of patronage and wealth, as it was during the Brezhnev era. And Jurabekov, the "Gray Cardinal" behind the regime, informally controlled the state mechanism for exporting cotton, the most lucrative export. Hence the government rejected necessary agricultural reform.

[97] Author's interview with B. Malikov, May 2004.

[98] Author's interview with Stanley Escadero, ambassador from the United States to Uzbekistan, Tashkent, July 1997.

[99] Author's conversations with economic and political elites representing powerful families in the Ferghana Valley, Tashkent, Uzbekistan, 1997, 1998.

[100] Author's interview with a representative of Human Rights Watch and with U.S. Embassy officers, Tashkent, 1997, 1998. For detailed reports of arrests and disappearances, see *Human Rights Watch World Report* (New York: Human Rights Watch, 1993), p. 241; and the *US Department of State Country Reports on Human Rights Practices for 1994* (Washington, DC: U.S. Government Printing Office, February 1995), pp. 1038–1047. Helsinki Watch Group was not even allowed to operate within the country until 1996.

[101] See the TACIS report on "Land Reform in Uzbekistan," unpublished document, Tashkent, 1997. The TACIS report actually significantly overestimates the progress of reform. Local farmers' NGOs complained in interviews with the author that reform was not only slow but haphazard, depending largely on the personal style of the regional *hokim*. The Uzbek Supreme Soviet's "*Polozhenie o zemle*" was passed in 1991, after an "*Ukaz o zemle*" (decree on land) by Karimov.

A New Ideology to Legitimize Uzbekistan's Autocracy

Karimov's campaign for legitimacy during the immediate post-independence period marks the post-Soviet Uzbek regime as fundamentally distinct from its Soviet predecessor. Despite the significant overlap of institutions and personnel, and despite the seeming superficiality of the post-1991 changes of names and slogans (e.g., the CPU became the NDPU, and posters and slogans of Karimov replaced those of Lenin), the new Karimov regime was not a communist one. Behind the regime lay no governing ideology, only a desire for power and its perquisites. No party (communist or otherwise) monopolized power. Karimov had sought distance from the political battles of Moscow while strategically increasing the executive presidency and setting up a new power base of his own.

Although before 1991 Karimov had allegedly crushed the opposition for demanding independence from the Union, after 1991 Karimov, not unlike Akaev, co-opted the opposition's platform and then sought to legitimize his regime by constructing a revised history of Uzbekistan's nationhood and statehood. Like Akaev, he also advocated a civic nationalism, so as to bolster his reputation for quelling interethnic instability.[102] For Karimov, however, a successful nationalist campaign was more critical, since he had neither a democratic basis of legitimacy nor great confidence in the permanence of the pact that had brought him to power. In the meantime, as we have seen, Karimov relied to a far greater extent than Akaev on the security forces, both to put down popular opposition and to monitor possible defectors from the 1989 pact. The result of his policies from 1990 through 1993 was the gradual transformation from a communist regime to an autocratic one, in which power belonged not to a hegemonic party, but to Karimov himself and the clique of clan elites who surrounded him.

IV. TAJIKISTAN'S TRAJECTORY: FROM REGIME COLLAPSE TO CIVIL WAR

The story of Tajikistan's transition from 1991 through 1994 is a story not of institution building, but of institutional breakdown and the collapse of order. As we noted in Chapter 3, during the later days of perestroika Tajikistan's neighbors had to varying degrees consolidated pacts incorporating the major clan players within the republic. The Tajik elite, however, had failed to do so. In fact, the Khodjentis and Kulyabis had even refused to do so. The conditions for instability within Tajikistan were ripe. The severe economic crisis plaguing all of Central Asia was merely the background. In the foreground was a serious imbalance of political power and resources among the major clan factions – groupings of smaller clans that usually came from the same region. One group of clans – commonly known as the Khodjentis – was

---

[102] Gregory Gleason, *Central Asia's New States* (Boulder, CO: Westview Press, 1997).

based primarily in the Leninabad region. They had dominated the system for decades. By some estimates, in late 1991 more than three-quarters of the key Communist Party positions in Tajikistan were in the hands of Khodjentis.[103] Unlike Akaev or Karimov, First Secretary Makhkamov and the Khodjenti elite felt so secure in their own power and backing from Moscow that they had failed either to redistribute power to their clients or to take such precautionary measures as merging the republic's various security and armed forces under their rule. Finally, the Tajik regime, despite the February 1990 demonstrations, had missed the opportunity to put a more legitimate individual at the head of the Tajik Communist Party. The August 1991 hard-liners' coup attempt took the Khodjentis by surprise; the subsequent months saw them abruptly cut off by their erstwhile patrons in Moscow. The Soviet subsidies disappeared, and the Khodjentis found themselves in desperate straits. Their already illegitimate and unrepresentative regime was poised for disaster, and the next few months witnessed the unraveling of its monopolistic grip.

The Shock of August 1991: The Communist Party Loses Power

The days following the coup were a whirlwind for Makhkamov. Discredited still further by his close association with and support of Boris Pugo and the GKChP, the Tajik leader was unable to reap the fruits of independence. Thus, following his reluctant declaration of independence, he adopted a somewhat more conciliatory stance toward his critics. Although the opposition was hardly united and did not engage in mass demonstrations, the DPT and the intelligentsia called for a ban on the Communist Party. The Supreme Soviet did not support this demand – unsurprisingly, since it was dominated by deputies from Khodjent and Dushanbe, who were loyal to Makhkamov. Nonetheless, Makhkamov sought to distance himself from the Party and to seek a new source of regime legitimization. Hence he convoked popular presidential elections, set for November 24, 1991.[104] Although all the conditions for elections were detrimental to the disorganized, disparate, and ill-funded opposition groups – they were announced in late September, leaving candidates less than two months to register and to collect the requisite number of signatures – the regime did make a major concession. Makhkamov "officially" stepped down from power while the campaign was under way, and Supreme Soviet Chairman Kadriddin Aslonov became "acting president." Aslonov, as a native of the Garm region, and particularly as a member of the Karategin clan, seemed an odd if not a risky choice for interim leader. Yet in the eyes of the Khodjenti, he was a long-time communist, a member of the *nomenklatura*, and, like most chairmen of the Tajik Supreme Soviet since

---

[103] A. Azamova, "*Tajikistan: agoniia nezavisimosti,*" *Moskovskie novosti,* September 13, 1992, p. 6. Cited in Muriel Atkin, "Thwarted Democratization in Tajikistan," in Dawisha and Parrott, eds., *Conflict and Change*, pp. 277–311.
[104] Bushkov and Mikul'skii, *Anatomiia.*

the 1960s, a client of the Khodjenti clans. Karateginis had traditionally been client clans of the Kulyabis – hence, subclients of Khodjent. For Makhkamov, Aslonov's appointment was to be brief and symbolic. Furthermore, his power would be tempered by its division with two other key transitional figures: the new acting chairman of the Supreme Soviet, who was a Pamiri, and the remaining premier, a Kulyabi and a client of Nabiev.[105]

In fact, the Khodjenti clan still controlled most state affairs, if indirectly. It focused its attention on the election of Rakhmon Nabiev, whom it had determined to revive as a presidential candidate in place of Makhkamov. Nabiev, the Communist Party first secretary until 1985, was the "strong hand" that the Khodjentis believed they needed in order to reassert control and to resubjugate their client clans to their governing will. In the meantime, however, the Khodjentis watched while Aslonov gave in to the intelligentsia's demands that the Communist Party be eliminated. On September 22, 1991, Aslonov signed a decree banning the Communist Party of Tajikistan (CPT) and its activities. Several days later, on September 30, 1991, he created the Socialist Party of Tajikistan (SPT), his version of the NDPU. The SPT was essentially a rebirth of the CPT, and merely another front for Khodjenti domination. It reflected the traditional ideology of the Communist Party. Aslonov had made a major concession of power to opposition forces. In a second radical blow to the Party, he allowed the democratic movement's demonstrators to remove a statue of Lenin from the capital's central square.[106] In a third and most serious strike at the regime's autocratic rule, Aslonov gave up a key post to a representative of the Pamiris. He turned over the ministry of internal affairs – a position traditionally run by the Kulyabis, in conjunction with their Khodjenti bosses – to the Pamiri police chief, Mamadayez Navzhuvanov. Although a serious attenuation of the security forces had already begun at the *oblast'* and local levels during the late 1980s, Aslonov's decision was a massive strike at the regime's monopoly on security in the republic's capital, and Navzhuvanov quickly began to replace his predominantly Kulyabi staff and troops with his Pamiri clan.[107] He also began to aid the opposition movement, La'li Badakhshan.[108]

Presidential Elections: The Khodjenti Attempt to Avoid a Transition

The November 24, 1991, elections took place, but as in Uzbekistan, they were widely considered rigged. Nabiev won only 57 percent of the vote, and his sole opponent, Davlat Khudonazar gathered 33 percent. The

[105] Trofimov, *Problemy etno-konfessionalnogo razvitiia*, pp. 23–24.
[106] Author's interview with an ORT journalist, Tashkent, July 1997.
[107] Author's interview with Dmitry Trofimov, first secretary, Embassy of Russia to Uzbekistan and specialist for Tajik/Afghan affairs, March 15, 1997. Interview with former U.S. ambassador to Tajikistan (1992–95) Stanley Escadero, Tashkent, July 1997.
[108] Irina Zviagelskaya, "The Tajik Conflict," *Central Asia and the Caucasus Journal of Social and Political Studies*, <http://www.ca-c.org/dataeng/st_09_zvjag_2.shtml>.

latter, representing the Pamiri-based Democratic Party of Tajikistan, was also an intellectual. He thus won the support of Rastokhez intellectuals from Leninabad and Dushanbe. Nabiev, however, used the election to re-assert the control of the Khodjentis. Unlike Akaev, who immediately began to court the West, Nabiev's first moves were concerned with neither the economy nor democracy. Instead, he was determined to reassert control over the security forces and to eliminate opposition from the executive ap-parat. Thus, he rapidly replaced the Pamiri minister of internal affairs with a traditional Kulyabi. He also created a new body, a transformation of the former Tajik KGB, called the National Security Service (SNB).[109] Removing Aslonov, Nabiev appointed a new chairman of the Supreme Soviet, a Kulyabi and a loyal client of Khodjent, Safarali Kenjaev. The latter had been respon-sible for running his electoral campaign, and he soon showed his prowess in other areas as he launched a "show trial" of the arrested minister, Navzhu-vanov. Finally, Nabiev arrested the mayor of Dushanbe, Maksud Ikramov. Thus obsessed with solidifying the Khodjenti grasp on power, Nabiev was barely able to formulate or impose a transitional strategy at all. Yet without a pact to hold competing clan elites together, and without the Soviet govern-ment to sustain Khodjent's power disparity vis-à-vis the rest of the country, Nabiev's strategy could no longer work. The Tajik regime became increas-ingly contested, not by intelligentsia-based demonstrations, but by assertive clan elites who had long been excluded from the center of power and who viewed Nabiev's actions with ever greater resentment.

The Cycle of Violence: Protest to Institutional Breakdown and War, 1992–1993

Nabiev's post-election crackdown did not go unchallenged. The balance of power and forces in the republic had changed, and regional clan leaders, as well as the more ideological opposition, were quick to seize the opportunities offered by the shift. The regime's repression thus incited a wave of mass demonstrations far beyond the scale of the 1990 riots. The protestors were an amalgam of the original intelligentsia-based civic groups along with Pamiri supporters of Khudonazar, Badakhshani supporters of Navzhuvanov, and Kulyabis inhabiting Dushanbe and the neighboring Kulyab *oblast'* who had decided to assert their own grievances against their Leninabad patrons. In fact, Russian and local journalists reported that busloads of regional clan supporters had arrived in Dushanbe from the Pamir and Badakhshan regions to join the protests.[110]

---

[109] Ibid.

[110] Rubin notes that "in the aftermath of the Soviet breakdown, patronage networks based on regionalism became key to political mobilization," in Barnett Rubin, "Russian Hege-mony and State Breakdown: Causes and Consequences of the Tajik Civil War," in Barnett Rubin and Jack Snyder, eds., *Post-Soviet Political Order* (London: Routledge Press, 1998), pp. 152–153.

The so-called opposition had come to be known by various names – the "democratic," "Islamic," or "nationalist" forces. The regime was simply painted as the "pro-Communist" forces. The outside world, as well as the Nabiev regime itself, thus came to view the escalating conflict in entirely misleading ideological terms.[111] Although the Khodjentis and Kulyabis had dominated the CPT, they were by no means committed to its goals or ideals. And as post-1994 events would demonstrate, the bond of communism would not prove strong enough to hold these disparate regional rivals together in the government. The "Islamic" front was led by IRP head Mullah Sayyid Abdullo Nuri; however it too fractured along clan and regional lines, with rivalries between the IRP of Garm, organized around Mullah Nuri's family lineage, the IRP of Kurgan-Tyube, and the "official Islam" of the *qaziyat* in Dushanbe.[112] Some also portrayed the conflict in ethnic terms, with Tajiks pitted against Russians and Uzbeks, when in fact the Uzbek population of Leninabad was largely not party to the demonstrations, while the Russian population, concentrated in the industrial and academic sector, had begun a mass exodus from the republic.[113] Between 1989 and 1992, almost 300,000 Russians emigrated.[114]

Despite its heterogeneity and regional divisions, the opposition merged against the regime in a steady and mounting series of protests from March through May of 1992. Meeting at the capital's central square, the demonstrators began by demanding (1) the release of Navzhuvanov, (2) the release of Ikramov, and (3) an end to the ban on the Communist Party.[115] These demands were limited, but far more concrete than those voiced by the DPT and IRP earlier in 1991 – cultural revival, a greater respect for Islamic values, and a general commitment to "Tajik identity." President Nabiev, however, responded with a show of executive force, making his clan crony Safarali Kenjaev not only chair of the Supreme Soviet but also head of the SNB, the renamed KGB. The demonstrators' demands grew louder and far more

[111] Government members repeatedly characterized the fragmented opposition groups by using the monolithic terms "opposition" and "Islamists." Author's interviews with first and second secretaries, Embassy of Tajikistan in Uzbekistan, Tashkent, September 1997 and April 1998. Russian government officials and scholars often use these labels. See Aleksei Malashenko, "Religioznoe ekho etnopoliticheskikh konfliktov," *Svobodnaia Mysl'* (1994).
[112] There were also debates among the Islamic clergy in Uzbekistan as to which Islam was the real Islam in Tajikistan. Most concluded that the "Islam" put forth by these political groups was a slogan with little substance, and not true Islam. Olivier Roy, who advised the OSCE mission in Tajikistan, noted the same phenomenon.
[113] Dmitry Trofimov, first secretary, Russian embassy in Uzbekistan, notes the same tendency. Author interview with Trofimov, Tashkent, March 1997.
[114] This figure was provided by the Russian embassy first consul in Uzbekistan, March 15, 1997. Prior to 1990, Russians had comprised about 8 percent of the population of Tajikistan. They were mainly concentrated in Dushanbe and Leninabad.
[115] See V. I. Bushkov and D. V. Mikul'skii, *Anatomiia grazhdanskoi voiny v Tadzhikistane* (Moscow: PAN, 1997), pp. 116–118, for detailed accounts of the breakdown of order.

serious: the nullification of the 1991 elections and the resignation of both Kenjaev and Nabiev. The wavering of the regime – Makhkamov's uncertainty and Nabiev's repression in the wake of the collapse of his Moscow patron – seemed to give the opposition greater coherence, at least momentarily, as it united, escalated its tactics, articulated its demands, and defined its goals.[116]

On May 3, 1992, the demonstrators and regime came head to head. When General Bahrom Rakhmonov, a Pamiri military advisor, deserted the regime and joined the Pamiri opposition, violence broke out. He threw open an arsenal outside Dushanbe and armed the demonstrators. Kenjaev responded by distributing Soviet Kalashnikov rifles to the MVD and KNB troops, as well as to Kulyabi supporters in Dushanbe. Shots were fired on the square, some civilians were killed, and perhaps hundreds more were wounded. The demonstrators named the place Shahidan (Martyrs') Square.[117]

Into the Maelstrom

Desperate to avoid chaos and civil war, Nabiev suddenly agreed to meet with the leaders of the opposition, under the auspices of the CIS commanding general in Tajikistan. On May 13, a document of reconciliation was signed, according to which a National Assembly was to be created in place of the Supreme Soviet, and a coalition government was immediately established. Akbarsho Iskanderov, a leading Pamiri elite, became chairman of the so-called coalition. The interim regime's problems were basic and twofold: first, the Khodjenti and Kulyabi clans refused to recognize the coalition government. Second, in the words of one Western diplomat, the so-called government of national reconciliation was "neither a government, nor national, nor one of reconciliation."[118] In fact, the coalition regime would not achieve a single concrete policy goal during its six months in power. It certainly did not bring even basic order to the republic. During the course of its rule, demonstrations gave way to full-fledged conflict, as each side (the opposition and the Nabiev regime) increasingly gave its supporters access to weapons.

A civil war had erupted and spread rapidly outside of the capital. As the war flowed from the Dushanbe intelligentsia to the rural peasant population,

---

[116] Social movement theory notes that it is the process of a social movement or protest that gives identity to the participants. The increased strength of the opposition's Islamic self-identification by 1997 and 1998 supports his argument. Interestingly, Islam in Chechnya has taken a similar direction.

[117] Author's interview with an ORT journalist who covered the demonstrations in person, Tashkent, July 1997. The interviewee noted the extreme uncertainty and contingency of the events from moment to moment.

[118] Author's interview with former U.S. ambassador to Tajikistan (1992–95) Stanley Escadero, July 1997.

ideological motives receded or disappeared altogether.[119] Likewise, the mass opposition movements disintegrated, and small, clan-based factions became the units of resistance. Their leaders were generally driven by a desire for increased resources and power, and their militias and support were mobilized through kin and fictive-kin networks.

Nearly six months of intensive village-to-village conflict ensued, warfare fueled by the rapid proliferation and increasing access to weapons due to unregulated cross-border smuggling from Afghanistan – which had plunged into its own conflict between the *mujahideen* and the Soviet-established communist government of the day.[120] Aided by Russian border troops, whose mission became continually more expansive, as well as by covert weapons transfers from Iran and Uzbekistan, the pro-Nabiev forces were well supplied and devastating. To the surprise of the regime, the Soviet 201st Motorized Rifle Division, staffed largely by Garmi Tajiks, initially deserted the government, exemplifying the Tajik regime's failure to assert control over a fractured military during 1990 and 1991.

Nabiev continued to foster clan-based militias. He enlisted the notorious Kulyabi ex-convict Sangak Safarov to form a special armed division, the Popular Front. Nabiev stacked the Presidential Guard with Kulyabis. Other individual Kulyabi forces included a militia under the control of the independent commander Langari Langariev. Another was a "secular" militia led by the popular leader Khaidar Sharifov, a Muslim cleric.[121] The latter group defied the general perception that the opposition was "Islamic" and that the government was "secular." Nabiev's militias committed some of the worst atrocities of the war, as they raided village after village of the Garmi, Badakhshani, Hissari, and Karategini clans; they executed or expelled entire local populations, and reportedly raped thousands of women.[122] Their actions brought the conflict to a deeply personal and tragic level. As refugees depicted the chaos, "We are all Tajiks, but one Tajik was killing another Tajik; and then brother was avenging brother. We never thought this could happen."[123] By the end of 1993, 50,000 to 100,000 were estimated dead,

---

[119] M. Olimov and S. Olimova, *Tadzhikistan na poroge peremen* (Moscow: Center for Strategic and Political Research, 1999).

[120] The Afghan conflict did not cause the Tajik war, but the breakdown of the Kabul regime made the flow of arms to Tajikistan easy and profitable. See Rubin, "The Fragmentation of Tajikistan," p. 213.

[121] Dmitry Trofimov, *Problemy etno-konfessional'nogo razvitiia* (Moscow: IMEMO, 1994), p. 25.

[122] Author's interview with Stanley Escadero and with U.S. military and civilian monitors of the conflict, Tashkent, Uzbekistan, May 1998. In interviews with UN military observers, Tashkent, February 1997, the interviewees noted the same phenomenon. They called it a war of personal revenge. "Everyone had a relative who had been killed, and often they knew who or from which village or clan the killer was." The UN personnel had been evacuated to Uzbekistan due to repeated kidnappings of foreign aid workers.

[123] Author's communication with a Tajik sociologist, Moscow, August 1998.

and 500,000 refugees had fled across the border to Afghanistan, Kyrgyzstan, and other parts of the CIS. Approximately one million people, almost one-fifth of the population, had suffered internal displacement.[124]

The violence did not spare Dushanbe. On September 7, 1993, Pamiri oppositionists chased Nabiev from the capital. Before escaping to Khodjent, Nabiev was compelled by his captors to sign a letter submitting his resignation from the office of president.[125] The opposition-led government at last took control in Dushanbe. Under the Pamiri chairman of the Supreme Soviet, Iskanderov, the presidency was abolished and a parliamentary regime established. And yet the Iskanderov regime could not control Dushanbe, much less the entire republic. Safarov and Kenjaev still mobilized their respective armed forces, as did dozens of other small, local clan-based and mafioso units.[126] Even the opposition became increasingly fractured and refused to surrender power to Iskanderov, who failed to represent the non-Pamiri clans and hence the larger and more populous regions of the republic.[127] By November, the opposition government was again losing to the pro-Khodjenti/Kulyabi forces.

The Elections of 1994: A New Pact?

On November 16, 1993, the Supreme Soviet, once again representing Khodjent, met in an emergency session to reject Nabiev's resignation; instead, the deputies simply abolished the office of president. Yet, in a move aimed at preserving their power and the Khodjenti-Kulyabi clan alliance, the session elected Imomali Rakhmonov to a newly created post – parliamentary chairman, now the highest executive post in the republic.[128] Rakhmonov was a former *kolkhoz* director and chairman of the Kulyab *oblast'* executive committee. For the first time in history, the primary position would go to a

---

[124] See the UNHCR report on Tajikistan, 1997 (unpublished internal report, made available to the author by the Tashkent headquarters). The Russian scholar Vladimir Mukomel' provides a much lower estimate: 20,000 casualties in 1992 and approximately 3,000 in subsequent years (1993–96). This is the lowest figure, and probably an underestimate. Mukomel' does claim that the number of rapes was far underreported and perhaps on the scale of the tragedy in Bosnia. See Vladimir Mukomel', "Vooruzhonnye mezhnatsional'nye i regional'nye konflikti: liudskie poteri, ekonomicheskii ushcherb i sotsial'nye posledtviia," in Martha Brill Olcott, Valery Tishkov, and Aleksei Malashenko, eds., *Identichnost' i konflikt v postsovetskikh gosudarstvakh* (Moscow: Carnegie Foundation Report, 1997), p. 301. ICG estimates up to 100,000 rapes, ICG report, December 24, 2001.

[125] Personal communication with a former member of Nabiev's apparat, Tashkent, Uzbekistan, May 1998.

[126] For a detailed look at the various clan and mafia elements involved in the conflict, see Bushkov and Mikul'skii, *Anatomiia*, pp. 141–150.

[127] Based on author's discussions with UN military observers, Tashkent, March 1997.

[128] Author's interview with Abdumalik Abdullajonov, former Prime Minister of Tajikistan (1992–94), Tashkent, Uzbekistan, August 1997.

Kulyabi, not a Khodjenti. In fact, the traditional relationship was reversed, with the Khodjenti leader Abdumalik Abdullajonov now in the position of prime minister. Abdullajonov was a powerful businessman and highly connected clan leader from Nabiev's Khodjenti clique. The Khodjentis were confident that he would successfully represent their interests in the regime, especially since they had selected Rakhmonov mainly for his lack of experience; the compromise was primarily symbolic. Meanwhile, the Khodjentis worked with the UN, Iran, and Russia to convoke a new presidential election in November 1994. Abdullajonov was already campaigning for the post. The elections of November 1994, however, turned out differently as international actors and neighboring countries became increasingly involved. Rakhmonov, with the external support of Uzbekistan and Russia, won a close election with 52 percent of the votes. Abdullajonov, declaring the vote invalid, resigned. By his estimates – he had organized his own electoral observers and vote counters – he had won in a landslide.[129] Once again, both sides alleged fraud, and minor armed skirmishes erupted throughout the country. Abdullajonov's forces resorted to extralegal measures to avenge him. Some of these would continue even after the peace agreement of 1997.

The Transition without Peace

The elections were hardly the end of the battle for power in Tajikistan. Instead, they indicated a deep and troublesome fault line in the Kulyabi-Khodjenti patron-client relationship, and the likelihood that these clans would initiate a new era of the violent interclan struggle for power and resources. Further, the elections highlighted the continuing lack of regime legitimacy, and consequently Tajikistan's increased reliance on outside forces and sources of revenue to prop up the weak and contested clan-based regime. What the elections did not foretell was the nature of the regime to follow. Democracy versus communism was not an electoral issue. Both candidates claimed to represent democracy. None of the players, however, seemed particularly concerned with what democracy might entail, and economic reform was not on the agenda. However, based on the precedent set by those in power already, it was highly unlikely that a democratic transition would follow the 1994 elections. Nonetheless, the elections did mark the conclusion of the full-scale civil conflict. They were a turning point in Tajikistan's trajectory.

SUMMARY

The regime transitions examined in the previous chapters present a number of challenges to the conventional theoretical arguments made about

---

[129] Author's interview with Abdumalik Abdullajonov, August 1997.

political transition and democratization in general, and to the rather static assumptions commonly made about the Central Asian transitions in particular. First, as argued earlier, the modernization and culturalist approaches, although admittedly not intended to explain democratization, do not shed light on the great diversity of transitional trajectories (democratization, neoautocracy, and civil conflict) that we find in the Central Asian cases. Analyses based on cultural and socioeconomic preconditions simply cannot explain why, from 1991 through 1994, rapid political democratization and economic liberalization took place and met with relative success in Kyrgyzstan, which by 1994 had not only met the basic criteria for an electoral and semiliberal democracy but showed strong signs of moving toward a full liberal democracy. In the political realm, Kyrgyzstan had far outpaced most of its neighbors in the CIS, and it even rivaled some countries in Eastern Europe. Its reforms proved short-term and easily reversible, but they were real while they lasted. The Kyrgyz Republic could not be dismissed as a mere "virtual" democracy. Further, introducing a democracy, even for a few years, does have some long-term positive effects, especially on civil society.

Second, the democratization and transitions literature does not explain the particular mode and phases of transition that the Kyrgyz, Uzbek, and Tajik cases underwent as they moved from colonial republics to independent states, and from communist regimes to something else. The literature's focus on pacts is misleading, for as we have argued, pacts of the kind that took place in Kyrgyzstan and Uzbekistan, while critical preconditions for a viable regime transition, do not guarantee a democratic one.[130] Furthermore, as I proposed in Chapter 2, clan interests are predominantly resource-driven in promotion of their kin networks. The pacts that Central Asians make are nonideological arrangements between social networks. Ideology is not even on the table. One would be hard-pressed to identify the hard-line versus soft-line clan elites. In contrast to Eastern Europe or Russia – and, in fact, more along the lines of Afghanistan or certain African cases – Central Asian societies and elites could boast only a few committed communists, and perhaps even fewer vocal and committed democrats. Instead, such pacts integrate competing clans into the governing apparatus, which in turn divides power and resources among them. In contrast to the central hypothesis of the transitions literature, elite pacting is not a "mode of transition"; it has not led to democratization in Kyrgyzstan. Yet a pact does make a durable transition more likely, and thus probably benefits democratization in the end.

---

[130] See Collins, "Clans, Pacts, and Politics: Understanding Regime Transition in Central Asia" (Ph.D. dissertation, Stanford University, 1999), Chapter 2, for a much more extensive discussion and critique of the hypotheses and indicators of each theory. Pacts are not a mode of transition to democracy in these cases. Also see Collins, "Clans, Pacts, and Politics," *Journal of Democracy*, vol. 13, no. 3 (July 2002), pp. 137–52.

Third, the historical comparison presented in this chapter suggests a different approach to analyzing transitions in Central Asia as well as in other places with clan-based social structures. First, as proposed in Chapter 2, clans do not determine ideological trajectories; rather, the discussion has highlighted certain *micro-level variables* – the very powerful and yet limited role of particular political actors, the transitional *elites*, and their *ideology* in shaping the emergent state's trajectory. These elite variables are highly contingent, and yet most critical during this most precarious moment of transition. Even when elite actors are most free of structure, their perceptions and decisions, and ultimately their breadth of choices, are highly influenced and constrained by *social structure*, by the structural nature of both the clan pacts and the clan societies within which they play the political game.

Fourth, elites can introduce an ideological agenda and impose that agenda for a limited period. And yet, as we saw in the previous chapter, the Central Asian transitions distinguished themselves from others by their very dearth of ideological discourse. This lack of an ideological agenda, however, has ideological consequences. The short-term transition becomes highly contingent upon the broker's ideology, if indeed he has one. Chapter 7 will demonstrate that as soon as clans realize that their resources are threatened by transitional reforms (part and parcel of democratization), they become antagonistic. Further, in pursuing their narrow group agendas, clans present challenges both for a democratic society and for any kind of state building. The Tajik case illuminates the destructive consequences of nonideological but resource-competing clan networks in the absence of a balancing clan pact.

In sum, these transitions highlight the complex and delicate interaction between structure and agency, and suggest the limits of the latter within certain types of dense and deep-seated social organizations.[131] As the next chapter will argue, clan-based societies severely constrict the influence of elite ideologies and individual elites' choices.

---

[131] On the relationship between structure and agency, see Alexander Wendt, *A Social Theory of International Politics* (New York: Cambridge University Press, 1999), Ch.2.

7

Central Asia's Regime Transformation (1995–2004)

Part I

> A Kyrgyz who doesn't know his clan and his fathers ten generations back must be ashamed. He is not a Kyrgyz.
>
> Kyrgyz woman, Bishkek, 1995

This remark was made by a Kyrgyz woman from the Soviet-educated intelligentsia in 1995. Chingiz Aitmatov wrote much the same in a story about a clan village on a *kolkhoz* in Talas in the 1940s. Probably the same was often said by *oqsoqol*s in the early Soviet and pre-Soviet days. Kin relations have powerful meaning, yet they are not purely social or cultural. One student, a citizen of the Kyrgyz Republic (with a prestigious U.S. degree), told me that if you do not have the right kin relations, then you will not find a good job. So, like so many other qualified young people, she wants to leave. Kin and clan have powerful aspects, both positive and negative. Why and how they affect the social and elite level of politics, even after the post-Soviet transitions, is the subject of this chapter.

I. FORMAL AND INFORMAL REGIMES IN THE POST-TRANSITION PERIOD

From 1991 to 1995, as Chapter 6 has shown, the Central Asian regime trajectories were clearly distinct. They differed both in terms of (1) their *durability* (the regime's ability to survive, that is, to avoid collapse or civil war during transition), and (2) their *regime type* (the ideological and institutional nature of the new post-Soviet regime). Subsequently, however, these political trajectories increasingly converged along the same two dimensions.[1] Studying these dimensions is complex; it involves explaining a dynamic process, not a

---

[1] On regime convergence during this period, see Philip Roeder, "The Revolution of 1989: Postcommunism and the Social Sciences," *Slavic Review*, vol. 58, no. 4 (Winter 1999), pp. 743–755.

fixed outcome. Where did these regimes stand from 1995 to 2004? All three are now widely recognized as super-presidential authoritarian systems. Although degrees of difference exist, Kyrgyzstan is no longer hailed as a democratizer, and little hope remains for the promised post-war democratization of Tajikistan. Uzbekistan's regime looks very much the same.[2] All three are temporarily durable, but none has become successfully consolidated (institutionalized and unlikely to collapse, given a shock to its system).[3] Uzbekistan's regime is somewhat stronger than the others, but fragile. Kyrgyzstan is increasingly precarious, and Tajikistan still relies enormously on Russia for its stability.[4] Lack of consolidation is surprising given that these regimes are formally super-presidential systems, and given that all have strong Soviet institutional roots; they have a much stronger institutional foundation than many other post-colonial regimes.

The previous chapter, in examining the divergence of post-Soviet trajectories in Central Asia, argued that in these cases particular elites, especially the presidents, made critical choices about democratization or nondemocratization. Yet focusing exclusively on individual elites ignores deeper empirical and theoretical puzzles: what happens after the transition, and why? Besides specifying the limited transitional role of presidential elites during the late Soviet and post-Soviet periods, I have also highlighted the central role of clan-based pacts in regime durability. Although clans determined neither the timing of the transition nor the type of regime institutions that were adopted, clans both shaped the pacts, thereby gaining influence with the regime, and affected the transitional leaders' decisions in critical ways. We should therefore ask what role these clan networks will have in the longer term, beyond the initial transition. We should wonder, in particular, whether and how these social networks might be linked to the nonconsolidation of the new regimes.

In this chapter and the next, I take up the fourth proposition set out in Chapter 2. I empirically argue that informal clan politics defines the new Central Asian regimes and prevents regime consolidation in all three cases. Clan politics causes the convergence of these three distinct trajectories to a common path characterized by the rise of informal clan networks that control, contest, and divide economic and political power, and by weak formal regime institutions. As clan elites and their networks pervade formal institutions and "capture" the state's resources, they prevent the consolidation of *both* democratic and authoritarian regimes and weaken their overall durability.

---

[2] See Freedom House indexes of political and civil liberties, Appendix, Table A.5.

[3] On defining durability and nonconsolidation, see Chapter 1. See also Deborah Yashar, "Democracy, Indigenous Movements, and the Postliberal Challenge in Latin America," *World Politics*, vol. 52, no. 1 (October 1999), pp. 76–104.

[4] On failures of consolidation, see International Crisis Group, "Tajikistan's Politics: Confrontation or Consolidation," *Asia Briefing*, May 19, 2004.

Second, I distinguish between two dimensions of these regimes: *formal and informal*. They are not simply authoritarian, neo-totalitarian, or neo-communist states, as the vast literature on the post-Soviet region suggests. The *formal regime*, which consists of the official, legal ordering of power and governmental institutions, has indeed become increasingly authoritarian in all three, especially since the 1999–2000 elections in Kyrgyzstan and Tajikistan. Moreover, although the new leaders make use of Soviet institutions, they have uniformly jettisoned communist ideology and the Party. The formal regimes face few mechanisms of accountability; they are based upon a super-presidential executive branch and a weak or fig-leaf legislature and judiciary. Only Kyrgyzstan retains any institutional checks upon the president. In theory, the presidencies are strong, and a strong, unified, centralized authoritarian state should have consolidated.

Third, I argue that an *informal regime* – the informal ordering of power and institutions of governance among informal actors and networks – exists behind the exterior façade. This regime is not readily transparent to its own subjects or outsiders, much less accountable to them. The interaction between informal actors and networks – especially clans – and the formal regime is substantial, especially during the transition, as the formal institutions of the old regime weaken or break down. Informal networks increasingly fill the power vacuum. Informal actors, especially clan elites, drive this process. In focusing on the post-transition trajectories, this chapter highlights the mechanisms by which clan networks penetrate the regime, creating an informal regime that shapes the political trajectory. Chapter 2 set out several key mechanisms. First, nepotism and patronage of one's kin and clan, in order to fulfill one's clan debts and duties and to surround oneself with loyal supporters, is a phenomenon that affects cadre choices and policies throughout the system. Clan patronage often occurs at the expense of transparency and effective policy formation and implementation. Second, the latter phenomenon allows clan asset stripping, or the dispersal of state goods to one's kin, clan, and clients. State jobs are doled out for personal gain. Third, clans within the regime or institutions of power use their networks either directly or indirectly to crowd out other forms of organization or representation. Clans, in short, monopolize the political and economic space, making alternative forms of organization unlikely. Clan elites grab power and resources, while clan members, followers, and clients accept dependence on these networks. Both elites and nonelites do so at the expense of the formal regime.

Fourth, this chapter and the next also show the decline during this period in "clan balancing," which had characterized the pre-transition period. Balancing had allowed the incorporation of various powerful clans within a pact, and had fostered a sharing of resources among them so as to preclude serious clan-based opposition. Clan balancing and pacts had taken place in the presence of an external threat, but as that threat declines or disappears during the post-Soviet period, the new Central Asian presidents – the managers of these pacts, charged with maintaining that balance – seem less inclined to maintain a balance of clan interests and increasingly prone to asserting hegemonic control. Together, these processes lead not only to a hollowing out of the formal regime, but also to declining regime durability. Under conditions of weak states and shrinking resources, clan politics is likely to significantly weaken the regime, risking collapse and conflict unless other factors intervene to stabilize the system.[5] Contestation over declining resources within clan pacts, and the exclusion of certain clans and other groups from the pacts altogether, has created friction in all three cases. This, in turn, creates greater potential for division or open conflict along clan-based lines.

This chapter demonstrates that clan politics pervades each case, inhibiting or preventing both democratization and regime consolidation. Although more rampant and visible in some cases, clan politics is present in each, in multiple realms: at the social level, within elite and national-level institutions, and within state-society linkages. As David Collier has argued, multiple observations of a phenomenon are important for establishing the importance of a variable and its causal effects.[6] Chapters 7 and 8 address all three levels in each case. In each realm, clans use common causal mechanisms to gain access and power. In each realm, we see that the informal institutions that typify clan behavior in the political realm in fact undermine the formal institutions of the regime in various ways. Clan politics furthermore undermines the legitimacy of the regime and drains state resources, a process that can lead to bankruptcy. Clan politics penetrates the regime and state at all levels, often with sponsorship from the very highest echelons of power. The president himself subverts the institution of the presidency by relying on clans and personalistic ties to rule, rather than on institutionalized executive power. Cabinet members, bureaucrats, local officials, and party leaders do the same. The use and abuse of clan networks to attain and keep power, and clans' use of informal institutions such as patronage and nepotism, lead to personalistic, particularistic, and exclusivist rule, the weakening of formal institutions, and the stripping of state resources. Competition between clans further weakens the regime and the state. Clan politics manifests itself somewhat differently in democratic and authoritarian regimes. Although more visible and immediately corrosive in the former, clan politics penetrates and undermines the key elements of each, resulting in a weakening, though not a complete destabilization, of these regimes.

[5] On the risk of collapse and conflict in personalistic, weakly institutionalized regimes under economic crisis, see Robert Rotberg, "Failed States, Collapsed States, Weak States: Causes and Indicators," in Robert Rotberg, ed., *State Failure and State Weakness in a Time of Terror* (Cambridge, MA: Brookings Institution Press, 2003); and Robert Rotberg, ed., *When States Fail: Causes and Consequences* (Princeton, NJ: Princeton University Press, 2004).

[6] David Collier and James Mahoney, "Insights and Pitfalls: Selection Bias in Qualitative Research," *World Politics*, vol. 49, no. 1 (1996), pp. 56–91.

In this chapter, I first examine the role of clans at the social level across the region. Then I explore the elite and state-society realms in the Kyrgyz case. Chapter 8 turns to clan politics within Uzbekistan and Tajikistan.

I. THE ROLE OF CLAN IDENTITY AND NETWORKS AT THE SOCIAL LEVEL

Apart from the elite and state-society levels of analysis, then, we should expect clans to function at the local, social level as well. Most political science scholarship, especially work concerned with post-Soviet Central Asia, has focused exclusively on elites and on formally institutionalized identities at the elite level. As a consequence, some have misunderstood the nature and roots of identities, attributing them exclusively to the Soviet period,[7] while others have focused only on those identities that can be more easily observed and are officially categorized.[8] Ronald Suny has critiqued such approaches, arguing that the repertoire of identities with which scholars have explained political behavior in Central Asia has been too limited.[9] My fieldwork in Central Asia in the 1990s, inspired by anthropological work on kinship and clans in other regions, included a significant social-level and rural component as well. Ethnographic research, in fact, powerfully suggests that kin-based networks continue to be operative at the local level, with somewhat less stigma than at the elite level, despite both Soviet and post-Soviet repression. Further, as I argued of clans in Chapter 2, this social-level research demonstrates that these networks embody an identity/cultural component, but at the same time are also "rational."

Clan networks, in various forms, existed throughout Central Asia at the social level long before the Soviet period, as Chapter 3 noted. Just as at the elite level, some variation in these identity networks exists from case to case and within cases, depending on the historical settlement pattern of the particular village or region. As they did during the pre-Soviet period, local networks in the late twentieth century took the form of *avlod, aul, qishloq,* and *mahalla.*[10] All share a culture of kinship bonds in the form of extended family, lineage, or clan, as well as fictive kin identity bonds in the form of village and *mahalla* ties, or "residence

---

[7] For example, see Jones Luong, *Institutional Change, and Political Continuity in Post-Soviet Central Asia: Power, Perceptions and Pacts* (Cambridge: Cambridge University Press, 2002), ch. 2.

[8] The extensive literature on nationality and ethnic conflict in Central Asia provides numerous examples.

[9] Ronald G. Suny, "Provisional Stabilities: The Politics of Identities in Post-Soviet Eurasia," *International Security*, vol. 24, no. 3 (Winter 1999/2000), pp. 139–178.

[10] See Oliver Roy, *The New Central Asia* (New York: New York University Press, 2000), pp. 87–89; and Saodat Olimova and Igor Bosc, *Labor Migration in Tajikistan* (Dushanbe: IOM, July 2003), pp. 49–50.

communities."[11] Whether in Kyrgyzstan, Uzbekistan, or Tajikistan, these bonds commonly exhibit a strong sense of "localism."

The cultural differences and implications of such local variation have been studied by ethnographers and anthropologists; they cannot be adequately addressed in the space here.[12] What is important for this study is to understand the importance of these ties and identities at the local and mass level, where they exist in a more traditional form. These networks pervade the social fabric of these states and constitute the social base that elite clan networks must control, govern, or mobilize, often through the creation of multiple layers of patronage ties. Local identity groups, furthermore, play important roles in stabilizing society by acting as a social safety net to meet the everyday needs of its citizens in the absence of effective state institutions.

Chapter 2 argued that the clan has rational, socioeconomic roots, and further that we should expect this network's importance to expand during times of political and economic transition, when its ties are necessary to daily survival. How do we address the third layer of identity at the social level? Ideally, a large-number random-sample survey, repeated over several years, would be used to get at mass attitudes, beliefs, and identities. However, in the post-Soviet context of authoritarian regimes and often reserved (to foreigners) Central Asian cultures, surveys seem to be a less-than-fruitful option. Survey instruments are especially problematic when studying informal identities. Local sociologists and ethnographers argue that clan and local network identities in rural and semirural Central Asia should be studied ethnographically, through in-depth interviews and participant observation.[13] A better understanding of the clan's social identity enables us to examine its role in fostering stability or fomenting conflict at the social level during the transitional and post-Soviet periods. Therefore, in the mid-1990s, in a series of trips to the villages, representing a sampling of regional variation across the Kyrgyz and Uzbek cases, I conducted ethnographic interviews and engaged in participant observation in order to better understand clan identity at the mass level.[14] In Tajikistan, the civil war prevented such fieldwork. However, separate research conducted by local Tajik sociologists supplements my findings in the other cases. Although qualitative and based upon smaller

[11] Paul Georg Geiss, *Pre-Tsarist and Tsarist Central Asia: Communal Commitment and Political Order in Change* (London: Routledge Curzon, 2003), pp. 86–96.
[12] See Sergei Abashin, "Tadzhikskii avlod tysiacheletiia spustia...," *Vostok*, no. 5 (1991), pp. 72–81; Geiss, *Pre-Tsarist and Tsarist*, pp. 38–60; V. V. Radlov, "Obraztsi narodnoi literaturi tiurkskikh' plemen, chast' 1," in S. Aliev et al., *Entsiklopedicheskii fenomen eposa Manas: sbornik statei* (Bishkek: Redaktsiia Kyrgyzskoi Entsiklopedii, 1995); M. Nazif Mohib Shahrani, *The Kirghiz and Wakhi of Afghanistan* (Seattle: University of Washington Press, 1979).
[13] Author's discussions with sociologists and ethnographers, including Valery Tishkov (Stanford, California, 1995), Alisher Ilkhamov (Tashkent, 1996), and several others.
[14] See the Appendix for a discussion of the advantages and disadvantages of such a method.

samples, this data provides an anthropological view of the cultural meaning and rational role of clan networks at the local level.

Such social-level research is critical to understanding to what extent clan identities, norms, and networks have operated in the rural areas during the post-Soviet period. The research focused on several indicators to assess the presence and relevance of clan identity networks. The first is language. As with other identities, it is important to note the use of language to express clan identity. Second, the presence and strength of clan and network identities is noted by observing their behavior within the local rural units – especially the village and *kolkhoz*. Such clan identities should incorporate and exhibit both rational and normative elements. I further attempted to assess the strength of clan presence by focusing questions on four main areas of concern: finances, living patterns, migration, and sociopolitical roles.

The Language of Clan Identity: Variations within the Region

The Central Asian populations express the concept of "clan" in both their native language and in Russian. However, as noted in Chapter 3, different groups (which vary in geographical location, socioeconomic base, and degree of urbanization) sometimes differ in the verbal terminology used to describe kinship networks, a phenomenon similar across these groups. Although the essential features of clan identity – kinship, identity, and a social network around those bonds – are present almost universally in rural areas, the nature and expression of clan identity varies from Kyrgyz villages (typically referred to as an *aul*, or sometimes as a *qishloq*) to Uzbek villages and residential communities (generally referred to as either a *qishloq* or a *mahalla*) to Tajik villages (alternately called *aul* or *qishloq*), as well as by the geography and specific economy (agricultural versus pastoral) of the regions within Kyrgyzstan and Uzbekistan. Language frequently reveals these differences.

Kyrgyz generally refer either to their historic tribe or to their more immediate lineage or clan (*rod* or *klan*, in Russian) or to their tribe (*plemia*). While the traditional Kyrgyz word is "*uruu*," Kyrgyz have widely incorporated the Russian terms into their local vocabulary.[15] Kyrgyz typically refer to a clan name, which defines their kin-based or semi-kin-based network – usually a small village (ranging in size from 1,000 to 3,000 inhabitants). Villages

---

[15] When Kyrgyz use the term *klan* they refer to a network with a strong kinship core; Uzbeks and Tajiks often use the term to refer to both kin-based groups and fictive kin networks (as discussed in Chapter 2) linked by other informal social, business, or marriage ties. The Russian use of the term, by contrast, refers almost exclusively to power cliques and mafia groups, generally with no kinship bonds. The Central Asian use of the term is far closer to the Middle Eastern usage and its genealogical connotation than to the Slavic usage. This is understandable, given that Central Asian family networks were typically much more extensive than Slavic ones. See Dale Eickelman, *The Middle East and Central Asia: An Anthropological Approach* (Upper Saddle River, NJ: Prentice Hall, 1998).

are frequently named after famous ancestors or lineages. Frequently, nearby villages on the same (former) *kolkhoz* are composed of extended kin or kin by marriage. (The *kolkhozes* have now been privatized in land reform.) Hence, the villagers are "fictively" members of the same clan. Respondents frequently answered about neighboring villages, "We marry each other. We are all related." When distinguishing themselves from others, at the national level or in the capital city, Kyrgyz often simply say, "I'm from Talas" or "I'm from Osh." Within their own region, however, they specifically refer to their village and clan or tribal lineage. One respondent said, "I'm from Chui, but I'm not Sarybagysh, like the president. I'm Solto." Kyrgyz respondents typically take pride in their tribal and clan ancestry, which they relate to their nomadic way of life. Although the Russian colloquialism "*klan*," with its implication of corruption, has increasingly replaced the use of the more traditional Russian word for clan (*rod*), Kyrgyz respondents in the villages do not dismiss clan as corruption. Most exhibit pride in their clan and tribal lineages. A common response to the question, "Does your clan matter, have meaning?" was "Of course." Several explained that "it would be a shame not to know your ancestors ten generations back." An elder in a village in Osh province retrieved a handwritten manuscript chronicling his clan ancestry. Another respondent said, "Our clan-tribal traditions are good. They are democratic. Our women never wore veils. We are very egalitarian." Clan and tribal ties were typically strongly and positively associated with the Kyrgyz nationality.

Ethnic Uzbeks tend to inhabit more populous, long-settled, intensively agricultural areas. They typically consider not only their village, in which most inhabitants are somehow related by blood or marriage, but also several neighboring villages to be part of that social network.[16] If a fellow Uzbek is from one's own region, he is part of that clan. At the most local level, for example, one is a Pop*lik* (from the village Pop). At the broader or national level, one from Namangan *oblast'* refers to himself as a Namangan*lik*[17] (from Namangan region, as opposed to another region). Their cognitive understanding of the clan and kinship is both more tied to the land and more fictive, probably reflecting their longer-settled roots in a particular village, as opposed to the typically more recently nomadic Kyrgyz. Explicitly political

[16] Ethnic Uzbeks in both Uzbekistan and Kyrgyzstan have generally been longer settled, and their "clan" has become associated less with a nomadic lineage than with their local network. This is typical of the Ferghana Valley. In other regions of Uzbekistan, however, both Uzbeks and many non-Uzbeks (e.g., the Tajiks of Surkhandarya and Kashkadarya and Namangan *oblast*'s, Kyrgyz of Andijan *oblast*', and Karakalpaks and Uzbeks of the Bukharan steppe), have more recent nomadic roots and still use more traditional identity terminology. It is an oversimplification to claim, as many nationalist Uzbek writers do, that the population of Uzbekistan was historically settled while the populations of Tajikistan and Kyrgyzstan were not. On Uzbek tribes, See Geiss, *Pre-Tsarist and Tsarist Central Asia*, pp. 43–45.

[17] The Turkic suffix *lik* refers to one who is of that place, and it is critical in defining the boundaries of that clan, boundaries that are primarily intra-ethnic, not interethnic.

factors also have influenced local understandings of the term "clan." Many Uzbeks take pride in their lineage, as do Kyrgyz. Indeed, in a village on the Uzbek side of the Ferghana Valley, an elder retrieved a written history of the clan's descendents, just as a Kyrgyz elder had done across the Kyrgyz border. However, Uzbek respondents more often associate the Russian word *klan* with the mafia, and thus are reluctant to refer to their local network as a clan. First the Andropov-Gorbachev purges, which hit the Uzbek Republic the hardest during the 1980s, and now Uzbek president Islam Karimov's frequent speeches against both clanism and regionalism as threats to the Uzbek nation, have vilified clans.[18] Uzbeks speak of their *rod*, and more typically of their *"urugh"* or *"avlod"* (clan and extended patrilineal family/lineage), although respondents frequently distinguish themselves from ethnic Kyrgyz, who do not share their "settled traditions."

Several studies of Tajikistan indicate that Tajik rural communities and identity networks have strong similarities to those in both Kyrgyzstan and Uzbekistan. Longer-settled Tajik areas are characterized by *mahalla* networks, as in Uzbekistan, and more recently settled or mountainous areas are characterized by more traditional clan ties, now based in the *qishloq*. The Tajik *avlod*, which also refers to "an extended family that can be developed into a clan based on patrilineage," is the root of both.[19] Despite state propaganda against clan identities since the civil war of the early 1990s, a survey conducted in 1996 found that 68.3 percent of respondents identified themselves as "members of a clan (*avlod*)."[20] As in Uzbekistan and Kyrgyzstan, clan identity did not preclude a sense of national identification as well. A high 42 percent of Tajiks claimed that ethnicity was more important than any regional or other differences.[21] Given that the conflict in Tajikistan has been almost entirely *intra*-ethnic (not involving Russians, Uzbeks, or Kyrgyz), this response may indicate the pervasiveness, but not necessarily the unifying force, of Soviet national identity policy. As in the other republics, local villages often take the name of an *avlod*.[22] In distinguishing themselves at the national level, clan groups may use the *oblast'* name. Clan divisions, however, frequently cut through Soviet *oblast'* boundaries and appear at the sub-*oblast'* level. For example, when Soviet settlement policies moved entire Garmi, Pamiri, and Badakhshani clan villages from Gorno-Badakhshan to regions in south central Tajikistan during the 1950s and 1960s, those

---

[18] Initiated by Andropov in 1983, the purges took full force under Gorbachev from 1985 to 1987.

[19] Kamoludin Abdullaev, "Current Local Government Policy Situation in Tajikistan," in *Tajikistan at a Crossroads*, p. 8. On the current role of the *avlod* in migration, see Olimova and Bosc, *Labor Migration*, pp. 48–50.

[20] IFES Survey, 1996, cited in Saodat Olimova, "Regionalism and Its Perception by Major Political and Social Powers of Tajikistan," in *Tajikistan at a Crossroads*, p. 93.

[21] IFES survey, pp. 104–106. The random sample survey was carried out in four regions of the country.

[22] Roy, *New Central Asia*.

villagers and their offspring retained their lineage ties and identities, and did not adopt the identity of the *oblast'* within which they now lived.[23] In survey results, 25 percent professed to have the greatest trust in their clan leader – a significantly higher figure than those trusting in either government or in Islamic entities.[24]

On the one hand, the Soviet regime and collectivization had some visibly homogenizing effects on the local social structure, such as settling most nomadic clans and preserving similar kin and fictive kin village clusters, and increasing their attachment to a particular community and land. Moreover, most Central Asians came to understand that their pre-Soviet clan or tribal identity was anathema to the Soviet regime, not to be openly discussed. On the other hand, variations in clan type persist, closely related to geography and historic settlement patterns. For example, Valentin Bushkov's ethnography of northern Tajikistan details forty local Uzbek clans in Leninabad *oblast'*. Still others are Kyrgyz and Tajik.[25] Their living patterns, however, are very similar. Likewise, respondents in several villages on the Uzbek side of the Ferghana Valley identified themselves as "from the Kipchak tribe." Some were Kyrgyz speakers and some Uzbek speakers. Their socioeconomic environments were very similar. Whether *rod, avlod, klan,* or *urugh,* located in the *mahalla, qishloq,* or *kolkhoz,* fundamentally these terms represent variations on a theme, embodying the qualities of kin-based identity networks. As the social anthropologist Johan Rasanayagam writes, "one way to think about the communal sphere is as an ideal type or moral framework which can be applied at a number of different levels simultaneously. It exists as an idea of how relations within a community of participant members should be organized, of what constitutes a community."[26] The traditional idea of community remains important across the cases.

[23] Valentin I. Bushkov, "Population Migration in Tajikistan: Past and Present," in Hisao Komatsu, Chika Obiya, and John Schoeberlein, eds., *Migration in Central Asia: Its History and Current Problems* (Osaka, Japan: JCAS, 2000), pp. 149–151; and Oliver Roy, *The New Central Asia* (New York: New York University Press, 2000), p. 96.

[24] IFES survey, p. 106. The question was phrased: "Which of these leaders do you trust the most to do what is right for the people? If you do not trust any, please tell me so." Of ten possible responses, the two other frequently chosen answers were the president (Rakhmonov) (28 percent) and "no one" (27 percent). The latter figure is credible, given the post-conflict situation and social trauma. Trust in Rakhmonov seems highly incredible, however, since many other sources indicate that Rakhmonov had almost no legitimacy and had done extremely little to improve the local situation (as other survey questions indicate). People are often extremely afraid of criticizing the president on surveys in Central Asia. Only 1 percent indicated primary trust in the *imam* of the mosque, and 1 percent in their parliamentary deputy.

[25] See Valentin I. Bushkov, *Naselenie severnogo Tadzhikistana: formirovanie i rasselenie* (Moscow: IEA, RAN, 1995).

[26] Johan Rasanayagam, "Market, State, and Community in Uzbekistan: Reworking the Concept of the Informal Economy," Max Planck Institute of Social Anthropology Working Paper No. 59 (2003), p. 9.

Financial Practices – Surviving the Transition

Financial practices are a revealing indicator of clan networks, especially since 100 percent of nonelites (that is, non-*kolkhoz* directors or deputies) expressed concern over their economic circumstances and their inability to sustain their large households and families (typically seven to thirteen persons). *Kolkhoz* workers in both Kyrgyzstan and Uzbekistan in 1997 and 1998 claimed a monthly salary of approximately six to ten dollars. Generally, they received no salary at all, but perhaps a sack of flour instead. When asked to enumerate their basic monthly expenses, they almost universally estimated at least four to five times their salary. Those expenses included purchasing whatever food they could not grow on their private plots, one to two meals of meat per month, medicine, materials for home repairs, and a few other incidental expenses. With that salary – the combined income of several male adults working in the bazaar and selling the produce of their private plot – a family could still only cover the bare minimum living expenses. Extraordinary expenses, or even ordinary expenses such as spring seed, demanded much more money. A simple wedding could cost a family $1,000 to $3,000, since norms demanded that one feed the entire village and extended clan (usually including 500 to 1,000 or more persons). Nonetheless, families insisted on financing such extensive weddings, as well as similarly expensive rituals such as *sunnat-toy*, because of their symbolic role in reinforcing clan and village relations.[27] Such expenses were also obligatory given that marriages frequently serve as political alliances and sources of economic advancement.[28] How did families meet these financial responsibilities? Almost 100 percent of nonelite respondents said that they had not received any loans – from banks, government programs, or *kolkhozes* – and that such loans were not available.[29]

Kolkhozniks generally elaborated several steps in their strategy to obtain financial assistance: (1) they turned to family members, especially to any "*bai kormiator*," a slang expression used by one respondent to refer to himself as a wealthy member of the kinship network, with responsibility for the welfare of others in his clan; (2) if they had no such relatives, they turned to a local *bai*, perhaps an *oqsoqol* or influential member of their village; (3) if the kin and clan network could not provide, then they requested aid from the *qishloq komiteti* (or *aul komiteti*, a nonstate village committee) composed of several *oqsoqols* who attempt to ensure harmony within the village;[30]

---

[27] Sergei Abashin, "*Vopreki 'zdravomy smysly'? (K voprosu o 'ratsional'nosti/irratsional'nosti' ritual'nykh raskhodov v Srednei Azii),*" *Vestnik Evrazii*, vol. 6–7 (May 1999), pp. 93–111.

[28] Author's interview with Alisher Khamidov, a journalist from Osh, May 2003.

[29] Olimova finds the same, "Regionalism," 2003; and Rasanayagam, "Market, State," pp. 9–12.

[30] According to Miksoz, the *mahalla* or *aul* committee is used by the poorest segment of society. Recent reforms in Uzbekistan put this committee under the state, and thus make it less trusted

(4) finally, a few turned to the *kolkhoz* director or *sel'sovet* (the committee of local elites who ran the collective farm). The *kolkhoz* committee was the last resort, for unless the individual seeking the loan was kin to, or belonged to the extended clan of, the *kolkhoz* director, he would be unlikely to receive a loan or would be put in a position of exploitative clientelism. If kin relations did exist, then one could get land or other favors from the director.[31] Numerous respondents implied that they had negative relations with the *kolkhoz* chairman, who during the 1990s was often appointed by the *raion hokim*, often his relative and not from their village network. In Tajikistan, survey results indicated that only 23 percent of respondents claimed to have received state subsidies, and even lower numbers expected to receive any such aid.[32] Financial issues thus enhanced the rationale for maintaining clan networks. Intra-clan, kin-based patronage and mutual exchange reciprocity enabled individuals to survive periods of economic instability. As Saodat Olimova's recent study in Tajikistan finds, "One of the most important factors in getting a good job is to have relatives or good friends from the same area.... Until today, Tajik employers preferred to base [hiring] on old, but very strong relative patrilineal ties (called '*avlod*' – clan) when making decisions of employment."[33] These relations are particularly beneficial to the lower-class members of the *avlod* and can provide a safety network for them.[34]

Living Patterns, Demography, and Rural Migration

Second, in response to concrete questions about living patterns and preferences, the Uzbekistani and Kyrgyzstani interviewees articulated traditional beliefs, as well as very rational arguments for holding those beliefs. Olimova argues that in Tajikistan, respondents overwhelmingly exhibit traditionalism, and that clan and subethnic groupings and loyalties conflict with both individualism and nationalism.[35] Except for married women (who usually came from a neighboring village), almost 100 percent of respondents were born in the village and on the *kolkhoz* where they were currently living and had worked their entire lives. Most men over the age of twenty-five had left their village to fulfill compulsory Soviet military service, but the majority had returned and settled near the home of their parents. Frequently, those who had married Russians brought those women back to the village, where they became part of the local unit. Yet, one elder claimed, in a typical response, "Our women can not marry a Russian, because he is not Muslim, but an

by the *mahalla* members. See David Mikosz, "Manual for Mahalla and Community-based Organization Leaders in Uzbekistan" (Tashkent: World Bank, 2003).
31 Rasanayagam, "Market, State, and Community in Uzbekistan," p. 20.
32 IFES survey, p. 71.
33 Olimova, "Regionalism," p. 92.
34 Ibid.; and Abdullaev, "Current Local Government," p. 9.
35 Olimova, "Regionalism," pp. 92–93.

Uzbek man can marry a Russian woman and bring her back to his family."[36] In addition to such social norms on marriage and migration, most respondents indicated that jobs were found through kin relations, so that in an economy in which at least 57.3 percent of Kyrgyz lived in poverty, leaving the kin group was risky. The kin network typically offered sustenance and informal employment of some form; only 3.1 percent had registered as "unemployed."[37]

Low migration in Kyrgyzstan and Uzbekistan – either into or out of the rural village – is worth noting. This trend continues despite a general freeing of Soviet-era restrictions on the former *kolkhozes*. In northern Kyrgyzstan, in the semirural areas surrounding the city of Bishkek, there has been some emigration to settlements closer to the city. Kyrgyz youth, in particular, are eager to join the bazaar in urban centers. The government estimates that a shanty town population of 50,000 to 100,000 has arisen around Bishkek, causing housing shortages and criminal problems. However, the rural population has remained attached to its traditional land and identity group. This population seldom permanently relocates even when there is clear economic motivation to do so. For instance, despite common perceptions in Kyrgyzstan that the economic situation in Uzbekistan is much more stable, *oqsoqol*s report almost no emigration (of either Kyrgyz or Uzbeks – who might have other, political reasons to prefer living in Uzbekistan) across the border to Uzbekistan. Similarly, Kyrgyz living in mountain *qishloq*s in Uzbekistan have not sought to move back to Kyrgyzstan for either ethnic or economic reasons. Data on migration illustrate this tendency.[38] In total, the out-migration rate in 1995 was equal to less than 1 percent of the rural population of Uzbekistan.[39] Even in Tajikistan, aside from the internal migration due to the war, 89 percent of survey respondents claimed that they did not plan to move from their native region.[40] By 1996, 98 percent

---

[36] On Tajik arranged marriages, see ibid., pp. 88–89.

[37] In actuality, poverty levels were likely higher; some local experts estimated that 80 percent of the population of Kyrgyzstan lived in poverty. Levels in Tajikistan are higher. Comparable data on Uzbekistan are unavailable. Official unemployment in Uzbekistan was similarly low: 5 percent in 1997, plus 10 percent "underemployed." In reality, these levels are also much higher.

[38] In 1995, for example, a total of 78,206 persons migrated from rural areas to urban areas. Of this group, less than 50 percent were Uzbek; the largest ethnic subgroups were Kazakh, Russian, and Tatar. At the same time, 50,870 persons – of whom the largest subgroup was Uzbek (39,540) – migrated *to* rural areas. These figures exhibit a large non-Uzbek out-migration, counterbalanced by a predominantly Uzbek in-migration. Comparable data on Kyrgyzstan are not available. As during the Soviet period, migration and ethnic data are highly sensitive. This author obtained Uzbek migration data through connections in the government; otherwise, it would not have been available. The secrecy surrounding such data suggests that it is more reliable than the data the Uzbek government makes public.

[39] See *Migratsiia naseleniia 1995: statisticheskii sbornik* (Tashkent: Goskomstat, 1996).

[40] IFES survey, p. 110. Of those surveyed, 86 percent were ethnic Uzbek or Tajik, groups that had a much lower propensity to move. As Bushkov's figures demonstrate, most of the Russian and Slavic population had already left (1997).

of the 600,000 internally displaced persons and 60,000 Tajik refugees in Afghanistan had returned to their home villages and begun to rebuild.[41] Strong Tajik networks – the *avlod*s – were a key factor in this unusually high rate of return.[42] Meanwhile, rural birth rates continued to be high during the 1990s (3 percent to 3.8 percent).[43] These patterns illustrate both traditional norms and practices of clannish localism, and its importance as the principle mechanism of survival in an economy of severe shortages. Although adequate data on migration does not exist, local sociologists note that especially since 2000, both permanent migration and seasonal labor migration have dramatically increased. In recent years, an estimated two to three million seasonal migrants from Kyrgyzstan, Tajikistan, and Uzbekistan go to Russia and Kazakhstan to work because of the poor economic conditions in their home country. In some cases, entire villages, lineages, or extended families relocate to Russia. Typically, however, seasonal migrants are specifically selected members of their *avlod*, returning to their families at home with their savings, and permanent migrants move with their extended networks, suggesting the strength of kinship networks.[44]

Clans as Informal Local Government

Political culture theories have described such behavior as symptomatic of "primordialist" attachment to the land, or as the manifestation of hierarchical and patrimonial "Asian values."[45] The evidence here, however, illustrates that clan identity, while changing over time, remains important because of the critical socioeconomic role of the clan unit in day-to-day survival. A culture emphasizing the importance of family unity and loyalty, bearing multiple children, and respect for one's elders – norms frequently iterated by Central Asians – arises from the centrality of the clan unit and the communal mode of life and reinforces that way of life. Committees composed of village patriarchs, and often including the *domla* or *imom*, take on most of the practical functions of governing daily life, functions normally performed by state or district administrative institutions.[46] The committees make decisions about marriage, divorce (which is generally discouraged as socially disruptive), internal family conflicts, conflicts between neighbors, migration, the distribution of land (together with the *kolkhoz*), informal (nonstate) taxes (for

---

[41] Figures are those of the *UNHCR Report on Tajikistan (January 1994–March 1996)* (Dushanbe: UNHCR, May 1996), pp. 10–19.

[42] Author's interview with James Lynch, Bishkek, Kyrgyzstan, January 2002.

[43] See UNDP Human Development Reports on Uzbekistan and Kyrgyzstan for 1997. This rate of birth over the past few decades has also led to high youth unemployment and child poverty.

[44] Author's discussions with sociologists in Kyrgyzstan, Uzbekistan, and Tajikistan, 2004.

[45] Lucian Pye (1961).

[46] Mikosz, "Manual," pp. 6–7. On Tajikistan, see Sergei Abashin, *"Tadzhikskii avlod,"* pp. 72–81.

redistribution to the poor), community activities and feasts, village relations with the *kolkhoz* director and committee, and sometimes even the appointment of local militia. Indeed, since 1992, Karimov and the other Central Asian presidents have attempted to enhance the regime's control and legitimacy by legalizing such practices.[47]

In the Uzbek system it is unsurprising that individuals avoid the procurator and the courts, organs considered the domain of the autocratic state. Yet, this informalization of law is common in Kyrgyzstan and Tajikistan as well. In a practice quietly present during the Soviet period, but increasingly vibrant since the Soviet regime's demise, village elders and notables govern according to local traditions, mores, and informal codes (*adab* and *adat*). Not one respondent claimed to have personally used the courts, and they almost unanimously viewed the courts as a last recourse, if one at all. Village or *oqsoqol* committees frequently usurp the role of the state courts and local administration by providing governance, a forum for participatory decision making, and communal mobilization.[48] Several *oqsoqol*s from the Ferghana Valley similarly described the transition to communism. In the words of one, "The Soviets changed nothing; we lived as we had always lived." On one level, certainly, this is an exaggeration. On another level, however, the elder's words reflected the degree to which their traditional way of life, customs, and beliefs had survived. The evidence suggests that the Soviet regime only superficially modernized the social, economic, and cultural system of rural Central Asia.[49]

In examining the social-level implications of clan identities, we see both their rationale and their normative content. In this multilayered and multifaceted society, although clans are not formally institutionalized identities, they are deeply embedded in the social fabric at the mass level. Just as Mancur Olson hypothesized of small organizations, clan elites can draw on dense ties of kinship, reciprocity, and patronage to mobilize and also to exploit their small groups to serve particularistic ends, whether in voting or in waging war.[50] At the local level, clan networks can and often do play a positive role in helping communities to survive social and economic crises; at the same time, they may buy into the hierarchical patronage system and thereby inhibit civic development; the socialist economy and constant shortages give them few options for breaking out of their traditional networks.[51]

---

[47] Each has adopted a law on the *mahalla* and local government.

[48] Abdullaev, "Current Local Government," p. 12; and Mikosz, "Mahalla and Community Based Organization."

[49] See also William Fierman, ed., *Soviet Central Asia: The Failed Transformation* (Bloomington, IN: Indiana University Press, 1991); and Sergei Poliakov, *Everyday Islam: Religion and Tradition in Rural Central Asia* (London: M.E. Sharpe, 1992).

[50] Mancur Olson, *The Logic of Collective Action: Public Goods and the Theory of Groups* (Cambridge, MA: Harvard University Press, 1965).

[51] On similar dynamics in southern Italy, see Judith Chubb, *Patronage, Power, and Poverty in Southern Italy* (New York: Cambridge University Press, 1984).

The strong and persistent role of clan networks – including kinship, fictive kinship, and residence networks – throughout the Soviet period and into the first decade of the post-Soviet period is remarkable. Policy makers and sociologists hypothesize that such local ties have provided something of a social safety net that has taken up the slack left by the government's retreat and failures after 1991.[52] Even migration during the civil war appears not to have broken down Tajik clan ties; to the contrary, argues Olimova, it seems to have strengthened them and increased group insularity.[53] In a recent ethnographic study of Kyrgyzstan, Irina Kostyukova finds that the *aul*-based community structures in the south have been under severe strain as a result of post-Soviet socioeconomic trends and migrant labor, causing the clan structure to fragment.[54] This process, in turn, has made the socioeconomic situation at the mass level more difficult, since no state program has filled the void of the traditional social safety net. In the north, however, she finds that kin-based ties remain intact throughout society, and are politically influential.

Indeed, massive economic and social change, declining living standards, and frustrated expectations are leading to social upheaval. The dramatic increase in labor migration is likely to transform clan relations at the social level. Meanwhile, in some urban areas the introduction of capitalism (especially in Kazakhstan) is shifting traditional network hierarchies as well. Further ethnographic research and monitoring needs to be done to evaluate how these processes of social transformation, which have escalated throughout Central Asia over the past three to five years, are affecting clan, kinship, and social ties at the mass level. Clan relationships are not static, and they will continue to be affected by, and to react to, changing political and economic circumstances. We now turn to clan relations at the meso and elite levels during the post-transition period; they too have adapted to new circumstances.

II. CLAN NETWORKS AT THE STATE-SOCIETY AND ELITE LEVELS IN KYRGYZSTAN

We marked the close of the Kyrgyz transition with the local, parliamentary, and presidential elections of 1994 and 1995.[55] Despite some minor

---

[52] See UNDP, *Kyrgyzstan Human Development Report* (Bishkek: UNDP, 2002); David Mikosz, "Mahalla and Community-Based Organization"; and Kathleen Collins, "The Political Role of Clans," *Comparative Politics* (January 2003): 171–190.

[53] Saodat Olimova and Igor Bosc, *Labor Migration from Tajikistan* (Dushanbe: Sharq and IOM, 2003), pp. 49–51.

[54] Irina Kostyukova, "A Surmountable Summit: Islam in Contemporary Kyrgyzstan," in Stephanie Duoignon and Komatsu Hisao, eds., *Islam in Politics in Russia and Central Asia* (London: Kegan Paul International, 2002), pp. 253–268.

[55] Chapter 1 discusses why it is useful to define the "transition" narrowly. The "transition" refers only to the immediate period of regime change, from initial liberalization of elections and participation until the end of the second free elections; this marks the period 1989 through 1995 in Kyrgyzstan, as discussed in Chapter 6.

violations – far more circumscribed than had been expected, given Akaev's uncertain chances – the elections were given a pass by the OSCE and other international observers. It is nonetheless necessary to take a deeper look at the phenomena that put Kyrgyzstan's democracy in question, for these events are critical to the post-electoral, post-transition developments of 1995 to the present.

In the case of Kyrgyzstan, where a more open political system in the 1990s allowed for a somewhat more public discussion of political problems, we can see the rampant rise of clan politics within the regime. The democratic ideology propounded by Akaev and the nascent Kyrgyz civil society in the early 1990s had only a limited effect on the regime; democratization begins to erode by 1995, actively driven by clans that have pervaded the regime and seek to consolidate their own power bases. Akaev's reaction to challenges from competing clans in defense of his own, as well as his reaction to criticism from other opposition groups, further undermines democratization.

By late 1994, Akaev's ability to transform the system from above by imposing a democratic ideology and democratic institutions had become increasingly limited as those clans that had brought him to power increasingly opposed reforms. In his speeches, Akaev publicly called for discarding the informal norms of clans and tribalism and instead adopting fair and transparent ones,[56] yet he found himself increasingly relying on clan support to keep himself in power. The pre-transition pact had embedded certain clans in an informal regime controlling the key economic resources of the country. Influential clans included the Kush'chu, Sarybagysh, Solto, Kochkor, and Buguu clan networks. The Kush'chu clan, led by Chingiz Aitmatov, quickly became one of the most powerful networks in the country. It also included Mrs. Akaev's family and relatives and the Sarygulov kin group. The Sarybagysh clan, the president's own clan, emerged as another very powerful network; it was represented by families from the Kemin village, including the Baekovas and Ashirkulovs. Those chiefly responsible for cadre appointments – the state secretary, Osmanakun Ibraimov, and the chief of presidential staff, Amanbek Karypkulov – came from this clan.[57] Several powerful Chui clans, such as the Solto, of which Feliks Kulov was a leading member, were included as well. Another powerful but "Sovietized" clan cut into the deal was a network including Apas Jumagulov and Daniyar Usmonov. Turdakun Usubaliev's clan, which was commonly known as the Kochkor network and had been the most powerful faction of the Sarybagysh clan during the Brezhnev era, was also included, despite Usubaliev's position as the former Communist Party first secretary. Finally, several important representatives of the Buguu clan also received lucrative posts in the regime.

---

[56] See Akaev's discussion of traditional norms, Askar Akaev, *Transition Economy through the Eyes of a Physicist* (Bishkek: Uchkun, 2001).

[57] Alisher Khamidov, "Kyrgyzstan's Unrest Linked to Clan Rivalries," *Eurasianet*, June 6, 2002.

These included Mukhtar Cholponbaev, speaker of parliament, and Tursun-bek Chinguishev, the first prime minister after 1991.[58] Insofar as political reform might challenge their interests, clan elites opposed it. And as they had done in 1990 in ousting party leader Absamat Masaliev, they wanted to keep southern clans, especially the large Ichkilik and Adygine clans, as well as the minority Uzbek population (mainly in the south), out of power.[59] Informal deals and power sharing arrangements among these clans in Akaev's circle initially kept stability. However, their use of nepotism, control of cadre appointments, patronage of their own group, and blatant asset stripping of state resources had destabilizing political and economic consequences by the late 1990s. As argued in Chapter 2, clan politics leads to a vicious cycle that undermines democratic institutions and weakens regime durability.

The rest of this chapter examines key dimensions of Kyrgyzstan's fledgling electoral democracy that have been undermined by clan politics[60] at the national/elite level and the meso level of state-society relations, including (1) the constitutional separation of powers and the effective autonomy of the legislature; (2a) participation, contestation, and representation through elections (presidential, parliamentary, and local) and (2b) the related sector of political party development; (3) horizontal accountability and the independence of the judiciary; (4) the development of civil society and the free media; and (5) transparency and accountability in controlling state resources and economic policy.[61]

Compromising Parliament and the Separation of Powers

Clan networks in Kyrgyzstan have undermined the constitutional separation of powers, and have prevented the parliamentary and court independence and accountability critical to democracy. Akaev's clan allies sought to prevent parliament from gaining too much power, since democratic opposition, old-guard communists, and their clan rivals together held a near-majority of its seats.

As noted earlier, those elected by virtue of their *nomenklatura* association with the Communist Party of Kyrgyzstan (CPK) – approximately one-third of the Supreme Soviet since 1990 – were unlikely to regain their seats, for the banning of the CPK had delegitimized the party, stripped its assets, and left

[58] Author's interview with a Kyrgyz journalist, Bishkek, August 2004.
[59] Khamidov, "Kyrgyzstan's Unrest."
[60] On measurement and key dimensions of democracy, see *Nations in Transit 2003* (New York: Freedom House, 2003) and *Freedom in the World 2003* (New York: Freedom House, 2003).
[61] These areas reflect the basic dimensions of democracy, defined by Dahl as participation, contestation, and representation. See Robert Dahl, *Polyarchy* (New Haven, CT: Yale University Press, 1971); and Linz and Stepan, *The Politics of Democratic Transition and Consolidation: Southern Europe, South America, and Post-Communist Europe* (Baltimore, MD: The Johns Hopkins University Press, 1996), p. 56.

its loyalists without a sponsor.[62] According to the 1993 Constitution, new elections would scale down the parliament from 450 to 300 seats, so many deputies sought to stall this event indefinitely.[63] They successfully did so despite sustained pressure from the president.[64] The impasse between the president and parliament was resolved in a highly controversial fashion when a faction of the latter refused to attend the September 10, 1994, opening session of the fall legislature. According to the constitution, without a standing quorum in parliament, the president had the right to dismiss the *Jogorku Kenesh* and convoke new elections. Within twenty-four hours, this was Akaev's course of action. Although the decision was technically in accord with the Constitution of 1993, Akaev's network of clan power brokers had reportedly engineered the walk-out and the new elections.[65] Manipulating patronage and kinship ties to key deputies, they had induced 100 legislators to boycott the opening session. Ironically, neither the "democrats," the old "communists," nor even Akaev's Osh opponents (Masaliev's supporters in the 1990 vote) took part in the supposed protest. According to a rumor circulating in government circles, the executive had promised them financial rewards.[66]

The September crisis, although not technically unconstitutional, cast doubt on Akaev's commitment to democracy. An action of more blatantly questionable legality, however, was Akaev's decision to use the parliamentary boycott to convoke a referendum to change the constitution. The referendum called for a new, even smaller, bicameral parliament: 105 seats divided into a full-time upper house of thirty-five members, the *zakonodatel'nyi palat* (Legislative House), and a lower *narodnyi palat* (People's Representative Assembly) of seventy deputies, who would meet several times a year to

---

[62] This assessment is based on author's interviews with journalists from *Vechernii Bishkek*, *Res Publica*, the *Kyrgyzstan Chronicle*, and *Delo Nomer*, September and October 1994, as well as on meetings with political party representatives seeking to contest seats in the new parliament. The interviewees represented a range of political figures, from supporters of Akaev to strong opponents. Although many did not agree with Akaev's method of calling new elections, they did agree that the old "communist" parliament had to be dissolved.

[63] The Kyrgyz Constitution was passed on May 5, 1993 – ironically, by the old Soviet-elected Kyrgyz Supreme Soviet. The Constitution was drafted by a Constitutional Assembly composed of representatives from every governmental branch and societal organization. The first Kyrgyz Constitution adopted a very American-style separation and balance of powers.

[64] Author's interview with a member of the legal department of the Presidential apparat, Bishkek, August 1994.

[65] Based on author's informal interviews and conversations with members of the government, Bishkek, fall 1994. Those in government, whether in the ministries or in the presidential apparat, did not want to discuss the topic openly. Journalists, by contrast, openly cried foul, and the foreign community seriously questioned Akaev's motives.

[66] The opposition paper *Res Publica* charged that massive corruption was involved in the scandal and printed a cartoon entitled "Democracy's Funeral." One official in the presidential apparat confided to the author, on the promise of anonymity, that a Mercedes had been promised to every deputy who supported Akaev in the walk-out. Since one of Akaev's wife's relatives controlled the government joint venture with Mercedes-Benz, this seemed plausible.

"approve" the work of the upper house.[67] Akaev called for a new Constitutional Assembly to convene in December 1994 as a way to incorporate – and legitimate – these "popularly demanded" changes to the Constitution of 1993.[68] Although he did have the constitutional power of referendum under special circumstances, Akaev had manipulated the ambiguously defined procedure by holding the referendum on both (1) the size and structure of the *Jogorku Kenesh* and (2) the electoral law.[69] The amendments were undoubtedly intended to weaken the parliament and give Akaev the upper hand in executive-legislative relations. On the one hand, these institutional changes did give the president greater power. On the other hand, they increased the influence of individual clan notables within the parliament and undercut the power of the Communist Party and of parties in general.

After the February 1995 elections, the democratic opposition largely faded from prominence. The remaining deputies, meanwhile, often treated their positions as sources of patronage for their narrow clan interests, rather than as a check upon the president or as a base for national policy making. The legislature increasingly factionalized along clan lines, as opposed to the communist-versus-reformist ideological division of the late perestroika and early independence years. The president's clan cronies consistently supported him and won personal benefits in exchange, from expensive cars to business licenses with tax exemptions for themselves and their relatives. The speaker of the new upper house, Mukhtar Cholponbaev, was a key clan ally of Akaev's. Akaev turned a blind eye to his corruption, even when he was called upon by Osh deputies to account for several hundred thousand dollars of legislative funds. Cholponbaev was removed as speaker in 1996 at the initiative of opposition deputies, but retained his deputy post.[70] In a similar major scandal within Akaev's close network, Prime Minister Chinguishev was exposed by opposition deputies for embezzling from the gold mining company; gold is Kyrgyzstan's only major natural resource and major export. Yet he did not lose his social or political standing within his clan, and in 1995 he was reelected to the People's Assembly of the parliament. Their

---

[67] "*Ukaz Prezidenta,*" *Slovo Kyrgyzstana,* September 23, 1994, p. 1.

[68] "*Demokratiia bez poderzhki narodovlastiia bessil'na,*" *Slovo Kyrgyzstana,* November 23, 1994, p. 2. Akaev also claimed the power to "appoint" the members of the Constitutional Assembly, although he did consciously include the leaders of all political parties, unions, cultural organizations, and other organs of civil society.

[69] The power to convoke a referendum was divided between the president and parliament, according to the provisions of the 1993 Constitution. The president needed 5,000 signatures in order to call a referendum against parliament's will. Under the 1996 amendments, the president now has the right to initiate changes by convoking a referendum. See Article 96, *Konstitutsiia Kyrgyzskoi Respubliki.*

[70] Nonetheless, bitter over his demotion, Cholponbaev claimed that the level of clan politics had been steadily increasing and influencing political decisions. He did not directly accuse Akaev of sidelining the Issyk-Kul clan, but he did claim that his removal was linked to clan rivalry. Author's interview with Mukhtar Cholponbaev, Bishkek, June 1998.

connection to the president probably saved them from prosecution, serious penalty, and imprisonment. Akaev merely appointed a different clan ally to the premiership. Apas Jumagulov, despite his record as an old guard communist. Several opposition deputies were given positions as rectors of universities, positions that enabled them to collect significant bribes from students.[71] This practice drew them into Akaev's patronage network. As the democratic movement has faded, the president's chief opponents in parliament (e.g., Adakhan Madumarov, Usen Sydykov, and Azimbek Beknazarov), who are leaders of southern clans, have mobilized support on the basis of strong kin and personalistic networks, not parties, unions, ideologies, or even open platforms.[72] Even Omurbek Tekebaev, one of the few active democratic party leaders, could mobilize only a narrow base of support and was seen as representing only his subregion, the Bazar-Kurgon area of Jalal-Abad. Consequently, the national press has repeatedly accused the parliament of tribal factionalism.[73]

Subverting the Judiciary and Horizontal Accountability

The undermining of judicial independence and, consequently, the court's role in providing horizontal accountability provide a flagrant example of Akaev's clan politics. The story of the Constitutional Court's relationship to the executive branch illustrates the subtle but crucial role of clan politics in attenuating the third pillar of the democratic regime's institutions and institutional separation of powers. In 1993, not long after the adoption of the new Kyrgyz Constitution, Akaev had nominated Cholpon Baekova, a prominent Soviet-era judge, to the highest position of judicial authority, chairman of the newly created Constitutional Court. Baekova had been a Gorbachev supporter and an early proponent of democratization. She was widely respected by international experts.[74] Yet, Akaev's opponents in the legislature rejected her nomination several times in 1994. Baekova was also known to be a kin relation of Akaev, from the Sarybagysh clan. The position remained empty until after the parliamentary election in 1995, when Akaev again put forward Baekova's nomination to a legislature now stacked with his cronies. This time the parliament approved it. Only then did the Court begin to operate.[75] Then, to the surprise of her international supporters, but in

---

[71] University rectors are named by the president.

[72] Author's interview with a journalist, Bishkek, Kyrgyzstan, January 2002.

[73] Ibid.

[74] Author's interview with Howard Ockman, ABA legal advisor, Bishkek, summer 1995.

[75] Between November 1995, when it began operating seriously, and November 1997, the Court made only 24 rulings. No rulings were issued until Baekova's chairmanship was confirmed in 1995.

accord with the expectations of Akaev's opponents, Baekova hardly played the role of an independent judge.[76] She kept the Court quiet during the executive's deliberations in the summer and fall of 1995, as it considered canceling the upcoming presidential election, even when a legislative delegation asked the Court to examine the constitutionality of the issue. Baekova artfully kept the Court out of the dispute. Her silence, however, implicitly supported the president. During the election campaign of 1995, the Court was almost blatantly partial to Akaev, readily approving the executive branch's decision to ban three candidates from the presidential electoral campaign. Although the charge against the candidates, forgery of voters' signatures, may have had some substance, the Court did not demand a serious investigation. Indeed, from 1995 through 1998, the Court issued twenty-four rulings that served primarily to approve executive decrees.[77]

A further test of the court's independence from Akaev came in mid-1998, when the third presidential election was looming on the horizon. Akaev's clique in the executive apparat, again led by the Aitmatovs, began to circulate rumors that President Akaev should be permitted to run for the office of president again. According to the Constitution of 1993, the president was restricted to two terms of office.[78] By spring of 1998, Akaev's closest clan supporters were already manipulating the rules to reelect him, and thereby to keep their own fiefdoms. In the pattern of 1995 – that is, without Akaev's active involvement – these clan elites, primarily from the Sarybagysh and Solto networks, circulated the argument that the 1991 elections "did not count," since they had taken place before the adoption of the new constitution. A traditional *kurultai* of village clan elders, *oqsoqols*, beseeched the president to run again. They attempted to bolster their position with a weaker but more pragmatic claim – that only Akaev could hold the state together, that only he could prevent clan and ethnic war.[79]

[76] The Court's first decision was taken on November 9, 1995. It was the decision to accept the changes to the Constitution, in the law "*O vnesenii izmenenii i dopolnenii v Konstitutsiiu Kyrgyzskoi Respubliki,*" submitted by the president of the Kyrgyz Republic. On December 22, 1995, the Court upheld the changes to the referendum process, also proposed by the executive branch. See Cholpon Baekova, *Sbornik reshenii konstitutsionnogo suda Kyrgyzskoi Respubliki* (Bishkek: Fond-Soros, 1998), pp. 39–40.
[77] Ibid.
[78] Article 20, *Konstitutsiia Kyrgyzskoi Respubliki* (1993). Akaev had been elected first in 1990 by the parliament, an election that at the time was not considered the beginning of a presidential term. He had been elected again in December 1991 in a popular vote, after the Kyrgyz Republic's full separation from the Soviet Union but still prior to the adoption of the new Constitution. Elected the third time in December 1995, by popular vote, Akaev was to serve his second term of office until December 2000.
[79] Author's interview with Askar Aitmatov, advisor to the president, and conversations with government officials from Talas, Chui, and Issyk-Kul, Bishkek, May and June 1998.

A core group of opposition deputies entreated the Constitutional Court to rule on the constitutionality of a third term.[80] In August 1998, even before the Russian court faced a similar issue, Baekova issued a decision: Akaev had the full constitutional right to run again, since his election in 2000 would technically be only a *second* term in office, under the 1993 Constitution. Baekova claimed political impartiality, but in the eyes of most, her decision blatantly ignored the relevant passages of the 1993 document, according to which all elections prior to May 1993 would be recognized as valid. Those officials were to complete their tenure under the rules of the new constitution.[81] The opposition interpreted the Court's decision as an unequivocal sign of its personal submission to Akaev, Baekova's kinsman.[82] Although a ruling against Akaev would have won her recognition and support both from the democratic opposition and from the international community, it would have guaranteed the passing of political power to another leader, and very likely to another clan.

As proposed in Chapter 2, the norms of kinship and the need to preserve the clan's power demanded Baekova's loyalty. In placing the interests of the clan before those of the constitution, Baekova thus undermined the juridical foundations of the Kyrgyz Republic's democracy. Her judgment in 1998 seemed rational, as the Akaev regime was solidly in control. Since 2000, however, repeated calls for Akaev's resignation and impeachment, demonstrations, and assassination attempts suggest that the Court's "defection" would be a better strategy.[83] Yet Baekova has continued to back Akaev, even as his regime faces ever greater domestic and international criticism. In mid-2004, Akaev's network was pressing for yet another court decision to allow a constitutional change that would permit Akaev to run for a fourth term. Clan norms have proved strong.

Participation, Contestation, and Representation: Elections and Parties

Participation and contestation in elections and representation through elected officials (in the legislature and executive) are the most basic elements of a democratic transition, but they have been severely weakened by clan politics. By late 1995, as presidential elections approached, acting on the advice of his clan elites behind the pact, the president determined to stay in

[80] Author's conversations with Western legal consultants to the Constitutional Court and Ministry of Justice, Bishkek, summer 1998.

[81] Author's interview with Cholpon Baekova, chairman of the Constitutional Court of Kyrgyzstan, Bishkek, June 1998.

[82] Author's interview with Omurbek Tekebaev, parliamentary deputy, Bishkek, June 1998; and with Bakyt Beshimov, parliamentary deputy, Osh, June 1998.

[83] Contrast this with the Argentinian case: Gretchen Helmke, "The Logic of Strategic Defection: Court-Executive Relations in Argentina under Dictatorship and Democracy," *American Political Science Review*, vol. 96, no. 2 (June 2002), pp. 291–304.

power to protect their interests. Having lost the support of his democratic constituency and the urban intelligentsia, Akaev's base shifted. He mobilized voters through his own clan network, that of his wife, and those of their closest clan allies. As opposed to the situation in 1991, when most people voted for Akaev as a national unifier and father figure, in 1995 this clan-based mobilization enabled the president to win reelection.[84] According to one local expert, "Akaev puts his kinsmen in positions of power, as the regional or local *akims* (governors). They promise things or put pressure on the clan elders or respected persons who have influence in the local community, and they get everyone out to vote as they say."[85] These hierarchical networks of clan patronage became an effective means of undermining open competition without the blatant use of force or the canceling of elections altogether.

Akaev's convocation of the first multicandidate, multiparty legislative elections had led to an immediate upsurge in party activity. A presidential decree had called for elections first to the local parliamentary bodies, the *keneshes* (October 22, 1994), and then to the national legislature, the *Jogorku Kenesh* (December 5, 1994).[86] The legislative elections were the first multiparty elections in Kyrgyzstan's history.[87] The electoral results, although "poorly and inefficiently organized," were internationally evaluated as "free and fair."[88] Minor electoral problems were blamed on the government's financial difficulties, not on intimidation or fraud. Parties had even pushed Akaev to delay the parliamentary elections by two months, from December 5, 1994, to February 5, 1995, so as to allow them more time to organize campaigns.

Although twelve registered parties competed, only 23 (21.9 percent) of the total of 105 deputy seats went to candidates running as party members. The Social Democrats (SDP), Akaev's strongest supporter, claimed only three seats. Another two each went to the Unity Party of Kyrgyzstan, Erkin Kyrgyzstan, and Ata-Meken. Only one seat each went to the People's Republican Party, the Agrarian Party, the Agrarian-Workers, and the DMK.[89]

---

[84] For more detail, see Kathleen Collins, "Clans, Pacts, and Politics: Understanding Regime Transition in Central Asia" (Ph.D. dissertation, Stanford University, 1999), Chapter 7.

[85] Author's interview with a local political expert from Kyrgyzstan, May 2003.

[86] "*Ukaz Prezidenta Askar Akaeva*," published in *Slovo Kyrgyzstana*, September 22, 1994, p. 1.

[87] The founding election was really the presidential contest of December 1991, in which parties were free to compete but no one stepped forth to challenge the incumbent president.

[88] Author's interviews with electoral observers, Bishkek, October 21, 1994. This author also participated in the electoral process as an observer. Although I was not entirely convinced that there was no room for fraud, especially outside the capital city, in general the voting process seemed open, free, and fair. No police presence or other threats intimidated voters. The turnout likewise seemed high.

[89] Report of the Central Electoral Commission, "Election Results for the Jogorku Kenesh as of February 25," *Kyrgyzstan Chronicle*, February 27, 1995. See also Central Electoral Commission, *Spravochnye materialy: chleny politicheskikh partii izbrannye v Jogorku Kenesh* (Bishkek: CEC, 1995), p. 129.

Interestingly, after the election, several deputies who had run as independent candidates identified themselves as Social Democrats. One deputy was even registered as a member of two parties, the SDP and Ata-Meken.[90] Eight of these party-affiliated deputies were not registered as party candidates on the CEC's list as of February 1995,[91] but they did appear as "party deputies" on the parliamentary list later that year.[92] Many registered as Social Democrats, giving that party the largest bloc in the legislature (9.5 percent).[93] Even the Communist Party – arguably the strongest, the best-off financially, and the bearer of the most popular economic agenda in a country reeling from the effects of shock therapy – failed abominably,[94] winning but two seats in the entire Kyrgyz legislature, a rather ironic outcome in one of the only former Soviet republics where Lenin's statue still towered over the parliament itself.[95] The remaining eighty-two seats went to mysterious "independents." Although each party had fielded multiple candidates and had participated in most districts, the new parliament was predominantly partyless.

Many factors could cause party weakness in a new democracy. Lack of financing, organization, and skill, as well as lack of sponsorship – for example, the absence of a presidential figurehead – have been conditions typical of neophyte parties in most post-communist states. The electoral law itself allowed independent candidates to run, did not establish a party list system, and did not encourage party development. Yet when the electoral law was initially discussed, few deputies or political leaders supported electoral rules

---

[90] Author's interview with Adilbek Kadirbekov, deputy chief of the information department of the Ministry of Defense and parliamentary deputy, Bishkek, June 1998. He represents Osh district nineteen, and is listed as a member of both Ata-Meken and the SDP. *Spravochnie materialy*, "*Chleny politicheskikh partii izbrannie v Jogorku Kenesh*," p. 112.

[91] Electoral results provided by the Central Electoral Commission, March 1995. Some seats were still being contested in a third round.

[92] *Spisok deputatov* (a list of deputies and party affiliations was provided by the Jogorku Kenesh), May 1995.

[93] Had the electoral law included a cut-off rule, as in most Eastern European countries and in Russia, it is unlikely that any party other than the SDP would have gained seats.

[94] According to a report in *Res Publica* in mid-1995, a sociologist's study of voter attitudes toward the economy and Akaev's program of economic reforms revealed sharply increasing negative opinions. From January to August of 1994, Raya Osmonalieva found that the percentage of respondents (from a pool of 8,000 surveyed) answering that the reforms were "good" declined from 26 percent to 14.5 percent among men, and from 23.9 percent to 13.3 percent among women. Those rating the economic reforms as "very bad" increased from 12.4 percent to 37.2 percent of men, and from 12 percent to 40.7 percent of women. "Economic reality gives everyone less basis for optimism," concludes Osmonalieva. See Raya Osmonalieva, "*Ekonomicheskie reformy v Kyrgyzstane: otsenki, mneniia naseleniia*," *Res Publica*, July 25, 1995.

[95] On the political economy of elections in Eastern Europe – i.e., the return of the communists and the rapid fluctuation of party strength due to declining economic conditions that are out of sync with voter expectations – see Andrew Janos, "Continuity and Change in Eastern Europe: Strategies of Change in Post-Communist Politics," in Beverly Crawford, ed., *Markets, States, and Democracy* (Boulder, CO: Westview Press, 1995), pp. 150–174.

TABLE 7.1. *Results of the 1995 elections to the Jogorku Kenesh of Kyrgyzstan (February 5 and 19, 1995)*

Party/Other	Seats	Percent
Social Democrats	8 (11)[a]	9.5%
Communist Party	2	1.9%
Agrarians	1	...
Agrarian-Workers	1	...
Erkin Kyrgyzstan	2	1.9%
Ata-Meken	2	1.9%
People's Republican Party	1	...
Unity Party of Kyrgyzstan	2	1.9%
DMK (Democratic Movement)	1	...
Total party seats	20 (23)	19.0% (21.9%)
Non-party independents	85 (82)	80.9% (78.1%)

[a] Three deputies joined the Social Democrats after the election. They ran and were elected as "independents."

that would strengthen parties rather than individual notables.[96] Parties were further debilitated by the underlying social structure of the region. It made more sense for clan leaders to use their informal patronage networks, not formal organizations with transparent rules, to get themselves into power.

Voter registration further suggests that few voters had begun to identify with party organizations. Even assuming that these registration lists were gathered legally, only 13,000 of the two and a half million Kyrgyz voters were registered party members in 1995.[97] In general, the intellectual cliques responsible for establishing most Kyrgyz parties had little following. Those few parties or party candidates who had local ties and won support (e.g., Asaba and Erkin Kyrgyzstan) had ties to a clan network based outside of the Russified capital city. Lacking a popular base, parties failed to act as an intermediary institution, as a linkage between society and the state.

The second presidential election, held on December 25, 1995, further exposed the clan-based cleavages underlying the Kyrgyz political system and the role of these networks in infiltrating the executive branch. Political parties fared no better than they had in the parliamentary contests. Several parties attempted to compete, but only three candidates gathered the requisite

[96] See the OSCE report on elections. This view was expressed both by deputies and by ABA advisor Howard Ockman. David Laitin and Said Samatar make a very similar observation about the failure of parties in Somalia after independence. David Laitin and Said Samatar, *Somalia: Nation in Search of a State* (Boulder, CO: Westview Press, 1987). On the electoral law in Kyrgyzstan, see Luong, *Power, Perception, and Pacts*, pp. 156–88.

[97] *Spisok politicheskikh partii* (obtained from the Ministry of Justice, Bishkek, Kyrgyzstan, November 1994). Since the elections in 1995, two more parties have registered, indicating yet greater fractionalization of intelligentsia-based parties. See the discussion in Turar Koichuev, ed., *Sovremennie politicheskie protsessi* (Bishkek: NAN, 1996), pp. 99–100.

TABLE 7.2. *Results of the 1995 presidential elections in Kyrgyzstan (December 25, 1995)*

Oblast'	Voter Turnout	Askar Akaev	Medetken Sherimkulov	Absamat Masaliev
City of Bishkek	335,646	83.69%	3.83%	10.75%
Chui	417,666	87.22%	3.7%	7.34%
Issyk-Kul	212,745	92.18%	.79%	4.27%
Naryn	121,837	97.03%	1.23%	0.72%
Jalal-Abad	349,257	61.27%	.73%	35.6%
Osh	680,370	50.01%	.58%	46.53%
Talas	98,035	85.62%	2.35%	10.43%
TOTAL	2,254,348	71.59%	1.72%	24.42%

Note: Data provided by the Central Electoral Commission, Bishkek, Kyrgyzia, December 1995.

number of signatures to be placed on the ballot:[98] Askar Akaev, Medetken Sherimkulov, and Absamat Masaliev. All three were independents. No CPK contender competed in the 1995 presidential race, although Sherimkulov was a northern party apparatchik and former speaker of the Supreme Soviet, and Masaliev, technically an "independent," was the former Party secretary.

Unlike electoral politics in Russia, where the 1995 parliamentary vote and presidential elections exhibited a polarization of reactionary and reformist candidates and voters,[99] in Kyrgyzstan the cultural and socioeconomic norms of clan politics pushed voters to coalesce behind major clan figures – either Akaev from the north or Masaliev from the south (see Table 7.2). Since Sherimkulov had little clan base of support, Masaliev was the only real challenger.[100] The latter, despite his debacle of 1990, when he had let the Osh riots spiral out of control, won a large portion of the southern vote from his native Osh (46.53 percent) and Jalal-Abad (35.6 percent) *oblast*'s. Indeed, Masaliev's support came entirely from Osh and Jalal-Abad *oblast*'s, although serious divisions among clan and ethnic factions prevented him from taking the entire region.[101] His success was due to his prominence within one Osh clan, not to the resources or ideology of the communists.

[98] See the "*Zakon o vybore prezidenta Kyrgyzskoi Respubliki.*"

[99] Michael McFaul, *Russia's 1996 Presidential Election: The End of Polarized Politics* (Stanford, CA: Hoover Institution Press, 1997).

[100] According to ethnographic studies of clan behavior, clans typically consolidated behind one key leader, distinguished not only by his seniority but also by his populist appeal. See S. M. Abramzon, *Kirgizy i ikh etnogeneticheskie i istoriko-kul'turnye sviazi* (Frunze: Kyrgyzstan, 1990).

[101] The journalist Dmitry Esenbai suggests that the best way to understand this irony is to see that Masaliev's clan connections, not his party or his record in office, are the basis of his electoral support. Author's interview with Dmitry Esenbai, Osh, July 1995. A journalist from *Ekho Osh* similarly argued that within Osh *oblast*', various clans supported Masaliev, as well as those who had won seats in parliament. According to a journalist from Radio Free

Akaev, without any party network, ran an even more successful campaign. He carried about 90 percent of the northern regions.[102] He swept the north, central, and northwest *oblast*'s, Naryn (97.03 percent) and Issyk-Kul (92.18 percent), where IMF reports indicate that economic reform had been harshest. Akaev likewise carried Talas (85.62 percent), with the exception of one district whose inhabitants were villagers relocated from part of Jalal-Abad. In Chui and Bishkek, where polls show that the democratic movement and intelligentsia had largely deserted the president, Akaev did slightly worse (Bishkek, 83.69 percent; Chui 87.22, percent). In Jalal-Abad and Osh, Akaev won a far lower, but still substantial, percentage of the vote (61.27 percent and 50.01 percent, respectively). Sherimkulov garnered less than 3 percent of the vote.[103] Voter turnout was high, except in Bishkek, where only about 60–65 percent went to the polls; in the less urbane, less Russified, and traditionally clan-dominated regions, voter turnout was about 90 percent.

Akaev's success in Osh and Jalal-Abad, where he had strategically placed his client *akims* (governors) several months before the election, invites skepticism. Since Masaliev still won a substantial percentage, the *akims* clearly had limited success in using fraud. The election was, however, declared "free and fair." Officially Akaev had lost 23 percent of the electorate between the two presidential elections (falling from 95 percent to 72 percent). Importantly, he had lost both the south, which had previously had no clan candidate to support, and also the democratic reformers, the intelligentsia. He had further lost the widespread support of the pro-democracy parties, and had neglected to establish his own party. However, Akaev had adopted a more savvy political strategy; he had generated stable support from Kyrgyz clans in the northern regions, who were pleased with the clan politics he and his wife had played when staffing their administration with kin and clan connections from the Chui, Talas, Naryn, and Issyk-Kul regions.[104]

The scale of political party failure in both the parliamentary and presidential elections was unprecedented elsewhere in the former communist space (where free elections had taken place). Moreover, the Kyrgyz elections had

Europe, Masaliev's clan was relatively small and weak. This may explain why he received such a small percentage of the vote.

[102] Of the three, Akaev's support was lowest in Talas (86 percent). This is surprising, since Akaev's wife has promoted many clan connections from this region. However, the district breakdown of the vote indicates that all but two districts gave Akaev well over 90 percent of the vote. The districts where the Sarybagysh clan is settled were the strongest for Akaev. The aberrant districts are on the border of Jalal-Abad and are populated by some Ichkilik and Adygine clan villages. Masaliev (not Sherimkulov) won 20 percent and 31 percent of the vote there.

[103] *Itogi vyborov prezidenta Kyrgyzskoi respubliki* (Bishkek: *Tsentrizbirkom*, unpublished statistical report, 1996).

[104] Author's interview with a journalist, Bishkek, August 1995.

defied political economy theories which argue that the negative effects of economic transformation cause a political backlash against new democratic governments during the second (or sometimes first) popular election.[105] Despite Kyrgyz "shock therapy" – including the slashing of state subsidies; price liberalization and hyperinflation in 1992 and 1993; failure to pay police, teachers, and pensioners for more than eight months in 1994 and 1995; and lack of a social safety net – no communist backlash had occurred. The re-registered Communist Party of Kyrgyzstan (CPK) had revived its economic agenda and looked well situated to win, as had its counterparts in the mid-1990s throughout much of Eastern Europe and Russia.[106] Yet unlike the LDPR and the KPRF, the CPK failed abominably in both elections, while Akaev, the perpetrator of painful economic reforms, won in a landslide.[107] Kyrgyzstan's elections marked a sharp break from the pattern in other former communist states. To Akaev's credit, his clan base successfully defied the political-economic cycle and clinched his victory. What was expected in return, however, did not bode well either for Akaev's independence or for the fate of Kyrgyz democracy.

If not party candidates, then, who did win the elections? Who were the "independents" who captured the presidency and almost 80 percent of parliament? The overall numbers of registered candidates did not reveal what was taking place at the district electoral level. Although candidate lists are not available for every one of the 105 districts, the CEC confirmed some interesting observations about the nature of the voting that took place. In Bishkek, the center of the intelligentsia, there were almost always ten candidates, and sometimes as many as seventeen, competing for one position in parliament. Some candidates were better connected than others, but at least

---

[105] Linz and Stepan, *Politics of Democratic Transition and Consolidation*, note that new democracies are often faced with severe economic problems. Typically, in the face of rapid economic decline, the first democratically elected government is ousted. A new one is then elected. This allows an "eight-year breathing space" for the regime, p. 79.

[106] In Russia especially, where shock therapy was initially pursued by Yeltsin and Gaidar, the communists made a strong and consistent comeback. In both 1993 and 1995 and in 1999, the Agrarians, communists, and fascists (the LDPR) garnered a total of 20–40 percent of the vote. In Moldova, the Communist Party won the 2001 election. Even in Poland, where society was perhaps most deeply committed to democracy, Solidarity was voted out and the communists brought back in 1995. The communists experienced a striking resurgence across the "postcommunist" region, almost everywhere but in Central Asia. On the communist parties in Eastern Europe, see Anna Gryzmala-Busse, *Redeeming the Past* (Cambridge: Cambridge University Press, 2002).

[107] In a survey conducted in 1996, in response to questions about which party "had significant power in Kyrgyzstan," 46.1 percent of respondents said the Communist Party did. Only 21.1 percent named the Social Democrats, and 19.7 percent named the DDK. Other parties were viewed as even less significant. Popular perceptions, however, do not coincide with how people actually voted. See A. Elebaeva, M. Karabaeva, and M. Bukhnyakh, "*Politicheskii pliuralizm v Kyrgyzstane,*" in T. Koichuev, ed., *Sovremennye politicheskie protsessy* (Bishkek: NAN, KR, 1996), pp. 23–24.

multiple candidates competed in the new democratic electoral process. In the rural regions outside Bishkek, however, far fewer candidates appeared on the ballot.[108] Several candidates competed for the national *kenesh* seats, but often only one candidate ran for the local *keneshes*. In Naryn and Talas, for example, where villages and even whole electoral districts are still composed of just one clan, the competition was negligible, and the village elders "selected the candidate as in Soviet times and before."[109] The primary candidate was generally a local "notable," whose lack of a platform and agenda suggests that he ran to maintain his position in his community and to represent the particularistic interests of his clan. Where several names appeared on one ballot in a rural district, competition among several notables, usually from different clans living within that district, took place. Ballots were typically cast along clan lines, just as had occured in *kolkhoz* votes during the Soviet era.[110] Although complete records of the voting are not available, family "patriarchs" reportedly appeared at polling stations with the "invitations to vote" of multiple registered voters – their extended family members – and simply signed their names and cast their votes. Rarely did an official interfere, and this "family voting" was often coupled with family ballot stuffing.[111] For example, in one Issyk-Kul district the competition among candidates from two rival clans was so intense, and the family ballot stuffing so open, that the election was canceled and rescheduled several times. Eventually, the more wealthy and powerful notable, Chinguishev, won the race.[112] In Naryn, the former Communist Party boss Usubaliev gathered 79 percent of the vote on the first round, despite having been ousted from power on corruption charges in 1986. Likewise, Masaliev claimed 84 percent in Osh after having been removed by the Kyrgyz Supreme Soviet for incompetency not five years earlier.[113] OSCE officials could not accurately document the extent of such voting practices,[114] but it is not unreasonable to hypothesize

---

[108] Author's interview with member of the Central Electoral Commission, Bishkek, August 1995.

[109] This was a response repeatedly given to the author during rural interviews in Talas, Issyk-Kul, Osh, Chui, and Jalal-Abad *oblast*'s.

[110] Based on author's ethnographic conversations with local notables, including *oqsoqols*, *kolkhoz* directors, *raion akims*, school authorities, enterprise directors, and prominent families – and journalists in a number of rural regions, 1997–98.

[111] The author's informal conversations in spring 1998 with rural inhabitants of five *oblast*'s (Talas, Issyk-Kul, Chui, Osh, and Jalal-Abad), about voting procedures echoed the OSCE findings. Most respondents thought that family voting was normal.

[112] Ironically, he was the prime minister who had been ousted by Akaev just a year earlier on massive corruption charges, for absconding with wealth from the nation's gold reserves.

[113] *Spravochnye materialy* (Bishkek, 1995), pp. 98–99.

[114] Unpublished reports on the elections, November 1994 and February 1995, provided by the Ministry of Foreign Affairs, Bishkek. In a published report on the elections in Azerbaijan (November 1995), OSCE advisor Michael Ochs points out that family voting and ballot stuffing were rampant among the Azeris as well. Azerbaijan is characterized by a social structure similar to that of the Central Asian republics, although greater urbanization has

that their impact was even stronger than the records suggest, and not limited to village backwaters. Even in Bishkek, monitors noticed multiple pages of voter signatures in the same handwriting. When questioned about the practice, one official responded: "This is our tradition. It's normal here."[115] Clan ties among voters appeared substantially stronger than respect for the democratic rule of law.

An examination of the professional status of the eighty-three independent deputies in the new parliament reveals the nature of their positions within the Kyrgyz social structure. Many of the deputies were *kolkhoz* directors or officials, positions of immense power and prestige under both Soviet and current rule.[116] If, as suggested in Chapter 3, the Soviet colonial system of agriculture preserved the *kolkhoz*, and froze in place, or even fostered, the pre-Soviet clan structures and identities, then the likelihood that the *kolkhoz* director would simultaneously be a clan patriarch was high. A *kolkhoz* director, even with limited financial resources, could rely on vertical clientelistic networks, already in place and reinforced by kin ties, to mobilize his power base and make his candidacy successful. Most other deputies were "businessmen" – either directors of state enterprises or owners of newly privatized firms. Those with financial means were very likely to have acquired their wealth through insider business transactions made possible by clan connections. Journalists and election observers reported that farm and enterprise directors were frequently relatives of political elites – appointees of regional and local *akims* who campaigned by doling out meat and rice on election day to remind their fictive kin networks (that is, the lower echelons of their clansmen) to whom they owed their livelihood.[117]

The upshot of this party failure to control parliament, much less the presidency, was the continued lack of adequate state-society linkages, a critical element of democratic governance, representation, and accountability. Further, the normal and legal process by which the national and local legislatures had become infiltrated by deputies who represented their own personal networks, at the expense of a broader ideological agenda, set the course of the

---

in part modernized society and weakened traditional networks. Also see Suny, "Provisional Stabilities."

[115] Author's interview with representative of the local election committee, Bishkek Technical Institute voting station, Bishkek, October 21, 1994.

[116] *Spisok deputatov*, obtained in July 1995 from the Ministry of Justice, Bishkek. A post-electoral review of parties can be found in N. J. Joldoshev, "*Politicheskie konflikty*" and "*Politicheskie partii Kyrgyzstana*," in T. Koichuev, ed., *Sovremennie politicheskie protsessy* (Bishkek: NAN, KR, 1996), p. 99. In a survey taken in 1996, only 5.3 percent of respondents claimed belief in the power of parties to "destabilize the country"; 32.9 percent claimed that "political power" could do so, and 14.5 percent claimed that "executive/administrative power" could. See A. Elebaeva, M. Karabaeva, and M. Bukhnyakh, "*Politicheskii pluralizm v Kyrgyzstane*," in the same volume, pp. 20–21.

[117] Author's meetings with Sabri Ergan, election monitor and second secretary, embassy of Turkey, Bishkek, October and November 1994, June and July 1995.

legislature's post-election behavior. Without a party to keep their behavior in check, deputies were bound only by personal ties, either to the president or to their clan.

In the February–March 2000 parliamentary elections, forty-two parties were registered, but independents – primarily clan notables – won 73 of 105 seats, despite an electoral law reformed so as to give parties more representation. Parties won thirty-two seats (30.4 percent), just a few more than they were guaranteed under the electoral law.[118] The president and his clan supporters subsequently began to form parties as well. In an election flawed by media bias and harassment of some opposition candidates, the pro-presidential parties did best. The Union of Democratic Forces won twelve seats, and its ally, "My Country," won another four seats. Aitmatov's personalistic party, "El" (the People's Party), was also pro-presidential and won two seats. Several other seats were scattered among democratic and communist parties. A few opposition clans have formed parties as well; for example, after breaking with Akaev, Feliks Kulov formed the Ar-Namys Party, and Daniyar Usenov became an opposition candidate. Most candidates still use their informal networks to mobilize support with little expense; they can thereby evade broader democratic oversight. Journalist Alisher Khamidov has observed that neither Islam nor parties typically mobilize people; rather, their clan affiliation remains most important in voting.[119] The Kyrgyz party system proved even weaker than Russia's, where at least the Communist Party developed a stable and substantial bloc during the 1990s.

Crowding out Civil Society and the Media

Third, the fledgling civil and political society has been crowded out by wider support for clan networks. Despite an active and free press and civic organizations in the early to mid-1990s, and despite numerous attempts at party formation and party coalitions, the democratic movement has failed to develop a wider constituency or to generate support for opposition parties. Numerous "civil society" groups have themselves been taken over by clan interests and do little to engage in democratic reform.[120] Moreover, clans usurp other forms of representation and competition that have reemerged in other areas of the former communist sphere: trade unions, social movements, and corporatist arrangements.[121]

---

[118] *Nations in Transit 2001: Kyrgyz Republic*, <www.freedomhouse.org/research/nitransit/ 2001/index.htm>. The report notes that independent deputies included government officials and clan leaders. There were also a handful of intellectuals, mostly from representing parties.

[119] Alisher Khamidov, "Kyrgyzstan: Organized Opposition and Civil Unrest," December 16, 2002, <www.eurasianet.org/departments/rights/articles/eav121602.shtml>.

[120] Author's conversation with a Kyrgyz journalist, January 2002.

[121] Author's interview with a trade union leader, Bishkek, Kyrgyzstan, August 1995.

Even more than civic organizations, the media, one of the pillars of the liberalization process of the early 1990s, have increasingly come under pressure from Akaev's network. *Res Publica* has persisted, despite a lengthy legal case waged by the government against its chief editor, Zamira Sydykova, because of her articles exposing corruption in the regime and in the Akaev family.[122] In 2002, Akaev's son-in-law, Adil Toigonbaev, bought one printing press and indirectly attained control of one of the major "independent" media complexes, which now sharply circumscribes access to information.[123] Akaev's daughter and son have been involved in other media ventures, and one of the Sarygulov brothers, also from the Sarybagysh clan, owns a major newspaper network.[124] The Akaev clan was reportedly frustrated at the U.S. government's funding of an independent printing press in 2002.[125] When informal politics are not sufficient to crowd out his opposition, Akaev increasingly has relied on authoritarian measures, such as jailing or threatening his most open critics.[126]

NGOs also fall victim to clan ties. Small NGOs tend to lack adequate management training, hiring informal networks of extended family and friends.[127] Nonetheless, there is a legacy of the democratization of the early 1990s. A handful of independent journalists and activists, drawing on the experiences and opportunities of the past fifteen years, as well as on international support and networks developed during that period, have continued to challenge Akaev's regime, calling for greater democratization and carefully monitoring elections, far more so than in any other Central Asian state.[128]

Undermining Transparency, Accountability, and Economic Reform

Fourth, clan nepotism, not transparency and accountability, has defined the allocation of public resources. Despite the mushrooming de jure power of the executive and the autonomy of the president, Akaev's attempts to implement his reformist agenda have been seriously thwarted. And the essence of this problem lay not in the legislature, which had relatively little power to interfere with Akaev's decrees. Instead, Akaev remained largely dependent upon the clans that had helped to bring him to power. Thus, he generously fed several northern Sarybagysh clans – especially the Kemin, Aitmatov, and

---

[122] Author's interview with Zamira Sydykova, editor, *Res Publica*, July 1998.
[123] Author's interview with a State Department official, January 2002. See also *The Economist*, August 2004.
[124] Author's interview with a journalist, Bishkek, August 2004.
[125] Author's interview with a journalist from *Internews*, Bishkek, January 2002.
[126] International Crisis Group, "Kyrgyzstan's Politics Crisis: An Exit Strategy," *Asia Report* No. 37, August 20, 2002.
[127] Abazov, "Kyrgyzstan," p. 340.
[128] Author's interview with a Kyrgyz democracy activist, South Bend, Indiana, February 2003; and with Cholpon Ergesheva, Jalal-Abad, August 2004.

Sarygulov networks and his wife's clan – while simultaneously doling out to rival clans just enough to prevent open conflict.[129]

According to one state advisor, during the early 1990s privatization of major state assets and key positions in government went to insider clans, which became entrenched in power and then resisted reform.[130] By 1995, as Akaev attempted to push through reforms, he hit a wall of opposition from the very clan elites who had all along backed his rise to power and electoral victories. In Akaev's State of the Republic address in late June 1996, he lashed out at corruption at all levels, beginning with his cabinet.[131] In 1997 and 1998, the government launched major anticorruption campaigns, but to little effect. Abazov describes the problem as connected to "a strong and deeply rooted tradition of patronage and an invisible web of patrimonial relations and loyalties" that come into play at the highest levels.[132] Yet, the problem is most vividly exemplified in the extensive business dealings of the presidential family network.

By 1996, Akaev was also under increasing pressure from international donors, who, after granting Kyrgyzstan $680 million in 1995, were now demanding privatization of the most valuable state assets as well as substantive land reform. Once small and medium-sized enterprises had been sold off in 1995, the *Gosfondimushchestvo* (State Property Fund, or GFI) had stalled.[133] Privatization of natural resources, major enterprises, land, and high-tech industry (formerly part of the Soviet military-industrial complex, although very limited) was blocked.[134]

The clan elites closest to Akaev, those bolstering executive power, had used their influence to shift power to key ministries and executive institutions from which they could enrich themselves and their extended networks; the more economically powerful they became, the more political clout they gained with Akaev. Given the small size of the Kyrgyz economy, the spoils to divide were few. At the central level, they included ministries and agencies controlling the flow of cash from trade, exports, and incoming loans and investment. The biggest prizes were Kyrgyzaltyn (the State Gold Company), GFI, *Goskominvest* (the State Committee on Investment, or GKI), the

---

[129] Matvei Chernykh, "*Velikii Askar i ego 'askoronostsy'*," May 22, 2003, <www.compromat. ru/main/akaev/velikij.htm>; and Alisher Khamidov, "Kyrgyzstan's Unrest Linked to Clan Rivalries," *Transitions Online*, June 6, 2002.

[130] Author's interview with Joormat Otorbaev, economic advisor to the president of Kyrgyzstan, Bishkek, Kyrgyzstan, January 2002.

[131] See the text of the address in *Slovo Kyrgyzstana*, June 1996.

[132] Abazov, "Kyrgyzstana," p. 350.

[133] Author's interviews with TACIS, World Bank, and USAID consultants to privatization programs in Kyrgyzstan, 1995, 1996, and 1997.

[134] Author's interview with a department head, Ministry of Industry, Kyrgyzstan, Bishkek, June 1998. Only in 1997 did the government begin to search for foreign investors in its high-tech enterprises; but it still refused to give up control of the enterprises, thus making new investment highly improbable.

Ministry of Finance and Economics, the Central Bank, the Tax Inspectorate, the Ministry of Emergency Situations, and the State Customs Committee. These posts went to his clan or his wife's. Akaev doled out other ministries like gifts in order to bolster his broader patronage ties. Such positions included the Ministry of Transport, which Akaev turned over to Kubanchibek Jumaliev, perhaps in a token gesture to an Osh clan. Although a southerner, and a former student of Akaev's in Leningrad, Jumaliev was more likely to be loyal to the president. Control of the small oil and gas industry went to Jumagulov, a northern clan ally, despite his Communist Party background. Each ministry was treated as the "personal property" of those who ran it. The post of state secretary, which controls all cadre appointments, was also critical, and has therefore always been filled by a trusted Akaev man, never by a rival clan member. Access to government ministries gave a person and his extended family the means to pursue private (and probably illegal) enterprises. While prime minister, for example, Jumagulov opened an import-export business and several high-end supermarkets. He also engaged in oil and gas station deals with Russia. Relatives of Akaev ran monopolies on sugar, cooking oil, bars, and minibuses. In short, public assets were informally treated as private within this regime of clan politics.

Akaev had established another set of patronage opportunities with the institutionalization of the *akimiat* (governorship) structures in 1992. This system of governorships was at once a return to pre-communist tribal and clan power arrangements and a transformation of the former Communist Party's regional and local structures. For seventy years, these Soviet institutions had largely been filled with "locals," cadres more loyal to their local networks than to the Party.[135] Now, however, these institutions could operate without a Party to oversee and limit their actions, and to relegate the practices of clan leaders to subversive backroom dealings. The *oblast' akims* (governors) held the most powerful regional posts. Akaev could directly appoint the province *akims*, with no oversight from either the cabinet or parliament; the *akims* in turn appointed district *akims*, who appointed local *akims*. At each level, *akims* controlled the appointment of the local procurator, judges, tax inspectors, customs officials, directors of state enterprises, and often MVD officials. They also influenced the privatization of land from former state farms. In short, the *akims*' networks controlled the most lucrative local-level positions.[136] The vast state bureaucracy was ripe for "the exploitation of political patronage, or the clan system."[137]

---

[135] For a more extensive discussion of the superficiality of Soviet colonialism in Central Asia, and of the Soviet system's inability to eliminate traditional clan networks and patterns of behavior, see Chapters 3 and 4. I discuss this issue in comparative perspective as well, drawing on anthropological accounts of clan and kinship networks in Georgia, Buryatia, the Middle East, and many African cases. See chapter 9.

[136] *Zakon o mestnoi vlasti* (Bishkek, 1994).

[137] Abazov, "Kyrgyzstan," p. 331.

During the early 1990s, the *oblast' akims* were almost invariably members of a powerful local clan. However, by 1995, Akaev began to appoint northerners, especially from his own clan, to control the southern regions – the base of his main rivals. Much friction resulted from such appointments, especially when Akaev's cronies attempted to change and control the appointment of local Osh cadres. In the four northern *oblast's*, by contrast, the *akims* were still powerful local notables. In Talas, the *akim* and *akimiat* cadre belonged almost exclusively to the clan of Akaev's wife, who was well known and increasingly criticized in the press for being of a more traditional Kyrgyz "clannish mentality" than Akaev himself.[138] In the Issyk-Kul and Naryn *oblast's*, the *akims* were related to the powerful local Aitmatov and Usubaliev networks.[139] By late 1997, realizing his slipping grasp on the levers of power and tenuous control over local resources, Akaev began more rapidly to shuffle *akims*, and even occasionally to send a Talas appointee to Naryn, and vice versa. This policy aroused the ire of the northern clans, but it did to some extent decrease their independent power base and increase their reliance upon and accountability to Akaev himself.

Broader north-south, provincial, and clan interests also rose to the fore in the legislature, especially when debating matters of economic policy, such as the tax code, the law of free economic zones, and the law on foreign direct investment. These issues became debates not about general policy but over control of capital. Those clan leaders closely tied to the president and executive power brokers won major concessions from the executive during such debates. The debate over the law on free economic zones (FEZs) exemplifies this clan-based opportunism. In 1996 and 1997, in order to attract rapid foreign direct investment and to boost and diversify the country's flailing economy, FEZs were created in particular districts of the Issyk-Kul, Chui, and Talas regions, as well as in Bishkek, all regions where Akaev's clan and allies lived.[140] No FEZs were established in the southern "opposition" regions, where more than 50 percent of the population lived, despite the attractive agricultural and industrial investments that the south offered, and despite its high unemployment.[141] Rather than engage in substantive representation and legislation, deputies from both houses focused their energies on using the

---

[138] By 1997, even *Vechernii Bishkek*, a widely circulated, and formerly state-controlled newspaper, began regularly to criticize the clan politics of the government.

[139] Aitmatov, as discussed in Chapters 4 and 5, was the leading figure of the Issyk-Kul clan and the broker of the 1990 pact. Usubaliev was the Communist Party first secretary removed by Gorbachev for corruption in 1985. He returned to Naryn, where he continued to be a powerful figure and to have a hand in the control of the hydroelectric power resources. He was elected to parliament in 1995.

[140] *Zakon o svobodnikh ekonomicheskikh zonakh* (Bishkek, 1997). A similar law was passed in Uzbekistan, privileging the Tashkent, Samarkand, and Ferghana regions. See *Zakon o svobodnikh ekonomicheskikh zonakh* (March 11, 1997).

[141] Author's interview with Usen Sydykov, parliamentary deputy from Jalal-Abad *oblast'*; author conversations with businessmen in Osh *oblast'*. Osh and Jalal-Abad are the two southern regions and comprise over 50 percent of the population.

Jogorku Kenesh to bring economic wealth to themselves and their network of supporters, as well as to their broader clan and regional base.

Shrinking Resources, Breaking the Pact, and Declining Durability

The blatant distribution of assets to clan cronies for their personal use has increasingly stressed Akaev's pact. Authoritarian control of the elections may not be enough to maintain stability. Realizing that the state is heavily indebted and nearing bankruptcy, clan elites – even those who support Akaev – have demanded more. The president's strategy for dealing with them is limited. Dividing shrinking resources while maintaining a pact and balance of clans has proven increasingly difficult.

The declining economy of the 1990s only enhanced already deep friction within the Kyrgyz pact (see Appendix, Table A.6 for economic indicators). In particular, dwindling state resources have caused tension among various northern clan networks who have been competing with each other rather than allying against the southern groups. In early 1998, the first major sign of such tension was Akaev's sudden sacking of one ally, Askar Sarygulov, a prominent representative of a powerful Talas clan. Kin of Akaev's wife, the Sarygulov clan had gained control of much of the republic's major resources. Sarygulov had been director of GKI since the early Akaev days and had expanded his control in 1996 to the GFI. Prima facie, Sarygulov's sacking was inexplicable; in fact, however, Akaev's decision was strategically designed to buy continued cooperation from rival clans of the Chui network, including Chui *akim* Kulov and Prime Minister Jumagulov, who resented the Sarygulovs' growing monopoly.[142] Although he removed Sarygulov from these posts, Akaev did not strip him of all economic assets or power. Sarygulov became chief of the Kyrgyz–Mercedes-Benz joint venture and remained active in other enterprises.[143] Akaev retained control of GKI and GFI by turning these institutions over to several extended kin from his own birthplace in Chui *oblast'*. Akaev's clan further controlled the tax inspectorate, the national guard, and the SNB (National Security Service),[144] and his connections staffed much of the executive branch. His apparat had grown astronomically since 1992, in numbers and in the

---

[142] Author's communications with government officials, including Askar Sarygulov, Bishkek, June 1998.

[143] Akaev gave him the ambassadorship to Malaysia, a country that had increasing trade and investment relations with Kyrgyzstan and hence was a potentially lucrative post.

[144] For biographies of every relevant political actor in contemporary Kyrgyz politics – where they come from and what positions they have held – see Igor Gusarov, *Kto est' Kto v Kyrgyzskoi Respublike* (Moscow, 1998). The publication was reportedly sponsored by the Russian mafia working in Central Asia. During the Soviet era, such biographical information was public. Since 1991, it has been secret. The publication exposes the degree to which all key positions in the regime have been held, and continue to be held, by Akaev's Kemin clan and by his wife's Talas clan. The book was not published or sold in Kyrgyzstan in 1998.

percentage of the budget it consumed – despite a declining GDP and budget crisis.[145]

The Sarygulov network did not endure such sidelining for long. In April 1998, they won significant revenge by convincing Akaev to oust both the prime minister and the Chui *akim*. Akaev, however, failed to exile Jumagulov, as planned, or even to strip him of his oil and gas enterprises. Instead, Jumagulov manipulated an appointment as *akim* of Jalal-Abad *oblast'*, which allowed him to retain control of major Kyrgyz energy reserves.[146] He also continued to operate monopolistic banking and other joint venture enterprises.[147] Shrinking resources even led Akaev to exclude certain members of the 1990 deal, thereby destabilizing the pact and his regime. Feliks Kulov, for example, was a powerful northern clan leader and one of the original parties to the 1990 pact, for which he had been awarded the lucrative posts of *akim* of Chui *oblast'* and the mayorship of Bishkek. In 1995, he claimed to be one of Akaev's strongest supporters.[148] By 1999, Kulov had split with Akaev over an undisclosed economic deal; the president cut Kulov's power, stripping him of his governorship and then of the mayoral post. Later Kulov was believed to have organized an unsuccessful coup attempt. Usubaliev and his clan were also increasingly sidelined; by 2001, Usubaliev had become an open critic of Akaev in parliament.

In addition to the split among the northern clan leaders, powerful southern clan networks, backed by their economically suffering *oblast'*s, were demanding a share of the spoils. When Dastan Sarygulov (Askar's brother) turned down Akaev's offer of the premiership, choosing instead to remain in his lucrative position as head of the state gold mining company, Akaev made a half-hearted gesture to the south. For the first time since 1992, Akaev appointed an Osh premier. Since the increasingly vocal legislature and media had repeatedly accused Akaev of employing a *"klannovaia sistema"* (clan system) in naming cadres,[149] the executive apparat widely paraded

---

[145] G. Kyz'min, *"Nam byi ministerstva vzyat' i otmenit'*," *Vechernii Bishkek*, June 1998. Kyz'min claims that much of the problem is due to the expanding police and security forces.

[146] Akaev sought to send him to the politically impotent post of ambassador to Germany, but Jumagulov refused.

[147] Jumagulov's joint ventures were primarily with German investors, which is reportedly why he negotiated the embassy post in Bonn. Akaev had originally sought to send him to London, a position that had less lucrative potential.

[148] Author's interviews with Feliks Kulov, former vice president, and *akim* of Chui *oblast'*, Bishkek, August 1995; and with other Kyrgyz officials, 1995–2001.

[149] Over time, the term *klan* (clan) has come to be commonly used in place of the Russian/Soviet term *rod* and the pre-Soviet Uzbek and Tajik terms *urugh* and *avlod*. *Klan* has a much harsher connotation, indicating familial and clan-based corruption. Author's interviews with Bakyt Beshimov, deputy of Osh *oblast'*, and with Mukhtar Cholponbaev, deputy of Issyk-Kul *oblast'*, Bishkek, July 1995 and July 1998. Even *Vechernii Bishkek*, a moderate newspaper, frequently made such accusations.

Jumaliev – as mentioned earlier, a native of Osh – as evidence of its unbiased cadre politics. The appointment thus satisfied neither the Osh power brokers nor the northern networks. Jumaliev was replaced in 1999, and succeeded by Kurmanbek Bakiev, also a southerner with weak clan ties.[150]

The split in the pact had become deeper, in part because in 1998, the government had defaulted on two international loans; by 2000, it then needed to delay its repayment schedule. Further, capital flight from Russia and from other foreign investors after the August 1998 Russian financial crisis had created bad debt and bankruptcy in many Kyrgyz enterprises. While the central bank has remained a stabilizing force, without further backing from the IMF, the Kyrgyz government will likely default on thousands of government bonds. The level of Kyrgyzstan's debt has left it highly exposed to external shocks.[151]

In the face of this bleak economic scenario, the spoils to divide in the nation's center have been steadily dwindling. Hence, competition to strip the state of what is left has sharply risen. Hoping to offset a crisis, in late 1998 Akaev appointed a new chief of the SNB, Misir Ashirkulov.[152] In March 1999, Ashirkulov directed the arrest of a number of members of Kulov's network who were believed to be connected to an attempted coup. Kulov's Chui connections and his former associates in the MVD were quietly accused and sentenced. Kulov himself, most likely too public and powerful a clan figure to arrest, was left untouched.[153] In April, however, Kulov resigned from his post as mayor of Bishkek, formed his own political party, and became a threat to Akaev in the December 2000 presidential elections. The Constitutional Court again rescued Akaev by finding grounds to disqualify Kulov from competing: Kulov had failed to demonstrate Kyrgyz language proficiency – as required by a new law. Finally, Kulov was arrested on politically motivated charges of corruption, and his family, network, and village were continually harassed.

---

[150] Jumaliev's appointment and term in office closely paralleled those of Sergei Kirienko in Russia, fostering speculation that Jumagulov's dismissal was connected to the ouster of Chernomyrdin. Jumagulov came from the northern region of Kyrgyzstan but not from Akaev's or his wife's clan, and hence Akaev had no familial or clan loyalty to him. In fact, the prime minister consistently interfered with Akaev's economic program. Jumagulov would probably have been ousted earlier (before April 1998) had his clan not been financially supported, beginning in the Soviet days, by clientelistic connections with the Soviet oil and gas enterprises, and particularly by Chernomyrdin and Lukoil. Lukoil was investing in Kyrgyz enterprises, and Jumagulov's sons and extended relations controlled much of this investment.

[151] IMF and World Bank, "Poverty Reduction, Growth, and Debt Sustainability in Low-Income CIS Countries," February 4, 2002, p. 43.

[152] The author met with Misir Ashirkulov in 1994, when he was rector of the UNDP International Business School, a prestigious and profitable post. He had no background in government, MVD, or KGB work.

[153] Author's communication with a diplomat, Bishkek, Kyrgyzstan, May 1999.

Increasingly, Akaev headed a government almost exclusively dominated by his clan cronies, and those of Mrs. Akaev.[154] Having lost of his popular legitimacy, Akaev's fortunes in the 2000 presidential election had depended on his remaining clan support and their ability to mobilize their networks. Increasingly, they did so by fixing the vote in contentious districts. The OSCE declared the election to have major problems, and by 2000 the international community began to brand Kyrgyzstan as an autocracy.

Clan tensions have further increased since September 11, 2001, as the overall economy remained stagnant, and growth uneven. Over half the population still lived below the poverty line in 2002, and Kyrgyzstan's Human Development Index rank slid to 102nd (of 173). (See Appendix, Table A.6.) Akaev used the fresh flow of resources from a deal with the United States (to allow the United States to base troops and antiterrorist operations in Kyrgyzstan) to feed his closest clan supporters, including his son, his son-in-law, and their family business networks.[155] Opposition was first vented by the Beknazarov clan in protest against Beknazarov's arrest by the regime. Other southern and eastern clans similarly excluded from power joined in protest. Demonstrations spiraled into a cycle of marches, arrests, and finally violence, when police fired on unarmed demonstrators in Ak-sy village of Jalal-Abad province. Confrontation continued from January through fall of 2002.[156] Negotiations between civil society leaders and the president after the Ak-sy conflict led to a referendum and several changes in the structure of parliament, which democratic activists hoped would allow for a more powerful legislature; however, since Ak-sy, opposition clans have reportedly begun arming themselves in the event of a future clash with the government.[157] According to one civil society activist, in mid-2004 "the president is already preparing nineteen of his relatives to run in the next parliamentary election. This way, he will have a bloc of control in the smaller new parliament."[158] In 2003, the president's daughter, Bermet Akaeva, established the new party "Alga Kyrgyzstan!" in anticipation of the next elections; Akaev's family began actively working to bolster the regime's image before the elections and to guarantee their victory in 2005. Yet the rise of the family may

---

[154] For a history of Akaev's clan genealogy, see T. Koichuev and M. Ploskikh, *Askar Akaev: Uchenyi Politik* (Bishkek: Ilim, 1996), pp. 8–9. Genealogy is used by Akaev's supporters as a source of legitimation; those excluded from his network of patronage accuse him of clan politics, corruption, and undermining democracy.

[155] Author's interview with a journalist, Bishkek, summer 2004. See also International Crisis Group, "Political Transition in Kyrgyzstan: Problems and Prospects," *Asia Report* No. 81, August 11, 2004.

[156] Alisher Khamidov, "Clan Politics at the Base of Kyrgyzstan's Political Crisis"; and author's interview with a Kyrgyz journalist, Osh, summer 2002.

[157] Author's interview with Raya Kadyrova, NGO leader and sociologist, Bishkek, Kyrgyzstan, Bishkek, August 2002.

[158] Author's interview with a civil society activist, Jalal-Abad, summer 2004.

only further alienate both clan and democratic opposition.[159] Tensions have remained high. After the 2000 election and then the Ak-sy crisis, it became clear that Akaev and his allies were excluding the south through both force and corruption. Consequently, prominent public figures and parliamentarians – including Beknazarov, Madumarov, Tekebaev, Sadyrbaev, Masaliev, Asanov, and Abdumomsunov – with clan ties to Osh, Batken and Jalal-Abad provinces have united in opposition. Their "common aim [is] ending the Sarybagysh clan's stranglehold on power."[160] One activist claimed that people are angry and will no longer stand for such abuses: "if the next elections are falsified, there will be a civil war."[161]

SUMMARY

The first part of this chapter examined the role of clans at the social level in facilitating transition by providing social safety networks for their kin. These local kin groups continue as affective ties embedded with meaning, especially for those who have not benefited from independence. In important ways, these networks have offered some stability in times of turmoil. Yet they also suggest the increasing distance between the local level and the state; nonelite clans are disaffected with the state and clan elites that have failed to provide for them.

The discussion then turned to the meso and elite levels of politics, where in post-Soviet Kyrgyzstan democratizing elites and ideology have proved short-lived. Key democratic institutions – elections, the separation of powers, parties, and civil society – have been steadily undermined, penetrated, or, one might say, crowded out of business by clan politics. Clan networks, which regularly make use of nepotism and corruption and strip public assets for their private benefit, have pervaded the regime. They have increasingly delegitimized it by rampant pursuit of their personal, short-term interests. The rise of vested clan interests has blocked or corrupted economic reforms, and has blocked further political reforms that might benefit society but undo their economic gains. Public knowledge of clannish corruption is significant. According to a summer 2004 survey, 70.3 percent of respondents agreed that the "central organs of power" were completely or close to completely "corrupted, and connected with family business and criminal activity."[162]

Furthermore, in discussing how and why the Kyrgyz clan networks arrived at a stabilizing pact during the pre-transition period (1990), I observed that three factors were essential to those pacts: (1) a relatively equal balance of

---

[159] Author's interview with Cholpon Ergeshova, director of the regional office, Coalition for Democracy and Civil Society, Jalal-Abad, August 24, 2004.
[160] Khamidov, "Kyrgyzstan's Unrest," p. 2.
[161] Author's interview with a civil society activist, Jalal-Abad, Kyrgyzstan, summer 2004.
[162] Bishkek Business Club and CIPE, Bulletin no. 2, p. 16.

power among the major clan networks, (2) the presence of a legitimate clan leader who could broker the pact and ensure compliance, and (3) stable and central control of the military and security forces. Having sufficient economic resources to divide among clan elites was a background condition. By the late 1990s, a decade after this pact had been formed, these conditions were disintegrating. Ironically, they were disintegrating largely because of the process by which clans within the pact had stripped the state of its assets. As resources declined and Akaev's family clans became greedier, Akaev cut rival clans from power. Yet, despite their nearly hegemonic control, they could not consolidate power and authority. Rather, Kyrgyzstan was spiraling into a vicious circle of decline. The consequences of this process for the longer-term durability of the regime will be significant.

Chapter 8 will continue this discussion with an examination of the role of clan networks at the elite and state-society levels in those regimes that did not experience significant political liberalization, Uzbekistan and Tajikistan. Like Kyrgyzstan, they too are increasingly penetrated by clan interests.

8

Central Asia's Regime Transformation (1995–2004)
Part II

> *Klannovnost'* is our biggest problem.
>
> Tajik taxicab driver, March 2001

One Uzbek scholar suggested to me several years ago that a social scientist could write a dissertation based on the views of taxicab drivers. One need only strike up a conversation with a cab driver in Central Asia to hear a tirade about whose clan controls the country. Eight to ten years ago, Kyrgyz cab drivers openly complained about clan politics, but in recent years Uzbek and Tajik cab drivers are often equally effusive. My Uzbek colleague was only partly joking. And even if not completely accurate, cab drivers' perceptions of their political system's problems often reflect public awareness of these issues.

I did not do a survey of cab drivers, but this chapter examines the rise of clan politics within the new, post-transitional authoritarian regimes of Uzbekistan and Tajikistan. Here, the politics of clans and their corrosive effects are not as plainly visible as in Kyrgyzstan, whose liberalizing regime was particularly susceptible to the effects of clan politics and made this phenomenon easier to observe. Nonetheless, clans are critical political and economic players that affect key institutions and policies of these authoritarian regimes as well. The previous chapter has already discussed local-level identity networks in these cases; this chapter turns to their elite and meso-level institutions. Uzbek and Tajik authoritarianism becomes penetrated and weakened by clan rivalries.

Explaining the nonconsolidation of an autocratic regime is not a task that comparative politics has typically attempted. The literature often implicitly assumes that autocracies are strong states, but in so doing, it leaves critical possibilities unexplored: first, that informal actors, such as clan networks, can inhibit consolidation; second, that clan interests can constrain the state even in countries where little or no reform has taken place;[1] and third, that a nonconsolidated autocracy is *not* on a trajectory leading to democratization.[2] The Uzbek and Tajik cases exemplify these possibilities. Like the Kyrgyz case, they suggest that "nonconsolidated" regimes may be viable and may persist in an unconsolidated condition for some time. We find that clans inhibit key elements of authoritarian regime consolidation, albeit to varying degrees.[3] A closer examination of the internal workings – of the very nerve system – of such regimes will better enable us to understand how clans penetrate and corrode these regimes. Under shrinking economic conditions and a transitional state, a vicious cycle of clan competition emerges and leads to declining durability. This decline may be temporarily halted by the strategic use of international funding (e.g., aid, loans, and foreign direct investment) to balance, appease, and constrain challengers; however, these regimes continue to be highly personalistic, weakly institutionalized, and fragile. The rest of this chapter will explore the nature of clan politics in Uzbekistan and Tajikistan, how clans affect authoritarian institutions, and the consequences for regime disability.

II. UZBEKISTAN: FORMAL AND INFORMAL AUTHORITARIAN POWER

Uzbekistan has been commonly portrayed by the Western media, scholars, and human rights organizations as a consolidated authoritarian state, even a totalitarian state. By the end of the transition, Karimov had cracked down on all known opposition parties and movements. The institutional restructuring of parliament and the electoral process marked the transition's conclusion. The OSCE's evaluation of the elections of fall 1994 and the referendum of spring 1995 was unequivocal: "not free and not fair."[4] The parliament itself, since 1992, when Karimov crushed the Mirsaidov clan's opposition bloc, had been under the strict supervision of a trusted client of Karimov's,

---

[1] For example, Joel Hellman's interesting work on the political economy of partial reform argues that vested interests that block reform arise only in states where partial political and economic liberalization has taken place. He does not find the rise of such interests in countries such as Uzbekistan, where there has been no reform. See Joel Hellman, "The Politics of Partial Reform," *World Politics*, vol. 5, no. 2 (February 1998), pp. 203–234.

[2] Guillermo O'Donnell and Philippe Schmitter, in *Transitions from Authoritarian Rule: Tentative Conclusions about Uncertain Democracies* (Baltimore: Johns Hopkins University Press, 1986), note other paths and modes of transition, but do little to explore them.

[3] The literature overoptimistically assumes that authoritarian regimes naturally consolidate, especially post-communist ones, since they inherit a strong institutional apparatus. These states did inherit a more developed institutional base than many post-colonial African states, yet independence and decolonization were much more rapid in the FSU (approximately five months!). The ex-Soviet republics were quickly cut off from Soviet support (e.g., budget transfers). Hence, they still needed to consolidate their new states, which often had no pre-Soviet history.

[4] Based on unpublished OSCE election material from 1996, accessed in Tashkent.

acting chairman Erkin Khalilov.[5] The referendum on the presidency, held on March 25, 1995, appeared to seal Uzbekistan's fate as an autocratic regime with Islam Karimov as its dictator.[6] Following the example of Saparmurat Niyazov in neighboring Turkmenistan, Karimov decreed that the 1995 presidential elections would be cancelled and replaced by a referendum on his presidency, allegedly to prevent further destabilization of the country during the transition.[7]

In contrast to Kyrgyzstan, whose democratization in the early 1990s fostered some decentralization of power, Uzbekistan's authoritarian transition has allowed the president to maintain a tighter grip on the regime and its resources. Karimov pursued authoritarian consolidation by recentralizing economic and political power. Karimov's rapid moves to build up security forces – the Ministry of Internal Affairs (MVD) and the National Security Service (SNB) – have been key factors in preserving some elements of a Soviet-style state. Nonetheless, Karimov has struggled to maintain state power apart from clan domains, and has waged an ongoing battle with clans who seek to disperse executive power and channel resources to their own control, and who use state positions to engage in backdoor deals that reek of corruption.[8]

Although Karimov's continued rule since 1989 has ensured continuity with the communist past, the sudden Soviet collapse and transition weakened the state. The military, security services, police, and Communist Party were hard hit by the departure of ethnic Russians and by the loss of Moscow's financing. Karimov himself banned the Party and seized its resources; even before that, Party membership had declined after Gorbachev eliminated its hegemony. Although Karimov later established the People's Democratic Party of Uzbekistan (NDPU) in its place, this new government party lacked the resources, legitimacy, and power of the old one. Karimov depended little on the party apparatus. Nor could he depend on Moscow. Instead, Karimov depended enormously on the clans that had brought him to his position as a broker of their interests. Hence, while attempting to control them, he also had to deal with and appease them. He had to play the game of clan politics.

In Uzbekistan, we find that clan politics affects the consolidation of six dimensions of authoritarianism: (1) institution building (e.g., executive control of parliament, political parties, and elections); (2) the president's ideology

---

[5] Author's communication with an "independent" former political party member, an intellectual and activist who was arrested in 1990 for his efforts to run for a seat in parliament, Tashkent, August 1997.

[6] On the importance of the referendum for consolidating Karimov's regime, see Rustam Jumaev, *Politicheskaia sistema Respubliki Uzbekistan: Stanovlenie i razvitie* (Tashkent: "FAN," 1996), p. 204.

[7] Author's interview with Rustam Jumaev, advisor and deputy director, Institute for Strategic Studies, Tashkent, October 1996.

[8] Author's interview with an Uzbek expert, Tashkent, January 2002.

of nationalism; (3) centralization of economic resources;[9] (4) presidential autonomy in policy making, vis-à-vis vested interests; (5) the *hokims* (governors); and (6) the state monopoly over the use of force. Failure to consolidate these spheres negatively affects regime and state durability.

Clan Structure in Post-Soviet Uzbekistan

As noted in Chapter 2, in contemporary Uzbekistan tribes no longer exist, and tribal lineages are typically not known. Identity groups are more fragmented along "local" or narrower family-clan lines. Uzbek clan networks can operate: (1) at the very local level of the *mahalla* or *qishloq*, already discussed in Chapter 7, and (2) at the provincial and national levels.

Identity and clan networks in Uzbekistan are complex, particularly among elites. Most Uzbeks identify themselves at the national level with reference to their provincial name. They typically refer to themselves as *Samarkandlik, Bukharalik, Tashkentlik, Ferghanalik,* or *Khorezmlik.* As discussed earlier, these identifications (with the exception of *Tashkentlik*) date back at least to the period of the khanates, when the settled populations developed ties to different pre-modern states and communities. Samarkand and Bukharan networks frequently intermarried in order to solidify relations, as Tashkent and Ferghana families did as well. The regional reference, however, does not imply that a region-wide social network, much less kin-based relations, incorporates the majority of people within those large territories. Rather, a regional network is based on a clan or on interrelated clans led by particular strongmen or notables. The norms of trust and personal loyalty bind them together.[10] Within these broad regional groupings, Uzbeks belong to familial-clan networks, centered around a particular individual, family, or neighborhood. In the case of elite families, the clan head is typically a wealthy businessman, a powerful government apparatchik, or a *kolkhoz* director. In the case of poorer families, the head may be a village *oqsoqol* or a respected religious leader.[11]

Clan elites use patronage to promote their own members, thus creating dependency networks and concentrating wealth and power in their own group. The term "clan" in contemporary Uzbekistan, as in Tajikistan, more accurately refers to these subregional networks, of which kin and fictive kin marriage and friendship relations are the key components. Personalist

---

[9] This is not an element of all authoritarian regimes, but it is a critical element in building "socialist" authoritarianism in Uzbekistan, which has sought to maintain a centrally planned economy.

[10] Dmitry Pashtun, "Structure and Practice of State Administration in Uzbekistan" (Local Government and Public Service Reform Initiative) (Budapest: Open Society Institute, 2003), p. 12. Refer also to the discussion of clans in Chapter 2.

[11] Based on author discussions with Uzbek and Tajik sociologists, 1996–1998. See also Demian Vaisman, "Regionalism and Clan Loyalty in the Political Life of Uzbekistan," in Yaacov Ro'I, ed., *Muslim Eurasia: Conflicting Legacies* (London: Frank Cass, 1995), pp. 109–113.

structures affect appointments in all spheres. According to one Uzbekistani scholar, "as a rule, the clan entrusted close relatives with the most prestigious positions."[12] From there, the networks extend outward.

As in Kyrgyzstan, extensive corruption is often involved with clan patronage at all levels, as the president often turns a blind eye to clan asset stripping. Further, during the post-Soviet period, as state power has waned, some mafias have also formed on the basis of clan networks. This phenomenon closely resembles mafia development in twentieth-century Italy.[13] Nonetheless, "clan" is not synonymous with the mafia or crime.[14]

In post-Soviet Uzbekistan, two groups of clans have emerged as the most powerful: the Tashkent clan, led by Timur Alimov (dubbed "the Grand Timur");[15] and the Samarkand clan, led by Ismoil Jurabekov, called "the Gray Cardinal" because of his role in masterminding Karimov's ascent.[16] Within these two groups, multiple smaller clans compete for influence. A somewhat less powerful grouping is the Ferghana clan; only a few Ferghana families actually have influence, and they are not representative of the region as a whole. Meanwhile, the Khorezm group, like some other regions (Kashkadarya, Surkhandarya, and Karakalpakistan), has had almost no economic or political power since 1991.

As in Kyrgyzstan, the clans infiltrating the post-Soviet regime have been those that engineered Karimov's rise to power in 1989. The Jurabekov and Rashidov clans of Samarkand, the Alimov clan of Tashkent, the Sultonov clan of Tashkent, the Gulomov clan of Tashkent/Ferghana, and the Azimov clan of Tashkent/Ferghana all backed Karimov's candidacy, and consequently benefited.[17] Two major clanlike mafias, the Gafur and Salim families, emerged as powers in the late 1980s. Once opposed to Karimov, they have now given the president limited backing in exchange for autonomy over their economic interests. The "balancing of clans" that clan elites entrusted Karimov to maintain has thus been limited to a small number of groups.[18]

Nonetheless, Karimov has faced increasing difficulties in maintaining that balance, in satisfying the demands of the power-hungry clan elites fighting over scarce resources, and in cutting their power when he deems they are gaining too much control and at the same time consolidating an

[12] Vaisman, "Regionalism and Clan Loyalty," p. 112.

[13] Judith Chubb, *Patronage, Power, and Poverty in Southern Italy: A Tale of Two Cities* (Cambridge: Cambridge University Press, 1982).

[14] Alisher Taksanov, "*Klany i korruptsiia v Uzbekistane,*" *Navigator*, September 10, 2002, <www.uzbekistanerk.org/Erkinfo100203-klans.ru.htm>.

[15] Usman Khaknazarov, "*Vozrozhdenie 'serogo kardinala' uzbekskoi politiki,*" February 21, 2003, <www.muslimuzbekistan.com>.

[16] Ibid.

[17] Based on author's interviews in Tashkent, 1997–2004. See also Usman Khaknazarov, "*Kandidaty v prezidenty Uzbekistana,*" February 21, 2003, <www.centrasia.ru>.

[18] Author's interview with Mukhammed-Babur Malikov, former minister of justice of Uzbekistan, Washington, D.C., May 2004.

authoritarian state run by his own cadre of technocrats. Throughout the 1990s Karimov often promoted those who lacked strong clan connections, had technocratic skills, and were likely to be loyal to him and to the Uzbek state. Originally, he was not seen as clannish or corrupt. Since 2001, however, local observers note the rise of "the Family," led by Karimov's elder daughter, Gulnora Karimova.[19] Her influence has both shaken the balance of power and increasingly alienated ordinary Uzbeks. Although the Uzbek state has greater force at its disposal than the Kyrgyz regime, Karimov has not clearly succeeded in institutionalizing the state's power or his personal power.

Authoritarian Institution Building: Executive Control of Parliament, Political Parties, and Elections

One significant area in which the battle between clans and the regime has evidently hurt the consolidation of authoritarianism is in institution building, especially in the creation of a parliament that mirrors the communist-style Supreme Soviet, which was a rubber stamp of executive decrees. After driving some prominent former communists from the parliament, Karimov seemed poised to consolidate a puppet legislature.[20] Yet clan interests have prevented the creation of a strong executive party, parties, or presidential bloc, as in Russia. In an authoritarian context, one would not expect institutions such as elections and the legislature to have even marginal significance. Karimov originally used the parliament as a venue for some clan representation. Since 1996, Karimov has manipulated electoral and party legislation in order to strengthen parties and thereby decrease clan representation. With that goal, he created five "pro-government" parties, each designated to represent different social sectors.

In chapter 6, we discussed the transformation of Uzbekistan from a single party communist regime to a non-ideological autocracy, in which no one party dominated the political, social, or economic sphere and in which Karimov sought to eliminate his opposition in the old Supreme Soviet. The process of drafting an electoral law, drafting a law on parties, convoking elections, and assembling the new national *Oliy Majlis* and the local soviets (the *majlislar*) was primarily directed at increasing the power of the central government, under Karimov.[21] It correspondingly aimed at decreasing the

---

[19] Author's interviews with a journalist, Tashkent, 2004; and with an Uzbek expert, South Bend, Indiana, June 2004.

[20] Yuri Kul'chick, *Respublika Uzbekistan v seredine 90-kh godov* (Moskva: RAN, 1995).

[21] On the first version of the electoral law, see Pauline Jones Luong, *Institutional Change and Political Continuity: Power, Perceptions, and Pacts* (New York: Cambridge University Press, 2002). The electoral law was subsequently changed several times. See Gregory Gleason, "Uzbekistan," in Freedom House, *Nations in Transit 2002* (New York: Freedom House, 2002), p. 419.

power of local and provincial clan bosses and their networks. Like Akaev, Karimov had originally supported a party-based electoral law, but he was unable to convince the factions that supported him to accept these impersonal electoral provisions. Like the Kyrgyz, both provincial and local Uzbek elites relied primarily on their extensive networks for their positions, and they did not want to trade a highly effective (for them) system of personalized politics for an impersonal party list system whose consequences were unknown and highly risky.[22]

The Uzbek parliament likewise did not care to submit itself to reelection under terms that would promote parties over individuals. As in Kyrgyzstan, the Uzbek Supreme Soviet had been elected in 1990 under the 1989 Soviet multicandidate electoral law, which had brought over 50 percent of deputies to power based on their personal ties, not on any party affiliation. A large faction was comprised of the Mirsaidov clan's opposition to Karimov.[23] Another faction was composed of Communist Party candidates, who could no longer rely on the CPU for their seats. Faced with this opposition, and with a tenuous political pact supporting him, Karimov had no choice but to engage in a negotiating process with various factions, many of which were based outside of Tashkent and had de facto, if not de jure, control over the agricultural economy and the rural population.[24] The upshot of these discussions was the creation of a "multiparty" system – albeit still without room for opposition parties – and an electoral law that allowed the continuation of nonparty, independent candidacies as well as party nominations.

On one level, electoral procedures ultimately did not matter, since parliament did not have the right of opposition. On another level, however, as in Kyrgyzstan, those elected to the *Oliy Majlis* had greater access to state resources; parliament was a source of patronage. From an economic perspective, then, the power of clans and of regional strongmen, outside of party control, increased with their election to parliament and created a drain upon the regime. The 1994 elections had given such independents a strong hold in parliament (see Table 8.1).

The president himself refused to become a party member or to found his own party. At the same time, he did encourage the formation of several parties, in part to appease Western agencies that were increasingly

---

[22] U.S. advisors in Kyrgyzstan who worked on the legal discussion of electoral laws noted similar propensities, and similar resistance to proportional representation laws. Author interview with Howard Ockman, CEELI advisor, Bishkek, Kyrgyzstan, June 1994. On Kyrgyz party politics, see Kathleen Collins, "The Failure of Political Parties in 'Democratic' Kyrgyzstan," unpublished manuscript, Association for the Study of Nationalities Convention, April 1996. Luong, *Institutional Change*, reports similar findings in a study of elite preferences for electoral institutions in Kazakhstan, Kyrgyzstan, and Uzbekistan.

[23] Author's interview with a former Uzbek government official, South Bend, Indiana, June 2004.

[24] See Luong, *Institutional Change*. Luong's book on electoral institutions argues that the electoral laws were the outcome of a bargaining process in each state.

TABLE 8.1. *Results of the 1994 elections to the Oliy Majlis of Uzbekistan (December 25, 1994)*

Affiliation/Nominating Body	Seats Won	Percentage of the Total Parliament
People's Democratic Party	69	27.6%
Vatan Tarakkioti	14	5.6%
Adolat	47	18.8%
Total party candidates	130	52.0%
Independents	120	48.0%
Total candidates elected	250	100%

Source: Uzbek Central Electoral Commission, 1995.

demanding political reform in exchange for economic aid, and in part to recreate a party organizational basis that his technocrats could control; after a law on parties was adopted in 1996, nearly twenty existed on paper by 1997. However, none of those officially registered were opposition parties. In part, this superficial institutionalization of parties was intended for Western consumption, to bolster Uzbekistan's claim to "Asian democratization." Yet Karimov was hardly so naive as to delude himself that the West would believe such propaganda. At a more critical level, Karimov's audience was domestic; he sought to create new party ideologies and organizations to replace the Communist Party. According to Article 15 of the party law, which was revised in 1998 in anticipation of new elections, the government had the right to subsidize parties in connection with elections.[25]

Party formation became a strategy for undercutting the power of clan elites. Initially, the main party sponsored by Karimov in the 1994 elections was the successor to the Communist Party, the NDPU.[26] Soon, however, Karimov lost confidence in this catch-all party's ability to bring in the vote, and he created other parties (Fidokorlar, Vatan Tarakkioti, Adolat, and Milliy Tiklanish), each with its own pro-Karimov message and target audience: youth, workers, pensioners, and businessmen. In 2003, in anticipation of the December 2004 election, two new parties, the Free Farmer Party and the Party of Agrarians and Entrepreneurs, announced plans to seek registration as well. Eventually, the National Democratic Institute (NDI) was even allowed to return to Uzbekistan to work on the development of the officially permitted political parties, and several government conferences were held to solicit the advice of Western experts. Nonetheless, party membership remains very low.

The first real test of the new party law and parties took place in the December 1999 elections. Although neither free nor fair, since no real opposition

[25] "The Law of the Republic of Uzbekistan on Political Parties," Tashkent, 1998, provided by the Central Electoral Commission.
[26] Author's interview with leaders of the NDPU, Tashkent, August 2000.

parties were allowed to compete and all candidates (party and independent) had to be vetted by the state (through the CEC), the election was a novel step for the Karimov regime. More candidates and parties were allowed to compete than in 1994. The results were surprising, both to the regime and to Western observers, who assumed that Karimov's authoritarian state would ensure his success in fixing the results. Despite government resources, advertising, intimidation, and pressure to vote – regular roundups occurred on election day in the universities, on the farms, and at places of work – the turnout for the official party candidates was weak. Only 49 percent of those elected were chosen through affiliation and promotion by the pro-Karimov parties (see Table 8.2), even though 70 percent of the competing candidates were party candidates. This was an even weaker performance than in 1994, despite the increased state support of parties. A substantial 51 percent of the deputies were still not affiliated with any party. Of these, 6 percent came from citizens' groups approved by the state. The bulk of these, 44 percent, were the nominees of executive bodies.[27] These candidates were nominated and successful due to their positions in local power networks run by the provincial and local *hokims* (governors), who were in such positions because of their status in the region as notables or strongmen.[28] Had the elections been legitimately democratic – or at least comparable to the Kyrgyz standard of "free and fair" – it is reasonable to believe that an even higher percentage of deputies would have likewise been "*bezpartinyi*" (partyless).[29] Meanwhile, one institutional reform that would further aid party candidates would be an exclusively party-list electoral law. Yet strong opposition from independents has prevented Karimov from adopting a party-list system, despite adoption of other changes intended to strengthen pro-Karimov parties.

As the state's preparation for the 2004 parliamentary elections geared up, the regime was clearly worried that its pro-regime parties would again fail to mobilize the population. According to Daniel Kimmage, President Karimov himself

offered unusually candid criticism of Uzbekistan's lackluster political arena at an April 29, 2004 press conference, saying, "[Uzbek political parties] have no independent platform or ideology and, regrettably, are still weak in terms of winning the hearts and minds of ordinary people and informing them of their aims, principles, and ideas. That is, now our country has no political parties like those in Europe, and in the East, for instance, Japan, South Korea, and others."[30]

[27] ODIHR, *Report on Election of Deputies to the Oliy Majlis 5 and 19 December 1999* (Warsaw: OSCE, April 2000).

[28] Author's meetings with Raphaelle Mathey, ODIHR, and Ambassador Ganchev, OSCE, Tashkent, June 2000. See also ODIHR, *Election of Deputies*. Kul'chick, *Respublika*, observes the same phenomenon in the 1994 elections.

[29] Author's interviews with rural and urban citizens outside of the capital indicated an extremely low level of knowledge about, and trust in, even the major political parties.

[30] Daniel Kimmage, RFE/RL Analytical Reports, July 28, 2004, vol. 4, no. 29, <http://www.rferl.org/reports/centralasia/2004/07/29-280704.asp>.

TABLE 8.2. *Results of the 1999 elections to the Oliy Majlis of Uzbekistan (December 5 and 19, 1999)*

Affiliation/Nominating Body	Number of Applications Submitted to the CEC	Number of Candidate Applications Registered	Percent of Candidate Applications Registered	Percent of Total Candidates Registered	Total Number of Elected Deputies	Percent of Elected Deputies
People's Democratic Party	250	180	72%	17.8%	48	19%
Fidokorlar Party	224	207	92%	20.4%	34	14%
Vatan Tarakkioti Party	136	108	79%	10.7%	20	8%
Adolat Party	161	119	74%	11.8%	11	4%
Milliy Tiklanish Party	116	93	80%	9.2%	10	4%
Total for all political parties	887	707	81%	70.0%	123	49%
Executive bodies	250	205	82%	20.3%	110	44%
Citizens' initiative groups	193	98	51%	9.7%	16	6%
Total of all candidates	1,330	1,010	76%	100%	249	100%

Sources: Uzbek Central Electoral Commission and ODIHR, election of deputies to the *Oliy Majlis* (parliament) 5 and 19, December, 1999: Limited Election Assessment Mission final report (Warsaw: OSCE, April 28, 2000).

In late 2003, however, a new pro-presidential party, the Liberal Democratic Party of Uzbekistan (LDPU), suddenly emerged, with Karimov's daughter, Gulnora Karimova, financing and directing it behind the scenes. With its goal of leading a pro-presidential bloc of parties, the LDPU is modeled on Putin's pro-presidential "Party of Power" in Russia.

Creating a New Ideology for Uzbekistan

Karimov's nationalist agenda directed enormous state resources into creating the symbols, legends, and history of the united "Uzbek nation." As in Kyrgyzstan, Uzbek nationalism was not openly directed against the Russian, Jewish, Tajik, or other minority populations. Nor was it the direct manifestation of anti-colonialism, as had been Birlik's program during the late 1980s.

In general, the regime's democratic and nationalist agenda amounted to an admission of its desperate need for broader popular legitimacy. As his speeches and publications repeatedly referred to the concrete threats of "regionalism," "separatism," and "clan conflict," it became clear that Karimov himself feared and sought to instill in the population the dread of a Tajik-like conflict, in which rival clans battled for central power.[31] As the Tajik conflict died down, Karimov turned to a new threat to mobilize the population behind him: Islamic fundamentalism, first in the form of the Taliban and later in the form of Uzbekistan's own underground radical movement.

A clear majority of the population strongly believed the unstated but widely propagated view that only Karimov could maintain political and economic stability and prevent a Tajik-like crisis. Competing regional and clan factions trusted Karimov more than they trusted each other, and hence preferred to have him at the center of the pact that held the state together, if by autocratic means. Meanwhile, the Tashkent intellectuals and Sovietized elite were at once Karimov's most likely source of democratic opposition and his strongest supporters. For them, the Karimov regime was better than the underground Islamic opposition, which they feared would follow the Taliban example.

Yet Karimov's dilemma has remained: he needs to consolidate an autocracy without inciting opposition from powerful clans. Whether or not making concessions to the "democratic" opposition would mitigate his other problems remains unclear. Hence his strategy has been mixed and hesitant. The scheduling of parliamentary and presidential elections in 1999–2000, and his continual attempts to create a national party or bloc of parties, in order to deliver the new ideology and mobilize the population, exemplify

---

[31] Islam Karimov, *Uzbekistan on the Threshold of the Twenty-First Century: Threats to Security, Conditions of Stability, and Guarantees for Progress* (Tashkent: Uzbekistan, 1997), pp. 88–89.

Karimov's attempts to legitimize his power and thereby to downsize various rival networks.

Control over Cadre Policy and the Allocation of Resources

The battle between the Karimov and Uzbek clan factions has also impeded the centralization of control over economic resources, an ironic outcome in a state that has steadfastly refused to reform its socialist, state-controlled economy. Like Akaev, Karimov needed to maintain the appearance of a neutral broker, merely managing the clan pact. Meanwhile, he was besieged by ever-increasing demands – primarily by two major clan groups from Samarkand and Tashkent, as well as by rival clan networks within each regional grouping – to be given control of a greater share of the state's resources.[32] They expected to be able to exploit these public resources for their networks' private gain. As a consequence, Karimov has been unable to consolidate state autonomy in policy making, vis-à-vis informal interests, despite his super-presidential decree power.[33] His attempts to control cadre politics and replace clan elites with technocrats, to introduce currency convertibility and privatization in line with IMF demands, to crack down on corruption and increase state revenues, and to control the governors and subnational clan and patronage networks have had limited success.

Contrary to most empirical and theoretical expectations of autocratic, post-communist regimes, the power ministries in Uzbekistan were not hegemonic party structures as in the Soviet era. Nor were they simply security structures. Rather, as in Kyrgyzstan, they were the institutions through which economic resources and capital flowed. Hence, clan fights to control and distribute these prizes were important issues; indeed, they were the most important political issues the regime was confronted with during the post-transition period. The principal sources of economic revenue included the state gold mining company, the ministry of oil and gas and the oil refineries (located in the Bukhara, Samarkand, and Ferghana *oblast*'s), the central bank, the National Bank (NBU), other banks, the ministry for foreign economic relations, the state cotton complex, the tax agency, and the customs agency. Control of the three major foreign investment projects, Coca-Cola, Daewoo, and Newmont Gold were key prizes. Rectorships of universities were also doled out.[34]

Karimov's cadre politics, much like Akaev's, had been founded upon a pact that included several major provincial players and clan networks.

---

[32] International Crisis Group (ICG), "Uzbekistan's Reform Program: Illusion or Reality?" *Asia Report* No. 46, February 18, 2003.

[33] Ravshan Mirzaev, "*Uzbekskie klany: nazhivaiutsia na kaznokradstve*," June 24, 2004.

[34] Author's interview with a former government bureaucrat and education expert, Tashkent, March 2004.

Hence, in order to keep each network satisfied, Karimov was careful not to allow any one to seize too much control. The head of cadre policy was therefore a critical post. The first head, Mavlan Umurzakov, was a representative of the Samarakand-Jizzak/Rashidov clan; he was arrested in 1994[35] amid talk that he might be a potential rival to Karimov.[36] Ismoil Jurabekov, the leader of another Samarkandi clan and the "Gray Cardinal" of Karimov's ascent to power, emerged as a power behind the throne, though he never became the official cadre chief. Umurzakov was replaced by Timur Alimov, the head of the Tashkent clans, who had steadily gained power in the 1990s. Karimov initially kept a balance of clans through cadre appointments, with the Jurabekov/Samarkandi and Alimov/Tashkenti factions as the major stakeholders in the informal political and economic regime, and the Azimov and Hamidov clans representing a presence for Ferghana. Karimov's own connections were most closely tied to the Samarkand clan. At the same time, Karimov sought to surround himself with loyal technocrats who had few clan connections.

In 1990, shortly after being appointed, Karimov released most of those imprisoned in the "Cotton Scandal" and began the "rehabilitation" of former Communist Party First Secretary Sharof Rashidov and of his extensive network. On a more concrete economic level, Karimov's rehabilitation of Rashidov returned control of many state assets, such as the Bukharan and Samarkandi *hokimiats*, to Rashidov's kin or more extended clan.[37] Rashidov's network was known to control the profitable tea trade. Yet by 1993, Karimov had judiciously begun to restrain the power of the Samarkand clan, both because his patronage had caused serious dissatisfaction among other powerful elites in Ferghana and Tashkent, and because he personally sought to establish a centralized autocratic regime in which he, not regional clan networks, controlled the levers of power. Hence, in 1994 Karimov reneged on a promise to put the Ministry of Foreign Economic Relations under Sayora Rashidova, the former Communist Party boss's daughter. Instead, he gave her license to "do business." In 1996, Rashidova was demoted to ombudsman for human rights. In 1995, Karimov moved Abdulaziz Komilov, another Rashidov relative, from his position as the longtime head of the Uzbek KGB to a less powerful and less lucrative position as foreign minister.[38]

[35] Author's interview with Bakhodir Musaev, sociologist, Tashkent, August 2004.

[36] Author's interview with a former Uzbek government official, New York, June 2004.

[37] Author's communications with relatives of powerful families in Samarkand and Bukhara, Samarkand, April 1998; Tashkent, May 1998. The Samarkand and Bukhara networks were large, and though often they represented one region, several very powerful families controlled most of the *oblast*'s resources. See Demian Vaisman, "Regionalism and Clan Loyalty in the Political Life of Uzbekistan," in Yaacov Ro'i, ed., *Muslim Eurasia: Conflicting Legacies* (London: Frank Cass, 1995), pp. 105–123.

[38] Research assistant's interview with a former Uzbek government official, New York, June 2004.

Karimov's sidelining of the Rashidov network in the early 1990s corresponded with the rise of another Samarkandi network, the Jurabekov clan. As deputy prime minister, Jurabekov officially had a fairly empty government portfolio. Yet, he actually controlled *Uzneftgaz* (the oil and gas complex), the bazaars, the vast cotton complex, and thus, much of the state's natural resource wealth and its largest export.[39] Jurabekov's network reportedly made millions of dollars manipulating the two to threefold difference between the official and unofficial currency rates. Jurabekov's clan was also believed to have a significant interest in the narcotics trade, to which the government turned a blind eye.[40]

The Tashkent clan, as noted earlier, is in fact a loose coalition of elite extended families, interrelated by marriage, business connections, and friendships going back to the Soviet period. The head of this clan, Timur Alimov, enhanced its well-being under his tenure as secretary for cadre politics. The central bank and many joint venture banks based in Tashkent were the booty of Tashkent elites, and the elaborate banking system that has emerged appears to be little more than a front for a prosperous shadow economy run by the same clans.[41] The Ministry of Foreign Economic Relations, the tax inspectorate, and the general procurator – all highly lucrative positions – were under the Alimov network's control. One of the wealthiest men in Alimov's clan was Deputy Prime Minister Mirabror Usmanov, who officially had few duties, but who unofficially controls the largest bazaar, a share of the dollar trade, most import-export businesses, and a chain of elite stores. His sons and relatives all have a piece of his business empire.

The appointment of the head of the NBU, whose assets are not on the scale of the natural resource enterprises but are still extensive, was a concession to the Ferghana Valley elite. Nonetheless, Karimov very selectively placed control of the NBU and its operations under the leadership of Rustam Azimov, a competent technocrat and businessman whose loyalty was split between his Russified and Soviet-educated base in Tashkent and his more traditional familial ties to the Ferghana/Kokand network.[42] The bulk of the regime's investment in the Ferghana Valley went to Ferghana city itself, not to other regions or networks. A Daewoo automobile factory went to Andijan in an attempt to alleviate severe unemployment and unrest

---

[39] Personal communications with a Uzbek businessmen, Tashkent, July 1997 and April 1998.

[40] Author's communications with representative of the United Nations Drug Control Program in Tashkent, Uzbekistan, September 1997 and May 1998.

[41] ICG, "The Failure of Reform in Uzbekistan: Ways Forward for the International Community," *Asia Report* No. 76, March 11, 2004.

[42] Azimov's clan basis was primarily in Kokand, Margilan, and Ferghana City, where he was seen as a "patron." Locals from the very distinct Ferghana Valley regions of Namangan and Andijan did not share that view. Based on author's ethnographic work in the Ferghana Valley, May–October 1997 and April–June 1998.

there.[43] Another deputy prime minister, Bakhtiyor Hamidov, came from a more powerful Ferghana family, but he had limited political influence with Karimov.[44] The president eventually removed Hamidov, whom he feared as a potential rival.

Two powerful mafias remain outside of Karimov's control. The Gafur and Salim networks have roots in Ferghana and Tashkent. They struck a deal with Karimov in the early 1990s; as long as they stay out of politics, they can operate their extensive businesses – including the wrestling and boxing federations and the narco and prostitution trade – with impunity. Local experts, however, suspect that they may be able to obtain arms.[45] Recently, these mafias have clashed with Gulnora Karimova's business interests.

Other groups were left out of the division of state assets. Khorezm, for instance, still suffered from Karimov's venom against his Khorezmi rival, Muhammad Salih, in the 1991 election. Ethnic discrimination tinged the division of resources as well, excluding not only Khorezm, historically a distinct Turkic tribe, but also Karakalpakistan, with its ethnic Kazakh and Karakalpak population.[46] The southern Surkhandarya and Kashkadarya regions, populated largely by mountain Tajiks, had played no role in the 1989 pact and received almost nothing in the subsequent division of spoils.

Vested Interests and Setting an Economic Policy Agenda

Clan networks that gained power during the late 1980s and early 1990s quickly established vested political interests in the political and economic status quo. Joel Hellman has argued that such interests arise in the context of "partial reform," such as in Kyrgyzstan; the Uzbek and Tajik cases, however, demonstrate that such interests can also arise in cases of no reform, at least in clan-based political systems. Hence, by 1995, when Karimov was considering IMF-backed reforms, the clans began to block his measures. Likewise, they opposed political reform that might either unseat Karimov, since they knew they had leverage with him, or that might lead to more transparent political and economic procedures. Led by Jurabekov, certain clans blocked agricultural reform, since it would undercut their cotton monopolies. Since Soviet times, cotton had been a major source of wealth and power for various clans.[47] When world cotton prices dropped in the mid-1990s, these networks sought new sources of revenue and pushed Karimov

---

[43] Author's interview with the deputy governor of Ferghana, Ferghana, August 1997.

[44] Khaknazarov, "*Kandidaty*"; and author's interview with journalists, Tashkent, March 2004.

[45] Author's interview with journalists, Tashkent, January 2003.

[46] Author's communication with Khorezm businessman, Tashkent, May 1998. This view was generally held by elite and nonelite informants in Khorezm, as well as by Tashkent elites.

[47] Mikhail Degtiar, "Clans, Cotton, and Currency," *Transitions Online*, October 2, 2002.

to cut off currency convertibility.[48] The subsequent convertibility crisis was one prominent example of the president's inability to define state policy in opposition to clan interests, even when top technocrats in the government were aware of the overall harm that the policy was causing the economy.[49] For over six years, the government consistently refused currency convertibility despite U.S., IMF, and World Bank pressure. Making the currency convertible would have undercut the clans' profitability. In 1999, Karimov announced that the som would become convertible by January 1, 2000; however, he faced considerable opposition from the Alimov, Ganiev, Jurabekov, and Sultonov clans, who had divvied up business monopolies over alcohol, sugar, oil, auto, and other import-export businesses. Restricted convertibility also enabled them to sell their hard currency from the gas, gold, and cotton sectors on the black market at exorbitant rates. In fact, some local experts suggest that Alimov himself controlled the black market. Although this is probably an exaggeration, certain well-connected networks did restrict who sold and bought dollars and made a large profit from the business.

The crackdown on convertibility, together with restrictions on privatization, further inhibited foreign investors from entering the market and posing competition to the local monopolies.[50] While certain clans used their informal networks to change their Uzbek currency profits into dollars, foreign businessmen could not do so without a special deal with the government, and therefore could not repatriate profits. According to an Institute for War and Peace Reporting (IWPR) report, "influential clan-based groups in power consider the new entrepreneurs competitors and a threat to their interests."[51] Because antagonizing these clans is too risky, Karimov has avoided taking the economic reforms necessary to attract investment and spur growth, despite foreign investor recommendations since 1997.[52] As of mid-2004, the government's failure to introduce full convertibility is one factor that has caused the international donor agencies, as well as the U.S. State Department, to cut aid to Uzbekistan. In the fall of 2003, when the banks did nominally introduce free convertibility, various informal restrictions emerged, limiting if not preventing currency conversion. Clans that suffered as a result began to pursue alternative sources of wealth, and successfully pushed through trade restrictions that gave them new monopolies and sources of rent seeking[53],

[48] Author's communication with an Uzbek economist, May 2004.
[49] Author's communication with an RFE Uzbek journalist, Washington, D.C., May 2004.
[50] Farangis Said, "Machinations Mar Uzbekistan's Banking System," *Central Asia-Caucasus Analyst*, November 8, 2000, <www.cacianalyst.org/view_article.php?articleid=308>. Author's conversations with Uzbek businessmen and journalists confirmed this.
[51] IWPR's Reporting Central Asia series, no. 290, "Banned Uzbek Demo Sign of Mounting Tensions," June 4, 2004.
[52] Author's interview with David Pearce, World Bank resident director, Tashkent, Uzbekistan, August 2002. See also ICG, "Uzbekistan," March 2004.
[53] Author's communication with economist, 2004.

in spite of Karimov's commitment to trade liberalization as a step toward facilitating a common market in the region.

Vested interests further blocked reforms intended to reduce corruption. Many international observers report that high-level corruption and the distribution of government positions take place in Uzbekistan "on the basis of family, clan, and regional cliques."[54] Karimov's campaign against corruption escalated in 2002 and 2003.[55] Yet it has not been implemented by his subordinates, and it has met with great resistance from clan elites as well as the mafia and regional strongmen. One major element in dealing with corruption entails dealing with the pervasiveness of clan nepotism, asset stripping, and the misuse of public goods for private ends. Administrative changes in early 2003, meant to dramatically cut the state bureaucracy's size and involvement in the economy, were part of this anti-corruption policy. Yet it is not clear to what extent these cuts have actually been implemented.[56] Action has been focused on low-level corruption (such as bribe taking in the airport), not on the higher levels, where it is often intertwined with clan interests. The crackdown on corruption has been implemented only against democratic opposition or against those bosses Karimov thinks weak enough to remove.

The Power of *Hokims*

One element of Karimov's struggle in consolidating the state and controlling economic policy has been the creation of the *hokimiat* (governorship) system.[57] Although the central bodies of the power ministries are located in Tashkent, their subsidiary institutions, as well as subsidiary branches of the banks and many state enterprises, are based in each region and under the control of the *hokims* (governors). Like Akaev, Karimov used the system to increase his control over the provinces. The system provided a convenient way to buy off and appease powerful, regionally based clan networks. Even though they controlled little at the center, they wielded near-ultimate control over local resources – including not only cadre selection, but also the collective farms and the profitable cotton crop, each *kolkhoz* bank (*Promstroibank* and *Pakhtabank*), and of course the local legal and judicial structures (the procurator, the judges, the local soviets, and, increasingly, the local security apparatus).[58] The *hokim* of each region was thus an enormously profitable

[54] Gregory Gleason, "Uzbekistan," in *Nations in Transit 2004* <www.freedomhouse.org/research/nitransit/2004/uzbekistan2004.pdf>.

[55] Author's communication with an Uzbek specialist, Tashkent, November 2003.

[56] Author's interview with an RFE journalist, Tashkent, August 2004.

[57] On the *hokimiat* system, see Paul Kubicek, "Regionalism, Nationalism, and Realpolitik in Central Asia," *Europe-Asia Studies*, vol. 49, no. 4 (June 1997), p. 647. On regional-center debates over election laws, see Luong, *Institutional Change*.

[58] On the threat to state unification posed by clan mentality and cadre politics, see Rustam Jumaev, *Politicheskaia Sistema Respubliki Uzbekistan: Stanovlenie i razvitie* (Tashkent:

post, and allegedly often given to the highest local bidder. In a relatively poor region like Khorezm, for example, the post was reportedly worth $600,000. The Khorezm *hokim* had used the post to promote his relatives and extended kin, who controlled every major position in the *oblast'*.[59] They made huge profits exporting cotton to Iran and India without the central control of Tashkent. The *hokim* himself, having become a client of Karimov, ran the *oblast'* like a totalitarian state, so as to ensure no dissent from the Erk Party or from Muhammad Salih's network.[60] A similar situation prevailed in Namangan and Kokand city, where Karimov had promoted smaller clans and allowed them total control and license to crush opposition forces (vocal during the 1989–92 period). This policy had, unsurprisingly, caused much local resentment.[61]

In other regions, the potential profits were larger and included natural resources, major state or joint venture enterprises, and a larger base for tax collection. In Ferghana, for example, a rich *oblast'*, the *hokim* was expected to turn over 40 percent of taxes to the center and use 60 percent for the *oblast*'s expenses. It is highly unlikely that the *hokims* actually did so. Just as during the Soviet period, underreporting of profits and production was rampant.[62] Karimov maintained a semblance of control by frequently and unexpectedly removing *hokims* and appointing new ones. Yet, the incentive structure was skewed. These local power brokers exploited the system and stripped the state's assets as quickly as possible before being replaced. Like Akaev, Karimov was continuously faced with the challenge of maintaining control despite de facto decentralization of power. For the short term, however – probably because Karimov's weak autocracy still had greater central control than Akaev's weak democracy – Karimov's cadre politics seemed more successful than Akaev's at maintaining a relative balance of clan networks. From 1995 through 1997, at least, the period of greatest foreign direct investment, Karimov skillfully directed foreign capital to various regions of the state. Although the bulk went by default to Tashkent and to Samarkand/Navoi gas and gold deposits, Karimov bought off the

"FAN," 1996), p. 77. Jumaev says traditional Uzbek "consciousness" may reanimate "clan connections" that affect the quality of government.
[59] Based on author's meetings with journalists (opposition and nonopposition), farmers, and businessmen in Khorezm *oblast'*, Khiva and Urgench and surrounding rural areas, October 1997. The *hokim* and his deputies refused to meet with the author. See also Pashtun, "Structure and Practice of State Administration," pp. 39–40.
[60] Khorezm was the regional base of Muhammad Salih, the Erk Party opposition candidate in the 1991 presidential election. See Chapters 5 and 6. Salih is now an active dissident from abroad. See "Letter of Salih to Amnesty International," July 1999, www.muslim-uzbekistan.org.
[61] Author interviews with elite and nonelite informants in Namangan and Kokand, Namangan, April 1998; Kokand, August 1997. Again, one networked family controlled all the major local resources and state positions.
[62] This problem is endemic throughout the former Soviet Union.

Ferghana Valley and Khorezm factions by directing the production centers for Daewoo and Coca-Cola to the major cities of these regions (Namangan, Andijan, and Urgench).

Challenges to Regime Durability and the Monopoly of Force

In Chapter 2, I set out the proposition that a pact incorporating powerful clan factions was key to maintaining regime durability in the absence of consolidated regime institutions. I also argued that a neutral broker who balanced power and resources was key to maintaining that pact, and that a shared external threat made it more likely that clan elites would support the pact and the regime. Since the late 1990s, Karimov (like Akaev and Rakhmonov) has been losing legitimacy by cutting some clans from power. Meanwhile, mutual threats from both Moscow and Afghanistan have gradually declined. Karimov has therefore turned to strengthening the security forces behind him and to increased repression to maintain power.

Shrinking Resources and a Shaky Pact. By the late 1990s, friction among the network that had long supported Karimov was increasing. As in Kyrgyzstan, that tension was fueled not by ideological concern about the nature of the regime and the rules of the game, but by conflict over resource division, the informal economic rules of the game, which were entirely detached from ideology. The government had cut off convertibility in 1996 because of dwindling hard currency reserves, resulting from poor agricultural conditions, falling export profits, low levels of foreign direct investment, and asset stripping of the state's coffers. But the move only exacerbated the problem; from 1997 onward, Uzbekistan saw an even further decline in the levels of direct foreign investment and export profits, and an even more serious crisis of elites' expectations.[63] The government had projected a significant increase in industrial and agricultural production, and yet both sectors continued to stagnate. The state's hopes for major oil and gas investment from Exxon and Texaco, in both the Bukhara and Ferghana regions, were dashed. World gold prices were falling, causing the Newmont Gold joint venture to be less profitable than anticipated. Meanwhile, world cotton prices had also dropped, cutting into the profits of the state and key elites. Moreover, with nothing to guarantee that they would receive their share of the state's cotton profits – de jure, all cotton was sold through a centralized state cotton agency under Jurabekov's control – regional *hokims*, local *hokims*, and *kolkhoz* directors were underreporting production and selling cotton on the black market.[64]

---

[63] Gleason, "Uzbekistan" (2002), pp. 426–427.

[64] Based on author's interviews with *dekhonlar* (private farmers) and *arendatory* (lessors) in the Syrdarya, Ferghana, Bukhara, and Khorezm *oblast*'s, 1997–98.

Corruption in Uzbekistan is rated among the worst in the former Soviet Union, and seventy-fourth of 102 countries in the world.[65] Lack of economic reform coupled with the political opportunity to allow the resurfacing of clan-based networks – conditions that reinforce each other – have led to the creation of a Rashidov-like regime, ridden with informal politics and corruption but without the central power and control from the Communist Party or elsewhere to ensure compliance. Corruption based on family, clan, and patronage networks is rarely prosecuted; this has hindered economic reform and shrunk the economy at large, while protecting the interests of ruling clans.[66] In contrast to the Soviet era, however, post-Soviet Uzbekistan's new "economy of shortages," as in Kyrgyzstan, has been characterized by growing inequality, rising poverty, lack of employment, frustrated expectations, and anger at corruption within the state. This scenario is likely to have destabilizing consequences (refer to Appendix, Table A.6).[67]

At the same time, Karimov has been locked in an ongoing struggle to maintain and increase his own personal autocratic control and to hold together powerful regional and clan elites without allowing them to strip the state of its capacity to survive. By late 1997, he had largely abandoned his attempt to harmonize clan interests by decentralizing certain state powers (budgetary authority, environmental and social policies, and even the local security and police forces). In truth, Karimov's decrees had only made de jure the processes that were, de facto, already under way. His decrees against corruption and his fortification of the security networks and tax inspectorate were directed at breaking the grip on the economy and polity of increasingly powerful clan networks.[68] Tensions with clan elites and with his ministers – as indicated earlier, these groups often overlapped – escalated.

Several members of the Ferghana network were purged, allegedly for corruption. Minister of Defense Akhmedov and Deputy Premier Bakhtiyor Hamidov were demoted.[69] Eventually, Prime Minister Sultonov, whose family businesses were growing very large, was removed as well. In late 1998, however, Karimov went after a bigger target and removed first deputy Prime

---

[65] Gleason, "Uzbekistan" (2002), p. 425. For other discussions of the notorious "cotton affair," see James Critchlow, "Corruption, Nationalism, and the Native Elites in Central Asia," *The Journal of Communist Studies*, vol. 4, no. 4 (June 1988), pp. 150–151. For corruption ratings, see Transparency International, <http://www.globalcorruptionreport.org> and Appendix Table A.7.

[66] Gregory Gleason, "Uzbekistan," in *Nations in Transit 2003* (New York: Freedom House, 2003), p. 647.

[67] ICG, "Uzbekistan's Reform"; and ICG, "The Failure of Reform," pp. 14–20. See also IMF and World Bank, "Poverty Reduction, Growth, and Sustainability in Low-Income CIS Countries" (February 4, 2002); and Gleason, "Uzbekistan" (2003).

[68] Karimov's "State of the Union" addresses in 1997 and 1998 were extensive monologues, broadcast on national television, in which the president repeatedly rebuked, sometimes by name, his ministers and government officials for inefficiency and corruption.

[69] Author's communication with a U.S. embassy official, Tashkent, Uzbekistan, June 1998.

Minister Jurabekov, the "Gray Cardinal," along with many from his clan. Jurabekov was well known for heading the most powerful clan in the country. Several months later, in February 1999, Karimov narrowly escaped an assassination attempt that most local experts believe Jurabekov to have organized. Karimov subsequently reinstated Jurabekov, a move many interpreted as an indication of Karimov's inability to crack down on the "Gray Cardinal's" clan. Other attempts to eliminate clan-based patronage and asset stripping in the cotton sector have had little success.[70]

While Karimov excludes former clan allies, he has promoted the rise of "the Family."[71] Both of the president's daughters have increasingly bought up Tashkent businesses. Gulnora Karimova took control of Uzdunrobita, the major state telecom company valued at approximately $51 million. She has increased control over key sectors of the economy, including the gold mining company, and was implicated in a major gold smuggling scandal in the spring of 2004. Gulnora also took part with Lukoil in a lucrative gas and oil deal in 2004. Like Akaev, Karimov has lost his legitimacy as a neutral broker of clan interests. He can control democratic dissent, the weakest form of opposition, but not clan dissent.

Rising Social Discontent. Karimov's limited reforms may be too little, too late to regain social legitimacy as well. A series of incidents in Namangan in the fall of 1997 reflected local dissatisfaction at the central government's continued attempts to control regional cadres. Namangan, as observed in Chapter 4, had been the strongest source of opposition during the late Soviet period. Left out of the central pact and kept from the levers of power in subsequent years, several local Namangani "clan mafias" avenged their discontent by murdering the chief of police and several other MVD and SNB personnel whom they perceived to be working against their local interests.[72] The Namangan incidents spurred a rapid, harsh, and prolonged regime reaction. From January 1998 through 1999, the regime arrested several thousand "opposition" figures.[73] The regime then accused the arrested of violently promulgating Islamic fundamentalism. The government also blamed the February 16, 1999 attempt to assassinate Karimov on the Islamists. In Kirov-like show trials, the accused gave public confessions of having received training and aid through ties to "Wahabbi" groups in Pakistan and Afghanistan, and of seeking to create an Islamic state. Some overlap between a regional, clan, and Islamic opposition has emerged.

---

[70] Author's interview with David Pierce, head of the World Bank, Tashkent, Uzbekistan, August 2002.

[71] ICG, "The Failure of Reform."

[72] Estimates are those of locals in both Tashkent and Namangan, April 1998. The U.S. embassy agreed.

[73] Author's interview with members of the opposition Erk Party, Urgench, October 1997; and with the U.S. Embassy official for human rights, Tashkent, October 1997 and May 1998.

This guerrilla group, led by some opposition leaders who had fled from Namangan in the early 1990s to Tajikistan and later to Afghanistan, had declared itself the Islamic Movement of Uzbekistan (IMU). The IMU invaded Uzbekistan and Kyrgyzstan, in the late summer of 1999 and 2000. Although ultimately unsuccessful, the IMU mortified both the Uzbek and Kyrgyz militaries, and its notoreity gained it some sympathy and adherents among militant youth. In part as a consequence of such repression, another underground Islamic party, Hizb ut-Tahrir al-Islami (HT), emerged in the late 1990s and has spread, gaining a following in the Ferghana Valley, Tashkent, and even in Khorezm and Kashkadarya. Some number HT's support in the tens of thousands.[74] More dissent, possibly related to the IMU or other Islamists, came with the first suicide bombings in Uzbekistan, in March and July of 2004. Little is known, but the March targets seem to have been the police and government. The July targets included the U.S. embassy, the Israeli embassy, and the general procurator's office.

Karimov's Strategy against Clans and the Use of Security Forces. Perhaps regretting his early cadre decisions after seeing their negative effects on the economy, and seeking to increase his personal power, since 2002 Karimov has increasingly adopted strategies intended not merely to balance clans but to minimize their informal role in politics and economics. He has appointed a cadre of technocrats who supposedly have few clan ties, but this has met with limited success. Rustam Azimov was originally one such "technocrat," but his own clan ties and his success in building a patronage network from the NBU's resources made his loyalty suspect, leading to his removal from the bank. A token few, such as Foreign Minister Sodyq Safaev, fill government posts, but have little real power to introduce change. Instead, Karimov's agenda and his cadre appointments have themselves been constrained by informal politics.

Constant shuffling of *hokims* is another of Karimov's strategies to prevent regionally based clan elites from consolidating their grasp on power. Yet the strategy has backfired; because *hokims* know that their time in power is short, they strip assets and line their pockets as fast as possible. And they rely on their tight-knit kin and clan to aid and abet them in doing so, before another rival clan replaces them. Just as Karimov surrounds himself with his most-trusted followers, the *hokims* do the same. Yet unlike Karimov, most *hokims* have an extensive kin and clan network. They appoint their inner circle to the key positions in the *oblast'*, to posts that are profitable and that will protect them from the state. In Khorezm, Samarkand, Namangan city, Kokand city, and most other regions, the *hokim* has placed clan members in key positions in the procurator's office, the police, the banks, the tax agency,

---

[74] ICG, "Radical Islam in Central Asia: Responding to Hizb ut-Tahrir," *Asia Report* No. 58, June 30, 2003.

in agriculture (as *shirkat* farm directors), and often as directors of the bread factory or other such profitable enterprises.[75] *Hokims* frequently appoint their relatives as rectors of universities or institutes, positions that give them access to significant bribes.[76]

Since 2000, the pace at which President Karimov has replaced *hokims* has intensified, and the president frequently exposes their clannishness and cadre abuses.[77] According to Daniel Kimmage, between January and July 2004 regional governors have been replaced in the Tashkent, Andijan, Surkhandarya, and Samarkand *oblast's*. The president harshly criticized Andijan governor Qobiljon Obidov. "On May 25, the official news agency UzA quoted President Karimov as saying: 'In recent years, cases of corruption and personal connections have intensified in the region.'"[78] Similarly, when Samarkand governor Rustam Kholmuradov was replaced in early July, "Uzbek TV quoted Karimov as criticizing him for allowing 'unworthy tendencies, criminal activities, abuses of power, violations of justice, and, worst of all, clannishness, regionalism, and serious errors in the training, selection, and assignment of staff.'"[79] Karimov clearly sees clannishness and clan-based patronage as persistent problems, often resulting in the central government's failure to implement reforms or collect revenues.

In spite of these attempts to undercut clans and corruption and to implement change, Karimov's actions should not simply be taken at face value. Unlike Gorbachev, Karimov understands the informal rules of the game. The symbiotic relationship between clans and the president continues, and makes long-term commitment to reform unlikely.[80] Karimov is dependent on clan support, and invested clan elites are highly dependent on his patronage. In fact, Karimov has continued the Soviet-era "stability of cadre" policy. "There has probably been less change in bureaucratic personnel in Uzbekistan than in any other Central Asian state. The use of patronage and dependence on state resources [are] a key source of loyalty that make any serious change very difficult under the present system."[81] According to one expert, "Karimov always makes speeches against clans...he tries to show that he's in a battle,

---

[75] Uzbek specialist, "*Klannovnost' v Uzbekistane*," unpublished manuscript, Tashkent, May 2002. My ethnographic work in Khorezm, Kokand, Namangan, and Samarkand replicated the manuscript's findings. ICG reports similar findings suggesting that these "close-knit" groups are akin to mafias and squeeze out honest officials. See ICG, "Failure of Reform," p. 11.

[76] Author's interview with an education specialist, Tashkent, March 2004.

[77] Author's interview with an RFE journalist, May 2004.

[78] Daniel Kimmage, RFE weekly report, July 2004.

[79] Ibid.

[80] Usmon Khaknazarov, "*Vozrozhdenie 'serogo kardinala' uzbekskoi politiki*," February 21, 2003, <www.centrasia.ru>.

[81] "Uzbekistan's Reform Program: Illusion or Reality," *Asia Report*, no. 46 (February 18, 2003), p. 25.

but we have no government plan against clans or corruption. The president himself is at the head of a pyramid of clans."[82]

In the meantime, since he came to power in 1989, Karimov has sought to bolster and tightly control the security services, placing them under his trusted cadre in order to guarantee his monopoly over force. Following the transition, Karimov increasingly centralized the military forces, purging many Russian officers and, more importantly, eventually removing any potential Uzbek rivals. One blatant example of this strategy came in early 1997, when Karimov removed General Akhmedov, the minister of defense and one of the only prominent members of Ferghana elite. A member of a prominent Tashkent clan, Kadyr Gulomov, although an historian by profession, eventually filled the post. He was promoted by his relative Timur Alimov, head of the major Tashkent clan.[83]

The MVD and the SNB were far more powerful institutions than the Ministry of Defense. Keeping these institutions out of clan control proved a challenge, so Karimov also established a personal presidential guard. All three were under his close supervision and control. No budgetary data are available, but the size and strength of these institutions has grown significantly since the late Soviet period. The sheer number of persons employed in the police and security forces has multiplied; it has been one of the largest employers in the country, estimated to be one-third of the employed labor force.[84]

In fact, Zokirjon Almatov, as the head of the MVD, controls an entire army of men and weapons in every *oblast'*.[85] With a reputation for being brutal, Almatov has maintained his powerful post in control of about 86,000 troops, of which 40,000 are based in Tashkent.[86] According to some sources, Almatov's clique now also includes the minister of emergency situations, the head of the customs inspectorate, and the prosecutor's office, three powerful and lucrative posts that give his network a financial base. Almatov's resources alone make him a potential threat; moreover, Almatov belongs to the Jurabekov clan, which no longer supports Karimov.

As in Kyrgyzstan, another problematic trend is police factionalization by *oblast'* and district. The central elite's control of cadre selection outside

[82] Author's interview with a political specialist, Tashkent, January 2003.
[83] Author's communication with an Uzbek analyst, March 2004.
[84] Political officer (a local Uzbek) of the U.S. embassy in Tashkent, June 1997. Although the police are paid relatively better than employees of other state institutions, the meager salary of approximately $50 per month almost ensured that the police would use their power and position to engage in corruption and exploit the populace, a situation fomenting unrest.
[85] See Almatov biography, <http://www.centrasia.ru/person.php4>; and Khaknazarov, "*Vozrozhdenie*."
[86] Khaknazarov, "*Vozrozhdenie*."

of Tashkent and Samarkand was unreliable. Although it did attempt to maintain key regional contacts and informants and even to buy their loyalty, the central regime was increasingly forced to allow limited decentralization of these institutions.[87] In attempting to appease the local clan elites and populace, who resisted police control from Tashkent, in mid-1997 Karimov had issued a decree allowing increased local control over the regional and local branches of the MVD.[88]

Karimov has sought to balance the MVD's power with the SNB and a recently formed elite Presidential Security Service (PSS). Little is known about the PSS, but it is believed to be heavily armed.[89] The SNB is headed by Rustam Inoyatov, a former KGB general from Surkhandarya *oblast'* who is not known for clan ties to either the Samarkandi or Tashkent networks.[90] Inoyatov gained favor with the president because of his competency in monitoring the Islamic opposition in Tajikistan prior to the Soviet collapse and the Islamic opposition in Uzbekistan, as well as in rebuilding the Uzbek army and security services after the Russian withdrawal. In particular, Karimov wanted an SNB immune to clan ties. However, Inoyatov also has allies in the Alimov clan, and makes use of his own clan. He has marriage and relative ties with members of the Russian SNB, and he has staffed his own institutions with relatives and the sons and daughters of his close connections.[91] The Uzbek SNB is no longer known for the professionalism of the Soviet days. It is a base for business operations of Inoyatov's wife and relatives.[92] Although the SNB remains loyal to the president, in a sense Inoyatov has created his own clan base of power.

For now, Karimov is still in control. A worrisome trend, however, is that these armed units are divided among themselves, mirroring other interclan conflicts.[93] The divisions allow Karimov to play them off against each other, and he increasingly pits the Jurabekov clan against the Alimov network. However, in the event of a succession crisis, they could come into violent conflict.

A Fragile Autocracy

Karimov's own concerns about his regime's stability led him to rig the presidential elections of 2000, to win by 92 percent of the vote. In a subsequent

---

[87] Author's interviews and personal communications in Ferghana *oblast'*, August 1997.
[88] Author's interview with political officers, U.S. Embassy, Tashkent, September 1997.
[89] Author's interview with a former Uzbek government official, Notre Dame, Indiana, June 2004.
[90] Artur Kasymkhodzhaev, "*Epizody upravliaemoi SNB 'Demokratii,'*" *Erkiniurt*, August 30, 2004.
[91] Ibid.
[92] Author's communication with a former government official, Tashkent, January 2002.
[93] Communication with an RFE journalist, Washington, D.C., May 2004.

referendum, an attempt to consolidate his gain, he extended his presidential term from five to seven years. With the formation of the Liberal Democratic Party of Uzbekistan (LDPU), many suspect that Gulnora Karimova will attempt to succeed her father, as did Ilham Aliev in Azerbaijan. At the very least, she will seek to control his successor. In late 2003, she backed the appointment of a powerful new prime minister, Shavkat Mirziyaev. Mirziyaev is reportedly a brutal apparatchik who has helped Karimov to demote both the Jurabekov and Alimov clans, and thereby to reassert presidential control. Mirziyaev, although from the Samarkand region, has no ties to Jurabekov; curiously, he comes from the Samarkand clan of the former first secretary Sharof Rashidov, which has had little power since it was ousted by Karimov and Jurabekov in the early 1990s.[94]

Despite Mirziyaev's recent changes, the regime remains unconsolidated. In fact, several important indicators point to declining durability and potential internal conflict in connection with clan competition and the president's increasing hegemony. While in 1991 and 1995 Karimov did not need to rig the elections, his legitimacy among clan elites as well as the population at large has now plummeted. Gulnora Karimova's blatant corruption has cut into the power and resources of many Tashkenti and Samarkandi clans and mafia groups, breeding enormous resentment on the part of these key interests and the population in general. Some external factors have mitigated the regime's financial state, which was nearing crisis by 2001. A sharp increase in international aid followed 9/11 and Uzbekistan's agreement to assist the United States in the war on terror. In fiscal year 2002, U.S. government assistance to Uzbekistan increased from approximately $85 million (in fiscal year 2001) to almost $300 million.[95] Still, aid was made partially contingent upon reform, and both the EBRD and the United States cut economic aid in 2004. International financial institution funds are still limited. Foreign direct investment remains minimal, apart from attempts by Russian government-backed companies to buy strategic resources. In short, clans' resource flows have been disrupted by a stifled economy. Although he possesses greater assets than Akaev, Karimov cannot indefinitely continue feeding and balancing clan demands. He incited instability in 1998–99 when he attempted to break the informal pact that had backed him. The president's subsequent strategy has wavered between a pattern of appeasement, which only delays critical economic reform, and occasional strikes at vested interests. The sudden appointment of the new prime minister led to the demotion of both the Jurabekov and Alimov clans. Yet, they still have significant economic power. Whether or not Mirziyaev can succeed where Karimov has failed for the

---

94 Author's interview with a former Uzbek government official, New York, June 2004.
95 Richard Giragosian, "An Overview of US Security Assistance to Central Asia" (manuscript), September 2004.

past fifteen years is unclear. A key factor will be whether the president or Mirziyaev can ensure that the MVD and SNB remain loyal.

III. TAJIKISTAN'S OPENLY CLAN-BASED REGIME

Tajikistan's trajectory since the mid-1990s has been a mix of liberalization, imposed in part by the international community, and renewed authoritarianism. As in Kyrgyzstan and Uzbekistan, the president has faced difficulties in consolidating the regime. Despite high hopes after the 1997 peace accord, liberalizing reforms have been undermined both by presidential power and by clan factionalism. Since 1997, Imomali Rakhmonov has taken a number of steps to strengthen the executive, to create a strong presidential (in fact, a super-presidential) system, and to undermine traditional patron-client and clan networks. On September 26, 1999, a national referendum extended the president's term from five to seven years and effectively allowed him to serve three terms; he may well continue in office until 2013. In the November 1999 presidential election, Rakhmonov won 96.91 percent of the vote, a greater victory than any Central Asian president other than Turkmenbashi. The IRP candidate took only 2.1 percent, and has played a much lesser role in politics since then. Like Karimov and Akaev, the president has further shifted executive power from the cabinet and prime minister into the president's office. Meanwhile, he has skillfully decreased parliament's power and created a party staffed by his clan. Legally, his regime could be described as a super-presidential autocracy.

Despite some successes, Rakhmonov has struggled to control various clan-based opposition factions and warlords, as well as a society locally organized around the *avlod* (clan) system and networked into a hierarchy of patron-client ties over which he has little control. His attempts to create a strong autocratic state have had limited success; as such, he increasingly uses an informal system of clan patronage to maintain control and hold the state together. As he has grown confident in support from Russia and the United States, Rakhmonov has shifted toward a more exclusionary informal politics and has created a new hegemonic system in which other clans are excluded from power and resources. This section examines the clan and social structure in Tajikistan, the challenges that clan politics have posed to Rakhmonov, and his own use of clan politics as a strategy of control since his election in 1994. The areas in which this section examines the rise of clan politics are similar to those highlighted in the other cases, including key dimensions of the fledgling Tajik regime: (1) the 1994 and 1999 presidential elections and the executive branch; (2) parties, the parliamentary elections, and parliament; (3) the regime monopoly over force, before and after the 1997 peace agreement was signed; (4) the allocation and distribution of resources; (5) external patronage and sovereignty; and (6) regime durability.

Tajikistan's social structure, much like Uzbekistan, is today divided into what the Tajik scholar Saodat Olimova describes as "ethno-regional groups and their leading clans."[96] As discussed in Chapter 3, these factions are historically rooted in different pre-Soviet ethnic and tribal settlement patterns and are closely associated with land. Sometimes they correspond to historically distinct regions (such as Khodjent, Garm, Kulyab, and Gorno-Badakhshan), and sometimes they do not. For example, both in the capital city and in Khatlon *oblast'*, multiple groups claim to be Garmi, Badakhshani, Hissari, Vaksh, Lakai, Khodjenti, or Dangharin and have fought along those lines during the war. Although some refer to these groups as ethnic or regional divisions, these predominantly intra-Tajik identity groups correspond more to settlement patterns and a strong localism rooted in kin, friendship, and patronage networks, rather than to ethnicity or language. "For example, in Gorno-Badakhshan Autonomous Oblast, like in other regions of Tajikistan, there is a clan, family, and ethnic fight for power. At present the key administrative posts are in the hands of the Shugnan people. They dominate in most regional organizations and agencies located in Khorog city. Meanwhile, these clans are distinct from Dormurukhti, Shokhdari, Suchani, Khorogi, Porshniyovi, etc."[97] Within each region, multiple clans form identity networks and compete for power. As in Uzbekistan, clans are comprised of extensive kin and fictive kin networks, typically led by prominent figures. When those subregional networks gain power, however, they do not necessarily promote the entire region or a broader tribe; their networks are typically much narrower.[98] For example, the Nabiev clan excluded many other groups from Leninabad, just as the Rakhmonov/Dangharin clan is currently excluding other Kulyabi clans.

Our focus here is mainly on interclan competition at the national level rather than at the intra-regional or local level, but it should be noted that surrounding oneself with one's trusted identity network is critical in politics at all levels. As one party leader observes, "In times of allotment of resources and control, administrators are trying to build a team of 'brothers.' This manner was also used in the Soviet system, but that government was trying to prevent regionalism and clanism. Today, the situation has changed. Sughd province (formerly Khodjent and Leninabad) is out of power. Relatives and 'brothers' of the president hold key positions."[99]

[96] Saodat Olimova, "Regionalism and Its Perception by Major Political and Social Forces in Tajikistan," in Luigi De Martino, ed., *Tajikistan at a Crossroad: The Politics of Decentralization* (Geneva: Cimera, 2003), p. 116.

[97] Olimova, "Regionalism," p. 103.

[98] Barnett Rubin, "Russian Hegemony and State Breakdown: Causes and Consequences of the Tajik Civil War," in Barnett Rubin and Jack Snyder, eds., *Post-Soviet Political Order* (London: Routledge Press, 1998), pp. 146–147.

[99] Political party member, cited in Olimova, "Regionalism," p. 96.

Both during the Soviet period and today, when these networks come to power in Dushanbe, they assist their clan networks by doling out positions to them and thereby creating circles of loyal supporters for themselves; they are also seen to represent their regions at large, although in reality they typically restrict their patronage to their kin, fictive kin, and allies. As we have seen, a network of Leninabadi/Khodjenti clans dominated Tajikistan for much of the Soviet period. During the post-Soviet period, state power has shifted to the Kulyabi clans of the Khatlon region. More specifically, power has primarily gone to one Kulyabi clan, the Dangharin clan of President Rakhmonov. Other subregional clans have emerged as powerful, mainly through their control of financial resources outside of government influence.[100] Clan networks in the post-Soviet, post-civil war period are more fragmented than in the neighboring states. The Ubaydulloyev and Iskanderov clans initially provided some balance in the regime, but they did not bring broad popular legitimacy to a primarily exclusivist system. Economic changes, in addition to the effects of war and the drug trade, have made other informal institutions and organizations, including bribery, corruption, and mafia activity, more salient elements of clan politics than in the past. As in Uzbekistan and Kyrgyzstan, together with clan politics, clannish corruption and the mafiosization of some clans pose challenges to regime consolidation and democratization.

Presidential Elections and the Executive's Power Base

The November 1994 presidential contest led to the election of Imomali Rakhmonov and marked a close, however flawed, to one phase of the post-Soviet transition. The most intense civil violence had ended, and a new regime and minimal stability appeared in the war-torn country. The presidential election, however, was little more than a token gesture toward democracy, meant to appease both the international community and certain opposition factions who had agreed to a cease-fire in August of that year. The temporary success of the regime's moves to achieve broader inclusiveness was, however, rapidly undone when Rakhmonov's allies engaged in massive and blatantly obvious falsification of the vote. The real contest was not between the communists and the democratic opposition, as the November 1991 election between Nabiev and Khudonazarov had been. By contrast, in 1994, as a result of the upsurge in interclan competition intensified by three years of war, the DPT and the other proto-parties of the perestroika era had largely been sidelined. Instead, the real competition came from Rakhmonov's main rival for the presidency, Abdumalik Abdullajonov – a leading member of an elite Khodjenti clan, and a man widely seen as the successor to Nabiev,

---

[100] "Elite Clan Groups in Tajikistan," unpublished report, Dushanbe, December 2003.

the former Khodjenti/communist boss. Despite endemic fraud, Rakhmonov won a close victory with 58 percent of the vote. Both Russia and Uzbekistan are believed to have played an influential role in his victory.

Rakhmonov had been a collective farm director and belonged to the minor Dangharin clan, one faction of the Kulyabi network.[101] In 1994, Rakhmonov himself had little legitimacy; he was not received by competing clans as a neutral broker, and he headed no formal or informal pact. Nor did he have much institutional power, as he had been elected in the midst of an ongoing, if low-scale, conflict. Since 1994, Russia has subsequently played the role of the Kulyabi external patron, a relationship not unlike Moscow's patronage of the Khodjentis during most of the Soviet era. Rakhmonov has also sought traditional sources of power. From the mid-1990s to the present, he has relied on a clan-based regime, stacked with his own Dangharin clan and close Kulyabi friends.

Surprisingly, given the causes of the war, Rakhmonov made little attempt to divide power and resources beyond this base. In an early gesture at balancing clan participation, he had appointed his Khodjenti rival Abdumalik Abdullajonov as the new prime minister. Yet by 1994 Rakhmonov had ousted Abdullajonov, ending any appearance of power sharing with the Khodjentis. The president then proceeded to cut off this entire Khodjenti network from access to political power and economic assets, making the Khodjentis the poorest faction in the state.[102] Rakhmonov's attempts to impose the hegemony of his clan have intensified in the past decade.

Parties, the Parliament, and Clan Factionalism

By 1993, the "national-democratic-Islamic" coalition – consisting of the Democratic Party of Tajikistan, Rastokhez, La'li Badakhshan, and the Islamic Renaissance Party – had essentially collapsed. With only a small intelligentsia-based membership and a weak social mandate to begin with, this neophyte movement had nearly evaporated not long after the onset of the civil war. Widely blamed for the deterioration of civil order, which began when fighting broke out during the coalition's 1992 protests in Dushanbe, the reformist coalition lost much of its limited popular support. With the exception of the Islamic Renaissance Party (IRP), the coalition parties simply faded into the background. Most of the movement leaders and individual party leaders became only peripheral political figures.[103] Although some parties continued activity as individual, independent political organizations, most experienced changes in leadership that only further weakened

---

[101] Author's interviews with a Tajik journalist, March 2001 and August 2004; see also biography of Rakhmonov, <www.ctaj.elcat.kg/tolstyi/c/co22.html>.

[102] Author's interview with a UNOCHA representative, Dushanbe, March 2001.

[103] Grigorii Kosach, "Tajikistan: Political Parties in an Inchoate National Space," in Yaacov Ro'i, ed., *Muslim Eurasia* (London: Frank Cass Publishers, 1995), pp. 123–142.

their capacity to act as a coherent civil political force. La'li Badakhshan was the most successful party in transforming itself, since many of its members have been drawn from the Ministry of Interior and the police, the clan network of the Pamiri leader Mamadayez Navzhuvanov.[104] Meanwhile, the disaffected populace instead backed various local clan-based militias engaged in the village-to-village fighting. Clan networks offered concrete material support, and their militias provided the guns that were essential to the protection of homes and lives.

With the cease-fire of 1994, parliamentary elections were put on the agenda; they were scheduled for February 26, 1995, pushed forward by the UN and other mediators in order to complete the process of regime transition.[105] Held in the wake of Rakhmonov's fraudulent election, however, the parliamentary contest was widely viewed with great cynicism. Many opposition figures simply refused to participate. Consequently, Rakhmonov had an even greater ability to manipulate the results. The post–civil war legislature thus became a mere extension of the Kulyabi clan's grasp on power. In this sense, despite the semicompetitive, multiparty elections, the legislature was even less independent than during the Soviet period.

The 1995 parliament, in contrast to the old Supreme Soviet, which had included a strong Pamiri opposition, was dominated by former communists, who had attained 55.5 percent of the vote. Yet the election did not signify a communist return to power. As Rubin observes, "communist" no longer meant (if it had ever meant) the ideological Soviet system of power.[106] The CPT's electoral victory could better be attributed to its interconnectedness with the Khodjenti and Kulyabi clans. As noted earlier, Soviet colonization in the Tajik SSR had unequivocally favored and recruited members from the Leninabad (Khodjent) and Kulyab power networks.[107] Like the parallel structures in Uzbekistan and Kyrgyzstan, these networks had monopolized the party in Tajikistan. Support for the party's relegalization under a different name had come primarily from these power networks, not from ideological hard-liners within the regime. Hence the appellation commonly given to these political figures – "neo-communist" – masks their true source of power. The name also misrepresents their economic agenda, which since 1995 has abandoned the ideology and economic policies of communism.[108]

---

[104] Irina Zviagelskaya, "The Tajik Conflict," *Central Asia and the Caucasus Journal of Social and Political Studies*, <http://www.ca-c.org/dataeng/st_09_zvjag_2.shtml>.

[105] The second round of the elections, the run-off, was held on March 12, 1995.

[106] Rubin, "Russian Hegemony."

[107] Teresa Rakowska-Harmstone's study of the Tajik SSR notes the Soviet failure to penetrate the social structures of Tajikistan, as well as its unbalanced development. See her *Russia and Nationalism in Central Asia: The Case of Tadzhikistan* (Baltimore: Johns Hopkins University Press, 1970); Yegor Ligachev, *Inside Gorbachev's Kremlin* (New York: Pantheon Press, 1993); and Zhores Medvedev, *Andropov* (London: W.W. Norton, 1983), pp. 65–70.

[108] Author's interview with a leader of the Communist Party of Tajikistan, Dushanbe, March 2001.

TABLE 8.3. *Results of the 1994 elections to the Majlisi
Oli of Tajikistan*

Party Affiliation	Seats	Percent
Communist Party of Tajikistan (CPT)[a]	100	55.5
People's Democratic Party (NDPT)	10	5.5
National Revival Bloc	6	3.3
PERPR	1	<1
Independents	64	35.4
TOTAL	181	100

[a] In the early to mid-1990s, this party supported Rakhmonov; by
1998, it had split with Rakhmonov, who had created his own presidential party (the NDPU) based on his clan.
Note: Numerical data provided by the Tajik Central Electoral
Commission.

A second element of the legislature's internal subversion can be traced to
Rakhmonov's decision, à la Islam Karimov, to adopt the Uzbek model of
stacking parliament with new "independent" deputies. Rakhmonov lacked
the support of a clan pact; unlike Karimov and Akaev, he needed a party to
bolster his weak legitimacy, and therefore, he founded the People's Democratic Party of Tajikistan (NDPT). The NDPT derived its support from the
Kulyabi clans, especially from Rakhmonov's own Dangharin clan.

The Tajik party system did, however, mimic the Uzbek pattern in other
ways. With the creation of approximately ten other parties, which together
won a negligible number of seats, the Rakhmonov regime could pride itself on multiparty pluralism without actually engaging the opposition.[109]
The cease-fire and 1994 elections produced neither a democratic division of
power among the branches of government, nor representative and effective
state-society linkages. Between the NDPT, some communists, and some independent candidates, the Kulyabi clan was estimated to control about half
of the 181 seats in parliament. Rakhmonov's growing network of clans and
clients was the real winner, not the political parties (see Table 8.3). The upshot, unsurprisingly, was a *Majlisi Oli* united with the executive presidency
in perpetuating the power of the Kulyabis, while simultaneously upsetting
the traditional role of other clan networks and regions in the parliament.[110]

In 1999, as Rakhmonov sought to circumvent the liberalization and free
elections demanded by the 1997 peace accord, he devised several ways, formal and informal, to assert even greater control over parliament. First, the
president restructured the parliament; it is now bicameral, consisting of a

[109] On the party system, see Kosach, "Tajikistan: Political Parties," pp. 139–140. Most parties
had little social base. Even the NDPT base was very narrow.
[110] The Garmis and Pamiris were largely excluded, although some Khodjentis were elected.

TABLE 8.4. *Results of the 2000 elections to the Majlisi Oli of Tajikistan (single republican constituency, twenty-two seats, based on party list)*

Party Affiliation	Percentage of Votes	Seats
Adolatkoh (PoJ)	1.32	0
Democratic Party of Tajikistan (DPT)	3.54	0
Communist Party of Tajikistan (CPT)	20.39	5
Islamic Renaissance Party (IRP)	7.31	2
Socialist Party of Tajikistan (SPT)	1.22	0
People's Democratic Party (NDPT)	64.91	15
Voted against all	0.83	–
TOTAL	100	22

Note: Data provided by the Tajik Central Electoral Commission and OSCE, 2000.

sixty-three-seat *Majlisi Namoyandagon* (MN, the assembly of representatives or lower chamber) and a forty-one-seat *Majlisi Melli* (MM, the national assembly or upper chamber). According to the new electoral law, in effect as of 1999, the MN is elected directly, 65 percent in single-member districts and 35 percent by party lists. Thirty-three deputies of the MM are elected indirectly, by local *majlisis* (councils) that the president informally controls through provincial patronage networks; the other eight are appointed by the president. Rakhmonov clearly wields greater control over this legislative structure. He has used his control over the legislature to manipulate local clan representation. For example, in the Gorno-Badakhshan region he has fostered the election of the Khorog and Shugnan clans; other clans in the region are not represented.[111]

Additionally, Rakhmonov acted earlier than the other Central Asian presidents to create a party on the basis of his clan. His NDPT grew significantly between the 1994 and 1999 elections, while other parties were stagnant and the Communist Party, with its Kulyabi clan base, declined (see Tables 8.4 and 8.5). The 1999 elections were a significant victory for Rakhmonov, even though six independent parties were allowed to compete. The NDPT won fifteen of the twenty-two party list seats and twenty-one of the forty-one single-member district seats; the NDPT now controlled 57 percent of the MN. The presidential party was by far the most successful in Central Asia. Violations were reported only in some districts, mainly against the IRP. However, ten seats, about one-sixth of the total, went to "independents," some of whom represented opposition clans.

---

[111] Saodat Olimova, "Regionalism and its Perception by Major Political and Social Powers of Tajikistan," in Luigi De Martino, ed., *Tajikistan at a Crossroad: The Politics of Decentralization* (Geneva: Cimera, 2003), p. 103.

TABLE 8.5. *Results of the 2000 elections to the Majlisi Oli of Tajikistan (single mandate constituency, forty-one seats)*

Party or Other Affiliation	Seats	Percent
Communist Party of Tajikistan (CPT)	8	19.5
People's Democratic Party (NDPT)	21	51.2
Independent	10	24.4
Election pending	2	4.8
Total elected	39	95.1
Total seats	41	100

Note: Data provided by the Tajik Central Electoral Commission and OSCE, 2000.

Opposition parties and candidates, as in Kyrgyzstan, are sometimes networked into clan or former warlords' factions (such as the Democratic Party of Iskanderov) as well. Those that lack a clan base, such as the Socialist Party and the Social Democratic Party, are "purely elitist," with an amorphous structure, and "devoid of the essential tool of a political organization in Tajikistan: the disposition of armed forces."[112]

Monopoly over Force? Continued Opposition, before and after the Peace Agreement

Rakhmonov has spent the past decade, 1994–2004, attempting to consolidate a monopoly over force. At first, various opposition factions, including the United Tajik Opposition (UTO) and multiple smaller, clan-based militias, were enraged by the electoral violations; the cease-fire, which had been extended to February 1995, began once again to deteriorate. The most virulent reaction came from Abdullajonov, who claimed to have won 70–80 percent of the vote rather than the 40 percent the government reported. Abdullajonov's monitors avowed that vote rigging had lost him the election by a narrow margin.[113] The election's results dramatically reversed the power relationship between the two clan groups (see Table 8.6). Under the power structure of the new regime, the Kulyabis were no longer consigned to the role of Khodjent's "little brother." They reversed the patron-client status between these power networks. Rakhmonov even used the election to justify ousting many suspect Khodjentis from the executive apparatus. Rakhmonov's internal coup against the leading Khodjenti clans ousted them from access to

---

[112] Stephane Dudoignon, "From Ambivalence to Ambiguity: Some Paradigms of Policymaking in Tajikistan," in Luigi De Martino, ed., *Tajikistan at a Crossroad: The Politics of Decentralization* (Geneva: Cimera, 2003), p. 124; and Kamoludin Abdullaev, "Current Local Government Policy Situation in Tajikistan," in De Martino, ed., *Tajikistan*, p. 5.

[113] Author's conversation with Abdumalik Abdullajonov, Tashkent, 1997.

TABLE 8.6. *Changing patterns of power in Tajikistan*

Period	Dominant Clan Faction and Leaders	Secondary Clan/Other Factions	Small Client Clans	External Patron
1930s–1992	Leninabadi,[a] Khodjenti *Nabiev,* *Makhkamov*[b]	Kulyabi	Others	Moscow
1992–93	National Reconciliation Commission of Pamiri and Garmi clans – civil war *Iskanderov*	Unclear	Unclear	None
1993–94	Kulyabi *Rakhmonov*	Khodjenti[a] *Abdullajonov*	Karategini, Hissari	Russia, Uzbekistan
1995–June 1997	Kulyabi *Rakhmonov*	None	None	Russia
1997–2000	Danghara, Kulyabi *Rakhmonov*	UTO (Karategini, Kurghanteppi) *Nuri,* *Turajonzoda*	Local militias	Russia, Iran
2001–03	Danghara *Rakhmonov*	Kulyabi	Former warlords	Russia, the United States

[a] During the Soviet period, the traditionally powerful Khodjenti clan from Khodjent, in the northern Tajik SSR, was referred to as the Leninabadi clan, after its (renamed) city Leninabad. By 1992, the city had been given its traditional name, and the clan was called Khodjenti as well.
[b] The italicized are the names of the leading elites of the clan.

power as well as to most central state resources. Now, by one count, as of 1995, sixteen of twenty-three cabinet posts had gone to Rakhmonov's kin and colleagues from the Kulyabi clan.[114] Token ministries, such as the Ministry of Foreign Affairs, were left for the Khodjentis and occasionally for representatives of other regions and clans. The power ministries, as in Uzbekistan and Kyrgyzstan, were under the tight control of Rakhmonov's network.

[114] Muriel Atkin, "Thwarted Democratization in Tajikistan," in Karen Dawisha and Bruce Parrott, eds., *Conflict, Cleavage, and Change in Central Asia and the Caucasus* (Cambridge: Cambridge University Press, 1997).

The Peace Agreement and the End to Major Violence. The Tajik president's break with Abdullajonov and his subsequent exclusion of the entire Khodjenti clan and Leninabad *oblast'* (renamed Khodjent, then Sughd) has had ongoing negative implications for the peace process.[115] The exclusion of a major clan and regional faction of Tajikistan nonetheless set the stage for a problematic peace agreement that would leave many issues unresolved. The Leninabad *oblast'*, with or without Uzbekistan's aid, has continued to be a major source of instability in the Tajik Republic and a prime spoiler of the cease-fire and peace implementation.

On June 27, 1997, an internationally brokered peace agreement was signed, bolstering Rakhmonov's government. The UTO and the government agreed to a cease-fire, a declaration of amnesty by Rakhmonov's regime, disarmament, and the integration of warring militias into a new Tajik national army. The major problem with the accord, as already mentioned, was its blatant exclusion of the largest opposition faction, the Khodjenti clans. The accord, the "General Agreement on the Establishment of Peace and National Accord in Tajikistan," in fact represented relatively few parties at the bargaining table. In essence, the agreement was a pact to share power between Rakhmonov and the UTO. The latter was to receive 30 percent of government posts. Only token positions, however, were in fact turned over.[116] The Ministry of Interior was now squarely under the Kulyabis who had been responsible for much of the violence since 1992. The Ministry of Defense was the one power institution designated for the opposition. Yet as of August 1999, Rakhmonov still controlled the defense forces. Demilitarization, as a result, has not been completed. The UTO leadership could not convince its own or other militias to disarm.[117] Gorno-Badakhshan, home to the former minister of defense, was also largely excluded from the agreement. The Badakhshan region, already an autonomous *oblast'*, has essentially become an autonomous state, for the damaged transportation routes have made the mountainous terrain of the region all but impossible to traverse. Tensions, nonetheless, have continued to run high. The level of violence in Dushanbe escalated. The execution of four UN workers in August 1998 was intended as a message from the "opposition" that it was displeased with an agreement that in its view was forced on the country by the UN and the United States. The accord in fact gave the UN's, and the international community's, legitimization to an exclusivist government of southern Tajiks, predominantly Kulyabis and representatives of Rakhmonov's Dangharin clan. The

---

[115] Catherine Barnes and Kamoludin Abdullaev, *Politics of Compromise: The Tajikistan Peace Process, Accord*, vol. 10 (London: Conciliation Resources, 2001).

[116] Author's interview with Muhiddin Kabiri, deputy representative of the IRP, Dushanbe, Tajikistan, April 2001. See also ICG, "Tajikistan: An Uncertain Peace," *Asia Report* No. 30, December 2001.

[117] Author's interview with UN and UNHCR officials, Tashkent, June 1998.

international community failed to compel Rakhmonov to share power as he had agreed to do.

Still, Rakhmonov's regime failed to restore order and rein in multiple warlords and clan militias until 2000–01, when increased Russian aid made this possible.[118] More than ten years of regime collapse and war, accompanied by massive social dislocation, have weakened many traditional clan networks and transformed powerful clans into the basis for militias and mafia-like organizations that deal in narcotics and profit from state instability.[119] The war did not, however, eradicate clan behavior from elite-level politics. In fact, Rakhmonov increasingly defied key provisions of the peace deal. The deal on power sharing was never fulfilled. Consequently, numerous regional warlords and their clan networks continued to fight, or remained outside state control. The situation perpetuated a low-level conflict, since it legitimated a regime that divided power between Rakhmonov's clan and the Islamic Renaissance Party, a narrowly based party that had risen to the leadership of the opposition during the war. Although the IRP had given up arms, other militias had not.[120]

Fragmented "Opposition" and "Regime" Forces. A key aspect and telling quality of the Tajik conflict from 1993 through 1997, and even to the present day, has been the factionalization of the "opposition movement." As noted already, this process has occurred with great rapidity since the outbreak of the conflict in 1992. As in similar cases of civil conflict in Chechnya, Yugoslavia, Georgia, Afghanistan, Somalia, and the Sudan, militias increasingly formed along localistic and clan lines, led by local warlords or clan elites. Some had long had local influence, through power in the *kolkhozes*, "the new tribe."[121] Others emerged as powerful during the anarchy of the war. Sangak Safarov, for example, the original leader of the Popular Front, had spent thirty years in jail under the communist regime, and yet his front fought in support of the Nabiev and then Rakhmonov, and their "neo-communist" regimes. Safarov's military success developed a personality cult within his Dangharin clan and Kulyab region. When the Kulyabis and Khodjentis split, Safarov's militia supported the Kulyabis. The rapid proliferation of cheap weapons, the access to and transport and trade of narcotics, and the tertiary involvement

[118] Nasrin Dadmehr, "Tajikistan: Regionalism and Weakness," in Robert Rotberg, ed., *State Failure and State Weakness in a Time of Terror* (Cambridge, MA: World Peace Foundation and Brookings Press, 2003).

[119] Author's interviews with Waldemar Rokoszewski, political affairs officer, United Nations Tajikistan Office of Peace-Building, Dushanbe, Tajikistan, August 2002 and October 2004. See also Shirin Akiner, *Tajikistan: Reconciliation or Disintegration?* (London: Royal Institute of International Affairs, 2001); and Dadmehr, "Tajikistan."

[120] Author's interview with ICG expert, August 2004.

[121] Author's interview with former U.S. ambassador to Tajikistan Stanley Escadero, Tashkent, May 1998. See also Roy, *The New Central Asia*, pp. 89–90.

of competing regional powers – including factions in Iran, Afghanistan, Russia, and Uzbekistan – have only enhanced such militias' ability to survive and their desire to perpetuate low-level conflict.[122]

The UTO, for its part, has proved incapable of controlling or even influencing the actions of the Khodjentis and their supporters. Ethnic Uzbek clans and militias from southern and western Uzbekistan, formerly supporters of the Kulyabi Popular Front militia and Rakhmonov, repeatedly engaged in assaults upon Dushanbe and seized various industrial sites outside of Dushanbe.[123] They reportedly had support from the Uzbek side of the Tajik-Uzbek border. One major violation of the peace agreement continued for several weeks in the fall and winter of 1998, when Colonel Makhmud Khudoberdiev, an ethnic Uzbek with ethnic Uzbek troops from the Lakai tribe of southwest Tajikistan, seized several industrial sites and attacked Kulyabi militias. When Rakhmonov's troops, with the aid of Russian peacekeepers, eventually drove the insurrectionists out of the region, the Uzbek militia took shelter across the border in Uzbekistan. Similarly, General Dostum's Uzbek militia from the Mazar-i-Sharif region of Afghanistan had harbored "opposition" Tajik refugees and reportedly provided arms and support to opposition militias as well.

Other elements of the opposition, not players in the UTO, have likewise refused to sign on to the peace agreement; many were excluded from the negotiations. The Garmis, Pamiris, and various Badakhshani groups, who suffered seriously during the conflict, have large stockpiles of weapons and ties to and support from some Afghan factions.[124] Having been purged from their former posts in the Ministry of Defense and Supreme Soviet, and from the villages to which the Soviet regime had relocated them (in the central and southern regions), they were the most bitter of the opposition, and had no incentive to comply with an accord that denied them both power and resources. Their underground opposition militia, though estimates are difficult, numbered approximately 4,500 in Dushanbe, 2,000 in the Kulyab *oblast'*, 3,500 in Kurgan-Tyube, and 7,000 in Gorno-Badakhshan.[125]

Most serious, however, has been the continued opposition of the Khodjentis. Although ethnic Tajik, Abdullajonov and his clan have long been supported by the Uzbek government, which saw the Khodjentis as a reliable

[122] Kathleen Collins, "Tajikistan: Bad Peace Agreements, and Prolonged Civil Conflict," in Chandra Sriram and Karen Wermerster, eds., *From Promise to Practice: Strengthening UN Capacities for the Prevention of Violent Conflict* (Boulder, CO: Lynne Reinner Press, 2003), pp. 281–287; and International Crisis Group, "Tajikistan: Confrontation or Consolidation," *Asia Briefing*, May 19, 2004. For comparative cases, see Chapter 9 of this volume.

[123] Based on author's interviews with Stanley Escadero, former U.S. ambassador to Tajikistan, Tashkent, May 1998, and Baku, July 1998.

[124] ICG, "Tajikistan: An Uncertain Peace," *Asia Report* No. 25, November 26, 2001.

[125] Ainura Elebaeva, *Mezhetnicheskie otnosheniia v postsovetskikh gosudarstvakh tsentral'noi azii: dinamika razvitiia* (Bishkek: Ilim, 1996), p. 38.

client. The Khodjent clan, unlike many other opposition factions and the UTO, was firmly opposed to any form of Islamic government and sought greater ties with the West. Since his ouster from the regime and electoral defeat, Abdullajonov has consistently sought political backing from Uzbekistan, and recognition and legitimization from the West as a major political figure in Tajikistan – if not as the legitimately elected president.[126] Although neither Uzbekistan nor the West has provided such open recognition, Karimov has quietly harbored Abdullajonov and his supporters. They have maintained a base and network in Tashkent, apparently undisturbed by the Uzbek security forces. An April 1997 assassination attempt on President Rakhmonov was linked to his network. The attempt on his life took place during Rakhmonov's visit to the Khodjent *oblast'*. Military incursions led by Colonel Makhmud Khudoberdiev in 1998 and 1999 were also linked to Abdullajonov. Khudoberdiev's militia is believed to have received safe haven in Uzbekistan while waiting for another opportunity to strike.

The assassination attempt incited a massive crackdown on the entire northern region, including the ethnic Uzbek population, although it did not actively support Abdullajonov. Rakhmonov's determination to exclude Abdullajonov, his Khodjenti clan, and the entire Khodjent *oblast'* has only hardened. Hence, the cycle of violence has continued. The regime's reaction triggered further insurrections in late 1998 and early 1999 in the Khodjent region. Militias armed across the border in Uzbekistan, perhaps with Uzbek government assistance, were reported to have caused violent outbreaks in and around the city of Khodjent.[127] Repeated delays in implementing the peace agreement have kept much of the UTO out.

Although some militias – those most directly under the control of Sayyid Abdullo Nuri, Akbar Turajonzoda, and the other leaders of the UTO – were disarmed or integrated into the newly constructed Tajik army as a result of the peace settlement, many local, clan-based militia groups have refused to go along.[128] In 2001, allegedly for budgetary reasons, Rakhmonov laid off about 4,000 members of the opposition militia who had been integrated. The "pro-government" forces, meanwhile, have been similarly fragmented and thus have produced their own spoiler elements. With the death of the nefarious warlord Safarov, the pro-government Popular Front also split into several smaller, local, clan-based militias that are beyond Rakhmonov's direct control.[129] Rakhmonov has, however, skillfully used his clan to control the key power ministries. He has therefore refused to share the MVD,

---

[126] Author's conversation with former prime minister Abdumallik Abdullajonov, Tashkent, Uzbekistan, July 1997.

[127] Author's interview with diplomat, OSCE, Dushanbe, March 2001.

[128] ICG, "Uncertain Peace." This was still true in 2004. Author interview with an ICG representative, Dushanbe, October 2004.

[129] Author's interview with Stanley Escadero, former U.S. ambassador to Tajikistan, Baku, July 1998. Russian embassy officials gave similar accounts, Tashkent, May 1998.

the SNB, and the presidential security forces with either the IRP or other opposition factions. In 2004, he even took back from the opposition the Ministry of Defense and the Ministry of Emergency Situations – two powerful posts that control weapons. While this has angered opponents and does not help to disarm opposition factions, his policy, with the support of Russia, has at least contributed to centralizing control of the official armed units.

Division of Resources, Rakhmonov's Cadre Politics, and Clan Strategy

Tajikistan was among the poorest of the Soviet republics before 1991, and the civil war devastated its economy; GNP per capita dropped precipitously from 1992 through 1998. Most factories as well as many collective farms and the infrastructure in the south and central part of the country were destroyed. Few resources were left, therefore, for Rakhmonov to divide among his clan and his allies, much less to give out as patronage to rivals. Although the economy has grown, after bottoming out during the war, the major sources of patronage are key posts within the administration and state. Investment and legitimate business are minimal, and access to donor aid and ministerial rents is coveted. As in Kyrgyzstan and Uzbekistan, cadre politics is a critical element of state control and patronage; cadre appointments are doled out by the president on the basis of one's clan, one's broader ethno-regional group, and personal loyalty – personal ties and relations with the president.[130] According to one Tajik scholar, "The president prefers contracting and patronage of real and potential opponents to direct competition and open debate."[131]

At the lower levels of power, this principle of cadre appointments holds as well, thus reinforcing the clan system. Clans use the administrative-territorial structures of the provincial governorships and deputies and the subprovincial mayorships, *raion*s, *kolkhoze*s, and *mahalla*s to solidify their power. During the civil war, state collapse was so severe that the central government lost control of most of these spheres. Rakhmonov has thereby sought to make these structures more dependent on himself, both financially and legally. While he has succeeded to some extent in subordinating the parliament, he has had less success outside of Dushanbe.[132] For example, the *kolkhoze*s continue to control one of the major assets, land, and continue to be organized around the *avlod*, whose identity network appears to have been strengthened due to its importance as the sole social safety net during

---

[130] G. Ileuova, B. Turekhanova, and D. Simakova, "Sociological Portrait of Elite of Tajikistan," *Central Asia Politics and Economics*, vol. 2 (November 2000), pp. 65–67.

[131] Kamoludin Abdullaev, "Current Local Government Policy Situation in Tajikistan," in De Martino, ed., *Ambivalence to Ambiguity*, p. 14.

[132] Boris Vokhonsky, "A Visit to Dushanbe," *Komersant*, <http://enews.ferghava.ru>.

the civil war and after.[133] Rakhmonov has taken legal measures to empower the local *jamoats*, (councils),[134] created in 1994 and accountable to the state, but in reality the *avlod* and *mahalla* committees, which are not state structures, continue to be the most influential local bodies. More broadly, local strongmen and warlords who emerged during the civil war have a following through extended kin, clan, local networks, and sometimes criminal gangs; these local elites often compete with the state structures, especially when Rakhmonov appoints regional governors who have no local legitimacy.[135]

Like Karimov, Rakhmonov initially sought to gain legitimacy among competing clans by "carefully balancing the relations with clans from other ethno-regional groups in order to reach a certain degree of stability.... [However,] the system is quite unstable."[136] He has done so only in the most superficial way, however, since he fears a strengthening of opposition clans. Turajonzoda was made deputy prime minister and has maintained that post, but at the price of being co-opted by the regime. In 1998, Davlat Usmon, another leading opposition figure, was made minister of economy, but was later removed from this lucrative post. After 1997, as noted earlier, another UTO leader was made minister of defense, but his appointment was later revoked and many UTO members were purged from the ministry in 2002.[137] The prime minister and minister of foreign affairs, although Khodjentis, are technocrats with few clan ties. Former UTO warlord Mirzo Ziyoev was made Minister of Emergency Situtions. General Gaffor Mirzoyev, another major warlord who once supported Rakhmonov by mobilizing support in southern areas of Kurgan-Tyube, demanded to be named as head of the powerful Presidental Guard. Rakhmonov appeased Mirzoyev at first, but later demoted him to a lesser but still profitable position as head of the Tajik border guards. In 2004, however, fearful that Mirzoyev's clan was gaining too much power, Rakhmonov had Mirzoyev arrested for corruption and murder. Mahmadruzi Iskanderov, another former UTO warlord with strong clan backing, was given control of the Ministry of Oil and Gas, but he subsequently fled the country after a near-violent showdown with Rakhmonov in summer 2003 after he began building an opposition in the Democratic Party. Only Makhmadsaid Ubaydulloyev has continued successfully to demand that Rakhmonov share power with his network. Ubaydulloyev was appointed mayor of Dushanbe, one of the most powerful and lucrative positions in the country. He supported Rakhmonov against the UTO, and is also from Kulyab, but has a separate and rival clan base.[138]

---

[133] Olimova, "Regionalism," pp. 117–118.
[134] The *jamoat* is the official liason between the *mahalla* and the provincial government.
[135] Author's communication with Tajik journalist, August 2004.
[136] Olimova, "Regionalism," p. 117.
[137] Author's interview with an UNTOP representative, Dushanbe, Tajikistan, March 2001.
[138] Ibid.

Meanwhile, Garmi, Pamiri, Hissari, Lakai, ethic Uzbek, and other clans still have no power. By 1999, about 10 percent of government posts had gone to the UTO, who represented only minor factions and parties from the south. The far more politically adept Khodjenti clan was again left out of the division of power. As the peace agreement receded into the past and the UTO and IRP lost their popular base, the semblance of power sharing disappeared, and Rakhmonov pursued hegemonic control.

For Rakhmonov, hegemony comes through his own clan's monopoly. Between 1999 and 2004, Rakhmonov gave key regime posts to his family, relatives, and friends.[139] According to one political party leader, "Danghara is in power now and other clans are dissatisfied with it."[140] The Dangharin clan has divided what was left of the economy – some cotton contracts, a major aluminum plant, hydroelectric power, a newly discovered oil field – both "privatized" and state.[141] Dangharis also have control over the Ministry of Finance and thus over internationally sponsored loans. Rakhmonov's network also controls the flow of most funds (e.g., the procurator, the banks, customs, the police, and the tax agency) and potential for taking bribes.[142] In flagrant violation of the peace accord, an estimated 80–90 percent of government posts have gone to Kulyabis.[143] Both diplomats and journalists further report that the regime has patronized and even actively been involved in the narcotics trade.[144] Key government posts and positions in the Tajik-Afghan border guards have been given to family and friends of Rakhmonov. International agencies believe that some well-connected persons profit from the narco trade, so the government does not crack down on it. Local experts in Tajikistan estimate that the bulk of the economy now relies on the narco trade. Indeed, Tajikistan verges on becoming a narco state.[145]

As in the other cases, clan interests are widely mixed with patronage, nepotism, and corruption. The effect on economic reform and the economy overall is negative. Privatization in Tajikistan, to the extent that it has taken place, has been flawed by insider connections. Land distribution causes particular tension, since the relatives and friends of *kolkhoz* directors or local elites

---

[139] Multiple sources report this. Author interview with an independent journalist, Dushanbe, July 2002. See also "Rakhmonov Emomali Sharipovich – Prezident Respubliki Tajikistan," <www.ctaj.elcat.kg/tolstyi/c/co22.html>; and Tajik expert, "Elite Clans in Tajikistan," and Payam Foroughi, "Tajikistan," in *Nations in Transit 2003* (New York: Freedom House, 2003), pp. 581–582.

[140] Political party leader, cited in Olimova, "Regionalism," p. 108.

[141] Tajik expert, "Elite Clans"; and Dudoignon, "From Ambivalence," p. 125.

[142] Foroughi, "Tajikistan," p. 589.

[143] Zviagelskaya, "The Tajik Conflict."

[144] Foroughi, "Tajikistan," p. 588. Author's interview with a Western diplomat, Dushanbe, October 2004.

[145] ICG, "Tajikistan: Confrontation or Consolidation?," *Asia Briefing*, May 19, 2004.

receive the best land.[146] The executive's putative battle against corruption since 1999 has made little progress, especially since Rakhmonov's own clan politics, buying support from both allies and opposition, undermines it.

External Patronage: The Russian Role

Unlike the other Central Asian states, Tajikistan has both benefited and suffered from the external patronage of Russia. As noted in Chapters 4 and 5, the abrupt end to Russian patronage of the Leninabadi clan's hegemony in 1991, after the Soviet collapse, triggered Tajikistan's regime collapse. Then, in the mid-1990s, Russia's renewed aid helped to stabilize the war-torn country. Primary support for Rakhmonov came from the Russian government, which after a brief hiatus had reengaged in the politics of its southern neighbors.[147] Russia played a critical role in bringing Rakhmonov to power in 1994.[148] Russia's continued patronage became the main source of the Rakhmonov regime's capacity to survive after 1995.[149] Indeed, dependency on Russian involvement was the consequence of the Tajik regime's failure to reach an acceptable division of power and resources with opposition clans (see Table 8.6). The regime's base of power, therefore, continues to be military aid and foreign capital provided by outside states.

Russia has bolstered Tajik military and security services, and the 201st Division remains in an expanded base. Even with Russia's help, however, Rakhmonov's regime failed to establish a monopoly over the use of force. The proliferation of arms was already beyond its control, and a constant flow of weapons crossed the Tajik-Afghan border. The UTO and multiple other militias, even those that had once supported Rakhmonov, remained at large. Just as importantly, however, Russian patronage means that Rakhmonov and Tajikistan have little real sovereignty. Consequently, Tajikistan's regime remains largely at Russia's mercy. Rakhmonov cannot claim to have consolidated power or gained the ability to pursue his own agenda apart from the direction of Tajikistan's big brother.

A Weak Autocracy: Tajikistan's Shaky Regime

Because of increased Russian patronage, Rakhmonov's strategy has become increasingly exclusionary; he has not attempted to balance clan interests

---

[146] Foroughi, "Tajikistan," in *Nations in Transit 2002* (New York: Freedom House, 2002), p. 383.

[147] Yeltsin's appointment of Yevgennii Primakov to the post of foreign minister of Russia marked a turning point in Russian relations with Central Asia. Known as an "Orientalist," Primakov adopted not only a colder line towards the West but a more proactive and engaged, even hegemonic, position in Russian–Central Asian relations.

[148] Uzbekistan is also believed to have supported Rakhmonov's candidacy.

[149] ICG, "Uncertain Peace."

informally, much less to represent them formally in the government.[150] The internationally sponsored elections in 1999 and 2000 were intended to initiate a democratic transition. Instead, Rakhmonov used the elections to stack the new government members with the Kulyabi network. According to one study, already in 2000, about 42 percent of the presidential apparat and 31 percent of the government positions (of those known) had gone to Kulyab and Danghara. Since then, their numbers have increased.[151] Furthermore, he has created a presidential party, the NDPT, which is dominated by his network but draws little broader support.[152] The Rakhmonov family and Dangharin clan now control not only the party and most lucrative and powerful positions, but also Orienbank (run by the First Lady's brother), most cotton-processing factories (run by the sons-in-law), and the aluminum and hydro-power plants. Rakhmonov has nine children, and his clan is becoming greedier.

The Communist Party remains legal, but it is excluded from the levers of power. The regime continues to shortchange not only the Khodjentis, but also most Garmi, Pamiri, Hissari, Lakai, and ethnic Uzbek clans.[153] As one political party activist put it, "Now we have elections, but the whole government is controlled by Rakhmonov's clan, and it's not even a large and important clan. It's a small Kulyabi clan that rose to power because of the war."[154] The government's own use of clan politics is ironically undermining Rakhmonov's goal of creating a strong and coherent authoritarian state. As the Tajik scholar Saodat Olimova writes, "the Soviet command-administrative control was substituted by a state with no political will, but with a strong clan system."[155] Local UN observers report that the problems with the functioning of Tajikistan's institutional structures, its system of public administration, and its economic programs "can be understood only in the context of underlying traditional and informal practices such as regionalism and clan politics."[156] This in turn fosters conflicting ethno-regional identities organized around the leading clans, rather than a unified Tajik nation-state.[157]

Stability is dependent upon Russia's continued backing of Rakhmonov. In short, the Rakhmonov regime has as much difficulty controlling its own fractionalized supporters as it does the UTO. Russia's estimated 25,000 peacekeepers (technically, "CIS peacekeepers") and its substantial financial

---

[150] Author's conversation with Abdullajonov.
[151] Ileuova, Turekhanova, and Simakova, "Sociological Portrait," p. 67.
[152] Author's interviews with a Tajik journalist and an OSCE representative, Dushanbe, August 2002.
[153] See Roy, *New Central Asia*; and Rubin, "Russian Hegemony."
[154] Author's interview with M. Kabiri, deputy head of the Islamic Renaissance Party, Dushanbe, March 2001.
[155] Olimova, "Regionalism," p. 117.
[156] Foroughi, "Tajikistan" (2002), p. 380.
[157] Olimova, "Regionalism," p. 116.

assistance have enabled Rakhmonov to stay in power.[158] Even so, UN military observers report that the regime has little control over the rest of the country.[159]

Although authoritarian, the regime is not consolidated. On the surface, Rakhmonov and his clan have asserted hegemonic control since 2001, and especially in 2003–2004, with the arrest of several former warlords, including some from the "government" side, such as General Gaffor Mirzoyev. Yet at a deeper level, the Tajik regime has exhibited little success in implementing its policies – such as the campaign against corruption, centralization of the economy, disarmament, and rebuilding state control outside of the capital.[160] Several assassination attempts have challenged this exclusivist clan politics.[161] Shirin Akiner has described the Tajik state under Rakhmonov as embodying the "semi-institutionalization of power struggles among different individuals and/or interest groups."[162]

Increased U.S. funding of Tajikistan in the wake of 9/11 created a new stream of resources, but the U.S. presence is limited. Although aid nearly tripled in 2002 to an estimated $163 million, by 2003 it was declining sharply, as was the short-term flurry of business brought by coalition military and humanitarian workers based in Dushanbe. International attention seems only to have encouraged Rakhmonov to thwart democratization and refuse to negotiate a more equitable pact with clan elites and other opposition forces. The economy relies more on the narcotics trade than on investment, which remains extremely limited. Despite some growth, after bottoming out in the mid-1990s, poverty is very high. Meanwhile, market-based growth is severely constrained by the regime. (See Appendix, Tables A.6, A.7.) According to Luigi De Martino, "the government's tactics of exclusion of opposition or potential opposition forces is nearing its limits."[163] The Tajik regime's stability remains highly dependent upon Russia's continued backing.[164]

---

[158] Russian aid has been far more substantial than Western aid, which totaled an average of $9.5 million annually from 1993 through 1995; Tajikistan, UNHCR Report, 1996.

[159] Meetings with UNMOT personnel and U.S. embassy military attachés, Tashkent, Uzbekistan, March 1997 and May 1998.

[160] Author's interview with Waldemar Rokoszewski, political affairs officer, United Nations Tajikistan Office of Peace-Building, Dushanbe, Tajikistan, August 2002. See also Roger McDermott, "The Army in Tajikistan: Ten Years of Independence," *Central Asia-Caucasus Analyst*, March 12, 2003 <www.cacianalyst.org/view_article.php?articleid=1143>. See also former ambassador R. Grant Smith, "Dealing With Warlords," *Central Asia-Caucasus Analyst*, January 30, 2002, <www.cacianalyst.org/view_article.php?articleid=45>.

[161] According to one Tajik journalist, clans have become increasingly criminalized since the war. Author's interview with a journalist, Moscow, August 2000.

[162] Akiner, *Tajikistan*, p. 88, cited in De Martino, p. 158.

[163] De Martino, *Tajikistan at a Crossroads*, p. 158.

[164] Author's interviews with a Tajik journalist and with Waldemar Rokoszewski, political affairs officer, United Nations Tajikistan Office of Peace-Building, Dushanbe, October 2004.

SUMMARY

Of the three regimes examined in Chapters 7 and 8, Uzbekistan remains the strongest: a weak pact is still in place, largely because clans supported Karimov in response to mutual, albeit declining, threats – Russia and then Afghanistan (until 2002). Now internal Islamism may be seen as a new common threat. Moreover, everyone fears an alternative leader. Karimov has made greater attempts than neighboring leaders to balance competing clan interests. Even though Karimov has cut their political power, he has allowed the most important networks to preserve their economic assets. Nonetheless, the recent rise of "the Family" is increasing both mass and clan-based discontent.

Tajikistan is certainly more stable now than in the 1990s, when it went through regime collapse and a brutal civil war. The 1997 peace agreement has for the most part held the peace. Yet it did not result in complete disarmament and a government monopoly over the use of force. Furthermore, its pact was very limited; it did not include numerous clan factions, such as the Khodjentis, Pamiris, Lakai, and multiple opposition warlords, and the agreement itself was never fully implemented. While President Rakhmonov initially gave some government positions to competing clan factions, he has not balanced power, and his "Family" has become increasingly hegemonic. Russia has helped him to regain control, but his regime remains precariously contingent upon Russian military support and international aid.

A leadership change in any of these cases would threaten most clan interests, since positions, power, and resources are not institutionalized; they depend on personal loyalties and connections. The succession question thus remains a likely source of conflict.[165] According to one analyst, "if something happens to Karimov, there is not a mechanism for the transfer of power; there could well be inter-clan war."[166] The same can probably be said of the other cases, where the increasing hegemony of the presidents' clans, under conditions of general economic decline, has fed interclan competition and rising resentment by those excluded from insider deals. The greatest threats to all three presidents, and to regime durability, come not from a democratic or even Islamist opposition, but from competing clan elites demanding their share of a shrinking pie.

Uzbekistan and Tajikistan are two cases of seemingly strong autocracies by powerful presidents, each with a Communist Party background. Kyrgyzstan has shifted from a democratizing state to a similarly super-presidential system in which even limited democratic freedoms are no longer guaranteed,

---

[165] Usman Khaknazarov, "*Vozrozhdenie 'serogo kardinala' uzbekskoi politiki,*" *Tsentr Aziia*, January 2, 2003, <www.centrasia.ru>; and Alisher Taksanov, "*Kanonizirovanie klanov,*" *Internet-gazeta* (Kazakhstan), December 20, 2002, <www.navi.kz/articles/?artid+21176>. The articles were quickly blocked in Uzbekistan.

[166] Author's interview, Tashkent, Uzbekistan, January 2002.

especially since the 2000 elections. Yet in none of these cases is the president able to assert control over the informal politics and deals that pervade both society and state. Presidential appointments and policy decisions are sharply constrained by clan interests and clan competition for resources. Once appointed, clan elites actively engage in nepotism and patronage of their kin and fictive kin networks. They strip state assets, creating a wealth and power base for their clan networks and protection for themselves, since the state provides no guarantees for their future. The overall economy and governance has consequently suffered (refer to Appendix, Tables A.6, A.7). A vicious cycle of clan politics has ensued, continuing to weaken institutions and prevent regime consolidation, and leaving the future of the regimes highly uncertain (refer to Appendix, Table A.7).

Authoritarian law has been strong when repressing democratic dissent, but weak when controlling its own cadre of clan elites with their vested interests in rent seeking, corruption, and blocking reform. Mafia organizations have taken advantage of this environment, and some elite clans have themselves engaged in illegal and violent activities to promote their economic or political interests. Despite the seeming autonomy of these presidents, the informal level of politics has increasingly shaped and constrained their formal powers. These once-strong communist republics have become weak states, run by personalistic networks and susceptible to sudden shocks. All three show signs of declining durability and possible failure.

9

Positive and Negative Political Trajectories
in Clan-Based Societies

It is not within the scope of this book to explain the rise and fall of clans as social and political organizations on a global scale. Yet some observations can be made here, so as to put the Central Asian states in a broader comparative framework. This chapter addresses two main issues. First, I ask whether this book's central argument, about the importance of clans and clan politics under the conditions discussed in earlier chapters, is unique to the three cases I have explored, or whether clans matter in other countries as well. While not a universal phenomenon, clans are certainly not a social organization unique to Central Asia, either historically or today. Where they have persisted, then, do they manifest themselves in ways similar to their role in Central Asia? Are the propositions of this book – about the political role of clan networks, their adaptability and persistence, the importance of clan pacts in promoting political stability, and the reemergence and deleterious effects of clans under transitional/new regimes – useful in explaining other cases in and beyond Central Asia?

Second, despite the persistence of clans in Central Asia, and despite the negative role that they generally play in contemporary Central Asian politics, I do not argue that clans always persist. This book does not accept the culturalist or "Orientalist" view that paints Central Asia as an unchanging, tribal, politically and economically backward society, in contrast with the developed, individualist, democratic, and capitalist West. The second key question addressed in this chapter is this: why have clans declined or disappeared in some cases, while they have persisted in others? Further, what conditions are likely to foster clan decline, or at least the transformation of clans into forms of particularistic politics more conducive to democratization and political stability?

This chapter will pursue these questions first by looking at the role of clans in several other cases in the former Soviet Union, including Kazakhstan and Turkmenistan in Central Asia, and Georgia, Azerbaijan, and Chechnya in the Caucasus. In applying the argument about the rise of clan politics to these additional cases, I ask why Kazakhstan has been somewhat more stable than the others, despite its clan-based society. The chapter will then go beyond the Soviet bloc to demonstrate that clans are neither simply Soviet artifacts nor Central Asian cultural constructs. Clans have in fact been important forms of social organization in other regions throughout history. Lisa Anderson and Mounira Charrad have demonstrated the power of kin groups in North African politics and society, states that have not yet undergone a regime transition. In this chapter, I will compare and contrast the role of clans in the political development of parts of Europe and Africa, focusing especially on the cases of Italy and Somalia, where, as in Central Asia, regime transitions of some kind have occurred. These comparisons, though brief, will provide some confirmation of the propositions in this book about the conditions under which clans persist and negatively affect political trajectories. Cross-regional comparison will also offer insight into the question of why clans break down, both historically and today. We can then begin to understand how clans can be transformed, and how their effects upon the political regime can be mitigated. Although this book argues against quick-fix elite-level and institutionalist answers to the problem of creating democracy in clan-based societies, it does not subscribe to social determinism. Rather, scholars and policy makers should be aware of the inevitable difficulties and complications of the long-term process of democratization in countries characterized by the strong informal institutions of a tribal, clan, or kin-based social structure, whether in Kyrgyzstan and Tajikistan in 1991, in Afghanistan and Iraq in 2004, or in Italy in 1919.

I. THE ROLE OF CLANS IN OTHER POST-SOVIET CASES

The most similar cases for further comparison are those that have shared the twentieth-century history of the Soviet experience and the political and economic legacies it created. Within the post-Soviet cases, there are several other examples of the persistence of clan networks and the rise of clan politics during the post-Soviet era. All of these cases are found on the southern edge of the former Soviet (and Russian) empire, where tribes, clans, and localist networks had persisted into the 1920s.[1] In the absence of formal states and in a pre-modern economy, these groups formed the core of sociopolitical organization before Soviet rule. Under the Soviet system, collectivization, nationality policies, and cadre politics fostered clan persistence by giving clans access to resources. As in Central Asia, the state advanced some clans at the expense of others and modernized these networks in some ways.

---

[1] Francine Hirsch, "Empire of Nations: Colonial Technologies and the Meaning of the Soviet Union, 1917–1939" (Ph.D. dissertation, Princeton University, 1998).

The Kazakh and Turkmen Cases

Does this work's hypothesis about the persistence of clans under the Soviet state, their reemergence, and the negative effect of clan politics on regime durability help to explain the political trajectories of the other Central Asian cases? A brief look at the cases of post-Soviet Turkmenistan and Kazakhstan give further support for the argument presented here. The Kazakh and Turkmen trajectories have also been shaped by informal clan politics. Informal pacts have facilitated durable but not democratic transitions: limited political but significant economic liberalization in Kazakhstan, and the creation of post-communist authoritarianism in Turkmenistan. Unlike the Kyrgyz, Uzbek, and Tajik cases, however, Kazakhstan and Turkmenistan are rich in energy resources. Both experienced the political and economic uncertainty of the transition, and both emerged with weakened states. Kazakhstan, however, liberalized some economic sectors quickly and experienced significant growth. Turkmenistan had positive prospects in the 1990s, but lack of liberalization has thwarted development. These cases thus enable us to better specify the role of economic conditions in fostering or preventing the emergence of clan politics.[2]

Formally, Kazakhstan's political trajectory has fallen somewhere between the Kyrgyz and Uzbek paths; informally, it is still plagued by the politics of clans, although the president himself has much greater power, sustained primarily through foreign direct investment in the oil sector. Nursultan Nazarbaev, like his neighbors, initially needed to maintain the appearance of a neutral *podesta* (a neutral executive broker) in managing the clan pact. Nazarbaev faced historical divisions between three hordes (tribal groupings) and among smaller clan lineages.[3] Despite his brief liberalization of the media and parties, Nazarbaev's regime has employed some elements of clan-based authoritarianism, using oil rents to appease rival clans and offering to include all three hordes in the system to some extent.[4] At the same time, Nazarbaev has sought to consolidate a super-presidential system in which his network controls power and resources.

Like his neighbors, however, Nazarbaev has faced a number of challenges. First, parliament became an arena for clan notables, as well as democrats, to gain access to state resources and form a potential opposition. Second,

[2] Kathleen Collins, "The Logic of Clan Politics: Evidence from the Central Asian Trajectories," *World Politics*, vol. 5, no. 2 (January 2004): 224–261.

[3] On tribalism, or competition between the three hordes in Kazakhstan, and problems for nation building, see Martha Olcott, *The Kazakhs* (Stanford, CA: Hoover Institution Press, 1988, 2nd ed. 1995); Edward Schatz, "The Politics of Multiple Identities: Lineage and Ethnicity in Kazakhstan," *Europe-Asia Studies*, vol. 52 (2000), pp. 498–506. Schatz argues that state efforts to address ethnic issues in fact rekindle lineage identities. See also Shirin Akiner, *The Formation of Kazak Identity: From Tribe to Nation-State* (London: Royal Institute of International Affairs, 1995).

[4] Olcott, *The Kazakhs*, pp. 202–203.

although Nazarbaev has manipulated electoral and party legislation in order to strengthen pro-government parties and decrease clan representation, the first two parliamentary elections were no more successful for Nazarbaev's parties than for Karimov's; individual notables won a plurality of seats, crowding out both state-sponsored parties and other forms of political mobilization. By 2004, a shift in power was evident, as Nazarbaev's family party had gained greater control. Third, rivals want their share of foreign investment and energy wealth, which has been diverted disproportionately to Nazarbaev's clan.[5] Some observers have described this horde- and clan-based battle for resource control as a return to pre-Soviet tribalism; in fact, however, it is simply a modern form of identity-based factionalism, organized along the group lines that still matter for political support and security.[6]

Meanwhile, as in Kyrgyzstan, Nazarbaev has used his clan to undermine the main area of regime liberalization, the media. The president's daughter Dariga Nazarbaeva and his son-in-law Rakhat Aliev now control most of the "independent" media as well as major business interests.[7] Nazarbaev has centralized the strong presidency around his family and clan connections. Aliev also headed Almaty's taxation department, another powerful post. Nazarbaev's other son-in-law is the director of a monopolistic pipeline company and is influential in the lucrative oil and gas sectors. Nazarbaev's clan has also gained control of the country's leading bank.[8] Energy wealth, together with rapidly rising oil prices in recent years, has bolstered his regime more than it has the neighboring regimes, allowing Nazarbaev to invest in his power structures. The national security service (SNB) is headed by his son-in-law. His family uses the SNB to control or buy off oligarchic rivals and the democratic opposition. While a wealthy regime and rising GDP per capita (refer to Appendix, Table A.6) insulate the regime for now, rival factions resent the Nazarbaev clan's usurpation of most major state assets. They could be a threat over the longer term if Nazarbaev does not preserve some balance.[9]

In Turkmenistan, President Niyazov acted more quickly than his neighbors to strengthen the security forces behind him during the early years of independence, and to use them to control clan and larger tribal rivalries,

---

[5] Author's conversation with a lawyer based in Kazakhstan, August 2003. See also Bhavna Dhave, "Kazakhstan," *Nations in Transit Report* (Lanham, MD: Rowman and Littlefield and Freedom House, 2003).

[6] Alshyn Zhalantos, "*Kazakhskoe obshchestvo vozvrashchaetsia k srednevekovym rodoplemmenym otnosheniiam...*," *Navigator-II*, March 5, 2003 <http://www.navi.kz/articles/?artid=2788>. On Kazakh tribes, Schatz, "Politics of Multiple Identities."

[7] RFE/RL, *Kazakh News*, October 10, 2001.

[8] Aldar Kusainov, "Kazakhstan's Critical Choice," January 1, 2003 <www.eurasia-net.org/departments/rights/articles/eavo11303.shtml www.eurasianet.org/departments/rights/articles/eavo11303.shtml>.

[9] Ibid.

which were more traditional in form and more salient politically in both pre-Soviet and Soviet Turkmenistan than elsewhere in Central Asia.[10] Although the parliament declared Niyazov "president for life" in 1999, and although many Western scholars and policy makers have portrayed Turkmenistan as a consolidated sultanistic or even totalitarian regime,[11] Niyazov's dictatorship is highly personalistic and erratic; yet, despite his image, Niyazov is not entirely autonomous. During his first decade in power, Niyazov was very careful to maintain a balance of clan representation in the government.[12] In the mid-1990s, he was careful to appoint regional *hokim*s (governors) and administrators from the respective local tribes rather than appointing outsiders, as Karimov has often done. This was a deliberate attempt to maintain a tribal balance, much as Soviet policy had done.[13] More recently, however, Niyazov has increasingly placed only Tekke clans in key positions.[14]

Reports of clan struggles over resources – with each other and/or against the president – are difficult to verify. Yet various clan and economic elites found to be stealing a share of the state pie are periodically purged.[15] In recent years, the Turkmen regime and state have become increasingly precarious. Reports by dissidents and journalists suggest that a struggle for power is ongoing, beneath the veneer of totalitarian control. Niyazov has broken ties with the network of supporters who backed his presidency during the immediate transition.[16] In the words of one dissident, "he is no longer balancing clans as under the traditional system."[17]

Nonetheless, extreme centralization of power has not consolidated or *institutionalized* Niyazov's regime. Now titled "Turkmenbashi the Great," Niyazov rules through informal ties with his cronies, not through institutions. Turkmenbashi's method of continually reshuffling or sacking his

[10] See Adrienne Edgar, *Tribal Nation* (Princeton, NJ: Princeton University Press, 2004); and Paul Georg Geiss, "Turkmen Tribalism," *Central Asia Survey*, vol 18, no. 3 (1999), pp. 347–357.

[11] Charles Fairbanks, "Disillusionment in the Caucasus and Central Asia," *Journal of Democracy*, vol. 12 (October 2001).

[12] Michael Ochs, "Turkmenistan," in Karen Dawisha and Bruce Parrott, eds., *Conflict, Cleavage, and Change in Central Asia and the Caucasus* (Cambridge: Cambridge University Press, 1997), p. 317; Olivier Roy, *The New Central Asia: The Creation of Nations* (New York: New York University Press, 2000), p. 13; and Shokhrat Kadyrov, *Turkmenistan: chetyre goda bez SSR* (Moscow: Panorama, 1996).

[13] Roy, *New Central Asia*, p. 115.

[14] International Crisis Group, "Turkmenistan: Cracks in the Marble: Turkmenistan's Failing Dictatorship," *Asia Report*, no. 44 <www.crisisgroup.org/home/index.cfm?id=14458/5/>. January 17, 2003, p. 21.

[15] Rustem Safronov, "Turkmenistan Purge Indicative of Instability," March 12, 2002 <www.eurasianet.org/ departments/insight/articles/eav031202.shtml>.

[16] International Crisis Group, "Turkmenistan," pp. 7–9.

[17] Author's interview with a Turkmen dissident, Moscow, August 2000.

ministers, advisors, and even his security service and military indicates a near-paranoia in his attempt to keep power. One expert stated: "People I talked to told me, 'if we go into any kind of clannish or civil war, it is very unlikely that the military would obey [presidential] orders.'"[18] Rumors of coup attempts abound. One attempt, believed to have been led by Boris Shikmuradov, a former foreign minister representing a powerful Yomut clan,[19] ended in a failed assassination attempt in November 2002.

In attempting to consolidate his power, Turkmenbashi has eliminated presidential elections and rarely convenes parliament. There is no institutional mechanism for leadership succession. It is increasingly unclear how long the police and military will support him.[20] The expert Viktor Ponomaryov recently observed that the president's decision to imprison former leaders of the SNB was risky, and that there would probably be no orderly succession of power in the event of a successful coup: "The regime is so brittle that whenever [Niyazov] goes, nobody will be able to assume power the way that he has, and the system will collapse."[21] Turkmenistan is an extreme case of the personalization and de-institutionalization of the regimes in Central Asia, but it shares the common risks of instability and breakdown present across the region.[22]

Energy wealth has not made Kazakhstan or Turkmenistan immune to clan politics. Instead, Nazarbaev and Niyazov have been able to use their greater state revenues to appease clan rivals and to increase their personal power. Nonetheless, they govern through informal, personalistic networks, allowing kin patronage and asset stripping of the state for personal ends. While their regimes are temporarily more durable than their neighbors, increasing GDP alone has not transformed clan politics or consolidated the regimes. In fact, energy-based economies appear to be particularly susceptible to clan-based corruption.[23] The "resource curse"[24] may foster instability between clans and hinder democratization over the longer term, and Kazakhstan and Turkmenistan are particularly susceptible to this problem.[25] Kazakhstan,

---

[18] "Turkmenistan Faces Multiple Sources of Domestic Strife," February 12, 2003 <www.eurasianet.org/departments/recaps/articles/ eav021203.shtml>.

[19] Rustem Safronov, "Opposition in Exile: Turkmenistan," December 9, 2002 <www.eurasianet.org/departments/rights/articles/ eav120902.shtml>.

[20] Roger McDermott, "Shake-up in Turkmen Spy Agency Hints at Pending Crisis," September 30, 2002 <www.eurasianet.org/departments/insight/articles/eav093002_pr.shtml>.

[21] "Analyst Predicts 'Radical Change' Near for Turkmenistan," October 21, 2002 <www.eurasianet.org/departments/recaps/articles/eav102102.shtml>.

[22] International Crisis Group, "Turkmenistan," pp. 3–7.

[23] Ariel Cohen, "Confronting Kazakhstan's 'Dutch Disease'," *Central Asia-Caucasus Analyst*, March 26, 2003 <www.cacianalyst.org/view_article.php?articleid=1263>; Terry Karl, *The Paradox of Plenty* (Berkeley: University of California Press, 1999).

[24] Michael Ross, "Does Oil Hinder Democracy?," *World Politics*, vol. 53 (April 2001), pp. 325–361.

[25] Author's conversation with Central Asian economists, Bishkek, 2004.

however, has seen some positive developments by allowing a narrow, entrepreneurial, market-oriented business sector to develop. This new sector is in some ways competing with and attenuating entrenched clan politics. It has also become the basis of a political opposition to the regime, the Democratic Choice of Kazakhstan (DCK). In February 2004, the DCK political manifesto openly attacked the regime's hegemonic clan politics: "In our country, money, power, newspapers, and television belong not to the people, but only and exclusively to the ruling clan headed by President Nazarbaev. For this reason, all the so-called pro-presidential parties have been created with the ruling clan's money and to defend its interests...."[26] The Kazakh and Turkmen cases strongly suggest, as I proposed in Chapter 2, that a growing market economy and dispersed wealth – not an increasing GDP per se – are more likely prevent the centralization of wealth under authoritarian leaders and their clan and patronage networks, thereby transforming clan politics and stabilizing these regimes.

Elements of Clan Politics in the Caucasus

Other scholars have observed the role of clan and familial patronage networks in the post-Soviet Caucasus, although both greater nationalism and industrialization have served to weaken clan identities in much of the Caucasus during the twentieth century. As centers of oil production and transport, the Caucasus received significant investment during the Soviet period. Only Georgia had as low a level of development as Central Asia. National identity in the Caucasian republics was also more developed. Armenian identity, in particular, was centuries old, rooted in the ancient language and religion of its people. A sense of nationalism was further consolidated during the genocide of 1915–18,[27] before the Soviets defined the republic's borders. Even so, in the early twentieth century rural Armenians were organized into autonomous, patriarchal extended families.[28] Furthermore, the dynamics of ethno-nationalist–inspired secessionist movements and conflicts in the Caucasus (the Armenian-Azeri conflict over Nagorno-Karabagh;[29] the South Ossetian and Abkhaz conflicts in Georgia; the Chechen conflict against Russia) initially subsume clan factionalization in this region, so that clan politics does not emerge in ways

[26] DCK cited in "Party of Kazakh President's Daughter Is Election Front-runner," *Transitions Online*, March 9–15, 2004.

[27] Ronald Suny, "Provisional Stabilities: The Politics of Identity in Post-Soviet Eurasia," *International Security*, vol. 24 (Winter 2000), pp. 139–178; Valery Tishkov, *Chechnya: Life in a War-Torn Society* (Berkeley: University of California Press, 2004), p. 219.

[28] Nora Dudwick, "Political Transformations in Postcommunist Armenia: Images and Realities," in Dawisha and Parrott, eds., *Conflict, Cleavage, and Change*, p. 72.

[29] Audrey Alstadt, "Azerbaijan's Struggle Toward Democracy," in Dawisha and Parrott, eds., *Conflict, Cleavage, and Change*, pp. 110–155.

parallel to the paths described in Central Asia. Nonetheless, the social, cultural, and economic conditions of the Caucasus, as well as the path of imperial conquest by the Russian and Soviet empires, made the social structure and political development of these republics very similar to that of Central Asia. Brezhnev's cadre politics propped up clan patronage networks throughout the Caucasus.[30] A renewed clan politics does emerge in various forms during the post-Soviet period, especially in Azerbaijan, Georgia, and Chechnya, where national and state formation occurred much later and socialist economic conditions prevailed in the twentieth century.

Azeri identity was a construct of the Soviet period; Azeris, like Uzbeks and Kazakhs, were a Turkic, seminomadic, tribal people on the eve of the Russian conquest.[31] Clan and familial networks were critical elements of social organization. Soviet industrialization, based on the oil industry in Baku, modernized Azerbaijan to a greater extent than Central Asia, and conflict with Armenia in the late 1980s also forged national unity. At the same time, First Secretary (later president) Heidar Aliev skillfully played and perpetuated the game of clan politics during his two long periods of rule (1969–82; 1993–2003).[32] He extensively used patronage to balance factional interests and solidify his control. As in Kazakhstan, energy wealth has ensured a modicum of stability in Azerbaijan. Increasing returns from massive foreign direct investment in the oil industry – following the "contract of the century" with a British Petroleum–led consortium in 1994 – enabled the president to consolidate significant control, in large part by providing a source of patronage for the Aliev clan and others.[33] The ongoing war with Armenia, a clear external threat, further consolidated popular and clan support behind Aliev, who was seen as the only candidate strong enough to deal with the threat. A small democratic opposition has organized parties and protests. The real challenges, however, as in Central Asia, have come from excluded rival factions, who have engineered several assassination attempts.[34] Nonetheless, the Aliev clan, which has had a strong kin and factional network based in Nakhichevan since Soviet days, has used its monopoly of oil wealth to bolster its control of competing factions through a combination of patronage and force, made possible by large and growing oil revenues, as in Kazakhstan. GDP grew by more than 10 percent in 2002 and 2003. Aliev's family tightly controls the security services, the major political party (the Yeni Azerbaycan Party), all the strategic state assets, key positions

---

[30] Ronald Grigor Suny, *The Revenge of the Past* (Stanford, CA: Hoover Institution Press, 1993).

[31] Audrey Alstadt, *The Azerbaijani Turks* (Stanford, CA: Hoover Institution Press, 1992), pp. 8–9.

[32] Suny, *The Revenge of the Past.*

[33] International Crisis Group, "Azerbaijan: Turning Over a New Leaf?" *Europe Report* No. 156, p. 11.

[34] Roy, *New Central Asia*, p. 138.

in parliament, and multiple profitable businesses.[35] The military, however, has remained a counter-elite.[36] Still, the dying Heidar Aliev effectively handed over power to his son, Ilham, in October 2003 with little serious challenge from rivals.[37] As in Kazakhstan, increasing resources have made possible greater regime consolidation. Even so, insider observers warn that Ilham is less capable of controlling and balancing clan factions than his father was.

Other examples of clan politics from both the north and the south Caucasus resemble the Tajik trajectory, where an exogenous shock from the Soviet collapse led to state breakdown and civil conflict. Although of varying initial causes – mostly related to ethno-national secessionist movements – the conflicts have largely taken the form of violence between clan-based militias. The emergence of clan factions, with their increasing involvement in the narcotics and arms trade and increasing demands for a share of state resources, strongly resembles the pattern of state breakdown and cycle of violence in Tajikistan. Charles Fairbanks argues that the rise of personalized militias was common throughout the post-communist south – not only in Tajikistan but also in Georgia, Chechnya, Dagestan, Albania, and Bosnia – as the regime and state power broke down during the transition.[38] In all of these cases, clan and kinship networks had historically pervaded society and were mobilized during the period of state collapse. The breakdown of the state invigorated a return to such networks as a way to gain protection and a share of, or control over, resources. These groups were not bound by an ideological cause, as are many guerilla movements, nor did they represent a state or public good. Rather, they were organized "on the basis of families, clans, residential quarters, and patron-client networks."[39]

Georgia, for example, had no informal pact in place to stabilize the regime transition; it witnessed both ethnic and clan conflict during the 1990s. Until late 2003, it followed a trajectory similar to Tajikistan's. Like Armenian identity, Georgian ethno-national identity was far older than Tajik identity; like the Armenians', the Georgians' ethnicity was characterized by an ancient written language and Christian religion that pre-dated the Soviet period by centuries.[40] Indeed, both Georgian and Armenian national identities were successfully mobilized against the Soviet region in secessionist

[35] International Crisis Group, "Azerbaijan," pp. 9–12; BBC Monitoring Central Asia, "Azeri Paper Publishes List of President's High Ranking Relatives," July 19, 2002.
[36] Richard Giragosian, "Generational Change and Leadership Succession in Azerbaijan: The Outsiders" (manuscript, 2004), p. 7.
[37] International Crisis Group, "Azerbaijan," pp. 12–14.
[38] Charles Fairbanks, "Weak States and Private Armies," in Mark Beissinger and Crawford Young, eds., *Beyond State Crisis? Postcolonial Africa and Post-Soviet Eurasia in Comparative Perspective* (Washington, DC: Woodrow Wilson Center Press, 2002), pp. 129–160.
[39] Ibid.
[40] Ronald Grigor Suny, *The Making of the Georgian Nation* (Bloomington: Indiana University Press, 1988).

movements. Demands by other ethnic enclaves within Georgia further complicated the process of decolonization and transition. The anthropologist Tamara Dragazde argues that Georgian social organization was also characterized by extensive familial and clan networks, both prior to and during the period of Soviet rule.[41] As in Central Asia, we see the mafiosization of some clannish networks as they became associated with criminal groups during the Soviet period and after; many powerful party or state figures used their own clan as a protection network.[42] Although the Georgian nationalist movement was gaining momentum in 1989–90, strengthened in opposition to both Russia and several ethnic enclaves, various clanlike networks also existed at the end of the Soviet era and formed a basis for smaller-group mobilization. As in Tajikistan, the Georgian state's military units had traditionally been based on the rural clans of central Georgia.[43] While ethnic nationalism was a major element of the civil conflict, opposition to Zviad Gamsakhurdia's attempts to disrupt local clan and patronage networks also played a role in inciting and perpetuating the violence. Competing clans quickly entered the power vacuum and became the basis of militias and mafia groups during the Georgian civil war of the early 1990s.[44] No informal pact created a basis for power sharing among Georgian clans and other factions; competing clans fought over resources in the chaos of state collapse. Only the strong-handed leadership of Eduard Shevardnadze recentralized state control. A decade later, however, contradictory tendencies remain; the "Rose Revolution" of November 2003, led by Western-backed urban intellectuals, is a hopeful sign for the entire region, although full democratization and consolidation of the Georgian regime remain in the distance. The pull of the West has been strong, but personalistic networks remain significant, albeit weakened.

Chechnya has similarly experienced both ethno-national war and inter-clan violence. Chechen national identity, which was mobilized by Dzhokar Dudayev in the sovereignty movement that emerged in 1990, was formed only in the twentieth century; "Chechen identity" was a construct of the Soviet era as a result of Soviet nationalities policy, which sought to consolidate various Caucasian clans and tribes into a more socially advanced "Chechen nation."[45] Chechen national identity was forged, however, primarily as a result of Stalin's deportation and attempted genocide in 1944.[46]

[41] Tamara Dragazde, *Rural Families in Soviet Georgia* (London: Routledge, 1988).

[42] Darrell Slider, "Democratization in Georgia," in Dawisha and Parrott, eds., *Conflict, Cleavage, and Change*, pp. 156–200.

[43] See Fairbanks, "Weak States."

[44] Ghia Nodia, "Putting the State Back Together in Post-Soviet Georgia," in Beissinger and Young, eds., *Beyond State Crisis?*, pp. 413–444; Georgi Derlugian, panel presentation, University of North Carolina, April 12, 2003.

[45] Hirsch, "Empire of Nations," and Tishkov, *Chechnya*, p. 21–27.

[46] Norman M. Naimark, *Fires of Hatred: Ethnic Cleansing in Twentieth-Century Europe* (Cambridge, MA: Harvard University Press, 2001), pp. 92–97.

Valery Tishkov even argues that for many, a sense of "Chechenness" came only in the 1990s, during the war against Russia.[47] Even so, clan ties remain powerful bonds and networks in the north Caucasus, especially in rural and mountainous areas, and continue to coexist with Chechen nationalism.[48] Norman Naimark writes that "the strength of clan ties to their neighbors and their villages in the mountains and valleys of the region are deep and abiding, more so than to any idea of Chechen or Ingush 'nationhood,' separately or individually, or to particular territorial boundaries."[49] Like Akaev and Karimov, Dzhokar Dudayev emerged as the leader of the Chechen Congress in large part because he was seen as a good compromise candidate by various Chechen clans.[50] Anatol Lieven has discussed the sociocultural aspects of clan solidarities in Chechnya in great depth, noting both the meaningfulness of these social ties as well as the critical role that clan factionalism plays in exacerbating conflict *within* Chechnya, among Chechens, even as a larger national-secessionist war with Russia rages.[51] The intra-Chechen civil conflict became especially acute from 1997 to 1999, during the period between the first and second war with Russia, as the external threat that had united Chechen clans briefly receded. As in Tajikistan, the strength of clan identities also served a critical role in mobilizing and organizing groups, both in opposition to Russia and to each other. Their role in Chechnya mirrors the role that local clan networks played during the Tajik war. William Reno further argues that "in Chechnya, the collapse of state authority and its substitution by clan-based mafia and militias bear a close resemblance to African warlord conditions."[52]

Clans and clan politics are clearly not unique to Central Asia. Yet the question remains: are clans socially or politically relevant outside of the post-Soviet space, either historically or today? Addressing this question is important to understanding that clans and clan politics were not simply created by the Soviet state. Further, if clans are no longer relevant in other cases – as, for example, in Western Europe – then why and how have they been transformed or broken down? How might they be transformed today? Conclusive answers to these questions are beyond the scope of this study, since the empirical cases explored here are all cases of clan persistence and reemergence under colonial and post-colonial conditions. Moreover, cross-regional comparison risks stretching the concept of clan and not recognizing the specific peculiarities of these identity networks in each region. A brief

---

[47] Valery Tishkov, *Life in a War-Torn Society.*

[48] Nabi Abdullaev, "Letter from Dagestan: Guardians of the Peace," *Transitions Online*, February 13, 2002.

[49] Naimark, *Fires of Hatred*, p. 92.

[50] Anatol Lieven, *Chechnya: Tombstone of Russian Power* (New Haven, CT: Yale University Press, 1998), p. 58.

[51] Lieven, *Chechnya.*

[52] William Reno, "Mafia Troubles, Warlord Crises," in Beissinger and Young, eds., *Beyond State Crisis?*, pp. 105–129.

cross-regional comparison with those cases where the secondary literature discusses the role of clans, however, offers some insight into the questions just posed.

II. CLAN AND KINSHIP NETWORK PERSISTENCE IN PARTS OF AFRICA AND THE MIDDLE EAST

Some striking similarities in both the social organization and political trajectories of Central Asia and many African and Middle Eastern countries can be identified. A cross-regional comparison highlighting the role of clans and the mechanisms by which clan politics affects political regimes suggests the cross-regional relevance of this study for students of the developing world. This comparison contradicts the view of many policy makers, both inside and outside Central Asia, who have opted to view Central Asia as "European" (or at least "Eurasian"), and to apply to it the same lenses used to understand Poland, Hungary, or Lithuania. Such a comparison has also been resisted by most scholars, since it challenges the far more typical view of the former Soviet Union as a communist bloc with a unified cultural and political legacy. A noteworthy exception to this view is the recent volume by Mark Beissinger and Crawford Young, who stress the problems with state building common to post-colonial Africa and Eurasia, both regions shaped by their colonial legacies at both the formal and informal institutional levels.[53] One can push their comparison further and look at the similar pre-colonial, colonial, and post-colonial trajectories of these states in terms of state building, nation building, democratization, and political order. The Central Asian cases are arguably the most similar of the Eurasian set to Africa, in that they share many features of exploitative colonialism, including late state and national development and an economy of shortages.

In the 1960s and 1970s, Thomas Hodgekin and James S. Coleman powerfully argued that post-colonial Africa has been plagued by problems of particularistic tribal loyalties that have undermined nascent ideas of nationhood and weakened Africa's new states.[54] At the time, this view was seen by many

[53] Mark Beissinger and Crawford Young, "The Effective State in Postcolonial Africa and Post-Soviet Eurasia: Hopeless Chimera or Possible Dream," in Beissinger and Young, eds., *Beyond State Crisis?*, pp. 465–487.

[54] See Thomas Hodgekin, *Nationalism in Colonial Africa* (London: Frederick Muller, 1956); James Coleman, "Nationalism in Tropical Africa," *American Political Science Review*, vol. 48 (June 1954), pp. 404–426; James Coleman and Carl Rosberg, eds., *Political Parties and National Integration in Tropical Africa* (Berkeley: University of California, 1964); James Coleman, *Nigeria: Background to Nationalism* (Berkeley: University of California Press, 1958); Aristide Zolberg, *Creating Political Order* (Chicago: Rand McNally, 1966); James Coleman, *Nationalism and Development in Africa: Selected Essays*, ed. Richard Sklar (Berkeley: University of California Press, 1994); and Abner Cohen, *Custom and Politics in Urban Africa* (Berkeley: University of California Press, 1969).

scholars and policy makers – those who championed the new African nationalism and democratization – as exceedingly pessimistic, even as cultural primordialism.[55] Later generations of scholars, however, have acknowledged the importance of Coleman's stress on social organization, and have renewed the discussion of the role of tribes and social organization in political and economic development.[56] "Tribe" varies in meaning across Africa and the Middle East, but clans similar to the *subethnic* networks of Central Asia are relevant social and political actors in some cases. As I. M. Lewis has argued, to ignore the "clan system" is to impose a "Eurocentric ideological view of the world" on social phenomena in Africa.[57] However, rather than view these regions as culturally destined to a "tribal" disorder and authoritarianism, we can identify certain conditions, common also to the Central Asian cases, under which clan politics emerges and has a negative impact on political development. Moreover, in looking at African and Middle Eastern cases nearly half a century after decolonization, we become more aware of the potential downfalls and crises that may lie ahead for Central Asia if policy makers are not aware of them.

For the purposes of this study, we are primarily interested in those cases in which clans were a predominant social structure during the precolonial period. We can then explore the propositions set out in Chapter 2. Do clans persist in other regions under similar conditions? Does clan politics emerge and affect formal institutions and regime durability in similar patterns, through similar mechanisms? Not all African or Middle Eastern cases are relevant for this cross-regional analysis; because most states in sub-Saharan Africa are characterized by great ethnic and linguistic as well as tribal diversity, it would be an oversimplification to study all these cases primarily in terms of clan organization. The Middle Eastern cases, on the other

---

[55] More culturally determinist treatments include Colin Legum, "The Dangers of Independence," *Transition*, vol. 6/7 (October 1962), pp. 11–12; David Apter, *Ghana in Transition* (New York: Atheneum Publishers, 1963); and Aristide Zolberg, "The Structure of Political Conflict in the New States of Tropical Africa," *American Political Science Review*, vol. 62 (March 1968), pp. 70–87.

[56] See Atul Kohli, ed., *The State and Development in the Third World* (Princeton, NJ: Princeton University Press, 1986); David Laitin and Said Samatar, *Somalia: Nation in Search of a State* (Boulder, CO: Westview Press, 1986); Francis Deng, "Beyond Cultural Domination," in Beissinger and Young, eds., *Beyond State Crisis?*, pp. 359–384; William Reno, *Warlord Politics and African States* (Boulder, CO: Lynne Reinner Press, 1998). Historical economists studying Africa and the Middle East have likewise stressed the importance of communal identities and social organization. See Avner Greif, "Historical and Comparative Institutional Analysis," *The American Economic Review*, vol. 88, no. 2 (1998), pp. 80–84. For a recent institutionalist treatment of tribes and ethnicity in Africa, see Daniel Posner, "The Colonial Origins of Ethnic Cleavages," *Comparative Politics*, vol. 35, no. 2 (January 2003), pp. 127–146.

[57] I. M. Lewis, *A Pastoral Democracy* (London: Oxford University Press, 1961); I. M. Lewis, *A Modern History of the Somali*, rev. ed. (Athens: Ohio University Press, 2002), p. viii.

hand, are characterized by great ethnic homogeneity and by a social organization of subethnic (i.e., intra-Arab), tribal, and subtribal clan groups. Lisa Anderson and Mounira Charrad have studied the persistence and powerful effect of tribal groups on post-colonial political organization in Arab North Africa.[58] Andrew Shryock has examined the difficulties of creating a modern national identity in Jordan, because of powerful subethnic tribal factions.[59] However, the Middle Eastern cases are limited ones for comparison here, since they have generally not experienced regime transitions. Moreover, their oil resources make many Middle Eastern cases less comparable to the Central Asian ones (with the exception of Kazakhstan). Moreover, African and Middle Eastern decolonization and state building took place in an earlier historical context than decolonization in Eurasia. Nonetheless, two appropriate cases for comparison are Somalia and the Sudan, two countries in the horn of Africa, often seen as a bridge between the Middle East and Africa.

Both Somalia and the Sudan have historically been characterized by a clan and tribal social structure.[60] Somalia and northern (Arab) Sudan are more ethnically (culturally and linguistically) homogenous than most African states.[61] All Somalis trace their heritage to one common ancestor and nation and divide themselves into multiple intra-ethnic tribes and clans. In the Sudan, the north consists of various Arab tribes, while the south and West consist of an array of non-Arab tribes.[62] Both countries have experienced colonization, independence, and post-colonial political transition. Like Kyrgyzstan and Tajikistan, both have undergone decolonization followed by political liberalization and failed democratization. Like Uzbekistan, both experienced renewed socialist authoritarianism. And both later experienced regime breakdown and civil conflict, largely along clan and tribal

---

[58] Lisa Anderson, *The State and Social Transformation in Tunisia and Libya, 1830–1980* (Princeton, NJ: Princeton University Press, 1986); Mounira Charrad, *States and Women's Rights: The Making of Postcolonial Tunisia, Algeria, and Morocco* (Berkeley: University of California Press, 2001).

[59] Andrew Shryock, *Nationalism and the Genealogical Imagination* (Berkeley: University of California, 1997). See Philip Khoury and Joseph Kostiner, eds., *Tribes and State Formation in the Middle East* (Berkeley: University of California Press, 1990).

[60] See E. E. Evans-Pritchard, *The Nuer: A Description of the Modes of Livelihood and Political Institutions among a Nilotic People* (Oxford: Clarendon Press, 1940); Lewis, *A Pastoral Democracy*; Francis Deng, *War of Visions: Conflict of Identities in the Sudan* (Washington, DC: Brookings Institution Press, 1995); and Lewis, *A Modern History*.

[61] The case of Sudan is somewhat more complex, since the overarching conflict is a campaign of racial, ethnic, and religious cleansing as the northern government has attempted to Arabize and Islamicize the country since 1989. See Deng, *War of Visions*; and International Crisis Group, "God, Oil and Country: Changing the Logic of War in the Sudan," *Africa Report* No. 39, January 28, 2002 <http://www.icg.org/home/index.cfm?id=1230&l=1>.

[62] Douglas Hamilton Johnson, *The Root Causes of Sudan's Civil Wars* (Bloomington: Indiana University Press, 2003).

lines.[63] Due to space constraints, we will focus on the case of Somalia
here.

A Deeper Look at Somalia

Somalia has been studied extensively by anthropologists, ethnographers,
and political scientists, who generally agree that the clan-based social
organization of the country has presented special challenges for its political
development.[64] Like Central Asia's, Somalia's clan structure was not a creation of the colonial regime, but is rooted in centuries of pre-colonial social
and economic development. According to Lewis, the Somali people consist
of various levels of kin-based affective units, from large tribes to subtribes,
clans, subclans, and families.[65] Post-colonial Somalia consists of approximately six large tribes, some numbering about one million people. Although
tribal affiliations are well known, the subtribal clans and subclan units are
typically the groups that matter for political, social, and economic purposes.
The smaller units are characterized by dense ties, mutual reciprocity, and
trust, and can thus be more easily mobilized.[66] As Lewis notes, kin-based
networks were a fundamental part of pre-colonial Somalia, both in the pastoral and agricultural regions, and even in the urban commercial centers.
The tribal and clan structure had both rational and normative elements; it
reflected both economic necessity and deeply ingrained cultural, social, and
political norms based on kinship loyalties.[67]

Beginning in the latter nineteenth century, European colonialism forced
distinct regimes upon the Somali tribes and divided their land into Italian
and British territories.[68] Some colonizers ignored clans, while others utilized
them. British rule fostered clans, advancing some at the expense of others
by explicitly creating salaried state positions for clan leaders. The British
used these leaders as a source of control over the indigenous population, but

---

[63] Author discussions with UNDP personnel, Khartoum, Sudan, July 2003. In the Sudan, the
civil war has various other dimensions, including ethnic and religious discrimination on the
part of the Arab and Islamic fundamentalist regime of General Bashir. Nonetheless, intertribal
conflict, in both the north and the south, has pitted kin-based tribal groups against each other
as they compete for land and herds. The government, moreover, has exploited, intensified,
and even created intertribal conflict by arming various pro-government Arab tribes. On the
tribal dimension, see International Crisis Group, "Sudan's Other Wars," *Africa Briefing*,
June 25, 2003 <http://www.icg.org/home/index.cfm?id=1230&l=1>.

[64] David D. Laitin and Said S. Samatar, *Somalia: Nation in Search of a State* (Boulder, CO:
Westview, 1987); Catherine Besteman, *Unraveling Somalia* (Philadelphia: University of Penn-
sylvania Press, 1999).

[65] On affective ties in Africa and Asia, see Donald Horowitz, *Ethnic Groups in Conflict*
Berkeley: University of California Press, 1985), pp. 55–63.

[66] Lewis, *A Modern History*.

[67] Ibid.

[68] The French also controlled part of Somali territory; after independence, it became the republic
of Djibouti, not part of a unified Somalia.

also – like the Soviets – gave clan elites access to state resources. In doing so, they created a system of "indirect rule" that allowed the clan system to adapt and persist.[69] Since the British rulers were not interested in economic, social, or political development, clans generally continued to live according to their traditional way of life. The Italians, on the other hand, attempted to introduce some limited elements of industrialization and agriculture. In preparation for independence, they imposed Western political institutions, ignoring the contradictions with underlying Somali clan traditions.[70] Italian development, however, was far less extensive than Soviet modernization. Clan networks in urban areas were weakened, as a class of state bureaucrats and commercial traders developed. In other areas, more traditional clan ties remained central to the social fabric. Unlike the Soviets, the colonial rulers did not seek to destroy clans. Across Somalia, to varying degrees, clan organization continued to maintain many of its traditional roles in providing both sustenance in poor and uncertain economic conditions and an informal but stable political order. As anticipated in Chapter 2, late state and national development, especially under conditions of weak colonial rule and an economy of shortages, enabled and fostered clan persistence into the modern era; in the case of Somalia, clans persisted well into the second half of the twentieth century without experiencing any repression of traditional practices. That only came with the post-colonial regimes. We should anticipate, therefore, that clan identity would play an even greater role in post-colonial Somalia than in Central Asia.

Decolonization and statehood, mandated by the United Nations in 1960, initiated major changes for Somalia, just as for Central Asia. Somali nationalism, however, did not begin with independence. David Laitin and Said Samatar note that a deep cultural sense of the "Somali nation," based on kinship ties, was historically rooted in the Somali people of all tribes.[71] In this sense, the Somali nation had more indigenous, historical roots than did the Soviet-created nations of Central Asia. Somali nationalism first manifested itself politically in the anti-colonial Dervish movement of the early 1900s, although it failed to attract a mass following. It again emerged in the wake of World War II, as Somalis demanded independence and unification. However, political nationalism was largely the product of urban elites. For ordinary Somalis, nationalism only provided a temporary call to unity during the transition from colonial rule. "In the heady days prior to independence, it became fashionable to speak of a man's ex-clan[,] ... nationalist solidarity became a *façon de parler*," and the pre-independence

[69] Deng, "Beyond Cultural," p. 377.
[70] Robert L. Hess, *Italian Colonialism in Somalia* (Chicago: University of Chicago Press, 1966); Paolo Tripodi, *The Colonial Legacy in Somalia* (London: Macmillan Press, 1999), pp. 104–105.
[71] Laitin and Samatar, *Somalia*.

habit of reference to one's clan affiliation was extirpated from political discourse.[72]

Clan loyalties coexisted with the new nationalism even after independence. Indeed, the British urged careful attention to balancing clan interests and representation within the new government.[73] An informal agreement to include the major clan factions within the new government, and to preserve the traditional Somali principle of "balancing" clans, was critical to transitional and post-transitional stability, just as in Central Asia. Yet clan balancing became a substitute for solving the country's economic and political problems.[74] However, not long after independence and unification in the new Somalia, clan divisions emerged as a major source of political factionalism, despite the overarching idea of Somali nationhood. During the post-colonial period, clan and tribal divisions reemerged. This first occurred very openly under the democratizing regime of the 1960s. Political parties, whose development had been encouraged by the departing Italian colonial power, were typically based on clans. These "clan-parties" proliferated and created a chaos of particularistic factionalism in the new parliament.[75] While clan loyalties did not replace nationalism and were not overtly antithetical to democracy, they did weaken the fledgling institutions in many respects.[76] As in Kyrgyzstan in the early 1990s, new democratic institutions were imposed upon Somali culture and social organization in the early post-colonial years, and did not quickly or evenly transform it. Although elements of pluralism initially flourished, the democratizing system allowed clan factionalism and its traditional mechanisms of clan patronage and nepotism to penetrate the new state and regime.[77] Those clans and elites with access to power did not evenly distribute resources to those without access. Under the national democratic system, such practices were increasingly viewed as corrupt pillaging of the desperately poor state.

On October 21, 1969, General Siyaad Barre rose to power in a military coup, backed by popular disgust with the chaos, corruption, and nepotism of clan factionalism masked as democracy.[78] Barre promised to create order and a fair, transparent system. He did so, however, by creating a brutal military dictatorship that banned clan identities and nepotistic practices and attempted to forcibly modernize society according to the principle of "scientific socialism," drawn from the Soviet model. Just as the Soviet

[72] Lewis, *A Modern History*, p. 92.
[73] Laitin and Samatar, *Somalia*, p. 76.
[74] Ibid., p. 70; A. A. Castagno, "The Political Party System in the Somali Republic: A Balancing Coalitional Approach," in James S. Coleman and C. G. Rosberg, eds., *Political Parties and National Integration in Tropical Africa* (Berkeley: University of California Press, 1964), pp. 512–559.
[75] Lewis, *A Modern History*, p. 146–147; Laitin and Samatar, *Somalia*, p. 76.
[76] Laitin and Samatar, *Somalia*, pp. 90–91.
[77] Ibid., pp. 70–76.
[78] Lewis, *A Modern History*, pp. 402–403; Laitin and Samatar, *Somalia*, pp. 76, 90.

model had failed, so too did Barre's modernization schemes and socialist dictatorship; in fact, Barre's did so more quickly. His socialist plans imposed an unprofitable economic system upon an economy already characterized by chronic shortages. The political system engendered informal resistance. In facing the reality of governing Somalia, Barre himself retreated from socialist principles. Barre eventually moved from "class rule" to "clan rule," from Soviet-style *nomenklatura* to "clan-kultura."[79] Thus, unlike the Central Asian republics, where clans remained repressed or in the informal and underground realm until socialism collapsed, Barre informally adopted a system of clan rule well before a formal regime transition. Barre's dictatorship was based upon a coalition of three clans to which he was related by blood or marriage. Known as the MOD, this coalition included the Mareehaan, the Ogaadeen, and the Dulbahante. Like the Central Asian leaders, Barre ensured that the military and security services were under his clan connections.[80] Like Karimov, Barre also skillfully appointed individuals from other clans, so long as they were removed from the elite political networks of those competing clans.[81] This gave the regime an outward semblance of balancing clan interests. Kinship and particularism, not ideology or bureaucratic institutions, defined Somali rule. In rural areas, meanwhile, Barre encouraged clan conflict as a means of weakening any opposition; this policy would have serious repercussions after Barre's fall from power.[82]

As Barre became increasingly worried about opposition and threats of a coup, he relied ever more on his own personal clan, edging others from power. His clan captured the regime and state, not unlike the situation in Tajikistan under Nabiev in 1991. Although this system lasted for twenty years, it was fragile and unstable. No mechanism of succession was in place. But his monopoly was precarious. With the end of the cold war and the collapse of the Soviet Union, Somalia, like Tajikistan, lost a significant source of its regime patronage. Somalia too would experience a shock to its regime that would unseat Barre's hegemony and ultimately catapult the fragile system into civil war.

The post-Barre era has been one of regime and state collapse and intense interclan conflict.[83] The clan coalition that had formed in opposition to Barre in the 1980s broke down, and different clans backed or formed militia groups.[84] The war from 1989 to 2000 exhibited the most negative political

---

[79] Hussein Adam, "Somalia: A Terrible Beauty Being Born?" in William Zartman, ed., *Collapsed States: The Disintegration and Restoration of Legitimate Authority* (Boulder, CO: Lynne Rienner Press, 1997), p. 76.

[80] Adam, "Somalia," p. 72.

[81] Laitin and Samatar, *Somalia*, pp. 156–157.

[82] Adam, "Somalia," p. 77.

[83] I. M. Lewis, "Clan Conflict and Ethnicity in Somalia," in David Turton, ed., *War and Ethnicity: Global Connections and Local Violence* (San Marino, CA: Center for Interdisciplinary Research on Social Stress, 1997), pp. 179–200.

[84] Tripodi, *Colonial Legacy*, pp. 138–139.

trajectory to appear under conditions of a weak state and declining economic conditions; as in Tajikistan, clan elites increasingly competed for declining resources, manipulated interclan relations, and mobilized their clan followings to violence.[85] Warlordism came to rule Somalia. While Russia played a major stabilizing role in Tajikistan in 1997 and after, in Somalia the regional powers have exacerbated the conflict. Despite extensive international intervention and peace negotiations involving both the United States and the UN, and despite internationally sponsored presidential elections in 2003, political order has still not been restored.[86]

Somalia, although one of the clearest cases of clan politics in Africa, is not the only one. Many other African cases have exhibited similar phenomena, as post-colonial democratizing regimes have become patronage systems in which "elected politicians become benefactors to their kin group or ethnic constituencies,"[87] depending on the social structure of the case. Moreover, this patronage of kin ties occurs "as a response to the objective realities of the socioeconomic conditions of Africa today."[88] These particularistic patronage relationships have become a principal mechanism by which clans can penetrate the regime and strip state assets. Post-colonial African systems have widely been weakened by the informal politics of patronage and the related rise in corruption. Many have factionalized and divided along clan, tribal, or ethnic lines.[89] Somalia, like Tajikistan, represents the path from clan hegemony to regime breakdown. Not all clan-based societies and states, however, end in negative political outcomes, as the following contrast with early modern Europe demonstrates.

III. THE DECLINE OF CLANS IN WESTERN EUROPE

Early State Formation, Nation Building, and Market Development

This study has empirically focused primarily on the Central Asian cases, which have exhibited the persistence of clans, the rise of clan politics, and, to varying extents, negative political trajectories. Hence, while this work

---

[85] Florence Ssereo, "Clan Politics, Clan Democracy, and Conflict Regulation in Africa: The Experience of Somalia," *The Global Review of Ethnopolitics*, vol. 2, no. 3–4 (March/June 2003), pp. 25–40.

[86] International Crisis Group, "Somaliland: Democratisation and Its Discontents," *Africa Report* No. 66, July 28, 2003 <http://www.icg.org/home/index.cfm?id=1232&l=1>.

[87] Deng, "Beyond Cultural," p. 379. Robert Price observes this phenomenon and its negative effect on state building in Ghana. See Robert Price, *Society and Bureaucracy in Contemporary Ghana* (Berkeley: University of California Press, 1975).

[88] Deng, "Beyond Cultural," p. 379.

[89] Donald Rothchild, *Managing Ethnic Conflict in Africa* (Washington, DC: Brookings Institution Press, 1997). See also Michael Bratton and Nicholas Van deWalle, *Democratic Experiments in Africa: Regime Transitions in Comparative Perspective* (Cambridge: Cambridge University Press, 1997).

opens up the question of "what breaks clans down," it cannot fully answer it. Nonetheless, the propositions advanced here offer a partial answer, in that they enable us to contrast the path of Central Asia (and the Caucasus, Africa, and the Middle East), where we find clan persistence, with that of Europe, where subnational clan identities and networks and their informal politics generally disappeared under strong states well before the twentieth century. The conditions that allowed and fostered clan persistence in the Central Asian cases, Somalia, and the Sudan – late state formation, late national identity formation, and an economy of shortages – differ sharply from the conditions in cases where clans did not persist into the twentieth century, or only weakly persisted, as in early modern Western Europe. Just as the rise of clan politics is an historically path-dependent process, so too is clan breakdown or transformation.

In order to explain better why clans persist into the modern period in Central Asia, I look briefly at clans in Western Europe in an effort to understand the conditions under which clans break down. As argued in Chapter 1, it is not simply modernization – in the form of literacy and urbanization – that causes clan ties to decline or disappear. If this were true, we should have seen their demise in Soviet Central Asia and their persistence in southern Italy.

Historians have observed that clans and kinship networks were once a form of social organization in contemporary Great Britain (especially Scotland), Ireland, France, Greece, and Italy. Comparing the Central Asian states to those of Western Europe highlights three factors that contributed to the decline of kinship networks in the latter region but not in the former. First, in contrast to Central Asia, the West European cases noted here each underwent an earlier process of state building and state formation that generally preceded democratization. The monarchies and imperial dynasties that characterized these political systems had deep, indigenous roots that developed over the course of centuries.[90] In Western Europe, state consolidation – including the establishment of state boundaries and the collection of tax revenues – was beginning as early as the fifteenth and sixteenth centuries.[91] State making was driven by wars of territorial conquest, because land and resources were scarce and population density was high.[92] Boundaries were formed by military consolidation, not by the whims of colonial powers.

---

[90] Charles Tilly, *Coercion, Capital, and European States, 990–1990* (Cambridge, MA: Blackwell, 1990); Benedict Anderson, *Imagined Communities*, 2nd ed. (London: Verso, 1991).

[91] Charles Tilly, "Reflections on the History of European State-Making," in Charles Tilly, ed., *The Formation of National States in Western Europe* (Princeton, NJ: Princeton University Press, 1975), pp. 3–83. To some extent, this argument could be made of several East Asian cases, such as South Korea and Japan, where kinship networks also declined with the rise of strong states and national identities.

[92] Herbst, *State and Power*, pp. 13–15, contrasts these conditions in Europe with those in sub-Saharan Africa, where population density was low and land plentiful. Herbst's characterization of Africa applies in large part to Central Asia as well.

State making through war making linked urban centers and rural territories and gradually forged national-state formation. As Charles Tilly writes, "the Europe of 1500 had a kind of cultural homogeneity only rivaled, at such a geographic scale, by that of China. The unification of the Roman Empire had produced some convergence of language, law, religion, administrative practice, agriculture, landholding, and perhaps kinship as well."[93] By contrast, Tilly continues, "in 1500 Celts and Basques held out in the north and west, Magyars and Mongols in the east, Turks and other Muslims in the south."[94] Already by the early modern period, the imperial states of Europe had emerged as relatively autonomous from the peasants and urban traders who comprised the majority of the society.[95] By contrast, state formation in Central Asia, as in Africa and parts of the Middle East, began in the twentieth century. To some extent, state formation began in 1924, with the national delimitation of the Central Asian republics by the Soviet government. In most respects, however, state formation began in 1991, after the Soviet collapse, when these states were given independence for the first time in modern history.

Second, in Europe, early state formation together with early industrialization also fostered the decline of pre-national forms of social organization and the relatively early formation of nation states and national identities. Tilly writes that the peoples of Europe already shared "fragments of a common political tradition" and culturally and socially differed from the nomadic and tribal peoples in other regions. "In a large part of the area [Europe] a single family system predominated; bilateral descent leading to the diffuse kindred (rather than a corporate group like the lineage) as the chief larger kinship unit, tendency towards a nuclear family residence, small households, relatively late marriage, frequent celibacy, and consequently moderate birth rates."[96] Together with the decline of pre-modern social organization, nationality formation was associated with a homogenization of language and culture throughout the population. As Benedict Anderson has argued, a strong state was increasingly able to impose linguistic unity through the use of capitalism, technology, and mass print media, which led to the rise of "national print-languages." Over time, a shared language and culture emerged, together with a myth – forged by elites and intellectuals – of an ancient ethnic lineage and ancestral rights to the land of the nation-state. The formation of British, French, Dutch, Spanish, Portugese, German, and

---

[93] Tilly, "European State-Making," p. 18.
[94] Ibid.
[95] Theda Skocpol, *States and Social Revolutions* (Cambridge: Cambridge University Press, 1979); Peter Evans, *Embedded Autonomy: States and Industrial Transformation* (Princeton, NJ: Princeton University Press, 1995).
[96] Tilly, "European State-Making," p. 18. On post-Enlightenment changes in the family and kinship in Western Europe, see Eileen Hunt, *Family Feuds: Wollstonecraft, Burke and Rousseau on the Transformation of the Family*, in press, 2004.

Irish national identities began approximately four centuries ago.[97] Even the Scots, infamous for being a fragmented nation of rival highlander clans, often the basis of internecine warfare, saw the decline of clan identities. By the late seventeenth century, high literacy, nationalism, and economic modernization and social transformation had fostered this change. By the nineteenth century, Scottish clans had declined in influence and become little more than the subject of culture and Walter Scott's fiction.[98]

A third factor that led to social change and clan breakdown in the West was the early development of a capitalist economy. According to Tilly, the growth of trade links between cities and rural and urban centers in Europe, and an increasingly commercialized European economy, were the foundation of early, strong states.[99] Although Tilly does not write specifically of market economies as opposed to socialist ones, implicit in his discussion of European state development is the assumption that a growing market economy provided the basis for tax revenue, which in turn supported military development and state consolidation. Furthermore, political liberalization was often linked to the desire of economic elites to find protection via a state that could guarantee economic rights through "credible commitments."[100] Barrington Moore's classic argument about the importance of the bourgeoisie comes to mind. In Europe, to a greater or lesser extent, the state emerged as the protector of economic interests and capitalist growth. "As rulers bargained directly with the subject populations for taxes, military service, and cooperation in state programs, most states took further steps of profound importance: a movement toward direct rule that reduced the role of local or regional patrons and placed representatives of the national state in every community, and expansion of popular consultation in the form of elections, plebiscites, and legislatures."[101] In doing so, the state usurped the traditional functions of clans and their patronage networks in an economy of scarcity and a political system where institutions could not guarantee credible commitments.

---

[97] See Benedict Anderson, *Imagined Communities* (London: Verso, 1991), especially Chapter 3; Eugen Weber, *Peasants into Frenchmen* (London: Chatto and Windus, 1979); and E. J. Hobsbawm, *Nations and Nationalism Since 1780* (Cambridge: Cambridge University Press, 1990). Bruce Cummings makes a similar argument about early national identity formation in Korea, where clan lineages were also once pervasive. Korea had formed a national identity based on shared language and culture well before the colonization of the Japanese.

[98] See Arthur Herman, *How the Scots Invented the Modern World* (New York: Crown Business Press, 2001); and Thomas Cairney, *Clans and Families of Ireland and Scotland: An Ethnography of the Gael, 500–1750* (Jefferson, NC: McFarland Press, 1989). Thanks to Phil Coustopolous for this point.

[99] See Tilly, *Coercion*; and Herbst, *State and Power*, pp. 13–15.

[100] Avner Greif, Paul Milgrom, and Barry R. Weingast, "Coordination, Commitment and Enforcement: The Case of the Merchant Guild," *The Journal of Political Economy*, vol. 102, no. 4 (August 1994), pp. 745–776.

[101] Tilly, *Coercion*, p. 63, cited in Herbst, *State and Power*, p. 14.

To some extent, the informal norms of clannish ties and extensive familial networks remain important even in democratic and capitalist states. Politics in the later-developing European states, such as Greece and Italy (especially southern Italy),[102] and likewise in South Korea and Taiwan in East Asia, is rife with patronage and clientelism, often on the basis of kin and per- sonalistic networks.[103] These states share some features of the late political development seen in Central Asia. I will trace the case of Italy here, since it exemplifies the conditions for clan persistence into the modern era as well as their transformation and decline. On the one hand, Italy's process of political and economic development represents one hopeful scenario for the future of Central Asia. On the other hand, Italy's low-quality democracy, plagued by clientelism in the south, emerged by a long and arduous path.

A Deeper Look at Italy, North and South

Medieval and early modern Italian history, both of the north and of the south, was characterized by strong family ties and clan networks that pervaded both economics and politics. Historical studies of the north have focused on the role of clan networks in politics and economics, even in Florence and Genoa, cities known both then and today to be among the most developed and ad- vanced in Italy. In the south, clans pervaded the more rural social structure, with elite clans dominating the landed estates of a feudal agricultural sys- tem, and poor kinship and village networks working as serfs. Clan patronage of their own kin kept wealth and political power within a restricted class. Despite the severe social inequalities, patronage and the creation of fictive identity ties between wealthy and poorer clans within an estate or village defined the social system. Change in these social networks occurred slowly.

---

[102] Italy is also a case of relatively late nation-state formation. Southern Italy, in particular, retained a more fragmented and traditional social structure. See Sidney Tarrow, *Peasant Communism in Southern Italy* (New Haven, CT: Yale University Press, 1967); and Robert Putnam, *Making Democracy Work* (Princeton, NJ: Princeton University Press, 1993). On the continued influence of clan-based clientelism and mafias, see Judith Chubb, *The Mafia and Politics: The Italian State under Siege* (Ithaca, NY: Cornell University Press, 1989); and Diego Gambetta, *The Sicilian Mafia* (Cambridge, MA: Harvard University Press, 1993). Susan Rose-Ackerman, *Corruption and Government* (Cambridge: Cambridge University Press, 1999), pp. 121–122, notes that kinship and trust strengthens mafia organizations.

[103] Although Korea has a centuries-old history of an ethno-national identity and pre-modern state development, Japan's colonization interrupted Korea's state development until the mid-twentieth century, when decolonization took place. Economic sociologists and politi- cal scientists have observed the importance of clannish familial networks in contemporary Korean politics and business. See Marco Orru, Nicole Biggart, and Gary Hamilton, eds., *The Economic Organization of East Asian Capitalism* (Thousand Oaks, CA: Sage Publica- tions, 1997); Larry Diamond and Doh Chull Shin, eds., *Institutional Reform and Demo- cratic Consolidation in Korea* (Stanford, CA: Hoover Institution Press, 2000); and David Kang, *Crony Capitalism: Corruption and Development in South Korea and the Philippines* (Cambridge: Cambridge University Press, 2002), pp. 53–54.

Indeed, the disappearance of clans in some areas and their decline and transformation into more narrow particularistic ties took place over centuries. It did so in the context of the growth of capitalism and the end of feudalism, national unification, state building, and ultimately Italy's post–World War II integration into Western Europe. Still, political and economic change occurred more rapidly in northern than in southern Italy.

Late State Development, National Formation, and Market Development. Italy lagged behind Western Europe in nation-state formation. Much like Central Asia, Italy, especially southern Italy, experienced frequent invasion and colonization that thwarted state formation and political and economic development. Greeks, Romans, Vandals, Goths, Byzantines, Arabs, Normans, Germans, Angevins, Catalans, the Hapsburgs, the Bourbons, and the Papacy invaded or controlled southern Italy at various points through the mid-nineteenth century.[104] The church also maintained a feudal-like grasp over large parts of the south-central Italian peninsula. The northern regions of Italy, by contrast, developed as independent city-states during much of the medieval and early modern period. Different dialects of Italian and French were spoken in distinct parts of the peninsula in the 1800s; indeed, Italy lacked a strong national identity until Mussolini came to power. The birth of the Italian state, which at last integrated the fragmented city-states of the north and the former "Kingdom of the Two Sicilies" and church territories of central-southern Italy, occurred in 1861, later than state formation in the rest of Western Europe. Rome was finally annexed in 1870. At that time, literacy levels were low and industrialization virtually nonexistent. Although the north was more economically advanced than the south, and had been at least since the medieval period, only in the mid to late 1800s did industrialization begin in the commercial and trading centers of the north. As the contrast between the north and the south illustrates, even within a nation-state we see the persistence of a fractured social system into the twentieth century. Feudal economic conditions in the south, as in Central Asia, would facilitate clan transformation into particularistic patronage networks and mafias that continue to inhibit economic growth and political (especially democratic) equality and representation. Thriving market economic conditions in the north led to social transformation and fostered the development of a civic culture.

The Decline of Clan Politics and the Rise of Republicanism in the North. A brief discussion of northern Italy highlights the conditions under which clan networks declined. Exhaustive research by John Padgett on the medieval and early modern period has shown that "in the late medieval era

---

[104] Clifford Backman, *The Decline and Fall of Medieval Sicily* (Cambridge: Cambridge University Press, 1995), pp. 13–16.

[1200s–1348], patrilineage (aggregated into fluid factions) was the core recruitment network into Florentine political office" as well as in the flourishing banking system.[105] Interclan struggles and intrigue often led to bloody
strife.[106] Guild succeeded patrilineage during the so-called guild-corporatist
regime of the early Florentine republic (1349–78).[107] The subsequent era of
politics was defined by the *popolani* social class logic, known in part for
oligarchic networks and in part for an emphasis on state service. These reformed network ties consisted not only of kin but also of close friendship
and marital alliances. Avner Greif's analysis of Genoese and Pisan Italian
clans complements Padgett's study of evolving kinship networks. The decline of clan politics and interclan warfare took place in conditions of both
mutual threat (from other clans or from northern invaders) and the potential for mutually increasing economic gains. Clan elites sought to preserve
and protect their gains, and therefore made pacts with each other to protect themselves and their resources. As the external threat declined, interclan
competition over resource accumulation resumed, and interclan war again
erupted, leading to "disorder, disintegration, and large economic cost,"[108] as
in Tajikistan in 1992. Not until a new balance of clans and renewed external
threat coincided did interclan cooperation resume.

Having learned from their previous experience of breakdown, Greif
demonstrates that clans, in a new pact, created a novel political institution, the *podesteria* (governing institution of the executive broker), designed to peacefully manage conflict and balance the interests and financial resources of each main clan faction. The *podesta* – like the presidents informally appointed by the perestroika-era pacts in Central Asia –
should have no internal clan ties, so that he could bargain between clans and
be trusted to establish a mutual defense force. As the conditions for cooperation continued, the *podesteria* fostered economic growth and eventually
became institutionalized as a political system throughout the communes of
northern Italy.[109] The need for clans to represent or defend the individual
declined.[110] The *podesteria*, as in Kazakhstan, had the potential to consolidate its own power by reaping the wealth of military victory or economic
growth, and in turn to undermine clan power. In Florence, for example, the

[105] John Padgett and Christopher Ansell, "Robust Action and the Rise of the Medici, 1400–
    1434," *American Journal of Sociology*, vol. 98, no. 6 (May 1993), pp. 1265–1267; John
    Padgett, "Organizational Genesis, Identity, and Control: The Transformation of Banking
    in Renaissance Florence," in James Rauch and Alessandra Casella, eds., *Networks and
    Markets* (New York: Russell Sage Foundation, 2001), pp. 237.
[106] Putnam, *Making Democracy Work*, pp. 131–132.
[107] Padgett, "Organizational Genesis."
[108] Avner Greif, "Self-Enforcing Political Systems and Economic Growth: Late Medieval
    Genoa," in Robert Bates et al., *Analytic Narratives* (Princeton, NJ: Princeton University
    Press, 1998), p. 43.
[109] Daniel Waley, *The Italian City-Republics* (New York: Longman, 1988).
[110] Giovanni Tabacco, *The Struggle for Power in Medieval Italy* (Cambridge: Cambridge Uni-
    versity Press, 1989).

Medici clan filled the role of *podesta* and used the threat of war to unite clans behind the regime. The Medici clan created a personalistic family oligarchy and used "extreme patronage" through the Medici party to gain loyalty and exert control over the populace.[111] A growing economy helped consolidate Medici power. In Genoa, by contrast, the ruling clans chose a *podesta* from outside Genoa, paid him a high salary, instituted a term limit, and forbade him to marry a Genoese; the Genoese governor had no clan ties, and thus had less ability to gain control of the regime.[112] In both these republics, the new governors brought in "new men" of the bourgeoisie as their clients, and thereby undermined the traditional clan notables.

The decline of clan organization and conflict was far from even or unilinear in northern Italy. Yet between the fifteenth and nineteenth centuries, the north continued to develop economically as a trading center for Europe under a liberal market. Clan and kinship ties were increasingly supplanted by weaker oligarchical networks.[113] By the 1800s, a flourishing private economy and the dispersal of wealth furthered individualism and social transformation. "Mutual aid societies" and other individualistic, autonomous, and "horizontal" ties developed, and republican norms flourished.[114] In short, the north, a region once characterized by pervasive clan networks, saw "revolutionary changes in the fundamental institutions of politics and economics."[115] Gradual social and political liberalization continued in the north, in marked contrast to the south. By the time of the twentieth-century democratic transition, the north was fertile ground for a democratic civil society and government.[116]

From Patrilineal Clans to Clientelism in the South. Southern Italian clans were historically known for their grasp on the land. Frederick III's colonial rule of the "Kingdom of Sicily" during the thirteenth and fourteenth centuries reinforced a feudal system characterized by elite kin and clan rivalries and their exploitation of the peasantry, at a time when clan politics was declining in the north. In Sicily's urban and rural areas, certain powerful networks became embedded in court and baronial politics, bolstered by the king's support. The practice of collective patrimony and intermarriage among powerful families solidified the power of certain clans. As in Central Asia today, "economic strength and political influence amounted to much the same thing."[117] Clans developed self-defense mechanisms as well. For example, one particularly powerful kin group, "the Rossos, showed this

[111] Padgett and Ansell, "Rise of Medici," pp. 1262, 1304–1306; and Padgett, "Organizational Genesis," pp. 237–38. Eventually, the Medici clan system broke down into conflict.
[112] Greif, "Self-Enforcing Political Systems," pp. 53–54.
[113] Waley, *Italian City*.
[114] Putnam, *Making Democracy*, p. 138.
[115] Ibid., p. 129.
[116] Ibid.
[117] Backman, *Decline and Fall*, p. 136.

intense spirit of protecting themselves by any means available.... the Rosso clan were notorious landlords who never hesitated ... to capitalize on their access to privileged information and local channels of power. During the last two decades of Frederick's reign they kept a large corps of armed thugs who served as bodyguards."[118] Frederick maintained a weakly institutionalized stability, but his death was followed by a savage series of civil wars among the petty lords for control of the resources of the countryside. Most historians agree that Sicily never recovered prior to unification, and that its economic backwardness, internecine family rivalries, and mafia are rooted in this period.[119] Even after unification, the south remained a primarily agricultural, feudal system.

Although feudalism had been officially abolished under Napoleonic rule (1805–15), feudal relations, patriarchal village networks, and intense localism persisted in the south. Moreover, a severe economy of shortages emerged as a result of the liquidation of feudalism. Chubb writes that "the peasant found his plight under freedom, if anything, more desperate."[120] The introduction of a market economy, without social or economic modernization, reinforced the already substantial obstacles to industrialization, class formation, and the transformation of social relations.[121] A new bourgeoisie was too small to compete with the post-feudal notables. Although mobility and urbanization led to the gradual decline of the traditional patrilineal village by the 1860s, patron-client ties intensified. The post-colonial, post-feudal "liberal era" of 1860–1922 was characterized by the development of "cliques or factions built around the figure of a 'notable' and his personal following."[122] Notables with access to parliament and the state doled out particularistic benefits and rewards to their kin and clientele, while the masses were largely excluded. Like traditional notables, they had little incentive to change the system. The state became an "immense spoils system for the maintenance and enrichment of personal clienteles.... The organization of politics around personality and patronage rather than ideas and practical programs not only absorbed and neutralized the opposition, but ultimately emptied the concept of 'party' of any meaning beyond that of a loose congeries of personal clienteles."[123] Exclusivist and often exploitative "vertical networks" continued to characterize the south's political economy and inhibited the development of alternative social organization or mass movements.[124] According to Robert Putnam, even under the initial democratization of 1919–22 parties were

[118] Backman, *Decline and Fall*, p. 136.
[119] Ibid.
[120] Judith Chubb, *Patronage, Power, and Poverty in Southern Italy: A Tale of Two Cities* (Cambridge: Cambridge University Press, 1982).
[121] Chubb, *Patronage*, pp. 18–19; Tarrow, *Peasant Communism*.
[122] Ibid.
[123] Chubb, *Patronage*, pp. 20–21.
[124] Putnam, *Making Democracy Work*, p. 138.

weakest in the south, where clientelism was strongest and "state patronage was bartered (via local notables) [not democratic parties] for electoral support."[125] Chubb and Putnam could have been writing of Kyrgyzstan in the 1990s. Conditions in southern Italy had changed little by the 1940s, when a full democratic system was first introduced.

Italy's Transition to Democracy. The failure of democratization during the early interwar period and the subsequent rise of fascism are not subjects that can be treated in depth here. Scholars note that the lack of a social base for democracy facilitated the rise of the fascist regime.[126] Ultimately, fascism delayed democratization until after Mussolini's defeat in World War II. This time democracy survived, albeit with many problems. The post-war era proved to be a fruitful time for democratization, as economic growth throughout Western Europe took off. Italy in 1945 was a fledgling democracy and agrarian economy with industrial enclaves, mostly in the north. By 1980, Italy was a stable democracy with an advanced industrial economy, albeit one plagued by inefficiency and corruption. Thirty-five years of rapid economic growth led to socioeconomic change in both the north and the south – growth fed in large part by the Marshall Plan after 1945, and later by Italy's integration into the European market. Along with economic modernization and agrarian reform in the 1950s came higher levels of education, improved living standards, and a decline in the birth rate.[127] Changes in culture and social structure followed; Italy saw a decline in religiosity and a decline in traditional extended family, kin, and village networks. Sidney Tarrow writes that "however unbalanced the Italian growth mechanism, it moved millions of people into roles in urban society in which they were released from the control of the landlord, the parish priest, and the weight of inherited traditions."[128] At the same time, social networks were slow to change; Joseph La Palombara observed in the 1960s that "primary associations are still dominant; family, kinship, neighborhood, village are still the associational forms that have the greatest call to individual loyalty."[129] Gabriel Almond

---

[125] Ibid., p. 142.
[126] See Sidney Tarrow, "Mass Mobilization and Regime Change: Pacts, Reform, and Popular Power in Italy (1918–1922)," in Richard Gunther, P. Nikiforos Diamandouros, and Jürgen Puhle, eds., *The Politics of Democratic Consolidation* (Baltimore, MD: The Johns Hopkins University Press, 1995), pp. 204–230; and Paolo Farneti, "Social Conflict, Parliamentary Fragmentation, Institutional Shift, and the Rise of Fascism: Italy," in Juan Linz and Alfred Stepan, eds., *The Breakdown of Democratic Regimes* (Baltimore: Johns Hopkins University Press, 1978), pp. 3–33.
[127] Sidney Tarrow, "Crisis, Crises, or Transition?" in Peter Lange and Sidney Tarrow, eds., *Italy in Transition* (London: Frank Cass, 1980), p. 168.
[128] Ibid., p. 169.
[129] Joseph La Palombara, *Interest Groups in Italian Politics* (Princeton, NJ: Princeton University Press, 1964), p. 38, cited in Tarrow, *Peasant Communism*, p. 54. In contrast to Edward Banfield's "amoral familism," both Tarrow and La Palombara find, as I have argued of

and Sidney Verba's cross-national study *The Civic Culture* of the late 1950s "found little sign of a 'civic' political culture in Italy" about ten years after its democratic constitution had been adopted; but by 1980, civic involvement, especially of the younger generation, had significantly increased.[130] The post–World War II generation experienced modernization, Western European style (not Soviet style!). This social change has been instrumental in supporting democracy, though not so dramatic as to force Italian politicians to eliminate deeply embedded clientelism in many state sectors and regions, especially in the south.

While the regime change from fascism to democracy that took place after Italy's defeat in 1945 was largely elite-driven, society also played a crucial role. Disillusioned by fascism and war, a broad stratum of society and social change supported the new regime and the Christian Democratic Party (DC), which would emerge as its leader for the next four decades. The Italian democratization process was successful in many respects; indeed, its very stability was surprising, especially given how few of the social, economic, cultural, and historical "preconditions" (at least in the south) for democracy were present. Nonetheless, Italy's democratic government has been widely criticized for its pervasive personalism. In the south especially, the government in post–World War II Italy was characterized not by ideology but by "personal, clientelistic linkages and a huge well-oiled patronage machine."[131] The DC merely substituted a new clientele system for that of the old one, and in so doing incorporated many of the same "notables." Traditional notables in Italy, as in Central Asia, survived because they had an institutional source of power, and thē regime either turned a blind eye or openly fostered them.

The democracy that emerged from the 1950s to the 1980s was by most indicators a low-quality democracy in which there was much continuity with the past. The informal mechanisms of patronage of family, kin, friends, and clientele, and the asset stripping of state resources to serve those ends, continued and even expanded at the national level, although traditional clans no longer existed. The DC drew on these well-established mechanisms for gaining political support and became a "democratic" organization of massive patronage and clientelism, both at the national level and at the regional and local levels throughout the south. A continued economy of shortages, especially in the rural south, allowed the DC's clientelism to succeed; southerners

Central Asia, that southern Italians had extensive kin and social networks that were not culturally undemocratic; rather, individuals were simply rationally operating within the constraints of the social networks, economic conditions, and political structure that had long characterized the south.

[130] Tarrow, "Crisis, Crises, or Transition?" p. 169; and Leonardo Morlino and José Montero, "Legitimacy and Democracy in Southern Europe," in Gunther et al., *Politics of Democratic Consolidation*, p. 252.

[131] Sondra Koff and Stephen Koff, *Italy from the First to the Second Republic* (London: Routledge, 2000), p. 4.

depended upon it for access to jobs. Patronage politics flourished, albeit within the confines of a democratic system, with negative consequences. Patronage politics arrested bureaucratic and economic reforms and led to an oversized and "permeable state," stalled growth in the south (its base), allowed massive and debilitating corruption, and threatened to bankrupt the state by the 1970s.[132]

In many of the areas just described, Italy might be seen as similar to Kyrgyzstan in 1991. Why, then, did Italian democracy succeed in avoiding subversion by clan politics or similar informal politics, while Kyrgyzstan and Central Asia did not successfully democratize? First, Italy's political and nation-state development in 1945, when democracy was first introduced from above (and outside) – while not as advanced as in other areas of Western Europe – was still significantly ahead of Central Asia in 1991, when the Soviet collapse forced transition. The birth of democracy, then, took place in very different historical conditions. By 1945, despite ongoing differences between the north and the south, Italy's national identity and state formation had been consolidated in an indigenous political process that had already spanned almost a century since Italian unification. Second, although Italy's socioeconomic conditions were relatively undeveloped compared to the rest of Western Europe, traditional clan organizations and networks had declined or been transformed into a less exclusivist type of informal politics based on clientelism. Third, a market economy, albeit with significant state intervention, did exist and had fostered the dispersion of wealth and power. Clientelist ties existed on an individualist basis and on a mass party basis (the DC), rather than on the kin-group basis of clans in earlier centuries. DC clientelism was based on inequality, dependency, and exploitation of the lower classes, but it was a more inclusive phenomenon in that it created mass access to the state through the party's organization. And the DC did not formally block participation in other parties or interest groups. A leftist opposition existed. Some Italian clan networks, especially in the south, became the basis for powerful mafias.[133] Both old and new mafia families are bound by the tight norms and informal institutions of kinship. Such mafias resemble certain elite clans of Central Asia, which, as Chapter 8 noted, have also undergone a mafiosization as their political and economic interests have become increasingly criminal. The Italian mafia's control of construction, agricultural and rural cooperatives, credit institutions, banks, and public works had a noxious effect upon the political economy. As in Central Asia, the mafia was not a band of street thugs; it was based on familial networks that often had close ties with government officials and the state bureaucracy.[134]

---

[132] Giuseppe Di Palma, "The Available State: Problems of Reform," in Lange and Tarrow, eds., *Italy in Transition*, pp. 148–149, 153–155, 157–159.

[133] Backman, *Decline and Fall*; Putnam, *Making Democracy*.

[134] Chubb, *Patronage*, pp. 140–141; Gambetta, *Sicilian Mafia*.

At the same time, a number of other factors, largely absent in Central Asia, facilitated democratic sustainability, in spite of the social structure and related corruption that have inhibited democratic deepening. Extensive Western support and pressure, both domestic and international anticommunism, Italy's new role in NATO, and its fortunate position within the new Europe, which was experiencing significant economic growth, all favored democracy's success.[135] Scholars further argue that the popular legitimacy of the new regime – based more on opposition to the past than on the efficacy of the new government – was a major factor in enabling democratic consolidation. As Sidney Tarrow puts it, "democracy has grown in Italy, not because of the legitimacy of democracy per se, but because it appears as the *modus vivendi* least likely to threaten the survival of any one of the country's major social or ideological groupings."[136] In Italy, the overarching commitment of elites and pressure from society to maintain a democratic regime prevented the patronage system from completely undermining the institutions of democracy.

The Italian case also demonstrates that not only Western rhetorical pressure and loans – also present in Kyrgyzstan and many post-colonial African cases – but also the incentives and sanctions of international organizations (such as the EU), trade, and a network of economic and cultural ties with Western Europe were critical at both the social and elite levels. This would also be a critical factor in post-communist Eastern Europe, which had the possibility of joining the EU and NATO; by contrast, such ties were almost entirely absent in Central Asia in the 1990s.[137]

In sum, as Chubb writes, in the case of Italy "modernity and backwardness are inextricably intertwined," even in the twentieth century.[138] Clans have broken down, especially in the north of the country, as a result of capitalist economic development and democratic and economic conditions fostered by integration into the West. In the south, clanlike ties may have transformed in some cases into mafia families and clientelism of a more generalized form. Unfortunately, the conditions present in Italy are not yet present in Central Asia, and are unlikely to be created there in the near future. Italy's path of clan transformation and relatively successful democratization is not likely to be easily, much less quickly, replicated in parts of Africa and Central Asia, where ties with growing market economies and democratic systems are negligible. Italy's path does at least highlight the importance of a market

---

[135] Koff and Koff, *Italy from the First.*
[136] Tarrow, "Crisis, Crises, or Transition?," p. 174; and Leonardo Morlino, "Parties, Groups and Democratic Consolidation in Italy," in H. E. Chelabi and Alfred Stepan, eds., *Politics, Society, and Democracy* (Boulder, CO: Westview Press, 1995), p. 276.
[137] On the importance of the international factor (or its absence) in democratization, see Jeffrey Kopstein and David Reilly, "Geographic Diffusion and the Transformation of the Postcommunist World," *World Politics*, vol. 53, no. 1 (October 2000), pp. 1–37.
[138] Chubb, *Patronage*, p. 251.

economy and society – factors I have earlier argued are key to changing the socioeconomic foundations of clan politics.

Charles Tilly has written that multiple paths of political development are possible, especially at different times and in different historical contexts. It is more difficult to predict the factors that will lead to the breakdown of clans in the contemporary period, in regions of late state formation and late development. Furthermore, a path-dependent approach would suggest that the conditions that facilitated clan breakdown in earlier eras may not be present, or might not have the same effect, in the twenty-first century.[139] In post-Soviet Central Asia, other factors – such as civil war, intense poverty, and migration, on the one hand, and economic development and the rise of an individualist and market economy, on the other hand – may be more likely to transform clan identities and clan politics than the factors that were central to the decline of clans in the Western European context.

SUMMARY

This chapter has shown that neither the social phenomenon of clans, nor the political phenomenon of rising clan politics under transitional or post-colonial states, is unique to Central Asia. Clan types vary across cases, but the concept is similar. In exploring comparisons within the post-Soviet region – Kazakhstan and Turkmenistan and some parts of the Caucasus – I found that clan networks in these cases are similar, and that they share similar political dynamics with clans in the three Central Asian cases that have been the focus of this book and its argument about clan politics. This chapter further sketched comparisons with parts of Africa and the Middle East, and looked briefly at the Sudan and more deeply at Somalia. Even beyond the Soviet region, I found that clans have similar dynamics. Regime collapse in Somalia has significant parallels with Tajikistan; one clan's hegemony set the stage for conflict between challenging clans elites and was a major factor in regime collapse and civil war. Warlords in Somalia and the Sudan have further drawn on and intensified clan identities in order to mobilize a loyal following.

In this chapter, I also showed cases where clans once thrived, but where alternative trajectories were possible; there, clan politics has broken down. Certain Western European cases exemplify this transformation and break-down, in the context of early state formation, early national formation, and a growing market economy. I used the case of Italy, and the differences in development between the Italian north and south, to portray the difficult but eventually successful path to democracy for clan-based societies. The Italian

---

[139] On path dependency, see Paul Pierson, "Increasing Returns, Path Dependence and the Study of Politics," *The American Political Science Review*, vol. 94, no. 2 (June 2000), pp. 251–267.

case, while hardly lauded by scholars as a successful model of political and economic reform, does offer some hope to Central Asia.[140]

The path of clan breakdown will probably be different, however, and more difficult in Central Asia than in Europe. In Central Asia, empires (Russian and Soviet) delayed the process of state formation until the late twentieth century. National identity formation and nationalism were also part of the Soviet imperial project, as opposed to other cases where they emerged together with print capitalism and literacy in an earlier period. In Central Asia, as in much of Africa, states and nations were imposed from outside and remain weak. A shortage economy, typical both of pre-modern (e.g., nomadic or feudal) and state socialist societies, also reinforces clan organization and clan politics. Such economies have characterized the Central Asian, Somali, Sudanese, and Caucasian (Georgian, Azerbaijani, and Chechen) experiences under colonial/Soviet rule, and during the post-colonial/post-Soviet period. There is greater hope for clan breakdown in cases such as Georgia, Armenia, and Kazakhstan (if it avoids creating a clan-based rentier oil state), where greater economic reforms have fostered more economic growth, some dispersion of wealth, and a business sector opposed to clan politics.[141] As in Italy, reforms may foster a social base independent of clan networks, as well as incentives for clan elites to invest in a stable, institutionalized political system.

---

[140] On persistent problems of clientelism, see Rossetti, "Constitutionalism and Clientelism in Italy," pp. 99–101.

[141] Armenia and Italy, for example, have much better economic freedom rankings than Uzbekistan or Tajikistan, or the Sudan or Somalia, where individual economic freedoms are negligible and market economies are highly restricted or nonexistent. See Heritage Foundation, Ranks of Economic Freedom, <www.heritage.org/research/featrues/index/countries> (Appendix Table A.7). Nations in Transit scores provide further indicators of economic liberalization.

10

Conclusions

All the road cannot be smooth.

Kyrgyz proverb

This book has explored the social and political meaning of clans, and the logic and dynamics of clan politics over the course of the past century in Central Asia. More broadly, this book has sought to contribute to an understanding and explanation of the rise and fall of clans, and of the impact of clan politics on political regimes and political order. In the preceding pages, I have shed light on an informal level of social organization and politics that is seldom studied, and on a poorly understood but politically important region of the world. The findings of this work suggest that we rethink and broaden our theoretical approaches to studying democratization, regime transition, and institutions, both in Central Asia and in other societies – in the Middle East, Africa, and parts of Asia – where kin, clan, and other informal identity networks are historically strong. This work has further contributed some insight to our understanding of identity and modernity. We need to understand the informal organizations and networks that can powerfully affect regimes, even in the modern era. Clans are not pre-modern phenomena, but socially embedded identity networks that exist in many societies and states, even in the twentieth and twenty-first centuries. What role they play in politics, and whether they survive, is historically contingent. In the Central Asian cases, these networks have changed gradually over time; they have adapted to and continue to adapt to the modern state, Soviet and post-Soviet.

A BROADER APPROACH TO UNDERSTANDING TRANSITION IN CENTRAL ASIA

This work has broadened the scholarly discussion of democratization and political transition beyond the political and economic spheres and the elite level of analysis. The post-communist cases are distinct from earlier transitions in Latin America and southern Europe in that they involve a "triple transition":[1] political, economic, and national. In post-Soviet Central Asia, the "national" transition was essentially one of decolonization and state building in a region where modern states had not existed prior to the Soviet period. National identities and nation-states were far more recent phenomena in Central Asia than in Eastern Europe or the Baltics, which had a pre-communist history of nationness and stateness. We have seen that the Central Asian regimes are instead faced with many of the same challenges that faced African and Middle Eastern states after decolonization: defining and legitimizing the state, defining and creating a nation from various sub-national groups, and imposing formal state institutions and rules upon a predominantly informally organized but strong society.

In contrast to other regions and earlier eras of democratization, however, these multiple transitions were taking place rapidly and simultaneously, at all levels of society and state. Focusing narrowly on elites or on formal political and economic institutions misses much of the story. One cannot assume a strong Weberian state or autonomous state elites, even given the Soviet legacy of state building. In the Central Asian context especially, where so much political and economic activity is informal, one must take into account society and informal social organization and institutions.

UNDERSTANDING THE RATIONALITY AND CULTURE OF CLANS

We have seen that clans are a powerful type of informal social organization. They persist over time because they are identity networks with cultural capital, rooted in both real kinship and the idea of kinship that incorporates one's trusted friends. Because clans are tight-knit identity groups, which carry meaning, clan elites can trust the members of their networks, and nonelites can rely on clan patrons to assist them in times of need. Clans are not some fixed, primordial identity. They are identity networks reflecting ideas of kinship and community in a primarily collectivist society, but they are also rational networks that foster individual survival in an environment characterized by failing, inadequate, or repressive formal institutions. Clans provided one means of resistance against the Soviet state. By adapting to and using Soviet institutions, and loopholes in Communist Party governance, in some ways they beat the Party at its own game. During the post-Soviet period, clan ties provide social safety nets at the local level, when state institutions fail to provide promised public goods. At the elite level, mobilizing and reinforcing clan networks guarantees their members both wealth and some security in

---

[1] See Philip G. Roeder, "The Revolution of 1989: Postcommunism and the Social Sciences," *Slavic Review*, vol. 58, no. 4 (Winter 1999), p. 744. See also Valerie Bunce, "Regional Differences in Democratization: The East versus the South," *Post-Soviet Affairs*, vol. 14, no. 3 (July–September 1998), pp. 187–211.

an unpredictable political and economic environment. You cannot trust the state to protect your property (legally or illegally gained) in Soviet and post-Soviet Central Asia, but you can trust your clan to use its informal levels of power and influence to do so.

We have also seen these networks operate both at the elite level of politics and at the mass, social level. For example, during the 1990s, Ismoil Jurabekov, one of the most powerful clan figures in Uzbekistan, and the "Gray Cardinal" behind Karimov's rise to power, placed his clan – his relatives through blood and marriage ties, and close friendships – in positions of wealth and influence, including jobs in the cotton complex, the water and agricultural ministries, an extensive network of private business monopolies, and, critically, the Ministry of Internal Affairs. From this inner circle of power, Jurabekov and his clan created a broader network of patronage, thereby building a substantial political and economic power base. In Kyrgyzstan, President Akaev and his wife, since the mid-1990s, have directly and increasingly used their clan ties, which are rooted in a recently nomadic-tribal tradition, to build a network of power. Their family, relatives, and extended clan fill the power ministries, the Ministry of Finance, the banks, the media, protected businesses, and what is now the strongest political party. In the case of Akaev, a Soviet physicist who in 1990 had long been outside of both clan networks and Kyrgyz politics, drawing on clan ties seemed unusual, but it was a politically expedient means of creating a trusted power base. Moreover, since his clan had initiated his rise to power, he was greatly indebted to them.

Clan politics also operates at the subnational level, as *hokim*s appoint relatives and clan members to key positions within the regional or *raion* government structures. Within the rural sector, the *kolkhoz* (or *shirkat*) directors give land or prized positions on the farms to their relatives and friends. During the Soviet period, brigades on the collective farms incorporated wholesale the *avlod*, *urugh*, or *aul*, the most traditional kin-based form of clan network. During the initial post-Soviet period, these local networks have provided critical social safety nets, although economic out-migration may be changing their role in recent years. Variation certainly exists across and within regions, but the essence of these informal networks, and the mechanisms that clan elites use to preserve and strengthen them – a combination of mutual reciprocity through patronage relations and informal sanctions – are fundamentally similar. When a clan elite, such as the local *hokim*, gives the state bread factory to his cousin, and his cousin appoints his sons and their friends, they all remain dependent upon and loyal to the *hokim*. Given that a *hokim* in Uzbekistan or Kyrgyzstan is likely to have dozens of cousins and extended relatives – typically referred to as "my brother" – he has a large network of dependents and supporters. We have seen throughout this study, during both the Soviet and post-Soviet periods, that at both the elite and social levels these networks provide identities and circles of trust, which can be essential for survival as well as for successful exploitation and exclusion of other groups in the political or economic sphere.

In tracing their evolution from the late nineteenth century to the present, we found that clans change and adapt to the external environment, both economic and political. In the twentieth century, clans were significantly transformed by the Soviet state. Talking about clan identity became illegal, for the Soviet regime viewed clans as antithetical to socialist modernity. The common practice of promoting one's kin and clan became illegal and was branded as corruption. Clan ties thus were driven underground and into the strictly informal sphere, including the shadow economy. Many traditional clan elites from the pre-Soviet era fled or were eliminated. The Communist Party promoted new elites, educated in the Soviet system. Yet many Central Asians still preserved a sense of kin and clan identity. They used and promoted those ties when the Soviet state was not looking, both in the cultural sphere of marriage alliances and in the political-economic sphere of cadre appointments. Twentieth-century Central Asia did not witness either Leninist or Weberian modernization of individual and state. Instead, a mutual transformation of clans and state has continually been under way; that transformation is sometimes dominated by the state (as in the Stalinist era) and sometimes dominated by clans (as in the post-Soviet era). Clans continue to evolve in a dynamic relationship with the political system today. Some clans are promoted and others excluded. Moreover, the past decade has been one of societal upheaval; broader social and economic forces, including war, migration, and crony capitalism, are changing the nature of clan networks within each state.

The approach and findings of this book's exploration of clans touch more broadly on one of the emerging fault lines in the social sciences today – the debate between culturalist and rationalist theories, whether of economics, of international relations, or of political behavior and political development.[2] After several decades of research, in which the primacy of the micro level and of rational strategic actors and institutions was often unchallenged, many social scientists are now gravitating toward, or perhaps back to, a discourse about culture and norms.[3] Yet still scholars too often assume that these paradigms for understanding the world are categorically distinct, and that good theory is incapable of synthesis.[4] As Ernest Gellner has argued,

---

[2] Peter Katzenstein, Robert O. Keohane, and Steven Krasner, "International Organization and the Study of World Politics," *International Organization*, vol. 52, no. 3 (Summer 1998), pp. 645–685.

[3] On norms, see Peter Katzenstein, *Culture, Norms and National Security: Police and Military in Post-War Japan* (Ithaca, NY: Cornell University Press, 1996). On culture, see Ernest Gellner, *Nationalism* (New York: New York University Press, 1997).

[4] Attempts to bridge this methodological divide include Robert Bates, Avner Greif, Margaret Levi, and Barry Weingast, *Analytic Narratives* (Princeton, NJ: Princeton University Press, 1998); and Sidney Tarrow, *Power in Movement* (Cambridge: Cambridge University Press, 2000).

"Culture and social organization are universal and perennial."[5] We must have theories to explain their role in politics. This study contributes to the rationalist–culturalist debate by challenging a false dichotomy between these research paradigms. My approach has acknowledged the critical importance of culture and identity, and indeed their centrality to the processes of regime transition and consolidation in Central Asia, while seeking to understand the fundamental and often *rational* basis of these phenomena.[6] A study of clans illuminates what Aristotle long ago observed in both the *Politics* and the *Nichomachean Ethics*: human beings are creatures not only of reason but also of habit and norms formed by their social environment. Hence, this work has aspired to bridge rationalist and cultural understandings of politics in the study of political transition.

THE PERSISTENCE OF CLANS IN THE TWENTIETH CENTURY

While clans as a social form are hardly unique to Central Asia, clans do not survive and persist in all cases. In fact, in some regions clans as a social form disappeared in earlier centuries. Why, then, do clans sometimes survive into and through the twentieth century, despite the modernizing forces seemingly at work against them? And when do they gain momentum as political actors that can pervade and transform regimes?

This book has found support for several propositions about clan persistence or decline, and about the conditions under which we see the rise of clan politics in Central Asia, comparing these cases to forms of clan politics in parts of Africa, the Middle East, and the Caucasus, in contrast to clan decline in Western Europe. The story of Central Asia in the twentieth century highlighted three conditions facilitating clan persistence. The first is late state formation. A modern state, with a defined territory, borders, citizenship, and a monopoly over force, did not exist across Central Asia until the Soviet conquest and Stalin's 1924 demarcation of the Central Asian republics. Clan and kin-based or localist identity networks, even nomadic clans and tribes in many areas, existed throughout most of Central Asia until the eve of the Soviet state. The Soviet state that dominated the region for most of the twentieth century, moreover, was an imperial one; the Central Asian republics became a new form of colony. Despite its communist ideology and affirmative action empire, the Soviet regime denied any real federal rights and delayed state formation in Central Asia for seventy years. A second and closely related condition for clan persistence into the twentieth century was the late formation of national identities. The current Central Asian borders and ethno-national identities have been in place only since

---

[5] Gellner, *Nationalism*, p. 4.
[6] David Laitin, *Hegemony and Culture: Politics among the Yoruba* (Chicago: University of Chicago Press, 1986).

the 1920s; they were imposed by Stalin on a populace organized around other subnational identities. Soviet nationality policy added another layer, creating the basis for the ethno-national identities of the post-Soviet Central Asian states, but did not successfully eradicate the traditions, loyalties, and identities and patterns of social organization already there. Third, we have seen that clan networks offer a social response to economic conditions of shortage, which characterize both pre-modern and socialist economies as well as the semisocialist or imperfect markets of Central Asia today. As discussed in the previous chapter, these conditions characterized Central Asia, much as they have the Sudan, Somalia, and parts of the Caucasus, well into the twentieth century.

Other conditions – absent in the just-mentioned cases – foster clan decline, as I demonstrated in Chapter 9's discussion of formerly clan-based societies in Western Europe. In northern Italy, for example, the early formation of independent city-states, and the early introduction of a market economy and consequent economic growth, led to deals between clans to create and bolster state institutions in order to protect that growth, and fostered the decline of clans in politics. In southern Italy, meanwhile, later decolonialization, the later formation of a national identity, and a feudal economy characterized by shortages delayed such a process. Even so, an overarching process of state and national formation and market-based growth during the mid-twentieth century did cause the decline of informal identity networks over a long period. Nonetheless, weaker clientelist networks persisted well into the post-war era. Indeed, many scholars have argued that the pervasiveness of particularistic ties has led to a low-quality and highly corrupt democracy that endures in large part because of pressure and incentives from its neighbors.

Beyond the issue of clan persistence in some regions and not in others, we must ask a more puzzling question: how did clans survive the Soviet state – which was led by one of the most repressive regimes in history, capable of sending tens of millions to their deaths, capable of eliminating dissent for seventy years, capable of industrializing a peasant economy in under three decades, and capable of creating a military-industrial superpower from the corpus of the Russian empire? Addressing this question has caused us to rethink the nature of Soviet power. James Scott's telling analysis in *Seeing Like a State* gives us a window into the thinking of the Soviet regime. Like many modernizing authoritarian states, the Soviet regime was partially blinded by its ideological and imperial struggle to create "high modernism,"[7] and Soviet measures to eliminate clans in the 1920s and 1930s were part of this goal. This policy, however, engendered both overt and veiled resistance. Kin ties and clan solidarity networks became a means for preserving Central Asian culture and identity, and for resisting Soviet rule and Soviet versions

---

[7] James Scott, *Seeing Like a State* (New Haven, CT: Yale University Press, 1999).

of modernity. Second, the Soviet state then provided the institutional means for clans to survive within the Soviet system. As we saw in Chapters 3 and 4, mass sedentarization and forced collectivization, together with the internal passport system, initially froze clans in place by ending their ability to migrate. Yet these policies also inadvertently gave clans access to significant resources, allowing them to feed their networks. Likewise, at the elite level, both nationality policy and cadre policy gave clans new access to high levels in the Communist Party and state. Insufficient regime monitoring of Central Asia in the early decades, and later Brezhnev's deliberate blindness to the development of wealthy clan networks, led to the initial rise of clan politics *within* the very Soviet system that sought to eradicate clans! In particular, Brezhnev's policy of "cadre stability" throughout the Soviet Union fit well with the local politics and practices of Central Asia. The Brezhnev era represented an informal social contract between the Soviet regime and Central Asian clan elites. Under Brezhnev's watch, an extensive system of clan-based nepotism, patronage, and corruption thrived.

The Soviet state denied the existence of clans, repressed them, and then fed them well. From the story of twentieth-century Central Asia, we not only learn about the survival power of society through social organizations, we also get a different view of Soviet power and the Soviet system. We see not only the repression but also the weaknesses, incompetence, and corruption of the Soviet state, its unintended consequences. Soviet policy led to clan survival in a more informal and often more corrupt form, not to clan demise.

THE RISE OF CLAN POLITICS

This work has often stressed the role of clans in organizing intergroup competition over resources and political power. Yet I also proposed in Chapter 2 that clans would unify in an informal pact at the initiative of key clan elites in some circumstances: if they shared a mutual threat, if a relative balance of power existed among them, and if a legitimate interclan broker could manage that balance. In Central Asia, clan pacts during the perestroika era initiated the rise of post-Soviet clan politics at the elite level. In Kyrgyzstan and Uzbekistan, clans unified against Gorbachev, who after Brezhnev's death had initiated a massive purge of thousands of Kyrgyz and Uzbek elites. Those purges and the infamous "red landing" of Gorbachev's new cadre had ended a quarter-century of hegemonic rule by the Usubaliev clan in Kyrgyzstan and the Rashidov clan in Uzbekistan, and thereby had balanced clan power. The purges had then unified clan elites in informal pacts against the regime, leading to the rise of both Akaev and Karimov, shortly before independence was thrust upon them. These pacts, however, as I have argued, against the central hypothesis of the transitions literature, do not lead to democratization. Rather, they foster regime durability. Both Akaev and Karimov have an informal but powerful base of support, and both successfully managed the transition, controlled the armed forces, and set about building new regime institutions during the early 1990s. In Tajikistan, by contrast, there was no purge, and thus no threat and no balancing. No pact took place, and no legitimate leader emerged. Instead, the continued hegemony of the Khodjenti clan ripened the conditions for regime collapse and civil war. With the sudden shock of independence came the end of massive Soviet budget subsidies and Moscow/KGB patronage. The Tajik regime could not resist the mobilization of a mix of Islamic, democratic, and clan-based opposition forces demanding a share of power.

Durable regimes emerge where pacts have preserved stability. Yet limited democratization has occurred in only one case, in Kyrgyzstan, largely at the initiative of Akaev's leadership and a handful of civil society activists. Here we do see that elite ideology matters, at least in a limited form, in the short term. For the most part, in Central Asia clan elites are nonideological, and their debates both before and after independence have had little to do with democracy, communism, or Islamism. They want resources. The Sarybagysh, Kochkor, and other clans in the pact behind Akaev support democratization, which they expect will bring foreign aid and investment and lucrative opportunities for them to monopolize. Elsewhere in Central Asia, the new presidents choose to form noncommunist but authoritarian regimes. They try to consolidate presidential control while also buying in – or in some cases, buying off – competing clan factions by informally ceding them control of state assets for their private use. As I proposed in Chapter 2, however, the transition is relatively short-lived, and a more rampant clan politics emerges in each case.

CLAN-BASED REGIMES AND PROSPECTS FOR DURABILITY

Guillermo O'Donnell has referred to the type of regime we see in Kyrgyzstan in the early 1990s as "delegative democracy."[8] While O'Donnell stresses that consolidation is unlikely, he argues that delegative democracies may be stable. Others, meanwhile, have simply assumed the consolidation of authoritarian regimes elsewhere in the region.[9] In 1994, in Bishkek, I stumbled across a copy of O'Donnell's article on delegative democracy and wondered if Kyrgyzstan could maintain its semiliberal, delegative, but clearly unconsolidated democracy.

Rather than concluding the analysis at 1994–95, with the end of the transition, however, I have sought to show that clans undermine the new regime institutions in each case, transforming the very system of governance

[8] Guillermo O'Donnell, "Delegative Democracy," *Journal of Democracy*, vol. 5, no. 1 (January 1994), pp. 55–69; and Guillermo O'Donnell, "Illusions about Consolidation," *Journal of Democracy*, vol. 7, no. 2 (April 1996), pp. 34–51.
[9] See *Nations in Transit* (New York: Freedom House, 2003).

and de-institutionalizing and thereby weakening the state in the process. While regime collapse is not imminent, these regimes have been transformed. Delegative democracy in a clan-based society has not proven stable; it has quickly deteriorated under the pressure of clan interests. Nor is clan-based autocracy a stable political system over the longer term.

Thirteen to fifteen years after independence from communism and the Soviet Union, the East Central Europeans have generally thrived under consolidated democracies. Even Russia (with the major exception of Chechnya) has made significant strides in consolidating authoritarian power. Yet according to most sources, the Central Asian regimes have ranked among the worst in the post-communist sphere, both politically and economically.[10] Despite the establishment of super-presidential systems across the region, in none of these cases is the president able to assert control over the informal politics and deals that pervade both society and state. We have seen that in each case, presidential appointments and policy decisions are defined or sharply constrained by clan interests and their competition for resources. Clan elites actively engage in nepotism and patronage of their kin and clan network, and they strip state assets. They create a wealth and power base largely independent of the state. Authoritarian law has been strong when repressing democracy, but weak when controlling its own cadre of increasingly corrupt clan elites. Moreover, in this environment, broader corruption and mafia organizations have thrived, further weakening the state.

Robert Rotberg has highlighted several key indicators of weak and failing states,[11] including the governance flaws of greed and despotism; external attacks; ethnic, linguistic, or intercommunal tension and violence; rising crime and mafia networks; deteriorating physical infrastructure; excessive corruption; and falling GDP per capita and other indicators of economic crisis. Weak states do not or cannot provide public goods and services. One might add that they do not provide a rule of law. Informal or illegal activity is commonplace, and formal institutions – both authoritarian and democratic – are often hollow. Failed states can no longer

---

[10] Freedom House *Nations in Transit* reports and Transparency International all rank these countries as among the least free and most corrupt. See Appendix, Tables A.5 and A.6. Except for Kazakhstan, assessments of economic freedom are among the lowest in the post-communist sphere as well. See Appendix, Tables A. 5 and A. 6.

[11] Robert Rotberg, "Failed States, Collapsed States, Weak States: Causes and Indicators," in Robert Rotberg, ed., *State Failure and State Weakness in a Time of Terror* (Washington, DC: Brookings Institution Press, 2003), pp. 2–9. See also William Reno, "Mafia Troubles, Warlord Crises," in Mark Beissinger and Crawford Young, eds., *Beyond State Crisis? Postcolonial Africa and Post-Soviet Eurasia in Comparative Perspective* (Washington, DC: Woodrow Wilson Center Press, 2002), pp. 105–129; Charles Fairbanks, "Weak States and Private Armies," in Beissinger and Young, eds., *Beyond State Crisis?*, pp. 129–160; and Mark Beissinger and Crawford Young, "The Effective State in Postcolonial Africa and Post-Soviet Eurasia: Hopeless Chimera or Possible Dream?" in Beissinger and Young, eds., *Beyond State Crisis?*, pp. 465–487.

control internal violence, solidify their borders, or monopolize the use of force.

Certainly the Central Asian states exemplify degrees of failure, and their regimes degrees of weakness. Kyrgyzstan may be an openly impotent leviathan, Tajikistan a grossly inept one, and Uzbekistan a Machiavellian one whose leader refuses to acknowledge the web of informal networks that handicap its power. Kyrgyzstan and Tajikistan have faced small-scale public protests, open clan-based opposition, and occasional armed clashes in recent years. Each regime has survived coup and assassination attempts.

Once part of a strong socialist system, now these states fail to deliver basic public goods, from education to health care. Kyrgyzstan and Tajikistan have been the least successful in providing goods (from gas and electricity to education and food) and in controlling open clan corruption. Uzbekistan and Turkmenistan have continued to provide a minimal level of public goods, such as subsidized gas. Yet as Rotberg's study of state failure finds, the latter cases are "hiding the underlying conditions of failure" and face the "possibility of implosion." Each one is set on a negative political trajectory that may well end in state failure and regime collapse, as have too many post-colonial African cases, absent significant reform or economic growth.[12] The one attempt at democratization has reverted to a weak, clan-run autocracy, undermining public trust in democracy in the process. All the regimes have become increasingly personalistic autocracies in which the presidents compete with rival clans for power, build their own clans, and undermine genuine economic reform that would threaten their vested interests. Formal institutions do not function properly; they have been hollowed out and to a large extent stripped of assets. There is no rule of law. Clan-based challenges exist within and outside the system. Brittle authoritarian structures remain, leaving the Central Asian regimes weak and potentially failing.[13]

What has driven this decline, and where might it lead? This book has argued that the rise of clans in politics during the post-Soviet period, characterized by the informal deals of clan elites, has been the major factor driving this decline. In pursuing their short-term interests through rampant nepotism and asset stripping, clan elites – including the presidents' own clans, clan allies, and clan opponents – have in fact weakened the regime and state as a whole and are thus undermining their own future interests. In anticipation of regime or even state collapse, they may in fact be precipitating that collapse.

[12] Kazakhstan, as noted in Chapter 9, has instituted greater market reforms than the other regimes.

[13] Robert Rotberg, "The Failure and Collapse of Nation-States: Breakdown, Prevention, and Repair," in Robert Rotberg, ed., *When States Fail: Causes and Consequences* (Princeton, NJ: Princeton University Press, 2004), pp. 17–18. The study rates Kyrgyzstan as a weak and "near-failing state." Tajikistan "harbors the possibility of failure."

They have also undermined the formal regime; these cases can be better understood as informal regimes of clan politics than as authoritarian, communist, or totalitarian regimes, which are typically understood by both scholars and policy makers as institutionalized and consolidated systems. I have referred to this process as the vicious circle of clan politics (see Chapter 2, Figure 2.1). Across Central Asia, against a backdrop of weak national unity, strong clan-based loyalties, the crushing of democratic opposition, declining economies, a crumbling infrastructure, intense popular frustration with poverty, repression, corruption, and minimal regime legitimacy, this vicious cycle may well lead to an impending crisis. The informal decentralization of power and assets, potentially including access to arms, among clan elites and along group identity lines, raises the likelihood of clan elites instigating intergroup conflict to defend their interests.

Mass protest and demands for revolution, especially for democracy, are unlikely to shake these regimes from below, given both the weakness and the factionalized nature of the democratic opposition and these states' propensity to use force to crush democratic opponents. An Islamic revolution also seems unlikely. Despite growing sympathy for political Islam in Uzbekistan, Islamist organizations are also fragmented; their activities are deeply underground, and the majority of Islamist leaders may already be in exile or in jail. In Kyrgyzstan, some forms of Islamism have growing support, especially in the south. In Tajikistan, the Islamic Renaissance Party has been widely blamed for the war or discredited as incompetent. In part because of disillusionment with failed democratization, radical versions of Islam, articulated by Hizb ut-Tahrir or by the Islamic Movement of Uzbekistan, have replaced calls for democracy as the most widespread form of opposition since the late 1990s.

The absence of an open social opposition movement does not indicate a lack of regime contenders. A more informal threat has emerged, in large part from clan elites who once supported the current presidents' rise to power but are increasingly excluded. Coup attempts, although they have failed thus far, could lead to instability. It is therefore worthwhile to keep in mind the lessons of the Tajik regime collapse of 1992. For decades, with Soviet backing, the Khodjenti clans actively created an insular, hegemonic regime, devoid of popular legitimacy, and refused to share power when opposition clans and a democratic/Islamist movement demanded reform. Ultimately, when they lost their external patron and financing, the regime fell. The Central Asian states today, with the possible exception of Kazakhstan, are at risk of repeating that scenario. Even if they avoid bloodshed, the transition of power to yet other clan factions is likely to result in more insider corruption and bad governance.

Clan division and competition over shrinking resources have intensified. Resentment against the increasing hegemony of the "family" or presidential clan has heightened at all levels. A shock to the fragile system of power, perhaps in the form of the president's death or an internal coup, might well spin these regimes into collapse. Regime collapse does not necessarily mean violence and civil war; guns are a necessary ingredient. When guns fall into the hands of opposing clan elites, they can use those weapons to mobilize their following and to pursue their interests through violence. In Tajikistan, weapons still appear to be plentiful within the country, and they could easily be brought across the border from Afghanistan. In Kyrgyzstan and Uzbekistan, there is little evidence to date of a proliferation of weapons. As long as the power ministries – the Ministry of Interior, the national security agency, the president's special guards, and the Ministry of Defense – are kept unified and behind the regime, then violence and state breakdown seem unlikely. As we saw in Chapters 7 and 8, however, these ministries are neither clearly behind the president nor united under one clan. Given the background conditions for failure, a powerful external shock could trigger crisis and collapse. Competition between clans, especially those trying to preserve their hegemonic power, and the dispersion of weapons among them might well lead to civil violence.

In recent months, as they resist the need to cut their own share of resources and/or to balance resources with other factions, the Central Asian presidents have adopted new strategies to preserve their hold on power and to undermine both democratic and clan opponents. In Uzbekistan, Kyrgyzstan, and Kazakhstan, their relatives are creating presidential parties, following the Putin "party of power" model. In all three, as the current leaders age they seem to be preparing their children for succession in another few years. In Kyrgyzstan and Kazakhstan, the presidents' relatives are buying up the independent media. In 2002, during the Ak-sy crisis, Akaev resolved the conflict by buying off clan opposition. Karimov and Rakhmonov have similarly "patronized" both clan and mafia networks who have challenged their power. It is not clear how much longer they can do so; foreign debt is high, investment low, and growth stagnant. Only Kazakhstan, like oil-rich Azerbaijan, clearly has the resources to continue such a practice to maintain stability. There, however, as we saw in Chapter 9, the greatest hope for clan transformation lies not in oil but in greater strides toward a market economy.

Perhaps because of this, each Central Asian country is preparing to hold parliamentary and presidential elections from 2004 to 2006, in part to appease the international community and win greater financial aid and loan concessions from the international donors, and in part to create a semblance of legality and legitimacy for their regimes. They argue that stability can be maintained only under their watch. Few international or local observers, however, expect the elections to be free and fair. Hence, the regimes seek somehow to avoid the Georgian scenario. A far more likely threat to them, however, is a form of the Tajik scenario.

Although this book has primarily focused on internal political dynamics, in Chapter 4 I pointed to several important external factors that affect internal stability and the durability of political pacts: an external patron and a shared external threat. Through much of the 1990s, the Central Asian pacts were bolstered by the shared threat from Afghanistan. Since the decline of the Taliban threat, the presidents themselves have been personally bolstered, vis-à-vis the pacts they led and their populations, by external actors. External patronage and increased aid from the United States and Russia as a result of the war on terror have provided a new source of rents as well as of military strength that bolsters the power of regime elites.

As a new round of elections across the region approaches, the prospects for democratization look bleak. The Central Asian presidents themselves and the clans that surround them have little interest in liberalization that will threaten their assets, and conflicting signals from the West, especially after 9/11, have further undermined Western leverage in promoting democratization. The hard stand that the European Bank for Reconstruction and Development and the United States took against Uzbekistan in cutting some economic and political aid in 2004 caught the attention of the region. Yet it may be too weak a response, too late, and too likely to be counterbalanced by the West's short-term security interests and desire to have stable regimes in the region.

In concluding this discussion, we should recall that not all clan networks breed corruption and bad governance. We saw in Chapters 3 and 7 that clans can in many ways provide the basis for strong local communities and self-help networks. Central Asian sociologists have noted the resilience of clans and their strong role in such sectors, despite the strains of poverty and labor migration over the past decade. Nor does democratization in clan-based societies necessarily end in corrupt and brittle autocratic regimes or failed states. As shown in Chapter 9, the integration and transformation of clans in the process of Western European state development, although difficult to replicate in the post-Soviet conditions of Central Asia, does suggest that a positive trajectory is possible. The conditions of post-colonial and post-Soviet state development allowed clan elites to entrench themselves in political and economic power while their new nation-states were still weak. Meanwhile, the regimes' political and economic legacy of the past fifteen years has made clan transformation more difficult and a positive economic and political trajectory less likely.

Ultimately, both a growing market economy and good governance, including different strategies to deal with clans, are needed to empower individual citizens, to provide them opportunities, and to breed faith in the regime, so that elites invest in institutions rather than stripping them of assets. These factors will undermine the informal politics of clans. How to introduce these conditions, when both the regime and the economy are now pervaded by

clan elites, is not clear. A younger generation with new ideas, a deeper understanding of democracy, and greater hope for the future may be necessary
to transform both society and the regime from below.

The history of Central Asia during the past century suggests that we should
not underestimate the power of human beings or their motivations, good and
evil, in resisting the regime. Human beings have transformed both the Soviet
and post-Soviet states by their daily actions, even as they were repressed by
those very states. Too often, as we have seen in these pages, they do so for
selfish ends – the pursuit of wealth and power for themselves and their group,
and the exclusion of others. Yet we have also seen, both during the Soviet
period and after, that they can do so for noble reasons – to protect their
family, kin, and identity. And there are even some who continue to resist
repression, to defend their society, to demand democracy, and to pave the
way for better lives for their children.

Epilogue

On March 24, 2005, after nearly a decade and a half of independence, people power finally made a breakthrough in Central Asia, a region many observers had believed to be a bastion of stable authoritarian regimes. Over 10,000 demonstrators turned out in the capital city of Kyrgyzstan to protest falsified elections. Within hours they had overrun the government house, shouting "Down with the Akaev clans," and forced the Kyrgyz president to flee.[1] The regime had tampered with elections several times before, but this time the democratic opposition and dozens of others, inspired by the successful examples of peaceful democratic revolutions in Georgia in November 2003, and in the Ukraine in December 2004, led protests around the country, and thousands followed. Because I submitted the final draft of this book in the fall of 2004, this epilogue will briefly address these recent dramatic events.

Several lessons can be learned from the recent events. First, clan-based systems corrupt regime institutions and become highly unstable when resources are declining and one clan strives for hegemony. The February 2005 elections were merely the catalyst. The fundamental cause of the political crisis was the Akaev regime's excessive, clan-based corruption. As argued in previous chapters, for the past decade Akaev has stripped state coffers and "privatized" state enterprises in order to feed his clan of relatives and friends, his wife's clan, and their closest cronies. Recent reports have documented the Akaev clan's extensive state and private assets – including over forty of the most lucrative businesses in the country, from the cement plant, to the telecommunications company, to the newspaper/television complexes, to the alcohol trade, to the company that "won" the multimillion-dollar fuel

[1] BBC Monitoring, "Kyrgyz Opposition Takes Control," <http://news.bbc.co.uk/go/pr/fr/-/l/hl/world/asia-pacific/4381555.stm>.

345

contract for the American military base.² Beyond stealing the nation's assets, the president and his clan had taken over the parliament. Many believed that with the help of the new parliament and his court, Akaev was initiating steps to manipulate the constitution yet once more, to allow him to be reelected in October 2005. If not, the president's children, who appear to have bought two parliamentary seats in the recent election, just as they had illegally taken control of many state and private assets, had been positioning themselves to succeed their father and preserve the dynasty.

Since 1995, members of Akaev's clique had become increasingly authoritarian in order to preserve their spoils and cover up their back-door dealings. For years, cab drivers and bazaar traders in Bishkek have expressed virulent animosity toward the opulent and clannish regime. Transparency International today ranks Kyrgyzstan as one of the world's most corrupt regimes. Despite official government statistics claiming significant economic growth, unemployment and poverty remain high, migrant labor keeps families alive, and socioeconomic disparities have sharply escalated. Many of the protestors in March were just angry, hungry young men, a fact that does not bode well for stability in the months and years ahead.

A second lesson is that the West plays a powerful role in either promoting or disillusioning democratic movements. Opposition parties, civil society activists, and independent journalists, although far weaker than their Georgian and Ukrainian neighbors, have made strides in recent years, in large part because of Western aid for democracy-building programs. The one free printing press that allowed independent journalists to disseminate information about Akaev's misdeeds was paid for with a U.S. grant. However, the West also shares some of the blame for Akaev's fifteen-year tenure, and for the long rule of his neighbors. Western governments and international organizations have too frequently turned a blind eye to Akaev's blatant abuses of power, or have preferred to soft-peddle their criticism. Throughout Central Asia and Azerbaijan, opposition leaders claim that the West has let them down. Especially since 9/11, the U.S. has sought to appease stable dictators who are allies in the War on Terror. The West should take note of its short-sighted policies; the Kyrgyz events make clear that corrupt authoritarian regimes in Central Asia are far more fragile than they look.

Several notes of caution are also in order. First, Kyrgyz protests differed in important ways from the revolutions in Ukraine and Georgia. The "democratic opposition" is far from united and not clearly democratic. The March protesters were a motley coalition of disparate factions and leaders, including a handful of democrats, such as the Ata-Jurt Movement and the Coalition NGO for Democracy and Civil Society, as well as various clan,

² "Kyrgyzstan: Weak Economy, Nepotism Seen as Factors in Akayev Fall," *Nezavissimaia Gazeta*, March 28, 2005, pp. 9, 11, reprinted in BBC Monitoring, April 11, 2005, <www.ft.com/search>.

regional, ethnic, and ideological factions that had not united previously and will likely continue to spar for a share of power. The revolutionaries could not even agree on the color or flower of their revolution. Some wore yellow and carried daffodils; others wore pink and carried tulips. Most were peaceful, though a few in the south used Molotov cocktails. The veneer of unity quickly shattered. Within days, two interim presidents and two parliaments claimed power, although the southern leader Kurmanbek Bakiev soon took control. In an attempt to stabilize the situation, he recognized the new pro-Akaev parliament.

Second, the weakness of democratic civil society – especially in contrast with Georgia and Ukraine – is evident; the revolutionary crowds turned quickly from civic demonstrations to pillaging. In fact, many of the same protesters, after ransacking the government house, later looted the capital city, causing over $100 million worth of damage. Moreover, the demonstrators were not all advocating a secular revolution. An extremist Islamist group, Hizb ut-Tahrir, which has gained ground among disaffected youth in the southern regions, called for the revolution to take a religious direction.

Third, significant clan divisions remain, and who controls the guns remains uncertain. Many in the police and security services, who were led by people very close to Akaev, have disappeared and could return to play a destabilizing role. Meanwhile, Feliks Kulov, the leader of one opposition faction, was released from prison during the events, and was initially named the interim head of all security forces. As discussed in previous chapters, Kulov is a former Akaev ally, with a shadowy background in the police. Kulov and Bakiev represent different factions, and have never before been united. Kulov quickly resigned from the interim government to declare his candidacy for the presidency in the elections scheduled for summer 2005. Shortly thereafter, his close ally and head of the people's militias, Usen Kudaibergenov, was mysteriously assassinated. Meanwhile, many in Akaev's ruling clique have simply disappeared, although thousands from his clan network have staged counterprotests. Akaev waited several weeks to resign from the presidency, and speaking from his haven in Moscow, denied any culpability. His daughter returned and assumed her position in parliament.

Fourth, transitional leadership is crucial, yet in Kyrgyzstan today it is lacking. Bakiev and his faction have never been clearly oriented toward democracy. Bakiev is also a former Akaev ally, although his brief stint as premier under Akaev was more of a bone Akaev threw to the south. Consumed with the struggle for power, Bakiev has so far failed to set forth a message of unity and democracy. His agenda and loyalties are unclear, and he lacks the charisma of a Mikhail Saakashvili or even a Viktor Yushchenko.

The lack of both political order and legitimacy is worrying. By late April, many protestors, angered by Bakiev's poor leadership and the slow pace of change once Akaev had fled, began taking things again into their own hands. Some have continued to demonstrate in front of parliament. One village clan mobilized protests in front of the police ministry, demanding a redress of their grievances. Still other protesters staged a sit-in in the Supreme Court, forcing the chairman of the court to resign. Many have little faith in the possibility of change. "Nothing has changed. Some come. Others go," said a disillusioned Kyrgyz mathematics professor interviewed on the events. "It's just a fight between clans."[3]

The situation is reminiscent of neighboring Tajikistan in 1992. Then, antiregime demonstrations went on for several months, and also included a ragtag coalition of democrats, Islamists, clan factions, and regional factions, all demanding a share of state resources. They too forced the president to flee. Yet what had begun with democratic slogans turned violent as the fragmented regime and opposition fought for power. The result was a brutal five-year civil war that devastated the already poor economy and created a haven for mafias, narcotics traders, and extremists. Such a scenario is not impossible in Kyrgyzstan today. Even after the elections, both domestic and international pressure for reform must continue in order to prevent a lapse into just another version of the Akaev regime, and to preclude the Tajik scenario. In one important step to date, a committee of government and civic leaders has recommended the adoption of a law that prevents the hiring of government employees on a clan basis, and instead demands review on the basis of professional qualifications.[4]

Neighboring Uzbekistan and Tajikistan are showing signs of growing instability as well. Their elections (in December 2004 and February 2005, respectively) went much more smoothly. In Uzbekistan, no opposition parties were even allowed to compete. The elections resulted in clear government victories, and the presidential parties took a large percentage of the vote. Nonetheless, as argued in Chapter 8, dissatisfaction remains high, and was evident well before the Kyrgyz events. Uzbekistan, in particular, has witnessed unprecedented signs of stress on Karimov's regime, and on the clan politics and corruption in which it is embedded. In early November 2004, multiple demonstrations took place in the Ferghana Valley (in Kokand, Andijan, and Margilan) and in Kashkadarya. According to various estimates, an unheard of 6,000 to 10,000 protesters turned out at one rally, where they burned cars and threw stones at police. The people were mostly traders demanding an end to new restrictions on the bazaar and their shuttle trade. Still other demonstrations took place in the towns of Bakht and Shakhrikhan in early December. In early April 2005, an antigovernment rally erupted in Jizzak, to protest poverty and the abduction of an opposition

[3] Mara Bellaby, "Many in Kyrgyzstan Unsure of Future," AP Online, March 30, 2005.
[4] "Kyrgyz Forum Insists on Sacking Security, Emergency Chiefs," *Kabar* news agency, April 20, 2005, reprinted in BBC Monitoring, April 20, 2005, <http://search.ft.com/search/article.html>.

leader; the provincial authorities planned to use force but backed down.[5] Meanwhile, the competition for power has heightened, pitting Karimov's family/clan against the Alimov clan and its Tashkent network, which controls the SNB forces, and the Jurabekov clan and its vast Samarkand network, which still controls the Ministry of Interior's vast army.[6]

In Tajikistan, popular disillusionment with both the government and the opposition, together with a fear of relapsing into civil war, leaves little faith in demonstrations, and de facto gives the Rakhmonov clan greater power. Still, rumblings followed the recent elections there as well. Both the Tajik and Uzbek presidents have been shaken by the Kyrgyz drama. Although less publicized, their own clannishness and corruption, and their increasingly hegemonic control of the state, have sown deep seeds of resentment – both among the populace and among rival clans. However, it is not yet clear what the Kyrgyz revolution will teach them: that power sharing and wealth sharing are essential for legitimacy or, more likely, that only increased repression will prevent regime challengers.

The Kyrgyz revolution was largely a popular reaction against clan politics, but unfortunately it does not guarantee a transcendence of clan politics. Still, despite the many risks ahead, the events of spring 2005 have produced more than a glimmer of hope for democracy in the region. As Vaclav Havel would say, many Kyrgyz have at last demanded that they "live in the truth." They have at last exposed "the lie" behind their regime. A new democratic regime will face many challenges in reestablishing and consolidating democracy in the Kyrgyz Republic. What they need now is a leader who will stand up for democracy and justice in order to keep the country united. Hopefully the next government and the younger generation will learn from the mistakes of Akaev's rule. With strong aid from the West and a renewed Kyrgyz society, this time it may succeed.

---

[5] Andrei Kudryashov, "Jizzakh Regional Authorities Handled an Impromptu Rally by Treating the Protestors to Pilau," *www.ferghana.ru*, April 4, 2005, <http://enews.ferghana.ru/4>.

[6] "Uzbekistan: A Power Struggle Brews," *Transitions Online*, January 14, 2005, <http://www.tol.cz/look/TOL/print.tpl?IdLanguage=I&IdPublication=4&NrIssue=98 &Nrs>.

Appendix

I. GLOSSARY OF FOREIGN TERMS[1]

adab	custom, tradition, norm
adat (Uzbek, Kyrgyz)	customary law
aga bii (Kyrgyz)	tribal leader
akim (Kyrgyz)	governor, provincial ruler
akimiat	governorship
aiyl (Kyrgyz)	village
arendator	lessor
autonomnaia oblast'	autonomous province
auyl (Kazakh)	village
aul (Russian spelling)	village
aksakal (Kyrgyz, Russian spelling)	elder of local community
aqsaqal (Kazakh)	elder of local community
aksakgal (Turkmen)	elder of local community
arbob (Tajik)	elder
avlod (Uzbek, Tajik)	clan, descent group
awlad	kinship group, clan
bedniak	poor
bek (Uzbek, Kyrgyz)	ruler of a province (also *bey*, *beg*)
bai (Kyrgyz)	wealthy person
bezpartinyi	partyless, independent
bi (Kazakh)	chieftain, tribal leader
bii (Kyrgyz, Uzbek, Karakalpak)	chieftain, tribal leader
blat	practice of informally exchanging favors

[1] Terms compiled from Russian, Uzbek–Russian, Kyrgyz–Russian and Tajik–Russian dictionaries, *Dictionary of Turkic Languages*, and Paul Georg Geiss, *Pre-Tsarist and Tsarist Central Asia* (London: Routledge Curzon, 2004).

byt	way of life
chistka	purge
chomry (Turkmen)	a settled tribesman
charva (Turkmen)	a nomadic tribesman
dekhonlar	private farmers
demokratizatsiia	democratization
ob'kom'partiia	oblast' communist party branch
domla	religious teacher
el (Kazakh, Kyrgyz)	tribe
elbegi (Uzbek)	tribal leader
hokim (Tajik, Uzbek)	governor, provincial ruler (sometimes spelled *hakim*)
hokimiat	governorship/provincial rulership
imom	Islamic religious and prayer leader
jamoat (Tajik)	council
Jogorku Kenesh (Kyrgyz)	national parliament
kadrovaia politika	cadre politics
kenesh	parliamentary body
khalk (Turkmen)	people, tribal confederacy
Khlopnii scandal	cotton scandal
khoja (Tajik, Uzbek)	person/caste descended from the caliph
kishlak	village
klan (Russian)	clan
klannovnost'	clannishness, clan system
kolkhoz (Russian)	collective farm
kolkhoznik	worker on a collective farm
kombedy	community of the poor
komitet	committee
korenizatsiia (Russian)	nativization policy
krasnyi desant	red landing
kulak (Russian)	wealthy peasant
kurultai	traditional Kyrgyz assembly (usually of elders)
madrassa	Islamic school (also *madrassah*, *madrassa*)
mahalla (Uzbek, Tajik)	neighborhood
mahalla komiteti (Uzbek)	mahalla committee
majlis (Uzbek, Tajik)	council, soviet
Majlisi Oli (Tajik)	National Assembly (parliament)
manap	clan and tribal leaders
mestnichestvo	localism
mufti (Kyrgyz, Uzbek, Tajik)	central Islamic leader of the republic
muftiat (Kyrgyz, Uzbek, Tajik)	hierarchical organization of Islamic clergy and mosques

mujahideen	Afghan freedom fighters
namoz (Uzbek, Tajik)	religious prayer
narodnost'	a people, nationality
narod	people
narodnyi palat (Kyrgyz)	people's assembly
nomenklatura	Soviet-era elite
novoe myshlenie	new thinking
oblast' (Russian)	province
Oliy Majlis (Uzbek)	National Assembly (parliament)
oqsoqol (Uzbek, Tajik)	elder of local community (literally, "white beard")
Orgbiuro	organizational bureau
osh	food, meal
otaliq (Uzbek)	tribal leader
plemia (Russian)	tribe
podesta (Italian)	broker, neutral executive leader
podesteria (Italian)	office/institution of broker, executive governing apparatus
propiska	residency permit
qawm (Tajik, Uzbek)	clan, descent group
qazi (Uzbek, Tajik)	judge
qaziyat (Tajik)	religious hierarchy
qishloq (Uzbek, Tajik)	village
qishloq komiteti (Uzbek)	village committee
qymyz (Kazakh, Kyrgyz)	Kumuz, fermented mare's milk
raion (Russian)	administrative unit
rakhat	renaissance
rod (Russian)	clan, descent group
ru (Kazakh)	clan, descent group
Sayyid (or *Saiid*) (Uzbek)	honorary title, or person/caste claiming descent from Muhammad's grandson Hussein
selo	village
sel'sovet	rural/village council
shahid	martyr
shirkat (Uzbek)	private farms
sovkhoz	state farm
toy or *toi* (Uzbek, Kyrgyz)	feast
tuzriki	indigenous executive committees
uezd (Russian)	administrative unit
ukaz	decree
ulema	Muslim scholars
urugh (Uzbek, Turkmen)	clan, descent group
uruu (Kyrgyz)	clan, descent group

uruw (Karakalpak)	clan, descent group
ustoz	respected teacher/elder
Uzneftgaz	Uzbek state oil and gas company
vatan	motherland
viloyat (Uzbek)	province
viloiat (Tajik)	province
volost'	smallest administrative division of Tsarist Russia
zakonodatel'nyi palat	legislative house of parliament
zemliachestvo	practice of appointing and promoting one's trusted friends and kinsmen

II. ACRONYMS

CIS	Commonwealth of Independent States
CEC	Central Electoral Commission
CPD	Congress of People's Deputies
CPK	Communist Party of Kyrgyzstan
CPSU	Communist Party of the Soviet Union
CPT	Communist Party of Tajikistan
CPU	Communist Party of Uzbekistan
DCK	Democratic Choice of Kazakhstan
DMK (also DDK)	Democratic Movement of Kyrgyzstan
DPT	Democratic Party of Tajikistan
EBRD	European Bank for Reconstruction and Development
FEZ	free economic zone
GFI	State Property Fund
GKChP	State Emergency Committee
GKI	State Investment Committee
GOSPLAN	state planning institution (responsible for the state central economic plan)
HT	Hizb ut-Tahrir al-Islami
IFI	International financial institutions
IMF	International Monetary Fund
IMU	Islamic Movement of Uzbekistan
IRP	Islamic Renaissance Party
KGB	secret police in the Soviet era
KPFR	Communist Party of the Russian Federation
LDPR	Liberal Democratic Party of Russia
LDPU	Liberal Democratic Party of Uzbekistan

MM	Majlisi Melli (national assembly/upper chamber, Tajikistan parliament)
MN	Majlisi Namoyandagon (assembly of representatives/lower chamber, Tajikistan parliament)
MO	Ministry of Defense
MVD	Ministry of Internal Affairs (the police)
NBU	National Bank of Uzbekistan
NDI	National Democratic Institute
NDPT	People's Democratic Party of Tajikistan
NDPU	People's Democratic Party of Uzbekistan
NGO	nongovernmental organization
OMON	Special Operations State Militia
OSCE	Organization for Security and Cooperation in Europe
PSS	presidential security service (Uzbekistan)
RAN	Russian Academy of Science
SADUM	Spiritual Directorate of Muslims of Central Asia
SDP	Social Democratic Party of Tajikistan
SNB (also NSS)	National Security Service (former KGB)
SPT	Socialist Party of Tajikistan
SSR	Soviet Socialist Republic
UN	United Nations
USAID	United States Agency for International Development
USSR	Union of Soviet Socialist Republics
UTO	United Tajik Opposition
WB	World Bank

Acronyms are based on transliteration from the foreign spelling, except when duplication made it necessary to use the English abbreviation, or when an English form is commonly used (e.g., by the United Nations).

III. RESEARCH METHOD AND SOURCES

I draw on field research and primary data accumulated during my three years of work in Central Asia. The book is a small-n study, a comparison of three cases. I chose this strategy for several reasons. First, choosing these cases enabled me to explain the variation in transitions while controlling for, and thereby eliminating, a range of other explanatory variables – such as mode of decolonization, timing of transition, even ethnic variation and external Russian influence (two important factors that distinguish the Kazakh case from the other Central Asian cases). Kyrgyzstan, Uzbekistan, and Tajikistan shared extremely similar social, economic, colonial, institutional, ethnic, cultural, ideological, and political legacies and levels of development. Yet their transitions varied dramatically for five years. They shared similar clan structures, and those clan structures played similar roles during the post-transition period. Critically, these cases expand the typical scope of transition studies. I explain transition both to democracy and to nondemocracy, as well as transition that ends in civil war.

Second, I am seeking to explain a complex process and mechanisms in cases about which we have little primary and limited secondary source data. Lack of good measurements of the critical variables poses problems for a large-n study. We quantify regime types, but measuring dynamic regime trajectories is more difficult. For this reason, I adopt a small-n qualitative and comparative historical approach. In a structured-focus comparison, I trace the role of clans and the specific propositions about clans (laid out in Chapter 2) in three cases. I analyze each case diachronically as well, looking at several periods from the early Soviet era to the post-Soviet era, and thereby demonstrate when and how clans are more successful in infiltrating the state and shaping its political trajectory.

Third, I analyze the social, political, and economic meaning and role of clans using both ethnographic and interview data, as well as published sources from Central Asia. Unlike ethnicity or political parties, clans are not registered and counted by the state. They are underground, a taboo subject in Central Asia. The Soviets denied them because they were a threat to communism's control; the current Central Asian regimes deny them primarily because they do not want to admit the extensive clan-based corruption that pervades their regimes. Quantitative measures are thus difficult. I therefore employ careful process tracing to examine the role of clans from the early twentieth century to the present, and their dynamic relationship to the state and regime trajectories.

Finally, my study avoids either an elite and urban bias or a rural, social one. Most studies of transition suffer from the former flaw. Society is critically important in questions of political stability and regime durability. In Central Asia especially, where the population is overwhelmingly rural, one cannot ignore this factor. Between 1994 and 2004, I carried out over three years of field work in Kyrgyzstan, Uzbekistan, and Tajikistan. The bulk of the work was done between 1994 and 2000, but I made several follow-up trips from 2001 to 2004. I draw on a variety of sources, including over 200 in-depth interviews in the Central Asian cases with government officials and other "elites," including journalists, academic specialists, policy analysts, clerical elites, nongovernmental organizations, representatives of foreign embassies and organizations, and political party members and civic activists. The sources also include new archival documents from the Central Asia Bureau and the Politburo files in the Communist Party Archive in Moscow. Both sources give a unique picture of both national and subnational politics and the role of clans during the Soviet and post-Soviet periods. I complement the elite-level analysis with a social-level analysis of clans, based on in-depth ethnographic interviews with over 300 respondents in a sampling of the rural and semirural regions of Kyrgyzstan (including Bishkek, Chu, Talas, Issyk-Kul, Osh, and Jalal-Abad) and Uzbekistan (including Tashkent, Khorezm, Samarkand, Bukhara, Syrdarya, Ferghana, Namangan, and Andijan). I also made trips to Dushanbe, Hissar, and Khodjent. Ethnographic methods are critical for understanding identity issues and for avoiding elite bias focused only on capital cities, in countries where approximately 70 percent of the population is rural. Rather than adopt a quantitative measure of clan identity, I used anthropological techniques. I posed a semistructured list of questions, while allowing open-ended responses in a conversational and informal, nonthreatening format. These regional, social-level interviews sought to assess the strength of clan identity at the local, nonelite level. I also draw on several oral histories and extensive participant observation conducted during many months traveling to villages and collective farms, as well as in urban areas.

There are certainly drawbacks to this methodology as well. A small-n study lacks the generalizability of a large-n study, although I try to correct for this by exploring cross-regional cases in Chapter 9. Admittedly, the discussion is based primarily on secondary sources, so it does not carry the same weight. An anthropologist would demand language ability in all the Central Asian languages in order to do interviews there. Unfortunately, I have a moderate grasp of Uzbek, very basic Kyrgyz, and no Tajik, so I could not do interviews in all these languages. I relied primarily upon Russian, in which I am fluent, or a mix of Russian and Uzbek, and occasionally had local help in translating from Uzbek to Russian when I did not fully understand. With limited funds, I could not afford a full-time translator. Ideally, one would do a survey or tape record interviews for content analysis, and thereby generate significant quantifiable data, but these techniques are highly problematic in closed cultures under political conditions in which people are often afraid to talk to scholars or to anyone asking them questions that relate to politics in any way. Clans became a taboo subject during the Soviet era, and continue to be taboo today. Respondents were more willing to answer questions in an informal setting, usually over a meal, provided that you did not tape record or quote them. With these difficulties, there was certainly a loss of data, but I have strived to understand and interpret properly the views of those I spoke with. As part of human subjects review, I agreed not to include names or identifiable information about respondents in rural areas, so as

to protect their anonymity. Some elite respondents did give me permission
to quote them, but I have not done so, because political conditions have
worsened in the years since I met with them. I did obtain an Uzbek government letter of support to pursue my research, but conditions are constantly
fluctuating, so I have chosen to take precautions. The result is a qualitative,
ethnographic picture. Since it is neither large enough nor sufficiently formal
to provide statistical evidence, I use the data to give an ethnographic picture
of networks and identity at the social level, and thereby to complement the
discussion of elite and meso-level networks. Although research on Central
Asia is increasingly important, it is also becoming increasingly difficult.

TABLE A.1. *Ethno-national composition of Kyrgyzstan, Tajikistan, and Uzbekistan, 1989 (percent of total population)*

Ethno-National Group	Kyrgyzstan 4.29 million	Tajikistan 5.11 million	Uzbekistan 19.9 million
Kyrgyz	52.4%[a]	1%	<2%
Russian	21.4%	8%	8.3%
Tajik	<2%	62%[a]	4.7%
Uzbek	12.9%	24%	71.4%[a]
Other (Turkmen, Jewish, Turkish, Tatar, Korean)	<12.3%	<4%	15.6%

[a] Titular ethnic group.

Source: 1989 census figures, *Goskomstat SSSR, 1990, 1991*. Last official Soviet census; data may not be accurate; percentage of Tajik population is very likely to be significantly underestimated because of underreporting by Tajiks on passports. 1996 figures from *Goskomprognostat Uzbekistan 1996, Goskomstat Rossii 1996, Statkomitet SNG 1995, Natskomstat Kyrgyzskoi Respubliki 1996*. Cited in Tim Heleniak, "The Changing Nationality Composition of the Central Asian and Transcaucasian States," *Post-Soviet Geography and Economics*, no. 6 (1997), pp. 371–375.

TABLE A.2. *Ethno-national composition of Kyrgyzstan, Tajikistan, and Uzbekistan, 1997 (percent of total population)*

Ethno-National Group	Kyrgyzstan 4.6 million[a]	Tajikistan 5.95 million[a]	Uzbekistan 23.5 million[a]
Kyrgyz	59.9%	<1%	0.9%
Russian	15.6%	3.4%	5.6%
Tajik	0.8%	68.1%	4.8%
Uzbek	14.1%	24.4%	76.6%
Other (Turkmen, Jewish, Turkish, Tatar, Korean)	9.6%	4.1%	12.1%

[a] Total population figure is for 1997; percentage by ethnic group is based on 1996 figures.

Source: CIA *World Factbook* data, 2003; figures are estimates, since no new census has been done.

TABLE A.3. *Indicators of development level in the former Soviet republics at independence/beginning of transition*

Former Soviet Republic	Population, 1989 census (in millions of persons)	GDP per capita ($ PPP, 1992)	Real GDP as % of (1991)	Adult Literacy, 1992 (% population)	HDI Rank, 1992[a] (1= highest; 175 = lowest)
Armenia	3.7	$4,469	58.2%	98.80%	90
Azerbaijan	7.4	$2,880	77.4%	96.30%	99
Belarus	10.2	$5,006	98.8%	97.90%	42
Estonia	1.6	$4,377	87.3%	99%	43
Georgia	5.5	$3,251	55.1%	94.90%	92
Kazakhstan	17.0	$4,304	89.0%	98%	64
Kyrgyzstan	4.5	$2,524	86.1%	97%	89
Latvia	2.6	$5,119	100.0%	99%	48
Lithuania	3.8	$8,032	99.0%	98.40%	71
Moldova	4.4	$3,195	71.0%	98.90%	81
Russia	149.0	$5,835	85.5%	98.70%	52
Tajikistan	5.6	$1,770	83.7%[a]	97%	103
Turkmenistan	3.9	$2,808	101.5%[b]	98%	86
Ukraine	52.1	$3,978	90.1%	98.80%	54
Uzbekistan	21.5	$2,342	88.9%	97%	94
Comparative sets:					
All developing countries				68.40%	
Least developed countries		$886		46.50%	
Low developed countries		$1,290			
(excluding India)		$1,356			
Medium developed countries		$2,605		58%	
High developed countries		$7,057		54.40%	
Industrial countries		$15,324			

[a] HDI = Human Development Index, a multivariate indicator of the overall modernization and socio-economic well-being of a state. States are rated from best (1) to worst (175). The index includes three components: (1) life expectancy at birth, (2) educational attainment, and (3) income. The HDI is compiled by the United Nations Development Program.

[b] Figure is from 1993.

Source: Human Development Report (New York: UNDP, 1992); *World Development Report* (1992).

TABLE A.4. *GDP, 1992–2002: Central Asia and regional comparisons*

Country or Region	GDP (Current US$ Billions)		GDP Growth (Annual %)		GDP per Capita (PPP $)	
	1992	2002	1992	2002	1992	2002
Kazakhstan	24.91	24.64	−5.30	9.80	4,190	5,870
Kyrgyz Republic	2.32	1.60	−13.89	−0.49	1,620	1,620
Tajikistan	1.90	1.21	−29.00	9.10	1,250	980
Turkmenistan	3.20	7.67	−5.30	14.90	5,910	43,00
Uzbekistan	12.95	7.93	−11.20	4.20	1,340	1,670
Russian Federation	460.21	346.52	−14.53	4.30	7,500	8,230
Europe and Central Asia	1011.91	1132.84	−9.25	4.62	5,687	7,022
Low and middle income	4204.89	6259.15	1.32	3.29	2,602	4,107
World	24302.49	32312.15	1.84	1.90	5,428	7,868

Source: World Development Indicators, World Bank, 2004.

TABLE A.5. *Freedom House ratings: Central Asia and the post-Soviet region*

Former Soviet Republic	1992	1993	1994	1995	1996	1997	1998	1999	2000	2001	2002	2003
Armenia	3.5	3.5	3.5	4	4.5	4.5	4	4	4	4	4	4
Azerbaijan	5	6	6	6	5.5	5	5	5	5.5	5.5	5.5	5.5
Belarus	3.5	4.5	4	5	6	6	6	6	6	6	6	6
Estonia	3	2.5	2.5	2	1.5	1.5	1.5	1.5	1.5	1.5	1.5	1.5
Georgia	4.5	5	5	4.5	4	3.5	3.5	3.5	4	4	4	4
Kazakhstan	5	5	5.5	5.5	5.5	5.5	5.5	5.5	5.5	5.5	5.5	5.5
Kyrgyz Republic	3	4	3.5	4	4	4	5	5	5.5	5.5	5.5	5.5
Latvia	3	3	2.5	2	2	1.5	1.5	1.5	1.5	1.5	1.5	1.5
Lithuania	2.5	2	2	1.5	1.5	1.5	1.5	1.5	1.5	1.5	1.5	1.5
Moldova	5	4	4	4	3.5	3.5	3	3	3	3	3.5	3.5
Russia	3.5	3.5	3.5	3.5	3.5	3.5	4	4.5	5	5	5	5
Tajikistan	6	7	7	7	6	6	6	6	6	6	5.5	5.5
Turkmenistan	6.5	7	7	7	7	7	7	7	7	7	7	7
Ukraine	3	4	3.5	3.5	3.5	3.5	3.5	3.5	4	4	4	4
Uzbekistan	6	7	7	7	6.5	6.5	6.5	6.5	6.5	6.5	6.5	6.5

Note: Ratings are combined FH scores of political rights and civil liberties.
Key: Free: 1–2.5; partly free: 3–4.5; not free: 5–7.

TABLE A.6. *Key economic and social indicators*

Country	Real GDP Growth (1996–2003 Average,%) (a)	GDP/Cap ($2003) (b)	GDP as % of 1990 Real GDP (c)	Foreign Direct Investment (% of GDP, 2003) (d)	External Debt (% of GDP, 2003) (e)	Budget Deficit (Cash Basis, % of GDP, 2003) (f)	Human Development Index Ranking 2002 (g)	Gini Coefficient (1996–98) (h)
Kazakhstan	5.7	1780	94.5	7.4	76.8	2.1	78	0.35
Kyrgyzstan	5.0	330	74.8	2.4	102.7	−3.7	110	0.47
Tajikistan	5.4	190	50.5	2.1	64.7	−1.8	116	0.47
Turkmenistan	10.1	1120ᵃ	128.3ᵇ	3.6	31.2	−1.4	86	0.45
Uzbekistan	4.0	420	111.1ᶜ	0.7	47.2	−1.5	107	–

[a] Preliminary estimate.
[b] Alternative estimates of real GDP growth by international finance organizations are 10 percent lower than the official government report.
[c] Alternative estimates of real GDP growth by international finance organizations are lower than the official government report.

Sources:

(a) World Bank Development Indicators, World Bank, 2004
(b) Word Bank regional statistical database
(c) World Bank regional statistical database
(d) World Bank Development Indicators, World Bank, 2004
(e) World Bank Development Indicators, World Bank, 2004
(f) World Bank Development Indicators, World Bank, 2004
(g) Human Development Report, UNDP, 2003
(h) World Bank Reports: "Transition: The First Ten Years"

TABLE A.7. *Key governance and political stability indicators.*

Country	Index of Economic Freedom (2003) (a)	Global Ranking of Economic Freedom (b)	Corruption Index (2003) (c)	Global Corruption Ranking (2003) (d)	Governance Index (2003) (e)	Government Effectiveness Rank (f)	Political Stability Index (g)
Kazakhstan	3.55	131	6.25	100	6.25	21.6	62.2
Kyrgyzstan	3.41	103	6.0	118	6.0	20.6	16.2
Tajikistan	4.10	146	6.0	124	6.0	8.8	17.8
Turkmenistan	4.21	150	6.25	n.a.	6.75	3.6	37.8
Uzbekistan	4.29	149	6.0	100	6.25	11.9	18.9

Sources:

(a) 2003 Index of Economic Freedom, the Heritage Foundation, and the *Wall Street Journal*; scores are rated from 1 to 5, with 1 being the best and 5 the worst.

(b) 2003 Index of Economic Freedom, the Heritage Foundation, and the *Wall Street Journal*; scores are rated from 1 to 5, with 1 being the best and 155 the worst.

(c) Nations in Transit report, 2004. This corruption index is based on expert opinions that rank the CIS states on a scale from 1 to 7; 1 is lowest corruption level, 7 is the highest corruption level.

(d) Transparency International. Note that TI rates Kyrgyzstan slightly more severely than the Nations in Transit report. TI is based on survey data.

(e) Nations in Transit report, 2004. This governance index is based on expert opinions that rank the CIS states on a scale from 1 to 7; 1 is the best, 7 is the worst.

(f) D. Kafman, A. Kraay, and M. Mastruzzi, World Bank governance dataset, <www.info.worldbank.org/governance/kkz2002/mc.region.asp>, 2003. Percentile rank is out of 100; 100th percentile is most effective regime, 0 is the least.

(g) D. Kafman, A. Kraay, and M. Mastruzzi, World Bank governance dataset, <www.info.worldbank.org/governance/kkz2002/mc.region.asp>, 2003. Percentile rank is out of 100; 100th percentile is the most stable regime, 0 is the least.

Index

Note: Page numbers followed by *f*, *t*, or *n* indicate figures, tables, or notes, respectively.